# MERCEDES-BENZ | C-CLASS 2001-07 REPAIR MANUAL

**CHILTON'S**

Covers U.S. and Canadian models of
**Mercedes-Benz C-Class C230, C240, C280, C320 and C350**

*Does not include information specific to AMG models*

**by Alan Ahlstrand**

**CHILTON** *Automotive Books*

PUBLISHED BY **HAYNES NORTH AMERICA.** Inc.

Manufactured in USA
©2008 Haynes North America, Inc.
ISBN-13: 978-1-56392-737-9
ISBN-10: 1-56392-737-3
Library of Congress Control Number 2008937128

**Haynes Publishing Group**
Sparkford Nr Yeovil
Somerset BA22 7JJ England

**Haynes North America, Inc**
861 Lawrence Drive
Newbury Park
California 91320 USA

ABCDE
FGHIJ
KLMNO
PQRST

# Contents

**Mechanic and photographer with a 2005 Mercedes-Benz C240**

## ACKNOWLEDGEMENTS

Technical writers who contributed to this project include John Wegmann, Mike Stubblefield and Joe Hamilton. Wiring diagrams originated exclusively for Haynes North America, Inc. by Solution Builders.

## About this manual

### ITS PURPOSE

The purpose of this manual is to help you get the best value from your vehicle. It can do so in several ways. It can help you decide what work must be done, even if you choose to have it done by a dealer service department or a repair shop; it provides information and procedures for routine maintenance and servicing; and it offers diagnostic and repair procedures to follow when trouble occurs.

We hope you use the manual to tackle the work yourself. For many simpler jobs, doing it yourself may be quicker than arranging an appointment to get the vehicle into a shop and making the trips to leave it and pick it up. More importantly, a lot of money can be saved by avoiding the expense the shop must pass on to you to cover its labor and overhead costs. An added benefit is the sense of satisfaction and accomplishment that you feel after doing the job yourself.

### USING THE MANUAL

The manual is divided into Chapters. Each Chapter is divided into numbered Sections, which are headed in bold type between horizontal lines. Each Section consists of consecutively numbered paragraphs.

At the beginning of each numbered Section you will be referred to any illustrations which apply to the procedures in that Section. The reference numbers used in illustration captions pinpoint the pertinent Section and the Step within that Section. That is, illustration 3.2 means the illustration refers to Section 3 and Step (or paragraph) 2 within that Section.

Procedures, once described in the text, are not normally repeated. When it's necessary to refer to another Chapter, the reference will be given as Chapter and Section number. Cross references given without use of the word "Chapter" apply to Sections and/or paragraphs in the same Chapter. For example, "see Section 8" means in the same Chapter.

References to the left or right side of the vehicle assume you are sitting in the driver's seat, facing forward.

Even though we have prepared this manual with extreme care, neither the publisher nor the author can accept responsibility for any errors in, or omissions from, the information given.

**➥NOTE**

A *Note* provides information necessary to properly complete a procedure or information which will make the procedure easier to understand.

### ✳✳ CAUTION

A *Caution* provides a special procedure or special steps which must be taken while completing the procedure where the Caution is found. Not heeding a Caution can result in damage to the assembly being worked on.

### ✳✳ WARNING

A *Warning* provides a special procedure or special steps which must be taken while completing the procedure where the Warning is found. Not heeding a Warning can result in personal injury.

## Introduction

Mercedes C-Class models are available in either a four-door sedan body style, two-door sport coupe or a four-door wagon body style.

Depending on year and model, C-Class vehicles are powered by either a 1.8L or 2.3L four-cylinder engine equipped with a belt-driven supercharger to provide more power. The C-Class may also be powered by a 2.5L, 2.6L, 3.0L, 3.2L or 3.5L V6 engine.

Automatic transmission models come equipped with either a five-speed or seven-speed automatic transmission, while manual transmission models are equipped with a six-speed manual transmission.

Most models are equipped with an independent, multi-link, front suspension system with McPherson strut type assemblies. All models are equipped with an independent, multi-link rear suspension.

The steering system consists of a rack-and-pinion steering gear and two adjustable tie-rods. Power assist is standard.

## Vehicle identification numbers

Modifications are a continuing and unpublicized process in vehicle manufacturing. Since spare parts lists and manuals are compiled on a numerical basis, the individual vehicle numbers are necessary to correctly identify the component required.

## VEHICLE IDENTIFICATION NUMBER (VIN)

This very important identification number is stamped on a plate attached to the dashboard inside the windshield on the driver's side of the vehicle (see illustration). The VIN also appears on the Vehicle Certificate of Title and Registration. It contains information such as where and when the vehicle was manufactured, the model year and the body style.

## VIN ENGINE AND MODEL YEAR CODES

Two particularly important pieces of information found in the VIN are the engine code and the model year code. Counting from the left, the engine code letter designation is the 8th digit and the model year code letter designation is the 10th digit.

**On the models covered by this manual, the model year codes are:**

1 ...................... 2001
2 ...................... 2002
3 ...................... 2003
4 ...................... 2004
5 ...................... 2005
6 ...................... 2006
7 ...................... 2007

## VEHICLE CERTIFICATION LABEL

The Vehicle Certification Label is attached to the driver's side door post (see illustration). Information on this label includes the name of the manufacturer, the month and year of production, as well as information on the options with which it is equipped. This label is especially useful for matching the color and type of paint for repair work.

## ENGINE IDENTIFICATION NUMBER

The engine number is stamped onto a machined pad on the top right of the flange next to the transmission.

## VEHICLE EMISSIONS CONTROL INFORMATION LABEL

This label is found in the engine compartment. See Chapter 6 for more information on this label.

**The VIN number is visible through the windshield on the driver's side**

**The vehicle certification label is affixed the to the driver's side door post**

## Recall information

Vehicle recalls are carried out by the manufacturer in the rare event of a possible safety-related defect. The vehicle's registered owner is contacted at the address on file at the Department of Motor Vehicles and given the details of the recall. Remedial work is carried out free of charge at a dealer service department.

If you are the new owner of a used vehicle which was subject to a recall and you want to be sure that the work has been carried out, it's best to contact a dealer service department and ask about your individual vehicle - you'll need to furnish them your Vehicle Identification Number (VIN).

The table below is based on information provided by the National Highway Traffic Safety Administration (NHTSA), the body which oversees vehicle recalls in the United States. The recall database is updated constantly. For the latest information on vehicle recalls, check the NHTSA website at www.nhtsa.gov, or call the NHTSA hotline at 1 888-327-4236.

| Recall date | Recall campaign number | Model(s) affected | Concern |
|---|---|---|---|
| Dec 17, 2003 | 03V534000 | 2004 C-Class | On certain passenger vehicles, some seat belt buckles may have a burr on a metal component of the locking mechanism. The presence of the burr could prevent the seat belt from locking under certain circumstances. |
| Dec 15, 2005 | 05V560000 | 2005 and 2006 C-Class | Certain passenger vehicles equipped with sport model steering wheels fail to comply with the requirements of Federal Motor Vehicle Safety Standard no. 208, "Occupant Crash Protection." In certain low-risk air bag deployment tests conducted by NHTSA, using an out-of-position unbelted 5th percentile female crash test dummy, irregularities were demonstrated indicating that occupants may not be properly protected in a crash. |

## Buying parts

Replacement parts are available from many sources, which generally fall into one of two categories - authorized dealer parts departments and independent retail auto parts stores. Our advice concerning these parts is as follows:

**Retail auto parts stores:** Good auto parts stores will stock frequently needed components which wear out relatively fast, such as clutch components, exhaust systems, brake parts, tune-up parts, etc. These stores often supply new or reconditioned parts on an exchange basis, which can save a considerable amount of money. Discount auto parts stores are often very good places to buy materials and parts needed for general vehicle maintenance such as oil, grease, filters, spark plugs, belts, touch-up paint, bulbs, etc. They also usually sell tools and general accessories, have convenient hours, charge lower prices and can often be found not far from home.

**Authorized dealer parts department:** This is the best source for parts which are unique to the vehicle and not generally available elsewhere (such as major engine parts, transmission parts, trim pieces, etc.).

**Warranty information:** If the vehicle is still covered under warranty, be sure that any replacement parts purchased - regardless of the source - do not invalidate the warranty!

To be sure of obtaining the correct parts, have engine and chassis numbers available and, if possible, take the old parts along for positive identification.

## MAINTENANCE TECHNIQUES

There are a number of techniques involved in maintenance and repair that will be referred to throughout this manual. Application of these techniques will enable the home mechanic to be more efficient, better organized and capable of performing the various tasks properly, which will ensure that the repair job is thorough and complete.

### Fasteners

Fasteners are nuts, bolts, studs and screws used to hold two or more parts together. There are a few things to keep in mind when working with fasteners. Almost all of them use a locking device of some type, either a lockwasher, locknut, locking tab or thread adhesive. All threaded fasteners should be clean and straight, with undamaged threads and undamaged corners on the hex head where the wrench fits. Develop the habit of replacing all damaged nuts and bolts with new ones. Special locknuts with nylon or fiber inserts can only be used once. If they are removed, they lose their locking ability and must be replaced with new ones.

Rusted nuts and bolts should be treated with a penetrating fluid to ease removal and prevent breakage. Some mechanics use turpentine in a spout-type oil can, which works quite well. After applying the rust penetrant, let it work for a few minutes before trying to loosen the nut or bolt. Badly rusted fasteners may have to be chiseled or sawed off or removed with a special nut breaker, available at tool stores.

If a bolt or stud breaks off in an assembly, it can be drilled and removed with a special tool commonly available for this purpose. Most automotive machine shops can perform this task, as well as other repair procedures, such as the repair of threaded holes that have been stripped out.

Flat washers and lockwashers, when removed from an assembly, should always be replaced exactly as removed. Replace any damaged washers with new ones. Never use a lockwasher on any soft metal surface (such as aluminum), thin sheet metal or plastic.

### Fastener sizes

For a number of reasons, automobile manufacturers are making wider and wider use of metric fasteners. Therefore, it is important to be able to tell the difference between standard (sometimes called U.S.

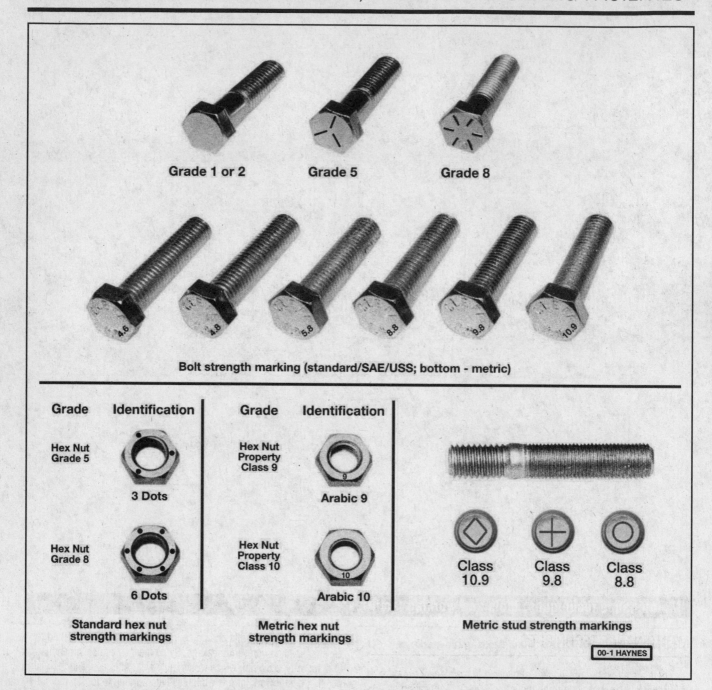

Grade 1 or 2          Grade 5          Grade 8

Bolt strength marking (standard/SAE/USS; bottom - metric)

| Grade | Identification | Grade | Identification |
|-------|----------------|-------|----------------|
| Hex Nut Grade 5 | 3 Dots | Hex Nut Property Class 9 | Arabic 9 |
| Hex Nut Grade 8 | 6 Dots | Hex Nut Property Class 10 | Arabic 10 |

Standard hex nut strength markings

Metric hex nut strength markings

Class 10.9          Class 9.8          Class 8.8

Metric stud strength markings

00-1 HAYNES

or SAE) and metric hardware, since they cannot be interchanged.

All bolts, whether standard or metric, are sized according to diameter, thread pitch and length. For example, a standard 1/2 - 13 x 1 bolt is 1/2 inch in diameter, has 13 threads per inch and is 1 inch long. An M12 - 1.75 x 25 metric bolt is 12 mm in diameter, has a thread pitch of 1.75 mm (the distance between threads) and is 25 mm long. The two bolts are nearly identical, and easily confused, but they are not interchangeable.

In addition to the differences in diameter, thread pitch and length, metric and standard bolts can also be distinguished by examining the bolt heads. To begin with, the distance across the flats on a standard bolt head is measured in inches, while the same dimension on a metric bolt is sized in millimeters (the same is true for nuts). As a result, a standard wrench should not be used on a metric bolt and a metric wrench should not be used on a standard bolt. Also, most standard bolts have slashes

radiating out from the center of the head to denote the grade or strength of the bolt, which is an indication of the amount of torque that can be applied to it. The greater the number of slashes, the greater the strength of the bolt. Grades 0 through 5 are commonly used on automobiles. Metric bolts have a property class (grade) number, rather than a slash, molded into their heads to indicate bolt strength. In this case, the higher the number, the stronger the bolt. Property class numbers 8.8, 9.8 and 10.9 are commonly used on automobiles.

Strength markings can also be used to distinguish standard hex nuts from metric hex nuts. Many standard nuts have dots stamped into one side, while metric nuts are marked with a number. The greater the number of dots, or the higher the number, the greater the strength of the nut.

Metric studs are also marked on their ends according to property class (grade). Larger studs are numbered (the same as metric bolts), while smaller studs carry a geometric code to denote grade.

### Metric thread sizes

| | Ft-lbs | Nm |
|---|---|---|
| M-6 | 6 to 9 | 9 to 12 |
| M-8 | 14 to 21 | 19 to 28 |
| M-10 | 28 to 40 | 38 to 54 |
| M-12 | 50 to 71 | 68 to 96 |
| M-14 | 80 to 140 | 109 to 154 |

### Pipe thread sizes

| | Ft-lbs | Nm |
|---|---|---|
| 1/8 | 5 to 8 | 7 to 10 |
| 1/4 | 12 to 18 | 17 to 24 |
| 3/8 | 22 to 33 | 30 to 44 |
| 1/2 | 25 to 35 | 34 to 47 |

### U.S. thread sizes

| | Ft-lbs | Nm |
|---|---|---|
| 1/4 - 20 | 6 to 9 | 9 to 12 |
| 5/16 - 18 | 12 to 18 | 17 to 24 |
| 5/16 - 24 | 14 to 20 | 19 to 27 |
| 3/8 - 16 | 22 to 32 | 30 to 43 |
| 3/8 - 24 | 27 to 38 | 37 to 51 |
| 7/16 - 14 | 40 to 55 | 55 to 74 |
| 7/10 - 20 | 40 to 60 | 55 to 81 |
| 1/2 - 13 | 55 to 80 | 75 to 108 |

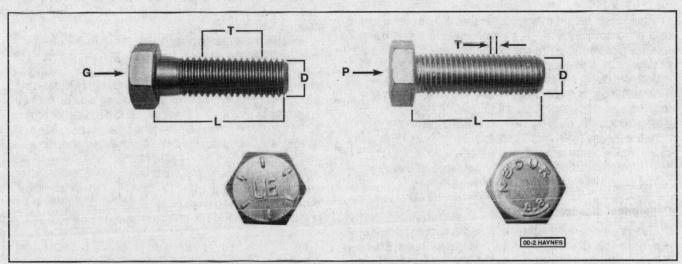

00-2 HAYNES

**Standard (SAE and USS) bolt dimensions/grade marks**

G   Grade marks (bolt strength)
L   Length (in inches)
T   Thread pitch (number of threads per inch)
D   Nominal diameter (in inches)

**Metric bolt dimensions/grade marks**

P   Property class (bolt strength)
L   Length (in millimeters)
T   Thread pitch (distance between threads in millimeters)
D   Diameter

It should be noted that many fasteners, especially Grades 0 through 2, have no distinguishing marks on them. When such is the case, the only way to determine whether it is standard or metric is to measure the thread pitch or compare it to a known fastener of the same size.

Standard fasteners are often referred to as SAE, as opposed to metric. However, it should be noted that SAE technically refers to a non-metric fine thread fastener only. Coarse thread non-metric fasteners are referred to as USS sizes.

Since fasteners of the same size (both standard and metric) may have different strength ratings, be sure to reinstall any bolts, studs or nuts removed from your vehicle in their original locations. Also, when replacing a fastener with a new one, make sure that the new one has a strength rating equal to or greater than the original.

### Tightening sequences and procedures

Most threaded fasteners should be tightened to a specific torque value (torque is the twisting force applied to a threaded component such as a nut or bolt). Overtightening the fastener can weaken it and cause it to break, while undertightening can cause it to eventually come loose. Bolts, screws and studs, depending on the material they are made of and their thread diameters, have specific torque values, many of which are noted in the Specifications at the end of each Chapter. Be sure to follow the torque recommendations closely. For fasteners not assigned a specific torque, a general torque value chart is presented here as a guide. These torque values are for dry (unlubricated) fasteners threaded into steel or cast iron (not aluminum). As was previously mentioned, the size and grade of a fastener determine the amount of torque that can

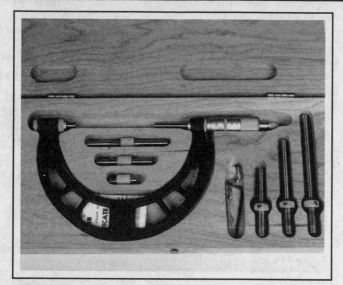

**Micrometer set**

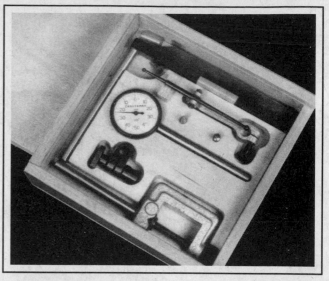

**Dial indicator set**

safely be applied to it. The figures listed here are approximate for Grade 2 and Grade 3 fasteners. Higher grades can tolerate higher torque values.

Fasteners laid out in a pattern, such as cylinder head bolts, oil pan bolts, differential cover bolts, etc., must be loosened or tightened in sequence to avoid warping the component. This sequence will normally be shown in the appropriate Chapter. If a specific pattern is not given, the following procedures can be used to prevent warping.

Initially, the bolts or nuts should be assembled finger-tight only. Next, they should be tightened one full turn each, in a criss-cross or diagonal pattern. After each one has been tightened one full turn, return to the first one and tighten them all one-half turn, following the same pattern. Finally, tighten each of them one-quarter turn at a time until each fastener has been tightened to the proper torque. To loosen and remove the fasteners, the procedure would be reversed.

## Component disassembly

Component disassembly should be done with care and purpose to help ensure that the parts go back together properly. Always keep track of the sequence in which parts are removed. Make note of special characteristics or marks on parts that can be installed more than one way, such as a grooved thrust washer on a shaft. It is a good idea to lay the disassembled parts out on a clean surface in the order that they were removed. It may also be helpful to make sketches or take instant photos of components before removal.

When removing fasteners from a component, keep track of their locations. Sometimes threading a bolt back in a part, or putting the washers and nut back on a stud, can prevent mix-ups later. If nuts and bolts cannot be returned to their original locations, they should be kept in a compartmented box or a series of small boxes. A cupcake or muffin tin is ideal for this purpose, since each cavity can hold the bolts and nuts from a particular area (i.e. oil pan bolts, valve cover bolts, engine mount bolts, etc.). A pan of this type is especially helpful when working on assemblies with very small parts, such as the carburetor, alternator, valve train or interior dash and trim pieces. The cavities can be marked with paint or tape to identify the contents.

Whenever wiring looms, harnesses or connectors are separated, it is a good idea to identify the two halves with numbered pieces of masking tape so they can be easily reconnected.

## Gasket sealing surfaces

Throughout any vehicle, gaskets are used to seal the mating surfaces between two parts and keep lubricants, fluids, vacuum or pressure contained in an assembly.

Many times these gaskets are coated with a liquid or paste-type gasket sealing compound before assembly. Age, heat and pressure can sometimes cause the two parts to stick together so tightly that they are very difficult to separate. Often, the assembly can be loosened by striking it with a soft-face hammer near the mating surfaces. A regular hammer can be used if a block of wood is placed between the hammer and the part. Do not hammer on cast parts or parts that could be easily damaged. With any particularly stubborn part, always recheck to make sure that every fastener has been removed.

Avoid using a screwdriver or bar to pry apart an assembly, as they can easily mar the gasket sealing surfaces of the parts, which must remain smooth. If prying is absolutely necessary, use an old broom handle, but keep in mind that extra clean up will be necessary if the wood splinters.

After the parts are separated, the old gasket must be carefully scraped off and the gasket surfaces cleaned. Stubborn gasket material can be soaked with rust penetrant or treated with a special chemical to soften it so it can be easily scraped off.

**※※ CAUTION:**

**Never use gasket removal solutions or caustic chemicals on plastic or other composite components.**

A scraper can be fashioned from a piece of copper tubing by flattening and sharpening one end. Copper is recommended because it is usually softer than the surfaces to be scraped, which reduces the chance of gouging the part. Some gaskets can be removed with a wire brush, but regardless of the method used, the mating surfaces must be left clean and smooth. If for some reason the gasket surface is gouged, then a gasket sealer thick enough to fill scratches will have to be used during reassembly of the components. For most applications, a non-drying (or semi-drying) gasket sealer should be used.

**Dial caliper**

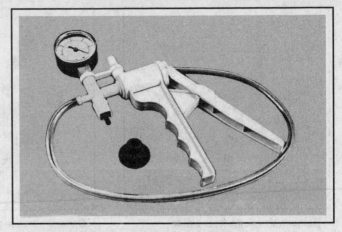

**Hand-operated vacuum pump**

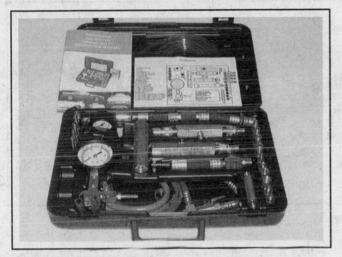

**Fuel pressure gauge set**

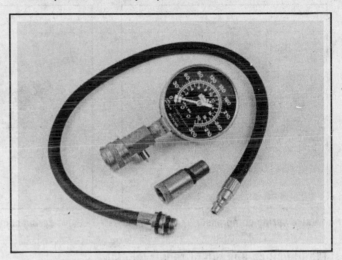

**Compression gauge with spark plug hole adapter**

## Hose removal tips

> ✳✳ **WARNING:**
>
> **If the vehicle is equipped with air conditioning, do not disconnect any of the A/C hoses without first having the system depressurized by a dealer service department or a service station.**

Hose removal precautions closely parallel gasket removal precautions. Avoid scratching or gouging the surface that the hose mates against or the connection may leak. This is especially true for radiator hoses. Because of various chemical reactions, the rubber in hoses can bond itself to the metal spigot that the hose fits over. To remove a hose, first loosen the hose clamps that secure it to the spigot. Then, with slip-joint pliers, grab the hose at the clamp and rotate it around the spigot. Work it back and forth until it is completely free, then pull it off. Silicone or other lubricants will ease removal if they can be applied between the hose and the outside of the spigot. Apply the same lubricant to the inside of the hose and the outside of the spigot to simplify installation.

As a last resort (and if the hose is to be replaced with a new one anyway), the rubber can be slit with a knife and the hose peeled from the spigot. If this must be done, be careful that the metal connection is not damaged.

If a hose clamp is broken or damaged, do not reuse it. Wire-type clamps usually weaken with age, so it is a good idea to replace them with screw-type clamps whenever a hose is removed.

## TOOLS

A selection of good tools is a basic requirement for anyone who plans to maintain and repair his or her own vehicle. For the owner who has few tools, the initial investment might seem high, but when compared to the spiraling costs of professional auto maintenance and repair, it is a wise one.

To help the owner decide which tools are needed to perform the tasks detailed in this manual, the following tool lists are offered: *Maintenance and minor repair, Repair/overhaul* and *Special*.

The newcomer to practical mechanics should start off with the *maintenance and minor repair* tool kit, which is adequate for the simpler jobs performed on a vehicle. Then, as confidence and experience grow, the owner can tackle more difficult tasks, buying additional tools as they are needed. Eventually the basic kit will be expanded into the *repair and overhaul* tool set. Over a period of time, the experienced do-it-yourselfer will assemble a tool set complete enough for most repair and overhaul procedures and will add tools from the special category when it is felt that the expense is justified by the frequency of use.

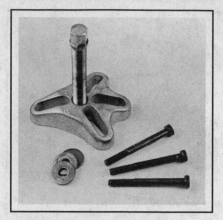

**Damper/steering wheel puller**

**General purpose puller**

**Hydraulic lifter removal tool**

**Valve spring compressor**

**Valve spring compressor**

**Ridge reamer**

## Maintenance and minor repair tool kit

The tools in this list should be considered the minimum required for performance of routine maintenance, servicing and minor repair work. We recommend the purchase of combination wrenches (box-end and open-end combined in one wrench). While more expensive than open end wrenches, they offer the advantages of both types of wrench.

> *Combination wrench set (1/4-inch to 1 inch or 6 mm to 19 mm)*
> *Adjustable wrench, 8 inch*
> *Spark plug wrench with rubber insert*
> *Spark plug gap adjusting tool*
> *Feeler gauge set*
> *Brake bleeder wrench*
> *Standard screwdriver (5/16-inch x 6 inch)*
> *Phillips screwdriver (No. 2 x 6 inch)*
> *Combination pliers - 6 inch*
> *Hacksaw and assortment of blades*
> *Tire pressure gauge*
> *Grease gun*
> *Oil can*
> *Fine emery cloth*
> *Wire brush*
> *Battery post and cable cleaning tool*
> *Oil filter wrench*
> *Funnel (medium size)*
> *Safety goggles*
> *Jackstands (2)*
> *Drain pan*

➡️**Note: If basic tune-ups are going to be part of routine maintenance, it will be necessary to purchase a good quality stroboscopic timing light and combination tachometer/dwell meter. Although they are included in the list of special tools, it is mentioned here because they are absolutely necessary for tuning most vehicles properly.**

## Repair and overhaul tool set

These tools are essential for anyone who plans to perform major repairs and are in addition to those in the maintenance and minor repair tool kit. Included is a comprehensive set of sockets which, though expensive, are invaluable because of their versatility, especially when various extensions and drives are available. We recommend the 1/2-inch drive over the 3/8-inch drive. Although the larger drive is bulky and more expensive, it has the capacity of accepting a very wide range of large sockets. Ideally, however, the mechanic should have a 3/8-inch drive set and a 1/2-inch drive set.

> *Socket set(s)*
> *Reversible ratchet*
> *Extension - 10 inch*
> *Universal joint*
> *Torque wrench (same size drive as sockets)*
> *Ball peen hammer - 8 ounce*
> *Soft-face hammer (plastic/rubber)*
> *Standard screwdriver (1/4-inch x 6 inch)*
> *Standard screwdriver (stubby - 5/16-inch)*
> *Phillips screwdriver (No. 3 x 8 inch)*
> *Phillips screwdriver (stubby - No. 2)*
> *Pliers - vise grip*

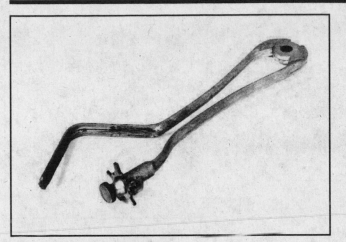

**Piston ring groove cleaning tool**

**Ring removal/installation tool**

**Ring compressor**

**Cylinder hone**

**Brake hold-down spring tool**

Pliers - lineman's
Pliers - needle nose
Pliers - snap-ring (internal and external)
Cold chisel - 1/2-inch
Scribe
Scraper (made from flattened copper tubing)
Centerpunch
Pin punches (1/16, 1/8, 3/16-inch)
Steel rule/straightedge - 12 inch
Allen wrench set (1/8 to 3/8 inch or 4 mm to 10 mm)
A selection of files
Wire brush (large)
Jackstands (second set)
Jack (scissor or hydraulic type)

➡**Note: Another tool which is often useful is an electric drill with a chuck capacity of 3/8-inch and a set of good quality drill bits.**

## Special tools

The tools in this list include those which are not used regularly, are expensive to buy, or which need to be used in accordance with their manufacturer's instructions. Unless these tools will be used frequently, it is not very economical to purchase many of them. A consideration would be to split the cost and use between yourself and a friend or friends. In addition, most of these tools can be obtained from a tool rental shop on a temporary basis.

This list primarily contains only those tools and instruments widely available to the public, and not those special tools produced by the vehicle manufacturer for distribution to dealer service depart-ments. Occasionally, references to the manufacturer's special tools are included in the text of this manual. Generally, an alternative method of doing the job without the special tool is offered. However, sometimes there is no alternative to their use. Where this is the case, and the tool cannot be purchased or borrowed, the work should be turned over to the dealer service department or an automotive repair shop.

Valve spring compressor
Piston ring groove cleaning tool
Piston ring compressor
Piston ring installation tool
Cylinder compression gauge
Cylinder ridge reamer
Cylinder surfacing hone
Cylinder bore gauge
Micrometers and/or dial calipers
Hydraulic lifter removal tool
Balljoint separator
Universal-type puller
Impact screwdriver
Dial indicator set
Stroboscopic timing light (inductive pick-up)
Hand operated vacuum/pressure pump
Tachometer/dwell meter
Universal electrical multimeter
Cable hoist
Brake spring removal and installation tools
Floor jack

**Torque angle gauge**

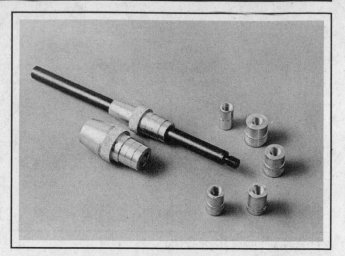

**Clutch plate alignment tool**

## Buying tools

For the do-it-yourselfer who is just starting to get involved in vehicle maintenance and repair, there are a number of options available when purchasing tools. If maintenance and minor repair is the extent of the work to be done, the purchase of individual tools is satisfactory. If, on the other hand, extensive work is planned, it would be a good idea to purchase a modest tool set from one of the large retail chain stores. A set can usually be bought at a substantial savings over the individual tool prices, and they often come with a tool box. As additional tools are needed, add-on sets, individual tools and a larger tool box can be purchased to expand the tool selection. Building a tool set gradually allows the cost of the tools to be spread over a longer period of time and gives the mechanic the freedom to choose only those tools that will actually be used.

Tool stores will often be the only source of some of the special tools that are needed, but regardless of where tools are bought, try to avoid cheap ones, especially when buying screwdrivers and sockets, because they won't last very long. The expense involved in replacing cheap tools will eventually be greater than the initial cost of quality tools.

## Care and maintenance of tools

Good tools are expensive, so it makes sense to treat them with respect. Keep them clean and in usable condition and store them properly when not in use. Always wipe off any dirt, grease or metal chips before putting them away. Never leave tools lying around in the work area. Upon completion of a job, always check closely under the hood for tools that may have been left there so they won't get lost during a test drive.

Some tools, such as screwdrivers, pliers, wrenches and sockets, can be hung on a panel mounted on the garage or workshop wall, while others should be kept in a tool box or tray. Measuring instruments, gauges, meters, etc. must be carefully stored where they cannot be damaged by weather or impact from other tools.

When tools are used with care and stored properly, they will last a very long time. Even with the best of care, though, tools will wear out if used frequently. When a tool is damaged or worn out, replace it. Subsequent jobs will be safer and more enjoyable if you do.

## HOW TO REPAIR DAMAGED THREADS

Sometimes, the internal threads of a nut or bolt hole can become stripped, usually from overtightening. Stripping threads is an all-too-

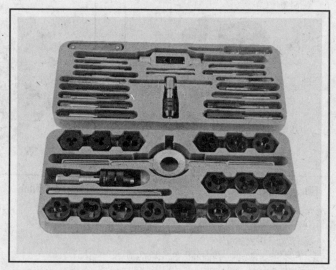

**Tap and die set**

common occurrence, especially when working with aluminum parts, because aluminum is so soft that it easily strips out.

Usually, external or internal threads are only partially stripped. After they've been cleaned up with a tap or die, they'll still work. Sometimes, however, threads are badly damaged. When this happens, you've got three choices:

1) *Drill and tap the hole to the next suitable oversize and install a larger diameter bolt, screw or stud.*
2) *Drill and tap the hole to accept a threaded plug, then drill and tap the plug to the original screw size. You can also buy a plug already threaded to the original size. Then you simply drill a hole to the specified size, then run the threaded plug into the hole with a bolt and jam nut. Once the plug is fully seated, remove the jam nut and bolt.*
3) *The third method uses a patented thread repair kit like Heli-Coil or Slimsert. These easy-to-use kits are designed to repair damaged threads in straight-through holes and blind holes. Both are available as kits which can handle a variety of sizes and thread patterns. Drill the hole, then tap it with the special included tap. Install the Heli-Coil and the hole is back to its original diameter and thread pitch.*

Regardless of which method you use, be sure to proceed calmly and carefully. A little impatience or carelessness during one of these relatively simple procedures can ruin your whole day's work and cost you a bundle if you wreck an expensive part.

## WORKING FACILITIES

Not to be overlooked when discussing tools is the workshop. If anything more than routine maintenance is to be carried out, some sort of suitable work area is essential.

It is understood, and appreciated, that many home mechanics do not have a good workshop or garage available, and end up removing an engine or doing major repairs outside. It is recommended, however, that the overhaul or repair be completed under the cover of a roof.

A clean, flat workbench or table of comfortable working height is an absolute necessity. The workbench should be equipped with a vise that has a jaw opening of at least four inches.

As mentioned previously, some clean, dry storage space is also required for tools, as well as the lubricants, fluids, cleaning solvents, etc. which soon become necessary.

Sometimes waste oil and fluids, drained from the engine or cooling system during normal maintenance or repairs, present a disposal problem. To avoid pouring them on the ground or into a sewage system, pour the used fluids into large containers, seal them with caps and take them to an authorized disposal site or recycling center. Plastic jugs, such as old antifreeze containers, are ideal for this purpose.

Always keep a supply of old newspapers and clean rags available. Old towels are excellent for mopping up spills. Many mechanics use rolls of paper towels for most work because they are readily available and disposable. To help keep the area under the vehicle clean, a large cardboard box can be cut open and flattened to protect the garage or shop floor.

Whenever working over a painted surface, such as when leaning over a fender to service something under the hood, always cover it with an old blanket or bedspread to protect the finish. Vinyl covered pads, made especially for this purpose, are available at auto parts stores.

## Booster battery (jump) starting

Observe the following precautions when using a booster battery to start a vehicle:

a) *Before connecting the booster battery, make sure the ignition switch is in the Off position.*

b) *Turn off the lights, heater and other electrical loads.*

c) *Your eyes should be shielded. Safety goggles are a good idea.*

d) *Make sure the booster battery is the same voltage as the dead one in the vehicle.*

e) *The two vehicles MUST NOT TOUCH each other!*

f) *Make sure the transmission is in Neutral (manual) or Park (automatic).*

g) *If the booster battery is not a maintenance-free type, remove the vent caps and lay a cloth over the vent holes.*

Connect one jumper lead between the positive (+) terminals of the two batteries (see illustration).

➡**Note: These vehicles are equipped with a remote positive terminal located on the side of the underhood fuse/relay box, to make jumper cable connection easier (see illustration).**

Connect the other jumper lead first to the negative (-) terminal of the booster battery, then to a good engine ground on the vehicle to be started.

➡**Note: These vehicles are also equipped with a remote grounding point, located on the right shock tower (near the remote positive terminal).**

Attach the lead at least 10 inches from the battery, if possible. Make sure the that the jumper leads will not contact the fan, drivebelt or other moving parts of the engine.

Start the engine using the booster battery, then, with the engine running at idle speed, disconnect the jumper cables in the reverse order of connection.

**Make the booster battery cable connections in the numerical order shown (note that the negative cable of the booster battery is NOT attached to the negative terminal of the dead battery)**

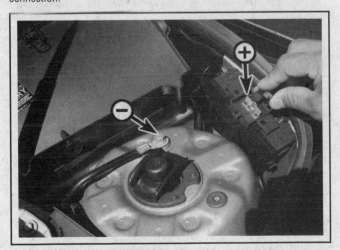

**Remote jump starting terminals**

**Jacking and towing**

## JACKING

**❋❋ WARNING:**

**The jack supplied with the vehicle should only be used for changing a tire or placing jackstands under the frame. Never work under the vehicle or start the engine while this jack is being used as the only means of support.**

The vehicle should be on level ground. Place the shift lever in Park, and block the wheel diagonally opposite the wheel being changed. Set the parking brake.

Remove the spare tire and jack from stowage. Remove the wheel cover and trim ring (if so equipped) with the tapered end of the wheel bolt wrench by inserting and twisting the handle and then prying against the back of the wheel cover. Loosen the wheel bolts about 1/4-to-1/2 turn each.

Place the scissors-type jack under the side of the vehicle and adjust the jack height until it fits in the notch in the vertical rocker panel flange nearest the wheel to be changed. There is a front and rear jacking point on each side of the vehicle (see illustration).

Turn the jack handle clockwise until the tire clears the ground. Remove the wheel bolts and pull the wheel off, then install the spare.

Install the wheel bolts and tighten them snugly. Don't attempt to tighten them completely until the vehicle is lowered or it could slip off the jack. Turn the jack handle counterclockwise to lower the vehicle. Remove the jack and tighten the wheel bolts in a diagonal pattern.

Install the cover (and trim ring, if used) and be sure it's snapped into place all the way around.

Stow the tire, jack and wrench. Unblock the wheels.

## TOWING

The manufacturer states that the only safe way to tow these vehicles is with a flatbed-type car carrier. Other methods could cause damage to the drivetrain.

**Place the jack so it engages the flange (between the two notches) rocker panel nearest the wheel to be raised**

## Automotive chemicals and lubricants

A number of automotive chemicals and lubricants are available for use during vehicle maintenance and repair. They include a wide variety of products ranging from cleaning solvents and degreasers to lubricants and protective sprays for rubber, plastic and vinyl.

## CLEANERS

*Carburetor cleaner and choke cleaner* is a strong solvent for gum, varnish and carbon. Most carburetor cleaners leave a dry-type lubricant film which will not harden or gum up. Because of this film it is not recommended for use on electrical components.

*Brake system cleaner* is used to remove brake dust, grease and brake fluid from the brake system, where clean surfaces are absolutely necessary. It leaves no residue and often eliminates brake squeal caused by contaminants.

*Electrical cleaner* removes oxidation, corrosion and carbon deposits from electrical contacts, restoring full current flow. It can also be used to clean spark plugs, carburetor jets, voltage regulators and other parts where an oil-free surface is desired.

*Demoisturants* remove water and moisture from electrical components such as alternators, voltage regulators, electrical connectors and fuse blocks. They are non-conductive and non-corrosive.

*Degreasers* are heavy-duty solvents used to remove grease from the outside of the engine and from chassis components. They can be sprayed or brushed on and, depending on the type, are rinsed off either with water or solvent.

## LUBRICANTS

*Motor oil* is the lubricant formulated for use in engines. It normally contains a wide variety of additives to prevent corrosion and reduce foaming and wear. Motor oil comes in various weights (viscosity ratings) from 0 to 50. The recommended weight of the oil depends on the season, temperature and the demands on the engine. Light oil is used in cold climates and under light load conditions. Heavy oil is used in hot climates and where high loads are encountered. Multi-viscosity oils are designed to have characteristics of both light and heavy oils and are available in a number of weights from 5W-20 to 20W-50.

*Gear oil* is designed to be used in differentials, manual transmissions and other areas where high-temperature lubrication is required.

*Chassis and wheel bearing grease* is a heavy grease used where increased loads and friction are encountered, such as for wheel bearings, ball-joints, tie-rod ends and universal joints.

*High-temperature wheel bearing grease* is designed to withstand the extreme temperatures encountered by wheel bearings in disc brake equipped vehicles. It usually contains molybdenum disulfide (moly), which is a dry-type lubricant.

*White grease* is a heavy grease for metal-to-metal applications where water is a problem. White grease stays soft under both low and high temperatures (usually from -100 to +190-degrees F), and will not wash off or dilute in the presence of water.

*Assembly lube* is a special extreme pressure lubricant, usually containing moly, used to lubricate high-load parts (such as main and rod bearings and cam lobes) for initial start-up of a new engine. The assembly lube lubricates the parts without being squeezed out or washed away until the engine oiling system begins to function.

*Silicone lubricants* are used to protect rubber, plastic, vinyl and nylon parts.

*Graphite lubricants* are used where oils cannot be used due to contamination problems, such as in locks. The dry graphite will lubricate metal parts while remaining uncontaminated by dirt, water, oil or acids. It is electrically conductive and will not foul electrical contacts in locks such as the ignition switch.

*Moly penetrants* loosen and lubricate frozen, rusted and corroded fasteners and prevent future rusting or freezing.

*Heat-sink grease* is a special electrically non-conductive grease that is used for mounting electronic ignition modules where it is essential that heat is transferred away from the module.

## SEALANTS

*RTV sealant* is one of the most widely used gasket compounds. Made from silicone, RTV is air curing, it seals, bonds, waterproofs, fills surface irregularities, remains flexible, doesn't shrink, is relatively easy to remove, and is used as a supplementary sealer with almost all low and medium temperature gaskets.

*Anaerobic sealant* is much like RTV in that it can be used either to seal gaskets or to form gaskets by itself. It remains flexible, is solvent resistant and fills surface imperfections. The difference between an anaerobic sealant and an RTV-type sealant is in the curing. RTV cures when exposed to air, while an anaerobic sealant cures only in the absence of air. This means that an anaerobic sealant cures only after the assembly of parts, sealing them together.

*Thread and pipe sealant* is used for sealing hydraulic and pneumatic fittings and vacuum lines. It is usually made from a Teflon compound, and comes in a spray, a paint-on liquid and as a wrap-around tape.

## CHEMICALS

*Anti-seize compound* prevents seizing, galling, cold welding, rust and corrosion in fasteners. High-temperature anti-seize, usually made with copper and graphite lubricants, is used for exhaust system and exhaust manifold bolts.

*Anaerobic locking compounds* are used to keep fasteners from vibrating or working loose and cure only after installation, in the absence of air. Medium strength locking compound is used for small nuts, bolts and screws that may be removed later. High-strength locking compound is for large nuts, bolts and studs which aren't removed on a regular basis.

*Oil additives* range from viscosity index improvers to chemical treatments that claim to reduce internal engine friction. It should be noted that most oil manufacturers caution against using additives with their oils.

*Gas additives* perform several functions, depending on their chemical makeup. They usually contain solvents that help dissolve gum and varnish that build up on carburetor, fuel injection and intake parts. They also serve to break down carbon deposits that form on the inside surfaces of the combustion chambers. Some additives contain upper cylinder lubricants for valves and piston rings, and others contain chemicals to remove condensation from the gas tank.

## MISCELLANEOUS

*Brake fluid* is specially formulated hydraulic fluid that can withstand the heat and pressure encountered in brake systems. Care must be taken so this fluid does not come in contact with painted surfaces or plastics. An opened container should always be resealed to prevent contamination by water or dirt.

*Weatherstrip adhesive* is used to bond weatherstripping around doors, windows and trunk lids. It is sometimes used to attach trim pieces.

*Undercoating* is a petroleum-based, tar-like substance that is designed to protect metal surfaces on the underside of the vehicle from corrosion. It also acts as a sound-deadening agent by insulating the bottom of the vehicle.

*Waxes and polishes* are used to help protect painted and plated surfaces from the weather. Different types of paint may require the use of different types of wax and polish. Some polishes utilize a chemical or abrasive cleaner to help remove the top layer of oxidized (dull) paint on older vehicles. In recent years many non-wax polishes that contain a wide variety of chemicals such as polymers and silicones have been introduced. These non-wax polishes are usually easier to apply and last longer than conventional waxes and polishes.

## CONVERSION FACTORS

### LENGTH (distance)

| | | | | | |
|---|---|---|---|---|---|
| Inches (in) | X 25.4 | = Millimeters (mm) | X 0.0394 | = Inches (in) |
| Feet (ft) | X 0.305 | = Meters (m) | X 3.281 | = Feet (ft) |
| Miles | X 1.609 | = Kilometers (km) | X 0.621 | = Miles |

### VOLUME (capacity)

| | | | | |
|---|---|---|---|---|
| Cubic inches (cu in; In³) | X 16.387 | = Cubic centimeters (cc; cm³) | X 0.061 | = Cubic inches (cu in; in³) |
| Imperial pints (Imp pt) | X 0.568 | = Liters (l) | X 1.76 | = Imperial pints (Imp pt) |
| Imperial quarts (Imp qt) | X 1.137 | = Liters (l) | X 0.88 | = Imperial quarts (Imp qt) |
| Imperial quarts (Imp qt) | X 1.201 | = US quarts (US qt) | X 0.833 | = Imperial quarts (Imp qt) |
| US quarts (US qt) | X 0.946 | = Liters (l) | X 1.057 | = US quarts (US qt) |
| Imperial gallons (Imp gal) | X 4.546 | = Liters (l) | X 0.22 | = Imperial gallons (Imp gal) |
| Imperial gallons (Imp gal) | X 1.201 | = US gallons (US gal) | X 0.833 | = Imperial gallons (Imp gal) |
| US gallons (US gal) | X 3.785 | = Liters (l) | X 0.264 | = US gallons (US gal) |

### MASS (weight)

| | | | | |
|---|---|---|---|---|
| Ounces (oz) | X 28.35 | = Grams (g) | X 0.035 | = Ounces (oz) |
| Pounds (lb) | X 0.454 | = Kilograms (kg) | X 2.205 | = Pounds (lb) |

### FORCE

| | | | | |
|---|---|---|---|---|
| Ounces-force (ozf; oz) | X 0.278 | = Newtons (N) | X 3.6 | = Ounces-force (ozf; oz) |
| Pounds-force (lbf; lb) | X 4.448 | = Newtons (N) | X 0.225 | = Pounds-force (lbf; lb) |
| Newtons (N) | X 0.1 | = Kilograms-force (kgf; kg) | X 9.81 | = Newtons (N) |

### PRESSURE

| | | | | |
|---|---|---|---|---|
| Pounds-force per square inch (psi; lbf/in²; lb/in²) | X 0.070 | = Kilograms-force per square centimeter (kgf/cm²; kg/cm²) | X 14.223 | = Pounds-force per square inch (psi; lbf/in²; lb/in²) |
| Pounds-force per square inch (psi; lbf/in²; lb/in²) | X 0.068 | = Atmospheres (atm) | X 14.696 | = Pounds-force per square inch (psi; lbf/in²; lb/in²) |
| Pounds-force per square inch (psi; lbf/in²; lb/in²) | X 0.069 | = Bars | X 14.5 | = Pounds-force per square inch (psi; lbf/in²; lb/in²) |
| Pounds-force per square inch (psi; lbf/in²; lb/in²) | X 6.895 | = Kilopascals (kPa) | X 0.145 | = Pounds-force per square inch (psi; lbf/in²; lb/in²) |
| Kilopascals (kPa) | X 0.01 | = Kilograms-force per square centimeter (kgf/cm²; kg/cm²) | X 98.1 | = Kilopascals (kPa) |

### TORQUE (moment of force)

| | | | | |
|---|---|---|---|---|
| Pounds-force inches (lbf in; lb in) | X 1.152 | = Kilograms-force centimeter (kgf cm; kg cm) | X 0.868 | = Pounds-force inches (lbf in; lb in) |
| Pounds-force inches (lbf in; lb in) | X 0.113 | = Newton meters (Nm) | X 8.85 | = Pounds-force inches (lbf in; lb in) |
| Pounds-force inches (lbf in; lb in) | X 0.083 | = Pounds-force feet (lbf ft; lb ft) | X 12 | = Pounds-force inches (lbf in; lb in) |
| Pounds-force feet (lbf ft; lb ft) | X 0.138 | = Kilograms-force meters (kgf m; kg m) | X 7.233 | = Pounds-force feet (lbf ft; lb ft) |
| Pounds-force feet (lbf ft; lb ft) | X 1.356 | = Newton meters (Nm) | X 0.738 | = Pounds-force feet (lbf ft; lb ft) |
| Newton meters (Nm) | X 0.102 | = Kilograms-force meters (kgf m; kg m) | X 9.804 | = Newton meters (Nm) |

### VACUUM

| | | | | |
|---|---|---|---|---|
| Inches mercury (in. Hg) | X 3.377 | = Kilopascals (kPa) | X 0.2961 | = Inches mercury |
| Inches mercury (in. Hg) | X 25.4 | = Millimeters mercury (mm Hg) | X 0.0394 | = Inches mercury |

### POWER

| | | | | |
|---|---|---|---|---|
| Horsepower (hp) | X 745.7 | = Watts (W) | X 0.0013 | = Horsepower (hp) |

### VELOCITY (speed)

| | | | | |
|---|---|---|---|---|
| Miles per hour (miles/hr; mph) | X 1.609 | = Kilometers per hour (km/hr; kph) | X 0.621 | = Miles per hour (miles/hr; mph) |

### FUEL CONSUMPTION *

| | | | | |
|---|---|---|---|---|
| Miles per gallon, Imperial (mpg) | X 0.354 | = Kilometers per liter (km/l) | X 2.825 | = Miles per gallon, Imperial (mpg) |
| Miles per gallon, US (mpg) | X 0.425 | = Kilometers per liter (km/l) | X 2.352 | = Miles per gallon, US (mpg) |

### TEMPERATURE

Degrees Fahrenheit = (°C x 1.8) + 32      Degrees Celsius (Degrees Centigrade; °C) = (°F - 32) x 0.56

*It is common practice to convert from miles per gallon (mpg) to liters/100 kilometers (l/100km),
where mpg (Imperial) x l/100 km = 282 and mpg (US) x l/100 km = 235

## FRACTION/DECIMAL/MILLIMETER EQUIVALENTS

### DECIMALS TO MILLIMETERS

| Decimal | mm | Decimal | mm |
|---|---|---|---|
| 0.001 | 0.0254 | 0.500 | 12.7000 |
| 0.002 | 0.0508 | 0.510 | 12.9540 |
| 0.003 | 0.0762 | 0.520 | 13.2080 |
| 0.004 | 0.1016 | 0.530 | 13.4620 |
| 0.005 | 0.1270 | 0.540 | 13.7160 |
| 0.006 | 0.1524 | 0.550 | 13.9700 |
| 0.007 | 0.1778 | 0.560 | 14.2240 |
| 0.008 | 0.2032 | 0.570 | 14.4780 |
| 0.009 | 0.2286 | 0.580 | 14.7320 |
| | | 0.590 | 14.9860 |
| 0.010 | 0.2540 | | |
| 0.020 | 0.5080 | | |
| 0.030 | 0.7620 | | |
| 0.040 | 1.0160 | 0.600 | 15.2400 |
| 0.050 | 1.2700 | 0.610 | 15.4940 |
| 0.060 | 1.5240 | 0.620 | 15.7480 |
| 0.070 | 1.7780 | 0.630 | 16.0020 |
| 0.080 | 2.0320 | 0.640 | 16.2560 |
| 0.090 | 2.2860 | 0.650 | 16.5100 |
| | | 0.660 | 16.7640 |
| 0.100 | 2.5400 | 0.670 | 17.0180 |
| 0.110 | 2.7940 | 0.680 | 17.2720 |
| 0.120 | 3.0480 | 0.690 | 17.5260 |
| 0.130 | 3.3020 | | |
| 0.140 | 3.5560 | | |
| 0.150 | 3.8100 | | |
| 0.160 | 4.0640 | 0.700 | 17.7800 |
| 0.170 | 4.3180 | 0.710 | 18.0340 |
| 0.180 | 4.5720 | 0.720 | 18.2880 |
| 0.190 | 4.8260 | 0.730 | 18.5420 |
| | | 0.740 | 18.7960 |
| 0.200 | 5.0800 | 0.750 | 19.0500 |
| 0.210 | 5.3340 | 0.760 | 19.3040 |
| 0.220 | 5.5880 | 0.770 | 19.5580 |
| 0.230 | 5.8420 | 0.780 | 19.8120 |
| 0.240 | 6.0960 | 0.790 | 20.0000 |
| 0.250 | 6.3500 | | |
| 0.260 | 6.6040 | | |
| 0.270 | 6.8580 | 0.800 | 20.3200 |
| 0.280 | 7.1120 | 0.810 | 20.5740 |
| 0.290 | 7.3660 | 0.820 | 20.8280 |
| | | 0.830 | 21.0820 |
| 0.300 | 7.6200 | 0.840 | 21.3360 |
| 0.310 | 7.8740 | 0.850 | 21.5900 |
| 0.320 | 8.1280 | 0.860 | 21.8440 |
| 0.330 | 8.3820 | 0.870 | 22.0980 |
| 0.340 | 8.6360 | 0.880 | 22.3520 |
| 0.350 | 8.8900 | 0.890 | 22.6060 |
| 0.360 | 9.1440 | | |
| 0.370 | 9.3980 | | |
| 0.380 | 9.6520 | | |
| 0.390 | 9.9060 | 0.900 | 22.8600 |
| 0.400 | 10.1600 | 0.910 | 23.1140 |
| 0.410 | 10.4140 | 0.920 | 23.3680 |
| 0.420 | 10.6680 | 0.930 | 23.6220 |
| 0.430 | 10.9220 | 0.940 | 23.8760 |
| 0.440 | 11.1760 | 0.950 | 24.1300 |
| 0.450 | 11.4300 | 0.960 | 24.3840 |
| 0.460 | 11.6840 | 0.970 | 24.6380 |
| 0.470 | 11.9380 | 0.980 | 24.8920 |
| 0.480 | 12.1920 | 0.990 | 25.1460 |
| 0.490 | 12.4460 | 1.000 | 25.4000 |

### FRACTIONS TO DECIMALS TO MILLIMETERS

| Fraction | Decimal | mm | Fraction | Decimal | mm |
|---|---|---|---|---|---|
| 1/64 | 0.0156 | 0.3969 | 33/64 | 0.5156 | 13.0969 |
| 1/32 | 0.0312 | 0.7938 | 17/32 | 0.5312 | 13.4938 |
| 3/64 | 0.0469 | 1.1906 | 35/64 | 0.5469 | 13.8906 |
| 1/16 | 0.0625 | 1.5875 | 9/16 | 0.5625 | 14.2875 |
| 5/64 | 0.0781 | 1.9844 | 37/64 | 0.5781 | 14.6844 |
| 3/32 | 0.0938 | 2.3812 | 19/32 | 0.5938 | 15.0812 |
| 7/64 | 0.1094 | 2.7781 | 39/64 | 0.6094 | 15.4781 |
| 1/8 | 0.1250 | 3.1750 | 5/8 | 0.6250 | 15.8750 |
| 9/64 | 0.1406 | 3.5719 | 41/64 | 0.6406 | 16.2719 |
| 5/32 | 0.1562 | 3.9688 | 21/32 | 0.6562 | 16.6688 |
| 11/64 | 0.1719 | 4.3656 | 43/64 | 0.6719 | 17.0656 |
| 3/16 | 0.1875 | 4.7625 | 11/16 | 0.6875 | 17.4625 |
| 13/64 | 0.2031 | 5.1594 | 45/64 | 0.7031 | 17.8594 |
| 7/32 | 0.2188 | 5.5562 | 23/32 | 0.7188 | 18.2562 |
| 15/64 | 0.2344 | 5.9531 | 47/64 | 0.7344 | 18.6531 |
| 1/4 | 0.2500 | 6.3500 | 3/4 | 0.7500 | 19.0500 |
| 17/64 | 0.2656 | 6.7469 | 49/64 | 0.7656 | 19.4469 |
| 9/32 | 0.2812 | 7.1438 | 25/32 | 0.7812 | 19.8438 |
| 19/64 | 0.2969 | 7.5406 | 51/64 | 0.7969 | 20.2406 |
| 5/16 | 0.3125 | 7.9375 | 13/16 | 0.8125 | 20.6375 |
| 21/64 | 0.3281 | 8.3344 | 53/64 | 0.8281 | 21.0344 |
| 11/32 | 0.3438 | 8.7312 | 27/32 | 0.8438 | 21.4312 |
| 23/64 | 0.3594 | 9.1281 | 55/64 | 0.8594 | 21.8281 |
| 3/8 | 0.3750 | 9.5250 | 7/8 | 0.8750 | 22.2250 |
| 25/64 | 0.3906 | 9.9219 | 57/64 | 0.8906 | 22.6219 |
| 13/32 | 0.4062 | 10.3188 | 29/32 | 0.9062 | 23.0188 |
| 27/64 | 0.4219 | 10.7156 | 59/64 | 0.9219 | 23.4156 |
| 7/16 | 0.4375 | 11.1125 | 15/16 | 0.9375 | 23.8125 |
| 29/64 | 0.4531 | 11.5094 | 61/64 | 0.9531 | 24.2094 |
| 15/32 | 0.4688 | 11.9062 | 31/32 | 0.9688 | 24.6062 |
| 31/64 | 0.4844 | 12.3031 | 63/64 | 0.9844 | 25.0031 |
| 1/2 | 0.5000 | 12.7000 | 1 | 1.0000 | 25.4000 |

## Safety first!

Regardless of how enthusiastic you may be about getting on with the job at hand, take the time to ensure that your safety is not jeopardized. A moment's lack of attention can result in an accident, as can failure to observe certain simple safety precautions. The possibility of an accident will always exist, and the following points should not be considered a comprehensive list of all dangers. Rather, they are intended to make you aware of the risks and to encourage a safety conscious approach to all work you carry out on your vehicle.

## ESSENTIAL DOS AND DON'TS

**DON'T** rely on a jack when working under the vehicle. Always use approved jackstands to support the weight of the vehicle and place them under the recommended lift or support points.

**DON'T** attempt to loosen extremely tight fasteners (i.e. wheel lug nuts) while the vehicle is on a jack - it may fall.

**DON'T** start the engine without first making sure that the transmission is in Neutral (or Park where applicable) and the parking brake is set.

**DON'T** remove the radiator cap from a hot cooling system - let it cool or cover it with a cloth and release the pressure gradually.

**DON'T** attempt to drain the engine oil until you are sure it has cooled to the point that it will not burn you.

**DON'T** touch any part of the engine or exhaust system until it has cooled sufficiently to avoid burns.

**DON'T** siphon toxic liquids such as gasoline, antifreeze and brake fluid by mouth, or allow them to remain on your skin.

**DON'T** inhale brake lining dust - it is potentially hazardous (see Asbestos below).

**DON'T** allow spilled oil or grease to remain on the floor - wipe it up before someone slips on it.

**DON'T** use loose fitting wrenches or other tools which may slip and cause injury.

**DON'T** push on wrenches when loosening or tightening nuts or bolts. Always try to pull the wrench toward you. If the situation calls for pushing the wrench away, push with an open hand to avoid scraped knuckles if the wrench should slip.

**DON'T** attempt to lift a heavy component alone - get someone to help you.

**DON'T** rush or take unsafe shortcuts to finish a job.

**DON'T** allow children or animals in or around the vehicle while you are working on it.

**DO** wear eye protection when using power tools such as a drill, sander, bench grinder, etc. and when working under a vehicle.

**DO** keep loose clothing and long hair well out of the way of moving parts.

**DO** make sure that any hoist used has a safe working load rating adequate for the job.

**DO** get someone to check on you periodically when working alone on a vehicle.

**DO** carry out work in a logical sequence and make sure that everything is correctly assembled and tightened.

**DO** keep chemicals and fluids tightly capped and out of the reach of children and pets.

**DO** remember that your vehicle's safety affects that of yourself and others. If in doubt on any point, get professional advice.

## STEERING, SUSPENSION AND BRAKES

These systems are essential to driving safety, so make sure you have a qualified shop or individual check your work. Also, compressed suspension springs can cause injury if released suddenly - be sure to use a spring compressor.

## AIRBAGS

Airbags are explosive devices that can CAUSE injury if they deploy while you're working on the vehicle. Follow the manufacturer's instructions to disable the airbag whenever you're working in the vicinity of airbag components.

## ASBESTOS

Certain friction, insulating, sealing, and other products - such as brake linings, brake bands, clutch linings, torque converters, gaskets, etc. - may contain asbestos or other hazardous friction material. Extreme care must be taken to avoid inhalation of dust from such products, since it is hazardous to health. If in doubt, assume that they do contain asbestos.

## FIRE

Remember at all times that gasoline is highly flammable. Never smoke or have any kind of open flame around when working on a vehicle. But the risk does not end there. A spark caused by an electrical short circuit, by two metal surfaces contacting each other, or even by static electricity built up in your body under certain conditions, can ignite gasoline vapors, which in a confined space are highly explosive. Do not, under any circumstances, use gasoline for cleaning parts. Use an approved safety solvent.

Always disconnect the battery ground (-) cable at the battery before working on any part of the fuel system or electrical system. Never risk spilling fuel on a hot engine or exhaust component. It is strongly recommended that a fire extinguisher suitable for use on fuel and electrical fires be kept handy in the garage or workshop at all times. Never try to extinguish a fuel or electrical fire with water.

## FUMES

Certain fumes are highly toxic and can quickly cause unconsciousness and even death if inhaled to any extent. Gasoline vapor falls into this category, as do the vapors from some cleaning solvents. Any draining or pouring of such volatile fluids should be done in a well ventilated area.

When using cleaning fluids and solvents, read the instructions on the container carefully. Never use materials from unmarked containers.

Never run the engine in an enclosed space, such as a garage. Exhaust fumes contain carbon monoxide, which is extremely poisonous. If you need to run the engine, always do so in the open air, or at least have the rear of the vehicle outside the work area.

## THE BATTERY

Never create a spark or allow a bare light bulb near a battery. They normally give off a certain amount of hydrogen gas, which is highly explosive.

Always disconnect the battery ground (-) cable at the battery before working on the fuel or electrical systems.

If possible, loosen the filler caps or cover when charging the battery from an external source (this does not apply to sealed or maintenance-free batteries). Do not charge at an excessive rate or the battery may burst.

Take care when adding water to a non maintenance-free battery and when carrying a battery. The electrolyte, even when diluted, is very corrosive and should not be allowed to contact clothing or skin.

Always wear eye protection when cleaning the battery to prevent the caustic deposits from entering your eyes.

## HOUSEHOLD CURRENT

When using an electric power tool, inspection light, etc., which operates on household current, always make sure that the tool is correctly connected to its plug and that, where necessary, it is properly grounded. Do not use such items in damp conditions and, again, do not create a spark or apply excessive heat in the vicinity of fuel or fuel vapor.

## SECONDARY IGNITION SYSTEM VOLTAGE

A severe electric shock can result from touching certain parts of the ignition system (such as the spark plug wires) when the engine is running or being cranked, particularly if components are damp or the insulation is defective. In the case of an electronic ignition system, the secondary system voltage is much higher and could prove fatal.

## HYDROFLUORIC ACID

This extremely corrosive acid is formed when certain types of synthetic rubber, found in some O-rings, oil seals, fuel hoses, etc. are exposed to temperatures above 750-degrees F (400-degrees C). The rubber changes into a charred or sticky substance containing the acid. *Once formed, the acid remains dangerous for years. If it gets onto the skin, it may be necessary to amputate the limb concerned.*

When dealing with a vehicle which has suffered a fire, or with components salvaged from such a vehicle, wear protective gloves and discard them after use.

## Troubleshooting

## CONTENTS

This Section provides an easy reference guide to the more common problems which may occur during the operation of your vehicle. These problems and their possible causes are grouped under headings denoting various components or systems, such as Engine, Cooling system, etc. They also refer you to the Chapter and/or Section which deals with the problem.

Remember that successful troubleshooting is not a mysterious art practiced only by professional mechanics. It is simply the result of the right knowledge combined with an intelligent, systematic approach to the problem. Always work by a process of elimination, starting with the simplest solution and working through to the most complex - and never overlook the obvious. Anyone can run the gas tank dry or leave the lights on overnight, so don't assume that you are exempt from such oversights.

Finally, always establish a clear idea of why a problem has occurred and take steps to ensure that it doesn't happen again. If the electrical system fails because of a poor connection, check the other connections in the system to make sure that they don't fail as well. If a particular fuse continues to blow, find out why - don't just replace one fuse after another. Remember, failure of a small component can often be indicative of potential failure or incorrect functioning of a more important component or system.

## ENGINE

### 1    Engine will not rotate when attempting to start

1    Battery terminal connections loose or corroded. Check the cable terminals at the battery; tighten cable clamp and/or clean off corrosion as necessary (see Chapter 1).

2    Battery discharged or faulty. If the cable ends are clean and tight on the battery posts, turn the key to the On position and switch on the headlights or windshield wipers. If they won't run, the battery is discharged.

3    Automatic transmission not engaged in Park (P) or Neutral (N).

4    Broken, loose or disconnected wires in the starting circuit. Inspect all wires and connectors at the battery, starter solenoid and ignition switch (on steering column).

5    Starter motor pinion jammed in flywheel/driveplate ring gear. Remove the starter (Chapter 5) and inspect the pinion and ring gear (Chapter 2).

6    Starter solenoid faulty (Chapter 5).

7    Starter motor faulty (Chapter 5).

8    Ignition switch faulty (Chapter 12).

9    Engine seized. Try to turn the crankshaft with a large socket and breaker bar on the pulley bolt.

10    Starter relay faulty (Chapter 4).

### 2    Engine rotates but will not start

1    Fuel tank empty.

2    Battery discharged (engine rotates slowly).

3    Battery terminal connections loose or corroded.

4    Fuel not reaching fuel injectors. Check for clogged fuel filter or lines and defective fuel pump. Also make sure the tank vent lines aren't clogged (Chapter 4).

5    Low cylinder compression. Check as described in Chapter 2.

6    Water in fuel. Drain tank and fill with new fuel.

7    Defective ignition coil(s) (Chapter 5).

8    Dirty or clogged fuel injector(s) (Chapter 4).

9    Wet or damaged ignition components (Chapters 1 and 5).

10    Worn, faulty or incorrectly gapped spark plugs (Chapter 1).

11    Broken, loose or disconnected wires in the starting circuit (see previous Section).

12    Broken, loose or disconnected wires at the ignition coil or faulty coil (Chapter 5).

13    Timing chain failure or wear affecting valve timing (Chapter 2).

14    Fuel injection or engine control systems failure (Chapters 4 and 6).

15    Defective MAF sensor (Chapter 6)

### 3    Starter motor operates without turning engine

1    Starter pinion sticking. Remove the starter (Chapter 5) and inspect.

2    Starter pinion or flywheel/driveplate teeth worn or broken. Remove the inspection cover and inspect.

### 4    Engine hard to start when cold

1    Battery discharged or low. Check as described in Chapter 1.

2    Fuel not reaching the fuel injectors. Check the fuel filter, lines and fuel pump (Chapters 1 and 4).

3    Defective spark plugs (Chapter 1).

4    Defective engine coolant temperature sensor (Chapter 6).

5    Fuel injection or engine control systems malfunction (Chapters 4 and 6).

### 5    Engine hard to start when hot

1    Air filter dirty (Chapter 1).

2    Fuel not reaching the fuel injection (see Section 4). Check for a vapor lock situation, brought about by clogged fuel tank vent lines.

3    Bad engine ground connection.

4    Fuel injection or engine control systems malfunction (Chapters 4 and 6).

### 6    Starter motor noisy or engages roughly

1    Pinion or driveplate teeth worn or broken. Remove the inspection cover on the left side of the engine and inspect.

2    Starter motor mounting bolts loose or missing.

### 7    Engine starts but stops immediately

1    Loose or damaged wire harness connections at coil or alternator.

2    Intake manifold vacuum leaks. Make sure all mounting bolts/nuts are tight and all vacuum hoses connected to the manifold are attached properly and in good condition.

3    Insufficient fuel pressure (see Chapter 4).

4    Fuel injection or engine control systems malfunction (Chapters 4 and 6).

## 8  Engine 'lopes' while idling or idles erratically

1  Vacuum leaks. Check mounting bolts at the intake manifold for tightness. Make sure that all vacuum hoses are connected and in good condition. Use a stethoscope or a length of fuel hose held against your ear to listen for vacuum leaks while the engine is running. A hissing sound will be heard. A soapy water solution will also detect leaks. Check the intake manifold gasket surfaces.
2  Leaking EGR valve or plugged PCV valve (see Chapter 6).
3  Air filter clogged (Chapter 1).
4  Fuel pump not delivering sufficient fuel (Chapter 4).
5  Leaking head gasket. Perform a cylinder compression check (Chapter 2).
6  Timing chain worn (Chapter 2).
7  Camshaft lobes worn (Chapter 2).
8  Valves burned or otherwise leaking (Chapter 2).
9  Ignition system not operating properly (Chapters 1 and 5).
10  Fuel injection or engine control systems malfunction (Chapters 4 and 6).

## 9  Engine misses at idle speed

1  Spark plugs faulty or not gapped properly (Chapter 1).
2  Faulty spark plug wires (Chapter 1).
3  Short circuits in ignition, coil or spark plug wires.
4  Sticking or faulty emissions systems (see Chapter 6).
5  Clogged fuel filter and/or foreign matter in fuel.
6  Vacuum leaks at intake manifold or hose connections. Check as described in Section 8.
7  Low or uneven cylinder compression. Check as described in Chapter 2.
8  Fuel injection or engine control systems malfunction (Chapters 4 and 6).

## 10  Excessively high idle speed

1  Vacuum leaks at intake manifold or hose connections. Check as described in Section 8.
2  Fuel injection or engine control systems malfunction (Chapters 4 and 6).

## 11  Battery will not hold a charge

1  Alternator drivebelt defective or not adjusted properly (Chapter 1).
2  Battery cables loose or corroded (Chapter 1).
3  Alternator not charging properly (Chapter 5).
4  Loose, broken or faulty wires in the charging circuit (Chapter 5).
5  Short circuit causing a continuous drain on the battery.
6  Battery defective internally.

## 12  Alternator light stays on

1  Fault in alternator or charging circuit (Chapter 5).
2  Alternator drivebelt defective or not properly adjusted (Chapter 1).

## 13  Alternator light fails to come on when key is turned on

1  Faulty bulb (Chapter 12).

2  Defective alternator (Chapter 5).
3  Fault in the printed circuit, dash wiring or bulb holder (Chapter 12).

## 14  Engine misses throughout driving speed range

1  Fuel filter clogged and/or impurities in the fuel system.
2  Faulty or incorrectly gapped spark plugs (Chapter 1).
3  Defective spark plug wires (Chapter 1).
4  Emissions system components faulty (Chapter 6).
5  Low or uneven cylinder compression pressures. Check as described in Chapter 2.
6  Weak or faulty ignition coil(s) (Chapter 5).
7  Weak or faulty ignition system (Chapter 5).
8  Vacuum leaks at intake manifold or vacuum hoses (see Section 8).
9  Dirty or clogged fuel injector(s) (Chapter 4).
10  Leaky EGR valve (Chapter 6).
11  Fuel injection or engine control systems malfunction (Chapters 4 and 6).

## 15  Hesitation or stumble during acceleration

1  Ignition system not operating properly (Chapter 5).
2  Dirty or clogged fuel injector(s) (Chapter 4).
3  Low fuel pressure. Check for proper operation of the fuel pump and for restrictions in the fuel filter and lines (Chapter 4).
4  Fuel injection or engine control systems malfunction (Chapters 4 and 6).

## 16  Engine stalls

1  Fuel filter clogged and/or water and impurities in the fuel system (Chapter 1).
2  Emissions system components faulty (Chapter 6).
3  Faulty or incorrectly gapped spark plugs (Chapter 1).
4  Vacuum leak at the intake manifold or vacuum hoses. Check as described in Section 8.
5  Fuel injection or engine control systems malfunction (Chapters 4 and 6).

## 17  Engine lacks power

1  Faulty or incorrectly gapped spark plugs (Chapter 1).
2  Air filter dirty (Chapter 1).
3  Faulty ignition coil(s) (Chapter 5).
4  Brakes binding (Chapters 1 and 9).
5  Automatic transmission fluid level incorrect, causing slippage (Chapter 1).
6  Fuel filter clogged and/or impurities in the fuel system (Chapter 4).
7  EGR system not functioning properly (Chapter 6).
8  Use of sub-standard fuel. Fill tank with proper octane fuel.
9  Low or uneven cylinder compression pressures. Check as described in Chapter 2.
10  Vacuum leak at intake manifold or vacuum hoses (check as described in Section 8).
11  Dirty or clogged fuel injector(s) (Chapters 1 and 4).
12  Fuel injection or engine control systems malfunction (Chapters 4 and 6).
13  Restricted exhaust system (Chapter 4).

## 18  Engine backfires

1   EGR system not functioning properly (Chapter 6).
2   Vacuum leak (refer to Section 8).
3   Damaged valve springs or sticking valves (Chapter 2).
4   Vacuum leak at the intake manifold or vacuum hoses (see Section 8).

## 19  Engine surges while holding accelerator steady

1   Vacuum leak at the intake manifold or vacuum hoses (see Section 8).
2   Restricted air filter (Chapter 1).
3   Fuel pump or pressure regulator defective (Chapter 4).
4   Fuel injection or engine control systems malfunction (Chapters 4 and 6).

## 20  Pinging or knocking engine sounds when engine is under load

1   Incorrect grade of fuel. Fill tank with fuel of the proper octane rating.
2   Carbon build-up in combustion chambers. Remove cylinder head(s) and clean combustion chambers (Chapter 2).
3   Incorrect spark plugs (Chapter 1).
4   Fuel injection or engine control systems malfunction (Chapters 4 and 6).
5   Restricted exhaust system (Chapter 4).

## 21  Engine diesels (continues to run) after being turned off

1   Incorrect spark plug heat range (Chapter 1).
2   Vacuum leak at the intake manifold or vacuum hoses (see Section 8).
3   Carbon build-up in combustion chambers. Remove the cylinder head(s) and clean the combustion chambers (Chapter 2).
4   Valves sticking (Chapter 2).
5   EGR system not operating properly (Chapter 6).
6   Fuel injection or engine control systems malfunction (Chapters 4 and 6).
7   Check for causes of overheating (Section 27).

## 22  Low oil pressure

1   Improper grade of oil.
2   Oil pump worn or damaged (Chapter 2).
3   Engine overheating (refer to Section 27).
4   Clogged oil filter (Chapter 1).
5   Clogged oil strainer (Chapter 2).
6   Oil pressure gauge not working properly (Chapter 2).

## 23  Excessive oil consumption

1   Pistons and cylinders excessively worn (Chapter 2).
2   Piston rings not installed correctly on pistons (Chapter 2).
3   Worn or damaged piston rings (Chapter 2).
4   Intake and/or exhaust valve oil seals worn or damaged.
5   Worn valve stems or guides.
6   Worn or damaged valves/guides.
7   Faulty or incorrect PCV valve allowing too much crankcase airflow.

## 24  Excessive fuel consumption

1   Dirty or clogged air filter element (Chapter 1).
2   Low tire pressure or incorrect tire size (Chapter 10).
3   Inspect for binding brakes.
4   Fuel leakage. Check all connections, lines and components in the fuel system (Chapter 4).
5   Dirty or clogged fuel injectors (Chapter 4).
6   Fuel injection or engine control systems malfunction (Chapters 4 and 6).
7   Thermostat stuck open or not installed.
8   Improperly operating transmission.

## 25  Fuel odor

1   Fuel leakage. Check all connections, lines and components in the fuel system (Chapter 4).
2   Fuel tank overfilled. Fill only to automatic shut-off.
3   Charcoal canister filter in Evaporative Emissions Control system clogged (Chapter 1).
4   Vapor leaks from Evaporative Emissions Control system lines (Chapter 6).

## 26  Miscellaneous engine noises

1   A strong dull noise that becomes more rapid as the engine accelerates indicates worn or damaged crankshaft bearings or an unevenly worn crankshaft. To pinpoint the trouble spot, disconnect the electrical connector from one coil at a time and crank the engine over. If the noise stops, the cylinder with the removed plug wire or disconnected coil indicates the problem area. Replace the bearing and/or service or replace the crankshaft (Chapter 2).
2   A similar (yet slightly higher pitched) noise to the crankshaft knocking described in the previous paragraph, that becomes more rapid as the engine accelerates, indicates worn or damaged connecting rod bearings (Chapter 2). The procedure for locating the problem cylinder is the same as described in Paragraph 1.
3   An overlapping metallic noise that increases in intensity as the engine speed increases, yet diminishes as the engine warms up indicates abnormal piston and cylinder wear (Chapter 2). To locate the problem cylinder, use the procedure described in Paragraph 1.
4   A rapid clicking noise that becomes faster as the engine accelerates indicates a worn piston pin or piston pin hole. This sound will happen each time the piston hits the highest and lowest points in the stroke (Chapter 2). The procedure for locating the problem piston is described in Paragraph 1.
5   A metallic clicking noise coming from the water pump indicates worn or damaged water pump bearings or pump. Replace the water pump with a new one (Chapter 3).
6   A rapid tapping sound or clicking sound that becomes faster as the engine speed increases indicates "valve tapping." This can be identified by holding one end of a section of hose to your ear and placing the other end at different spots along the valve cover. The point where the sound is loudest indicates the problem valve. If the pushrod and rocker arm components are in good shape, you likely have a collapsed valve lifter. Changing the engine oil and adding a high viscosity oil treatment will sometimes cure a stuck lifter problem. If the problem persists, the lifters, pushrods and rocker arms must be removed for inspection (see Chapter 2).
7   A steady metallic rattling or rapping sound coming from the area of the timing chain cover indicates a worn, damaged or out-of-adjust-

ment timing chain. Service or replace the chain and related components (Chapter 2).

# COOLING SYSTEM

### 27  Overheating

1   Insufficient coolant in system (Chapter 1).
2   Drivebelt defective or not adjusted properly (Chapter 1).
3   Radiator core blocked or dirty and restricted (Chapter 3).
4   Thermostat faulty (Chapter 3).
5   Cooling fan not functioning properly (Chapter 3).
6   Expansion tank cap not maintaining proper pressure. Have cap pressure tested by gas station or repair shop.
7   Defective water pump (Chapter 3).
8   Improper grade of engine oil.
9   Inaccurate temperature gauge (Chapter 12).

### 28  Overcooling

1   Thermostat faulty (Chapter 3).
2   Inaccurate temperature gauge (Chapter 12).

### 29  External coolant leakage

1   Deteriorated or damaged hoses. Loose clamps at hose connections (Chapter 1).
2   Water pump seals defective. If this is the case, water will drip from the weep hole in the water pump body (Chapter 3).
3   Leakage from radiator core or header tank. This will require the radiator to be professionally repaired (see Chapter 3 for removal procedures).
4   Leakage from the expansion tank or cap.
5   Engine drain plugs or water jacket freeze plugs leaking (see Chapters 1 and 2).
6   Leak from coolant temperature switch (Chapter 3).
7   Leak from damaged gaskets or small cracks (Chapter 2).

### 30  Internal coolant leakage

→Note: Internal coolant leaks can usually be detected by examining the oil. Check the dipstick and the underside of the engine oil filler cap for water deposits and an oil consistency like that of a milkshake.

1   Leaking cylinder head gasket. Have the system pressure tested or remove the cylinder head (Chapter 2) and inspect.
2   Cracked cylinder bore or cylinder head. Dismantle engine and inspect (Chapter 2).

### 31  Abnormal coolant loss

1   Overfilled cooling system (Chapter 1).
2   Coolant boiling away due to overheating (see causes in Section 27).
3   Internal or external leakage (see Sections 29 and 30).
4   Faulty expansion tank cap. Have the cap pressure tested.
5   Cooling system being pressurized by engine compression. This could be due to a cracked head or block or leaking head gasket(s). Have

the system tested for the presence of combustion gas in the coolant at a shop. (Combustion leak detectors are also available at some auto parts stores.)

### 32  Poor coolant circulation

1   Inoperative water pump. A quick test is to pinch the top radiator hose closed with your hand while the engine is idling, then release it. You should feel a surge of
coolant if the pump is working properly (Chapter 3).
2   Restriction in cooling system. Drain, flush and refill the system (Chapter 1). If necessary, remove the radiator (Chapter 3) and have it reverse flushed or professionally cleaned.
3   Loose water pump drivebelt (Chapter 1).
4   Thermostat sticking (Chapter 3).
5   Insufficient coolant (Chapter 1).

### 33  Corrosion

1   Excessive impurities in the water. Soft, clean water is recommended. Distilled or rainwater is satisfactory.
2   Insufficient antifreeze solution (refer to Chapter 1 for the proper ratio of water to antifreeze).
3   Infrequent flushing and draining of system. Regular flushing of the cooling system should be carried out at the specified intervals as described in (Chapter 1).

# CLUTCH

→Note: All clutch service information is located in Chapter 8, unless otherwise noted.

### 34  Fails to release (pedal pressed to the floor - shift lever does not move freely in and out of Reverse)

1   Clutch plate warped, distorted or otherwise damaged.
2   Diaphragm spring fatigued. Remove clutch cover/pressure plate assembly and inspect.
3   Seized pilot bearing.

### 35  Clutch slips (engine speed increases with no increase in vehicle speed)

1   Worn or oil soaked clutch plate.
2   Clutch plate not broken in. It may take 30 or 40 normal starts for a new clutch to seat.

### 36  Grabbing (chattering) as clutch is engaged

1   Oil on clutch plate. Remove and inspect. Repair any leaks.
2   Worn or loose engine or transmission mounts. They may move slightly when clutch is released. Inspect mounts and bolts.
3   Worn splines on transmission input shaft. Remove clutch components and inspect.
4   Warped pressure plate or flywheel. Remove clutch components and inspect.

5   Diaphragm spring fatigued. Remove clutch cover/pressure plate assembly and inspect.
6   Clutch linings hardened or warped.
7   Clutch lining rivets loose.

### 37   Squeal or rumble with clutch engaged (pedal released)

1   Release bearing binding on transmission shaft. Remove clutch components and check bearing. Remove any burrs or nicks, clean and relubricate before reinstallation.
2   Clutch plate cracked.
3   Fatigued clutch plate torsion springs. Replace clutch plate.

### 38   Squeal or rumble with clutch disengaged (pedal depressed)

1   Worn or damaged release bearing.
2   Worn or broken pressure plate diaphragm fingers.
3   Defective pilot bearing.

### 39   Clutch pedal stays on floor when disengaged

Defective release system.

## MANUAL TRANSMISSION

➡Note: All manual transmission service information is located in Chapter 7A, unless otherwise noted.

### 40   Noisy in Neutral with engine running

1   Input shaft bearing worn.
2   Damaged main drive gear bearing.
3   Insufficient transmission oil (Chapter 1).
4   Transmission oil in poor condition. Drain and fill with proper grade oil. Check old oil for water and debris (Chapter 1).

### 41   Noisy in all gears

1   Any of the above causes, and/or:
2   Worn or damaged output gear bearings or shaft.

### 42   Noisy in one particular gear

1   Worn, damaged or chipped gear teeth.
2   Worn or damaged synchronizer.

### 43   Slips out of gear

1   Shift linkage binding.
2   Broken or loose input gear bearing retainer.
3   Worn linkage.
4   Damaged or worn check balls, fork rod ball grooves or check springs.
5   Worn mainshaft or countershaft bearings.

6   Excessive gear end play.
7   Worn synchronizers.
8   Chipped or worn gear teeth.

### 44   Oil leaks

1   Excessive amount of lubricant in transmission (see Chapter 1 for correct checking procedures). Drain lubricant as required.
2   Oil seal damaged.
3   To pinpoint a leak, first remove all built-up dirt and grime from the transmission. Degreasing agents and/or steam cleaning will achieve this. With the underside clean, drive the vehicle at low speeds so the air flow will not blow the leak far from its source. Raise the vehicle and determine where the leak is located.

### 45   Difficulty engaging gears

1   Clutch not releasing completely.
2   Insufficient transmission oil (Chapter 1).
3   Transmission oil in poor condition. Drain and fill with proper grade oil. Check oil for water and debris (Chapter 1).
4   Damaged shift fork.
5   Worn or damaged synchronizer.

### 46   Noise occurs while shifting gears

1   Check for proper operation of the clutch (Chapter 8).
2   Faulty synchronizer assemblies.

## AUTOMATIC TRANSMISSION

➡Note: Due to the complexity of the automatic transmission, it's difficult for the home mechanic to properly diagnose and service. For problems other than the following, the vehicle should be taken to a reputable mechanic.

### 47   Fluid leakage

1   Automatic transmission fluid is a deep red color, and fluid leaks should not be confused with engine oil which can easily be blown by air flow to the transmission.
2   To pinpoint a leak, first remove all built-up dirt and grime from the transmission. Degreasing agents and/or steam cleaning will achieve this. With the underside clean, drive the vehicle at low speeds so the air flow will not blow the leak far from its source. Raise the vehicle and determine where the leak is located. Common areas of leakage are:

   a)   *Fluid pan: tighten mounting bolts and/or replace pan gasket as necessary (Chapter 1).*

   b)   *Rear extension: tighten bolts and/or replace oil seal as necessary.*

   c)   *Filler pipe: replace the rubber oil seal where pipe enters transmission case.*

   d)   *Transmission oil lines: tighten fittings where lines enter transmission case and/or replace lines.*

   e)   *Vent pipe: transmission overfilled and/or water in fluid (see checking procedures, Chapter 1).*

f) *Vehicle speed sensor: replace the O-ring where speed sensor enters transmission case.*

## 48   General shift mechanism problems

Chapter 7B deals with checking and adjusting the shift linkage on automatic transmissions. Common problems which may be caused by out of adjustment linkage are:

a) *Engine starting in gears other than P (park) or N (Neutral).*
b) *Indicator pointing to a gear other than the one actually engaged.*
c) *Vehicle moves with transmission in P (Park) position.*

## 49   Transmission will not downshift with the accelerator pedal pressed to the floor

Since these transmissions are electronically controlled, check for any diagnostic trouble codes stored in the PCM. The actual repair will most likely have to be performed by a qualified repair shop with the proper equipment.

## 50   Engine will start in gears other than Park or without brake pedal being depressed

Brake Transmission Shift Interlock (BTSI) system out of adjustment (Chapter 7B).

## 51   Transmission slips, shifts rough, is noisy or has no drive in forward or Reverse gears

1  There are many probable causes for the above problems, but the home mechanic should concern himself only with one possibility: fluid level.
2  Before taking the vehicle to a shop, check the fluid level and condition as described in Chapter 1. Add fluid, if necessary, or change the fluid and filter if needed. If problems persist, have a professional diagnose the transmission.
3  Transmission fluid break down after 30,000 miles.

# DRIVESHAFT

→Note: Refer to Chapter 8, unless otherwise specified, for service information.

## 52   Leaks at front of driveshaft

Defective transmission or transfer case seal. See Chapter 7 for replacement procedure. As this is done, check the splined yoke for burrs or roughness that could damage the new seal. Remove burrs with a fine file or whetstone.

## 53   Knock or clunk when transmission is under initial load (just after transmission is put into gear)

1  Loose or disconnected rear suspension components. Check all mounting bolts and bushings (Chapters 7 and 10).

2  Loose driveshaft bolts. Inspect all bolts and nuts and tighten them securely.
3  Worn or damaged universal joint bearings (Chapter 8).
4  Worn sleeve yoke and mainshaft spline.

## 54   Metallic grating sound consistent with vehicle speed

Pronounced wear in the universal joints or driveshaft center support bearing. Replace driveshaft or center support bearing, as necessary.

## 55   Vibration

→Note: Before blaming the driveshaft, make sure the tires are perfectly balanced and perform the following test.

1  Install a tachometer inside the vehicle to monitor engine speed as the vehicle is driven. Drive the vehicle and note the engine speed at which the vibration (roughness) is most pronounced. Now shift the transmission to a different gear and bring the engine speed to the same point.
2  If the vibration occurs at the same engine speed (rpm) regardless of which gear the transmission is in, the driveshaft is NOT at fault since the driveshaft speed varies.
3  If the vibration decreases or is eliminated when the transmission is in a different gear at the same engine speed, refer to the following probable causes:

a) *Bent or dented driveshaft. Inspect and replace as necessary.*
b) *Undercoating or built-up dirt, etc. on the driveshaft. Clean the shaft thoroughly.*
c) *Worn universal joint bearings. Replace the U-joints or driveshaft as necessary.*
d) *Driveshaft and/or companion flange out of balance. Check for missing weights on the shaft. Remove driveshaft and reinstall 180-degrees from original position, then recheck. Have the driveshaft balanced if problem persists.*
e) *Loose driveshaft mounting bolts/nuts.*
f) *Worn transmission rear bushing (Chapter 7).*

## 56   Scraping noise

Make sure there is nothing, such as an exhaust heat shield, rubbing on the driveshaft.

# AXLE(S) AND DIFFERENTIAL

→Note: For differential servicing information, refer to Chapter 8, unless otherwise specified.

## 57   Noise - same when in drive as when vehicle is coasting

1  Road noise. No corrective action available.
2  Tire noise. Inspect tires and check tire pressures (Chapter 1).
3  Front wheel bearings loose, worn or damaged (Chapter 1).
4  Insufficient differential oil (Chapter 1).
5  Defective differential.

## 58   Knocking sound when starting or shifting gears

Defective or incorrectly adjusted differential.

## 59   Noise when turning

Defective differential.

## 60   Vibration

See probable causes under Driveshaft. Proceed under the guidelines listed for the driveshaft. If the problem persists, check the rear wheel bearings by raising the rear of the vehicle and spinning the wheels by hand. Listen for evidence of rough (noisy) bearings. Remove and inspect (Chapter 8).

## 61   Oil leaks

1   Pinion oil seal damaged (Chapter 8).
2   Driveaxle oil seals damaged (Chapter 8).
3   Differential cover leaking. Tighten mounting bolts or replace the gasket as required.
4   Loose filler plug on differential (Chapter 1).
5   Clogged or damaged breather on differential.

# BRAKES

➡ Note: Before assuming a brake problem exists, make sure the tires are in good condition and inflated properly, the front end alignment is correct and the vehicle is not loaded with weight in an unequal manner. All service procedures for the brakes are included in Chapter 9, unless otherwise noted.

## 62   Vehicle pulls to one side during braking

1   Defective, damaged or contaminated brake pad on one side. Inspect as described in Chapter 1. Refer to Chapter 9 if replacement is required.
2   Excessive wear of brake pad material or disc on one side. Inspect and repair as necessary.
3   Loose or disconnected front suspension components. Inspect and tighten all bolts securely (Chapters 1 and 10).
4   Defective front brake caliper assembly. Remove caliper and inspect for stuck piston or damage.
5   Scored or out-of-round disc.
6   Loose brake caliper mounting bolts.

## 63   Noise (high-pitched squeal or scraping sound)

1   Brake pads worn out. Replace pads with new ones immediately!
2   Glazed or contaminated pads.
3   Dirty or scored disc.

## 64   Excessive brake pedal travel

1   Partial brake system failure. Inspect entire system (Chapter 1) and correct as required.
2   Insufficient fluid in master cylinder. Check (Chapter 1) and add fluid - bleed system if necessary.
3   Air in system. Bleed system.
4   Defective master cylinder.

## 65   Brake pedal feels spongy when depressed

1   Air in brake lines. Bleed the brake system.
2   Deteriorated rubber brake hoses. Inspect all system hoses and lines. Replace parts as necessary.
3   Master cylinder mounting nuts loose. Inspect master cylinder bolts (nuts) and tighten them securely.
4   Master cylinder faulty.
5   Incorrect brake pad clearance.
6   Clogged reservoir cap vent hole.
7   Deformed rubber brake lines.
8   Soft or swollen caliper seals.
9   Poor quality brake fluid. Bleed entire system and fill with new approved fluid.

## 66   Excessive effort required to stop vehicle

1   Power brake booster not operating properly.
2   Excessively worn brake pads. Check and replace if necessary.
3   One or more caliper pistons seized or sticking. Inspect and rebuild as required.
4   Brake pads contaminated with oil or grease. Inspect and replace as required.
5   Worn or damaged master cylinder or caliper assemblies. Check particularly for frozen pistons.

## 67   Pedal travels to the floor with little resistance

Little or no fluid in the master cylinder reservoir caused by leaking caliper piston(s) or loose, damaged or disconnected brake lines. Inspect entire system and repair as necessary.

## 68   Brake pedal pulsates during brake application

1   Wheel bearings damaged, worn or out of adjustment.
2   Caliper not sliding properly due to improper installation or obstructions. Remove and inspect.
3   Disc not within specifications. Check for excessive lateral runout and parallelism. Have the discs resurfaced or replace them with new ones. Also make sure that all discs are the same thickness.

## 69   Brakes drag (indicated by sluggish engine performance or wheels being very hot after driving)

1   Master cylinder piston seized in bore. Replace master cylinder.
2   Caliper piston seized in bore.
3   Parking brake assembly will not release.
4   Clogged or internally split brake lines.
5   Brake pedal height improperly adjusted.

### 70 Rear brakes lock up under light brake application

1 Tire pressures too high.
2 Tires excessively worn (Chapter 1).

### 71 Rear brakes lock up under heavy brake application

1 Tire pressures too high.
2 Tires excessively worn (Chapter 1).
3 Front brake pads contaminated with oil, mud or water. Clean or replace the pads.
4 Front brake pads excessively worn.

## SUSPENSION AND STEERING

➡**Note: All service procedures for the suspension and steering systems are included in Chapter 10, unless otherwise noted.**

### 72 Vehicle pulls to one side

1 Tire pressures uneven (Chapter 1).
2 Defective tire (Chapter 1).
3 Excessive wear in suspension or steering components (Chapter 1).
4 Front end alignment incorrect
5 Front brakes dragging. Inspect as described in Section 71.
6 Wheel bearings improperly adjusted (Chapter 1).
7 Wheel bolts loose.

### 73 Shimmy, shake or vibration

1 Tire or wheel out of balance or out of round.
2 Loose, worn or out of adjustment wheel bearings (Chapter 1).
3 Shock absorbers and/or suspension components worn or damaged (see Chapter 10).

### 74 Excessive pitching and/or rolling around corners or during braking

1 Defective shock absorbers. Replace as a set.
2 Sagging springs.
3 Worn or damaged stabilizer bar or bushings.

### 75 Wandering or general instability

1 Improper tire pressures.
2 Incorrect front end alignment.
3 Worn or damaged steering linkage or suspension components.
4 Improperly adjusted steering gear.
5 Out-of-balance wheels.
6 Loose wheel bolts.
7 Worn rear shock absorbers.

### 76 Excessively stiff steering

1 Lack of fluid in the power steering fluid reservoir, where appropriate (Chapter 1).
2 Incorrect tire pressures (Chapter 1).
3 Front end out of alignment.
4 Steering gear out of adjustment or lacking lubrication.
5 Worn or damaged steering gear.
6 Low tire pressures.
7 Worn or damaged balljoints.
8 Worn or damaged tie-rod ends.

### 77 Excessive play in steering

1 Worn wheel bearings (Chapter 1).
2 Excessive wear in suspension bushings (Chapter 1).
3 Steering gear worn.
4 Incorrect front end alignment.
5 Steering gear mounting bolts loose.
6 Worn or damaged tie-rod ends.

### 78 Lack of power assistance

1 Steering pump drivebelt faulty or tensioner defective (Chapter 1).
2 Fluid level low (Chapter 1).
3 Hoses or pipes restricting the flow. Inspect and replace parts as necessary.
4 Air in power steering system. Bleed system.
5 Defective power steering pump.

### 79 Steering wheel fails to return to straight-ahead position

1 Incorrect front end alignment.
2 Tire pressures low.
3 Worn or damaged balljoint.
4 Worn or damaged tie-rod end.
5 Lack of fluid in power steering pump.

### 80 Steering effort not the same in both directions

1 Leaks in steering gear.
2 Clogged fluid passage in steering gear.

### 81 Noisy power steering pump

1 Insufficient fluid in pump.
2 Clogged hoses or oil filter in pump.
3 Loose pulley.
4 Drivebelt faulty or tensioner defective (Chapter 1).
5 Defective pump.

### 82 Miscellaneous noises

1 Improper tire pressures.
2 Defective balljoint or tie-rod end.
3 Loose or worn steering gear or suspension components.
4 Defective shock absorber.
5 Defective wheel bearing.

6 Worn or damaged suspension bushings.
7 Loose wheel lug nuts.
8 Worn or damaged shock absorber mounting bushing.
9 Worn stabilizer bar bushings.
10 Incorrect rear axle endplay.
11 See also causes of noises at the rear axle and driveshaft.

## 83 Excessive tire wear (not specific to one area)

1 Incorrect tire pressures.
2 Tires out of balance.
3 Wheels damaged. Inspect and replace as necessary.
4 Suspension or steering components worn (Chapter 1).
5 Front end alignment incorrect.
6 Lack of proper tire rotation routine. See *Routine Maintenance Schedule*, Chapter 1.

## 84 Excessive tire wear on outside edge

1 Incorrect tire pressure.
2 Excessive speed in turns.
3 Front end alignment incorrect.

## 85 Excessive tire wear on inside edge

1 Incorrect tire pressure.
2 Front end alignment incorrect.

## 86 Tire tread worn in one place

1 Tires out of balance.
2 Damaged or buckled wheel. Inspect and replace if necessary.
3 Defective tire.

**Section**

1 TUNE-UP AND ROUTINE MAINTENANCE

**Engine compartment layout (four-cylinder model)**

1  Coolant expansion tank
2  Automatic transmission fluid filler tube
3  Engine oil dipstick tube
4  Air filter housing
5  Power steering fluid reservoir
6  Windshield washer fluid reservoir
7  Engine oil filler cap
8  Oil filter housing

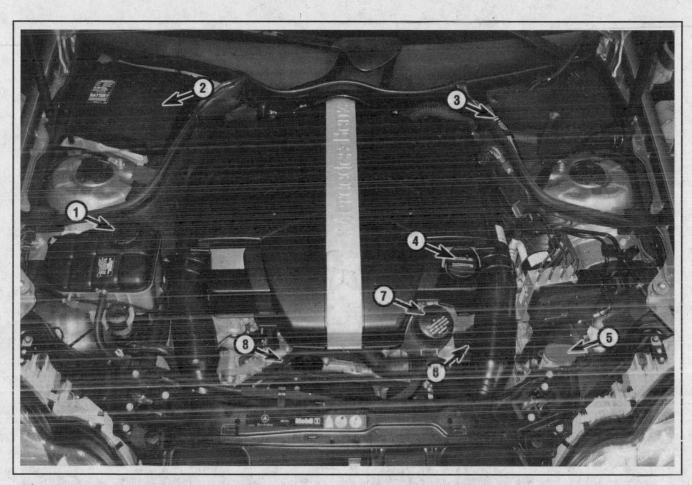

**Engine compartment layout (V6 model)**

1  Coolant expansion tank (pressure cap)
2  Interior ventilation filter/battery
   access cover
3  Brake fluid reservoir access cover
4  Engine oil filler cap
5  Windshield washer fluid reservoir
6  Power steering fluid reservoir
7  Oil filter housing
8  Serpentine drivebelt

**Typical front underside components (V6 shown, others similar)**

| | | | | | |
|---|---|---|---|---|---|
| 1 | Engine oil drain plug | 3 | Exhaust pipe | 5 | Radiator drain plug |
| 2 | Front disc brake caliper | 4 | Automatic transmission fluid drain plug | 6 | Steering gear boot |

**Typical rear underside components**

1   Rear disc brake caliper
2   Rear shock absorber
3   Driveaxle boot
4   Exhaust pipe
5   Muffler
6   Rear differential

## 1 Maintenance schedule

The maintenance intervals in this manual are provided with the assumption that you, not the dealer, will be doing the work. These are the minimum maintenance intervals recommended by the factory for vehicles that are driven daily. If you wish to keep your vehicle in peak condition at all times, you may wish to perform some of these procedures even more often. Because frequent maintenance enhances the efficiency, performance and resale value of your car, we encourage you to do so. If you drive in dusty areas, tow a trailer, idle or drive at low speeds for extended periods or drive for short distances (less than four miles) in below freezing temperatures, shorter intervals are also recommended.

When your vehicle is new, it should be serviced by a factory authorized dealer service department to protect the factory warranty. In many cases, the initial maintenance check is done at no cost to the owner.

### EVERY 250 MILES (400 KM) OR WEEKLY, WHICHEVER COMES FIRST

Check the engine oil level (see Section 4)
Check the engine coolant level (see Section 4)
Check the brake fluid level (see Section 4)
Check the power steering fluid level (see Section 4)
Check the windshield washer fluid level (see Section 4)
Check the automatic transmission fluid level (see Section 4)
Check the tires and tire pressures (see Section 5)
Check the operation of all lights
Check the horn operation

### EVERY 3,000 MILES (4800 KM) OR 3 MONTHS, WHICHEVER COMES FIRST

All items listed above, plus:
Change the engine oil and filter (see Section 6)
Check and replace, if necessary, the air filter element (Section 7)

### EVERY 6,000 MILES (9600 KM) OR 6 MONTHS, WHICHEVER COMES FIRST

All items listed above, plus:
Check the wiper blade condition (see Section 8)
Check and clean the battery and terminals (see Section 9)
Rotate the tires (see Section 10)
Check the seatbelts (see Section 11)
Inspect underhood hoses (see Section 12)

Check the cooling system hoses and connections for leaks and damage (see Section 13)
Check the exhaust pipes and hangers (see Section 14)

### EVERY 15,000 MILES (24,000 KM) OR 12 MONTHS, WHICHEVER COMES FIRST

All items listed above, plus:
Check the differential lubricant level (Section 4)
Check the manual transmission lubricant level (see Section 4)
Check the transfer case lubricant level (see Section 4)
Replace the interior ventilation filter and charcoal filter (see Section 15)
Check the brake system (see Section 16)
Check the suspension/steering components and driveaxle boots (see Section 17)
Check the fuel system hoses and connections for leaks and damage (see Section 18)
Check the drivebelts and replace if necessary (see Section 19)

### EVERY 30,000 MILES (48,000 KM) OR 24 MONTHS, WHICHEVER COMES FIRST

All items listed above, plus:
Replace the air filter element (see Section 7)
Change the brake fluid (see Section 20)
Replace the spark plugs (see Section 21)
Check the spark plug wires (see Section 22)
Check the ignition coil(s) (see Chapter 5)
Change the automatic transmission fluid and filter (Section 24)

### EVERY 60,000 MILES (96,000 KM) OR 48 MONTHS, WHICHEVER COMES FIRST

All items listed above, plus:
Replace the fuel filter (see Chapter 4)
Change the differential lubricant (see Section 23)
Change the manual transmission fluid (see Section 25)
Change the transfer case lubricant (see Section 27)

### EVERY 60 MONTHS (REGARDLESS OF MILEAGE)

Service the cooling system (drain, flush and refill) (Section 26)

## 2 Introduction

This Chapter is designed to help the home mechanic maintain the Mercedes-Benz C-Class with the goals of maximum performance, economy, safety and reliability in mind.

Included is a master maintenance schedule, followed by procedures dealing specifically with each item on the schedule. Visual checks, adjustments, component replacement and other helpful items are included. Refer to the accompanying illustrations of the engine compartment and the underside of the vehicle for the locations of various components.

Servicing your vehicle in accordance with the mileage/time maintenance schedule and the step-by-step procedures will result in a planned maintenance program that should produce a long and reliable service life. Keep in mind that it's a comprehensive plan, so maintaining some items but not others at the specified intervals will not produce the same results.

As you service your vehicle, you will discover that many of the procedures can - and should - be grouped together because of the nature of the particular procedure you're performing or because of the close proximity of two otherwise unrelated components to one another.

For example, if the vehicle is raised for chassis lubrication, you should inspect the exhaust, suspension, steering and fuel systems while you're under the vehicle. When you're rotating the tires, it makes good sense to check the brakes since the wheels are already removed. Finally, let's suppose you have to borrow or rent a torque wrench. Even if you only need it to tighten the spark plugs, you might as well check the torque of as many critical fasteners as time allows.

The first step in this maintenance program is to prepare yourself before the actual work begins. Read through all the procedures you're planning to do, then gather up all the parts and tools needed. If it looks like you might run into problems during a particular job, seek advice from a mechanic or an experienced do-it-yourselfer.

### OWNER'S MANUAL AND VECI LABEL INFORMATION

Your vehicle owner's manual was written for your year and model and contains very specific information on component locations, specifications, fuse ratings, part numbers, etc. The Owner's Manual is an important resource for the do-it-yourselfer to have; if one was not supplied with your vehicle, it can generally be ordered from a dealer parts department.

Among other important information, the Vehicle Emissions Control Information (VECI) label contains specifications and procedures for applicable tune-up adjustments and, in some instances, spark plugs. The information on this label is the exact maintenance data recommended by the manufacturer. This data often varies by intended operating altitude, local emissions regulations, month of manufacture, etc.

This Chapter contains procedural details, safety information and more ambitious maintenance intervals than you might find in manufacturer's literature. However, you may also find procedures or specifications in your Owner's Manual or VECI label that differ with what's printed here. In these cases, the Owner's Manual or VECI label can be considered correct, since it is specific to your particular vehicle.

## 3 Tune-up general information

The term tune-up is used in this manual to represent a combination of individual operations rather than one specific procedure.

If, from the time the vehicle is new, the routine maintenance schedule is followed closely and frequent checks are made of fluid levels and high wear items, as suggested throughout this manual, the engine will be kept in relatively good running condition and the need for additional work will be minimized.

More likely than not, however, there will be times when the engine is running poorly due to lack of regular maintenance. This is even more likely if a used vehicle, which has not received regular and frequent maintenance checks, is purchased. In such cases, an engine tune-up will be needed outside of the regular routine maintenance intervals.

The first step in any tune-up or diagnostic procedure to help correct a poor running engine is a cylinder compression check. A compression check (see Chapter 2C) will help determine the condition of internal engine components and should be used as a guide for tune-up and repair procedures. If, for instance, a compression check indicates serious internal engine wear, a conventional tune-up will not improve the performance of the engine and would be a waste of time and money. Because of its importance, the compression check should be done by

someone with the right equipment and the knowledge to use it properly.

The following procedures are those most often needed to bring a generally poor running engine back into a proper state of tune.

### MINOR TUNE-UP

Check all engine-related fluids (Section 4)
Clean, inspect and test the battery (Section 9)
Check all underhood hoses (Section 12)
Check the cooling system (Section 13)

### MAJOR TUNE-UP

*All items listed under Minor tune-up, plus . . .*
Replace the air filter (Section 7)
Check the drivebelt (Section 19)
Replace the spark plugs (Section 21)
Check the charging system (Chapter 5)

## 4  Fluid level checks (every 250 miles or weekly)

1   Fluids are an essential part of the lubrication, cooling, brake and windshield washer systems. Because the fluids gradually become depleted and/or contaminated during normal operation of the vehicle, they must be periodically replenished. See *Recommended lubricants and fluids* at the of this Chapter before adding fluid to any of the following components.

➡Note: The vehicle must be on level ground when fluid levels are checked.

### ENGINE OIL

◆ Refer to illustrations 4.2a, 4.2b, 4.4, 4.6a and 4.6b

➡Note: To perform this procedure on 2005 and earlier models, you'll have to obtain a dipstick (part number 120 589 07 21 00) from a dealer parts department or an aftermarket tool supplier (unlike most vehicles, a dipstick is not present in the oil filler tube).

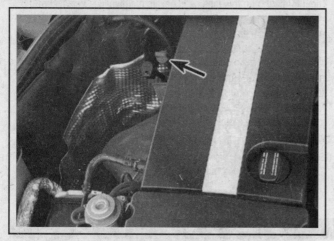

4.2a  Engine oil dipstick tube cap (four-cylinder engines)

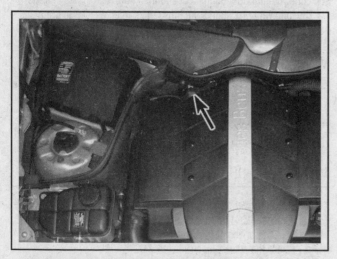

4.2b  Engine oil dipstick/dipstick tube cap location (V6 engines)

## ❋❋ CAUTION:

**The dipstick used for checking the oil level on 2005 and earlier models is only a tool; it should never be left in the dipstick tube when the vehicle is operated.**

2   On 2006 and later models, the oil level is checked with a dipstick, which is located on the side of the engine (see illustrations). The dipstick extends through a metal tube down into the oil pan. On 2005 and earlier models there's a dipstick tube, but it has a cap on the top and no dipstick inside.

3   The oil level should be checked before the vehicle has been driven, or about 5 minutes after the engine has been shut off. If the oil is checked immediately after driving the vehicle, some of the oil will remain in the upper part of the engine, resulting in an inaccurate reading on the dipstick.

4   Pull the dipstick out of the tube and wipe all the oil from the end with a clean rag or paper towel. Insert the clean dipstick all the way back into the tube and pull it out again. Note the oil at the end of the dipstick; on 2006 and later models, the level should be between the MIN and MAX marks (see illustration). On 2005 and earlier models, the level on the temporary dipstick should be as follows:

   Four-cylinder engines - between 118 mm and 120 mm on the dipstick
   V6 engines
      Rear-wheel drive models - between 170 mm and 173 mm on the dipstick
      4MATIC (all-wheel drive) models - between 123 mm and 126 mm on the dipstick

➡Note: After checking the oil and adjusting the level (if necessary), be sure to remove the temporary dipstick and reinstall the cap on the dipstick tube.

5   Do not allow the level to drop below the minimum mark, or oil starvation may cause engine damage. Conversely, overfilling the engine (adding oil above the MAX mark) may cause oil fouled spark plugs, oil leaks or oil seal failures. The oil could also be whipped by the crank-

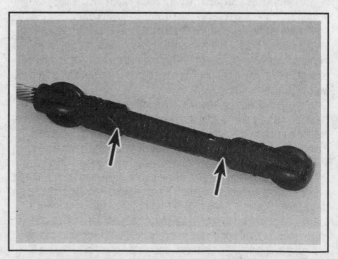

4.4  On 2006 and later models, at its highest point, the level should be between the MIN and MAX marks on the dipstick

shaft, causing it to foam, which could cause accelerated wear of the friction surfaces in the engine due to lack of proper lubrication.

6   To add oil, remove the filler cap from the valve cover (see illustrations). After adding oil, wait a few minutes to allow the level to stabilize, then pull out the dipstick and check the level again. Add more oil if required. Install the filler cap and tighten it by hand only.

7   Checking the oil level is an important preventive maintenance step. A consistently low oil level indicates oil leakage through damaged seals, defective gaskets or past worn rings or valve guides. If the oil looks milky in color or has water droplets in it, the cylinder head gasket(s) may be blown or the head(s) or block may be cracked. The engine should be checked immediately. The condition of the oil should also be checked. Whenever you check the oil level, slide your thumb and index finger up the dipstick before wiping off the oil. If you see small dirt or metal particles clinging to the dipstick, the oil should be changed (see Section 6).

## ENGINE COOLANT

▶ **Refer to illustration 4.9**

> ❊❊ **WARNING:**
>
> **Do not allow antifreeze to come in contact with your skin or painted surfaces of the vehicle. Flush contaminated areas immediately with plenty of water. Don't store new coolant or leave old coolant lying around where it's accessible to children or pets - they're attracted by its sweet smell. Ingestion of even a small amount of coolant can be fatal! Wipe up garage floor and drip pan spills immediately. Keep antifreeze containers covered and repair cooling system leaks as soon as they're noticed.**

8   All vehicles covered by this manual are equipped with a pressurized coolant recovery system. An expansion tank is located in the right side of the engine compartment.

9   The coolant level in the tank should be checked regularly.

> ❊❊ **WARNING:**
>
> **Never remove the expansion tank cap when the engine is warm!**

The level in the tank varies with the temperature of the engine. When the engine is cold, the coolant level should reach the black top part of the reservoir on the expansion tank (see illustration). If it doesn't, remove the cap from the tank and add a 50/50 mixture of MB 325.0 Anticorrosion/antifreeze agent (or equivalent) and water.

> ❊❊ **WARNING:**
>
> **Remove the cap slowly. If you hear a hissing sound when unscrewing the cap, wait until it stops, then proceed.**

10  Drive the vehicle and recheck the coolant level. If only a small amount of coolant is required to bring the system up to the proper level, water can be used. However, repeated additions of water will dilute the

**4.6a  Engine oil filler cap (four-cylinder engines)**

**4.6b  Engine oil filler cap (V6 engines)**

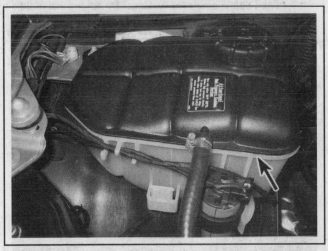

**4.9  When the engine is cold, the coolant level should reach the black part of the expansion tank**

antifreeze and water solution. In order to maintain the proper ratio of antifreeze and water, always top up the coolant level with the correct mixture. Don't use rust inhibitors or additives. An empty plastic milk jug or bleach bottle makes an excellent container for mixing coolant.

11 If the coolant level drops consistently, there may be a leak in the system. Inspect the radiator, hoses, filler cap, drain plugs and water pump (see Section 13). If no leaks are noted, have the expansion tank cap pressure tested by a service station.

12 If you have to remove the expansion tank cap, wait until the engine has cooled completely, then wrap a thick cloth around the cap and turn it to the first stop. If coolant or steam escapes, or if you hear a hissing noise, let the engine cool down longer, then remove the cap.

13 Check the condition of the coolant as well. It should be relatively clear. If it's brown or rust colored, the system should be drained, flushed and refilled. Even if the coolant appears to be normal, the corrosion inhibitors wear out, so it must be replaced at the specified intervals.

## BRAKE FLUID

▶ **Refer to illustrations 4.14 and 4.15**

14 The brake master cylinder is located in the driver's side of the engine compartment, near the firewall (see illustration).

15 To check the fluid level of the brake master cylinder, remove the access cover from the left cowl cover, then look at the MAX and MIN marks on the reservoir (see illustration). The level should be within the specified distance from the maximum fill line.

16 If the level is low, wipe the top of the reservoir cover with a clean rag to prevent contamination of the brake system before lifting the cover.

17 Add only the specified brake fluid to the brake reservoir (refer to *Recommended lubricants and fluids* at the end of this Chapter, or to your owner's manual). Mixing different types of brake fluid can damage the system. Fill the brake master cylinder reservoir only to the MAX line.

**✳✳ WARNING:**

**Use caution when filling either reservoir - brake fluid can harm your eyes and damage painted surfaces. Do not use brake fluid that is more than one year old or has been left open. Brake fluid absorbs moisture from the air. Excess moisture can cause a dangerous loss of braking.**

18 While the reservoir cap is removed, inspect the master cylinder reservoir for contamination. If deposits, dirt particles or water droplets are present, the fluid should be changed (see Section 20).

19 After filling the reservoir to the proper level, make sure the lid is properly seated to prevent fluid leakage and/or system pressure loss.

20 The fluid in the brake master cylinder will drop slightly as the brake pads at each wheel wear down during normal operation. If the master cylinder requires repeated replenishing to keep it at the proper level, this is an indication of leakage in the brake system, which should be corrected immediately. If the brake system shows an indication of leakage, check all brake lines and connections, along with the calipers and master cylinder (see Section 16 for more information).

21 If, upon checking the brake master cylinder fluid level, you discover the reservoir empty or nearly empty, the system should be thoroughly inspected (see Chapter 9).

## POWER STEERING FLUID

▶ **Refer to illustrations 4.23 and 4.27**

22 Check the power steering fluid level periodically to avoid steering system problems, such as damage to the pump.

**✳✳ CAUTION:**

**DO NOT hold the steering wheel against either stop (extreme left or right turn) for more than five seconds. If you do, the power steering pump could be damaged.**

23 The power steering reservoir, is located at the right side of the engine compartment (see illustration).

24 For the check, the front wheels should be pointed straight ahead and the engine should be off.

25 Use a clean rag to wipe off the reservoir cap and the area around the cap. This will help prevent any foreign matter from entering the reservoir during the check.

26 Twist off the cap and check the temperature of the fluid at the end of the dipstick with your finger.

27 Wipe off the fluid with a clean rag, reinsert the dipstick, then withdraw it and read the fluid level. The fluid should be at the proper level, depending on whether it was checked hot or cold (see illustration).

**4.14  Release the clips by turning them 1/4-turn, then remove the cover to access the brake fluid reservoir**

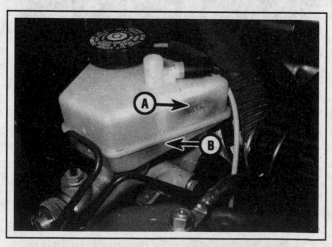

**4.15  Never let the brake fluid level drop below the MIN mark**

*A  MAX mark*          *B  MIN mark*

4.23 Power steering fluid reservoir

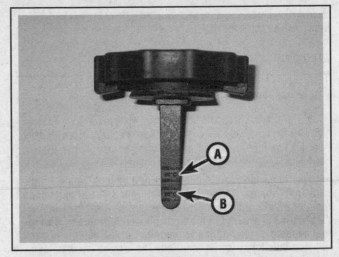

4.27 The fluid should be at the proper level, depending on whether it was checked hot (A) or cold (B)

Never allow the fluid level to drop below the lower mark on the dipstick.

28  If additional fluid is required, pour the specified type directly into the reservoir, using a funnel to prevent spills.

29  If the reservoir requires frequent fluid additions, all power steering hoses, hose connections, steering gear and the power steering pump should be carefully checked for leaks.

## WINDSHIELD WASHER FLUID

♦ Refer to illustration 4.30

30  Fluid for the windshield washer system is stored in a plastic reservoir located at the left front of the engine compartment (see illustration).

31  In milder climates, plain water can be used in the reservoir, but it should be kept no more than 2/3 full to allow for expansion if the water freezes. In colder climates, use windshield washer system antifreeze, available at any auto parts store, to lower the freezing point of the fluid. Mix the antifreeze with water in accordance with the manufacturer's directions on the container.

**❋❋ CAUTION:**

**Do not use cooling system antifreeze - it will damage the vehicle's paint.**

## DIFFERENTIAL LUBRICANT

♦ Refer to illustration 4.32

➡Note: It isn't necessary to check this lubricant weekly; every 15,000 miles or 12 months will be adequate.

32  To check the fluid level, raise the vehicle and support it securely on jackstands. On the axle housing, remove the check/fill plug (see illustration). If the lubricant level is correct, it should be up to the lower edge of the hole.

33  If the differential needs more lubricant (if the level is not up to the hole), use a syringe or a gear oil pump to add more. Stop filling the differential when the lubricant begins to run out the hole.

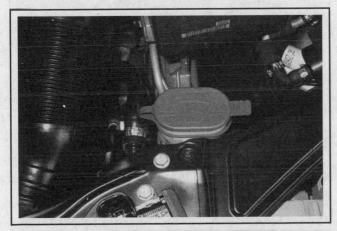

4.30  The windshield washer fluid reservoir is located in the left front corner of the engine compartment

4.32  Differential check/fill plug (A) and drain plug (B)

34 Install the plug and tighten it securely. Drive the vehicle a short distance, then check for leaks.

## AUTOMATIC TRANSMISSION FLUID

▶ **Refer to illustration 4.38**

35 This procedure should only be used when refilling the transmission after the fluid has been drained, unless an obvious leak has been detected. Low fluid level can lead to slipping or loss of drive, while overfilling can cause foaming and loss of fluid.

➡**Note: To perform this procedure you'll have to obtain a dipstick (part number 140 589 15 21 00) from a dealer parts department or an aftermarket tool supplier (unlike most vehicles, a dipstick is not present in the transmission filler tube). A scan tool capable of reading the temperature of the automatic transmission fluid will also be required. The alternative is to take the vehicle to a dealer for the fluid level check. You'll also need a new locking clip for the tamperproof cap on the dipstick tube.**

36 In order to check the automatic transmission fluid level, the transmission must be at operating temperature (fluid temperature 176-degrees F). Operating temperature is reached after driving for approximately 10 miles. Do not attempt to check the fluid level on a cold transmission. Using a scan tool capable of reading the temperature of the automatic transmission fluid, check the temperature of the automatic transmission fluid.

37 With the transmission at operating temperature, ensure that the vehicle is parked on level ground. Remove the engine cover/air filter housing on models where it interferes with access to the dipstick tube (see Chapter 4).

38 The top of the filler tube is equipped with a tamperproof cap incorporating a red plastic clip. The clip is broken when the cap is removed, and a new clip must be installed when the cap is installed. Pry out the locking clip securing the filler tube cap (see illustration).

39 With the engine running at idle speed and the parking brake applied, ensure that the transmission selector lever is in position P.

40 Insert the dipstick into the filler tube and pull out again, and note the fluid level. With a fluid temperature of 176-degrees F, the level on the dipstick must be in the "B" range on the dipstick.

41 If topping-up is necessary, top-up through the filler tube using fluid of the specified type (see *Recommended lubricants and fluids* at

the end of this Chapter). Do not overfill the transmission - the fluid level must not be above the "B" mark.

42 On completion, reinstall the filler tube cap. Install a new tamper-proof clip.

## MANUAL TRANSMISSION LUBRICANT

➡**Note: It isn't necessary to check this lubricant weekly; every 15,000 miles or 12 months will be adequate.**

43 The manual transmission has a filler plug which must be removed to check the lubricant level. If the vehicle is raised to gain access to the plug, be sure to support it safely on jackstands - DO NOT crawl under a vehicle that is supported only by a jack! Be sure the vehicle is level or the check may be inaccurate.

44 Using the appropriate wrench, unscrew the fill plug from the transmission.

45 Use your finger to reach inside the housing to feel the lubricant level. The level should be at or near the bottom of the plug hole. If it isn't, add the recommended lubricant through the plug hole with a syringe or squeeze bottle.

46 Install and tighten the plug. Check for leaks after the first few miles of driving.

## TRANSFER CASE LUBRICANT (AWD MODELS)

▶ **Refer to illustration 4.48**

➡**Note: It isn't necessary to check this lubricant weekly; every 30,000 miles (48,000 km) or 24 months will be adequate (unless leakage is noted).**

47 The transfer case has a filler plug and a check plug which must be removed to check the lubricant level. To gain access to the plugs, the engine rear crossmember and mount (see Chapter 2B), and the front driveshaft (see Chapter 8) must be removed.

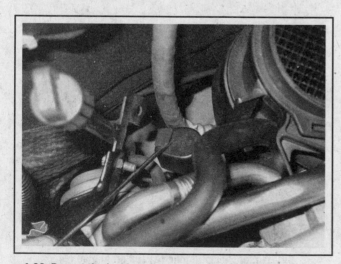

**4.38  Pry out the locking clip securing the filler tube cap**

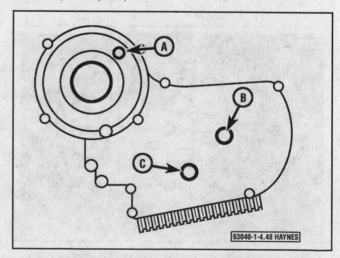

**4.48  Transfer case filler plug (A), check plug (B) and drain plug (C)**

48 Raise the transmission/transfer case with the floor jack until they are at their installed height. Remove the filler plug and the check plug (see illustration). Using a squeeze bottle or lubricant pump, add the recommended lubricant to the filler plug hole until lubricant starts to flow from the check plug hole.

➡ Note: This is the only way to accurately verify that the transfer case is properly filled, since there is another chamber (behind the one that the check plug screws into) that must be full.

49 Allow the lubricant to drip from the check plug hole for a couple of minutes, then install the check and filler plugs and tighten them to the torque value listed in this Chapter's Specifications.

➡ Note: Be sure to install new sealing rings on the check and filler plugs.

50 Install the front driveshaft and the engine crossmember.
51 Check for leaks after the first few miles of driving.

## 5  Tire and tire pressure checks (every 250 miles or weekly)

▶ Refer to illustrations 5.2, 5.3, 5.4a, 5.4b and 5.8

1  Periodic inspection of the tires may spare you the inconvenience of being stranded with a flat tire. It can also provide you with vital information regarding possible problems in the steering and suspension systems before major damage occurs.

2  The original tires on this vehicle are equipped with 1/2-inch wide bands that will appear when tread depth reaches 1/16-inch, at which point they can be considered worn out. Tread wear can be monitored with a simple, inexpensive device known as a tread depth indicator (see illustration).

3  Note any abnormal tread wear (see illustration). Tread pattern irregularities such as cupping, flat spots and more wear on one side than the other are indications of front end alignment and/or balance problems. If any of these conditions are noted, take the vehicle to a tire shop or service station to correct the problem.

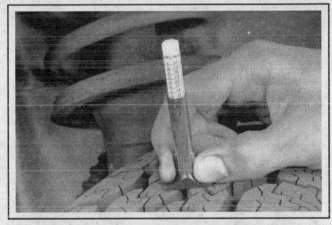

5.2 A tire tread depth indicator should be used to monitor tire wear - they are available at auto parts stores and service stations and cost very little

UNDERINFLATION

CUPPING

Cupping may be caused by:
• Underinflation and/or mechanical irregularities such as out-of-balance condition of wheel and/or tire, and bent or damaged wheel.
• Loose or worn steering tie-rod or steering idler arm.
• Loose, damaged or worn front suspension parts.

OVERINFLATION

INCORRECT TOE-IN OR EXTREME CAMBER

FEATHERING DUE TO MISALIGNMENT

5.3 This chart will help you determine the condition of your tires, the probable cause(s) of abnormal wear and the corrective action necessary

4   Look closely for cuts, punctures and embedded nails or tacks. Sometimes a tire will hold air pressure for a short time or leak down very slowly after a nail has embedded itself in the tread. If a slow leak persists, check the valve stem core to make sure it is tight (see illustration). Examine the tread for an object that may have embedded itself in the tire or for a plug that may have begun to leak (radial tire punctures are repaired with a plug that is installed in a puncture). If a puncture is suspected, it can be easily verified by spraying a solution of soapy water onto the puncture area (see illustration). The soapy solution will bubble if there is a leak. Unless the puncture is unusually large, a tire shop or service station can usually repair the tire.

5   Carefully inspect the inner sidewall of each tire for evidence of brake fluid leakage. If you see any, inspect the brakes immediately.

6   Correct air pressure adds miles to the life span of the tires, improves mileage and enhances overall ride quality. Tire pressure cannot be accurately estimated by looking at a tire, especially if it's a radial. A tire pressure gauge is essential. Keep an accurate gauge in the glove compartment. The pressure gauges attached to the nozzles of air hoses at gas stations are often inaccurate.

7   Always check tire pressure when the tires are cold. Cold, in this case, means the vehicle has not been driven over a mile in the three hours preceding a tire pressure check. A pressure rise of four to eight pounds is not uncommon once the tires are warm.

8   Unscrew the valve cap protruding from the wheel or hubcap and push the gauge firmly onto the valve stem (see illustration). Note the reading on the gauge and compare the figure to the recommended tire pressure shown on the tire placard on the driver's side door. Be sure to reinstall the valve cap to keep dirt and moisture out of the valve stem mechanism. Check all four tires and, if necessary, add enough air to bring them up to the recommended pressure.

9   Don't forget to keep the spare tire inflated to the specified pressure (refer to the pressure molded into the tire sidewall).

**5.4a  If a tire loses air on a steady basis, check the valve core first to make sure it's snug (special inexpensive wrenches are commonly available at auto parts stores)**

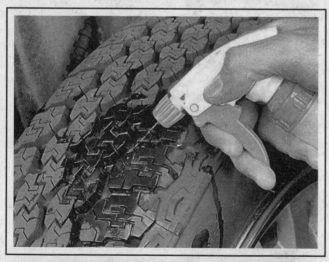

**5.4b  If the valve core is tight, raise the corner of the vehicle with the low tire and spray a soapy water solution onto the tread as the tire is turned slowly - slow leaks will cause small bubbles to appear**

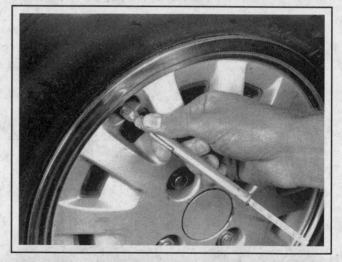

**5.8  To extend the life of your tires, check the air pressure at least once a week with an accurate gauge (don't forget the spare!)**

## 6   Engine oil and filter change (every 3000 miles or 3 months)

▶ Refer to illustrations 6.2, 6.6a, 6.6b, 6.6c, 6.8, 6.13a, 6.13b
and 6.14

1   Frequent oil changes are the best preventive maintenance the
home mechanic can give the engine, because aging oil becomes diluted
and contaminated, which leads to premature engine wear.
2   Make sure you have all the necessary tools before you begin
this procedure (see illustration). You should also have plenty of rags or
newspapers handy for mopping up any spills.
3   Access to the underside of the vehicle is greatly improved if the
vehicle can be lifted on a hoist, driven onto ramps or supported by
jackstands.

### ✳✳ WARNING:

**Do not work under a vehicle which is supported only by a jack.**

4   If this is your first oil change, get under the vehicle and familiarize yourself with the location of the oil drain plug. The engine and
exhaust components will be warm during the actual work, so try to
anticipate any potential problems before the engine and accessories are
hot.
5   Park the vehicle on a level spot. Start the engine and allow it to
reach its normal operating temperature. Warm oil and sludge will flow
out more easily. Turn off the engine when it's warmed up. Remove the
filler cap from the valve cover.
6   Working in the engine compartment, locate the oil filter/housing
on the front left-hand side of the engine. Place a rag around the housing
to absorb any spilt oil, then unscrew the oil filter cap (see illustrations).
The element is withdrawn with the oil filter cap, and can then be separated and discarded (see illustration)
7   Raise the vehicle and support it securely on jackstands.

### ✳✳ WARNING:

**Never get beneath the vehicle when it is supported only by a
jack. The jack provided with your vehicle is designed solely for
raising the vehicle to remove and replace the wheels. Always
use jackstands to support the vehicle when it becomes necessary to place your body underneath the vehicle.**

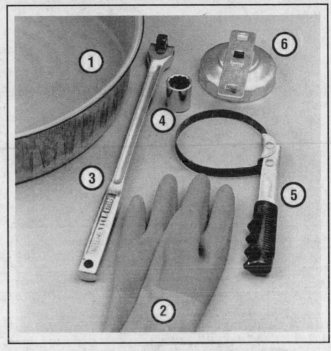

**6.2  These tools are required when changing the engine oil
and filter**

1   *Drain pan* - It should be fairly shallow in depth, but wide in order
to prevent spills
2   *Rubber gloves* - When removing the drain plug and filter, it is
inevitable that you will get oil on your hands (the gloves will prevent
burns)
3   *Breaker bar* - Sometimes the oil drain plug is pretty tight and a
long breaker bar is needed to loosen it
4   *Socket* - To be used with the breaker bar or a ratchet (must be the
correct size to fit the drain plug)
5   *Filter wrench* - This is a metal band-type wrench, which requires
clearance around the filter to be effective
6   *Filter wrench* - This type fits on the bottom of the filter and can
be turned with a ratchet or beaker bar (different size wrenches are
available for different types of filters)

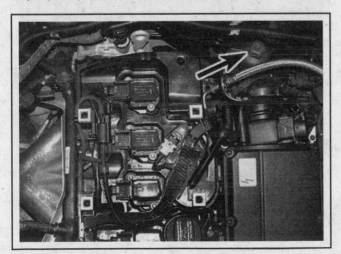

**6.6a  Oil filter location - four-cylinder models**

**6.6b  On V6 engines, use an oil filter wrench to remove the
filter cap**

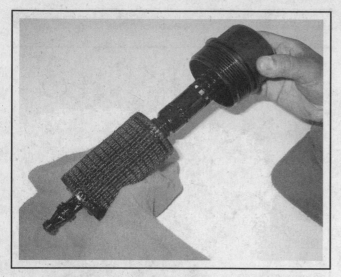

**6.6c Pull the used element off of the filter cap stem**

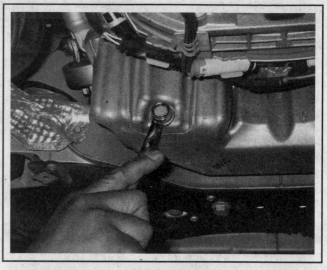

**6.8 Use a proper size box-end wrench or socket to remove the oil drain plug and avoid rounding it off**

**6.13a Install a new O-ring on the cap . . .**

**6.13b . . . and stem**

**6.14 Install the new filter element**

8 Being careful not to touch the hot exhaust components, place the drain pan under the drain plug in the bottom of the pan and remove the plug (see illustration). You may want to wear gloves while unscrewing the plug the final few turns if the engine is hot.

9 Allow the old oil to drain into the pan. It may be necessary to move the pan farther under the engine as the oil flow slows to a trickle. Inspect the old oil for the presence of metal shavings and chips.

10 After all the oil has drained, wipe off the drain plug with a clean rag. Even minute metal particles clinging to the plug would immediately contaminate the new oil.

11 Clean the area around the drain plug opening, reinstall the plug and tighten it securely, but do not strip the threads.

12 Remove all tools, rags, etc. from under the vehicle, being careful not to spill the oil in the drain pan, then lower the vehicle.

13 Wipe out the oil filter housing and cap using a clean rag, then install a new O-ring on the cap and stem (see illustrations).

14 Install the filter element onto the cap (see illustration).

15 Screw on and tighten the cap securely.

16 Add new oil to the engine through the oil filler cap in the valve cover. Use a funnel, if necessary, to prevent oil from spilling onto the top of the engine. Pour the specified type and amount of fresh oil into the engine (refer to *Recommended lubricants and fluids* and *Capacities* at the end of this Chapter). Wait a few minutes to allow the oil to drain into the pan, then check the level (see Section 4). If the oil level is correct, install the filler cap hand tight, start the engine and allow the new oil to circulate.

17 Allow the engine to run for about a minute. While the engine is running, look under the vehicle and check for leaks at the oil pan drain plug and around the oil filter. If either is leaking, stop the engine and tighten the plug or filter.

18 Wait a few minutes to allow the oil to trickle down into the pan, then recheck the level on the dipstick and, if necessary, add enough oil to bring it to the correct level.

19 During the first few trips after an oil change, make it a point to check frequently for leaks and proper oil level.

20 The old oil drained from the engine cannot be reused in its

present state and should be disposed of. Check with your local auto parts store, disposal facility or environmental agency to see if they will accept the oil for recycling. After the oil has cooled, it can be drained into a container (capped plastic jugs, topped bottles, milk cartons, etc.) for transport to one of these disposal sites. Don't dispose of the oil by pouring it on the ground or down a drain!

## SERVICE INDICATOR RESETTING

▶ **Refer to illustration 6.21**

➡**Note: After changing the engine oil, it's important to reset the service indicator so it can keep an accurate record of engine operating time/vehicle mileage.**

21  Several buttons on the steering wheel and instrument panel, as well as the display on the instrument cluster, are used to reset the service indicator (see illustration).

22  Begin the process by turning the ignition key to the no. 1 (On) position.

23  Push the system selection buttons until "Kilometer reading" appears on the multi-function display.

24  Push the dimmer knob ("R" button) three times; you should then hear a beep and voltage should read out on the multi-function display.

25  Turn the ignition key to the no. 2 (Run) position.

26  Push the forward/back scroll buttons until "Service display" appears on the multi-function display.

27  Push the dimmer knob ("R" button) once; "Oil type" should appear on the multi-function display. Use the +/- buttons to select the oil type that was added to the engine.

28  Push the forward/back scroll buttons until "Confirm oil reset,

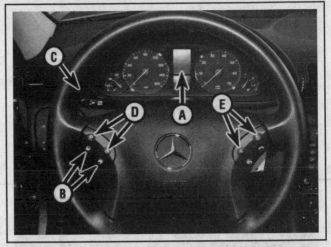

**6.21  Buttons and instrument cluster display used for resetting the service indicator**

| | |
|---|---|
| A    Multi-function display | D    Forward/back scroll buttons |
| D    System selection buttons | E    +/- buttons (for selecting |
| C    Dimmer knob ("R" button) | oil grade) |

press R button for 3s" appears on the multi-function display.

29  Push the dimmer knob ("R" button) in and hold it for three seconds; "Service confirmed" should appear on the multi-function display.

30  Push the forward/back scroll buttons until "Service display" appears on the multi-function display.

31  Push the system selection buttons until "Kilometer reading" appears on the multi-function display, then turn the ignition key to the Off position.

---

## 7  Air filter check and replacement (every 3000 miles or 3 months)

## V6 MODELS

### Vehicles with a remote air filter housing

➡**Note: On some 2001 through 2005 models, the air filter housing is located in the right front corner of the engine compartment.**

1  Loosen the connecting duct hose clamp.

2  Release the tabs or remove the fasteners that secure the two halves of the air cleaner housing together, then separate the cover halves and remove the air filter element.

3  Installation is the reverse of removal.

### Vehicles with an integral engine cover/air filter housing

▶ **Refer to illustrations 7.4, 7.5, 7.6, 7.7a and 7.7b**

4  Remove the front engine cover (see illustration).

**7.4  Pull up the front edge of the cover to disengage the front retaining clips and locator pin, then pull the cover forward to disengage the two rear retaining clips at the back of the cover**

5  Remove the fresh air intake ducts (see illustration).
6  Remove the air filter housing (see illustration).
7  Remove the fasteners that secure the two filter element covers on the air cleaner housing and remove the air filter element (see illustrations).

**7.5  Pull off the fresh air intake ducts from the air filter housing**

**7.6  Lift the engine cover/air filter housing up to disengage it from the mounting grommets**

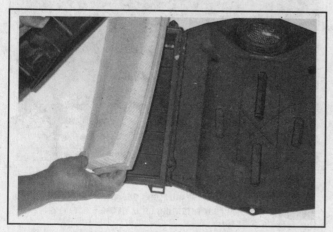

**7.7b . . . then remove the air filter elements**

## FOUR-CYLINDER MODELS

### 2002 models

➡**Note: The air filter housing on 2002 models is located at the front of the engine compartment, and is long and narrow so it can fit transversely, directly in front of the engine.**

8  Loosen the air intake duct hose clamp and disconnect the duct.
9  Release the tabs or remove the fasteners that secure the two halves of the air cleaner housing together, then separate the cover halves and remove the air filter element.
10  Installation is the reverse of removal.

### 2003 through 2005 models

▶ **Refer to illustration 7.11**

11  Remove the fasteners that secure the top of the air cleaner housing, then separate the cover and remove the air filter element (see illustration).
12  Installation is the reverse of removal.

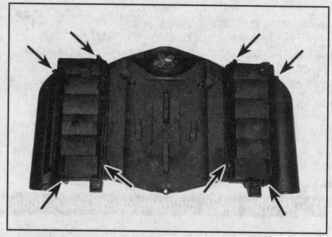

**7.7a  Remove the fasteners that secure the two filter element covers . . .**

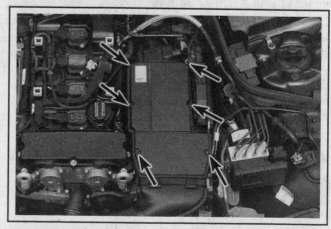

**7.11  Remove the fasteners securing the air filter element cover**

## 8    Windshield wiper blade inspection and replacement (every 6000 miles or 6 months)

▶ **Refer to illustration 8.5**

1   The windshield wiper and blade assembly should be inspected periodically for damage, loose components and cracked or worn blade elements.

2   Road film can build up on the wiper blades and affect their efficiency, so they should be washed regularly with a mild detergent solution.

3   The action of the wiping mechanism can loosen bolts, nuts and fasteners, so they should be checked and tightened, as necessary, at the same time the wiper blades are checked.

4   If the wiper blade elements are cracked, worn or warped, or no longer clean adequately, they should be replaced with new ones.

5   Lift the arm assembly away from the glass for clearance, pull the release lever, then slide the wiper blade assembly out of the hook at the end of the arm (see illustration).

6   Attach the new wiper to the arm. Connection can be confirmed by an audible click.

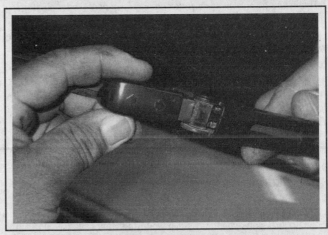

**8.5  To release the blade holder, pull the release latch and slide the wiper blade out of the hook at the end of the arm**

## 9    Battery check, maintenance and charging (every 6000 miles or 6 months)

▶ **Refer to illustrations 9.1, 9.6a, 9.6b, 9.7a and 9.7b**

Certain precautions must be followed when checking and servicing the battery. Hydrogen gas, which is highly flammable, is always present in the battery cells, so keep lighted tobacco and all other open flames and sparks away from the battery. The electrolyte the battery is actually diluted sulfuric acid, which will cause injury if splashed on your skin or in your eyes. It will also ruin clothes and painted surfaces. When removing

the battery cables, always detach the negative cable first and hook it up last!

➡**Note: The battery is located in the trunk, to the right of the spare tire.**

1   A routine preventive maintenance program for the battery in your vehicle is the only way to ensure quick and reliable starts. But before performing any battery maintenance, make sure that you have the proper equipment necessary to work safely around the battery (see illustration).

**9.1  Tools and materials required for battery maintenance**

1   *Face shield/safety goggles* - When removing corrosion with a brush, the acidic particles can easily fly up into your eyes

2   *Baking soda* - A solution of baking soda and water can be used to neutralize corrosion

3   *Petroleum jelly* - A layer of this on the battery posts will help prevent corrosion

4   *Battery post/cable cleaner* - This wire brush cleaning tool will remove all traces of corrosion from the battery posts and cable clamps

5   *Treated felt washers* - Placing one of these on each post, directly under the cable clamps, will help prevent corrosion

6   *Puller* - Sometimes the cable clamps are very difficult to pull off the posts, even after the nut/bolt has been completely loosened. This tool pulls the clamp straight up and off the post without damage

7   *Battery post/cable cleaner* - Here is another cleaning tool which is a slightly different version of number 4 above, but it does the same thing

8   *Rubber gloves* - Another safety item to consider when servicing the battery; remember that's acid inside the battery!

2   There are also several precautions that should be taken whenever battery maintenance is performed. Before servicing the battery, always turn the engine and all accessories off and disconnect the cable from the negative terminal of the battery (see Chapter 5, Section 1).

3   The battery produces hydrogen gas, which is both flammable and explosive. Never create a spark, smoke or light a match around the battery. Always charge the battery in a ventilated area.

4   Electrolyte contains poisonous and corrosive sulfuric acid. Do not allow it to get in your eyes, on your skin or on your clothes. Never ingest it. Wear protective safety glasses when working near the battery. Keep children away from the battery.

5   Note the external condition of the battery. If the positive terminal and cable clamp on your vehicle's battery is equipped with a rubber protector, make sure that it's not torn or damaged. It should completely cover the terminal. Look for any corroded or loose connections, cracks in the case or cover or loose hold-down clamps. Also check the entire length of each cable for cracks and frayed conductors.

6   If corrosion, which looks like white, fluffy deposits (see illustration) is evident, particularly around the terminals, the battery should be removed for cleaning. Loosen the cable clamp bolts with a wrench, being careful to remove the ground cable first, and slide them off the terminals (see illustration). Then disconnect the hold-down clamp bolt and nut, remove the clamp and lift the battery from the engine compartment.

7   Clean the cable clamps thoroughly with a battery brush or a terminal cleaner and a solution of warm water and baking soda (see illustration). Wash the terminals and the top of the battery case with the same solution but make sure that the solution doesn't get into the battery. When cleaning the cables, terminals and battery top, wear safety goggles and rubber gloves to prevent any solution from coming in contact with your eyes or hands. Wear old clothes too - even diluted, sulfuric acid splashed onto clothes will burn holes in them. If the terminals have been extensively corroded, clean them up with a terminal cleaner (see illustration). Thoroughly wash all cleaned areas with plain water.

8   Make sure that the battery tray is in good condition and the hold-down clamp fasteners are tight. If the battery is removed from the tray, make sure no parts remain in the bottom of the tray when the battery is reinstalled. When reinstalling the hold-down clamp bolts, do not over-tighten them.

9   Information on removing and installing the battery can be found in Chapter 5. If you disconnected the cable(s) from the negative and/ or positive battery terminals, see Chapter 5, Section 1. Information on jump starting can be found at the front of this manual.

## CLEANING

10  Corrosion on the hold-down components, battery case and surrounding areas can be removed with a solution of water and baking soda. Thoroughly rinse all cleaned areas with plain water.

11  Any metal parts of the vehicle damaged by corrosion should be covered with a zinc-based primer, then painted.

## CHARGING

### ✳✳ WARNING:

**When batteries are being charged, hydrogen gas, which is very explosive and flammable, is produced. Do not smoke or allow open flames near a charging or a recently charged battery. Wear eye protection when near the battery during charging. Also, make sure the charger is unplugged before connecting or disconnecting the battery from the charger.**

12  Slow-rate charging is the best way to restore a battery that's discharged to the point where it will not start the engine. It's also a good way to maintain the battery charge in a vehicle that's only driven a few miles between starts. Maintaining the battery charge is particularly important in the winter when the battery must work harder to start the engine and electrical accessories that drain the battery are in greater use.

13  It's best to use a one or two-amp battery charger (sometimes called a "trickle" charger). They are the safest and put the least strain on the battery. They are also the least expensive. For a faster charge, you can use a higher amperage charger, but don't use one rated more than 1/10th the amp/hour rating of the battery. Rapid boost charges that

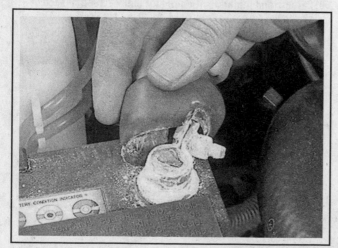

**9.6a  Battery terminal corrosion usually appears as light, fluffy powder**

**9.6b  Removing a cable from the battery post with a wrench - sometimes a pair of special battery pliers are required for this procedure if corrosion has caused deterioration of the nut hex (always remove the ground (-) cable first and hook it up last!)**

claim to restore the power of the battery in one to two hours are hardest on the battery and can damage batteries not in good condition. This type of charging should only be used in emergency situations.

14 The average time necessary to charge a battery should be listed in the instructions that come with the charger. As a general rule, a trickle charger will charge a battery in 12 to 16 hours.

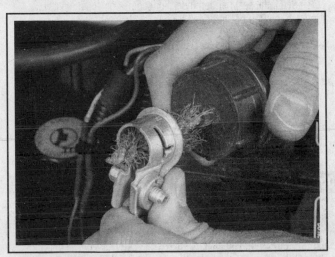

**9.7a When cleaning the cable clamps, all corrosion must be removed**

**9.7b Regardless of the type of tool used to clean the battery posts, a clean, shiny surface should be the result**

## 10 Tire rotation (every 6000 miles or 6 months)

**◆ Refer to illustrations 10.2a and 10.2b**

1 The tires should be rotated at the specified intervals and whenever uneven wear is noticed.

2 Refer to the accompanying illustrations for the preferred tire rotation pattern.

3 Refer to the information in *Jacking and towing* at the front of this manual for the proper procedures to follow when raising the vehicle and changing a tire. If the brakes are to be checked, don't apply the parking brake as stated. Make sure the tires are blocked to prevent the vehicle from rolling as it's raised.

4 Preferably, the entire vehicle should be raised at the same time. This can be done on a hoist or by jacking up each corner, then lowering the vehicle onto jackstands placed under the frame rails. Always use four jackstands and make sure the vehicle is safely supported.

5 After rotation, check and adjust the tire pressures as necessary. Tighten the lug nuts to the torque listed in this Chapter's Specifications.

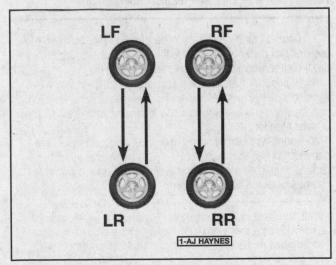

**10.2a The recommended four-tire rotation pattern for directional tires**

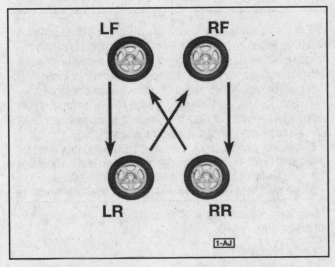

**10.2b The recommended four-tire rotation pattern for non-directional tires**

## 11 Seat belt check (every 6000 miles or 6 months)

1   Check seat belts, buckles, latch plates and guide loops for obvious damage and signs of wear.

2   Where the seat belt receptacle bolts to the floor of the vehicle, check that the bolts are secure.

3   See if the seat belt reminder light comes on when the key is turned to the Run or Start position.

## 12 Underhood hose check and replacement (every 6000 miles or 6 months)

### GENERAL

### ※※ CAUTION:

**Replacement of air conditioning hoses must be left to a dealer service department or air conditioning shop that has the equipment to depressurize the system safely and recover the refrigerant. Never remove air conditioning components or hoses until the system has been depressurized.**

1   High temperatures in the engine compartment can cause the deterioration of the rubber and plastic hoses used for engine, accessory and emission systems operation. Periodic inspection should be made for cracks, loose clamps, material hardening and leaks. Information specific to the cooling system hoses can be found in Section 13.

2   Some, but not all, hoses are secured to their fittings with clamps. Where clamps are used, check to be sure they haven't lost their tension, allowing the hose to leak. If clamps aren't used, make sure the hose has not expanded and/or hardened where it slips over the fitting, allowing it to leak.

### VACUUM HOSES

3   It's quite common for vacuum hoses, especially those in the emissions system, to be color-coded or identified by colored stripes molded into them. Various systems require hoses with different wall thickness, collapse resistance and temperature resistance. When replacing hoses, be sure the new ones are made of the same material.

4   Often the only effective way to check a hose is to remove it completely from the vehicle. If more than one hose is removed, be sure to label the hoses and fittings to ensure correct installation.

5   When checking vacuum hoses, be sure to include any plastic T-fittings in the check. Inspect the fittings for cracks and the hose where it fits over the fitting for distortion, which could cause leakage.

6   A small piece of vacuum hose (1/4-inch inside diameter) can be used as a stethoscope to detect vacuum leaks. Hold one end of the hose to your ear and probe around vacuum hoses and fittings, listening for the "hissing" sound characteristic of a vacuum leak.

### ※※ WARNING:

**When probing with the vacuum hose stethoscope, be very careful not to come into contact with moving engine components such as the drivebelt, cooling fan, etc.**

### FUEL HOSE

### ※※ WARNING:

**There are certain precautions that must be taken when inspecting or servicing fuel system components. Work in a well-ventilated area and do not allow open flames (cigarettes, appliances, etc.) or bare light bulbs near the work area. Mop up any spills immediately and do not store fuel soaked rags where they could ignite. The fuel system is under high pressure, so if any fuel lines are to be disconnected, the pressure in the system must be relieved first (see Chapter 4 for more information).**

7   Check all rubber fuel lines for deterioration and chafing. Check especially for cracks in areas where the hose bends and just before fittings, such as where a hose attaches to the fuel filter.

8   High quality fuel line, made specifically for high-pressure fuel injection systems, must be used for fuel line replacement. Never, under any circumstances, use unreinforced vacuum line, clear plastic tubing or water hose for fuel lines.

9   Spring-type clamps are commonly used on fuel lines. These clamps often lose their tension over a period of time, and can be "sprung" during removal. Replace all spring-type clamps with screw clamps whenever a hose is replaced.

## METAL LINES

10 Sections of metal line are routed along the frame, between the fuel tank and the engine. Check carefully to be sure the line has not been bent or crimped and that cracks have not started in the line.

11 If a section of metal fuel line must be replaced, only seamless steel tubing should be used, since copper and aluminum tubing don't have the strength necessary to withstand normal engine vibration.

12 Check the metal brake lines where they enter the master cylinder and brake proportioning unit for cracks in the lines or loose fittings. Any sign of brake fluid leakage calls for an immediate and thorough inspection of the brake system.

## 13  Cooling system check (every 6000 miles or 6 months)

▶ **Refer to illustration 13.4**

1   Many major engine failures can be attributed to a faulty cooling system. If the vehicle is equipped with an automatic transmission, the cooling system also cools the transmission fluid and thus plays an important role in prolonging transmission life.

2   The cooling system should be checked with the engine cold. Do this before the vehicle is driven for the day or after it has been shut off for at least three hours.

3   Remove the cooling system pressure cap and thoroughly clean the cap, inside and out, with clean water. Also clean the filler neck on the radiator. All traces of corrosion should be removed. The coolant inside the radiator should be relatively transparent. If it is rust-colored, the system should be drained, flushed and refilled (see Section 26). If the coolant level is not up to the top, add additional antifreeze/coolant mixture (see Section 4).

4   Carefully check the large upper and lower radiator hoses along with the smaller diameter heater hoses that run from the engine to the firewall. Inspect each hose along its entire length, replacing any hose that is cracked, swollen or shows signs of deterioration. Cracks may become more apparent if the hose is squeezed (see illustration). Regardless of condition, it's a good idea to replace hoses with new ones every two years.

5   Make sure all hose connections are tight. A leak in the cooling system will usually show up as white or rust-colored deposits on the areas adjoining the leak. If wire-type clamps are used at the ends of the hoses, it may be a good idea to replace them with more secure screw-type clamps.

6   Use compressed air or a soft brush to remove bugs, leaves, etc. from the front of the radiator or air conditioning condenser. Be careful not to damage the delicate cooling fins or cut yourself on them.

7   Every other inspection, or at the first indication of cooling system problems, have the cap and system pressure tested. If you don't have a pressure tester, most repair shops will do this for a minimal charge.

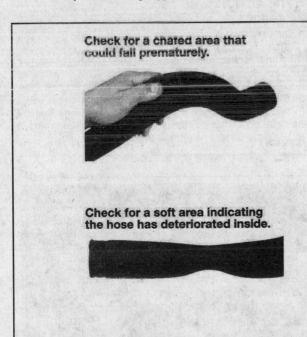
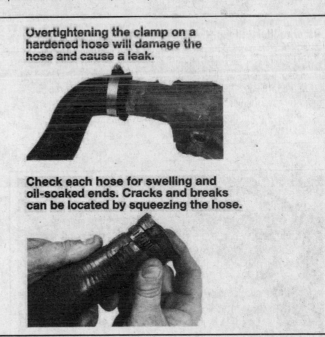

**13.4  Hoses, like drivebelts, have a habit of failing at the worst possible time - to prevent the inconvenience of a blown radiator or heater hose, inspect them carefully as shown here**

## 14  Exhaust system check (every 6000 miles or 6 months)

♦ **Refer to illustration 14.2**

1    With the engine cold (at least three hours after the vehicle has been driven), check the complete exhaust system from the manifold to the end of the tailpipe. Be careful around the catalytic converter, which may be hot even after three hours. The inspection should be done with the vehicle on a hoist to permit unrestricted access. If a hoist isn't available, raise the vehicle and support it securely on jackstands.

2    Check the exhaust pipes and connections for signs of leakage and/or corrosion indicating a potential failure. Make sure that all brackets and hangers are in good condition and tight (see illustration).

3    Inspect the underside of the body for holes, corrosion, open seams, etc. which may allow exhaust gasses to enter the passenger compartment. Seal all body openings with silicone sealant or body putty.

4    Rattles and other noises can often be traced to the exhaust system, especially the hangers, mounts and heat shields. Try to move the pipes, mufflers and catalytic converter. If the components can come in contact with the body or suspension parts, secure the exhaust system with new brackets and hangers.

**14.2  Inspect the muffler (A), and all hangers (B) for signs of deterioration**

## 15  Interior ventilation filter and charcoal filter replacement (every 15,000 miles or 12 months)

### INTERIOR VENTILATION FILTER

♦ **Refer to illustrations 15.1a and 15.1b**

1    The interior ventilation filter is located inside a housing at the right (passenger's) side of the engine compartment. To remove the ventilation filter, release the clips that secure the cover, then lift the cover off and remove the ventilation filter element (see illustrations).

2    Installation is the reverse of the removal procedure.

### CHARCOAL FILTER

3    Some models are equipped with charcoal air filtering elements in the air conditioning system, located in a housing under the right side of the instrument panel.

4    Remove the lower dash trim below the glove compartment (see the glove compartment removal procedure in Chapter 11).

5    On the bottom of the heater box, open the filter door by sliding it toward the seat.

6    Remove both charcoal filters.

7    Installation is the reverse of the removal procedure.

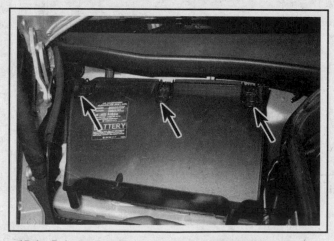

**15.1a  Release the clips to open the air inlet grille**

**15.1b  Remove the filter element**

## 16  Brake system check (every 15,000 miles or 12 months)

### ✳✳ WARNING:

**The dust created by the brake system is harmful to your health. Never blow it out with compressed air and don't inhale any of it. An approved filtering mask should be worn when working on the brakes. Do not, under any circumstances, use petroleum-based solvents to clean brake parts. Use brake system cleaner only!**

➡Note: For detailed photographs of the brake system, refer to Chapter 9.

1  In addition to the specified intervals, the brakes should be inspected every time the wheels are removed or whenever a defect is suspected.

2  Any of the following symptoms could indicate a potential brake system defect: The vehicle pulls to one side when the brake pedal is depressed; the brakes make squealing or dragging noises when applied; brake pedal travel is excessive; the pedal pulsates; or brake fluid leaks, usually onto the inside of the tire or wheel. A brake pedal that sinks slowly to the floor, with no apparent external fluid leakage, indicates a faulty master cylinder.

➡Note: A faulty master cylinder can leak fluid into the power brake booster.

3  Loosen the wheel lug nuts.
4  Raise the vehicle and place it securely on jackstands.
5  Remove the wheels (see *Jacking and towing* at the front of this book, or your owner's manual, if necessary).

## DISC BRAKES

▶ Refer to illustrations 16.7 and 16.9

6  There are two pads (an outer and an inner) in each caliper. The pads are visible with the wheels removed.

7  Check the pad thickness by looking at each end of the caliper and through the inspection window in the caliper body (see illustrations). If the lining material is less than the thickness listed in this Chapter's Specifications, replace the pads.

➡Note: Keep in mind that the lining material is riveted or bonded to a metal backing plate and the metal portion is not included in this measurement.

8  If it is difficult to determine the exact thickness of the remaining pad material by the above method, or if you are at all concerned about the condition of the pads, remove the caliper(s), then remove the pads from the calipers for further inspection (see Chapter 9).

9  Once the pads are removed from the calipers, clean them with brake cleaner and re-measure them with a ruler or a vernier caliper (see illustration).

10  Measure the disc thickness with a micrometer to make sure that it still has service life remaining. If any disc is thinner than the specified minimum thickness, replace it (see Chapter 9). Even if the disc has service life remaining, check its condition. Look for scoring, gouging and burned spots. If these conditions exist, remove the disc and have it resurfaced (see Chapter 9).

11  Before installing the wheels, check all brake lines and hoses for damage, wear, deformation, cracks, corrosion, leakage, bends and twists, particularly in the vicinity of the rubber hoses at the calipers. Check the clamps for tightness and the connections for leakage. Make sure that all hoses and lines are clear of sharp edges, moving parts and the exhaust system. If any of the above conditions are noted, repair, reroute or replace the lines and/or fittings as necessary (see Chapter 9).

## BRAKE BOOSTER CHECK

12  Sit in the driver's seat and perform the following sequence of tests.

13  With the brake fully depressed, start the engine - the pedal should

16.7  With the wheel off, check the thickness of the brake pads through the inspection hole (front disc shown, rear disc caliper similar)

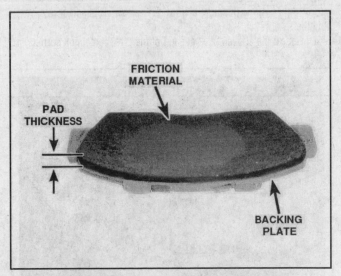

16.9  If a more precise measurement of pad thickness is necessary, remove the pads and measure the remaining friction material

move down a little when the engine starts.

14  With the engine running, depress the brake pedal several times - the travel distance should not change.

15  Depress the brake, stop the engine and hold the pedal in for about 30 seconds - the pedal should neither sink nor rise.

16  Restart the engine, run it for about a minute and turn it off. Then firmly depress the brake several times - the pedal travel should decrease with each application.

17  If your brakes do not operate as described, the brake booster has failed. Refer to Chapter 9 for the replacement procedure.

## PARKING BRAKE

18  One method of checking the parking brake is to park the vehicle on a steep hill with the parking brake set and the transmission in Neutral (be sure to stay in the vehicle for this check!). If the parking brake cannot prevent the vehicle from rolling, it's in need of adjustment (see Chapter 9).

## 17  Suspension, steering and driveaxle boot check (every 15,000 miles or 12 months)

→Note: The steering linkage and suspension components should be checked periodically. Worn or damaged suspension and steering linkage components can result in excessive and abnormal tire wear, poor ride quality and vehicle handling and reduced fuel economy. For detailed illustrations of the steering and suspension components, refer to Chapter 10.

### SHOCK ABSORBER CHECK

▶ Refer to illustration 17.6

1  Park the vehicle on level ground, turn the engine off and set the parking brake. Check the tire pressures.

2  Push down at one corner of the vehicle, then release it while noting the movement of the body. It should stop moving and come to rest in a level position within one or two bounces.

3  If the vehicle continues to move up-and-down or if it fails to return to its original position, a worn or weak shock absorber is probably the reason.

4  Repeat the above check at each of the three remaining corners of the vehicle.

5  Raise the vehicle and support it securely on jackstands.

6  Check the shock absorbers for evidence of fluid leakage (see illustration). A light film of fluid is no cause for concern. Make sure that any fluid noted is from the shocks and not from some other source. If leakage is noted, replace the shocks as a set.

7  Check the shocks to be sure that they are securely mounted and undamaged. Check the upper mounts for damage and wear. If damage or wear is noted, replace the shocks as a set (front or rear).

8  If the shocks must be replaced, refer to Chapter 10 for the procedure.

### STEERING AND SUSPENSION CHECK

▶ Refer to illustrations 17.9 and 17.11

9  Visually inspect the steering and suspension components (front and rear) for damage and distortion. Look for damaged seals, boots and bushings and leaks of any kind. Examine the bushings where the control arms meet the chassis (see illustration).

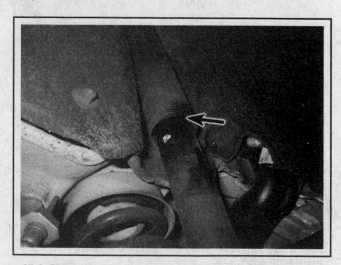

17.6  Check the shocks for leakage at the indicated area

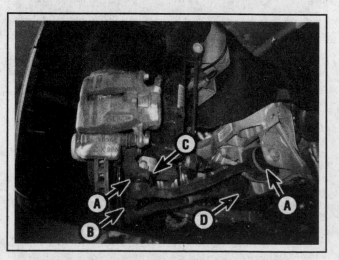

17.9  Examine the mounting points for the lower control arm on the front suspension (A), the tie-rod ends (B), the balljoints (C), and the steering gear boots (D)

**17.11 With the steering wheel in the locked position and the vehicle raised, grasp the front tire as shown and try to move it back-and-forth - if any play is noted, check the steering gear mounts and tie-rod ends for looseness**

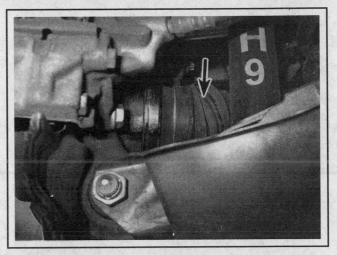

**17.14 Inspect the inner and outer driveaxle boots for loose clamps, cracks or signs of leaking lubricant**

10  Clean the lower end of the steering knuckle. Have an assistant grasp the lower edge of the tire and move the wheel in-and-out while you look for movement at the steering knuckle-to-control arm balljoint. If there is any movement the suspension balljoint(s) must be replaced.

11  Grasp each front tire at the front and rear edges, push in at the front, pull out at the rear and feel for play in the steering system components. If any freeplay is noted, check the idler arm and the tie-rod ends for looseness (see illustration).

12  Additional steering and suspension system information and illustrations can be found in Chapter 10.

## DRIVEAXLE BOOT CHECK

▶ **Refer to illustration 17.14**

13  The driveaxle boots are very important because they prevent dirt, water and foreign material from entering and damaging the constant velocity (CV) joints. Because it constantly pivots back and forth following the steering action of the front hub, the outer CV boot wears out sooner and should be inspected regularly.

14  Inspect the boots for tears and cracks as well as loose clamps (see illustration). If there is any evidence of cracks or leaking lubricant, they must be replaced as described in Chapter 8.

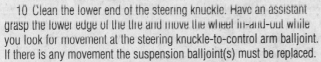

## 18  Fuel system check (every 15,000 miles or 12 months)

### ❊❊ WARNING:

**Gasoline is flammable, so take extra precautions when you work on any part of the fuel system. Don't smoke or allow open flames or bare light bulbs near the work area, and don't work in a garage where a gas-type appliance (such as a water heater or clothes dryer) is present. Since fuel is carcinogenic, wear fuel-resistant gloves when there's a possibility of being exposed to fuel, and, if you spill any fuel on your skin, rinse it off immediately with soap and water. Mop up any spills immediately and do not store fuel-soaked rags where they could ignite. When you perform any kind of work on the fuel system, wear safety glasses and have a Class B type fire extinguisher on hand. The fuel system is under constant pressure, so, before any lines are disconnected, the fuel system pressure must be relieved (see Chapter 4).**

1  If you smell fuel while driving or after the vehicle has been sitting in the sun, inspect the fuel system immediately.

2  Remove the fuel filler cap and inspect it for damage and corrosion. The gasket should have an unbroken sealing imprint. If the gasket is damaged or corroded, install a new cap.

3  Inspect the fuel feed line for cracks. Make sure that the connections between the fuel lines and the fuel injection system and between the fuel lines and the in-line fuel filter are tight.

### ❊❊ WARNING:

**Your vehicle is fuel injected, so you must relieve the fuel system pressure before servicing fuel system components. The fuel system pressure relief procedure is outlined in Chapter 4.**

4   Since some components of the fuel system - the fuel tank and part of the fuel feed and return lines, for example - are underneath the vehicle, they can be inspected more easily with the vehicle raised on a hoist. If that's not possible, raise the vehicle and support it on jackstands.

5   With the vehicle raised and safely supported, inspect the fuel tank and filler neck for punctures, cracks and other damage. The connection between the filler neck and the tank is particularly critical. Sometimes a rubber filler neck will leak because of loose clamps or deteriorated rubber. Inspect all fuel tank mounting brackets and straps to be sure that the tank is securely attached to the vehicle.

**❊❊ WARNING:**

Do not, under any circumstances, try to repair a fuel tank (except rubber components). A welding torch or any open flame can easily cause fuel vapors inside the tank to explode.

6   Carefully check all rubber hoses and metal lines leading away from the fuel tank. Check for loose connections, deteriorated hoses, crimped lines and other damage. Repair or replace damaged sections as necessary (see Chapter 4).

## 19  Drivebelt check and replacement (every 15,000 miles or 12 months)

1   The drivebelt is located at the front of the engine and plays an important role in the overall operation of the vehicle and its components. Due to its function and material make-up, the drivebelt is prone to failure after a period of time and should be inspected and adjusted periodically to prevent major engine damage.

2   The vehicles covered by this manual are equipped with a single self-adjusting serpentine drivebelt, which is used to drive all of the accessory components such as the alternator, power steering pump, water pump and air conditioning compressor.

## INSPECTION

▶ **Refer to illustration 19.4**

3   With the engine off, open the hood and locate the drivebelt at the front of the engine. Using your fingers (and a flashlight, if necessary),

move along the belts checking for cracks and separation of the belt plies. Also check for fraying and glazing, which gives the belt a shiny appearance. Both sides of each belt should be inspected, which means you will have to twist the belt to check the underside.

4   Check the ribs on the underside of the belt. They should all be the same depth, with none of the surface uneven (see illustration).

5   The tension of the belt is automatically adjusted by the belt tensioner and does not require any adjustments.

## REPLACEMENT

▶ **Refer to illustrations 19.6a and 19.6b**

6   To replace the belt, rotate the tensioner counterclockwise to relieve the tension on the belt (see illustration). Some models have a cast-in-hex on the tensioner arm that will accept a wrench or socket

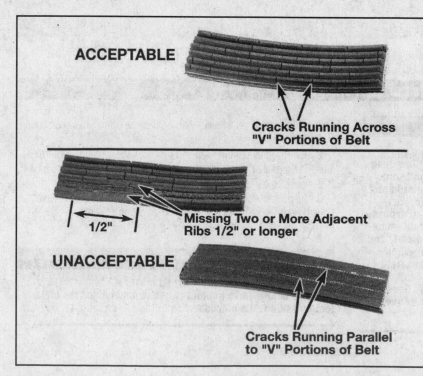

ACCEPTABLE

Cracks Running Across "V" Portions of Belt

1/2"

Missing Two or More Adjacent Ribs 1/2" or longer

UNACCEPTABLE

Cracks Running Parallel to "V" Portions of Belt

**19.4  Here are some of the more common problems associated with drivebelts (check the belts very carefully to prevent an untimely breakdown)**

19.6a Rotate the tensioner arm to relieve belt tension

19.6b Some models have a cast-in-hex on the tensioner arm

(see illustration). On other models, place a Torx-bit onto the fastener in the center of the pulley.

7  Remove the belt from the auxiliary components and carefully release the tensioner.

8  Route the new belt over the various pulleys, again rotating the tensioner to allow the belt to be installed, then release the belt tensioner. Make sure the belt fits properly into the pulley grooves - it must be completely engaged.

➡ **Note: Most models have a drivebelt routing decal on the upper radiator panel to help during drivebelt installation.**

9  Reconnect the battery.

## TENSIONER REPLACEMENT

10  Remove the drivebelt.

11  Remove the fasteners that secure the tensioner to the engine, then remove the tensioner.

12  Installation is the reverse of removal. Tighten the mounting bolt(s) to the torque listed in this Chapter's Specifications.

## 20  Brake fluid change (every 30,000 miles or 24 months)

### ❋❋ WARNING:

**Brake fluid can harm your eyes and damage painted surfaces, so use extreme caution when handling or pouring it. Do not use brake fluid that has been standing open or is more than one year old. Brake fluid absorbs moisture from the air. Excess moisture can cause a dangerous loss of braking effectiveness.**

➡ **Note: Used brake fluid is considered a hazardous waste and it must be disposed of in accordance with federal, state and local laws. DO NOT pour it down the sink, into septic tanks or storm drains, or on the ground.**

1  At the specified intervals, the brake fluid should be replaced. Since the brake fluid may drip or splash when pouring it, place plenty of rags around the master cylinder to protect any surrounding painted surfaces.

2  Before beginning work, purchase the specified brake fluid (see *Recommended lubricants and fluids* at the end of this Chapter).

3  Remove the cap from the master cylinder reservoir.

4  Using a hand suction pump or similar device, withdraw the fluid from the master cylinder reservoir.

5  Add new fluid to the master cylinder until the level of the fluid rises to the base of the filler neck.

6  Bleed the brake system as described in Chapter 9 at all four brakes until new and uncontaminated fluid is expelled from the bleeder screw. Be sure to maintain the fluid level in the master cylinder as you perform the bleeding process. If you allow the master cylinder to run dry, air will enter the system.

7  Refill the master cylinder with fluid and check the operation of the brakes. The pedal should feel solid when depressed, with no sponginess.

### ❋❋ WARNING:

**Do not operate the vehicle if you are in doubt about the effectiveness of the brake system.**

## 21 Spark plug check and replacement (every 30,000 miles or 24 months)

▶ Refer to illustrations 21.2, 21.5, 21.7, 21.10, 21.11, 21.12 and 21.13

1   The spark plugs are located in the cylinder head(s).

2   In most cases the tools necessary for spark plug replacement include a spark plug socket which fits onto a ratchet (this special socket is padded inside to protect the porcelain insulators on the new plugs and hold them in place), various extensions and a feeler gauge to check and adjust the spark plug gap (see illustration). Since these engines are equipped with an aluminum cylinder head, a torque wrench should be used when tightening the spark plugs.

3   The best approach when replacing the spark plugs is to purchase the new spark plugs beforehand, adjust them to the proper gap and then replace each plug one at a time. When buying the new spark plugs, be sure to obtain the correct plug for your specific engine. This information can be found in this Chapter's Specifications, or on the Vehicle Emissions Control Information (VECI) label located under the hood. If differences exist between the sources, purchase the spark plug type specified on the VECI label as it was printed for your specific engine.

4   Allow the engine to cool completely before attempting to remove any of the plugs. During this cooling off time, each of the new spark plugs can be inspected for defects and the gaps can be checked.

5   The gap is checked by inserting the proper thickness gauge between the electrodes at the tip of the plug (see illustration). The gap between the electrodes should be as listed in this Chapter's Specifications or in your owner's manual. The wire should touch each of the electrodes. Also, at this time check for cracks in the spark plug body (if any are found, the plug must not be used).

6   Cover the fender to prevent damage to the paint. Fender covers are available from auto parts stores but an old blanket will work just fine.

7   On 2001 through 2005 V6 engines, there are two spark plugs per cylinder. The coil packs are mounted on top of the valve covers with short spark plug leads connecting them to the plugs. With the engine cool, remove the spark plug wire from one spark plug. Pull on the boot at the end of the spark plug wire - do not pull on the wire (see illustration).

8   On 2006 and later V6 engines, and on all four-cylinder engines, there is one centrally mounted spark plug per cylinder. The ignition coils are mounted directly over the plugs. Remove each ignition coil from the spark plug (see Chapter 5).

9   If compressed air is available, use it to blow any dirt or foreign material away from the spark plug area.

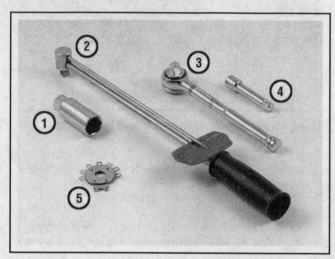

**21.2  Tools required for changing spark plugs**

*1   Spark plug socket* - This will have special padding inside to protect the spark plug porcelain insulator

*2   Torque wrench* - Although not mandatory, use of this tool is the best way to ensure that the plugs are tightened properly

*3   Ratchet* - Standard hand tool to fit the plug socket

*4   Extension* - Depending on model and accessories, you may need special extensions and universal joints to reach one or more of the plugs

*5   Spark plug gap gauge* - This gauge for checking the gap comes in a variety of styles. Make sure the gap for your engine is included

**21.5  Spark plug manufacturers recommend using a wire-type gauge when checking the gap - the wire should slide between the electrodes with a slight drag**

**21.7  When removing the spark plug wires, pull only on the boot**

**21.10  Use a socket and extension to unscrew the spark plugs**

10 Place the spark plug socket over the plug and remove it from the engine by turning it in a counterclockwise direction (see illustration).

11 Compare the spark plug with the chart (see illustration) to get an indication of the overall running condition of the engine.

12 It's a good idea to lightly coat the threads of the spark plugs with an anti-seize compound (see illustration) to insure that the spark plugs do not seize in the aluminum cylinder head.

13 It's often difficult to insert spark plugs into their holes without cross-threading them. To avoid this possibility, fit a piece of rubber hose over the end of the spark plug (see illustration). The flexible hose acts as a universal joint to help align the plug with the plug hole. Should the plug begin to cross-thread, the hose will slip on the spark plug, preventing thread damage. Install the spark plug and tighten it to the torque listed in this Chapter's Specifications.

14 Before pushing the spark plug wire onto the end of the plug, inspect the wires following the procedures outlined in Section 22.

15 Repeat the procedure for the remaining spark plugs.

A **normally worn** spark plug should have light tan or gray deposits on the firing tip.

A **carbon fouled** plug, identified by soft, sooty, black deposits, may indicate an improperly tuned vehicle. Check the air cleaner, ignition components and engine control system.

An **oil fouled** spark plug indicates an engine with worn piston rings and/or bad valve seals allowing excessive oil to enter the chamber.

This spark plug has been **left in the engine too long,** as evidenced by the extreme gap- Plugs with such an extreme gap can cause misfiring and stumbling accompanied by a noticeable lack of power.

A **physically damaged** spark plug may be evidence of severe detonation in that cylinder. Watch that cylinder carefully between services, as a continued detonation will not only damage the plug, but could also damage the engine.

A **bridged or almost bridged** spark plug, identified by a build-up between the electrodes caused by excessive carbon or oil build-up on the plug.

**21.11 Inspect the spark plug to determine engine running conditions**

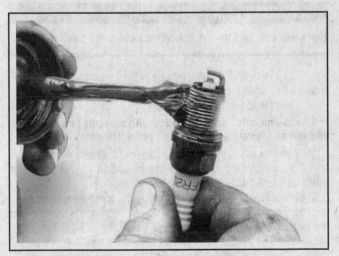
**21.12 Apply a thin film of anti-seize compound to the spark plug threads to prevent damage to the cylinder head**

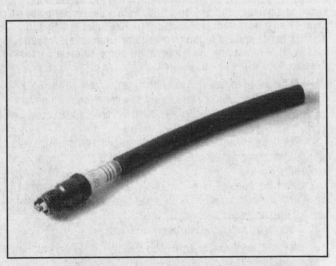
**21.13 A length of snug-fitting rubber hose will save time and prevent damaged threads when installing the spark plugs**

## 22  Spark plug wires - check (every 30,000 miles or 24 months)

➡**Note: This procedure applies to 2005 and earlier V6 models only.**

1  The spark plug wires should be checked at the recommended intervals or whenever new spark plugs are installed.

2  Begin this procedure by making a visual check of the spark plug wires while the engine is running. In a darkened garage (make sure there is adequate ventilation) or at night, start the engine and observe each plug wire. Be careful not to come into contact with any moving engine parts. If possible, use an insulated or non-conductive object to wiggle each wire. If there is a break in the wire, you will see arcing or a small blue spark coming from the damaged area. Secondary ignition voltage increases with engine speed and sometimes a damaged wire will not produce an arc at idle speed. Have an assistant press the accelerator pedal to raise the engine speed to approximately 2000 rpm. Check the spark plug wires for arcing as stated previously. If arcing is noticed, replace all spark plug wires.

## 23  Differential lubricant change (every 60,000 miles or 48 months)

1  This procedure should be performed after the vehicle has been driven so the lubricant will be warm and therefore will flow out of the differential more easily. Raise the vehicle and support it securely on jackstands.

2  Remove the check/fill plug, then remove the drain plug and drain the lubricant (see illustration 4.32).

3  Reinstall the drain plug and tighten it securely.

4  Use a hand pump, syringe or funnel to fill differential housing with the specified lubricant until the lubricant level is up to the bottom of the hole.

5  Install the filler plug and tighten it securely.

## 24  Automatic transmission fluid and filter change (every 30,000 miles or 24 months)

▶ **Refer to illustrations 24.5, 24.6, 24.8 and 24.9**

➡**Note: To perform this procedure you'll have to obtain a dipstick (part number 140 589 15 21 00) from a dealer parts department or an aftermarket tool supplier (unlike most vehicles, a dipstick is not present in the transmission filler tube). A scan tool capable of reading the temperature of the automatic transmission fluid will also be required.**

1  At the specified time intervals, the transmission fluid should be drained and replaced. Since the fluid will remain hot long after driving, perform this procedure only after everything has cooled down completely.

2  Before beginning work, purchase the specified transmission fluid (see *Recommended lubricants and fluids* at the end of this Chapter) and a new filter.

3  Other tools necessary for this job include jackstands to support the vehicle in a raised position, a drain pan capable of holding several quarts, newspapers and clean rags.

4  Raise and support the vehicle on jackstands.

5  Place the drain pan underneath the transmission pan. Remove the drain plug and allow the fluid to drain, then reinsert the plug and tighten it securely (see illustration). Measure the amount of fluid drained (the same amount will be added to the transmission later).

6  Remove the transmission pan bolts (see illustration), then remove the pan, prying gently if necessary.

### ※※ WARNING:

**There will still be some transmission fluid in the pan.**

7  Carefully clean the gasket surface of the transmission and pan to remove all traces of the old gasket and sealant.

8  Clean the pan with solvent and dry it.

➡**Note: Some models are equipped with magnets in the transmission pan to catch metal debris (see illustration).**

Clean the magnet thoroughly. A small amount of metal material is normal at the magnet. If there is considerable debris, consult a dealer or transmission specialist.

9  Remove the filter from the valve body inside the transmission (see illustration).

10  Install a new O-ring and filter.

11  Make sure the gasket surface on the transmission pan is clean, then install a new gasket on the pan. Put the pan in place against the transmission and install the bolts. Tighten each bolt a little at a time to the torque listed in this Chapter's Specifications.

**24.5  Remove the drain plug and allow the fluid to drain**

**24.6  Remove the transmission pan bolts**

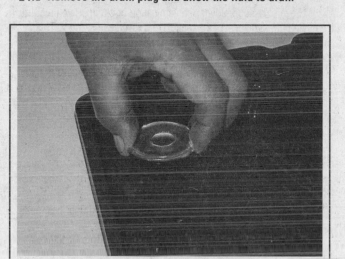

**24.8  Clean the transmission pan magnet thoroughly**

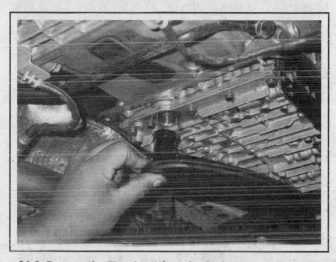

**24.9  Remove the filter from the valve body**

12  Lower the vehicle and add the specified type of automatic transmission fluid (the same amount that was drained in Step 5), through the filler tube (see Section 4).

13  With the transmission in Park and the parking brake set, run the engine at a fast idle, but don't race it.

14  Move the gear selector through each range and back to Park, then let the engine idle for a few minutes. Check the fluid level (see Section 4). It may be low. Add enough fluid to bring the level to the proper mark on the dipstick. Be careful not to overfill.

15  Check under the vehicle for leaks during the first few trips. Check the fluid level again when the transmission is hot (see Section 4).

## 25  Manual transmission lubricant change (every 60,000 miles or 48 months)

1  This procedure should be performed after the vehicle has been driven so the lubricant will be warm and therefore will flow out of the transmission more easily. Raise the vehicle and support it securely on jackstands.

2  Move a drain pan, rags, newspapers and wrenches under the transmission.

3  Remove the fill plug from the side of the transmission case, then remove the transmission drain plug at the bottom of the case and allow the lubricant to drain into the pan.

4  After the lubricant has drained completely, reinstall the drain plug and tighten it securely.

5  Using a hand pump, syringe or squeeze bottle, fill the transmission with the specified lubricant until it just reaches the bottom edge of the hole. Reinstall the fill plug and tighten it securely.

6  Lower the vehicle.

7  Drive the vehicle for a short distance, then check the drain and fill plugs for leakage.

## 26  Cooling system servicing (draining, flushing and refilling) (every 60 months)

### ✳✳ WARNING:

Do not allow antifreeze to come in contact with your skin or painted surfaces of the vehicle. Rinse off spills immediately with plenty of water. Antifreeze is highly toxic if ingested. Never leave antifreeze lying around in an open container or in puddles on the floor; children and pets are attracted by it's sweet smell and may drink it. Check with local authorities about disposing of used antifreeze. Many communities have collection centers which will see that antifreeze is disposed of safely.

1   Periodically, the cooling system should be drained, flushed and refilled to replenish the antifreeze mixture and prevent formation of rust and corrosion, which can impair the performance of the cooling system and cause engine damage. When the cooling system is serviced, all hoses and the expansion tank cap should be checked and replaced if necessary.

## DRAINING

▶ **Refer to illustration 26.4**

2   Apply the parking brake and block the wheels. If the vehicle has just been driven, wait several hours to allow the engine to cool down before beginning this procedure.

3   Once the engine is completely cool, remove the expansion tank cap.

4   Move a large container under the radiator drain to catch the coolant. Attach a length of hose to the drain fitting to direct the coolant into the container, then open the drain fitting (a pair of pliers may be required to turn it) (see illustration).

5   After the coolant stops flowing out of the radiator, move the container under the engine block drain plug and allow the coolant in the block to drain. The block drain plug is generally located about one to two inches above the oil pan - there is one on the side of the engine block.

6   While the coolant is draining, check the condition of the radiator hoses, heater hoses and clamps (refer to Section 13 if necessary). Replace any damaged clamps or hoses.

7   Apply thread sealant to the block drain plug. Reinstall the drain plug and tighten it securely.

## FLUSHING

▶ **Refer to illustration 26.10**

8   Once the system has completely drained, remove the thermostat housing from the engine (see Chapter 3), then reinstall the housing without the thermostat. This will allow the system to be thoroughly flushed.

9   Disconnect the upper hose from the radiator.

10  Place a garden hose in the upper radiator inlet and flush the system until the water runs clear at the upper radiator hose (see illustration).

11  Severe cases of radiator contamination or clogging will require removing the radiator (see Chapter 3) and reverse flushing it. This involves inserting the hose in the bottom radiator outlet to allow the clean water to run against the normal flow, draining out through the top. A radiator repair shop should be consulted if further cleaning or repair is necessary.

12  When the coolant is regularly drained and the system refilled with the correct coolant mixture, there should be no need to employ chemical cleaners or descalers.

## REFILLING

13  Close and tighten the radiator drain.

14  Place the heater temperature control in the maximum heat position.

15  Make sure to use the proper coolant listed in this Chapter's

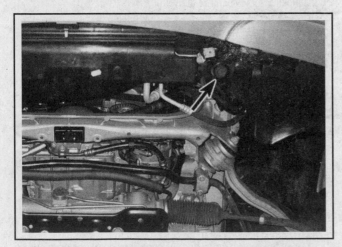

**26.4  The radiator drain fitting is located at the lower corner of the radiator**

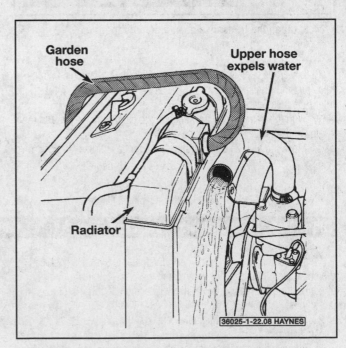

Garden hose

Upper hose expels water

Radiator

36025-1-22.08 HAYNES

**26.10  With the thermostat removed, disconnect the upper radiator hose and flush the radiator and engine block with a garden hose**

Specifications. Slowly fill the cooling system at the expansion tank with the recommended mixture of antifreeze and water.

16 Continue adding coolant to the expansion tank until the level is up to the black top part of the reservoir on the expansion tank. Wait five minutes and recheck the coolant level, adding if necessary.

17 Install the expansion tank cap and run the engine in a well-ventilated area until the thermostat opens (coolant will begin flowing through the radiator and the upper radiator hose will become hot).

18 Turn the engine off and let it cool. Add more coolant mixture to bring it up to the proper level on the expansion tank.

19 Squeeze the upper radiator hose to expel air, then add more coolant mixture if necessary. Install the expansion tank cap.

20 Start the engine, allow it to reach normal operating temperature and check for leaks. Also, set the heater and blower controls to the maximum setting and check to see that the heater output from the air ducts is warm. This is a good indication that all air has been purged from the cooling system.

## 27 Transfer case lubricant change (every 60,000 miles [96,000 km] or 48 months)

1 Changing the transfer case lubricant is only slightly more involved than checking the lubricant level. Refer to Section 4 and follow the procedure for checking the lubricant level, but also remove the drain plug and allow the lubricant to drain into a pan.

2 After the lubricant has finished draining, install the drain plug (be sure to use a new sealing ring) and tighten it to the torque listed in this Chapter's Specifications.

3 Add the proper lubricant through the filler plug hole until it flows out the check plug hole. Once the lubricant no longer drips from the check plug hole, install the check plug and filler plug (be sure to use new sealing rings) and tighten them to the torque listed in this Chapter's Specifications.

## Specifications

### Recommended lubricants and fluids

➡Note: Listed here are manufacturer recommendations at the time this manual was written. Manufacturers occasionally upgrade their fluid and lubricant specifications, so check with your local auto parts store for current recommendations.

| | |
|---|---|
| Engine oil | |
| Type | API grade "certified for gasoline engines," fully synthetic |
| Oil viscosity* | |
| Recommended (for most any operating temperature range) | SAE 0W-30, 0W-40, 5W-30, 5W-40, 5W-50 |
| Acceptable alternative | |
| Temperatures always above -4-degrees F (-20-degrees C) | SAE 10W-30, 10W-40, 10W-50, 10W-60 |
| Temperatures always above 5-degrees F (-15-degrees C) | SAE 15W-40, 15W-50 |
| Temperatures always above 23-degrees F (-5-degrees C) | SAE 20W-40, 20W-50 |
| Automatic transmission fluid type | Mercedes-Benz automatic transmission fluid or equivalent |
| Manual transmission fluid type | Mercedes-Benz manual transmission fluid or equivalent |
| Coolant | 50/50 mixture of Mercedes-Benz 325.0 Anticorrosion/antifreeze (or equivalent) and water |
| Differential lubricant type | |
| Front differential (AWD models) | SAE 85W-90 hypoid gear oil |
| Rear differential | SAE 85W-90 hypoid gear oil |
| Transfer case lubricant type (AWD models) | Mercedes-Benz automatic transmission fluid or equivalent |
| Brake fluid type | DOT 4 brake fluid |
| Power steering fluid | Mercedes-Benz power steering fluid (Pentosin CHF 11S) or equivalent |

*Choice of viscosity may be determined/limited by brand of oil.

## Specifications (continued)

### Capacities*

Cooling system

    Four-cylinder models

        2004 and earlier models        Up to 15.3 quarts (14.5 liters)

        2005 models        Up to 6 quarts (5.7 liters)

    V6 models

        2005 and earlier models        Up to 6.8 quarts (6.4 liters)

        2006 and later models        Up to 7.5 quarts (7.1 liters)

Engine oil (with filter change)

    Four-cylinder models

        2002        7.4 quarts (7 liters)

        2003 and later        5.8 quarts (5.5 liters)

    V6 models

        2002        8.5 quarts (8 liters)

        2003 through 2005        Up to 7.9 quarts (7.5 liters)

        2006 and later        8.5 quarts (8 liters)

    Automatic transmission        Up to 9 quarts (8.5 liters)**

    Manual transmission (drain and refill)        Up to 1.6 quarts (1.5 liters)**

    Rear axle        Up to 1.7 quarts (1.6 liters)

    Front axle (AWD models)        0.48 quarts (0.46 liters)

    Transfer case (AWD models)        0.56 quarts (0.59 liters)

*All capacities approximate. Add as necessary to bring the appropriate levels.*

**Note: This is a dry-fill capacity. The best way to determine the amount of fluid to add during a routine fluid change is to measure the amount drained. When refilling, add only 5.3 quarts (5 liters) initially, then check the fluid level and add a little at a time, as necessary. It is important not to overfill the transmission.**

### Ignition system

Spark plug type

    Four-cylinder engine

        2002 models        NGK IFR6D10 or equivalent

        2003 and later models        Bosch F6MPP332 or equivalent

    V6 engine

        2002 and earlier models        Bosch F8DPER or equivalent

        2003 through 2005 models        Bosch F8DPP332 or equivalent

        2006 and later models        Bosch Platinum Y7MPP33

Spark plug gap

    Four-cylinder engine

        2002        0.039 inch (1 mm)

        2003 and later models        0.031 inch (0.8 mm)

    V6 engine

        2005 and earlier models        0.039 inch (1 mm)

        2006 and later models        0.031 inch (0.8 mm)

Firing order

    Four-cylinder engines        1-3-4-2

    V6 engines        1-4-3-6-2-5

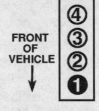

FRONT OF VEHICLE

72031-1-SPECS HAYNES

**Cylinder locations - 4-cylinder engine**

63040-2B-specs HAYNES

**Cylinder locations - V6 engines**

## Specifications (continued)

### Brakes

| | |
|---|---|
| Disc brake pad lining thickness (minimum) | 1/8 inch (3.2 mm) |
| Parking brake shoe lining thickness (minimum) | 1/16 inch (1.6 mm) |

| Torque specifications | Ft-lbs (unless otherwise indicated) | Nm |
|---|---|---|

➡Note: One foot-pound (ft-lb) of torque is equivalent to 12 inch-pounds (in-lbs) of torque. Torque values below approximately 15 ft-lbs are expressed in inch-pounds, since most foot-pound torque wrenches are not accurate at these smaller values.

| | | |
|---|---|---|
| Engine oil drain plug | 141 in-lbs | 16 |
| Automatic transmission pan bolts | | |
|     Type 722.6 transmission | 71 in-lbs | 8 |
|     Type 722.9 transmission | | |
|         Step 1 | 35.4 in-lbs | 4 |
|         Step 2 | Tighten an additional 180-degrees | |
| Automatic transmission drain plug | | |
|     Type 722.6 transmission | 177 in-lbs | 20 |
|     Type 722.9 transmission | 16.2 | 22 |
| Manual transmission | | |
|     Drain plug | 22 | 30 |
|     Fill plug | 25 | 35 |
| Differential drain and fill plugs | | |
|     Front (AWD models) | 22 | 30 |
|     Rear | 37 | 50 |
| Transfer case drain and fill plugs | 22 | 30 |
| Drivebelt tensioner | | |
|     Tensioner mounting bolts | | |
|         Threads pre-tapped | 18.5 | 25 |
|         Threads not pre-tapped | | |
|          (new timing chain case) | 25.8 | 35 |
|     Tensioner shock absorber | | |
|         To tensioner | 18.5 | 25 |
|         To water pump | 25.8 | 35 |
| Spark plugs | 18.5 | 25 |
| Wheel bolts | 80 | 108 |

**Notes**

# 2A
## FOUR-CYLINDER ENGINES

## Section

## Reference to other Chapters

## 1 General information

This Part of Chapter 2 is devoted to in-vehicle repair procedures for the 1.8L and 2.3L four-cylinder engines. These engines utilize two overhead-camshafts on an aluminum cylinder head. These engines are equipped with a belt-driven supercharger to provide more power. The 2002 2.3L engine is referred to as the "type 111," while the later 1.8L engine (2003 to 2005) is referred to as the "type 271" engine.

Information concerning engine removal and installation and engine overhaul can be found in Part C of this Chapter.

The following repair procedures are based on the assumption that the engine is installed in the vehicle. If the engine has been removed from the vehicle and mounted on a stand, many of the steps outlined in this Part of Chapter 2 will not apply.

## 2 Repair operations possible with the engine in the vehicle

Many major repair operations can be accomplished without removing the engine from the vehicle.

Clean the engine compartment and the exterior of the engine with some type of degreaser before any work is done. It will make the job easier and help keep dirt out of the internal areas of the engine.

Depending on the components involved, it may be helpful to raise the hood to its full-open position as repairs are performed; to do this, open the hood, then push the button on the left support strut and raise the hood until it is vertical. Cover the fenders to prevent damage to the paint. Special pads are available, but an old bedspread or blanket will also work.

If vacuum, exhaust, oil or coolant leaks develop, indicating a need for gasket or seal replacement, the repairs can generally be made with the engine in the vehicle. The intake and exhaust manifold gaskets, oil pan gasket, crankshaft oil seals and cylinder head gasket are all accessible with the engine in place.

Exterior engine components, such as the intake and exhaust manifolds, the oil pan, the oil pump, the water pump (see Chapter 3), the starter motor, the alternator and the fuel system components (see Chapter 4) can be removed for repair with the engine in place.

Since the cylinder head can be removed without pulling the engine, valve component servicing can also be accomplished with the engine in the vehicle. Replacement of the camshafts, timing chains and sprockets are also possible with the engine in the vehicle.

In extreme cases caused by a lack of necessary equipment, repair or replacement of piston rings, pistons, connecting rods and rod bearings is possible with the engine in the vehicle. However, this practice is not recommended because of the cleaning and preparation work that must be done to the components involved.

## 3 Top Dead Center (TDC) for number one piston - locating

◆ **Refer to illustration 3.8**

1 Top Dead Center (TDC) is the highest point in the cylinder that each piston reaches as it travels up the cylinder bore. Each piston reaches TDC on the compression stroke and again on the exhaust stroke, but TDC generally refers to piston position on the compression stroke.

2 Positioning the piston(s) at TDC is an essential part of certain procedures such as valve timing, camshaft and timing chain/sprocket removal.

3 Before beginning this procedure, be sure to place the transmission in Park or Neutral and apply the parking brake or block the rear wheels. Also, disconnect the cable from the negative terminal of the battery, then remove the ignition coils (see Chapter 5) and the spark plugs (see Chapter 1).

4 The preferred method is to turn the crankshaft with a socket and ratchet or breaker bar attached to the bolt threaded into the front of the crankshaft. When looking at the front of the engine, normal crankshaft rotation is clockwise. Turn the bolt in a clockwise direction only.

5 Install a compression pressure gauge in the number one spark plug hole (see Chapter 2C). It should be a gauge with a screw-in fitting and a hose at least six inches long.

6 Rotate the crankshaft while observing for pressure on the compression gauge. The moment the gauge shows pressure indicates that the number one cylinder is on the compression stroke.

7  Once the compression stroke has begun, TDC for the compression stroke of the number one cylinder is reached by bringing the piston to the top of the cylinder.

8  These engines are equipped with a vibration damper that has markings to identify the position of the crankshaft for timing purposes. When the compression gauge is showing pressure in cylinder number 1, turn the crankshaft front bolt until the "zero" or "OT" mark on the pulley aligns with the stationary pointer on the timing cover (see illustration).

9  After the number one piston has been positioned at TDC on the compression stroke, TDC for any of the remaining cylinders can be located by turning the crankshaft 180-degrees and following the firing order (refer to the Specifications). For example, rotating the engine 180-degrees past TDC #1 will put the engine at TDC compression for cylinder #3.

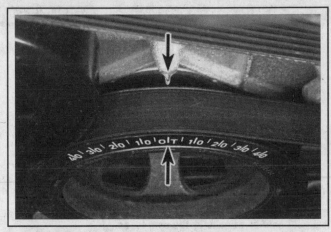

**3.8  Align the mark on the damper with the "OT" mark on the timing chain cover**

---

## 4  Valve cover - removal and installation

### REMOVAL

1  Disconnect the cable from the negative terminal of the battery (see Chapter 5, Section 1).

2  Remove the engine cover. On the type 111 engines (2002 models), it is secured by bolts, and the cover is clipped to studs on the engine. Simply pull the cover up to remove (see Chapter 1).

3  Remove the ignition coils and spark plugs (see Chapter 5).

4  Remove the PCV hose from the grommet on the valve cover (see Chapter 6).

5  Disconnect the electrical connector at the camshaft position sensor (see Chapter 6)

6  Loosen the valve cover mounting bolts a little at a time, then remove them.

7  Detach the valve cover.

➡ **Note: If the cover sticks to the cylinder head, use a block of wood and a hammer to dislodge it.**

### INSTALLATION

▸ **Refer to illustration 4.10**

8  The mating surfaces of each cylinder head and valve cover must be perfectly clean when the covers are installed. Inspect the rubber gaskets; if they're in good condition and there were no oil leaks, they can be re-used.

9  Clean the mounting bolt threads with a die (if necessary) to remove any corrosion and restore damaged threads. Use a tap to clean the threaded holes in the heads.

10  Place the valve cover in position, then install the bolts. Tighten the bolts in the recommended sequence (see illustration), in several steps, to the torque listed in this Chapter's Specifications.

11  Complete the installation by reversing the removal procedure. Start the engine and check carefully for oil leaks.

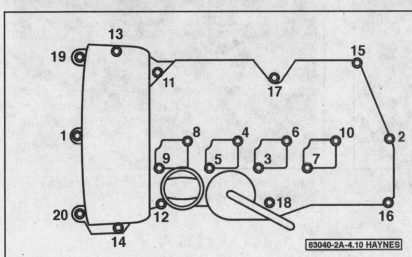

**4.10  Valve cover bolt TIGHTENING sequence - type 271 (2003 and later) shown, type 111 (2002) similar**

63040-2A-4.10 HAYNES

### 5  Cam followers/rocker arms and hydraulic lash adjusters - removal, inspection and installation

1  Before beginning this procedure, be sure to place the transmission in Park or Neutral, apply the parking brake and block the rear wheels. Disconnect the cable from the negative terminal of the battery (see Chapter 5, Section 1).

2  Remove the camshafts (see Section 7).

## 2002 MODELS (TYPE 111 ENGINE)

▶ **Refer to illustrations 5.4a and 5.4b**

➡**Note: The type 111 engine uses bucket-type hydraulic cam followers, actuated directly by the cam lobes.**

3  Before removing the cam followers, use a wooden dowel to push down on each follower and note its action. Each follower should feel solid; if any follower compresses more easily than the others, replace all of the followers as a set.

➡**Note: When pushing down on a follower, don't use too much force, or you'll wind up pushing the valve off its seat.**

4  Using a suction cup tool, remove the cam followers from the cylinder head (see illustrations). Store the cam followers in order, upright, in a container partially filled with clean engine oil (this will prevent them from bleeding down).

5  Inspect the surfaces of each cam follower for scoring or other signs of wear. Again, if one is bad, it's a good idea to replace all of them as a set.

6  Installation is the reverse of removal. Be sure to lubricate the followers with clean engine oil before installing them.

➡**Note: After the engine is started, there may be some temporary noise from the valvetrain until engine oil pressure fills the cam followers.**

## 2003 THROUGH 2005 MODELS (TYPE 271 ENGINE)

➡**Note: The valves on the type 271 engine are actuated by the camshafts via rocker arms, and hydraulic lash adjusters mounted in the valve-end of each rocker arm.**

7  Before the rocker arms and lash adjusters are removed, arrange to label and store them, so they can be kept separate and reinstalled on the same valve they were removed from.

8  Using moderate force, push on the lash adjuster end of each rocker arm. The lash adjuster should feel fairly solid; if any lash adjuster's plunger compresses more easily than the others, replace all of the lash adjusters as a set.

➡**Note: When pushing down on a lash adjuster, don't use too much force, or you'll wind up pushing the valve off its seat.**

9  Remove each rocker arm by lifting straight up. The hydraulic lash adjuster will come out of its bore along with the rocker arm.

10  Push the retaining clip off by hand, then remove the lash adjuster from the rocker arm. Store the lash adjusters, in order, in a container partially filled with clean engine oil (this will prevent them from bleeding down).

11  To separate the lash adjuster from the rocker arm, remove the retaining clip by hand.

12  Check the ends and the side friction surfaces of the lash adjusters for wear. Make sure the lash adjusters move up and down freely in their bores in the cylinder head without excessive side to side play. If one lash adjuster is worn, it's a good idea to replace all of them as a set.

13  Inspect each rocker arm for wear, cracks and other damage. Make sure the rollers turn freely and show no signs of wear. Also check the pivot area for wear, cracks and galling.

14  Installation is the reverse of removal. Be sure to lubricate the lash adjusters and rocker arm roller and pivot surfaces with clean engine oil before installing them.

15  Installation is the reverse of removal.

5.4a  Use a suction cup tool to pull the cam follower up . . .

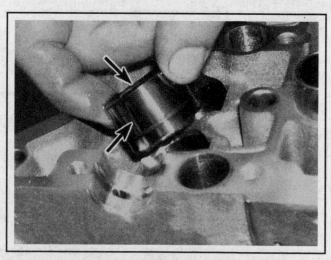

5.4b  . . . then remove it from its bore. Check the friction surfaces for signs of wear

## 6  Timing chain - replacement

This repair procedure requires several expensive special tools. Because of the difficulty of this repair procedure and the necessary special tools, it is recommended to have the timing chain replaced by a dealer service department or other qualified automotive repair facility.

## 7  Camshafts and sprockets - removal, inspection and installation

### REMOVAL

1  Disconnect the cable from the negative terminal of the battery (see Chapter 5, Section 1).

2  Remove the valve cover (see Section 4). Also remove the upper timing cover from the front of the cylinder head.

#### 2002 models (type 111 engine)

▶ Refer to illustrations 7.6 and 7.8

3  Rotate the engine to TDC for cylinder number 1 (see Section 3), then rotate further clockwise (seen from the front of the engine) until the "30" mark lines up with the pointer on the timing cover. This represents 30-degrees After TDC, which puts the camshafts in a position where there will be no interference between valves and pistons during the procedure.

4  Make matching paint marks on the sprockets and the chain links to aid in reassembly.

5  Remove the alternator (see Chapter 5).

6  Loosen the end piece of the timing chain tensioner one turn, then unscrew the timing chain tensioner (see illustration).

7  Remove the sprocket from the exhaust camshaft.

➡ **Note: Hold the camshaft from turning using a wrench on the hex portion of the camshaft (between the first two lobes), while using a socket and ratchet to loosen and remove the sprocket center bolt.**

With the exhaust camshaft sprocket removed, lift the timing chain off the intake camshaft sprocket. Support the timing chain with a length of wire to prevent it from dropping down into the timing chain case.

8  Turn the camshafts so that as many of the cam lobes as possible are positioned so that their base circles (low points) are facing the cam followers (this will relieve tension on the camshafts). Verify the markings on the camshaft bearing caps. The caps should be marked from 1 to 5, and with an "I" or an "E," to indicate intake or exhaust. Also verify that there are arrow marks on the caps indicating the front of the engine. Loosen the camshaft bearing caps in two or three steps, then detach the bearing caps (see illustration). Remove the camshafts.

**✳✳ CAUTION·**

**Keep the caps in order. They must go back in the same location they were removed from.**

**7.6  Timing chain tensioner removal - be sure to replace the sealing ring during installation**

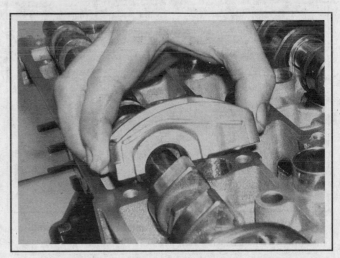

**7.8  Remove the camshaft bearing caps and store them in order for reassembly**

## 2003 through 2005 models (type 271 engine)

9  Rotate the engine to TDC for cylinder number 1 (see Section 3).

10  Make matching paint marks on the sprockets and the chain links to aid in reassembly.

11  Push on the tensioning rail to permit enough chain slack to slip the chain from the intake camshaft sprocket. This can be done with a large screwdriver or a prybar, or you can fabricate a wedge out of wood to insert between the two runs of the timing chain to push the tensioner rail back.

12  Loosen the bearing cap bridge bolts a little at a time, working in an order opposite that of the tightening sequence (see illustration 7.20). Detach the upper portion of the bearing cap bridge, then lift up the timing chain and remove the camshafts. Support the timing chain with a length of wire to prevent it from dropping down into the timing chain case.

➡️Note: If a wedge is being used to retract the tensioner, the chain will already be supported.

13  If the sprockets are to be removed from the camshafts, hold the camshaft with a wrench on the hex portion of the camshaft (between the first two lobes), while using a socket and ratchet to loosen and remove the sprocket center bolt.

## INSPECTION

▶ **Refer to illustrations 7.15 and 7.16**

14  Inspect the camshaft secondary sprockets for wear on the teeth. Inspect the chains for cracks or excessive wear of the rollers. Inspect the facing of the chain tensioner for excessive wear. If any of the components show signs of excessive wear, they must be replaced.

15  After the camshaft has been removed from the engine, cleaned with solvent and dried, inspect the bearing journals for uneven wear,

pitting and evidence of seizure (see illustration). If the camshaft journals are damaged, inspect the cylinder head and the camshaft bearing caps/bearing cap bridge.

16  Measure the lobe height of each cam lobe on the intake camshaft and record your measurements (see illustration). Compare the measurements for excessive variations. If the lobe heights vary more than 0.010 inch (0.254 mm), replace the camshaft. Compare the lobe height measurements on the exhaust camshaft and follow the same procedure. Do not compare intake camshaft lobe heights with exhaust camshaft lobe heights, as they are different. Only compare intake lobes with intake lobes and exhaust lobes with other exhaust lobes.

17  Check the camshaft lobes for heat discoloration, score marks, chipped areas, pitting and uneven wear. If the lobes are in good condition and if the lobe lift variation measurements recorded earlier are within the limits, the camshaft can be reused.

## INSTALLATION

▶ **Refer to illustration 7.20**

18  Oil the camshaft lobes and bearing journals and reinstall the camshafts in the bearing saddles of the head. If the sprockets were not removed from the camshafts before, you can angle the sprocket down under the timing chain as you install the camshaft, making sure the paint marks you made align. On type 271 engines, when you install the second camshaft, you will have to pull back on the camshaft guide (against the pressure of the tensioner) to allow the chain to fit over the second camshaft (unless a wedge was used to push the tensioner back).

➡️Note: On type 111 engines, if the sprockets were removed, new bolts should be used on reassembly.

If the sprockets were removed, install them, lining up the paint marks made before removal.

**7.15  Check the diameter of each camshaft bearing journal to pinpoint excessive wear and out-of-round conditions**

**7.16  Measure the camshaft lobe height (greatest dimension) with a micrometer**

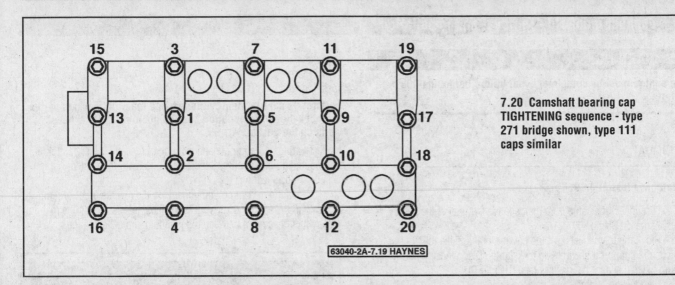

**7.20 Camshaft bearing cap TIGHTENING sequence - type 271 bridge shown, type 111 caps similar**

63040-2A-7.19 HAYNES

19 Install the bearing caps (type 111 engines) or bearing cap bridge (type 271 engines) and tighten the bolts hand tight.

20 On type 271 engines, tighten the bearing cap bridge bolts in several steps, to the torque listed in this Chapter's Specifications, using the proper tightening sequence (see illustration). On type 111 engines, tighten the bearing cap bolts, a little at a time, to the torque listed in this Chapter's Specifications.

21 On type 111 engines, install the tensioner body, using a new sealing ring. Tighten the tensioner body to the torque listed in this Chapter's Specifications. Next, install the tensioner end piece, using a new sealing ring, and tighten it to the torque listed in this Chapter's Specifications.

22 The remaining installation steps are the reverse of removal.

## 8  Intake manifold  removal and installation

### REMOVAL

1  Relieve the fuel system pressure (see Chapter 4).

2  Disconnect the cable from the negative terminal of the battery (see Chapter 5, Section 1). Remove the engine cover, on models so equipped.

3  Remove the air intake duct and the air filter housing (on models with an engine-mounted air filter housing) (see Chapter 4).

4  Label and disconnect the PCV hose, vacuum hoses and electrical connectors attached to the intake manifold and throttle body. Disconnect the electronic throttle control (ETC) system connector from the throttle body (see Chapter 4).

5  Remove the two bolts securing the fuel rail to the intake manifold, then carefully pry the injectors up and out of the manifold.

6  Remove the intake manifold bolts. Remove the intake manifold and the gasket.

➡ Note: You may have to remove some clamps on the engine wiring harness to provide enough room for the manifold to be removed.

### INSTALLATION

7  Clean and inspect the intake manifold to cylinder head sealing surfaces. Inspect the gasket for tears or cracks, replacing the gasket if necessary. The gasket can be reused if it isn't damaged.

8  Position the intake manifold onto the engine, making sure the gasket and manifold are aligned correctly over the cylinder head dowels. Tighten the manifold bolts to the torque listed in this Chapter's Specifications.

9  Install the fuel rail and injectors onto the manifold (see Chapter 4).

10  The remaining installation steps are the reverse of removal. Run the engine and check for fuel, vacuum and coolant leaks.

## 9   Exhaust manifold - removal and installation

**❊❊ WARNING:**

The engine must be completely cool before beginning this procedure.

### REMOVAL

**▶ Refer to illustration 9.7**

1   Disconnect the cable from the negative terminal of the battery (see Chapter 5, Section 1).

2   Block the rear wheels, set the parking brake, raise the front of the vehicle and support it securely on jackstands. Disconnect the downstream oxygen sensor connectors (see Chapter 6).

3   Remove the engine lower splash shield.

4   Unbolt the exhaust pipes at the exhaust manifolds (see Chapter 4).

5   Lower the vehicle. Working in the engine compartment, disconnect the oxygen sensor's electrical connector.

6   If equipped, remove the exhaust manifold heat shield mounting bolts and remove the heat shield.

7   Remove the mounting bolts and detach the manifold from the cylinder head (see illustration). Be sure to spray penetrating lubricant onto the bolts and threads before attempting to remove them.

### INSTALLATION

8   Clean the mating surfaces to remove all traces of old gasket material, then inspect the manifold for distortion and cracks. Warpage can be checked with a precision straightedge held against the mating flange. If a feeler gauge thicker than 0.030-inch can be inserted between the straightedge and flange surface, take the manifold to an automotive machine shop for resurfacing.

9   Place the exhaust manifold in position with a new gasket and install the mounting bolts finger tight.

**➡ Note: Be sure to identify the exhaust manifold gaskets by the correct cylinder designation and the position of the exhaust ports on the gasket.**

10   Starting in the middle and working out toward the ends, tighten the mounting bolts in several increments, to the torque listed in this Chapter's Specifications.

11   Install the remaining components in the reverse order of removal.

12   Start the engine and check for exhaust leaks between the manifold and cylinder head and between the manifold and exhaust pipe.

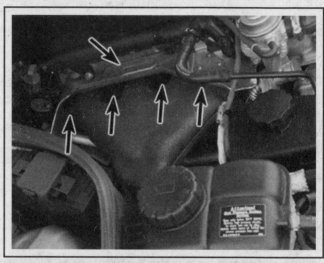

**9.7  Exhaust manifold bolts (not all are visible here) - upper arrow indicates heat shield**

## 10   Cylinder head - removal and installation

**❊❊ WARNING:**

The engine must be completely cool before beginning this procedure.

### REMOVAL

1   Disconnect the cable from the negative terminal of the battery (see Chapter 5, Section 1).

2   Remove the engine cover(s), on models so equipped.

3   Drain the cooling system and remove the water inlet at the cylinder head front cover (see Chapter 3).

4   Disconnect the electrical connector(s) at the camshaft solenoid(s) on the front cover, then remove the front cover bolts and the cover.

5   Tag and disconnect the engine harness electrical connectors and clamps securing the harness.

6   Remove the valve cover (see Section 4).

7   Remove the intake manifold (see Section 8).

8   Remove the exhaust manifold (see Section 9).

9   Remove the camshafts and sprockets (see Section 7).

10   On type 271 engines (2003 and later models), remove the rocker arms and hydraulic lash adjusters from the cylinder head (see Section 5). Before the rocker arms and lash adjusters are removed, arrange to label and store them, so they can be kept separate and reinstalled on the same valve from which they were removed.

11   Label and remove any remaining items attached to the cylinder head, such as coolant fittings, ground straps, cables, hoses, wires or brackets.

12   Using a breaker bar and the appropriate sized socket, loosen the cylinder head bolts in 1/4-turn increments until they can be removed by

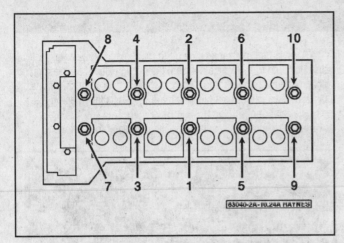

**10.23a Cylinder head bolt TIGHTENING sequence - 2002 models (type 111)**

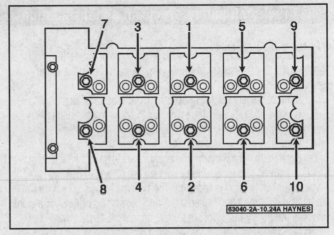

**10.23b Cylinder head bolt TIGHTENING sequence - 2003 through 2005 models (type 271)**

hand. Loosen the bolts in the reverse order of the tightening sequence (see illustrations 10.23a and 10.23b) to avoid warping or cracking the head.

13 Lift the cylinder head off the engine block with the exhaust manifold attached. If it's stuck, very carefully pry up at the transmission end, beyond the gasket surface, at a casting protrusion. After removal, set the head on wood blocks.

14 Remove all external components from the cylinder head to allow for thorough cleaning and inspection before having the cylinder head serviced at a qualified automotive machine shop.

## INSTALLATION

✦ **Refer to illustrations 10.23a, 10.23b and 10.23c**

15 The mating surfaces of the cylinder head and block must be perfectly clean when the head is installed.

16 Use a plastic abrasive pad to remove all traces of carbon and old gasket material from the cylinder head and engine block being careful not to gouge the aluminum, then clean the mating surfaces with brake system cleaner. If there's oil on the mating surfaces when the head is installed, the gasket may not seal correctly and leaks could develop. When working on the block, stuff the cylinders with clean shop rags to keep out debris. Use a vacuum cleaner to remove material that falls into the cylinders.

17 Use a tap of the correct size to chase the threads in the head bolt holes, then clean the holes with compressed air - make sure that nothing remains in the holes.

### ✳✳ WARNING:

**Wear eye protection when using compressed air!**

18 Check each cylinder head bolt for stretching by measuring the length of the bolt from below the head to the tip, comparing your measurements with the values listed in this Chapter's Specifications. Bolts that exceed the maximum length must be replaced.

➥**Note: Due to the work involved, it's a good idea to replace the head bolts with new ones regardless of the measurements.**

19 Install the components that were removed from the head.

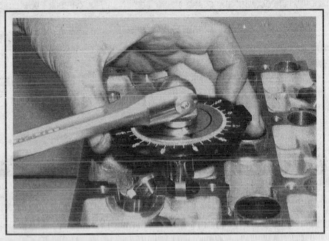

**10.23c Use an angle gauge to tighten the bolts the specified number of degrees**

20 Position the new cylinder head gasket over the dowel pins on the block, noting which direction on the gasket faces up.

21 Carefully set the head over the dowels on the block without disturbing the gasket.

22 Before installing the head bolts, apply a small amount of clean engine oil to the threads and under the bolt heads.

23 Install the bolts in their original locations and tighten them finger tight. Then tighten all the bolts in several steps, following the proper sequence (see illustrations), to the torque listed in this Chapter's Specifications.

24 Tighten the cylinder head-to-timing chain cover bolts to the torque listed in this Chapter's Specifications.

25 Install the cam followers (type 111) or lash adjusters and rocker arms (type 271) in the cylinder head (see Section 5), then install the camshafts as described in Section 7.

26 The remaining installation steps are the reverse of removal. When reinstalling the water outlet to the cylinder head front cover, install a new O-ring.

27 Refill the cooling system and change the engine oil and filter (see Chapter 1).

28 Start the engine and check for oil and coolant leaks.

## 11 Crankshaft pulley - removal and installation

▶ **Refer to illustration 11.5**

1  Disconnect the cable from the negative terminal of the battery (see Chapter 5, Section 1).

2  Remove the engine lower splash shield (see Chapter 1).

3  Remove the drivebelt (see Chapter 1) and position the belt tensioner away from the crankshaft pulley.

4  Remove the air intake duct from the supercharger (see Chapter 4).

5  Remove the crankshaft pulley center bolt. The crankshaft center bolt is tightened to a high torque, so a secure means of holding the crankshaft from turning is required. The best method is to remove the starter and position a tool against the ring gear teeth, while an assistant removes the pulley bolt. Note that there are several dished washers behind the center bolt, keep track of their order and position (see illustration).

6  Pull the damper off the crankshaft with a two-jaw puller. The jaws should face outward and clamp inside the holes in the damper, not on the outer edge of the pulley.

7  Check the surface on the pulley hub that the oil seal rides on. If the surface has been grooved from long-time contact with the seal, a new pulley will be required.

8  Make sure the Woodruff key is in position in its groove on the nose of the crankshaft. Lubricate the pulley hub with clean engine oil and reinstall the crankshaft pulley.

9  Apply a film of clean engine oil to the threads of the crankshaft pulley bolt, and to the washers. Install the crankshaft pulley retaining bolt and tighten it to the torque listed in this Chapter's Specifications. As with removal, an assistant is helpful during installation and tightening of the center bolt.

10  The remainder of installation is the reverse of the removal.

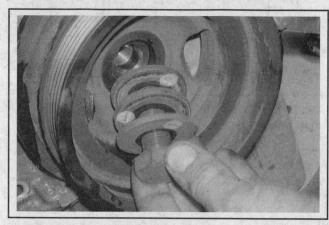

**11.5  Keep track of the order and position of the dished washers when removing the crankshaft pulley center bolt**

## 12 Crankshaft front oil seal - replacement

▶ **Refer to illustrations 12.2 and 12.4**

1  Remove the crankshaft pulley/damper from the engine (see Section 11).

2  Carefully pry the seal out of the cover with a seal removal tool or a large screwdriver (see illustration).

### ✳✳ CAUTION:

**Be careful not to scratch, gouge or distort the area that the seal fits into or an oil leak will develop.**

3  Clean the bore to remove any old seal material and corrosion.

Position the new seal in the bore with the seal lip (usually the side with the spring) facing IN (toward the engine). A small amount of oil applied to the outer edge of the new seal will make installation easier.

4  Drive the seal into the bore with a seal driver or a large socket and hammer until it's completely seated (see illustration). Select a socket that's the same outside diameter as the seal and make sure the new seal is pressed into place squarely until it bottoms against the cover flange.

5  Lubricate the seal lips with engine oil and reinstall the crankshaft pulley (see Section 11).

6  The remainder of installation is the reverse of removal. Run the engine and check for oil leaks.

**12.2  The seal can be removed carefully with a seal tool or large screwdriver - don't nick the cover**

**12.4  A seal driver or an appropriate-size socket can be used when tapping in the new seal**

## 13 Oil pan - removal and installation

### REMOVAL

1   Disconnect the cable from the negative terminal of the battery (see Chapter 5, Section 1). Remove the engine oil dipstick.

2   Apply the parking brake and block the rear wheels. Raise the front of the vehicle and place it securely on jackstands. Remove the engine lower splash shields (see Chapter 1).

3   Drain the engine oil and remove the oil filter (see Chapter 1).

4   Support the engine from above with an engine support cradle. Remove the engine mount-to-subframe bolts and lower the subframe with a transmission jack.

### ✳✳ WARNING:

**Chain the subframe to the transmission jack to prevent it from falling off.**

5   Detach any clips securing the transmission oil cooler lines that would interfere with removal of the oil pan (see Chapter 3).

6   Disconnect the oil sensor connector at the oil pan.

7   Remove the oil pan mounting bolts, then carefully separate the oil pan from the block. Don't pry between the block and the pan or damage to the sealing surfaces could occur and oil leaks may develop. Instead, pry at the casting protrusion at the front of the pan.

➡Note: There are various sizes of bolts securing the oil pan. Draw a sketch of their original locations for later identification.

### INSTALLATION

8   Clean the pan with solvent and remove all old sealant and gasket material from the block and pan mating surfaces. Clean the mating surfaces with brake system cleaner and make sure the bolt holes in the block are clear. Check the oil pan flange for distortion, particularly around the bolt holes.

9   Apply a bead of RTV sealant to the oil pan rail parting lines at the front cover and at the rear main oil seal retainer. Install the gasket on the block.

10   Place the oil pan in position on the block and install the nuts/bolts.

11   After the fasteners are installed, tighten them to the torque listed in this Chapter's Specifications. Starting at the center, follow a criss-cross pattern and work up to the final torque in three steps.

12   Raise the subframe and attach the engine mount bolts, steering gear and subframe-to-body bolts (see Chapter 10).

13   The remaining steps are the reverse of the removal procedure.

14   Refill the engine with oil (see Chapter 1), replace the filter, run it until normal operating temperature is reached and check for leaks.

## 14 Oil pump - removal and installation

### REMOVAL

1   Remove the oil pan (see Section 13).

### 2002 models (type 111 engines)

◆ **Refer to illustration 14.3**

2   Rotate the engine to TDC for number 1 piston (see Section 3). Make matching paint marks on the chain and the oil pump gear.

3   Reach up on the left side of the chain and push on the oil pump chain's tensioner, until you can release the chain from the oil pump sprocket (see illustration).

4   Remove the oil pump pick up tube from the pump and the one bolt at the main bearing cap.

5   Remove the bolts securing the oil pump housing to the bottom of the engine block.

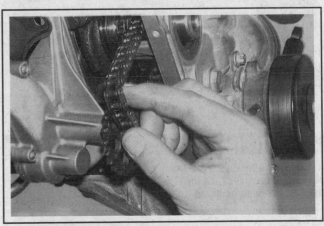

**14.3 Push against the oil pump chain tensioner and slip the chain from the pump sprocket**

### 2003 and later models (type 271 engines)

6   On type 271 engines, the oil pump is bolted to the rear of the balance-shaft assembly. The balance shaft assembly does not have to be removed, and the drive chain does not have to be disturbed. Simply remove the cover and access the oil pump gears.

7   To remove the drive gear, look under the right side of the balance shaft assembly and you will see a hex section on the balance shaft. Hold this with a wrench while unbolting the oil pump drive gear.

8   Remove the bolts securing the pump housing to the balance shaft assembly. One of the bolts is only accessible after removing the oil pump drive gear.

9   Gently pry the oil pump housing outward enough to clear the dowel pins on the engine block and remove it from the engine.

### INSTALLATION

10  Pack the pump with petroleum jelly to prime it. Assemble the oil pump and tighten all fasteners to the torque listed in this Chapter's Specifications.

11  On type 111 engines, push back the chain tensioner and slip the chain back on the oil pump drive sprocket, making sure the paint marks match up.

12  The remaining steps are the reverse of the removal procedure.

13  Refill the engine with oil (see Chapter 1), replace the filter, run the engine until normal operating temperature is reached and check for leaks.

## 15  Flywheel/driveplate - removal and installation

♦ **Refer to illustration 15.3**

1   Remove the transmission (see Chapter 7).

### ✳✳ WARNING:

**The engine must be supported from above with an engine hoist or an engine support fixture before working underneath the vehicle with the transmission removed.**

2   Now would be a good time to check and replace the transmission front pump seal on models with automatic transmissions. On manual-shift models, this is a good time to inspect and/or replace the clutch components (see Chapter 8).

3   Use paint or a center-punch to make alignment marks on the driveplate and crankshaft to ensure correct alignment during reinstallation (see illustration).

4   Remove the bolts that secure the driveplate to the crankshaft. If the crankshaft turns, jam a large screwdriver or prybar through the driveplate to keep the crankshaft from turning, then remove the mounting bolts and bolt plate.

5   Pull straight back on the driveplate to detach it from the crankshaft.

### ✳✳ CAUTION:

**If removing a flywheel on a manual transmission-equipped vehicle, wear gloves, as the flywheel is heavy and the teeth of the ring gear can be sharp.**

6   When installing, be sure to align the marks made prior to removal. Use thread-locking compound on the bolt threads and tighten them to the specified torque in a criss-cross pattern.

7   The remaining steps are the reverse of the removal procedure.

15.3  Before removing the flywheel bolts, make marks on the flywheel and crank flange for alignment

## 16  Rear main oil seal - replacement

▶ **Refer to illustration 16.4**

1   All models use a one-piece rear main oil seal which is installed in a bolt-on housing. Replacing this seal requires removal of the transmission and driveplate. The rear main seal and housing are serviced as one complete assembly. This procedure will require several special tools.

2   Remove the transmission (see Chapter 7) and the oil pan (see Section 13).

3   Remove the driveplate (see Section 15).

4   Remove the rear main oil seal housing bolts and the housing (see illustration).

5   Install the new oil seal housing onto the crankshaft using a special guide tool.

6   Once the oil seal housing is attached and bolts slightly tight, install a special alignment tool that centers the seal over the crankshaft.

7   While pressing the oil seal housing evenly, tighten the oil seal housing retainer bolts to the torque listed in this Chapter's Specifications. The housing must be flush with the plane of the oil pan mating surface of the block to prevent oil leaks.

8   The remainder of installation is the reverse of the removal procedure.

16.4  The rear oil seal and retainer are replaced as a unit

## 17  Engine mounts - check and replacement

1   There are three powertrain mounts; left and right engine mounts attached to the engine block and to the subframe and a rear mount attached to the transmission and the subframe. Refer to Chapter 7 for check and replacement procedures for the transmission mount.

### CHECK

2   During the check, the engine must be raised slightly to remove the weight from the mounts.

3   Raise the vehicle and support it securely on jackstands. Remove the front wheels and tires. Position two jacks, one under the crankshaft pulley and the other under the transmission bellhousing. Place a block of wood between the jack head and the crankshaft pulley or bellhousing, then carefully raise the engine/transmission just enough to take the weight off the mounts. The safest method is to use an engine support

cradle that raises the engine from above. These can be rented at most tool rental shops.

**✳✳ WARNING:**

**DO NOT** place any part of your body under the engine when it's supported only by a jack!

4   Check the mounts to see if the rubber is cracked, hardened or separated from the metal plates. Sometimes the rubber will split right down the center.

5   Check for relative movement between the mount brackets and the engine or subframe (use a large screwdriver or prybar to attempt to move the mounts). If movement is noted, lower the engine and tighten the mount fasteners.

### REPLACEMENT

▶ **Refer to illustration 17.9**

6   Disconnect the cable from the negative terminal of the battery (see Chapter 5, Section 1) then raise the vehicle and support it securely on jackstands.

7   Remove the engine splash shield (see Chapter 1).

8   Remove the bolts holding the engine mount to the subframe.

9   Raise the engine until the engine mount bracket clears the subframe, then remove the bracket-to-mount bolt from above (see illustration).

10  Remove one engine mount and replace it with a new one, then replace the other front mount. Install the bolts, then lower the engine. Tighten the bolts to the torque listed in this Chapter's Specifications.

17.9  Engine bracket-to-mount bolt

## Specifications

### General

2002 (type 111)

| | |
|---|---|
| Displacement | 140 cubic inches (2.3 liters) |
| Bore | 3.58 inches (90.9 mm) |
| Stroke | 3.48 inches (88.4 mm) |
| Cylinder compression pressure | |
|     Minimum | 174 to 217 psi |
|     Maximum variation between cylinders | 22 psi |

2003 and later (type 271)

| | |
|---|---|
| Displacement | 110 cubic inches (1.8 liters) |
| Bore | 3.23 inches (82.0 mm) |
| Stroke | 3.35 inches (85.0 mm) |
| Cylinder compression pressure | |
|     Minimum | 142 psi |
|     Maximum variation between cylinders | 15 psi |
| Oil pressure (minimum, warm engine) | |
|     Idle | 8 psi |
|     2000 rpm | 25 psi |
| Firing order | 1-3-4-2 |
| Cylinder head bolt length (maximum) | |
|     2002 (type 111) | 4.13 inches (105 mm) |
|     2003 and later (type 271) | 6.6 inches (167.5 mm) |

72031-1-SPECS HAYNES

**Cylinder identification diagram**

| Torque specifications | Ft-lbs (unless otherwise indicated) | Nm |
|---|---|---|

➡ **Note: One foot-pound (ft-lb) of torque is equivalent to 12 inch-pounds (in-lbs) of torque. Torque values below approximately 15 ft-lbs are expressed in inch-pounds, since most foot-pound torque wrenches are not accurate at these smaller values.**

| | | |
|---|---|---|
| Camshaft sprocket bolts | | |
|   Step 1 | 177 in-lbs | 20 |
|   Step 2 | Tighten an additional 60-degrees | |
| Camshaft adjuster-to-camshaft center bolt | | |
|   Step 1 | 44 in-lbs | 5 |
|   Step 2 | Tighten an additional 90-degrees | |
| Camshaft bearing cap bolts | 15 | 21 |
| Crankshaft pulley/damper bolt | | |
|   2002 (type 111) | 221 | 300 |
|   2003 and later (type 271) | | |
|     Step 1 | 148 | 200 |
|     Step 2 | Tighten an additional 90-degrees | |
| Cylinder head bolts | | |
|   Step 1 | | |
|     2002 (type 111) | 41 | 55 |
|     2003 and later (type 271) | 33 | 45 |
|   Step 2 | Tighten an additional 90-degrees | |
|   Step 3 | Tighten an additional 90-degrees | |

➡**Note: One foot-pound (ft-lb) of torque is equivalent to 12 inch-pounds (in-lbs) of torque. Torque values below approximately 15 ft-lbs are expressed in inch-pounds, since most foot-pound torque wrenches are not accurate at these smaller values.**

| | Ft-lbs (unless otherwise indicated) | Nm |
|---|---|---|
| Cylinder head-to-timing chain cover bolts | | |
|     2002 (type 111) | | |
|         Step 1 | 159 in-lbs | 18 |
|         Step 2 | Tighten an additional 90-degrees | |
|     2003 and later (type 271) | 177 in-lbs | 20 |
| Drivebelt tensioner | 22 | 30 |
| Driveplate bolts | | |
|     Step 1 | 33 | 45 |
|     Step 2 | Tighten an additional 90-degrees | |
| Exhaust manifold bolts | 15 | 20 |
| Engine front mount-to-crossmember bolts | 26 | 35 |
| Engine front mount bracket-to-engine bolts | 37 | 50 |
| Intake manifold bolts | 15 | 20 |
| Oil pan bolts | | |
|     6-mm bolts | 71 in-lbs | 8 |
|     8-mm bolts | 15 | 20 |
| Oil pan drain plug | 22 | 30 |
| Oil pump mounting bolts | 15 | 20 |
| Oil pump tube to main cap bolt | 35 in-lbs | 4 |
| Rear main oil seal retainer bolts | 86 in-lbs | 10 |
| Timing chain cover bolts | 18 | 25 |
| Timing chain tensioner | | |
|     2002 (type 111) | | |
|         Tensioner body | 59 | 80 |
|         Tensioner end piece | 26 | 40 |
|     2003 and later (type 271) | 26 | 40 |
| Valve cover bolts | 89 in-lbs | 10 |

**Notes**

# 2B

## V6 ENGINES

**Section**

**Reference to other Chapters**

## 1   General information

This Part of Chapter 2 is devoted to in-vehicle repair procedures for the 2.6L, 3.0L, 3.2L and 3.5L V6 engines. These engines utilize an aluminum block with six cylinders arranged in a V. The overhead camshaft aluminum cylinder heads are equipped with replaceable valve guides and seats. On 2005 and earlier models (type 112 engines) the design is a single overhead camshaft (SOHC) on each cylinder head. Roller rocker arms mounted on two shafts in each cylinder head are actuated by the camshaft and in turn operate the valves. These engines have three valves per cylinder, one exhaust and two intakes.

2006 and later models (type 272 engines) have dual overhead camshafts (DOHC) on each head, which directly operate the valves without rocker arms. These engines have four valves per cylinder, two intake and two exhaust.

Information concerning engine removal and installation and engine overhaul can be found in Part C of this Chapter. The following repair procedures are based on the assumption the engine is installed in the vehicle. If the engine has been removed from the vehicle and mounted on a stand, many of the steps outlined in this Part of Chapter 2 will not apply.

## 2   Repair operations possible with the engine in the vehicle

Many major repair operations can be accomplished without removing the engine from the vehicle.

Clean the engine compartment and the exterior of the engine with some type of degreaser before any work is done. It'll make the job easier and help keep dirt out of the internal areas of the engine.

Depending on the components involved, it may be helpful to remove the hood to improve access to the engine as repairs are performed (see Chapter 11 if necessary). Cover the fenders to prevent damage to the paint. Special pads are available, but an old bedspread or blanket will also work.

If vacuum, exhaust, oil or coolant leaks develop, indicating a need for gasket or seal replacement, the repairs can generally be done with the engine in the vehicle. The intake and exhaust manifold gaskets, timing belt cover gasket, oil pan gasket, crankshaft oil seals and cylinder head gaskets are all accessible with the engine in place.

Exterior engine components, such as the intake and exhaust manifolds, the oil pan (and the oil pump), the water pump, the starter motor, the alternator and the fuel system components can be removed for repair with the engine in place.

Since the cylinder heads can be removed without pulling the engine, valve component servicing can also be accomplished with the engine in the vehicle. Replacement of the camshafts, timing belt and sprockets is also possible with the engine in the vehicle, although the cylinder head must be removed from the engine to remove the camshafts.

In extreme cases caused by a lack of necessary equipment, repair or replacement of piston rings, pistons, connecting rods and rod bearings is possible with the engine in the vehicle. However, this practice is not recommended because of the cleaning and preparation work that must be done to the components involved.

## 3   Top Dead Center (TDC) for number one piston - locating

1   Top Dead Center (TDC) is the highest point in the cylinder that each piston reaches as it travels up the cylinder bore. Each piston reaches TDC on the compression stroke and again on the exhaust stroke, but TDC generally refers to piston position on the compression stroke.

2   Positioning the piston(s) at TDC is an essential part of certain procedures, such as camshaft and timing chain/sprocket removal.

3   Before beginning this procedure, be sure to place the transmission in Park (automatic) or Neutral (manual) and apply the parking brake or block the rear wheels. Disable the ignition system by disconnecting the primary electrical connectors at the ignition coil packs, then remove the coil packs and spark plugs (see Chapter 1). Also disable the fuel system (see Chapter 4, Section 2).

4   In order to bring any piston to TDC, the crankshaft must be turned using one of the methods outlined below. When looking at the front of the engine, normal crankshaft rotation is clockwise.

   a) *The preferred method is to turn the crankshaft with a socket and ratchet attached to the bolt threaded into the front of the crankshaft. Turn the bolt in a clockwise direction.*

   b) *A remote starter switch, which may save some time, can also be used. Follow the instructions included with the switch. Once the piston is close to TDC, use a socket and ratchet as described in the previous paragraph.*

   c) *If an assistant is available to turn the ignition switch to the Start position in short bursts, you can get the piston close to TDC without a remote starter switch. Make sure your assistant is out of the vehicle, away from the ignition switch, then use a socket and ratchet as described in Paragraph a) to complete the procedure.*

5   Install a compression pressure gauge in the number one spark plug hole (see Chapter 2C). It should be a gauge with a screw-in fitting and a hose at least six inches long.

6   Rotate the crankshaft using one of the methods described above while observing for pressure on the compression gauge. The moment the gauge shows pressure indicates that the number one cylinder has begun the compression stroke.

7   Once the compression stroke has begun, TDC for the compression stroke is reached by bringing the piston to the top of the cylinder.

8   Continue turning the crankshaft until the TDC notch in the crankshaft damper is aligned with the pointer on the front cover (mark "C" in illustration 5.9). At this point, the number one cylinder is at TDC on the compression stroke. If the marks are aligned but there was no compression, the piston was on the exhaust stroke. Continue rotating the crankshaft 360-degrees (1-turn).

9   After the number one piston has been positioned at TDC on the compression stroke, TDC for any of the remaining cylinders can be located by turning the crankshaft 120-degrees at a time and following the firing order (refer to the Specifications). Rotating the engine 120-degrees past TDC no. 1 will put the engine at TDC compression for cylinder no. 2.

## 4   Valve cover(s) - removal and installation

### REMOVAL

♦ **Refer to illustrations 4.5, 4.7a, 4.7b, 4.7c, 4.8a and 4.8b**

1   Disconnect the cable from the negative terminal of the battery (see Chapter 5, Section 1).

2   Refer to Chapter 4 and remove the engine cover/air filter assembly.

3   Remove the ignition coils (see Chapter 5).

➡**Note: Tag all the connectors and spark plug wires to simplify reassembly.**

4   On the right bank, unbolt the oil dipstick tube from the bracket at the rear of the cylinder head.

5   Disconnect the PCV hoses from each valve cover (see illustration).

6   On models with a rigid fuel line attached to the fuel rail, the line must be disconnected. Refer to Chapter 4 and note the **Cautions** and fuel pressure relief procedure.

7   On 272 model engines (2006 and later), remove the connectors and fasteners securing the engine harness assembly to the right valve cover (see illustration), and also remove the camshaft cover from the front of each cylinder head/valve cover (see illustration). Remove the mounting bolts for the round centrifuge cover at the rear of the right valve cover, then remove the center bolt and the centrifuge (see illustration). Have rags handy to catch oil that will drip out when the cover is removed.

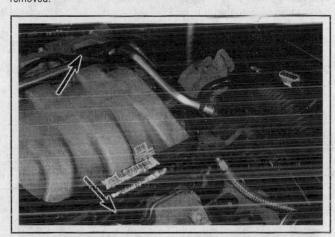

**4.5  PCV hoses at the valve covers (2005 model shown, others similar)**

**4.7a  Engine harness at right valve cover on type 272**

**4.7b  Tag and disconnect the hoses and connectors at the camshaft front cover, then unbolt the camshaft cover (2006 and later models)**

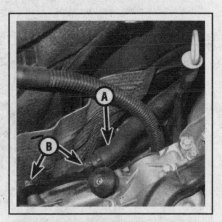

**4.7c  At the rear of the right valve cover on 2006 and later engines, disconnect the air hose (A), and remove the centrifuge mounting bolts (B, all bolts not visible here)**

➡Note: The centrifuge-to-camshaft bolt is a left-hand thread.

8  Remove the valve cover bolts (see illustrations). Note the locations of any stud bolts so they can be reinstalled in their proper locations.

9  Detach the valve cover.

➡Note: If the cover sticks to the cylinder head, use a block of wood and a hammer to dislodge it. If the cover still won't come loose, pry on it carefully, but don't distort the sealing flange.

## INSTALLATION

▸ **Refer to illustrations 4.10a and 4.10b**

10  The mating surfaces of each cylinder head and valve cover must be perfectly clean when the covers are installed. Inspect the rubber gaskets; if they're in good condition and there were no oil leaks, they can be re-used (see illustration). On 272 type engines (2006 and later), RTV sealant must be used in several locations under the valve cover (see illustration). Install the valve covers within 10 minutes of applying the sealant.

11  Clean the mounting bolt threads with a die (if necessary) to remove any corrosion and restore damaged threads. Use a tap to clean the threaded holes in the heads.

12  On 2005 and earlier models, place the valve cover and new gasket in position, then install the bolts. Tighten the bolts a little at a time to the torque listed in this Chapter's Specifications.

13  On 2006 and later models, place the valve cover and new gasket in position, then install the bolts. Tighten the bolts, in two stages and in the correct sequence (see illustration 4.8b), to the torque listed in this Chapter's Specifications. Reinstall the centrifuge to the camshaft on the right valve cover, aligning the dowel pin to the hole, and tighten the bolt to the torque listed in this Chapter's Specifications. Inspect the seal in the center of the centrifuge cover before installation and replace it if necessary.

14  The remaining installation steps are the reverse of removal. Start the engine and check carefully for oil leaks.

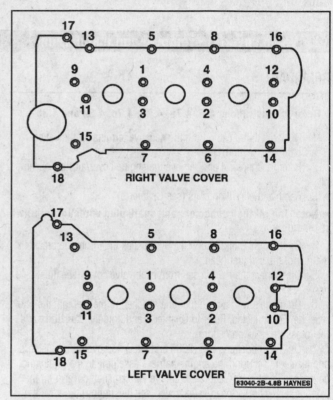

**4.8b  Valve cover bolt locations and tightening sequence (2006 and later models)**

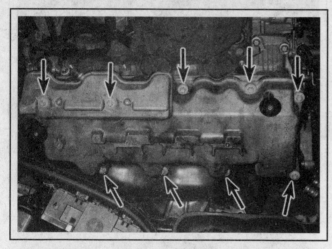

**4.8a  Valve cover bolt locations (2005 and earlier models)**

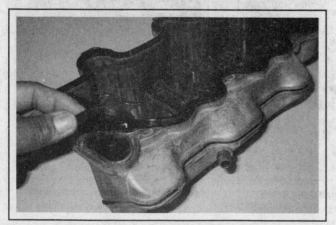

**4.10a  Clean and inspect the rubber valve cover gaskets - they can be reused if not cracked or damaged**

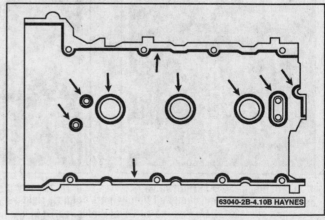

**4.10b  Areas of RTV sealant application - 2006 and later models**

## 5  Timing chain - replacement

This repair procedure requires several expensive special tools. Because of the difficulty of this repair procedure and the necessary special tools, it is recommended to have the timing chain replaced by a dealer service department or other qualified automotive repair facility.

## 6  Camshafts - removal, inspection and installation

### REMOVAL

#### 2001 through 2005 (112 model engines)

▸ Refer to illustrations 6.2, 6.4, 6.6a, 6.6b, 6.6c, 6.6d and 6.8

1   Remove the spark plugs (see Chapter 1) and the valve covers (see Section 4).

➡Note: On dual-plug engines, only one spark plug per cylinder need be removed.

2   Set the engine to TDC compression for cylinder number one (see Section 3). Using a socket and breaker bar on the crankshaft pulley bolt, continue to rotate the engine until the 40-degrees after TDC mark (on the crankshaft pulley) for cylinder number one lines up with the pointer on the engine (see illustration).

3   Remove the alternator (see Chapter 5).

4   Remove the timing chain tensioner from the right side of the block (see illustration).

5   Disconnect and remove the camshaft position sensor (see Chapter 6).

6   Secure the timing chain to the camshaft sprocket with plastic cable-ties (see illustrations).

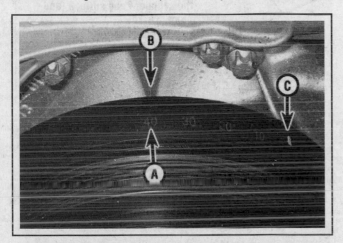

6.2  Set the type 112 engine to 40-degrees after TDC - here the 40-degree mark (A) is lined up with the pointer on the engine (B). Note that the TDC mark (C) is well past the pointer

6.4  Remove the timing chain tensioner from the right side of the timing chain case

6.6a  Timing chain and camshaft timing mark details - right camshaft sprocket. Note that the sprocket timing mark (A) is aligned with the center of the copper-colored link (B), C is the master link that will be removed with the chain tool

6.6b  Left camshaft sprocket timing mark and copper-colored link

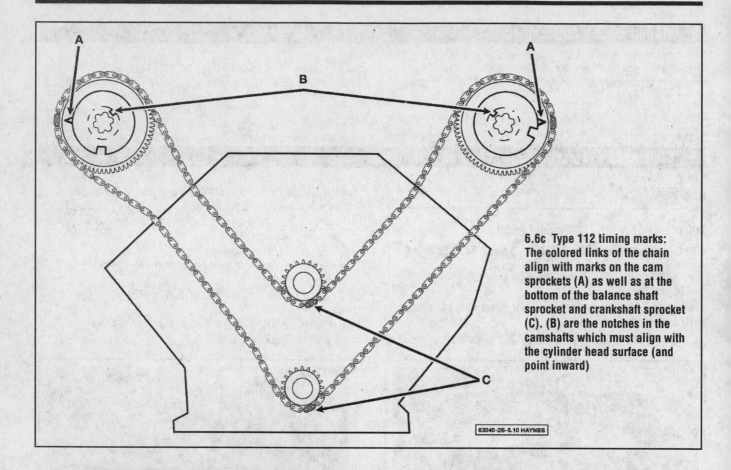

**6.6c  Type 112 timing marks: The colored links of the chain align with marks on the cam sprockets (A) as well as at the bottom of the balance shaft sprocket and crankshaft sprocket (C). (B) are the notches in the camshafts which must align with the cylinder head surface (and point inward)**

63040-2B-5.10 HAYNES

**6.6d  Secure the timing chain to the camshaft sprocket with cable-ties**

7  Hold the camshaft with an open-end wrench on the hex portion and remove the sprocket bolt. Remove the sprocket from the camshaft.

8  Loosen the camshaft bearing cap-bridge/rocker assembly mounting bolts in the reverse of the tightening sequence (see illustration). Remove the bolts and the bridge/rocker assembly.

9  Carefully remove the camshaft from the cylinder head, pulling it straight up out of the bearing saddles.

### 2006 and later (272 model engines)

▶ **Refer to illustrations 6.16a, 6.16b and 6.17**

10  Remove the spark plugs (see Chapter 1) and the valve covers (see Section 4).

➡**Note: On dual-plug engines, only one spark plug per cylinder need be removed.**

11  Set the engine to TDC compression for cylinder number one (see Section 3). Using a socket and breaker bar on the crankshaft pulley bolt, continue to rotate the engine until the 40-degrees after TDC mark (on the crankshaft pulley) for cylinder number one lines up with the pointer on the engine.

12  Unbolt and set aside the air pump shutoff valves at each camshaft front cover, but do not disconnect the air hose attached to the air pump switchover valve at the right camshaft front cover.

13  Remove the vacuum pump at the rear of the engine, if equipped.

14  Mark and disconnect the electrical connectors at the camshaft position sensors and camshaft solenoids, then remove the two camshaft position sensors from the front cover (see Chapter 6).

15  Through the holes where the CMPs were located, you should be able to see the marks on the pulse wheels of the sprockets (circular markings) line up directly in the center of the CMP holes.

16  Remove the front cover.

**When prying off the camshaft front covers, use a square tool only, and only in the area with two opposing flanges at the top. The three sets of marks on the camshaft adjusters/sprockets should align (see illustrations). Also note the marks on the backside of the camshaft adjuster/sprockets that align with the colored link on the timing chain (see illustration).**

17 Install a 3 mm punch in the alignment hole of the exhaust camshaft adjuster/sprocket (see illustration).

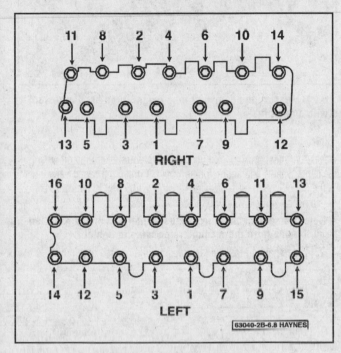

6.8  Camshaft cap/bridge/rocker assembly bolt TIGHTENING sequence

18 At the front of each camshaft to be removed, loosen the nut for the center valve in the middle of the adjuster/sprocket.

➡**Note: The exhaust cam center valve nuts have left-hand threads (turn them clockwise to loosen).**

Use a Torx tool at the rear of the camshaft to hold it while the center valve nut is loosened.

➡**Note: The alignment pin on the exhaust pulse wheel is under considerable pressure during tightening of the center valve, so the manufacturer recommends that when the exhaust camshaft adjuster/sprocket is removed for service, a new pulse wheel should be used on reassembly.**

19 After the exhaust camshaft is removed, secure the timing chain to keep it from falling once the intake camshaft is removed. The intake camshaft sprocket can be left on the engine secured to the timing chain.

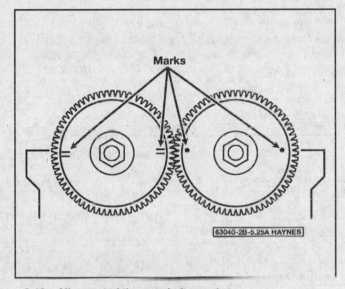

6.16a  Alignment of the camshaft sprockets

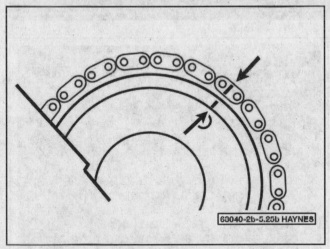

6.16b  The colored link on the chain aligns with the marks on the backside of the intake cam sprocket

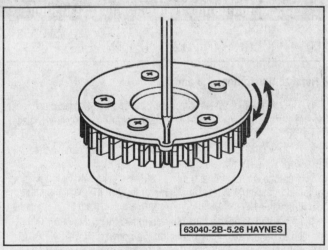

6.17  Before removing the timing chain, insert a punch in the exhaust cam adjuster/sprocket

## INSPECTION

▶ **Refer to illustration 6.21**

20  After the camshaft has been removed from the engine, cleaned with solvent and dried, inspect the bearing journals for uneven wear, pitting and evidence of seizure. If the camshaft journals are damaged, inspect the cylinder head also.

21  Measure the lobe height of each cam lobe on the intake camshaft and record your measurements (see illustration). Compare the measurements for excessive variations. Standard measurements should be within 0.001 inch (0.025 mm). If the lobe heights vary more than 0.010 inch (0.254 mm), replace the camshaft. Compare the lobe height measurements on the exhaust camshaft and follow the same procedure. Do not compare intake camshaft lobe heights with exhaust camshaft lobe heights, as they are different. Only compare intake lobes with intake lobes and exhaust lobes with other exhaust lobes.

22  Check the camshaft lobes for heat discoloration, score marks, chipped areas, pitting and uneven wear. If the lobes are in good condition and if the lobe lift variation measurements recorded earlier are within the limits, the camshaft can be reused.

## INSTALLATION

23  Lubricate the camshaft bearing journals and cam lobes with camshaft installation lube.

24  On 2006 and later models (type 272 engines), install new pulse

**6.21  Measure the camshaft lobe height (greatest dimension) with a micrometer**

wheels on the sprockets, and use a small amount of engine oil where the center valves contact the pulse wheel. Tighten the center valve nuts to the Specification in this Chapter, using a Torx tool to hold the rear of the camshaft while tightening the center valves.

➡**Note: Remember that the exhaust center valve nuts have left-hand threads (turn them counterclockwise to tighten).**

25  The remaining installation steps are the reverse of removal.

## 7  Intake manifold - removal and installation

### 2001 THROUGH 2005 (112 MODEL ENGINES)

▶ **Refer to illustrations 7.3 and 7.7**

1  Relieve the fuel system pressure (see Chapter 4), then disconnect the cable from the negative terminal of the battery (see Chapter 5, Section 1).

2  Remove the air filter housing/engine cover, then remove the MAF/IAT sensor with the intake air tube (see Chapter 6).

3  Remove the fuel rail and injectors (see Chapter 4). On engines so equipped, remove the electric air pump in front of the intake manifold (see illustration).

4  Label and disconnect the hoses and electrical connectors attached to the intake manifold and throttle body.

5  Disconnect the EGR hose at the rear of the intake manifold (see Chapter 6).

6  Disconnect the hoses and electrical connectors from the throttle body (see Chapter 4).

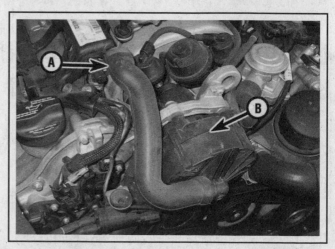

**7.3  On models so equipped, disconnect the air pump hose (A), and unbolt the electric air pump (B)**

7   Remove the intake manifold bolts and the manifold (see illustration).

> **❋❋ CAUTION:**
>
> **Remove the intake manifold as an assembly, do not separate the upper half of the manifold from the lower half.**

8   Clean the mounting surfaces of the intake manifold and cylinder heads.

9   Use alignment dowels (you can make these by cutting heads from bolts of the intake manifold-mounting size) to align the intake manifold to the gaskets and the cylinder heads. Install the manifold gaskets and manifold, then install the bolts hand tight. Remove the alignment dowels and install the remainder of the bolts. Tighten the bolts a little at a time, starting with the center bolts and working to the outer bolts using a circular pattern, to the torque listed in this Chapter's Specifications.

10  The remaining installation steps are the reverse of removal. Run the engine and check for fuel or vacuum leaks.

## 2006 AND LATER (272 MODEL ENGINES)

11  Relieve the fuel system pressure (see Chapter 4), then disconnect the cable from the negative terminal of the battery (see Chapter 5, Section 1).

12  Remove the air filter housing/engine cover, then remove the MAF/IAT sensor with the intake air tube (see Chapter 6).

13  Remove the fuel rail and injectors (see Chapter 4)

14  Label and disconnect the hoses and electrical connectors attached to the intake manifold and throttle body.

15  Disconnect the large connector from the right side of the PCM (see Chapter 6). Do not disconnect the left-side connector.

16  Release the PCM from its two holders and set the PCM aside, with the left connector still connected.

17  Remove the engine lifting bracket at the left rear of the engine.

18  Remove the intake manifold mounting bolts and remove the intake manifold.

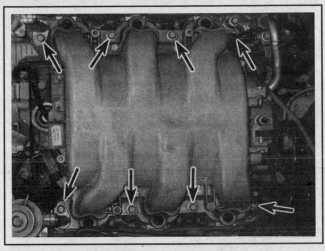

**7.7  Location of intake manifold mounting bolts - 2005 and earlier (type 112 engines)**

> **❋❋ CAUTION:**
>
> **Remove the intake manifold as an assembly; do not separate the upper half of the manifold from the lower half.**

19  Clean the mounting surfaces of the intake manifold and cylinder heads.

20  Use alignment dowels (you can make these by cutting heads from bolts of the intake manifold-mounting size) to align the intake manifold to the gaskets and the cylinder heads. Install the manifold gaskets and manifold, then install the bolts hand tight. Remove the alignment dowels and install the remainder of the bolts. Tighten the bolts a little at a time, starting with the center bolts and working to the outer bolts using a circular pattern, to the torque listed in this Chapter's Specifications.

21  The remaining installation steps are the reverse of removal. Run the engine and check for fuel or vacuum leaks.

## 8   Exhaust manifold(s) - removal and installation

> **❋❋ WARNING:**
>
> **The engine must be completely cool before beginning this procedure.**

## REMOVAL

▶ **Refer to illustrations 8.3 and 8.5**

1   Disconnect the cable from the negative terminal of the battery (see Chapter 5, Section 1).

2   Raise the front of the vehicle and support it securely on jackstands. Remove the engine splash shield.

3   Detach the exhaust pipes from the exhaust manifolds (see illustration).

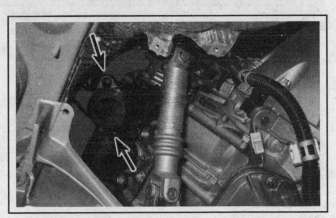

**8.3  Soak the flange bolts with penetrant, then disconnect the exhaust pipe-to-manifold bolts (shown with pipe removed for clarity)**

4   Lower the vehicle.

5   Remove the mounting nuts and detach the manifold from the cylinder head (see illustration).

➡Note: Be sure to spray penetrating oil on the bolts before attempting to remove them.

## INSTALLATION

6   Clean the mating surfaces to remove all traces of old gasket material, then inspect the manifold for distortion and cracks. Warpage can be checked with a precision straightedge held against the mating flange. If a feeler gauge thicker than 0.030-inch can be inserted between the straightedge and flange surface, take the manifold to an automotive machine shop for resurfacing.

7   Place the exhaust manifold in position with a new gasket (or gaskets, on 2005 and earlier models) and install the mounting bolts finger tight.

➡Note: Be sure to identify the exhaust manifold gaskets by the correct cylinder designation and the position of the exhaust ports on the gasket.

8   Starting in the middle and working out toward the ends, tighten the mounting bolts in several increments, to the torque listed in this

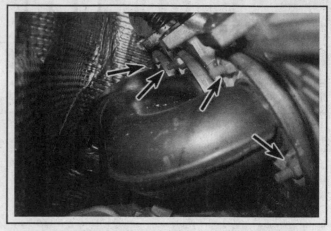

**8.5  Location of the exhaust manifold mounting nuts (not all nuts are visible here)**

Chapter's Specifications.

9   The remaining installation steps are the reverse of removal.

10  Start the engine and check for exhaust leaks between the manifold and cylinder head and between the manifold and exhaust pipe.

---

## 9   Cylinder heads - removal and installation

### ✳✳✳ WARNING:

The engine must be completely cool before beginning this procedure.

➡Note: Special tools are necessary to complete this procedure. Read through the entire procedure and obtain the special tools before beginning work.

## 2001 THROUGH 2005 (112 MODEL ENGINES)

### Removal

1   Relieve the fuel system pressure (see Chapter 4). Disconnect the cable from the negative terminal of the battery (see Chapter 5, Section 1).

2   Drain the cooling system (see Chapter 1).

3   Remove the drivebelt (see Chapter 1).

4   Remove the intake manifold (see Section 7).

5   Remove the valve covers (see Section 4).

6   Detach the exhaust pipe from the exhaust manifold (see Section 8).

7   Remove the cooling fan and shroud (see Chapter 3). It is suggested that the radiator be protected with a piece of wood paneling or heavy cardboard while the fan/shroud assembly is out of the vehicle.

8   Left cylinder head: On models equipped with an oil cooler, remove the oil filter/oil cooler assembly from in front of the intake manifold.

9   Remove the camshaft from the cylinder head being removed (see Section 6).

10  Remove the bolts securing the cylinder head to the timing case cover, then loosen each of the cylinder head mounting bolts 1/4-turn at a time until they can be removed by hand - work from bolt-to-bolt in a pattern that's the reverse of the tightening sequence (see illustration 9.16). Store the bolts in the cardboard holder as they're removed.

11  Lift the head(s) off the engine. If resistance is felt, don't pry between the head and block as damage to the mating surfaces will result. Recheck for head bolts that may have been overlooked, then use a hammer and block of wood to tap up on the head to break the gasket seal. Be careful because there are locating dowels in the block which position each head. After removal, place the head on blocks of wood to prevent damage to the gasket surfaces.

### Installation

▸ Refer to illustrations 9.13 and 9.16

12  The mating surfaces of each cylinder head and block must be perfectly clean when the head is installed. Clean the mating surfaces with dish soap and water. If there's oil on the mating surfaces when the head is installed, the gasket may not seal correctly and leaks may develop. When working on the block, it's a good idea to cover the valley with shop rags to keep debris out of the engine. Use a shop rag or vacuum cleaner to remove any debris that falls into the cylinders.

➡Note: The cylinder heads and block surface may have a factory-applied silicone coating. If so, do not remove it, but inspect the surfaces for any tears or low spots. Apply new coating (available at a dealership) to any low spots.

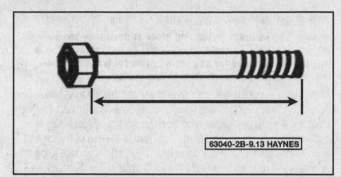

**9.13  Check the length of the head bolts, from the underside of the head to the end. Replace any bolt that exceeds the length listed in this Chapter's Specifications**

13  Use a tap of the correct size to chase the threads in the head bolt holes. Dirt, corrosion, sealant and damaged threads will affect torque readings. Check the cleaned head bolts for stretch by measuring the distance from the underside of the bolt head to the end of the threads (see illustration). Replace any head bolts with new ones if the measurement is over the value listed in this Chapter's Specifications.

14  Position the new gasket over the dowel pins in the block. Check the front edge of the old head gaskets. There are two types, depending on the engine's displacement:

  *2.6L, 2.8L and 3.2L engines use Type A gaskets.*
  *2.4L engines use Type B gaskets.*

Type A gaskets have one semi-circular notch at the front, while Type B gaskets have two notches.

### ✳✳ CAUTION:

**Use of the wrong head gasket can cause engine problems (the pistons can come in contact with the gaskets).**

15  Carefully position the head on the block without disturbing the gasket, and making sure the head fits down over the dowel pins.

16  Tighten the bolts in the recommended sequence (see illustration) to the torque listed in this Chapter's Specifications.

17  The remaining installation steps are the reverse of removal.

18  Change the oil and filter, refill the cooling system (see Chapter 1), run the engine and check for leaks.

## 2006 AND LATER (272 MODEL ENGINES)

### Removal

19  Relieve the fuel system pressure (see Chapter 4). Disconnect the cable from the negative terminal of the battery (see Chapter 5, Section 1).

20  Drain the cooling system (see Chapter 1).

21  Remove the drivebelt (see Chapter 1).

22  Remove the intake manifold (see Section 7).

23  Detach the catalytic converter from the exhaust manifold (see Section 8).

24  Remove the front cover from the cylinder head.

25  Remove the valve cover (see Section 4).

26  If you're removing the left cylinder head, remove the oil separator (see Chapter 6, Section 18).

27  Remove the aspirator shutoff valve (see Chapter 6, Section 19).

28  Remove the oil filter/oil cooler assembly from in front of the intake manifold.

29  Remove the alternator (see Chapter 5).

30  Remove the camshafts (see Section 6).

31  Remove the slide rail pins (left cylinder head) or slide rail pins and tensioning rail bolts (right cylinder head) from the front of the cylinder head. This will require a treaded adapter that fits into the pins/bolts and a puller to pull them out.

32  If you're removing the right cylinder head, remove the air pump and bracket. Also unbolt the dipstick tube from the head

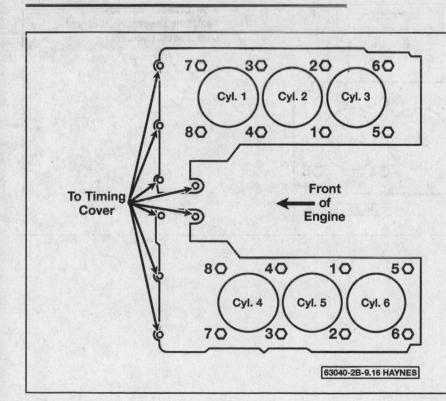

**9.16  Cylinder head bolt tightening sequence - 2005 and earlier models (type 112)**

33  Remove the bolts securing the cylinder head to the timing case cover, then loosen each of the cylinder head mounting bolts 1/4-turn at a time until they can be removed by hand - work from bolt-to-bolt in a pattern that's the reverse of the tightening sequence (see illustration 9.39). Store the bolts in the cardboard holder as they're removed.

34  Lift the head(s) off the engine. If resistance is felt, don't pry between the head and block as damage to the mating surfaces will result. Recheck for head bolts that may have been overlooked, then use a hammer and block of wood to tap up on the head to break the gasket seal. Be careful because there are locating dowels in the block which position each head. After removal, place the head on blocks of wood to prevent damage to the gasket surfaces.

## Installation

**▶ Refer to illustration 9.39**

35  The mating surfaces of each cylinder head and block must be perfectly clean when the head is installed. Clean the mating surfaces with dish soap and water. If there's oil on the mating surfaces when the head is installed, the gasket may not seal correctly and leaks may develop. When working on the block, it's a good idea to cover the valley with shop rags to keep debris out of the engine. Use a shop rag or vacuum cleaner to remove any debris that falls into the cylinders.

**➡Note: The cylinder heads and block surface may have a factory-applied silicone coating. If so, do not remove it, but inspect the surfaces for any tears or low spots. Apply new coating (available at a dealership) to any low spots.**

36  Use a tap of the correct size to chase the threads in the head bolt holes. Dirt, corrosion, sealant and damaged threads will affect torque readings. Check the cleaned head bolts for stretch by measuring the distance from the underside of the bolt head to the end of the threads (see illustration 9.13). Replace any head bolts with new ones if the measurement is over the value listed in this Chapter's Specifications.

37  Position the new gasket over the dowel pins in the block.

38  Carefully position the head on the block without disturbing the gasket, and making sure the head fits down over the dowel pins.

39  Tighten the bolts in the recommended sequence (see illustration) to the torque listed in this Chapter's Specifications.

40  The remaining installation steps are the reverse of removal.

**➡Note: When installing the slide rail pins/tensioning rail bolts, coat them with sealant (such as Loctite 5970).**

41  Change the oil and filter, refill the cooling system (see Chapter 1), run the engine and check for leaks.

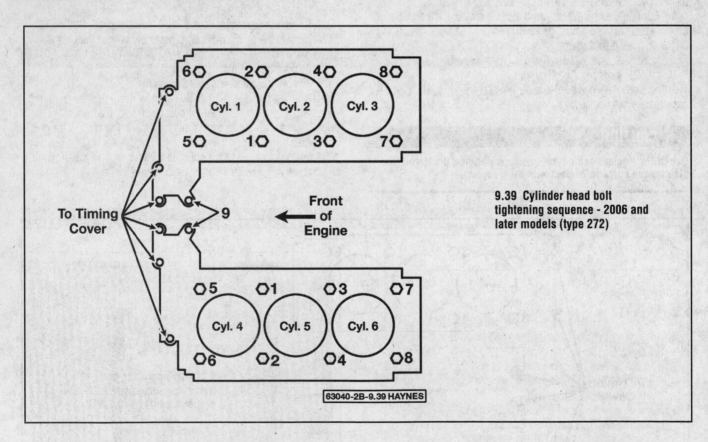

**9.39  Cylinder head bolt tightening sequence - 2006 and later models (type 272)**

63040-2B-9.39 HAYNES

## 10 Crankshaft pulley - removal and installation

▶ **Refer to illustration 10.3**

1    Disconnect the cable from the negative terminal of the battery (see Chapter 5, Section 1). Remove the accessory drivebelt (see Chapter 1).

2    Due to the large amount of torque required to remove/install the pulley center bolt, the engine must be held from turning by a substantial tool. It would be best to utilize a tool that locks into the teeth of the flywheel ring-gear. Remove the access cover in the bellhousing for installing such a tool on the flywheel.

3    If your model has a crankshaft pulley with large enough holes through it, an alternative is to position a large screwdriver or other tool through the crankshaft pulley and against the block to keep the crankshaft from turning and remove the pulley-to-crankshaft bolt (see illustration). It may require a helper to perform this procedure.

4    Install the crankshaft pulley retaining bolt and tighten it to the torque listed in this Chapter's Specifications.

5    The remaining installation steps are the reverse of removal.

**10.3  Use a chain wrench or insert a prybar through the pulley to hold it while you loosen the crankshaft pulley bolt**

## 11 Crankshaft front oil seal - replacement

1    Remove the crankshaft pulley (see Section 10).

2    Pry the old seal out with a hook-type seal tool, being very careful not to scratch the seal surface of the crankshaft. Note how the seal is installed - the new one must be installed to the same depth and facing the same way.

3    Lubricate the inner lip of the new seal with engine oil and drive it in with a seal driver or large deep socket and a hammer.

4    The remaining installation steps are the reverse of removal.

## 12 Oil pan - removal and installation

### REMOVAL

#### Lower pan

▶ **Refer to illustration 12.10**

1    Disconnect the cable from the negative terminal of the battery (see Chapter 5, Section 1).

2    Remove the engine cover (see Chapter 1).

3    Remove the MAF/IAT sensor and its intake tube (see Chapter 6).

4    Remove the engine oil dipstick.

5    Remove the bolt securing the oil dipstick tube at the top/rear of the engine, then pull the tube upward slightly.

6    Raise the front of the vehicle and support it securely on jackstands. Apply the parking brake and block the rear wheels to keep the vehicle from rolling off the stands.

7    If you're working on a 2005 or earlier model, remove the front suspension subframe (see Chapter 10).

8    Drain the engine oil and remove the oil filter (see Chapter 1).

9    On 2006 and later models, remove the bolt securing the power steering hose to the oil pan, and the bolt securing the electrical harness to the pan.

10   Remove the oil pan mounting bolts (see illustration).

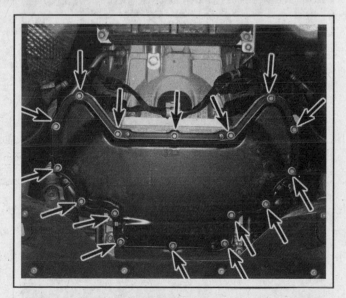

**12.10  Location of the lower oil pan bolts - type 272 shown**

11 Remove the front engine mount bolt (see Section 16).

12 Remove the oil pan bolts, then carefully separate the oil pan from the block. Don't pry between the block and the pan or damage to the sealing surfaces could occur and oil leaks may develop. Instead, tap the pan with a soft-face hammer to break the gasket seal. Tap a plastic wedge tool between the upper and lower pans to free the lower pan.

13 Raise the engine with the hoist just enough to allow oil pan removal, then guide the pan out rearward.

➡ **Note: On 112 engines, you may have to pull the dipstick tube up a little and pull the transmission fluid lines away from the pan rail for clearance.**

### Upper pan

▶ **Refer to illustrations 12.15, 12.16, 12.17 and 12.18**

14 Follow the Steps above and remove the lower oil pan.

15 Disconnect and remove the oil sensor at the rear of the upper pan (see illustration).

16 If equipped with an automatic transmission, unbolt the transmission fluid banjo bolts at the transmission and the fluid lines from the bracket at the oil pan mounting flange (see illustration).

17 Pry the oil dipstick tube from the upper oil pan (see illustration).

18 With the vehicle on a lift, support the engine from above with an engine support fixture (see illustration).

19 Refer to Chapter 10 and lower the front suspension subframe with a transmission jack. This allows room to remove the upper oil pan.

20 Remove the Torx bolts securing the upper oil pan to the engine.

➡ **Note: There are a number of different bolts lengths and sizes. Use a piece of cardboard with holes punched in it to store the bolts with reference marks to where they were used.**

## INSTALLATION

21 Clean the pan with solvent and remove all old sealant and gasket material from the block and pan mating surfaces. Clean the mating surfaces with brake system cleaner and make sure the bolt holes in the block are clear. Check the oil pan flange for distortion, particularly around the bolt holes.

22 Apply a 2 mm bead of RTV sealant around the pan rail, just inside the bolt holes.

23 Install the oil pan mounting bolts, tightening them to the torque listed in this Chapter's Specifications. Starting at the center, follow a criss-cross pattern and work up to the final torque in three steps.

24 Tighten the oil pan-to-engine bolts to the torque listed in this Chapter's Specifications.

25 The remaining installation steps are the reverse of removal.

26 Refill the engine with oil (see Chapter 1), replace the filter, run it until normal operating temperature is reached and check for leaks.

**12.15 Disconnect the oil sensor**

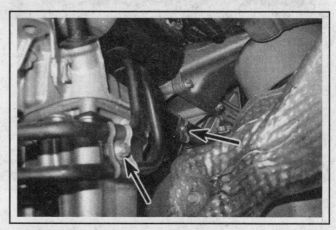

**12.16 Unbolt the transmission fluid lines and brackets attached to the upper oil pan (automatic transmission models)**

**12.17 Pry the engine oil dipstick tube from the flange on the upper oil pan**

**12.18 The engine must be secured with an engine support fixture to allow removal of the upper oil pan**

## 13 Oil pump - removal, inspection and installation

### ❊❊ CAUTION:

**Do not remove the oil pressure relief valve, spring and plunger from the oil pump. Replace the oil pump as one complete assembly if the oil pressure relief valve is damaged.**

1   Remove the lower and upper oil pans (see Section 12).
2   Remove the oil pump pick-up tube.
3   Push back the tensioner for the oil pump chain, and slip the chain from the oil pump sprocket.

4   Remove the oil pump-to-block bolts and pull the oil pump from the block.
5   During installation of the pump, prime it by filling the housing with engine oil.
6   To install the pump, slip the sprocket of the oil pump into the chain while supporting the pump to the block for installation of the mounting bolts.
7   When the bolts are finger-tight, torque the pump mounting bolts to the torque listed in this Chapter's Specifications.
8   The remaining installation steps are the reverse of removal.

## 14 Driveplate/flywheel - removal and installation

This procedure is essentially the same as for the four-cylinder engine. Refer to Part A and follow the procedure outlined there, but use

the bolt torque listed in this Chapter's Specifications.

## 15 Rear main oil seal - replacement

➡**Note: The rear main seal and housing are serviced as one complete assembly.**

1   This procedure is essentially the same as for the four-cylinder engine - refer to Chapter 2A.
2   On 2006 and later models (272 engines), apply a 2 mm bead of

RTV sealant at the cover-sealing area of the block, inside the bolt holes and around the bolt holes for the two bolts coming up from the upper oil pan. Refer to Part A and follow the procedure outlined there, but use the bolt torque value listed in this Chapter's Specifications.

## 16 Engine mounts - check and replacement

♦ **Refer to illustrations 16.1a and 16.1b**

This procedure is essentially the same as for the four-cylinder engine. Refer to Part A and follow the procedure outlined there, but refer

to the illustrations here and use the torque values listed in this Chapter's Specifications. The front mounts have an upper mounting bolt that secures them to the engine bracket and a lower bolt that fastens it to the subframe.

**16.1a  Location of the right engine mount-to-subframe mounting bolt (seen from below)**

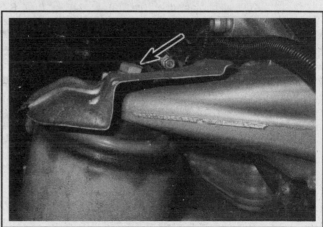

**16.1b  Location of the left engine mount-to-engine bracket mounting bolt**

## Specifications

### General

Engine designation
| | |
|---|---|
| 2001 through 2005 models | 112 |
| 2006 and later models | 272 |

C240 models, 2001 to 2005
| | |
|---|---|
| Displacement | 158 cubic inches (2.6 liters) |
| Bore | 3.54 inches (89.9 mm) |
| Stroke | 2.68 inches (68.2 mm) |

C320 models, 2001 to 2005
| | |
|---|---|
| Displacement | 195 cubic inches (3.2 liters) |
| Bore | 3.54 inches (89.9 mm) |
| Stroke | 3.30 inches (84.0 mm) |

C230 models, 2006 and later
| | |
|---|---|
| Displacement | 152 cubic inches (2.5 liters) |
| Bore | 3.46 inches (88.0 mm) |
| Stroke | 2.69 inches (68.4 mm) |

C280 models, 2006 and later
| | |
|---|---|
| Displacement | 183 cubic inches (3.0 liters) |
| Bore | 3.46 inches (88.0 mm) |
| Stroke | 3.23 inches (82.1 mm) |

C350 models, 2006 and later
| | |
|---|---|
| Displacement | 213 cubic inches (3.5 liters) |
| Bore | 3.65 inches (92.9 mm) |
| Stroke | 3.38 inches (86.0 mm) |

Cylinder compression pressure
| | |
|---|---|
| Minimum | 174 to 203 psi |
| Maximum variation between cylinders | 22 psi |

Oil pressure (minimum, warm engine)
| | |
|---|---|
| 700 rpm | 10 psi |
| 3000 rpm | 43 psi |
| Firing order | 1-4-3-6-2-5 |

**V6 engine
1-4-3-6-2-5**

63040-2B-specs HAYNES

**Cylinder identification diagram**

### Cylinder head bolt length (maximum) (see illustration 9.13)

| | |
|---|---|
| 2005 and earlier models (type 112) | 5.70 inches (144.5 mm) |
| 2006 and later models (type 272) | 6.77 inches (172 mm) |

| Torque specifications | Ft-lbs (unless otherwise indicated) | Nm |
|---|---|---|

➥**Note: One foot-pound (ft-lb) of torque is equivalent to 12 inch-pounds (in-lbs) of torque. Torque values below approximately 15 ft-lbs are expressed in inch-pounds, since most foot-pound torque wrenches are not accurate at these smaller values.**

| | | |
|---|---|---|
| Camshaft sprocket bolts | | |
| Step 1 | 37 | 50 |
| Step 2 | Tighten an additional 90-degrees | |
| Camshaft cap/bridge bolts | | |
| Short bolts | 133 in-lbs | 15 |
| Long bolts | | |
| Step 1 | 89 in-lbs | 10 |
| Step 2 | Tighten an additional 90-degrees | |

| Torque specifications | Ft-lbs (unless otherwise indicated) | Nm |
|---|---|---|

➡Note: One foot-pound (ft-lb) of torque is equivalent to 12 inch-pounds (in-lbs) of torque. Torque values below approximately 15 ft-lbs are expressed in inch-pounds, since most foot-pound torque wrenches are not accurate at these smaller values.

| | | |
|---|---|---|
| Centrifuge cover bolts and centrifuge-to-camshaft bolt (2006 and later models) | | |
| Step 1 | 53 in-lbs | 6 |
| Step 2 | Tighten an additional 90-degrees | |
| Crankshaft pulley bolt | | |
| Step 1 | 148 | 200 |
| Step 2 | Tighten an additional 95-degrees | |
| Cylinder head bolts | | |
| 2005 and earlier models | | |
| Step 1 | 89 in-lbs | 10 |
| Step 2 | 22 | 30 |
| Step 3 | Tighten an additional 90-degrees | |
| Step 4 | Tighten an additional 90-degrees | |
| 2006 and later models | | |
| Step 1 | 177 in-lbs | 20 |
| Step 2 | 30 | 40 |
| Step 3 | Tighten an additional 90-degrees | |
| Step 4 | Tighten an additional 90-degrees | |
| Drivebelt tensioner bolt | 18 | 25 |
| Driveplate-to-crankshaft bolts | | |
| Step 1 | 33 | 45 |
| Step 2 | Tighten an additional 90-degrees | |
| Engine mount bolts, front | 26 | 35 |
| Exhaust manifold-to-cylinder head bolts | 177 in-lbs | 20 |
| Exhaust pipe bolts | 177 in-lbs | 20 |
| Intake manifold bolts | 177 in-lbs | 20 |
| Oil pan drain plug | 22 | 30 |
| Oil pan bolts | | |
| Upper pan-to-engine | | |
| M6 bolts | 80 in-lbs | 9 |
| M8 bolts | 177 in-lbs | 20 |
| Lower pan-to-upper pan bolts | 80 in-lbs | 9 |
| Oil pump cover with pipe, mounting bolt | 89 in-lbs | 10 |
| Oil pump to engine bolts | 177 in-lbs | 20 |
| Valve cover bolts | | |
| 2005 and earlier models (type 112) | 70 in-lbs | 8 |
| 2006 and later models (type 272) - in sequence (see illustration 4.8b) | | |
| First pass | 106 in-lbs | 12 |
| Second pass | Tighten an additional 90-degrees | |

**Notes**

## Section

### Reference to other Chapters

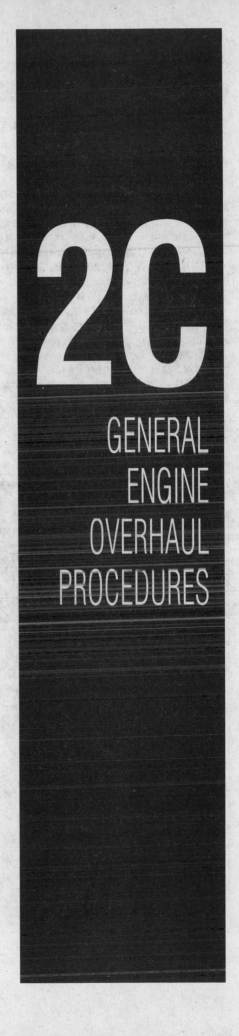

# 2C

GENERAL
ENGINE
OVERHAUL
PROCEDURES

### 1 General information - engine overhaul

◆ **Refer to illustrations 1.1, 1.2, 1.3, 1.4, 1.5 and 1.6**

Included in this portion of Chapter 2 are general information and diagnostic testing procedures for determining the overall mechanical condition of your engine.

The information ranges from advice concerning preparation for an overhaul and the purchase of replacement parts and/or components to detailed, step-by-step procedures covering removal and installation.

The following Sections have been written to help you determine whether your engine needs to be overhauled and how to remove and install it once you've determined it needs to be rebuilt. For information concerning in-vehicle engine repair, see Chapter 2A or 2B.

The Specifications included in this Part are general in nature and include only those necessary for testing the oil pressure and engine compression, and bottom-end torque specifications. Refer to Chapter 2A (four-cylinder engines) or 2B (V6 engines) for additional engine Specifications.

It's not always easy to determine when, or if, an engine should be completely overhauled, because a number of factors must be considered.

High mileage is not necessarily an indication that an overhaul is needed, while low mileage doesn't preclude the need for an overhaul. Frequency of servicing is probably the most important consideration.

An engine that's had regular and frequent oil and filter changes, as well as other required maintenance, will most likely give many thousands of miles of reliable service. Conversely, a neglected engine may require an overhaul very early in its service life.

Excessive oil consumption is an indication that piston rings, valve seals and/or valve guides are in need of attention. Make sure that oil leaks aren't responsible before deciding that the rings and/or guides are bad. Perform a cylinder compression check to determine the extent of the work required (see Section 3). Also, check the vacuum readings under various conditions (see Section 4).

Check the oil pressure with a gauge installed in place of the oil pressure sending unit and compare it to this Chapter's Specifications (see Section 2). If it's extremely low, the bearings and/or oil pump are probably worn out.

Loss of power, rough running, knocking or metallic engine noises, excessive valve train noise and high fuel consumption rates may also point to the need for an overhaul, especially if they're all present at the same time. If a complete tune-up doesn't remedy the situation, major mechanical work is the only solution.

An engine overhaul involves restoring the internal parts to the specifications of a new engine. During an overhaul, the piston rings are replaced and the cylinder walls are reconditioned (rebored and/or honed) (see illustrations 1.1 and 1.2). If a rebore is done by an

**1.1  An engine block being bored. An engine rebuilder will use special machinery to recondition the cylinder bores**

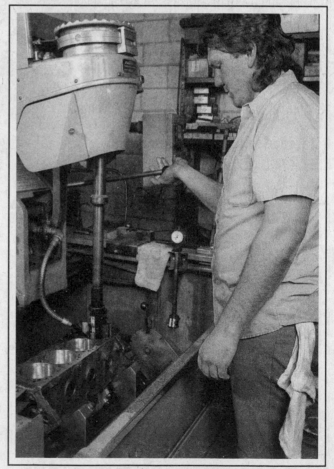

**1.2  If the cylinders are bored, the machine shop will normally hone the engine on a machine like this**

automotive machine shop, new oversize pistons will also be installed. The main bearings, connecting rod bearings and camshaft bearings are generally replaced with new ones and, if necessary, the crankshaft may be reground to restore the journals (see illustration 1.3). Generally, the valves are serviced as well, since they're usually in less-than-perfect condition at this point. While the engine is being overhauled, other components, such as the distributor, starter and alternator, can be rebuilt as well. The end result should be similar to a new engine that will give many trouble free miles.

➡ **Note: Critical cooling system components such as the hoses, drivebelts, thermostat and water pump should be replaced with new parts when an engine is overhauled. The radiator should be checked carefully to ensure that it isn't clogged or leaking (see Chapter 3). If you purchase a rebuilt engine or short block, some rebuilders will not warranty their engines unless the radiator has been professionally flushed. Also, we don't recommend overhauling the oil pump - always install a new one when an engine is rebuilt.**

Overhauling the internal components on today's engines is a difficult and time-consuming task which requires a significant amount of specialty tools and is best left to a professional engine rebuilder (see illustrations 1.4, 1.5 and 1.6). A competent engine rebuilder will handle the inspection of your old parts and offer advice concerning the reconditioning or replacement of the original engine, never purchase parts or have machine work done on other components until the block has been thoroughly inspected by a professional machine shop. As a general rule, time is the primary cost of an overhaul, especially since the vehicle may be tied up for a minimum of two weeks or more. Be aware that some engine builders only have the capability to rebuild the engine you bring them while other rebuilders have a large inventory of rebuilt exchange engines in stock. Also be aware that many machine shops could take as much as two weeks time to completely rebuild your engine depending on shop workload. Sometimes it makes more sense to simply exchange your engine for another engine that's already rebuilt to save time.

1.3 A crankshaft having a main bearing journal ground

1.4 A machinist checks for a bent connecting rod, using specialized equipment

1.5 A bore gauge being used to check the main bearing bore

1.6 Uneven piston wear like this indicates a bent connecting rod

## 2   Oil pressure check

▶ **Refer to illustration 2.2**

1   Low engine oil pressure can be a sign of an engine in need of rebuilding. A low oil pressure indicator (often called an "idiot light") is not a test of the oiling system. Such indicators only come on when the oil pressure is dangerously low. Even a factory oil pressure gauge in the instrument panel is only a relative indication, although much better for driver information than a warning light. A better test is with a mechanical (not electrical) oil pressure gauge.

2   Locate the oil pressure test port. On V6 engines, a plug with a sealing ring is located on the front of the timing cover (see illustration). Remove the plug. On four-cylinder engines, the cover of the oil filter housing has a threaded plug that can be removed for pressure testing.

3   Unscrew the plug and then screw in the hose for your oil pressure gauge. If necessary, install an adapter fitting. Use Teflon tape or thread sealant on the threads of the adapter and/or the fitting on the end of your gauge's hose.

4   Connect an accurate tachometer to the engine, according to the tachometer manufacturer's instructions.

5   Check the oil pressure with the engine running (normal operating temperature) at the specified engine speed, and compare it to this Chapter's Specifications. If it's extremely low, the bearings and/or oil pump are probably worn out.

6   Installation is the reverse of removal. Clean the threads on the sensor and use new sealant on the threads before installation.

**2.2   Oil pressure test location (2005 and earlier V6 engine shown, 2006 and later V6 similar) - remove this plug and insert your test pressure fitting**

## 3   Cylinder compression check

▶ **Refer to illustration 3.6**

1   A compression check will tell you what mechanical condition the upper end of your engine (pistons, rings, valves, head gaskets) is in. Specifically, it can tell you if the compression is down due to leakage caused by worn piston rings, defective valves and seats or a blown head gasket.

➡ **Note: The engine must be at normal operating temperature and the battery must be fully charged for this check.**

2   Begin by cleaning the area around the spark plugs before you remove them (compressed air should be used, if available). The idea is to prevent dirt from getting into the cylinders as the compression check is being done.

3   Remove the ignition coil assemblies (see Chapter 5). Also disable the fuel pump by removing the fuel pump fuse (see Chapter 4, Section 2).

4   Remove the spark plugs (see Chapter 1).

➡ **Note: On V6 engines with dual spark plugs, only remove one plug from each cylinder to perform the compression test.**

5   Gain access to the throttle body (see Chapter 4), then block the throttle wide open.

6   Install a compression gauge in the spark plug hole (see illustration).

**3.6   Use a compression gauge with a threaded fitting for the spark plug hole, not the type that requires hand pressure to maintain the seal**

7   Crank the engine over at least seven compression strokes and watch the gauge. The compression should build up quickly in a healthy engine. Low compression on the first stroke, followed by gradually increasing pressure on successive strokes, indicates worn piston rings. A low compression reading on the first stroke, which doesn't build up during successive strokes, indicates leaking valves or a blown head gasket (a cracked head could also be the cause). Deposits on the undersides of the valve heads can also cause low compression. Record the highest gauge reading obtained.

8   Repeat the procedure for the remaining cylinders and compare the results to this Chapter's Specifications.

9   Add some engine oil (about three squirts from a plunger-type oil can) to each cylinder, through the spark plug hole, and repeat the test.

10  If the compression increases after the oil is added, the piston rings are definitely worn. If the compression doesn't increase significantly, the leakage is occurring at the valves or head gasket. Leakage past the valves may be caused by burned valve seats and/or faces or warped, cracked or bent valves.

11  If two adjacent cylinders have equally low compression, there's a strong possibility that the head gasket between them is blown. The appearance of coolant in the combustion chambers or the crankcase would verify this condition.

12  If one cylinder is slightly lower than the others, and the engine has a slightly rough idle, a worn lobe on the camshaft could be the cause.

13  If the compression is unusually high, the combustion chambers are probably coated with carbon deposits. If that's the case, the cylinder head(s) should be removed and decarbonized.

14  If compression is way down or varies greatly between cylinders, it would be a good idea to have a leak-down test performed by an automotive repair shop. This test will pinpoint exactly where the leakage is occurring and how severe it is.

## 4   Vacuum gauge diagnostic checks

▶ Refer to illustrations 4.4 and 4.6

1   A vacuum gauge provides inexpensive but valuable information about what is going on in the engine. You can check for worn rings or cylinder walls, leaking head or intake manifold gaskets, incorrect carburetor adjustments, restricted exhaust, stuck or burned valves, weak valve springs, improper ignition or valve timing and ignition problems.

2   Unfortunately, vacuum gauge readings are easy to misinterpret, so they should be used in conjunction with other tests to confirm the diagnosis.

3   Both the absolute readings and the rate of needle movement are important for accurate interpretation. Most gauges measure vacuum in inches of mercury (in-Hg). The following references to vacuum assume the diagnosis is being performed at sea level. As elevation increases (or atmospheric pressure decreases), the reading will decrease. For every 1,000 foot increase in elevation above approximately 2,000 feet, the gauge readings will decrease about one inch of mercury.

4   Connect the vacuum gauge directly to the intake manifold vacuum, not to ported (throttle body) vacuum (see illustration). Some models are equipped with a vacuum fitting built into the brake booster vacuum hose grommet at the brake booster. Other models are equipped with a vacuum hose fitting on the intake manifold.

5   Before you begin the test, allow the engine to warm up completely. Block the wheels and set the parking brake. With the transmission in Park, start the engine and allow it to run at normal idle speed.

**✶✶ WARNING:**

**Keep your hands and the vacuum gauge clear of the fans.**

**4.4 A simple vacuum gauge can be handy in diagnosing engine condition and performance. Connect it to a manifold vacuum source (not ported, or in front of the throttle plate, vacuum source)**

6  Read the vacuum gauge; an average, healthy engine should normally produce about 17 to 22 in-Hg with a fairly steady needle (see illustration). Refer to the following vacuum gauge readings and what they indicate about the engine's condition:

7  A low, steady reading usually indicates a leaking gasket between the intake manifold and cylinder head(s) or throttle body, a leaky vacuum hose, late ignition timing or incorrect camshaft timing. Check ignition timing with a timing light and eliminate all other possible causes, utilizing the tests provided in this Chapter before you remove the timing chain cover to check the timing marks.

8  If the reading is three to eight inches below normal and it fluctuates at that low reading, suspect an intake manifold gasket leak at an intake port or a faulty fuel injector.

9  If the needle has regular drops of about two-to-four inches at a steady rate, the valves are probably leaking. Perform a compression check or leak-down test to confirm this.

10  An irregular drop or down-flick of the needle can be caused by a sticking valve or an ignition misfire. Perform a compression check or leak-down test and read the spark plugs.

11  A rapid vibration of about four in-Hg vibration at idle combined with exhaust smoke indicates worn valve guides. Perform a leak-down test to confirm this. If the rapid vibration occurs with an increase in engine speed, check for a leaking intake manifold gasket or head gasket, weak valve springs, burned valves or ignition misfire.

12  A slight fluctuation, say one inch up and down, may mean ignition problems. Check all the usual tune-up items and, if necessary, run the engine on an ignition analyzer.

13  If there is a large fluctuation, perform a compression or leak-down test to look for a weak or dead cylinder or a blown head gasket.

14  If the needle moves slowly through a wide range, check for a clogged PCV system, incorrect idle fuel mixture, throttle body or intake manifold gasket leaks.

15  Check for a slow return after revving the engine by quickly snapping the throttle open until the engine reaches about 2,500 rpm and let it shut. Normally the reading should drop to near zero, rise above normal idle reading (about 5 in-Hg over) and then return to the previous idle reading. If the vacuum returns slowly and doesn't peak when the throttle is snapped shut, the rings may be worn. If there is a long delay, look for a restricted exhaust system (often the muffler or catalytic converter). An easy way to check this is to temporarily disconnect the exhaust ahead of the suspected part and redo the test.

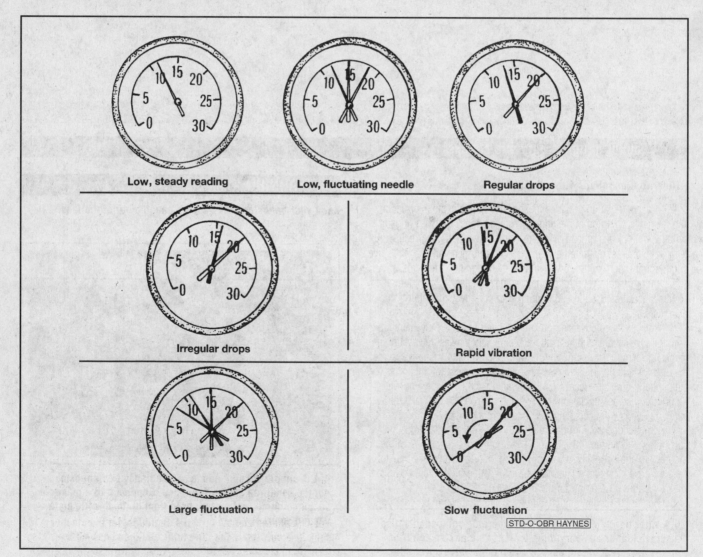

Low, steady reading     Low, fluctuating needle     Regular drops

Irregular drops     Rapid vibration

Large fluctuation     Slow fluctuation

STD-O-OBR HAYNES

**4.6 Typical vacuum gauge readings**

## 5   Engine rebuilding alternatives

The do-it-yourselfer is faced with a number of options when purchasing a rebuilt engine. The major considerations are cost, warranty, parts availability and the time required for the rebuilder to complete the project. The decision to replace the engine block, piston/connecting rod assemblies and crankshaft depends on the final inspection results of your engine. Only then can you make a cost effective decision whether to have your engine overhauled or simply purchase an exchange engine for your vehicle.

Some of the rebuilding alternatives include:

**Individual parts -** If the inspection procedures reveal that the engine block and most engine components are in reusable condition, purchasing individual parts and having a rebuilder rebuild your engine may be the most economical alternative. The block, crankshaft and piston/connecting rod assemblies should all be inspected carefully by a machine shop first.

**Short block -** A short block consists of an engine block with a crankshaft and piston/connecting rod assemblies already installed. All new bearings are incorporated and all clearances will be correct. The existing camshafts, valve train components, cylinder head and external parts can be bolted to the short block with little or no machine shop work necessary.

**Long block -** A long block consists of a short block plus an oil pump, oil pan, cylinder head, valve cover, camshaft and valve train components, timing sprockets and chain or gears and timing cover. All components are installed with new bearings, seals and gaskets incorporated throughout. The installation of manifolds and external parts is all that's necessary.

**Low mileage used engines -** Some companies now offer low mileage used engines which is a very cost effective way to get your vehicle up and running again. These engines often come from vehicles which have been in totaled in accidents or come from other countries which have a higher vehicle turn over rate. A low mileage used engine also usually has a warranty similar to the newly remanufactured engines.

Give careful thought to which alternative is best for you and discuss the situation with local automotive machine shops, auto parts dealers and experienced rebuilders before ordering or purchasing replacement parts.

## 6   Engine removal - methods and precautions

◆ **Refer to illustrations 6.1, 6.2, and 6.3**

If you've decided that an engine must be removed for overhaul or major repair work, several preliminary steps should be taken. Read all removal and installation procedures carefully prior to committing to this job. These engines are removed by lowering the engine to the floor, along with the transmission, and then raising the vehicle sufficiently to slide the assembly out; this will require a vehicle hoist as well as an engine hoist.

Locating a suitable place to work is extremely important. Adequate work space, along with storage space for the vehicle, will be needed. If a shop or garage isn't available, at the very least a flat, level, clean work surface made of concrete or asphalt is required.

Cleaning the engine compartment and engine before beginning the removal procedure will help keep tools clean and organized (see illustrations 6.1 and 6.2).

An engine hoist will also be necessary and a transmission jack

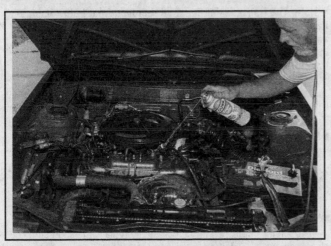

6.1  After tightly wrapping water-vulnerable components, use a spray cleaner on everything, with particular concentration on the greasiest areas, usually around the valve cover and lower edges of the block. If one section dries out, apply more cleaner

6.2  Depending on how dirty the engine is, let the cleaner soak in according to the directions and then hose off the grime and cleaner. Get the rinse water down into every area you can get at; then dry important components with a hair dryer or paper towels

is also very helpful. Make sure the hoist is rated in excess of the combined weight of the engine and transmission. Safety is of primary importance, considering the potential hazards involved in removing the engine from the vehicle.

If you're a novice at engine removal, get at least one helper. One person cannot easily do all the things you need to do to remove a big heavy engine and transmission assembly from the engine compartment. Also helpful is to seek advice and assistance from someone who's experienced in engine removal.

Plan the operation ahead of time. Arrange for or obtain all of the tools and equipment you'll need prior to beginning the job (see illustration 6.3). Some of the equipment necessary to perform engine removal and installation safely and with relative ease are (in addition to a vehicle hoist and an engine hoist) a heavy duty floor jack (preferably fitted with a transmission jack head adapter), complete sets of wrenches and sockets as described in the front of this manual, wooden blocks, plenty of rags and cleaning solvent for mopping up spilled oil, coolant and gasoline.

Plan for the vehicle to be out of use for quite a while. A machine shop can do the work that is beyond the scope of the home mechanic. Machine shops often have a busy schedule, so before removing the engine, consult the shop for an estimate of how long it will take to rebuild or repair the components that may need work.

**6.3 Get an engine stand sturdy enough to firmly support the engine while you're working on it. Stay away from three-wheeled models; they have a tendency to tip over more easily, so get a four-wheeled unit**

## 7   Engine - removal and installation

### ※※ WARNING 1:

**Gasoline is extremely flammable, so take extra precautions when you work on any part of the fuel system. Don't smoke or allow open flames or bare light bulbs near the work area, and don't work in a garage where a gas-type appliance (such as a water heater or clothes dryer) is present. Since gasoline is carcinogenic, wear fuel-resistant gloves when there's a possibility of being exposed to fuel, and, if you spill any fuel on your skin, rinse it off immediately with soap and water. Mop up any spills immediately and do not store fuel-soaked rags where they could ignite. The fuel system is under constant pressure, so, if any fuel lines are to be disconnected, the fuel pressure in the system must be relieved first (see Chapter 4 for more information). When you perform any kind of work on the fuel system, wear safety glasses and have a Class B type fire extinguisher on hand.**

### ※※ WARNING 2:

**The air conditioning system is under high pressure. Do not loosen any hose fittings or remove any components until after the system has been discharged. Air conditioning refrigerant must be properly discharged into an EPA-approved recovery/recycling unit at a dealer service department or an automotive air conditioning repair facility. Always wear eye protection when disconnecting air conditioning system fittings.**

### ※※ WARNING 3:

**The engine must be completely cool before beginning this procedure.**

➡Note: The transmission must be removed from below using a transmission jack, then the engine is removed from above with an engine hoist. A lift or other safe method of raising/supporting the vehicle must be used to raise the vehicle enough for the transmission to be rolled out from under the vehicle.

## REMOVAL

▶ Refer to illustrations 7.19, 7.26a and 7.26b

1   Have the air conditioning system discharged by an automotive air conditioning technician.

2   Relieve the fuel system pressure (see Chapter 4).

3   Disconnect the cables from the negative and positive battery terminals (see Chapter 5, Section 1).

4   Open the hood, then press the button on the left support strut and place the hood in the full-open position.

5   Remove the engine cover/air filter housing and the intake air ducts (see Chapter 4).

6   Loosen the front wheel bolts. With the vehicle raised and safely supported, remove the front wheels and the engine undercover(s).

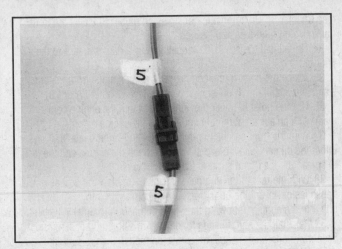

**7.19 Label both ends of each wire or vacuum connection before disconnecting them**

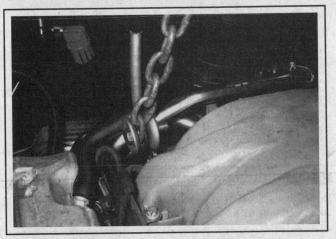

**7.26a Attach the chains of your engine hoist to the lifting brackets at the rear of the engine (right side shown, left side similar) . . .**

**7.26b . . . and at the front (V6 engine shown)**

7 Drain the cooling system and engine oil (see Chapter 1).

8 On models with automatic transmission, partially drain the automatic transmission fluid (see Chapter 1).

9 If you are working on a model with an automatic transmission, detach the transmission cooler lines from the engine brackets and the transmission (see Chapter 7B). If you are working on a model with a manual transmission, disconnect the clutch fluid line at the bellhousing and plug the line to prevent fluid loss.

10 Disconnect the oxygen sensors, then disconnect exhaust pipes from the exhaust manifolds and remove the pipes. From the exhaust manifold connections to the Y-pipe after the secondary converters, the whole exhaust system comes out as one unit. Refer to Chapter 4 and release the rubber hanger cushions, unbolt the pipes at the exhaust manifolds and at the rear Y, then remove the bolts securing the exhaust support crossmember (near the transmission crossmember) and remove the exhaust system.

11 Remove the starter (see Chapter 5).

12 On automatic transmission models, remove the torque converter-to-driveplate bolts (see Chapter 7B).

13 Remove the rear driveshaft (see Chapter 8). On AWD models, detach the ground cable from the transfer case, remove the front driveaxles, and detach the front driveshaft from the transfer case flange (see Chapter 8). Loosen the sleeves of the front driveshaft and push the driveshaft back.

14 Remove the drivebelt (see Chapter 1).

15 Remove the electric engine cooling fan (see Chapter 3). Also remove the heater hoses and the coolant reservoir.

→**Note: The manufacturer suggests making a radiator protector from a section of sheetmetal, plastic or wood paneling big enough to cover the entire engine side of the radiator. As the engine is removed, work slowly and carefully to avoid engine components damaging the radiator.**

16 Remove the alternator (see Chapter 5).

17 Drain the power steering reservoir and power steering pump, disconnect the hoses and remove the pump/reservoir (see Chapter 10). Plug or seal off the hose connections.

18 Remove the PCV hose (see Chapter 6).

19 Label and disconnect all wires from the engine (see illustration). Masking tape and/or a touch-up paint applicator work well for marking items. Disconnect the main engine harness connectors at the PCM, and with the passenger-side kick panel and lower instrument panel cover

removed, disconnect the engine harness connectors there. Remove the sealing material at the firewall and pull the interior ends of the harness through the firewall to the engine side.

→**Note: Take instant photos or sketch the locations of components and brackets to help with reassembly.**

20 Label and remove all vacuum lines between the engine and the firewall (or other components in the engine compartment).

21 Remove the engine oil dipstick tube.

22 Disconnect the engine block heater, if equipped.

23 Disconnect the crankshaft position sensor connector (see Chapter 6).

24 Remove the automatic transmission dipstick, then pull the dipstick tube from the transmission.

25 On V6 engines, disconnect the coolant hoses from the oil cooler mounted at the top front of the engine (see Chapter 3).

26 Support the engine from above with a hoist. Attach the hoist chain to the engine lifting brackets (see illustrations). If no brackets are present, you'll have to fasten the chains to some substantial part of the engine - one that is strong enough to take the weight, but in a location that will provide good balance. If you're attaching the chain to a stud on the engine, or are using a bolt passing through the chain and into a threaded hole, place a washer between the nut or bolt head and the chain, and tighten the nut or bolt securely.

27 Support the transmission from below with a transmission jack. Securely chain the transmission to the platform on the jack.

28 Remove the transmission crossmember, and lower the transmission enough to access the fasteners to disconnect the shifter linkage (see Chapter 7A or 7B). Remove the transmission-to-engine bolts.

29 With the weight of the engine supported by the engine hoist and slightly raised, remove the engine mount bolts and the mounts.

30 Check to make sure everything is disconnected, then lift the engine up out of the engine compartment. The engine will need to be tilted downward at the rear as it's raised, so have an assistant help you.

## ✳✳ WARNING:

**Do not place any part of your body under the engine when it is supported only by a hoist or other lifting device.**

31 Set the engine on the floor and support it so it doesn't tip over. Remove the flywheel/driveplate and mount the engine on an engine stand for disassembly, or on a wooden skid for transport to a rebuilding shop.

## INSTALLATION

32 Check the engine mounts. If they're worn or damaged, replace them (see Chapter 2A).

33 On manual transmission models, inspect the clutch components (see Chapter 8). On automatic transmission models, inspect the front transmission fluid seal and bearing.

34 On manual transmission models, apply a dab of grease to the pilot bearing.

35 Attach the hoist to the engine, remove the engine from the engine stand and install the flywheel or driveplate (see Chapter 2A or 2B).

36 Use the hoist to lower the engine back into the engine compartment, with an assistant to help you line up the engine mounts.

37 With the front engine mounts bolted hand-tight, use a floor jack under the oil pan (use a piece of wood between the engine and the jack to spread the load) and support the rear of the engine.

38 With the rear of the engine low enough to allow full access to the transmission-to-engine bolts, raise the transmission into position and bolt it to the engine, following the Steps outlined in Chapter 7A or 7B.

39 Reinstall the shift linkage to the transmission (and clutch fluid hose if working on a manual transmission model) then raise it into position and align it with the transmission crossmember and transmission mount.

40 Tighten all the bolts on the front engine mounts and transmission crossmember, then remove the hoist and jack.

41 Reinstall the remaining components in the reverse order of removal.

42 Add coolant, oil, power steering and transmission fluid as needed (see Chapter 1).

43 Run the engine and check for proper operation and leaks. Shut off the engine and recheck the fluid levels.

## 8  Engine overhaul - disassembly sequence

1 It's much easier to remove the external components if it's mounted on a portable engine stand. A stand can often be rented quite cheaply from an equipment rental yard. Before the engine is mounted on a stand, the flywheel/driveplate should be removed from the engine.

2 If a stand isn't available, it's possible to remove the external engine components with it blocked up on the floor. Be extra careful not to tip or drop the engine when working without a stand.

3 If you're going to obtain a rebuilt engine, all external components must come off first, to be transferred to the replacement engine. These components include:

*Flywheel/driveplate*
*Ignition system components*
*Emissions-related components*
*Engine mounts and mount brackets*
*Intake/exhaust manifolds*
*Supercharger (four-cylinder models)*
*Fuel injection components*
*Oil filter and oil cooler*
*Spark plug wires and spark plugs*
*Thermostat and housing assembly*
*Water pump*

➡**Note: When removing the external components from the engine, pay close attention to details that may be helpful or important during installation. Note the installed position of gaskets, seals, spacers, pins, brackets, washers, bolts and other small items.**

4 If you're going to obtain a short block (assembled engine block, crankshaft, pistons and connecting rods), then remove the timing chain, cylinder head(s), oil pan, oil pump pick-up tube, oil pump and water pump from your engine so that you can turn in your old short block to the rebuilder as a core. See *Engine rebuilding alternatives* for additional information regarding the different possibilities to be considered.

## 9 Pistons and connecting rods - removal and installation

### REMOVAL

▶ **Refer to illustrations 9.1, 9.3 and 9.4**

➡**Note: Prior to removing the piston/connecting rod assemblies, remove the cylinder head(s) and oil pan (see Chapter 2A). On four-cylinder engines, the balance shaft assembly must be removed for access to the rod and main bearing caps (see Section 12).**

1   Use your fingernail to feel if a ridge has formed at the upper limit of ring travel (about 1/4-inch down from the top of each cylinder). If carbon deposits or cylinder wear have produced ridges, they must be completely removed with a special tool (see illustration). Follow the manufacturer's instructions provided with the tool. Failure to remove the ridges before attempting to remove the piston/connecting rod assemblies may result in piston breakage. After the cylinder ridges have been removed, turn the engine so the crankshaft is facing up.

2   If you're working on a four-cylinder engine, remove the balance shaft assembly (see Section 12).

3   Before the main bearing cap assembly and connecting rods are removed, check the connecting rod endplay with feeler gauges. Slide them between the first connecting rod and the crankshaft throw until the play is removed (see illustration). Repeat this procedure for each connecting rod. The endplay is equal to the thickness of the feeler gauge(s). Check with an automotive machine shop for the endplay service limit (a typical endplay should measure from 0.005 to 0.015 inch [0.127 to 0.396 mm]). If the play exceeds the service limit, new connecting rods will be required. If new rods (or a new crankshaft) are installed, the endplay may fall under the minimum allowable. If it does, the rods will have to be machined to restore it. If necessary, consult an automotive machine shop for advice.

4   Check the connecting rods and caps for identification marks. If they aren't plainly marked, use paint or marker (see illustration) to clearly identify each rod and cap (1, 2, 3, etc., depending on the cylinder they're associated with). Do not interchange the rod caps. Install the exact same rod cap onto the same connecting rod.

**✳✳ CAUTION:**

**Do not use a punch and hammer to mark the connecting rods or they may be damaged.**

5   Loosen each of the connecting rod cap bolts or nuts 1/2-turn at a time until they can be removed by hand.

6   Remove the number one connecting rod cap and bearing insert. Don't drop the bearing insert out of the cap.

7   Remove the bearing insert and push the connecting rod/piston assembly out through the top of the engine. Use a wooden or plastic hammer handle to push on the upper bearing surface in the connecting rod. If resistance is felt, double-check to make sure that all of the ridge was removed from the cylinder.

8   Repeat the procedure for the remaining cylinders.

9   After removal, measure the length of the rod bolts, from the underside of the bolt head to the end, and compare your measurements

**9.1  Before you try to remove the pistons, use a ridge reamer to remove the raised material (ridge) from the top of the cylinders**

**9.3  Checking the connecting rod endplay (side clearance)**

**9.4  If the connecting rods or caps are not marked, use permanent ink or paint to mark the caps to the rods by cylinder number (for example, this would be number 4 cylinder connecting rod)**

with the values listed in this Chapter's Specifications. Replace any bolts that have stretched excessively. Reassemble the connecting rod caps and bearing inserts in their respective connecting rods and install the cap bolts finger tight. Leaving the old bearing inserts in place until reassembly will help prevent the connecting rod bearing surfaces from being accidentally nicked or gouged.

10 The pistons and connecting rods are now ready for inspection and overhaul at an automotive machine shop.

## PISTON RING INSTALLATION

▶ **Refer to illustrations 9.13, 9.14, 9.15, 9.19a, 9.19b and 9.22**

11 Before installing the new piston rings, the ring end gaps must be checked. It's assumed that the piston ring side clearance has been checked and verified correct.

12 Lay out the piston/connecting rod assemblies and the new ring sets so the ring sets will be matched with the same piston and cylinder during the end gap measurement and engine assembly.

13 Insert the top (number one) ring into the first cylinder and square

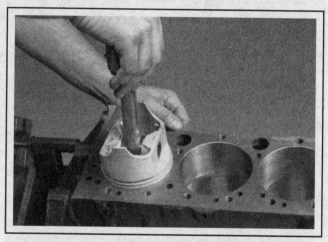

**9.13 Install the piston ring into the cylinder then push it down into position using a piston so the ring will be square in the cylinder**

it up with the cylinder walls by pushing it in with the top of the piston (see illustration). The ring should be near the bottom of the cylinder, at the lower limit of ring travel.

14 To measure the end gap, slip feeler gauges between the ends of the ring until a gauge equal to the gap width is found (see illustration). The feeler gauge should slide between the ring ends with a slight amount of drag. A typical ring gap should fall between 0.010 and 0.020 inch (0.25 to 0.50 mm) for compression rings and up to 0.030 inch (0.76 mm) for the oil ring steel rails. If the gap is larger or smaller than specified, double-check to make sure you have the correct rings before proceeding.

15 If the gap is too small, it must be enlarged or the ring ends may come in contact with each other during engine operation, which can cause serious damage to the engine. If necessary, increase the end gaps by filing the ring ends very carefully with a fine file. Mount the file in a vise equipped with soft jaws, slip the ring over the file with the ends contacting the file face and slowly move the ring to remove material from the ends. When performing this operation, file only by pushing the ring from the outside end of the file towards the vise (see illustration).

16 Excess end gap isn't critical unless it's greater than 0.040 inch (1.01 mm). Again, double-check to make sure you have the correct ring type.

17 Repeat the procedure for each ring that will be installed in the first cylinder and for each ring in the remaining cylinders. Remember to keep rings, pistons and cylinders matched up.

18 Once the ring end gaps have been checked/corrected, the rings can be installed on the pistons.

19 The oil control ring (lowest one on the piston) is usually installed first. It's composed of three separate components. Slip the spacer/expander into the groove (see illustration). If an anti-rotation tang is used, make sure it's inserted into the drilled hole in the ring groove. Next, install the lower side rail in the same manner (see illustration). Don't use a piston ring installation tool on the oil ring side rails, as they may be damaged. Instead, place one end of the side rail into the groove between the spacer/expander and the ring land, hold it firmly in place and slide a finger around the piston while pushing the rail into the groove. Finally, install the upper side rail.

20 After the three oil ring components have been installed, check to make sure that both the upper and lower side rails can be rotated smoothly inside the ring grooves.

**9.14 With the ring square in the cylinder, measure the ring end gap with a feeler gauge**

**9.15 If the ring end gap is too small, clamp a file in a vise as shown and file the piston ring ends - be sure to remove all raised material**

21 The number two (middle) ring is installed next. It's usually stamped with a mark which must face up, toward the top of the piston. Do not mix up the top and middle rings, as they have different cross-sections.

➡**Note: Always follow the instructions printed on the ring package or box - different manufacturers may require different approaches.**

22 Use a piston ring installation tool and make sure the identification mark is facing the top of the piston, then slip the ring into the middle groove on the piston (see illustration). Don't expand the ring any more than necessary to slide it over the piston.

➡**Note: Be careful not to confuse the number one and number two rings.**

23 Install the number one (top) ring in the same manner.
24 Repeat the procedure for the remaining pistons and rings.

## INSTALLATION

25 Before installing the piston/connecting rod assemblies, the cylinder walls must be perfectly clean, the top edge of each cylinder bore must be chamfered, and the crankshaft must be in place.

26 Remove the cap from the end of the number one connecting rod (refer to the marks made during removal). Remove the original bearing inserts and wipe the bearing surfaces of the connecting rod and cap with a clean, lint-free cloth. They must be kept spotlessly clean.

### Connecting rod bearing oil clearance check

▸ **Refer to illustrations 9.30, 9.35, 9.37 and 9.41**

27 Clean the back side of the new upper bearing insert, then lay it in place in the connecting rod.

28 Make sure the tab on the bearing fits into the recess in the rod. Don't hammer the bearing insert into place and be very careful not to nick or gouge the bearing face. Don't lubricate the bearing at this time.

29 Clean the back side of the other bearing insert and install it in the rod cap. Again, make sure the tab on the bearing fits into the recess in the cap, and don't apply any lubricant. It's critically important that the mating surfaces of the bearing and connecting rod are perfectly clean and oil free when they're assembled.

30 Position the piston ring gaps at the intervals around the piston as shown (see illustration).

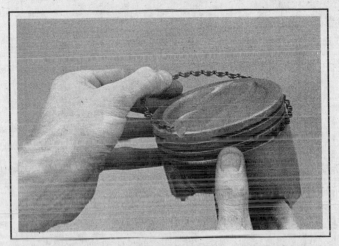

**9.19a  Installing the spacer/expander in the oil ring groove**

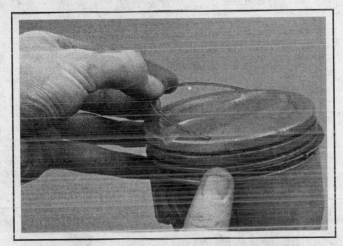

**9.19b  DO NOT use a piston ring installation tool when installing the oil control side rails**

**9.22  Use a piston ring installation tool to install the compression rings - on some engines the number two compression ring has a directional mark that must face toward the top of the piston**

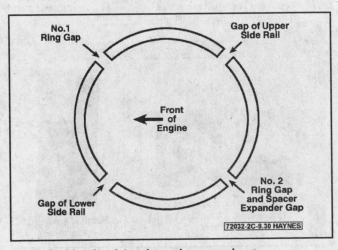

**9.30  Position the piston ring end gaps as shown**

# ENGINE BEARING ANALYSIS

## Debris

Babbitt bearing embedded with debris from machinings

**Microscopic detail of debris**

Microscopic detail of gouges

Overplated copper alloy bearing gouged by cast iron debris

Aluminum bearing embedded with glass beads

**Microscopic detail of glass beads**

Damaged lining caused by dirt left on the bearing back

## Misassembly

Result of a lower half assembled as an upper - blocking the oil flow

Excessive oil clearance is indicated by a short contact arc

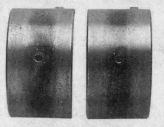

Polished and oil-stained backs are a result of a poor fit in the housing bore

Result of a wrong, reversed, or shifted cap

## Overloading

Damage from excessive idling which resulted in an oil film unable to support the load imposed

Damaged upper connecting rod bearings caused by engine lugging; the lower main bearings (not shown) were similarly affected

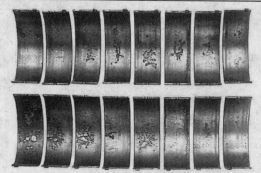

The damage shown in these upper and lower connecting rod bearings was caused by engine operation at a higher-than-rated speed under load

# Misalignment

A warped crankshaft caused this pattern of severe wear in the center, diminishing toward the ends

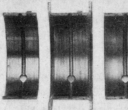

A poorly finished crankshaft caused the equally spaced scoring shown

A tapered housing bore caused the damage along one edge of this pair

A bent connecting rod led to the damage in the "V" pattern

# Lubrication

Result of dry start: The bearings on the left, farthest from the oil pump, show more damage

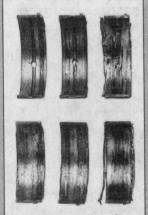

Result of a low oil supply or oil starvation

Severe wear as a result of inadequate oil clearance

# Corrosion

Microscopic detail of corrosion

Corrosion is an acid attack on the bearing lining generally caused by inadequate maintenance, extremely hot or cold operation, or inferior oils or fuels

Microscopic detail of cavitation

Example of cavitation - a surface erosion caused by pressure changes in the oil film

Damage from excessive thrust or insufficient axial clearance

Bearing affected by oil dilution caused by excessive blow-by or a rich mixture

31  Lubricate the piston and rings with clean engine oil and attach a piston ring compressor to the piston. Leave the skirt protruding about 1/4-inch to guide the piston into the cylinder. The rings must be compressed until they're flush with the piston.

32  Rotate the crankshaft until the number one connecting rod journal is at BDC (bottom dead center) and apply a liberal coat of engine oil to the cylinder walls. Refer to the TDC locating procedure in Chapter 2A for additional information.

33  With the "front" mark (letter F or arrow) on the piston facing the front (timing chain end) of the engine, gently insert the piston/connecting rod assembly into the number one cylinder bore and rest the bottom edge of the ring compressor on the engine block.

34  Tap the top edge of the ring compressor to make sure it's contacting the block around its entire circumference.

35  Gently tap on the top of the piston with the end of a wooden or plastic hammer handle (see illustration) while guiding the end of the connecting rod into place on the crankshaft journal. The piston rings may try to pop out of the ring compressor just before entering the cylinder bore, so keep some downward pressure on the ring compressor. Work slowly, and if any resistance is felt as the piston enters the cylinder, stop immediately. Find out what's hanging up and fix it before

proceeding. Do not, for any reason, force the piston into the cylinder - you might break a ring and/or the piston.

36  Once the piston/connecting rod assembly is installed, the connecting rod bearing oil clearance must be checked before the rod cap is permanently installed.

37  Cut a piece of the appropriate size Plastigage slightly shorter than the width of the connecting rod bearing and lay it in place on the number one connecting rod journal, parallel with the journal axis (see illustration).

38  Clean the connecting rod cap bearing face and install the rod cap. Make sure the mating mark on the cap is on the same side as the mark on the connecting rod (see illustration 9.4).

39  Install the rod bolts and tighten them to the torque listed in this Chapter's Specifications.

➡ **Note: Use a thin-wall socket to avoid erroneous torque readings that can result if the socket is wedged between the rod cap and the bolt or nut. If the socket tends to wedge itself between the fastener and the cap, lift up on it slightly until it no longer contacts the cap. DO NOT rotate the crankshaft at any time during this operation.**

40  Remove the fasteners and detach the rod cap, being very careful not to disturb the Plastigage.

41  Compare the width of the crushed Plastigage to the scale printed on the Plastigage envelope to obtain the oil clearance (see illustration). The connecting rod bearing oil clearance is usually about 0.001 to 0.002 inch. Consult an automotive machine shop for the clearance specified for the rod bearings on your engine.

42  If the clearance is not as specified, the bearing inserts may be the wrong size (which means different ones will be required). Before deciding that different inserts are needed, make sure that no dirt or oil was between the bearing inserts and the connecting rod or cap when the clearance was measured. Also, recheck the journal diameter. If the Plastigage was wider at one end than the other, the journal may be tapered. If the clearance still exceeds the limit specified, the bearing will have to be replaced with an undersize bearing.

✳✳ **CAUTION:**

When installing a new crankshaft always use a standard size bearing.

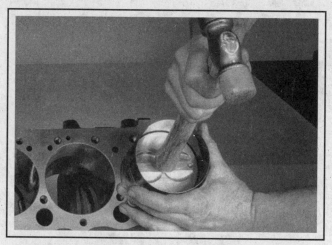

**9.35  Use a plastic or wooden hammer handle to push the piston into the cylinder**

**9.37  Place Plastigage on each connecting rod bearing journal parallel to the crankshaft centerline**

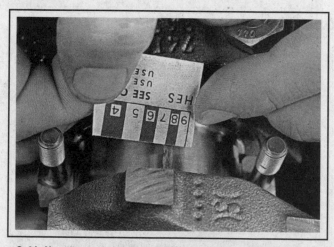

**9.41  Use the scale on the Plastigage package to determine the bearing oil clearance - be sure to measure the widest part of the Plastigage and use the correct scale; it comes with both standard and metric scales**

## Final installation

43  Carefully scrape all traces of the Plastigage material off the rod journal and/or bearing face. Be very careful not to scratch the bearing - use your fingernail or the edge of a plastic card.

44  Make sure the bearing faces are perfectly clean, then apply a uniform layer of clean moly-base grease or engine assembly lube to both of them. You'll have to push the piston into the cylinder to expose the face of the bearing insert in the connecting rod.

45  Slide the connecting rod back into place on the journal, install the rod cap, install the bolts and tighten them to the torque listed in this Chapter's Specifications.

46  Repeat the entire procedure for the remaining pistons/connecting rods.

47  The important points to remember are:

a)  Keep the back sides of the bearing inserts and the insides of the connecting rods and caps perfectly clean when assembling them.

b)  Make sure you have the correct piston/rod assembly for each cylinder.

c)  The mark on the piston must face the front (timing chain end) of the engine.

d)  Lubricate the cylinder walls liberally with clean oil.

e)  Lubricate the bearing faces when installing the rod caps after the oil clearance has been checked.

48  After all the piston/connecting rod assemblies have been correctly installed, rotate the crankshaft a number of times by hand to check for any obvious binding.

49  As a final step, check the connecting rod endplay again. If it was correct before disassembly and the original crankshaft and rods were reinstalled, it should still be correct. If new rods or a new crankshaft were installed, the endplay may be inadequate. If so, the rods will have to be removed and taken to an automotive machine shop for resizing.

## 10  Crankshaft - removal and installation

### REMOVAL

▶ **Refer to illustrations 10.1 and 10.3**

➡**Note: The crankshaft can be removed only after the engine has been removed from the vehicle. It's assumed that the flywheel or driveplate, crankshaft pulley, timing chain, oil pan, oil pump, oil filter, balance shaft assembly (four-cylinder models) and piston/connecting rod assemblies have already been removed. The rear main oil seal retainer must be unbolted and separated from the block before proceeding with crankshaft removal.**

1  Before the crankshaft is removed, measure the endplay. Mount a dial indicator with the indicator in line with the crankshaft and touching the end of the crankshaft (see illustration).

2  Pry the crankshaft all the way to the rear and zero the dial indicator. Next, pry the crankshaft to the front as far as possible and check the reading on the dial indicator. The distance traveled is the endplay. A typical crankshaft endplay will be from 0.003 to 0.010 inch (0.076 to 0.254 mm). If it is greater than that, check the crankshaft thrust washer/bearing assembly surfaces for wear after it's removed. If no wear is evident, new main bearings should correct the endplay.

3  If a dial indicator isn't available, feeler gauges can be used. Gently pry the crankshaft all the way to the front of the engine. Slip feeler gauges between the crankshaft and the front face of the thrust bearing or washer to determine the clearance (see illustration).

4  Loosen the main bearing cap/bedplate bolts 1/4-turn at a time

**10.1  Checking crankshaft endplay with a dial indicator**

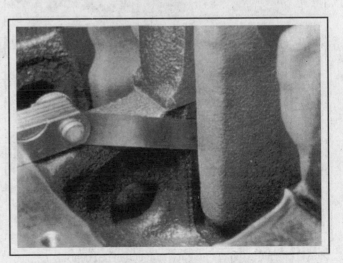

**10.3  Checking crankshaft endplay with feeler gauges at the thrust bearing journal**

each, until they can be removed by hand.

5   Gently tap the main bearing caps assembly with a soft-face hammer to loosen them. Pull the main bearing caps straight up and off the cylinder block. Try not to drop the bearing inserts if they come out with the assembly.

➡**Note: V6 engines have side bolts that go through the side of the block into the caps. Do not try to remove the caps until all cap and side bolts are removed.**

6   Carefully lift the crankshaft out of the engine. It may be a good idea to have an assistant available, since the crankshaft is quite heavy and awkward to handle. With the bearing inserts in place inside the engine block and main bearing caps, reinstall the main bearing caps onto the engine block and tighten the bolts finger tight. Make sure you install the main bearing caps with the arrows facing the front of the engine.

## INSTALLATION

7   Crankshaft installation is the first step in engine reassembly. It's assumed at this point that the engine block and crankshaft have been cleaned, inspected and repaired or reconditioned.

8   Position the engine block with the bottom facing up.

9   Remove the mounting bolts and lift off the main bearing cap.

10   If they're still in place, remove the original bearing inserts from the block and from the main bearing caps. Wipe the bearing surfaces of the block and main bearing caps with a clean, lint-free cloth. They must be kept spotlessly clean. This is critical for determining the correct bearing oil clearance.

## MAIN BEARING OIL CLEARANCE CHECK

♦ **Refer to illustrations 10.14, 10.17, 10.19a, 10.19b and 10.21**

11   Without mixing them up, clean the back sides of the new upper main bearing inserts (with grooves and oil holes) and lay one in each main bearing saddle in the block. Each upper bearing has an oil groove and oil hole in it.

### ✲✲ CAUTION:

**The oil holes in the block must line up with the oil holes in the upper bearing inserts.**

Clean the back sides of the lower main bearing inserts and lay them in the corresponding location in the main bearing caps. Make sure the tab on the bearing insert fits into the recess in the block or main bearing cap. The upper bearings with the oil holes are installed into the engine block while the lower bearings without the oil holes are installed in the caps.

### ✲✲ CAUTION:

**Do not hammer the bearing insert into place and don't nick or gouge the bearing faces. DO NOT apply any lubrication at this time.**

12   Clean the faces of the bearing inserts in the block and the crankshaft main bearing journals with a clean, lint-free cloth.

13   Check or clean the oil holes in the crankshaft, as any dirt here can go only one way - straight through the new bearings.

14   Once you're certain the crankshaft is clean, carefully lay it in position in the block. Lube and insert the thrust washers on either side of journal no. 3. The thrust washers must be installed in the correct journal.

➡**Note: Install the thrust washers with the groove in the thrust washer facing the crankshaft and the smooth sides facing the main bearing saddle.**

15   Before the crankshaft can be permanently installed, the main bearing oil clearance must be checked.

16   Cut several strips of the appropriate size of Plastigage. They must be slightly shorter than the width of the main bearing journal.

17   Place one piece on each crankshaft main bearing journal, parallel with the journal axis as shown (see illustration).

18   Clean the faces of the bearing inserts in the main bearing caps. Hold the bearing inserts in place and install the caps onto the crank-

**10.14  Insert the thrust washer into the machined surface between the crankshaft and the upper bearing saddle, then rotate it down into the block until it's flush with the parting line on the main bearing saddle - make sure the oil grooves on the thrust washer face the crankshaft**

**10.17  Place the Plastigage onto the crankshaft bearing journal as shown**

shaft and cylinder block. DO NOT disturb the Plastigage. Make sure you install the main bearing caps with the arrows facing the front (timing chain end) of the engine.

19  Apply clean engine oil to all bolt threads prior to installation, then install all bolts finger-tight. Tighten main bearing cap bolts in the sequence shown (see illustrations) progressing in steps, to the torque listed in this Chapter's Specifications. DO NOT rotate the crankshaft at any time during this operation.

20  Remove the bolts in the reverse order of the tightening sequence and carefully lift the main bearing caps straight up and off the block. Do not disturb the Plastigage or rotate the crankshaft. If the main bearing caps are difficult to remove, use the bolts, partially inserted into the caps, as a handle.

21  Compare the width of the crushed Plastigage on each journal to the scale printed on the Plastigage envelope to determine the main bearing oil clearance (see illustration). A typical main bearing oil clearance should fall between 0.0015 and 0.0023-inch. Check with an automotive machine shop for the clearance specified for your engine.

22  If the clearance is not as specified, the bearing inserts may be the wrong size (which means different ones will be required). Before deciding if different inserts are needed, make sure that no dirt or oil was between the bearing inserts and the caps or block when the clearance was measured. If the Plastigage was wider at one end than the other, the crankshaft journal may be tapered. If the clearance still exceeds the limit specified, the bearing insert(s) will have to be replaced with an undersize bearing insert(s).

---

**✳✳ CAUTION:**

**When installing a new crankshaft, always install a standard bearing insert set.**

---

23  Carefully scrape all traces of the Plastigage material off the main bearing journals and/or the bearing insert faces. Be sure to remove all residue from the oil holes. Use your fingernail or the edge of a plastic card - don't nick or scratch the bearing faces.

## FINAL INSTALLATION

24  Carefully lift the crankshaft out of the cylinder block.

25  Clean the bearing insert faces in the cylinder block, then apply a thin, uniform layer of moly-base grease or engine assembly lube to each of the bearing surfaces. Be sure to coat the thrust faces as well as the journal face of the thrust washers.

➡**Note: Install the thrust washers after the crankshaft has been installed.**

26  Make sure the crankshaft journals are clean, then lay the crankshaft back in place in the cylinder block.

27  Clean the bearing insert faces and then apply the same lubricant to them. Clean the engine block thoroughly. The surfaces must be free of oil residue. Install the thrust washers.

28  Install each main bearing cap onto the crankshaft and cylinder block.

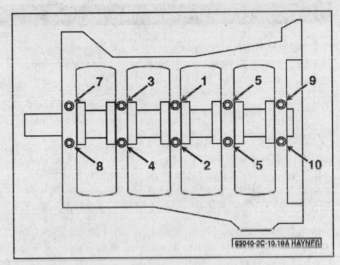

**10.19a  Main bearing cap bolt tightening sequence - four-cylinder models**

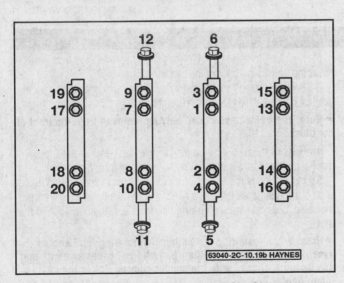

**10.19b  Main bearing cap and side bolt tightening sequence - V6 models**

**10.21  Use the scale on the Plastigage package to determine the bearing oil clearance - be sure to measure the widest part of the Plastigage and use the correct scale; it comes with both standard and metric scales**

29 Prior to installation, apply clean engine oil to all bolt threads and under the bolt heads, wiping off any excess, then install all bolts finger-tight.

➡ **Note: The manufacturer recommends using only NEW bolts for the main caps (and side bolts on V6 engines).**

30 Tighten the main bearing cap bolts to the torque listed in this Chapter's Specifications (in the proper sequence) (see illustrations 10.19a and 10.19b).

31 Recheck crankshaft endplay with a feeler gauge or a dial indicator. The endplay should be correct if the crankshaft thrust faces aren't worn or damaged and if new bearings have been installed.

32 Rotate the crankshaft a number of times by hand to check for any obvious binding. It should rotate with a running torque of 50 in-lbs or less. If the running torque is too high, identify and correct the problem at this time.

33 Install the new rear main oil seal (see Chapter 2A).

## 11 Engine overhaul - reassembly sequence

1 Before beginning engine reassembly, make sure you have all the necessary new parts, gaskets and seals as well as the following items on hand:

*Common hand tools*
*A 1/2-inch drive torque wrench*
*New engine oil*
*Gasket sealant*
*Thread locking compound*

2 If you obtained a short block, it will be necessary to install the cylinder heads, the oil pump and pick-up tube, the oil pans, the water pump, the timing chain and timing cover, and the valve covers (see Chapter 2A). In order to save time and avoid problems, the external components must be installed in the following general order:

*Thermostat and housing cover*
*Water pump*
*Intake and exhaust manifolds*
*Fuel injection components*
*Emission control components*
*Spark plugs*
*Ignition coils*
*Oil filter and oil cooler*
*Engine mounts and mount brackets*
*Flywheel/driveplate*

## 12 Balance shaft assembly

1 All covered engines have a balance shaft assembly designed to reduce engine vibrations. On V6 engines, the balance shaft assembly consists of a straight shaft passing through the block from front to rear, to which is fitted an offset balance weight at each end. In most cases this balance shaft assembly need not be removed to perform an overhaul. On four cylinder engines, the balance shaft assembly is inside a case bolted to the lower block, and it must be removed whenever access is needed to replace pistons, rods or crankshaft.

### V6 ENGINES

2 Assuming that the engine has been stripped down to the block and the timing chain has been removed, insert a suitable-size pin through the hole in the rear counterweight. It should fit into a corre-sponding hole in the back of the block.

3 Remove the bolt securing the rear counterweight to the balance shaft, and remove the rear counterweight.

➡ **Note: The balance shaft can only be removed from the front of the block.**

4 Remove the bolt securing the balance shaft retainer plate to the front of the block and withdraw the balance shaft from the engine.

5 Installation is the reverse of removal. Inspect the condition of the shaft bearing surfaces for uneven wear and replace the shaft if wear is indicated. Lubricate the shaft bearing surfaces during installation to the block.

➡ **Note: When installing the timing chain during final engine assembly, check that the balance shaft front counterweight gear has its mark aligned with the copper-colored link in the chain (see Chapter 2B).**

## FOUR-CYLINDER ENGINES

♦ **Refer to illustration 12.12**

6   On four-cylinder engines, the balance shaft assembly also incorporates the engine's oil pump. Refer to Chapter 2A if the oil pump is to be separated from the balance shaft assembly.

7   To remove the balance shaft assembly, the oil pan must be off, and the engine turned to TDC for number 1 cylinder. The procedure is best performed with the block on an engine stand with the bottom-side up.

8   Mark the timing chain links and balancer drive gears with matching paint marks (see Chapter 2A).

9   At the right-front of the balance shaft case, there is access to insert an open-end wrench to secure the square lobe on the balance shaft.

10  With the shaft held securely by the wrench, remove the sprocket bolt from the middle sprocket of the assembly.

11  Use a pry tool to force the chain tensioner toward the inside, and slip the timing chain from the sprockets.

12  Remove the 10 bolts securing the balance shaft assembly to the block, using the reverse of the tightening sequence (see illustration).

13  Lift the assembly from the block. You may have to rock the assembly somewhat to loosen the oil pump's tube from the block.

14  Installation is the reverse of the removal procedure. Make sure the oil pump's tube seats firmly into the block. Follow the timing chain procedure in Chapter 2A and align the mating marks on the balance shaft assembly sprockets.

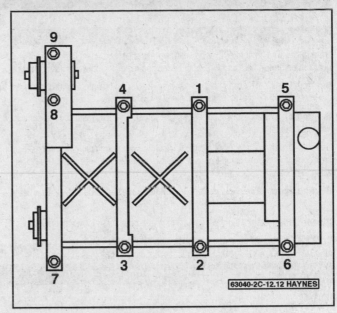

**12.12  Balance shaft assembly mounting bolt TIGHTENING sequence (four-cylinder engine)** -

## 13  Initial start-up and break-in after overhaul

### ☀ WARNING:

**Have a fire extinguisher handy when starting the engine for the first time.**

1   Once the engine has been installed in the vehicle, double-check the engine oil and coolant levels.

2   With the spark plugs out of the engine and the ignition system and fuel pump disabled, crank the engine until oil pressure registers on the gauge or the light goes out.

3   Install the spark plugs and ignition coils, and reinstall the fuel pump relay.

4   Start the engine. It may take a few moments for the fuel system to build up pressure, but the engine should start without a great deal of effort.

5   After the engine starts, it should be allowed to warm up to normal operating temperature. While the engine is warming up, make a thorough check for fuel, oil and coolant leaks.

6   Shut the engine off and recheck the engine oil and coolant levels.

7   Drive the vehicle to an area with minimum traffic, accelerate from 30 to 50 mph, then allow the vehicle to slow to 30 mph with the throttle closed. Repeat the procedure 10 or 12 times. This will load the piston rings and cause them to seat properly against the cylinder walls. Check again for oil and coolant leaks.

8   Drive the vehicle gently for the first 500 miles (no sustained high speeds) and keep a constant check on the oil level. It is not unusual for an engine to use oil during the break-in period.

9   At approximately 500 to 600 miles, change the oil and filter.

10  For the next few hundred miles, drive the vehicle normally. Do not pamper it or abuse it.

11  After 2000 miles, change the oil and filter again and consider the engine broken in.

# GLOSSARY

## B

**Backlash** - The amount of play between two parts. Usually refers to how much one gear can be moved back and forth without moving the gear with which it's meshed.

**Bearing Caps** - The caps held in place by nuts or bolts which, in turn, hold the bearing surface. This space is for lubricating oil to enter.

**Bearing clearance** - The amount of space left between shaft and bearing surface. This space is for lubricating oil to enter.

**Bearing crush** - The additional height which is purposely manufactured into each bearing half to ensure complete contact of the bearing back with the housing bore when the engine is assembled.

**Bearing knock** - The noise created by movement of a part in a loose or worn bearing.

**Blueprinting** - Dismantling an engine and reassembling it to EXACT specifications.

**Bore** - An engine cylinder, or any cylindrical hole; also used to describe the process of enlarging or accurately refinishing a hole with a cutting tool, as to bore an engine cylinder. The bore size is the diameter of the hole.

**Boring** - Renewing the cylinders by cutting them out to a specified size. A boring bar is used to make the cut.

**Bottom end** - A term which refers collectively to the engine block, crankshaft, main bearings and the big ends of the connecting rods.

**Break-in** - The period of operation between installation of new or rebuilt parts and time in which parts are worn to the correct fit. Driving at reduced and varying speed for a specified mileage to permit parts to wear to the correct fit.

**Bushing** - A one-piece sleeve placed in a bore to serve as a bearing surface for shaft, piston pin, etc. Usually replaceable.

## C

**Camshaft** - The shaft in the engine, on which a series of lobes are located for operating the valve mechanisms. The camshaft is driven by gears or sprockets and a timing chain. Usually referred to simply as the cam.

**Carbon** - Hard, or soft, black deposits found in combustion chamber, on plugs, under rings, on and under valve heads.

**Cast iron** - An alloy of iron and more than two percent carbon, used for engine blocks and heads because it's relatively inexpensive and easy to mold into complex shapes.

**Chamfer** - To bevel across (or a bevel on) the sharp edge of an object.

**Chase** - To repair damaged threads with a tap or die.

**Combustion chamber** - The space between the piston and the cylinder head, with the piston at top dead center, in which air-fuel mixture is burned.

**Compression ratio** - The relationship between cylinder volume (clearance volume) when the piston is at top dead center and cylinder volume when the piston is at bottom dead center.

**Connecting rod** - The rod that connects the crank on the crankshaft with the piston. Sometimes called a con rod.

**Connecting rod cap** - The part of the connecting rod assembly that attaches the rod to the crankpin.

**Core plug** - Soft metal plug used to plug the casting holes for the coolant passages in the block.

**Crankcase** - The lower part of the engine in which the crankshaft rotates; includes the lower section of the cylinder block and the oil pan.

**Crank kit** - A reground or reconditioned crankshaft and new main and connecting rod bearings.

**Crankpin** - The part of a crankshaft to which a connecting rod is attached.

**Crankshaft** - The main rotating member, or shaft, running the length of the crankcase, with offset throws to which the connecting rods are attached; changes the reciprocating motion of the pistons into rotating motion.

**Cylinder sleeve** - A replaceable sleeve, or liner, pressed into the cylinder block to form the cylinder bore.

## D

**Deburring** - Removing the burrs (rough edges or areas) from a bearing.

**Deglazer** - A tool, rotated by an electric motor, used to remove glaze from cylinder walls so a new set of rings will seat.

## E

**Endplay** - The amount of lengthwise movement between two parts. As applied to a crankshaft, the distance that the crankshaft can move forward and back in the cylinder block.

## F

**Face** - A machinist's term that refers to removing metal from the end of a shaft or the face of a larger part, such as a flywheel.

**Fatigue** - A breakdown of material through a large number of loading and unloading cycles. The first signs are cracks followed shortly by breaks.

**Feeler gauge** - A thin strip of hardened steel, ground to an exact thickness, used to check clearances between parts.

**Free height** - The unloaded length or height of a spring.

**Freeplay** - The looseness in a linkage, or an assembly of parts, between the initial application of force and actual movement. Usually perceived as slop or slight delay.

**Freeze plug** - See Core plug.

## G

**Gallery** - A large passage in the block that forms a reservoir for engine oil pressure.

**Glaze** - The very smooth, glassy finish that develops on cylinder walls while an engine is in service.

## H

**Heli-Coil** - A rethreading device used when threads are worn or damaged. The device is installed in a retapped hole to reduce the thread size to the original size.

## I

**Installed height** - The spring's measured length or height, as installed on the cylinder head. Installed height is measured from the spring seat to the underside of the spring retainer.

## J

**Journal** - The surface of a rotating shaft which turns in a bearing.

## K

**Keeper** - The split lock that holds the valve spring retainer in position on the valve stem.

**Key** - A small piece of metal inserted into matching grooves machined into two parts fitted together - such as a gear pressed onto a shaft - which prevents slippage between the two parts.

**Knock** - The heavy metallic engine sound, produced in the combustion chamber as a result of abnormal combustion - usually detonation. Knock is usually caused by a loose or worn bearing. Also referred to as detonation, pinging and spark knock. Connecting rod or main bearing knocks are created by too much oil clearance or insufficient lubrication.

## L

**Lands** - The portions of metal between the piston ring grooves.

**Lapping the valves** - Grinding a valve face and its seat together with lapping compound.

**Lash** - The amount of free motion in a gear train, between gears, or in a mechanical assembly, that occurs before movement can begin. Usually refers to the lash in a valve train.

**Lifter** - The part that rides against the cam to transfer motion to the rest of the valve train.

## M

**Machining** - The process of using a machine to remove metal from a metal part.

**Main bearings** - The plain, or babbitt, bearings that support the crankshaft.

**Main bearing caps** - The cast iron caps, bolted to the bottom of the block, that support the main bearings.

## O

**O.D.** - Outside diameter.

**Oil gallery** - A pipe or drilled passageway in the engine used to carry engine oil from one area to another.

**Oil ring** - The lower ring, or rings, of a piston; designed to prevent excessive amounts of oil from working up the cylinder walls and into the combustion chamber. Also called an oil-control ring.

**Oil seal** - A seal which keeps oil from leaking out of a compartment. Usually refers to a dynamic seal around a rotating shaft or other moving part.

**O-ring** - A type of sealing ring made of a special rubberlike material; in use, the O-ring is compressed into a groove to provide the sealing action.

**Overhaul** - To completely disassemble a unit, clean and inspect all parts, reassemble it with the original or new parts and make all adjustments necessary for proper operation.

## P

**Pilot bearing** - A small bearing installed in the center of the flywheel (or the rear end of the crankshaft) to support the front end of the input shaft of the transmission.

**Pip mark** - A little dot or indentation which indicates the top side of a compression ring.

**Piston** - The cylindrical part, attached to the connecting rod, that moves up and down in the cylinder as the crankshaft rotates. When the fuel charge is fired, the piston transfers the force of the explosion to the connecting rod, then to the crankshaft.

**Piston pin (or wrist pin)** - The cylindrical and usually hollow steel pin that passes through the piston. The piston pin fastens the piston to the upper end of the connecting rod.

**Piston ring** - The split ring fitted to the groove in a piston. The ring contacts the sides of the ring groove and also rubs against the cylinder wall, thus sealing space between piston and wall. There are two types of rings: Compression rings seal the compression pressure in the combustion chamber; oil rings scrape excessive oil off the cylinder wall.

**Piston ring groove** - The slots or grooves cut in piston heads to hold piston rings in position.

**Piston skirt** - The portion of the piston below the rings and the piston pin hole.

**Plastigage** - A thin strip of plastic thread, available in different sizes, used for measuring clearances. For example, a strip of plastigage is laid across a bearing journal and mashed as parts are assembled. Then parts are disassembled and the width of the strip is measured to determine clearance between journal and bearing. Commonly used to measure crankshaft main-bearing and connecting rod bearing clearances.

**Press-fit** - A tight fit between two parts that requires pressure to force the parts together. Also referred to as drive, or force, fit.

**Prussian blue** - A blue pigment; in solution, useful in determining the area of contact between two surfaces. Prussian blue is commonly used to determine the width and location of the contact area between the valve face and the valve seat.

## R

**Race (bearing)** - The inner or outer ring that provides a contact surface for balls or rollers in bearing.

**Ream** - To size, enlarge or smooth a hole by using a round cutting tool with fluted edges.

**Ring job** - The process of reconditioning the cylinders and installing new rings.

**Runout** - Wobble. The amount a shaft rotates out-of-true.

## S

**Saddle** - The upper main bearing seat.

**Scored** - Scratched or grooved, as a cylinder wall may be scored by abrasive particles moved up and down by the piston rings.

**Scuffing** - A type of wear in which there's a transfer of material between parts moving against each other; shows up as pits or grooves in the mating surfaces.

**Seat** - The surface upon which another part rests or seats. For example, the valve seat is the matched surface upon which the valve face rests. Also used to refer to wearing into a good fit; for example, piston rings seat after a few miles of driving.

**Short block** - An engine block complete with crankshaft and piston and, usually, camshaft assemblies.

**Static balance** - The balance of an object while it's stationary.

**Step** - The wear on the lower portion of a ring land caused by excessive side and back-clearance. The height of the step indicates the ring's extra side clearance and the length of the step projecting from the back wall of the groove represents the ring's back clearance.

**Stroke** - The distance the piston moves when traveling from top dead center to bottom dead center, or from bottom dead center to top dead center.

**Stud** - A metal rod with threads on both ends.

## T

**Tang** - A lip on the end of a plain bearing used to align the bearing during assembly.

**Tap** - To cut threads in a hole. Also refers to the fluted tool used to cut threads.

**Taper** - A gradual reduction in the width of a shaft or hole; in an engine cylinder, taper usually takes the form of uneven wear, more pronounced at the top than at the bottom.

**Throws** - The offset portions of the crankshaft to which the connecting rods are affixed.

**Thrust bearing** - The main bearing that has thrust faces to prevent excessive endplay, or forward and backward movement of the crankshaft

**Thrust washer** - A bronze or hardened steel washer placed between two moving parts. The washer prevents longitudinal movement and provides a bearing surface for thrust surfaces of parts.

**Tolerance** - The amount of variation permitted from an exact size of measurement. Actual amount from smallest acceptable dimension to largest acceptable dimension.

## U

**Umbrella** - An oil deflector placed near the valve tip to throw oil from the valve stem area.

**Undercut** - A machined groove below the normal surface.

**Undersize bearings** - Smaller diameter bearings used with re-ground crankshaft journals.

## V

**Valve grinding** - Refacing a valve in a valve-refacing machine.

**Valve train** - The valve-operating mechanism of an engine; includes all components from the camshaft to the valve.

**Vibration damper** - A cylindrical weight attached to the front of the crankshaft to minimize torsional vibration (the twist-untwist actions of the crankshaft caused by the cylinder firing impulses). Also called a harmonic balancer.

## W

**Water jacket** - The spaces around the cylinders, between the inner and outer shells of the cylinder block or head, through which coolant circulates.

**Web** - A supporting structure across a cavity.

**Woodruff key** - A key with a radiused backside (viewed from the side).

## Specifications

### FOUR-CYLINDER ENGINES

#### General

2002 (Type 111)

| | |
|---|---|
| Displacement | 140 cubic inches (2.3 liters) |
| Bore | 3.58 inches (90.9 mm) |
| Stroke | 3.48 inches (88.4 mm) |
| Cylinder compression pressure | |
| Minimum | 174 to 217 psi |
| Maximum variation between cylinders | 22 psi |

2003 through 2005 (Type 271)

| | |
|---|---|
| Displacement | 110 cubic inches (1.8 liters) |
| Bore | 3.23 inches (82.0 mm) |
| Stroke | 3.35 inches (85.0 mm) |
| Cylinder compression pressure | |
| Minimum | 142 psi |
| Maximum variation between cylinders | 15 psi |
| Oil pressure (minimum, warm engine) | |
| Idle | 8 psi |
| 2000 rpm | 25 psi |

Connecting rod bolt length (maximum)

| | |
|---|---|
| 2002 (Type 111) | N/A |
| 2003 through 2005 (Type 271) | 1.51 inches (38.4 mm) |

## Torque specifications*

| | Ft-lbs (unless otherwise indicated) | Nm |
|---|---|---|

**➡Note: One foot-pound (ft-lb) of torque is equivalent to 12 inch-pounds (in-lbs) of torque. Torque values below approximately 15 ft-lbs are expressed in inch-pounds, since most foot-pound torque wrenches are not accurate at these smaller values.**

2002 (Type 111)

| | Ft-lbs | Nm |
|---|---|---|
| Connecting rod cap bolts | | |
| Step 1 | 44 in-lbs | 5 |
| Step 2 | 18 | 25 |
| Step 2 | Tighten an additional 90 degrees | |
| Main bearing cap bolts | | |
| Step 1 | 41 | 55 |
| Step 2 | Tighten an additional 95-degrees | |

2003 through 2005 (Type 271)

| | Ft-lbs | Nm |
|---|---|---|
| Connecting rod cap bolts | | |
| Step 1 | 44 in-lbs | 5 |
| Step 2 | 133 in-lbs | 15 |
| Step 3 | Tighten an additional 90-degrees | |
| Main bearing cap bolts | | |
| Step 1 | 22 | 30 |
| Step 2 | Tighten an additional 90-degrees | |
| Balance shaft assembly | | |
| Assembly-to-block bolts | 71 in-lbs | 8 |
| Oil pump cover screw | 80 in-lbs | 9 |
| Screw at balance shaft housing | 80 in-lbs | 9 |
| Oil pump drive screw at shaft | 15 | 20 |

**\* Note: Refer to Part A for additional torque specifications.**

## V6 ENGINES

C240 models, 2001 to 2005 (Type 112)
  Displacement — 158 cubic inches (2.6 liters)
  Bore — 3.54 inches (89.9 mm)
  Stroke — 2.68 inches (68.2 mm)

C320 models, 2001 to 2005 (Type 112)
  Displacement — 195 cubic inches (3.2 liters)
  Bore — 3.54 inches (89.9 mm)
  Stroke — 3.30 inches (84.0 mm)

C230 models, 2006 and later (Type 272)
  Displacement — 152 cubic inches (2.5 liters)
  Bore — 3.46 inches (88.0 mm)
  Stroke — 2.69 inches (68.4 mm)

C350 models, 2006 and later (Type 272)
  Displacement — 213 cubic inches (3.5 liters)
  Bore — 3.65 inches (92.9 mm)
  Stroke — 3.38 inches (86.0 mm)

Cylinder compression pressure
  Minimum — 174 to 203 psi
  Maximum variation between cylinders — 22 psi

Oil pressure (minimum, warm engine)
  700 rpm — 10 psi
  3000 rpm — 43 psi

Connecting rod bolt length (maximum)
  2001 to 2005 (Type 112) — 1.87 inches (47.6 mm)
  2006 and later (Type 272) — 1.59 inches (40.5 mm)

| Torque specifications* | Ft-lbs (unless otherwise indicated) | Nm |
|---|---|---|

➡**Note: One foot-pound (ft-lb) of torque is equivalent to 12 inch-pounds (in-lbs) of torque. Torque values below approximately 15 ft-lbs are expressed in inch-pounds, since most foot-pound torque wrenches are not accurate at these smaller values.**

| 2001 to 2005 (Type 112) | | |
|---|---|---|
| Connecting rod cap bolts | | |
| Step 1 | 44 in-lbs | 5 |
| Step 2 | 18 | 25 |
| Step 2 | Tighten an additional 90 degrees | |
| Main bearing cap bolts | | |
| M8 bolts (new) | | |
| Step 1 | 15 | 20 |
| Step 2 | Tighten an additional 90-degrees | |
| M10 bolts (new) | | |
| Step 1 | 44 in-lbs | 5 |
| Step 2 | 22 | 30 |
| Step 3 | Tighten an additional 90-degrees | |
| Side bolts | 22 | 30 |

**\* Note: Refer to Part A for additional torque specifications.**

| Torque specifications*(continued) | Ft-lbs (unless otherwise indicated) | Nm |
|---|---|---|
| 2006 and later (Type 272) | | |
| Connecting rod cap bolts | | |
| Step 1 | 44 in-lbs | 5 |
| Step 2 | 15 | 20 |
| Step 3 | Tighten an additional 90-degrees | |
| Main bearing cap bolts | | |
| M8 bolts (new) | | |
| Step 1 | 15 | 20 |
| Step 2 | Tighten an additional 90-degrees | |
| M10 bolts (new) | | |
| Step 1 | 44 in-lbs | 5 |
| Step 2 | 22 | 30 |
| Step 3 | Tighten an additional 90-degrees | |
| Side bolts | 22 | 30 |
| Balance shaft bolts | | |
| Front retainer bolt | 15 | 20 |
| Rear counterweight bolt | | |
| Step 1 | 15 | 20 |
| Step 2 | Tighten an additional 90-degrees | |

**\* Note: Refer to Part B for additional torque specifications.**

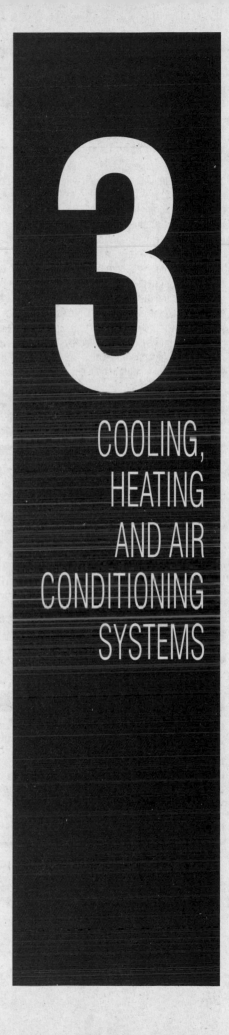

# 3

## COOLING, HEATING AND AIR CONDITIONING SYSTEMS

**Section**

**Reference to other Chapters**

## 1 General information

### ENGINE COOLING SYSTEM

All vehicles covered by this manual employ a pressurized engine cooling system with thermostatically controlled coolant circulation. An impeller-type water pump mounted on the engine pumps coolant through the engine. The coolant flows around each cylinder and toward the rear of the engine. Cast-in coolant passages direct coolant around the intake and exhaust ports, near the spark plug areas and in close proximity to the exhaust valve guides.

A wax-pellet type thermostat controls engine coolant temperature. During warm up, the closed thermostat prevents coolant from circulating through the radiator. As the engine nears normal operating temperature, the thermostat opens and allows hot coolant to travel through the radiator, where it's cooled before returning to the engine.

The cooling system is sealed by a pressure-type cap on the coolant reservoir/expansion tank, which raises the boiling point of the coolant and increases the cooling efficiency of the radiator.

### ❋❋ WARNING:

**Do not remove this cap unless the engine is completely cool.**

### HEATING SYSTEM

The heating system consists of a blower fan and heater core located in the heater unit, the hoses connecting the heater core to the engine cooling system and the heater/air conditioning control panel on the dashboard. Hot engine coolant is circulated through the heater core. When the heater mode is activated, a flap door opens to expose the heater unit to the passenger compartment. A fan switch on the control head activates the blower motor, which forces air through the core, heating the air.

### AIR CONDITIONING SYSTEM

The air conditioning system consists of a condenser mounted in front of the radiator, an evaporator mounted adjacent to the heater core, a compressor mounted on the engine, a receiver-drier which contains a high pressure relief valve and the plumbing connecting all of the above components.

A blower fan forces the warmer air of the passenger compartment through the evaporator core (sort of a radiator-in-reverse), transferring the heat from the air to the refrigerant. The liquid refrigerant boils off into low pressure vapor, taking the heat with it when it leaves the evaporator.

### ❋❋ WARNING:

**The models covered by this manual are equipped with Supplemental Restraint Systems (SRS), more commonly known as airbags. Always disable the airbag system before working in the vicinity of any airbag system components to avoid the possibility of accidental deployment of the airbag(s), which could cause personal injury (see Chapter 12).**

## 2 Antifreeze - general information

▶ **Refer to illustration 2.4**

### ❋❋ WARNING:

**Do not allow antifreeze to come in contact with your skin or painted surfaces of the vehicle. Rinse off spills immediately with plenty of water. Antifreeze is highly toxic if ingested. Never leave antifreeze lying around in an open container or in puddles on the floor; children and pets are attracted by its sweet smell and may drink it. Check with local authorities about disposing of used antifreeze. Many communities have collection centers, which will see that antifreeze is disposed of safely. Never dump used antifreeze on the ground or into drains.**

The cooling system should be filled with a water/ethylene glycol based antifreeze solution, which will prevent freezing down to at least -20-degrees F, or lower if local climate requires it. It also provides protection against corrosion and increases the coolant boiling point.

The cooling system should be drained, flushed and refilled at the specified intervals (see Chapter 1). Old or contaminated antifreeze solutions are likely to cause damage and encourage the formation of rust and scale in the system. Use distilled water with the antifreeze.

Before adding antifreeze, check all hose connections, because antifreeze tends to leak through very minute openings. Engines don't normally consume coolant, so if the level goes down, find the cause and correct it.

The exact mixture of antifreeze-to-water that you should use depends on the relative weather conditions. The mixture should contain at least 50-percent antifreeze, but should never contain more than 70-percent antifreeze. Consult the mixture ratio chart on the antifreeze container before adding coolant. Hydrometers are available at most auto parts stores to test the ratio of antifreeze to water (see illustration). Antifreeze test strips are available at some auto parts stores instead of the hydrometer gauge. Use antifreeze that meets the vehicle manufacturer's specifications.

**2.4  The condition of your coolant can easily be checked with this type of hydrometer, available at auto parts stores**

## 3   Thermostat - check and replacement

### ☀☀ WARNING:

**Do not attempt to remove the radiator cap, reservoir/expansion tank pressure cap, coolant or thermostat until the engine has cooled completely.**

## CHECK

▶ **Refer to illustration 3.6**

1   Before assuming the thermostat is responsible for a cooling system problem, check the coolant level (see Chapter 1), drivebelt tension (see Chapter 1) and temperature gauge (or light) operation.

2   If the engine takes a long time to warm up (as indicated by the temperature gauge or heater operation), the thermostat is probably stuck open. Replace the thermostat with a new one.

3   If the engine runs hot or overheats, a thorough test of the thermostat should be performed.

4   Testing of the thermostat can only be done when it is removed from the vehicle (see *Replacement*). If the thermostat is stuck in the open position at room temperature, it is faulty and must be replaced.

### ☀☀ CAUTION:

**Do not drive the vehicle without a thermostat. The computer may stay in open loop and emissions and fuel economy will suffer.**

5   To properly test a thermostat, suspend the (closed) thermostat on a length of string or wire in a container of cold water, with a thermometer (cooking type that reads beyond 212-degrees F [100-degrees C]).

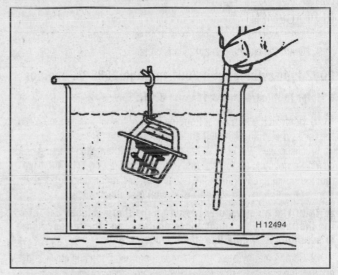

**3.6  A thermostat can be accurately checked by heating it in a container of water with a thermometer and observing the opening and fully open temperature**

6   Heat the water on a stove while observing the temperature and the thermostat. Neither should contact the sides of the container (see illustration).

7   Note the temperature when the thermostat begins to open and when it is fully open. Compare the temperatures to the Specifications in this Chapter.

8   If the thermostat doesn't open and close as specified, or sticks in any position, replace it.

**3.11a Unbolt and remove the thermostat housing cover from the housing (2002 four-cylinder engine)**

**3.11b Unbolt and remove the thermostat housing cover from the timing case cover (2005 and earlier V6 engines)**

## REPLACEMENT

9   Drain the engine coolant (see Chapter 1).

### 2002 four-cylinder and 2001 through 2005 V6 engines

▶ **Refer to illustrations 3.11a and 3.11b**

10   Remove the trim panel from the front of the engine and remove the forward section of the left engine trim panel.

11   Disconnect the coolant hose(s) from the thermostat housing cover. Remove the thermostat housing cover mounting bolts and separate the housing cover from the housing (four-cylinder engine) or the front of the timing case cover (V6 engine) (see illustrations).

➡**Note: The manufacturer considers the thermostat as part of the thermostat housing on these engines, and the replacement is available only as a thermostat/housing unit.**

12   Scrape off any old O-ring on the thermostat housing cover and engine, then clean them with brake system cleaner.

13   Install a new O-ring and bolt the housing cover in place.

14   Installation is the reverse of removal. Tighten the thermostat housing cover fasteners to the torque listed in this Chapter's Specifications, then reinstall the hoses.

15   Refill and bleed the cooling system (see Chapter 1). Run the engine and check for leaks and proper operation.

### 2003 and later four-cylinder engine

▶ **Refer to illustration 3.16**

16   If the radiator hose is to be replaced, disconnect the hose from the thermostat housing; otherwise the thermostat housing can be removed from the engine with the hose attached. Remove the thermostat housing cover mounting bolts and separate the cover from the engine (see illustration). Remove the thermostat from the cylinder head.

17   Scrape off any old gasket or sealant on the thermostat housing

**3.16 On 2003 and later four-cylinder engines, pry back the hose clip (right arrow) to loosen the hose, then remove the two thermostat housing cover bolts (left arrows; one bolt hidden)**

and the thermostat cover, then clean them with brake system cleaner.

18   Scrape off any old O-ring on the thermostat housing and engine, then clean them with brake system cleaner.

19   Install a new O-ring in the groove of the thermostat housing cover, then bolt the cover in place.

20   Installation is the reverse of removal. Tighten the thermostat housing cover fasteners to the torque listed in this Chapter's Specifications, then reinstall the hose.

21   Refill and bleed the cooling system (see Chapter 1). Run the engine and check for leaks and proper operation.

### 2006 and later V6 engine

▶ **Refer to illustration 3.23**

22  Remove the air cleaner duct and filter housing (see Chapter 4).

23  Disconnect the radiator hose from the thermostat housing (see illustration)

24  Remove the serpentine belt and its idler pulley (see Chapter 1).

25  Disconnect the electrical connector from the thermostat housing cover. Remove the thermostat housing cover mounting bolts and separate the cover from the engine.

➡**Note: The manufacturer considers the thermostat as part of the thermostat housing on these engines, and the replacement is available only as a thermostat/housing unit.**

26  Scrape off any old gasket or sealant on the thermostat housing and the thermostat cover, then clean them with lacquer thinner.

27  Install a new O-ring and gasket (both are used on these engines).

28  Installation is the reverse of removal. Tighten the thermostat cover fasteners to the torque listed in this Chapter's Specifications, then reinstall the hose.

29  Refill and bleed the cooling system (see Chapter 1). Run the engine and check for leaks and proper operation.

**3.23  Pry back the hose clip and detach the hose from the thermostat housing cover (2006 and later V6 engines)**

---

## 4  Engine cooling fan - check and replacement

**✳ WARNING:**

**To avoid possible injury or damage, DO NOT operate the engine with a damaged fan. Do not attempt to repair fan blades. Always replace a damaged fan with a new one.**

### CHECK

1  Disconnect the cable from the negative terminal of the battery (see Chapter 5, Section 1). Rock the fan back and forth by hand to check for excessive bearing play.

2  With the engine cold (and not running), turn the fan blades by hand. The fan should turn freely.

### REPLACEMENT

▶ **Refer to illustration 4.9, 4.11a, 4.11b, 4.13, 4.14a, 4.14b, 4.14c, 4.15 and 4.16**

3  Disconnect the cable from the negative terminal of the battery (see Chapter 5, Section 1).

4  Remove the air cleaner housing (four-cylinder engines) and air inlet duct(s) (all engines) (see Chapter 4).

5  On 4WD models, disconnect the power steering line bracket from the top rear of the radiator crossmember.

6  Follow the fan wiring harness to the connector and unplug it.

7  Remove the horn (see Chapter 12).

8  Detach the power steering oil cooler from the front of the radiator crossmember (see Chapter 10).

9  Free the coolant line from the clip at the top rear of the radiator crossmember (see illustration).

10  If the hood latch cable will block removal of the crossmember, disconnect it at the connector on the left side of the engine compartment (see Chapter 11).

**4.9  Free the coolant line from the clip on the radiator crossmember**

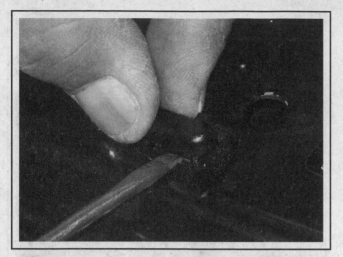

**4.11a  Pry out . . .**

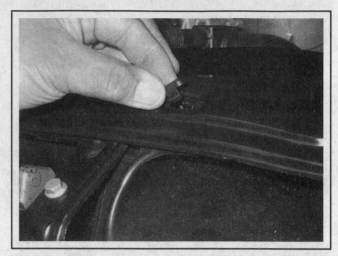

**4.11b  . . . and remove the air guide clips**

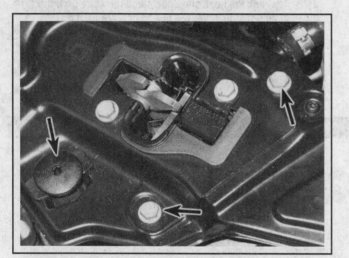

**4.13  Unscrew the radiator crossmember bolts and retaining pin from each end of the crossmember**

11  Detach the air guide clips and wiring harness ties from the crossmember at the upper front of the engine compartment (see illustrations).

12  Unbolt the bracket that secures the crossmember to the grille.

13  Remove the retaining pin and mounting bolts from each end of the crossmember (see illustration).

14  Squeeze the radiator retaining clips where they protrude upward through the crossmember to disengage them, then lift the crossmember off the vehicle (see illustration). Remove the clips that secure the air guide (located beneath the radiator crossmember) and remove it from the vehicle (see illustrations).

15  Follow the fan wiring harness to the connector and unplug it (see illustration).

16  Free the clips that secure the fan shroud to the radiator and lift the shroud off the radiator (see illustration), together with the fan motor. On vehicles with the fan motor controller mounted on the fan shroud,

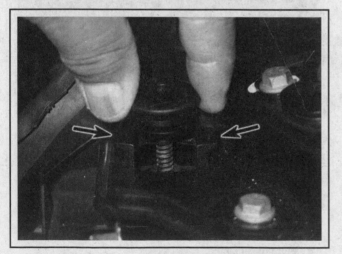

**4.14a  With the retaining pin out of the way, squeeze the clips that secure the radiator to the crossmember and lift the crossmember off**

**4.14b  The air duct beneath the crossmember is secured by plastic clips (arrow) . . .**

**4.14c . . . push them to one side to release them**

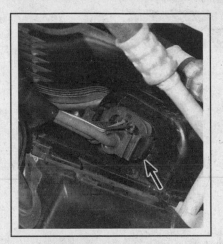

**4.15 Unplug the radiator fan electrical connector (this view is from below the vehicle)**

**4.16 Unclip the fan shroud from the radiator**

lift it out as well. Tilt the radiator forward for clearance as you lift the fan out.

17 Carefully inspect the fan blades for any damage. Replace if necessary. Inspect the fan motor and electronic controller for signs of damage (burned or melted wiring or connector terminals) or roughness when rotating the assembly.

18 At this point, the fan may be unbolted from the motor, if necessary, and the motor (and controller, if mounted on the shroud) unbolted from the fan shroud.

19 Installation is the reverse of removal. Be sure to tighten the fan and motor mounting bolts evenly and securely.

## 5 Radiator and coolant reservoir/expansion tank - removal and installation

### ⚠ WARNING.

**Wait until the engine is completely cool before beginning this procedure.**

### COOLANT RESERVOIR/EXPANSION TANK

▶ **Refer to illustration 5.2**

1 The coolant reservoir is mounted on the right side of the engine compartment.

2 Disengage the auxiliary coolant pump and wiring from the front of the reservoir, then detach the electrical connector from the sensor at the bottom of the reservoir. Detach the hoses from the reservoir, remove the reservoir retaining nut, pull the reservoir up to disengage the grommet at the bottom, then lift the reservoir out (see illustration).

3 Be careful not to spill coolant on painted surfaces. If it spills, clean the surface immediately with soapy water and rinse.

4 Pour the coolant into a container.

5 After washing the reservoir inside and out (use a household bottle brush to clean inside), inspect the reservoir for cracks and chafing. If it's damaged or so obscured by age as to make reading the water level difficult, replace it.

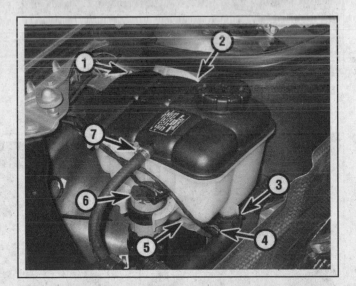

**5.2 Coolant reservoir details**

| | | | |
|---|---|---|---|
| 1 | Mounting nut | 5 | Grommet |
| 2 | Tang | 6 | Auxiliary coolant pump |
| 3 | Coolant hose (to lower radiator hose) | 7 | Coolant hose (to upper radiator hose) |
| 4 | Electrical connector | | |

6   Installation is the reverse of removal.

## RADIATOR

▶ **Refer to illustrations 5.10a, 5.10b, 5.11a, 5.11b, 5.11c, 5.12 and 5.16**

7   Disconnect the cable from the negative terminal of the battery.

8   Remove the fan and shroud (see Section 4). If you're working on a supercharged model, remove the air-to-air intercooler (see Chapter 4).

9   Drain the cooling system (see Chapter 1). If the coolant is relatively new or in good condition, save it and reuse it. Read the **Warning** in Section 2.

10  Disconnect the automatic transmission cooler lines from the radiator if equipped (see illustrations). Use a drip pan to catch spilled fluid and plug the lines and fittings.

11  These vehicles use non-standard cooling hose attachments in some locations. To detach the hoses, pry the hose clip out of its groove with a screwdriver until it locks, then work the metal-tipped end of the hose free of the fitting on the radiator (see illustrations). Remove the O-ring from the metal end of the hose.

12  Release the clips that attach the radiator to the vehicle and to the air conditioning condenser (see illustration). Carefully lift the radiator up and slightly rearward to separate it from the air conditioning condenser. Do not put stress on the connections at the condenser. Once the radiator is removed, the condenser will have to be tied up in place to the core support to prevent strain on the refrigerant connections. Take care not to spill coolant on the vehicle, as it can damage painted surfaces.

13  Inspect the radiator for leaks and damage. If it needs repair, have a radiator shop or dealer service department perform the work, as special tools and techniques are required.

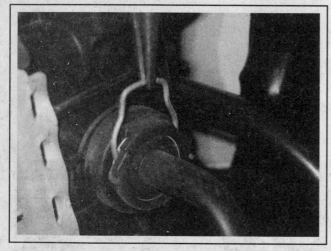

**5.10a  If the vehicle is equipped with an automatic transmission, pull up the clips to detach the cooler lines . . .**

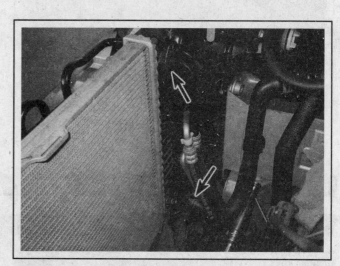

**5.10b  . . . then pull them out of the radiator - use new O-rings on installation**

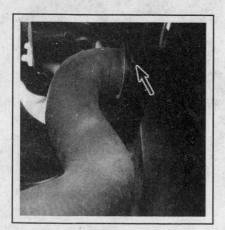

**5.11a  Pull back the clip to loosen the hose at the top of the radiator . . .**

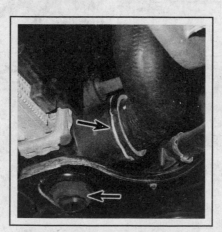

**5.11b  . . . and at the bottom (upper arrow) - the radiator is supported at the bottom by insulators (lower arrow) . . .**

**5.11c  . . . then disconnect the hoses and remove the O-rings**

14  Bugs and dirt can be removed from the radiator by spraying it with a garden hose nozzle from the back side. The radiator should be flushed out with a garden hose before reinstallation.

15  Check the radiator mounts for deterioration and replace if necessary.

16  Installation is the reverse of the removal procedure. Use new O-rings on the radiator hoses. Make sure the transmission fluid cooler hose clips are securely engaged (see illustration). Guide the radiator

into the mounts until it seats properly.

17  Refill and bleed the cooling system (see Chapter 1).

18  Start the engine and check for leaks. Allow the engine to reach normal operating temperature, indicated by the upper radiator hose becoming hot. Allow the engine to cool completely, then recheck the coolant level and add more if required.

19  Check and add automatic transmission fluid if needed (see Chapter 1).

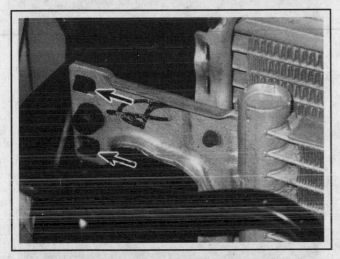

**5.12  Squeeze the clips and separate the condenser from the radiator**

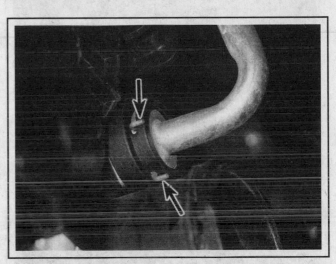

**5.16  After installation, make sure the clip is securely engaged**

## 6  Water pump - check and replacement

### CHECK

1  A failure in the water pump can cause serious engine damage due to overheating.

2  There are two ways to check the operation of the water pump while it's installed on the engine. If the pump is found to be defective, it should be replaced with a new or rebuilt unit.

3  Water pumps are equipped with weep (or vent) holes. If a failure occurs in the pump seal, coolant will leak from the hole.

4  If the water pump shaft bearings fail, there may be a howling sound at the pump while it's running. Shaft wear can be felt by relieving the serpentine belt tension (see Chapter 1) and rocking the water pump pulley up and down to detect shaft wear. Don't mistake drivebelt slippage, which causes a squealing sound, for water pump bearing failure.

5  Even a pump that exhibits no outward signs of a problem, such as noise or leakage, can still be due for replacement. Removal for close examination is the only sure way to tell. Sometimes the fins on the back of the impeller can corrode to the point that cooling efficiency is hampered.

### REPLACEMENT

#### Four-cylinder and 2001 through 2005 V6 engines

▶ **Refer to illustrations 6.10, 6.13, 6.14a and 6.14b**

6  Disconnect the cable from the negative terminal of the battery.

7  Remove the air cleaner housing (see Chapter 4). On supercharged models, remove the air intake silencer.

8  If you're working on a V6, remove the cooling fan (see Section 4) and engine shock absorber, if so equipped.

9  Drain the engine coolant from the block and the radiator (see Chapter 1). If the coolant is relatively new or in good condition, save it and reuse it.

**6.10  Loosen the water pump pulley bolts before removing the drivebelt (late four-cylinder shown)**

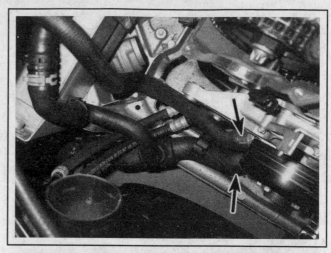

**6.13  Water pump coolant hoses (2001 through 2005 V6 engine)**

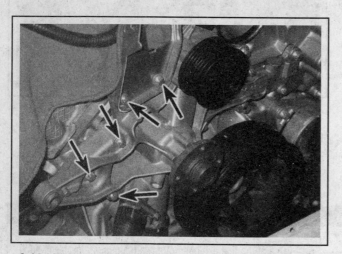

**6.14a  Water pump bolt locations - right side (2001 through 2005 V6 engine)**

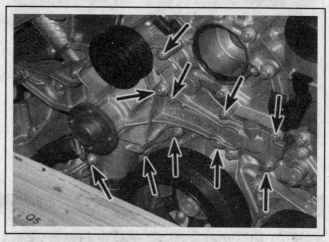

**6.14b  Water pump bolt locations - left side (2001 through 2005 V6 engine)**

10  Loosen the water pump pulley bolts while the drivebelt is still tight. Don't remove the bolts yet (see illustration).

11  Remove the drivebelt (see Chapter 1).

12  Remove the pulley mounting bolts and take the pulley off the pump.

13  Disconnect the coolant hose(s) (if equipped) from the water pump (see illustration).

14  Remove the bolts and detach the water pump from the engine (see illustrations). Check the impeller on the backside for evidence of corrosion or missing fins.

### 2006 and later V6 engines

▸ Refer to illustrations 6.18 and 6.21

15  Insert the key in the ignition and turn it to the 0 position.

16  Drain the engine coolant from the block and the radiator (see Chapter 1). If the coolant is relatively new or in good condition, save it and reuse it.

17  Remove the drivebelt (see Chapter 1).

18  Carefully pry the trim covers off the timing belt idler pulleys

(see illustration). Remove the pulley bolts and take the pulleys off their shafts.

19  Pry the wiring harness retainer off the pump and pull the harness out of the pump groove.

20  Disconnect the coolant hose from the water pump.

21  Loosen the pump bolts evenly, in the opposite of the tightening sequence (see illustration). Once all the bolts are loose, remove them and take the pump off the engine.

### All models

22  Clean the bolt threads and the threaded holes in the engine to remove corrosion and sealant.

23  Compare the new pump to the old one to make sure they're identical.

24  Remove all traces of old gasket sealant or O-ring material from the engine.

25  Clean the engine and new water pump mating surfaces with lacquer thinner or acetone.

26  Water pumps on 2003 through 2005 four-cylinder models are sealed with O-rings. Clean the O-ring grooves before replacing the

O-rings, and lubricate the groove with a little liquid soap to ease installation of the O-ring. On all other engines, the water pump is sealed with a gasket.

27 Carefully attach the pump to the engine and thread the bolts into the holes finger tight. Use a small amount of RTV sealant on the bolt threads, and make sure that the dowel pins, if used, are in their original locations.

28 Tighten the bolts to the torque listed in this Chapter's Specifications in 1/4-turn increments. Don't overtighten the bolts or the pump may be distorted. On 2006 and later V6 engines, tighten the bolts in the specified sequence (see illustration 6.21).

29 Reinstall all parts removed for access to the pump.

30 Wait at least one hour for the sealant to cure. Refill and bleed the cooling system (see Chapter 1). Run the engine and check for leaks and proper operation.

**6.18 Pry the trim cover from each of the idler pulleys (upper idler pulley shown)**

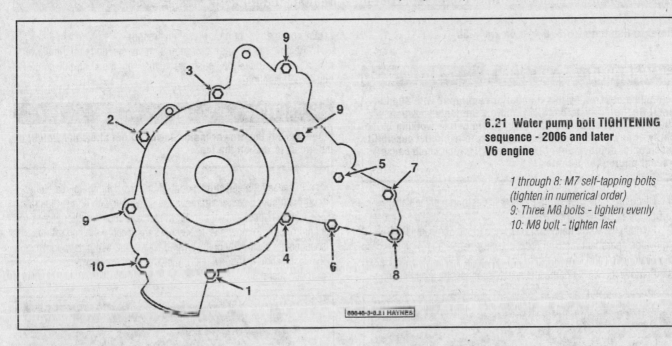

**6.21 Water pump bolt TIGHTENING sequence - 2006 and later V6 engine**

*1 through 8: M7 self-tapping bolts
(tighten in numerical order)
9: Three M8 bolts - tighten evenly
10: M8 bolt - tighten last*

## 7 Coolant temperature gauge sending unit - check and replacement

### ❋ WARNING:

**Wait until the engine is completely cool before beginning this procedure.**

### CHECK

▸ **Refer to illustration 7.1**

1 On all models covered by this manual, the Engine Coolant Temperature (ECT) sensor, which is an information sensor for the Powertrain Control Module (PCM), also functions as the coolant temperature sending unit (see Chapter 6). On all four-cylinder and 2001 through 2005 V6 engines, it's mounted on the thermostat housing (see illustration). On 2006 and later V6 engines, it's mounted on the back of the left cylinder head.

**7.1 On 2005 and earlier V6 engines, the coolant temperature sensor is mounted on the thermostat housing or the coolant passage at the front of the engine**

2   If an overheating indication occurs, check the coolant level in the system and then make sure all connectors in the wiring harness between the sending unit and the indicator light or gauge are tight.

3   When the ignition switch is turned to START and the starter motor is turning, the indicator light (if equipped) should come on. This doesn't mean the engine is overheated; it just means that the bulb is good.

4   If the light doesn't come on when the ignition key is turned to START, the bulb might be burned out, the ignition switch might be faulty or the circuit might be open.

5   As soon as the engine starts, the indicator light should go out

and remain off, unless the engine overheats. If the light doesn't go out, refer to Chapter 6 and check for any stored trouble codes in the Powertrain Control Module (PCM).

6   If the engine tends to overheat easily, check the coolant to make sure it's of the proper concentration (see Chapter 1).

## REPLACEMENT

7   See Chapter 6 for the ECT sensor replacement procedure.

## 8   Blower motor and electronic control unit - removal and installation

▶ **Refer to illustration 8.3, 8.4, 8.5a and 8.5b**

### ❋❋ WARNING:

**The models covered by this manual are equipped with Supplemental Restraint Systems (SRS), more commonly known as airbags. Always disable the airbag system before working in the vicinity of any airbag system components to avoid the possibility of accidental deployment of the airbag(s), which could cause personal injury (see Chapter 12).**

1   Disconnect the cable from the negative terminal of the battery (see Chapter 5, Section 1).

2   Remove the lower dash trim below the glove compartment (see the glove compartment removal procedure in Chapter 11) to gain access to the heater case and blower motor.

3   Remove the wiring harness cover. Disconnect the electrical con-

nector from the blower motor (see illustration).

4   Remove the blower motor mounting screws, and pull the blower motor carefully out of the housing, together with the electronic control unit (see illustration).

### ❋❋ CAUTION:

**When you set the blower motor down, do not allow the weight of the motor to rest on the fan.**

5   To separate the electronic control unit from the motor, carefully pry off the rubber cover and remove the screw beneath it (see illustration). Turn the housing over and lift the fan and motor out for access to the control unit. Remove the Torx screws that secure the control unit, disconnect its electrical connector and take it out (see illustration).

6   Installation is the reverse of removal. Run the blower and check for proper operation.

**8.3  Remove the wiring harness cover from the blower motor and unplug the connector**

**8.4  Remove the motor-to-housing bolts and lower the motor out of the housing, together with the fan**

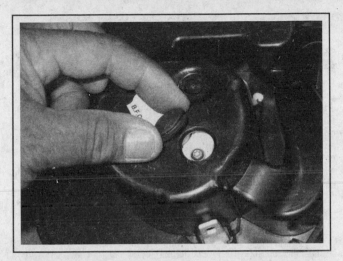

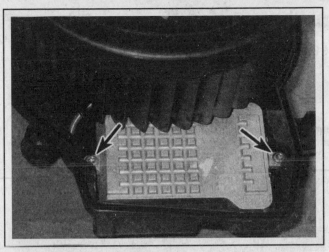

8.5a  Pry the rubber plug off the motor and remove the screw beneath it . . .

8.5b  . . . lift the fan up for access, remove the control unit's Torx screws and take the unit out

## 9   Heater and air conditioning control assembly - removal and installation

▶ Refer to illustrations 9.3a, 9.3b and 9.3c

### ❊ WARNING:

The models covered by this manual are equipped with Supplemental Restraint Systems (SRS), more commonly known as airbags. Always disable the airbag system before working in the vicinity of any airbag system components to avoid the possibility of accidental deployment of the airbag(s), which could cause personal injury (see Chapter 12).

1   Disconnect the negative cable from the battery (see Chapter 5, Section 1).

2   Refer to Chapter 11 for removal of the ashtray and upper console trim panels.

3   Remove the screws from the underside of the control assembly (see illustration). Carefully pry the heating/air conditioning control unit out of the center console cover with a trim stick and pull it out for access to the electrical connectors (see illustrations).

4   Disconnect the electrical connectors from the rear side of the control assembly and remove it from the vehicle.

5   Installation is the reverse of the removal procedure. Be sure the control unit clicks into position when you push it in.

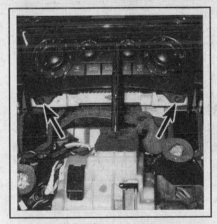

9.3a  Remove the air conditioning control unit mounting screws . . .

9.3b  . . . carefully pry the control unit out with a trim stick . . .

9.3c  . . . disengage the clips and unplug the electrical connectors

## 10  Heater core - replacement

▶ Refer to illustrations 10.7, 10.9 and 10.10

### ✳✳ WARNING 1:

The models covered by this manual are equipped with Supplemental Restraint Systems (SRS), more commonly known as airbags. Always disable the airbag system before working in the vicinity of any airbag system components to avoid the possibility of accidental deployment of the airbag(s), which could cause personal injury (see Chapter 12).

### ✳✳ WARNING 2:

Wait until the engine is completely cool before beginning this procedure.

➡Note: Replacement of the heater core is a difficult procedure for the home mechanic. If you attempt this procedure at home, keep track of the assemblies by taking notes and keeping screws and other hardware in small, marked plastic bags for reassembly.

1   Turn the heater control setting to HOT. Drain the cooling system (see Chapter 1). If the coolant is relatively new, or tests in good condition (see Section 2), save it and re-use it.

### ✳✳ WARNING:

Do not allow antifreeze to come in contact with your skin or painted surfaces of the vehicle. Rinse off spills immediately with plenty of water. Antifreeze is highly toxic if ingested. Never leave antifreeze lying around in an open container or in puddles on the floor; children and pets are attracted by its sweet smell and may drink it. Check with local authorities about disposing of used antifreeze. Many communities have collection centers which will see that antifreeze is disposed of safely. Never dump used antifreeze on the ground or into drains.

2   Disconnect the cable from the negative terminal of the battery.
3   Adjust the steering column as far back and down as it will go. Remove the steering wheel (see Chapter 10).
4   Remove the lower trim panel from the left side of the instrument panel (see Chapter 11).
5   Remove the instrument cluster (see Chapter 12).
6   Remove the accelerator pedal (see Chapter 4).
7   Peel back the carpet in the driver's footwell far enough to expose the air duct that runs to the back seat (see illustration).
8   Detach the steering column from the instrument panel and lower it into the driver's footwell (see Chapter 10). It isn't necessary to separate the steering shaft from the coupling.
9   Unhook the three springs that secure the upper end of the rear air duct, then remove the fitting at the upper end of the air duct (see illustration).

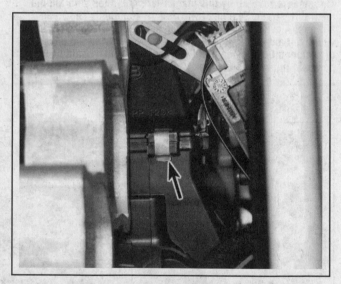

**10.7  Pull back the driver's side carpet to expose the top end of the rear air duct**

**10.9  Unhook the three clips (one clip shown) and detach the duct**

10 Place some plastic sheeting on the footwell floor, then pull the clips out of the heater hose fittings (see illustration).

➡**Note: Replace the clips with new ones on installation.**

11 Carefully pull the coolant tubes out of the heater core.

12 Remove the bracket bolts and take the bracket off the heater core (see illustration 10.10). Separate the heater core from the evaporator housing and take it out.

13 Wipe any spilled coolant from the inside of the housing.

14 Installation is the reverse order of removal. When attaching the steering column to the support bracket, tighten the nuts or bolts to the torque listed in the Chapter 10 Specifications.

15 Refill the cooling system (see Chapter 1), reconnect the battery and run the engine. Check for leaks and proper operation of the system.

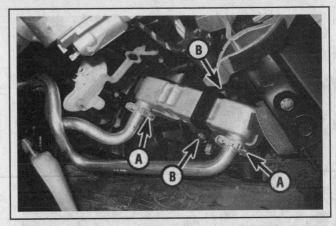

**10.10  Pull out the clips (A) to free the heater hoses, unbolt the bracket (B) and remove the heater core**

---

## 11  Air conditioning and heating system - check and maintenance

### AIR CONDITIONING SYSTEM

**✳✳ WARNING:**

The air conditioning system is under high pressure. Do not loosen any hose fittings or remove any components until after the system has been discharged. Air conditioning refrigerant should be properly discharged into an EPA-approved recovery/recycling unit at a dealer service department or an automotive air conditioning repair facility. Always wear eye protection when disconnecting air conditioning system fittings.

**✳✳ CAUTION 1:**

All models covered by this manual use environmentally friendly R-134a. This refrigerant (and its appropriate refrigerant oils) are not compatible with R-12 refrigerant system components and must never be mixed or the components will be damaged.

**✳✳ CAUTION 2:**

When replacing entire components, additional refrigerant oil should be added equal to the amount that is removed with the component being replaced. Be sure to read the can before adding any oil to the system, to make sure it is compatible with the R-134a system.

1  The following maintenance checks should be performed on a regular basis to ensure that the air conditioning continues to operate at peak efficiency.

 a) Inspect the condition of the compressor drivebelt. If it is worn or deteriorated, replace it (see Chapter 1).
 b) Check the drivebelt tension (see Chapter 1).
 c) Inspect the system hoses. Look for cracks, bubbles, hardening and deterioration. Inspect the hoses and all fittings for oil bubbles or seepage. If there is any evidence of wear, damage or leakage, replace the hose(s).
 d) Inspect the condenser fins for leaves, bugs and any other foreign material that may have embedded itself in the fins. Use a fin comb or compressed air to remove debris from the condenser.
 e) Make sure the system has the correct refrigerant charge.

2  It's a good idea to operate the system for about ten minutes at least once a month. This is particularly important during the winter months because long term non-use can cause hardening, and subsequent failure, of the seals. Note that using the Defrost function operates the compressor.

3  If the air conditioning system is not working properly, proceed to Step 6 and perform the general checks outlined below.

4  Because of the complexity of the air conditioning system and the special equipment necessary to service it, in-depth troubleshooting and repairs beyond checking the refrigerant charge and the compressor clutch operation are not included in this manual. However, simple checks and component replacement procedures are provided in this Chapter.

5  The most common cause of poor cooling is simply a low system

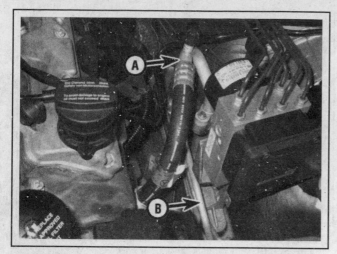

11.8 Refrigerant suction line (A) and discharge line (B)

11.10 Insert a thermometer in the center duct while operating the air conditioning system - the output air should be 35 to 40 degrees F less than the ambient temperature, depending on humidity

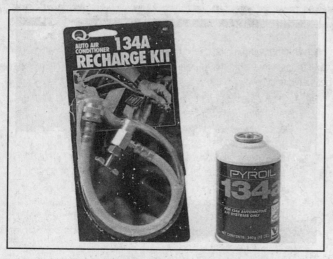

11.12 A basic charging kit for 134a systems is available at most auto parts stores - it must say 134a (not R-12) and so must the can of refrigerant

refrigerant charge. If a noticeable drop in system cooling ability occurs, one of the following quick checks will help you determine whether the refrigerant level is low. Should the system lose its cooling ability, the following procedure will help you pinpoint the cause.

### Checking the refrigerant charge

▶ Refer to illustrations 11.8 and 11.10

6  Warm the engine up to normal operating temperature.

7  Place the air conditioning temperature selector at the coldest setting and put the blower at the highest setting. Open the doors (to make sure the air conditioning system doesn't cycle off as soon as it cools the passenger compartment).

8  After the system reaches operating temperature, feel the suction line on the left side of the engine compartment (see illustration).

9  The suction line should be cold (the tubing that leads back to the compressor) and the discharge line should be warm or hot. If the

evaporator outlet is warm, the system probably needs a charge.

10  Insert a thermometer in the center air distribution duct (see illustration) while operating the air conditioning system at its maximum setting - the temperature of the output air should be 35 to 40 degrees F below the ambient air temperature (down to approximately 40 degrees F). If the ambient (outside) air temperature is very high, say 110 degrees F, the duct air temperature may be as high as 60 degrees F, but generally the air conditioning is 35 to 40 degrees F cooler than the ambient air.

11  Further inspection or testing of the system requires special tools and techniques and is beyond the scope of the home mechanic.

### Adding refrigerant

▶ Refer to illustrations 11.12, 11.15 and 11.16

> ❄❄ **CAUTION:**
>
> Make sure any refrigerant, refrigerant oil or replacement component your purchase is designated as compatible with environmentally friendly R-134a systems.

12  Purchase an R-134a automotive charging kit at an auto parts store (see illustration). A charging kit includes a can of refrigerant, a tap valve and a short section of hose that can be attached between the tap valve and the system low side service valve.

13  Hook up the charging kit by following the manufacturer's instructions.

> ❄❄ **WARNING:**
>
> DO NOT hook the charging kit hose to the system high side! The fittings on the charging kit are designed to fit only on the low side of the system.

14  Back off the valve handle on the charging kit and screw the kit onto the refrigerant can, making sure first that the O-ring or rubber seal inside the threaded portion of the kit is in place.

**11.15 Attach the refrigerant kit to the low-side charging port**

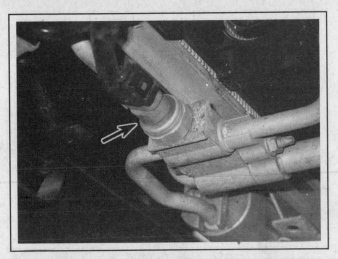

**11.16 The air conditioning pressure switch is located beneath the radiator - if the compressor will not stay engaged, disconnect the connector and bridge it with a jumper wire during the charging procedure**

15  Remove the dust cap from the low-side charging port and attach the quick-connect fitting on the kit hose (see illustration).

16  Warm up the engine and turn on the air conditioning. Keep the charging kit hose away from the fan and other moving parts.

➡ **Note 1: The charging process requires the compressor to be running. If the clutch cycles off, you can put the air conditioning switch on High and leave the car doors open to keep the clutch on and compressor working.**

➡ **Note 2: The compressor can be kept on during the charging by removing the connector from the dual-pressure switch and bridging it with a paper clip or jumper wire during the procedure (see illustration).**

17  Turn the valve handle on the kit until the stem pierces the can, then back the handle out to release the refrigerant. You should be able to hear the rush of gas. Add refrigerant to the low side of the system, keeping the can upright at all times, but shaking it occasionally. Allow stabilization time between each addition.

➡ **Note: The charging process will go faster if you wrap the can with a hot-water-soaked shop rag to keep the can from freezing up.**

18  If you have an accurate thermometer, you can place it in the center air conditioning duct inside the vehicle and keep track of the output air temperature. A charged system that is working properly should cool down to approximately 40 degrees F. If the ambient (outside) air temperature is very high, say 110 degrees F, the duct air temperature may be as high as 60 degrees F, but generally the air conditioning is 35-40 degrees F cooler than the ambient air.

19  When the can is empty, turn the valve handle to the closed position and release the connection from the low-side port. Reinstall the dust cap.

20  Remove the charging kit from the can and store the kit for future use with the piercing valve in the UP position, to prevent inadvertently piercing the can on the next use.

## HEATING SYSTEMS

21  If the carpet under the heater core is damp, or if antifreeze vapor or steam is coming through the vents, the heater core is leaking. Remove it (see Section 10) and install a new unit (most radiator shops will not repair a leaking heater core).

22  If the air coming out of the heater vents isn't hot, the problem could stem from any of the following causes:

a) *The thermostat is stuck open, preventing the engine coolant from warming up enough to carry heat to the heater core. Replace the thermostat (see Section 3).*

b) *There is a blockage in the system, preventing the flow of coolant through the heater core. Feel both heater hoses at the firewall. They should be hot. If one of them is cold, there is an obstruction in one of the hoses or in the heater core, or the heater control valve is shut. Detach the hoses and back flush the heater core with a water hose. If the heater core is clear but circulation is impeded, remove the two hoses and flush them out with a water hose.*

c) *If flushing fails to remove the blockage from the heater core, the core must be replaced (see Section 10).*

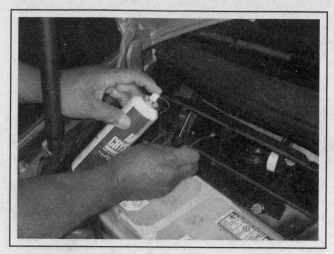

**11.26 With the cabin air filter removed and the blower set to its highest setting, spray the disinfectant into the opening**

## ELIMINATING AIR CONDITIONING ODORS

▶ **Refer to illustration 11.26**

23 Unpleasant odors that often develop in air conditioning systems are caused by the growth of a fungus, usually on the surface of the evaporator core. The warm, humid environment there is a perfect breeding ground for mildew to develop.

24 The evaporator core on most vehicles is difficult to access, and factory dealerships have a lengthy, expensive process for eliminating the fungus by opening up the evaporator case and using a powerful disinfectant and rinse on the core until the fungus is gone. You can service your own system at home, but it takes something much stronger than basic household germ-killers or deodorizers.

25 Aerosol disinfectants for automotive air conditioning systems are available in most auto parts stores, but remember when shopping for them that the most effective treatments are also the most expensive. The basic procedure for using these sprays is to start by running the system in the RECIRC mode for ten minutes with the blower on its highest speed. Use the highest heat mode to dry out the system and keep the compressor from engaging by disconnecting the wiring connector at the compressor (see Section 13).

26 The disinfectant can usually comes with a long spray hose. Remove the cabin air filter (see Chapter 1), turn the blower to the highest speed setting, point the nozzle inside the opening and spray according to the manufacturer's recommendations (see illustration). Follow the manufacturer's recommendations for the length of spray and waiting time between applications.

## AUTOMATIC HEATING AND AIR CONDITIONING SYSTEMS

27 Some models are equipped with an optional automatic climate control system. This system has its own computer that receives inputs from various sensors in the heating and air conditioning system. This computer, like the PCM, has self-diagnostic capabilities to help pinpoint problems or faults within the system. Vehicles equipped with automatic heating and air conditioning systems are very complex and considered beyond the scope of the home mechanic. Vehicles equipped with automatic heating and air conditioning systems should be taken to dealer service department or other qualified facility for repair.

---

## 12  Air conditioning receiver/drier - removal and installation

### ❄❄ WARNING:

**The air conditioning system is under high pressure. DO NOT loosen any fittings or remove any components until after the system has been discharged. Air conditioning refrigerant should be properly discharged into an EPA-approved container at a dealer service department or an automotive air conditioning repair facility. Always wear eye protection when disconnecting air conditioning system fittings.**

## REMOVAL

1  The receiver/drier stores refrigerant and removes moisture from the system. When any major air conditioning component (compressor, condenser, evaporator) is replaced, or the system has been apart and exposed to air for any length of time, the receiver/drier must be replaced. On vehicles built up to April 23, 2004, the receiver/drier is built into the right-hand side of the condenser. On later models, it's mounted beneath the front of the vehicle.

2  Take the vehicle to a dealer service department or automotive air conditioning shop and have the air conditioning system discharged and the refrigerant recovered (see the **Warning** at the beginning of this Section).

### Early models (up to April 23, 2004)

▶ **Refer to illustration 12.3**

3  Open the hood. Pull up the plastic cover to expose the receiver/drier plug (see illustration).

4  Unscrew the plug, then lift the receiver/drier cartridge out of the condenser.

### Later models

▶ **Refer to illustrations 12.6, 12.7 and 12.8**

5  Set the parking brake, block the rear wheels and raise the front of the vehicle, supporting it securely on jackstands and remove the splash cover from below the engine.

6  Remove the clips that retain the cover to the receiver/drier (see illustration).

7  Unbolt the retaining plate from the end of the receiver/drier (see illustration).

**12.3  On early models, remove the plastic cover and unscrew the plug to remove the receiver/drier**

**12.6  On later models, free the clips and remove the cover from the receiver/drier . . .**

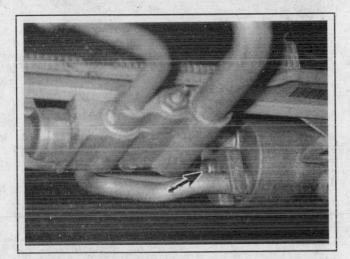

**12.7  . . . unbolt the retaining plate . . .**

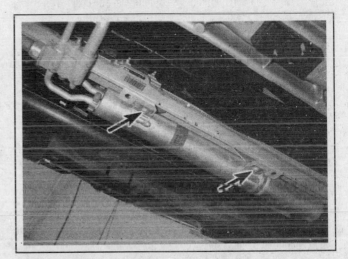

**12.8  . . . remove the mounting bolts, then detach the receiver/drier from the lines**

8  Remove the mounting bolts, then separate the receiver/drier from the refrigerant lines (see illustration). Cap or plug the open lines immediately.

9  Take the receiver/drier out of the vehicle.

## INSTALLATION

### All models

10  If you are replacing the receiver/drier, add 20 cc of clean refrigerant oil to the new receiver/drier. This will maintain the correct oil level in the system after the repairs are completed.

### Early models

11  Don't open the new receiver/drier's packaging until you're ready to install the unit in the condenser. Once you do open the packaging, install the receiver/drier within 20 minutes.

12  Insert the new receiver/drier into the condenser, cylinder end down (shaft end up). Install the threaded plug and tighten it to the torque listed in this Chapter's Specifications.

13  Install the plastic cover over the plug.

### Later models

14  Place the new receiver/drier into position, tighten the mounting bracket bolt lightly, still allowing the receiver/drier to be turned to align the line connections.

15  Lubricate the O-rings using clean refrigerant oil and reconnect the lines. Now tighten the mounting bracket bolt securely.

16  Install the receiver/drier cover and splash cover.

### All models

17  Have the system evacuated, recharged and leak tested by a dealer service department or an air conditioning repair facility.

## 13 Air conditioning compressor - removal and installation

➡Note: The receiver/drier should be replaced whenever the compressor is replaced (see Section 12).

## REMOVAL

◆ **Refer to illustration 13.5**

1   Have the air conditioning system refrigerant discharged and recycled by an air conditioning technician (see **Warning** above).
2   Disconnect the cable from the negative terminal of the battery (see Chapter 5, Section 1).
3   Remove the drivebelt (see Chapter 1).
4   Remove the air cleaner intake tube mounted above the compressor (see Chapter 4).
5   Disconnect the compressor clutch wiring harness (see illustration). Disconnect the refrigerant lines from the compressor. Plug the open fittings to prevent entry of dirt and moisture.
6   Unbolt the compressor from the mounting bracket and remove it from the vehicle.

## INSTALLATION

7   The clutch may have to be transferred from the old compressor to the new unit.

8   Add the proper amount of refrigerant oil to the new compressor using the following calculations:
  a)  *Drain the refrigerant oil from the old compressor through the suction fitting and measure it in cubic centimeters.*
  b)  *Drain any new oil from the new compressor.*
  c)  *Add an amount of clean, new oil, equal to the drained amount, to the new compressor. Add an additional 20 cc.*

9   Installation is the reverse of removal, using new O-rings where the lines attach to the compressor.
10  Have the system evacuated, recharged and leak tested by an air conditioning technician.

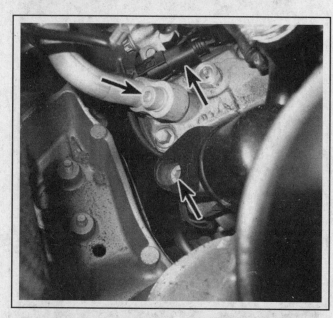

**13.5 Disconnect the wiring and refrigerant lines from the compressor**

## 14 Air conditioning condenser - removal and installation

## REMOVAL

1   Have the refrigerant discharged and recycled by an air conditioning technician (see **Warning 1** above).

2   Disconnect the cable from the negative terminal of the battery and drain the cooling system (see Chapter 1).

3   On early models with the receiver/drier mounted inside the condenser, remove the receiver/drier from the condenser (see Section 12).

4   Disconnect the condenser line and discharge line from the condenser. On early models, unplug the electrical connector from the pressure switch and remove the nut that secures the refrigerant line junction block to the condenser. On later models (with the receiver/drier mounted beneath the condenser), remove the receiver/drier, referring to Section 12. Cap the fittings on the condenser and lines to prevent entry of dirt or moisture.

5   Release the clips that secure the condenser to the radiator (see illustration 5.12).

6   Lift the condenser out of the vehicle.

## INSTALLATION

7   Installation is the reverse of removal.

8   Have the system evacuated, charged and leak tested by an air conditioning technician.

## Specifications

### General

| | |
|---|---|
| Coolant capacity | See Chapter 1 |
| Drivebelt tension | See Chapter 1 |
| Radiator cap pressure rating | 19 to 22 psi |
| Thermostat rating | |
|   Four-cylinde engines | |
|     Valve opens | 185 to 192 degrees F (85 to 89 degrees C) |
|     Fully open | 226 degrees F (102 degrees C) |
|   2001 through 2005 V6 engines | |
|     Valve opens | 190 to 197 degrees F (88 to 92 degrees C) |
|     Fully open | 215 degrees F (105 degrees C) |
|   2006 and later V6 engines | |
|     Main valve opens | 149 degrees F (65 degrees C) |
|     Shutoff valve opens | 130 degrees F (40 degrees C) |
|     Fully open | 212 degrees F (100 degrees C) |
| Amount of opening | 5/16 inch (8 mm) |
| Refrigerant | R-134a |

## Torque specifications

| | In-lbs* | Nm |
|---|---|---|

➡**Note: One foot-pound (ft-lb) of torque is equivalent to 12 inch-pounds (in-lbs) of torque. Torque values below approximately 15 ft-lbs are expressed in inch-pounds, since most foot-pound torque wrenches are not accurate at these smaller values.**

| | In-lbs* | Nm |
|---|---|---|
| Thermostat housing cover bolts | | |
|   2002 four-cylinder engine | | |
|     M6 bolts | 106 | 10 |
|     M8 bolts | 265 | 25 |
|   2003 through 2005 four-cylinder engine | 95 | 9 |
|   2001 through 2005 V6 engine | 148 | 14 |
|   2006 and later V6 engine | 265 | 25 |
| Water pump retaining bolts | | |
|   2002 four-cylinder engine | | |
|     M6 bolts | 106 | 10 |
|     M8 bolts | 265 | 25 |

## Section

## Reference to other Chapters

# 4

# FUEL AND
# EXHAUST
# SYSTEMS

## 1   General information

All models covered by this manual are equipped with a sequential multi-port fuel injection system. This type of fuel injection system uses timed impulses to sequentially inject the fuel directly into the intake ports of each cylinder in the same sequence as the firing order. The Powertrain Control Module (PCM) controls the injectors. The PCM monitors various engine parameters and delivers the exact amount of fuel, in firing order sequence, into the intake ports. For more information about the fuel injection system, see Section 10.

The fuel pump/fuel level sensor module consists of the fuel inlet strainer, the pump and the fuel level sensor for the right part of the tank, and can be accessed by removing the rear seat cushion, an access cover in the floor and a retainer on top of the fuel tank. A second fuel level sensor, which is located in the left part of the fuel tank, has its own access cover and retainer, and is accessed in the same manner as the fuel pump module. Neither of these modules is serviceable. If anything malfunctions on either module, you must replace the entire unit.

The fuel filter is located at the rear of the left half of the fuel tank. The fuel pressure regulator is an integral component of the fuel filter. If the fuel filter or the fuel pressure regulator fails, you must replace the entire unit.

The exhaust system consists of the two exhaust manifolds, the front part of the exhaust system (which includes a pair of catalytic converters, the pipes connecting the exhaust manifolds to the converters and the converters to the rear part of the exhaust system), and the rear part of the exhaust system (which includes a resonator [or pre-muffler] and the muffler/tailpipe assembly). Each of the catalysts and their inlet and outlet pipes can be replaced separately from the other exhaust pipe/catalyst assembly. The rear part of the exhaust system is a one-piece assembly. For information regarding removal of the various parts of the exhaust system, see Section 16. For information regarding removal/replacement of the catalytic converters, refer to Chapter 6.

## 2   Fuel pressure relief procedure

▶ **Refer to illustration 2.1**

✻✻ **WARNING:**

**See the Warning in Section 1.**

1   The fuel pump fuse and fuel pump relay (see illustration) are both located on the fuse and relay box in the trunk.

2   Open the trunk and remove the fuse and relay box cover, which is located on the left side of the trunk.

3   Remove the fuel pump fuse.

4   Turn the ignition key to START and crank over the engine for several seconds. It will either start momentarily and immediately stall, or it won't start at all.

5   Turn the ignition key to the OFF position.

6   Disconnect the cable from the negative battery terminal before beginning work on the fuel system (see Chapter 5, Section 1).

7   Install the fuel pump fuse and the fuse and relay box cover.

8   After all work on the fuel system has been completed, reconnect the battery (see Chapter 5, Section 1).

9   When the engine is started, the CHECK ENGINE light or Malfunction Indicator Light (MIL) might come on because the engine was cranked while the fuel pump fuse was pulled. The light should go out after a period of normal operation. If it does not go out, refer to Chapter 6.

**2.1  The fuel pump fuse (A) and the fuel pump relay (B) are both located in the fuse and relay box inside the left side of the trunk.**

## 3   Fuel pump/fuel pressure - check

### ✵✵ WARNING:

**See the Warning in Section 1.**

## PRELIMINARY CHECK

1   The fuel pump is located inside the fuel tank. Turn the ignition key to ON (not START) and listen carefully for the soft whirring sound made by the fuel pump as it's briefly turned on by the PCM to pressurize the fuel system prior to starting the engine. You will only hear a soft whirring sound for a second or two, but that sound tells you that the pump is working. If you can't hear the pump from inside the vehicle, remove the fuel filler cap and have an assistant turn the ignition switch to ON while you listen for the sound of the pump. If the pump does not come on when the ignition key is turned to ON, check the fuel pump fuse and relay, both of which are located in the fuse and relay box in the right rear corner of the engine compartment (see illustration 2.1). If the fuse and relay are okay, check the wiring back to the fuel pump. See Section 5 for the location of the fuel pump electrical connector. If the fuse, relay and wiring are okay, the fuel pump is probably defective. If the pump runs continuously with the ignition key in the ON position, the Powertrain Control Module (PCM) is probably defective. Have the PCM checked by a dealer service department or other qualified repair shop.

## PRESSURE CHECK

⯈ **Refer to illustrations 3.3, 3.4a, 3.4b and 3.4c**

➡Note: In order to perform the fuel pressure test, you will need a fuel pressure gauge capable of measuring high fuel pressure. You'll also need an adapter to connect your fuel pressure testing rig to the Schrader service valve on the fuel rail.

2   Relieve the fuel system pressure (see Section 2).
3   For this check, you'll need to obtain a fuel pressure gauge (see illustration) with a hose and an adapter suitable for connecting it to the Schrader valve on the fuel rail.

4   Remove the Schrader valve cap and connect your fuel pressure gauge to the fuel rail (see illustrations).
5   Start the engine and check the pressure on the gauge, comparing your reading with the pressure listed in this Chapter's Specifications.
6   If the fuel pressure is not within specifications, check the following:

a) If the pressure is lower than specified, check for a restriction in the fuel system. One likely cause is a clogged fuel inlet strainer at the base of the fuel pump/fuel level sensor module in the right fuel tank chamber.

➡Note: The strainer cannot be replaced separately from the fuel pump. If you're unable to clean the strainer, replace the fuel pump/fuel level sensor module (see Section 5).

b) If the fuel pressure is higher than specified, replace the fuel pressure regulator (see Section 6), which is an integral component of the fuel filter, which is located behind the left chamber of the fuel tank.

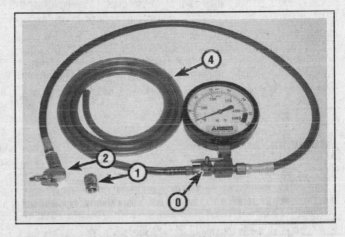

**3.3  A typical fuel pressure gauge set up**

1   *Screw-on adapter for the*
    *Schrader valve on the fuel rail*
2   *Hose with fitting to connect*
    *to the adapter*
3   *Bleeder valve (optional)*
4   *Bleeder hose (optional)*

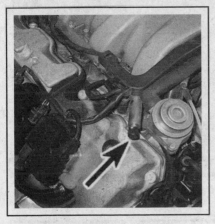  

**3.4a  The fuel rails on all models are equipped with a Schrader valve test port like this one. To access the valve, simply unscrew the cap (2005 and earlier V6 engine shown)**

**3.4b  Schrader valve test port location on a four-cylinder engine**

**3.4c  To connect your fuel pressure gauge to the Schrader valve test port, simply screw it on**

## 4  Fuel lines and fittings - repair and replacement

Gasoline is extremely flammable, so take extra precautions when you work on any part of the fuel system. See the Warning in Section 2.

1   Always relieve the fuel pressure before servicing fuel lines or fittings on fuel-injected vehicles (see Section 2).

2   The fuel supply line connects the fuel tank to the fuel rail on the engine. Be sure to inspect the fuel and the Evaporative Emission Control (EVAP) system lines for leaks, kinks and dents whenever you're servicing something underneath the vehicle. All of these lines are secured to the vehicle underbody by plastic clips. To disengage fuel and EVAP lines from these clips, simply pry the clip down and pull out the lines from above.

3   Whenever you're working under the vehicle, be sure to inspect all fuel and EVAP lines for leaks, kinks, dents and other damage. Always replace a damaged fuel line or EVAP line immediately. Leaking fuel and EVAP lines will result in loss of fuel and excessive air pollution (leaking raw fuel emits unburned hydrocarbon vapors into the atmosphere).

4   If you find signs of dirt in the lines during disassembly, disconnect all lines and blow them out with compressed air. If the fuel lines are particularly dirty, you might also have to replace the fuel pump module and the fuel filter module (see Sections 5 and 6). (Neither the inlet strainer at the inlet end of the pump nor the main fuel filter can be inspected for contamination.)

## STEEL TUBING

5   Because fuel lines used on fuel-injected vehicles are under fairly high pressure, it is critical that they be replaced with lines of equivalent specification. If you have to replace a steel line, make sure that you use steel tubing that meets the manufacturer's specifications. Don't use copper or aluminum tubing to replace steel tubing. These materials cannot withstand normal vehicle vibration.

6   Some steel fuel lines have threaded fittings. When loosening these fittings to service or replace components:

a) *Use a backup wrench on the stationary portion of the fitting while loosening and tightening the fitting nuts.*

b) *If you're going to replace one of these fittings, use original equipment parts or parts that meet original equipment standards.*

## PLASTIC TUBING

7   If you ever have to replace a plastic line, use only the original equipment plastic tubing.

When removing or installing plastic fuel line tubing, be careful not to bend or twist it too much, which can damage it. Damaged fuel lines MUST be replaced! Also, be aware that the plastic fuel tubing is NOT heat resistant, so keep it away from excessive heat. Nor is it acid-proof, so don't wipe it off with a shop rag that has been used to wipe off battery electrolyte. If you accidentally spill or wipe electrolyte on plastic fuel or emissions tubing, replace the tubing.

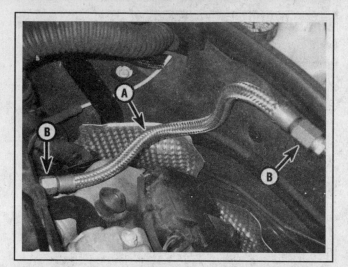

4.10  The fuel supply hose (A) uses threaded fittings (B) at both ends

## FLEXIBLE HOSES

Use only original equipment replacement hoses or their equivalent. Unapproved hoses might fail when subjected to the high operating pressures of the fuel system.

8   Don't route fuel hoses within four inches of exhaust system components or within ten inches of a catalytic converter. Make sure that no flexible hoses are installed directly against the vehicle, particularly in places where there is any vibration. If allowed to touch some vibrating part of the vehicle, a hose can easily become chafed and it might start leaking. A good rule of thumb is to maintain a minimum of 1/4-inch clearance around a hose (or metal line) to prevent contact with the vehicle underbody.

## FUEL LINE FITTINGS

9   The vehicles covered in this manual use two kinds of fittings for fuel lines: threaded fittings and a special type of hose-clamp, which requires a special crimping tool to install.

**Threaded fittings**

▶ **Refer to illustration 4.10**

ALWAYS relieve the fuel system pressure (see Section 2) before disconnecting a fuel line fitting.

10  Threaded fittings (see illustration) are used at both ends of the braided-steel-covered supply hose, in the engine compartment, that connects the fuel supply line to the fuel rail.

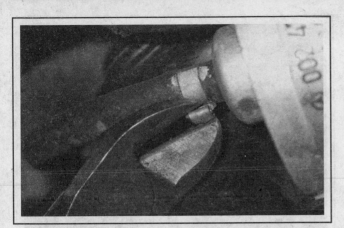

**4.12  To remove a fuel hose clamp, simply cut it off with a pair of diagonal cutters**

**4.13  Here's a typical crimping tool for these types of clamps. This tool, and similar tools, are available at most auto parts stores**

### Hose clamps

➡ **Refer to illustrations 4.12 and 4.13**

---

❋❋ **WARNING:**

---

**ALWAYS relieve the fuel system pressure (see Section 2) before disconnecting a fuel line fitting.**

---

11  Special hose clamps are used at the fuel pump, at the fuel filter and at other locations in the fuel system where fuel hoses are connected to plastic or metal fuel lines or pipes.

12  To remove one of these clamps, simply cut it off with a pair of diagonal cutters (see illustration).

13  Install the new hose clamp and crimp it tightly with the special tool (see illustration).

---

**5    Fuel pump/fuel level sensor and fuel level sensor modules - removal and installation**

---

❋❋ **WARNING:**

---

**See the Warning in Section 1.**

---

1    Relieve the fuel system pressure (see Section 2), then disconnect the cable from the negative battery terminal (see Chapter 5, Section 1).

2    The fuel tank doesn't have to be empty for either of the following procedures, but it shouldn't be full. If the fuel level is too high, you will have to disconnect fuel hoses that will be submerged in gasoline. If you don't want to immerse your hands in gasoline, drain fuel out of the tank with a hose routed through the fuel filler neck. Use a hard nylon tube

with a 30-degree cut on the end to push open the check valve in the fuel filler neck. If you're unable to extract any fuel from the tank because you can't work the siphon hose through the filler neck into the tank, then siphon fuel from the tank after you remove the retainer ring for the fuel pump/fuel level sensor module or fuel level sensor module.

---

❋❋ **WARNING:**

---

**Do NOT start the siphoning action by mouth! Use a siphoning kit (available at most auto parts stores).**

---

3    Remove the rear seat cushion (see Chapter 11).

## FUEL LEVEL SENSOR MODULE

▶ **Refer to illustrations 5.4, 5.5, 5.6, 5.7, 5.8a, 5.8b, 5.8c and 5.9**

---

❋❋ **WARNING:**

---

**See the Warning in Section 1.**

---

➡**Note: The fuel level sensor module is located in the left compartment of the fuel tank. This Section covers the removal and installation of the complete module, which is replaced as a single assembly.**

4    Remove the metal access cover (see illustration).

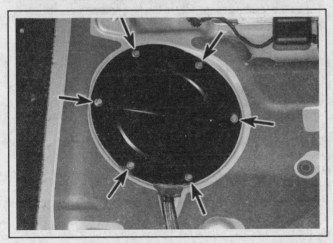

**5.4  To detach the metal access cover, remove these bolts (left access cover shown, right similar)**

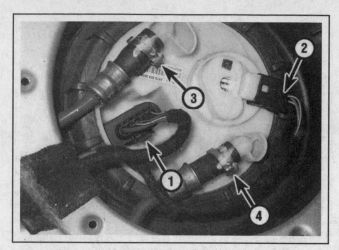

**5.5 Before removing the fuel level sensor, disconnect the following:**

1   *Fuel level sensor/fuel pump connector (depress the tab and pull it off)*
2   *Fuel pressure sensor connector (depress the tab and pull it off)*
3   *Hose clamp - fuel supply hose*
4   *Hose clamp - fuel return hose*

5   Disconnect the electrical connectors from the fuel level sensor module (see illustration). Cut off and discard the special hose clamps that secure the fuel supply and return hoses to the fuel level sensor locating cover, then disconnect the fuel supply and return hoses from the module (these hoses go to the fuel filter/fuel pressure regulator on the back of the fuel tank).

**❊❊ WARNING:**

**Do NOT attempt to re-use the special hose clamps used to secure the fuel supply and return hoses to the fuel level sensor locating cover. These clamps must be replaced! Failure to do so could allow fuel to leak out and could cause a fire.**

6   To prevent dirt from entering the fuel tank, clean the area surrounding the retainer that secures the mounting flange for the fuel level sensor module. Then, using a special fuel pump retainer tool (available at most auto parts stores), unscrew the retainer (see illustration).

➡Note: If you don't have a special fuel pump retainer tool, use very large water pump pliers. Use some clean shop rags to protect the nylon retainer from damage from the teeth on the pliers. These rings can be so tight that you might not be able to loosen the ring on your vehicle with pliers. If so, we recommend buying or borrowing the correct tool.

7   Before removing the fuel level sensor module from the fuel tank, be sure to mark the orientation of the module to the tank (see illustration). There's a raised arrow on the locating cover, next to the fuel pressure regulator, but it's difficult to see. You can fix that by coloring it black with a permanent marker. There is also a raised alignment mark on top of the fuel tank, but it's also difficult to see, because it's located too far from the arrow on the locating cover to be of much use; in fact, it's located beyond the circumference of the fuel level sensor access hole in the floor. So, make your own mark next to the arrow on the locating cover. This step is critical, because if the fuel level sensor module is incorrectly aligned when you install it, the float arm could be restricted or damaged.

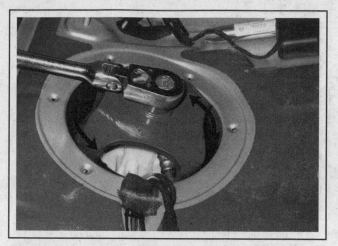

**5.6 Use a fuel pump retainer tool to loosen and unscrew the fuel level sensor. If you don't have this tool, try using large water pump pliers instead (use shop rags to protect the retainer from the teeth on the pliers)**

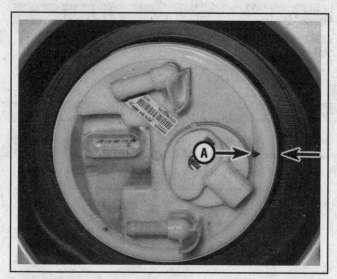

**5.7 Before removing the fuel level sensor module, be sure to mark the orientation of the locating cover. There is an arrow (A) on the locating cover next to the fuel pressure sensor - make a corresponding alignment mark on the tank**

8   Lift the fuel level sensor module up out of the fuel tank far enough to disconnect the electrical connector underneath (see illustration). Then disconnect the fuel supply hose (the upper hose) and the fuel return hose (lower hose) from the module (see illustrations). Remove the fuel level sensor module from the fuel tank. Tilt the sensor module as necessary to protect the fuel level sensor float arm from damage. Remove and discard the old sealing ring.

9   When installing the fuel level sensor module, be sure to install a new sealing ring (see illustration) and a new O-ring for the fuel supply hose elbow.

10  Before securing the fuel level sensor with the retaining ring, make sure that the arrow on the locating cover is aligned with the mark that you made before removing the fuel level sensor module. Installation is otherwise the reverse of removal.

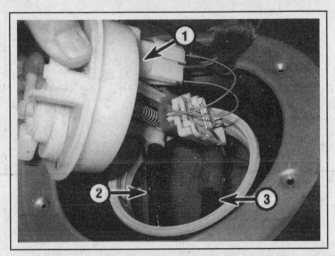

**5.8a** Lift up the fuel level sensor module far enough to disconnect the electrical connector (1), then release the tabs and disconnect the fuel supply hose (2) and return hose (3) from the module

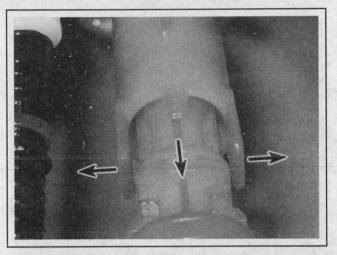

**5.8b** To disconnect the fuel return hose, spread these two tangs apart and pull the hose out of the fitting (this hose is routed through the fuel tank back to the fuel pump/fuel level sensor module in the right half of the tank)

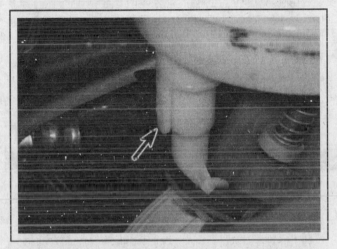

**5.8c** To disconnect the fuel supply hose, release the tab from the hose elbow. Be sure to replace the O-ring on the hose elbow

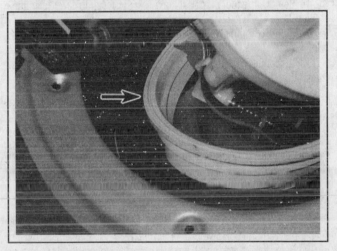

**5.9** Be sure to install a new sealing ring before installing the fuel level sensor module

## FUEL PUMP/FUEL LEVEL SENSOR MODULE

▶ **Refer to illustrations 5.14 and 5.16**

➡**Note: The fuel pump/fuel level sensor module is located in the right compartment of the fuel tank. This module includes the fuel pump inlet strainer, the fuel pump and the fuel level sensor for the right fuel tank compartment. This Section covers the removal and installation of the complete module, which is removed as a single assembly. None of the components on the fuel pump module can be replaced individually. If one of these components is defective, you must replace the fuel pump/fuel level sensor module.**

11  Remove the metal access cover (see illustration 5.4).

12  To prevent dirt from entering the fuel tank, clean the area surrounding the retainer that secures the mounting flange for the fuel pump/fuel level sensor module. Then using a special fuel pump retainer tool (available at most auto parts stores), unscrew the retainer (see illustration 5.6).

➡**Note: If you don't have a special fuel pump retainer tool, use very large water pump pliers.**

Use some clean shop rags to protect the nylon retainer from damage from the teeth on the pliers. These rings can be so tight that you might not be able to loosen the ring on your vehicle with pliers. If so, we recommend buying or borrowing the correct tool.

13  Before removing the fuel pump/fuel level sensor module from the fuel tank, be sure to mark the orientation of the module to the tank (see illustration 5.7). There's a raised arrow on the locating cover, next to the fuel pressure regulator, but it's difficult to see. You can fix that by coloring it black with a permanent marker. There is also a raised alignment mark on top of the fuel tank, but it's also difficult to see, because it's located too far from the arrow on the locating cover to be of much use; in fact, it's located beyond the circumference of the fuel level sensor access hole in the floor. So, make your own mark next to the arrow on the locating cover. This step is critical, because if the fuel level sensor module is incorrectly aligned when you install it, the float arm could be restricted or damaged.

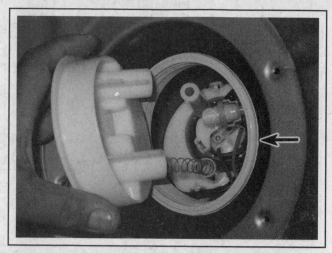

**5.14  Remove the locating cover from the fuel pump/fuel level sensor module, then remove and discard the old sealing ring**

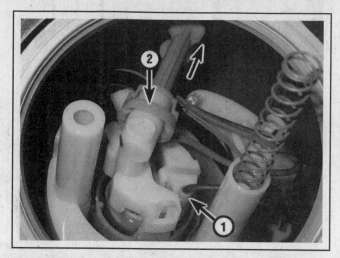

**5.16  Disconnect the electrical connector (1) from the fuel pump/fuel level sensor, then disconnect the fuel supply line fitting (2)**

14  Remove the fuel pump/fuel level sensor locating cover (see illustration).

15  Remove and discard the old fuel pump/fuel level sensor sealing ring.

16  Disconnect the electrical connector from the fuel pump/fuel level sensor module (see illustration), then place the harness safely out of the way.

17  Disconnect the fuel supply hose then lift up the fuel pump/fuel level sensor module far enough to disconnect the fuel return hose underneath.

18  Remove the fuel pump/fuel level sensor module from the tank. Tilt the pump/sensor module as necessary to protect the fuel level sensor float arm from damage.

19  Installation is the reverse of removal.

## 6  Fuel filter/fuel pressure regulator - replacement

▶ **Refer to illustrations 6.3a, 6.3b and 6.4**

1  Relieve the fuel system pressure (see Section 2), then disconnect the cable from the negative battery terminal (see Chapter 5, Section 1).

2  Raise the vehicle and support it securely on jackstands.

3  Remove the left under-cover (see illustrations).

4  Disconnect the fuel hoses from both ends of the fuel filter (see illustration). If you're unfamiliar with the special hose clamps used to secure the fuel hoses to the fuel filter, refer to Section 4.

5  Remove the fuel filter clamp bolt (see illustration 6.4) and remove the filter.

6  Installation is the reverse of removal.

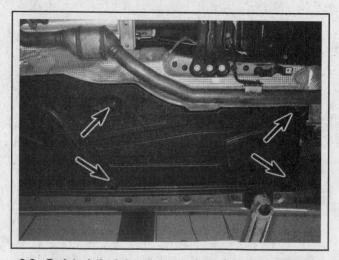

**6.3a  To detach the left under-cover from the vehicle, remove these nuts from the front . . .**

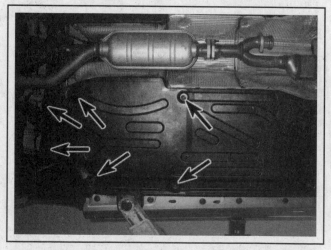

**6.3b  . . . and these nuts from the rear, then pull the cover straight down**

**6.4 Fuel filter/fuel pressure regulator details:**

1   *Fuel supply hose (from fuel pump)*
2   *Fuel return hose (back to fuel tank)*
3   *Vent hose (for fuel pressure regulator diaphragm)*
4   *Fuel supply hose (to fuel rail)*
5   *Mounting clamp bolt*

## 7 Fuel tank - removal and installation

▶ Refer to illustrations 7.11, 7.14, 7.19 and 7.21

### ✳✳ WARNING:

See the Warning in Section 1.

### ✳✳ WARNING:

Removing and installing the fuel tank on these vehicles is difficult - and could be dangerous - because you must lower the entire rear suspension assembly before you can remove the tank. To lower the suspension assembly, you must devise a way to firmly support the entire rear suspension assembly, and you must lower it far enough to allow sufficient clearance to lower the fuel tank. If you're working at home, you're probably going to be working under the vehicle while it's on jackstands, which means that you won't have a lot of room to work. We therefore don't recommend tackling this job at home. It's much easier to do when the vehicle is raised on a vehicle hoist, which allows you enough room to get a transmission jack under the rear suspension assembly.

1   Relieve the fuel system pressure (see Section 2).
2   Disconnect the cable from the negative battery terminal (see Chapter 5, Section 1).
3   Remove the rear seat cushion (see Chapter 11).
4   Remove the access panels for the fuel level sensor and for the fuel pump/fuel level sensor module, then remove the retaining rings for both modules (see Section 5). Working through the access hole for the fuel level sensor, disconnect the electrical connector from the sensor assembly.
5   Lift up the fuel level sensor from the left side of the fuel tank and siphon out as much fuel as possible. Then lift up the fuel pump/fuel level sensor from the right side of the tank and siphon out as much fuel out as possible.

### ✳✳ WARNING:

Never start the siphoning action by mouth!

6   Loosen the rear wheel bolts. Raise the vehicle and place it securely on jackstands. Remove the rear wheels.
7   Remove the two under covers (see illustrations 6.3a and 6.3b).
8   Remove the entire rear exhaust system from the flange in front of the pre-muffler to the muffler/tailpipe (see Section 16).
9   Remove the retaining nuts that secure the exhaust pipe heat shields and remove the heat shields.
10   Detach the driveshaft from the rear differential flange (see Chapter 8).
11   Remove the parking brake cable cover (see illustration 11.9 in Chapter 9), then disconnect the parking brake cables from the equalizer (see illustration) and pull the cables out of the cable bracket.

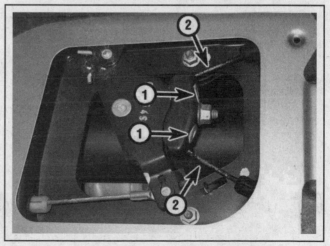

**7.11 To disconnect the parking brake cables from the equalizer, remove the plugs (1), then remove each parking brake cable (2) end plug through the hole and detach the cable**

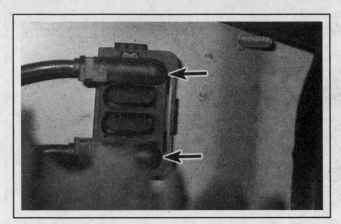

**7.14  These two wheel speed sensor electrical connectors are plugged into a terminal located directly above the right inner CV joint. Clearly label both connectors, then disconnect them**

12  If the rear brake calipers are equipped with rear brake pad wear sensors, disconnect the sensors from the calipers, then trace the sensor leads and disengage them from any clips on the rear suspension assembly and carefully set aside the leads. Unbolt and remove the rear brake calipers and support them with lengths of wire (see Chapter 9).

➡**Note: It's not necessary to disconnect the brake hoses from the calipers.**

13  Remove the rear stabilizer bar (see Chapter 10).

14  Locate the electrical terminal for the rear wheel speed sensor leads in the underside of the vehicle body, directly above the right inner CV joint (see illustration), and disconnect the two wheel speed sensor leads from the terminal.

15  Remove the coil springs (see Chapter 10).

16  Support the rear suspension assembly, preferably with an adjustable-head transmission jack. The crossmember must be securely supported on each side, front and rear. It might be necessary to fabricate a fixture to supplement the jack in order to accomplish this.

17  Remove the four large bolts that attach the rear suspension crossmembers and carefully lower the rear suspension assembly.

18  Remove the splash shield from the right rear wheel well (see Chapter 11).

19  Loosen the hose clamps for the fuel filler neck hose, fuel overflow shutoff hose and fuel tank vent hoses and disconnect all three hoses (see illustration).

20  Support the fuel tank.

21  Remove the fuel tank strap nuts (see illustration) and remove the fuel tank straps.

22  Lower the tank slightly and disconnect any remaining electrical harnesses and EVAP hoses.

23  Once everything is disconnected, lower and remove the fuel tank.

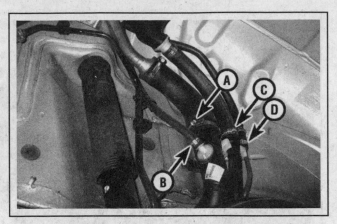

**7.19  Disconnect all four of these fuel and EVAP hoses:**

*A   Fuel filler neck hose clamp*
*B   On-Board Refueling Vapor Recovery (ORVR) hose clamp*
*C   Fuel shutoff hose clamp*
*D   Fuel tank vent hose clamp*

**7.21  To detach the fuel tank straps, remove the strap nuts**

24  Installation is the reverse of removal, noting the following points:

*a)  If you're replacing the fuel tank, remove all components from the old fuel tank and install them on the new tank. If you need help with the fuel pump/fuel level sensor module (in the right fuel tank chamber) and/or the fuel level sensor (left fuel tank chamber), refer to Section 5.*
*b)  Tighten the fuel tank strap nuts securely.*
*c)  Be sure to adjust the parking brake cables when you're done (see Chapter 9).*

## 8  Fuel tank cleaning and repair - general information

1  The fuel tank installed in the vehicles covered by this manual is not repairable. If it becomes damaged, it must be replaced.

2  Cleaning the fuel tank (due to fuel contamination) should be performed by a professional with the proper training to carry out this critical and potentially dangerous work. Even after cleaning and flushing, explosive fumes may remain inside the fuel tank.

3  If the fuel tank is removed from the vehicle, it should not be placed in an area where sparks or open flames could ignite the fumes coming out of the tank. Be especially careful inside a garage where a gas-type appliance is located.

## 9 Air filter housing and air intake duct - removal and installation

### V6 MODELS

#### Vehicles with a remote air filter housing

➡ Note: On some 2001 through 2005 models, the air filter housing is located in the right front corner of the engine compartment and is connected to the throttle body by an air intake duct equipped with a resonator that is bolted to the engine.

#### Air intake duct

1  Disconnect the PCV fresh air inlet hose from the air intake duct.
2  Unbolt the resonator from the engine.
3  Loosen the hose clamps at both ends of the air intake duct and remove the duct.

#### Air filter housing

4  Remove the air intake duct.

5  Disconnect the electrical connector from the Mass Air Flow/Intake Air Temperature (MAF/IAT) sensor.
6  Remove the air filter housing.
7  Installation is the reverse of removal.

#### Vehicles with an integral engine cover/air filter housing

▶ Refer to illustrations 9.8, 9.9, 9.10a and 9.10b

➡ Note: On most 2001 and later V6 models, the two air filter housings (one above each valve cover) are integrated into the main engine cover. On 2006 and later V6 models, the housing has a large opening in the center for the Powertrain Control Module (PCM), which is mounted on top of the intake manifold.

8  Remove the front engine cover (see illustration).
9  Remove the fresh air intake ducts (see illustration).
10  Remove the air filter housing (see illustrations).
11  Installation is the reverse of removal.

9.8  Pull up the front edge of the cover to disengage the front retaining clips and locator pin, then pull the cover forward to disengage the two rear retaining clips at the back of the cover (2001 through 2005 V6 models)

9.9  Pull off the fresh air intake ducts from the air filter housing

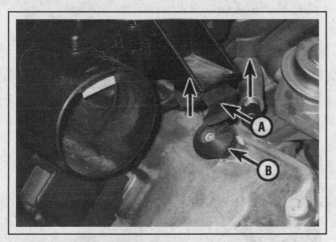

9.10a  To remove the engine cover/air filter housing on 2001 through 2005 V6 models, disengage the two front retaining clips (A) from their mounting grommets (B) . . .

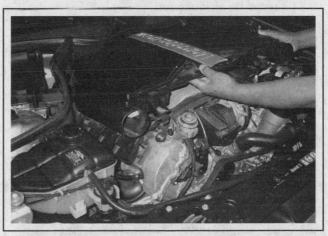

9.10b  . . . then lift up the front of the cover/filter housing and disengage the two rear retaining clips from their mounting grommets and remove the cover/filter housing as a single assembly (see Chapter 1 for filter replacement)

## FOUR-CYLINDER MODELS

### 2002 models

→Note: **There are two different air filter housings used on the 2002 models. They're both located at the front of the engine compartment, and are long and narrow so they can fit transversely, directly in front of the engine. The two filter housings look similar, but they're not.**

### Early air filter housing (engine type 111.951)

12 Rotate the air inlet pipe lock counterclockwise and disconnect the air inlet pipe from the air filter housing.

13 Disconnect the electrical connector from the MAF/IAT sensor.

14 Loosen the air intake duct hose clamp and disconnect the duct.

15 Push aside the inlet pipe and lift the air filter housing up and off. Installation is the reverse of removal.

### Later air filter housing (engine type 111.955)

16 Remove the air filter housing retaining screw.

17 Rotate the air inlet pipe lock counterclockwise (and disconnect the air inlet pipe from the air filter housing).

18 Loosen the connecting duct hose clamp and disconnect the connecting duct from the air filter housing. (The connecting duct connects the air filter housing to the recirculating air flap actuator.)

19 Lift the air filter housing up and off.

20 Installation is the reverse of removal.

### 2003 through 2005 four-cylinder models

♦ Refer to illustrations 9.22, 9.24a, 9.24b, 9.24c, 9.27 and 9.28

21 Disconnect the cable from the negative terminal of the battery (see Chapter 5, Section 1).

22 Disconnect the air duct from the air filter housing (see illustration).

23 Disconnect the hose from the back of the air filter housing.

24 Disconnect the electrical connectors from the Powertrain Control Module, the Mass Air Flow (MAF) sensor and the altitude sensor (see illustrations).

25 Disconnect the PCV crankcase ventilation hose from the back of the air filter housing.

26 Loosen the hose clamp that secures the air intake duct to the back of the air filter housing.

27 Remove the two air filter housing bolts (see illustration).

28 To remove the air filter housing, pull the rear part of the housing up and toward the firewall, then lift the air filter housing out of its rubber mounts (see illustration).

29 Installation is the reverse of removal.

**9.22  Remove the air intake duct**

**9.24a  Flip up the lock and disconnect the electrical connectors from the PCM**

**9.24b  Disconnect the electrical connector from the Mass Airflow (MAF) sensor**

**9.24c  Disconnect the electrical connector from the altitude sensor**

**9.27 Air filter housing mounting bolt locations - 2003 and later four cylinder engine (housing removed for clarity)**

**9.28 Pull the filter housing up at the rear and move it toward the firewall, then lift it from its rubber mounts**

## 10 Fuel injection system - general information

The injectors are small computer-controlled solenoids that inject fuel into the air intake passages. In a sequential multiport fuel injection (ME-SFI) system, the injectors squirt fuel in the cylinder firing order. The Powertrain Control Module (PCM) turns the injectors on and off. When the engine is running, the PCM constantly monitors engine operating conditions with an array of information sensors, calculates the correct amount of fuel, then varies the pulse width (the interval of time during which the injectors are open). Sequential MFI systems provide good power, decent mileage and lower emissions.

The ME-SFI system uses the PCM and information sensors to determine and deliver the correct air/fuel ratio under all operating conditions. The ME-SFI system consists of three sub-systems: air induction, electronic control and fuel delivery. The ME-SFI system is integrated with many PCM-controlled emission control systems. (For information about the PCM, information sensors and emission control systems, refer to Chapter 6.)

### AIR INDUCTION SYSTEM

The air induction system consists of the air filter housing, the Mass Air Flow/Intake Air Temperature (MAF/IAT) sensor, the air intake duct, the intake resonator (on models with a remote air filter housing), the throttle body and the intake manifold. On V6 models, there are two air filter elements housed in an integral engine cover/air filter housing mounted on top of the engine. On four-cylinder models, only one filter element is used. The throttle body contains a throttle plate that regulates the amount of air entering the intake manifold. There is no accelerator cable. The throttle plate is opened and closed in response to input from the Accelerator Pedal Position (APP) sensor. When you depress the accelerator pedal, the APP sensor measures the angle of the pedal and sends a voltage signal to the Powertrain Control Module (PCM) that's proportional to the pedal angle. The PCM processes this input, then commands a solenoid motor inside the throttle body to open or close the throttle plate accordingly.

The Mass Air Flow/Intake Air Temperature (MAF/IAT) sensor is located between the air filter housing and the air intake duct. The MAF sensor measures the mass of air entering the engine. The Intake Air Temperature (IAT) sensor, which is an integral component of the MAF sensor, relays a voltage signal to the PCM that varies in accordance with the temperature of the incoming air. The PCM uses this data from the MAF and IAT sensors to calculate how rich or lean the air/fuel mixture should be.

All of the air induction components are covered in this Chapter, except for the intake manifold, which is covered in Chapter 2, and the information sensors, which are covered in Chapter 6.

There is no Idle Air Control (IAC) valve on these engines. When the engine is idling, the PCM maintains the correct idle speed by regulating the angle of the throttle plate. The idle speed is controlled by the PCM in response to the running conditions of the engine (cold or warm running, power steering pressure high or low, air conditioning system on or off, etc.). As the PCM receives data from the information sensors (vehicle speed, coolant temperature, air conditioning and/or power steering load, etc.) it adjusts the idle according to the demands of the engine and driver. The idle control system consists of the PCM, the throttle plate solenoid motor inside the throttle body, and several information sensors, including the Engine Coolant Temperature (ECT) sensor, the Intake Air Temperature (IAT) sensor and the Mass Air Flow (MAF) sensor.

### ELECTRONIC CONTROL SYSTEM

For more information about the electronic control system, including the PCM, its information sensors and output actuators, refer to Chapter 6.

### FUEL DELIVERY SYSTEM

The fuel delivery system consists of the fuel pump/fuel level sensor module, the fuel rail and fuel injectors, and the hoses, lines and pipes that carry fuel between all of these components. This is a returnless system; there is no fuel return line from the fuel rail back to the fuel tank. For more information about the fuel lines and fittings, refer to Section 4.

Because of the tunnel in the fuel tank for the driveshaft and the exhaust system, the tank is essentially divided into two tanks, although it's a one-piece assembly. The two halves of the fuel tank are connected by a crossover tube which utilizes a siphon effect produced by the fuel pump to ensure that the two sides of the fuel tank contain an equal amount of fuel.

There are two fuel level sensors, one for each side of the tank. The fuel level sensor for the left half of the tank is a stand-alone unit. The fuel level sensor for the right half of the tank is an integral component of the fuel pump/fuel level sensor module. The fuel pump/fuel level sensor module cannot be disassembled. If either component is defective, you must replace the entire assembly.

The fuel filter/fuel pressure regulator is located directly behind the left half of the fuel tank. The fuel pressure regulator maintains the fuel pressure within the specified operating range. When the fuel pressure inside the fuel filter housing exceeds the design threshold, the fuel pressure regulator opens and dumps the excess fuel back into the fuel tank (there is no fuel return line from the fuel rail back to the tank). Excess fuel is sent back to the left fuel level sensor, and from there it's routed through a hose over to the fuel pump/fuel level sensor in the right half of the fuel tank where it's dumped back into the tank. The fuel pump provides the siphoning action that pulls the excess fuel back into the tank.

The fuel rail, which is bolted to the intake manifold, functions as a reservoir for pressurized fuel so that there's always enough fuel available for acceleration and high speed operation. The upper end of each injector is inserted into the fuel rail and the lower end of each injector is inserted into the intake manifold. The upper and lower ends of each injector are sealed by O-rings.

Each fuel injector is a solenoid-actuated, pintle-type design consisting of a solenoid, plunger, valve, and housing. When the engine is running, there is always voltage on the hot side of each injector terminal. Injector drivers inside the PCM turn the injectors on and off by switching their ground paths on and off. When the ground path for an injector is closed by the PCM, current flows through the solenoid coil, a valve inside the injector opens and pressurized fuel squirts out the nozzle into the intake port above the intake valves. The quantity of fuel injected each time an injector opens is determined by its pulse width, which is the interval of time during which the valve is open.

## 11  Fuel injection system - check

▶ **Refer to illustration 11.7**

➡**Note: The following procedure is based on the assumption that the fuel pressure is adequate (see Section 3).**

1  Inspect all electrical connectors that are related to the system. Check the ground wire connections on the intake manifold for tightness. Loose connectors and poor grounds can cause many problems that resemble more serious malfunctions.

2  Verify that the battery is fully charged, as the control unit and sensors depend on an accurate supply of voltage in order to properly meter the fuel.

3  Inspect the air filter element (see Chapter 1). A dirty or partially blocked filter will severely impede performance and economy.

4  Check the related fuses. If a blown fuse is found, replace it and see if it blows again. If it does, search for a grounded wire in the harness.

5  Inspect the condition of all vacuum hoses connected to the intake manifold.

6  Remove the air intake duct and air resonator box (if equipped) and inspect the mouth of the throttle body for dirt, carbon or other residue build-up. If it's dirty, wipe it clean with a shop towel.

7  With the engine running, place an automotive stethoscope against each injector, one at a time, and listen for a clicking sound, indicating operation (see illustration).

8  If an injector doesn't make a clicking sound, disconnect the electrical connector and measure the resistance of that injector, then measure the resistance of the other injectors and compare the resistance of all six injectors.

    a) *If the resistance of the silent injector is well outside the range of indicated resistance for the other injectors, the injector is defective.*

    b) *If the indicated resistance of all the injectors is within the same range, the Powertrain Control Module (PCM) or the injector wiring harness could be the cause of the injector not operating.*

9  Any further testing of the fuel injection system should be performed at a dealer service department or other qualified repair shop.

10  For more information about the engine control system, refer to Chapter 6.

**11.7 Use an automotive stethoscope to listen to each fuel injector, which should make a clicking sound that rises and falls with engine speed changes**

## 12  Throttle body - removal and installation

### V6 MODELS

♦ **Refer to illustrations 12.3, 12.4a, 12.4b, 12.4c, 12.5 and 12.6**

➡**Note:** The throttle body is located below the back of the engine cover/air filter housing, on the back end of the intake manifold, between the Mass Air Flow/Intake Air Temperature (MAF/IAT) sensor and the intake manifold. The accompanying photos depict a typical throttle body on a 2001 through 2005 V6 model, but the throttle body used on later models is virtually identical.

1   Remove the engine cover/air filter housing (see Section 9).
2   Remove the Mass Air Flow/Intake Air Temperature (MAF/IAT) sensor (see Chapter 6).
3   Disconnect the PCV hose/EVAP purge hose connection from the throttle body (see illustration).
4   Remove the elbow-shaped air intake duct (see illustrations).
5   Remove the four throttle body mounting bolts (see illustration) and remove the throttle body from the intake manifold.
6   Disconnect the electrical connector from the throttle body (see illustration).

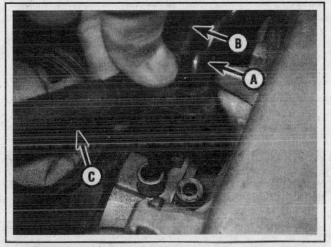

**12.3  To disconnect the connection for the EVAP purge line and the PCV hoses from the throttle body, simply pull it straight up**

A   EVAP purge line
B   PCV hose from left valve cover
C   PCV hose from right valve cover

**12.4a  To remove the elbow-shaped air intake duct from the throttle body, lift up and disengage the upper tab from its lug . . .**

**12.4b  . . . push down and disengage the lower tab from its lug . . .**

**12.4c  . . . and remove the air intake duct (intake manifold removed for clarity)**

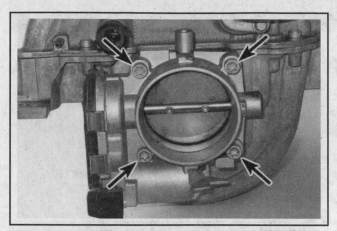

**12.5 To detach the throttle body from the intake manifold, remove these four bolts (intake manifold removed for clarity)**

7    Remove the throttle body gasket and discard it. Always use a new gasket when installing the throttle body.

8    Wipe off the gasket mating surfaces of the throttle body and the intake manifold.

**✳✳ CAUTION:**

**Never soak the throttle body in solvent or in any type of carburetor cleaner. Do not even use spray carburetor cleaners or silicone lubricants on any part of the throttle body.**

9    Installation is the reverse of removal. Be sure to tighten the throttle body mounting bolts to the torque listed in this Chapter's Specifications.

## FOUR-CYLINDER MODELS

### 2002 models

10   Remove the engine trim panels.

11   Loosen the hose clamp that connects the air scoop (the short horn-shaped air intake duct between the MAF/IAT sensor and the throttle body to the MAF/IAT sensor, unbolt the air scoop from the throttle body and remove the scoop.

12   Disconnect the electrical connector from the throttle body.

13   Remove the throttle body mounting bolts and remove the throttle

**12.18 Depress the tabs and detach the electrical connector from the throttle body (2003 and later four-cylinder engines)**

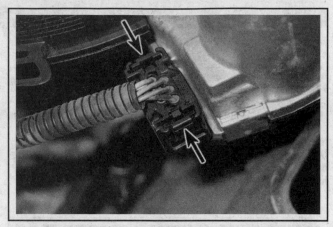

**12.6 To disconnect the electrical connector from the throttle body, depress these release tabs and pull off the connector**

body.

14   Remove and discard the throttle body gasket. Always use a new gasket when installing the throttle body.

15   Wipe off the gasket mating surfaces of the throttle body and the intake manifold.

**✳✳ CAUTION:**

**Never soak the throttle body in solvent or in any type of carburetor cleaner. Do not even use spray carburetor cleaners or silicone lubricants on any part of the throttle body.**

16   Installation is the reverse of removal. Be sure to use a new throttle body gasket and tighten the throttle body mounting bolts to the torque listed in this Chapter's Specifications.

### 2003 through 2005 four-cylinder models

▶ **Refer to illustrations 12.18, 12.19a, 12.19b, 12.21a, 12.21b and 12.22**

17   Remove the air filter housing (see Section 9).

18   Disconnect the electrical connector from the throttle body (see illustration).

19   Disconnect the pressure connection (the pressurized air intake duct coming up from the outlet side of the intercooler) (see illustrations).

20   Disconnect the purge valve vacuum line from the throttle body.

21   Remove the throttle body mounting bolts and remove the throttle body (see illustrations).

22   Remove the throttle body gasket and discard it. Always use a new gasket when installing the throttle body.

23   Wipe off the gasket mating surfaces of the throttle body and the intake manifold.

**✳✳ CAUTION:**

**Never soak the throttle body in solvent or in any type of carburetor cleaner. Do not even use spray carburetor cleaners or silicone lubricants on any part of the throttle body.**

24   Installation is the reverse of removal. Be sure to tighten the throttle body mounting bolts to the torque listed in this Chapter's Specifications.

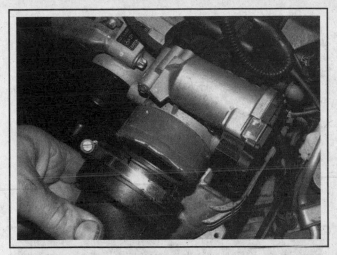

12.19a  Disconnect the pressure duct connection . . .

12.19b  . . . and remove the sealing collar

12.21a  Unscrew the throttle body
mounting bolts . . .

12.21b  . . . and remove the throttle
body (2003 and later four-cylinder
engines)

12.22  Remove the old throttle body
gasket and install a new one

## 13  Fuel rail and injectors - removal and installation

### V6 MODELS

▶ Refer to illustrations 13.6, 13.8, 13.9, 13.10, 13.11, 13.12, 13.13 and 13.14

❋❋ **WARNING 1:**

See the Warning in Section 1.

❋❋ **WARNING 2:**

The engine must be completely cool before beginning this procedure.

➡Note: The photos accompanying this Section depict the fuel rail and injector assembly used on 2001 through 2005 models. 2006 and later models use a slightly different fuel rail assembly, but it's similar enough that you will have no problem using this procedure to remove, disassemble, reassemble and install it.

1  Remove the engine cover/air filter housing (see Section 9).
2  Relieve the fuel system pressure (see Section 2), then disconnect the cable from the negative terminal of the battery (see Chapter 5, Section 1).
3  On models with a remote air filter housing, remove the air intake duct and resonator (see Section 9).
4  Disconnect the Exhaust Gas Recirculation (EGR) purge line from the throttle body (see illustration 12.3).
5  Detach the plastic covers from the fuel injector/ignition coil harness.

6   On 2001 through 2005 models, disconnect the engine harness from the following components, then set the harness aside:

    *Fuel injectors (see illustration)*
    *Ignition coils (see Chapter 5)*
    *Air injection pump (see Chapter 6)*
    *Exhaust Gas Recirculation (EGR) purge valve (see Chapter 6)*
    *Camshaft Position (CMP) sensor (see Chapter 6)*
    *Manifold Absolute Pressure (MAP) sensor (see Chapter 6)*
    *Engine Coolant Temperature (ECT) sensor (see Chapter 6)*
    *Air injection switchover valve and shutoff valves (see Chapter 6)*
    *Alternator (see Chapter 5)*
    *Starter (see Chapter 5)*
    *Oil sensor (see Chapter 2)*

7   On 2006 and later models, disconnect the right electrical connector from the Powertrain Control Module (PCM) (see Chapter 6), but do NOT disconnect the left electrical connector from the PCM. Then detach the PCM from its left and right mounting brackets (see Chapter 6) and carefully lay the PCM and harness aside. Also disconnect the two large electrical connectors and detach the larger of these two connectors from the fuel rail.

8   Disconnect the fuel supply hose fitting from the fuel rail (see illustration). On 2006 and later models, also disconnect the PCV hoses.

9   Remove the fuel rail mounting bolts (see illustration).

10  Remove the fuel rail and injectors as a single assembly (see illustration).

**13.6  To disconnect the electrical connector from each fuel injector, squeeze the wire retainers and pull off the connector (2001 through 2005 V6 model shown, 2006 and later V6 models similar)**

**13.8  Fuel supply hose fitting at the fuel rail (2006 and later V6 models shown, earlier V6 models similar)**

**13.9  Fuel rail mounting bolts (2001 through 2005 V6 model shown, 2006 and later V6 models similar)**

**13.10  Remove the fuel rail and injectors as a single assembly**

11 Remove each injector retainer clip (see illustration) and remove the injector from the fuel rail.

12 Remove and discard the old injector O-rings (see illustration).

13 Install the retainer clip on each injector, then align the slots on the retainer with the flared edges of the injector mounting hole (see illustration) and insert the injector into the fuel rail until the retainer snaps into place.

14 Push each injector down into its mounting hole until the slots on each retainer are fully engaged with the flared edges of the injector mounting hole (see illustration).

15 Installation is the reverse of removal.

## FOUR-CYLINDER MODELS

### 2002 models

16 Remove the engine trim panels.

17 Relieve the fuel system pressure (see Section 2), then disconnect the cable from the negative battery terminal (see Chapter 5, Section 1).

### Pulsation damper

18 Remove the locking clamp (and pull out the pulsation damper).

19 Remove the pulsation damper O-ring.

20 Installation is the reverse of removal. Be sure to use a new O-ring.

13.11  Note how the retainers are installed, then remove each retainer with needle nose pliers

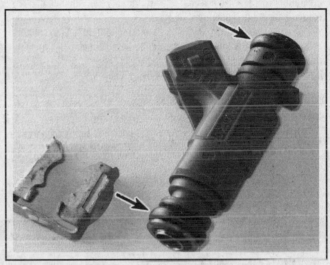

13.12  Remove and discard the old injector O-rings. Use new O-rings even if you're planning to install the old injectors

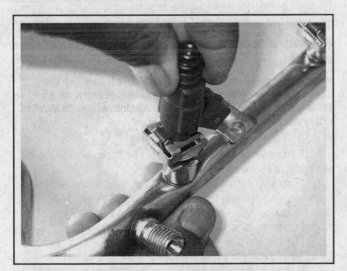

13.13  To install each injector, install the retainer on the injector, then align the slots in the retainer with the flared edges of the injector mounting hole and insert the injector into the fuel rail

13.14  Push the injector down into its mounting hole until the slots on each retainer are fully engaged with the flared edges of the injector mounting hole

### Fuel rail and injectors

21 Disconnect the fuel supply line from the fuel rail.

22 Disconnect the electrical connectors from the fuel injectors.

23 Remove the two fuel rail mounting bolts.

24 Remove the fuel rail and injectors as a single assembly.

25 Remove the injector retainer clip (and remove the injector from the fuel rail).

26 Remove each injector retainer clip (see illustration 13.11) and remove the injector from the fuel rail.

27 Remove and discard the old injector O-rings (see illustration 13.12).

28 Install the retainer clip on each injector, then align the slots on the retainer with the flared edges of the injector mounting hole (see illustration 13.13) and insert the injector into the fuel rail until the retainer snaps into place.

29 Push each injector down into its mounting hole until the slots on each retainer are fully engaged with the flared edges of the injector mounting hole (see illustration 13.14).

30 Installation is the reverse of removal.

### 2003 through 2005 models

31 Remove the air filter housing (see Section 9).

32 Relieve fuel system pressure (see Section 2), then disconnect the cable from the negative battery terminal (see Chapter 5, Section 1).

### Pulsation damper

33 This procedure is virtually identical to the procedure for removing and installing the pulsation damper on 2002 models (see Steps 18 through 20).

### Fuel rail and injectors

34 Disconnect the fuel supply line from the fuel rail.

35 Detach the fuel injector harness clip.

36 Disconnect the electrical connectors from the fuel injectors.

37 Remove the two fuel rail mounting bolts.

38 Remove the fuel rail and injectors as a single assembly.

39 Remove each injector retainer clip (see illustration 13.11) and remove the injector from the fuel rail.

40 Remove and discard the old injector O-rings (see illustration 13.12).

41 Install the retainer clip on each injector, then align the slots on the retainer with the flared edges of the injector mounting hole (see illustration 13.13) and insert the injector into the fuel rail until the retainer snaps into place.

42 Push each injector down into its mounting hole until the slots on each retainer are fully engaged with the flared edges of the injector mounting hole (see illustration 13.14).

43 Installation is the reverse of removal.

## 14 Supercharger system (2002 four-cylinder models) - description and component replacement

## DESCRIPTION

1 On early 2002 models with the 2.3L four-cylinder engine (111.951), the belt-driven supercharger is mounted on the right side of the engine block. An electromagnetic clutch (like the clutch used on an air conditioning compressor) disengages the supercharger when no boost is needed, and engages it when boost is needed. The system is intercooled; the intercooler is located across the lower front part of the engine compartment. Outside air is routed from the air filter housing into the supercharger, where it's pressurized before traveling through the intercooler. From the intercooler, the compressed air is routed through the Mass Air Flow/Intake Air Temperature (MAF/IAT) sensor, then through the throttle body and into the intake manifold.

2 On later 2002 models with the same 2.3L four-cylinder engine (111.955), the supercharger is still mounted on the right side of the engine block, but the plumbing is different. This system includes the air filter housing, the resonance body, the electronic air flap actuator, the inlet and pressure connection (manifold), the supercharger, the intercooler and the air ducts connecting these components.

3 The important difference between the two systems is the means by which boost is controlled. The early 2002 system uses a clutching device to disengage the supercharger when it's not needed. On the later 2002 system, the supercharger runs all the time and boost is controlled by the PCM-controlled air flap actuator. When the air flap actuator is closed, all boosted air goes through the intercooler to the intake manifold. When the flap is open, boosted air coming out of the blower is recirculated back into the resonance body, which is sort of like a resonator on an air intake duct on a normally aspirated system. When the flap is anywhere between fully closed and fully open, the amount of boost is proportional to the angle of the flap, which means that the manifold pressure can be anywhere between almost full boost and intake manifold vacuum. The PCM determines the position of the flap in relation to engine load, engine speed, etc.

## COMPONENT REPLACEMENT

### Resonance body and recirculated air flap actuator assembly

➡**Note: The recirculated air flap actuator is located on the underside of the forward end of the resonance body, which functions as an accumulator or reservoir for redirected boosted intake air when the air flap is open.**

4 Remove the engine cover.

5 Remove the two bolts that secure the resonance body to the inlet and pressure connection.

6 Disconnect the two vent lines from the resonance body. (One of these vent lines connects the resonance body to the valve cover; the other line connects the resonance body to the engine block.)

7 Loosen the hose clamp that secures the recirculated air flap actuator to the inlet and pressure connection. (You might have to remove the air filter housing to access the screw for this clamp.)

8 Pull up on the recirculated air flap actuator until you can disconnect the electrical connector from the air flap actuator (then remove the resonance body and air flap actuator as a single assembly).

9 Remove and inspect the O-ring that seals the connection between the air flap actuator and the inlet and pressure connection.

10 Installation is the reverse of removal.

### Recirculated air flap actuator

11  Remove the resonance body and recirculated air flap actuator assembly (see Steps 4 through 9).

12  Separate the air flap actuator from the resonance body.

13  Installation is the reverse of removal.

### Inlet and pressure connection

14  Remove the resonance body and recirculated flap actuator assembly (see Steps 4 through 9).

15  Remove the bolt that secures the coolant line to the inlet and pressure connection.

16  Disconnect the air duct that connects the output end of the inlet and pressure connection to the inlet pipe of the intercooler.

17  Disconnect the vent line from the inlet and pressure connection.

18  Remove the four inlet and pressure connection mounting bolts, then remove the inlet and pressure connection.

19  Remove and replace the gasket between the inlet and pressure connection and the supercharger.

20  Installation is the reverse of removal.

### Supercharger

21  Remove the air filter housing (see Section 9).

22  Remove the resonance body and recirculated air flap actuator assembly and remove the inlet and pressure connection (see Steps 4 through 9 and 14 through 19).

23  Remove the supercharger drivebelt (see Chapter 1).

24  Remove the supercharger mounting bolts, then remove the supercharger.

25  Installation is the reverse of removal.

### Intercooler

26  Raise the vehicle and remove the engine under-cover.

27  Loosen the hose clamp and disconnect the inlet air duct from the intercooler.

28  Loosen the hose clamp and disconnect the outlet air duct from the intercooler.

29  Remove the intercooler mounting bolts, then remove the intercooler.

30  Installation is the reverse of removal.

### Charge air duct

➡Note: The charge air duct is the long L-shaped air duct that connects the outlet pipe of the intercooler to the Mass Air Flow/Intake Air Temperature (MAF/IAT) sensor.

31  Remove the air filter housing (see Section 9).

32  Disconnect the electrical connector from the MAF/IAT sensor.

33  Loosen the hose clamp that secures the short connection hose on the downstream side of the MAF/IAT sensor to the air scoop.

34  Disengage the spring clip or clamp from the lower (inlet) end of the charge air duct (down at the outlet pipe of the intercooler) and remove the charge air duct.

35  Remove the MAF/IAT sensor mounting bolts (and remove the MAF/IAT sensor from the charge air duct)

36  Remove and inspect the O-ring at the inlet end of the air charge duct.

37  Remove and inspect the O-ring at the outlet end of the air charge duct

38  Installation is the reverse of removal.

## 15  Supercharger system (2003 through 2005 four-cylinder models) - description and component replacement

## DESCRIPTION

1  The supercharging system used on 2003 through 2005 four-cylinder models uses a recirculated air flap like later 2002 models, but is otherwise completely different. The intake manifold, recirculated air flap actuator, inlet and pressure connection and supercharger are all mounted on the left side of the engine. The plumbing on this system is considerably more complex than either of the 2002 systems.

2  The supercharging system consists of the suction damper, the recirculated air flap, the supercharger, the wideband noise damper, the intercooler and the various ducts connecting these components.

## COMPONENT REPLACEMENT

### Supercharger

3  Relieve the system fuel pressure and disconnect the cable from the negative terminal of the battery.

4  Remove the engine cover and the intake manifold.

5  Remove the supercharger drivebelt (see Chapter 1).

6  Remove the upper supercharger mounting bolts.

7  Disconnect the ground cable from the inlet and pressure connection.

8  Disconnect the electrical connector from the recirculated air flap actuator.

9  Raise the front of the vehicle and place it securely on jackstands.

10  Remove the engine under-cover.

11  Remove the two intake muffler bolts, pry the intake muffler off the supercharger inlet fitting and lift the muffler up and out.

12  Remove the lower supercharger mounting bolt.

13  Detach the supercharger, rotate it 180 degrees and remove the clutch.

14  Remove the supercharger, intake and pressure connection and air flap actuator as a single assembly.

### Intake and pressure connection

15  Remove the supercharger/intake and pressure connection/air flap actuator assembly (see Steps 4 through 14).

16  Loosen the hose clamp screw and pull off the rubber boot that connects the intake and pressure connection to the supercharger.

17  Remove the (four) intake and pressure connection mounting bolts (and remove the intake and pressure connection).

18  Remove and replace the gasket between the intake and pressure connection and the supercharger.

19  Installation is the reverse of removal.

### Air recirculation flap actuator

20 Remove the supercharger/intake and pressure connection/air flap actuator assembly (see Steps 4 through 14).

21 Remove the pressure muffler.

22 Remove the four Torx mounting bolts (and remove the recirculated air flap actuator).

23 Remove and discard the old actuator gasket.

24 Installation is the reverse of removal.

### Wide band silencer

**→Note: The wide band silencer is a noise damper installed inline in the charge air duct (the pressurized duct that takes boosted air from the supercharger's pressure damper to the intercooler). The charge air duct/wide band silencer assembly is located in front of the engine. The upper end, on the left side of the engine compartment, is connected to the supercharger. The right end, in the lower right part of the engine compartment, is connected to the inlet end of the intercooler.**

25 Remove the fresh air inlet duct.

26 Loosen the hose clamp and disconnect the hose from the pipe at the lower right end of the wide band silencer (next to the mounting bolt).

27 Loosen the hose clamp that secures the lower charge air duct to the wide band silencer, then disconnect the lower charge air duct.

28 Loosen the hose clamp that secures the upper charge air hose to the wide band silencer, then disconnect the upper charge air duct.

29 Remove the two wide band silencer retaining bolts (and remove the wide band silencer).

30 Installation is the reverse of removal.

### Intercooler

**→Note: The intercooler is located at the lower front end of the vehicle, directly behind the bumper cover.**

31 Raise the vehicle and remove the engine under-cover.

32 Remove the front bumper cover (see Chapter 11).

33 Loosen the spring type clamp and disconnect the inlet charge air duct from the intercooler.

34 Remove the O-ring.

35 Loosen the spring type clamp and disconnect the outlet charge air duct from the intercooler.

36 Remove the O-ring.

37 Unclip the intercooler from the underside of the radiator.

38 Disengage the two intercooler lugs from the radiator sleeves.

39 Remove the intercooler and air scoop as a single assembly.

40 Remove the air scoop from the intercooler.

41 Installation is the reverse of removal.

## 16  Exhaust system servicing - general information

▶ **Refer to illustrations 16.1a, 16.1b, 16.1c, 16.4a and 16.4b**

**✻✻ WARNING:**

**The vehicle's exhaust system generates very high temperatures and must be allowed to cool down completely before touching any of the components. Be especially careful around the catalytic converter, which stays hot longer than other exhaust components.**

1  The exhaust system consists of the exhaust manifolds, the exhaust pipes, the catalytic converter(s), the resonator (or pre-muffler), the muffler/tailpipe assembly, various exhaust heat shields and the exhaust pipes and flanges that connect these components together. The exhaust system is isolated from the vehicle body and from chassis components by a series of rubber hangers (see illustrations). Inspect these hangers periodically for cracks or other signs of deterioration, and replace them as necessary. Some exhaust components are also supported by brackets bolted to the underside of the vehicle (see illustration). Make sure that these brackets are tightly fastened to the exhaust

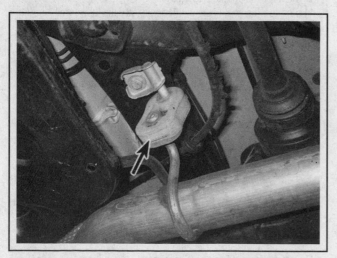

**16.1a  A typical rubber exhaust hanger for suspending the exhaust system**

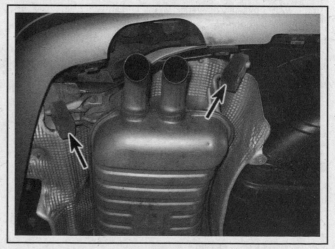

**16.1b  Sometimes two rubber exhaust hangers are used to immobilize some part of the system, such as the muffler**

**16.1c  Some parts of the exhaust system are suspended by brackets bolted to the underside of the vehicle**

**16.4a  Use penetrating oil to loosen up bolts and nuts that secure the flanges between exhaust manifolds and exhaust pipes . . .**

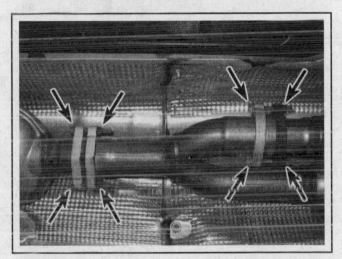

**16.4b  . . . and on the fasteners used to secure flanges farther downstream**

system and to the vehicle and that they're neither cracked nor corroded.

2   Conduct regular inspections of the exhaust system to keep it safe and quiet. Look for any damaged or bent parts, open seams, holes, loose connections, excessive corrosion or other defects which could allow exhaust fumes to enter the vehicle. Do not repair deteriorated exhaust system components; replace them with new parts.

3   If the exhaust system components are extremely corroded, or rusted together, you'll need welding equipment and a cutting torch to remove them. The convenient strategy at this point is to have a muffler repair shop remove the corroded sections with a cutting torch. If you want to save money by doing it yourself, but you don't have a welding outfit and cutting torch, simply cut off the old components with a hacksaw. If you have compressed air, there are special pneumatic cut-

ting chisels (available from specialty tool manufacturers) that can also be used. If you decide to tackle the job at home, be sure to wear safety goggles to protect your eyes from metal chips and wear work gloves to protect your hands.

4   Replacement of exhaust system components is basically a matter of removing the heat shields, disconnecting the component and installing a new one. The heat shields and exhaust system hangers must be reinstalled in the original locations or damage could result. Due to the high temperatures and exposed locations of the exhaust system components, rust and corrosion can seize parts together. Penetrating oils are available to help loosen frozen fasteners. However, in some cases it may be necessary to cut the pieces apart with a hacksaw or cutting torch only persons experienced in this work should employ this latter method. Here are some simple guidelines to follow when repairing the exhaust system:

a) Work from the back to the front when removing exhaust system components.

b) Apply penetrating oil to the exhaust system component fasteners (see illustrations) to make them easier to remove.

c) While you're waiting for the penetrant to loosen up the exhaust system fasteners, always disconnect the electrical connectors for the downstream oxygen sensors and remove the sensors before removing the exhaust pipe section that includes the catalytic converter (see Catalytic converter - description, check and replacement in Chapter 6).

c) Use new gaskets, fasteners and rubber hangers when installing exhaust systems components.

d) Apply anti-seize compound to the threads of all exhaust system fasteners during reassembly.

e) Be sure to allow sufficient clearance between newly installed parts and all points on the underbody to avoid overheating the floor pan and possibly damaging the interior carpet and insulation. Pay particularly close attention to the catalytic converter and heat shield.

## Specifications

### General

| | | |
|---|---|---|
| Fuel pressure | 54 to 59.5 psi | 3.7 to 4.1 bar |
| Fuel injector resistance | 14 to 17 ohms* | |

*Approximate values, depending on temperature*

| Torque specifications | Ft-lbs (unless otherwise indicated) | Nm |
|---|---|---|

**Note: One foot-pound (ft-lb) of torque is equivalent to 12 inch-pounds (in-lbs) of torque. Torque values below approximately 15 ft-lbs are expressed in inch-pounds, since most foot-pound torque wrenches are not accurate at these smaller values.**

| | | |
|---|---|---|
| Throttle body mounting bolts (all engines, all models) | 80 in-lbs | 9 |

**Section**

**Reference to other Chapters**

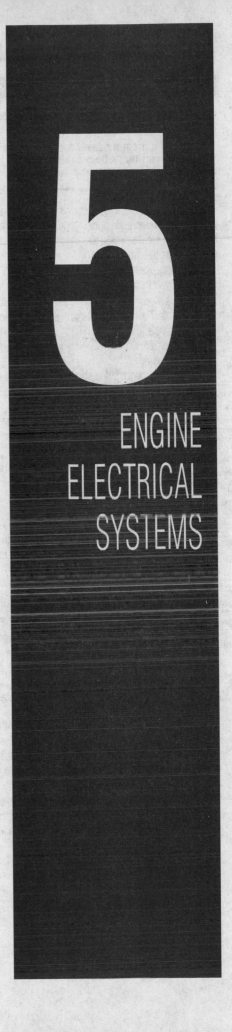

# 5

ENGINE
ELECTRICAL
SYSTEMS

## 1 General information

> ✳✳ **CAUTION:**
>
> **You'll need a memory saver for battery disconnection. Before you disconnect the battery cables, always hook up the memory saver in accordance with the manufacturer's instructions**

1  The engine electrical systems include all ignition, charging and starting components. Because of their engine-related functions, these components are discussed separately from chassis electrical devices such as the lights, the instruments, etc. (which are included in Chapter 12).

2  Always observe the following precautions when working on the electrical systems:

a) *Be extremely careful when servicing engine electrical components. They are easily damaged if checked, connected or handled improperly.*

b) *Never leave the ignition switch on for long periods of time with the engine off.*

c) *Don't disconnect the battery cables while the engine is running.*

d) *Maintain correct polarity when connecting a battery cable from another vehicle during jump-starting.*

e) *Always disconnect the negative cable first and hook it up last or the battery may be shorted by the tool being used to loosen the cable clamps.*

3  It's also a good idea to review the safety-related information regarding the engine electrical systems located in the *Safety First!* Section near the front of this manual before beginning any operation included in this Chapter.

4  Before you disconnect the battery, be sure to connect a memory saver in accordance with the manufacturer's instructions. You must also carry out certain procedures after reconnecting the battery (see Steps 8 through 20).

## BATTERY DISCONNECTION

5  The battery is located in the engine compartment on all vehicles covered by this manual. To disconnect the battery for service procedures that require battery disconnection, simply disconnect the cable from the negative battery terminal. Make sure that you isolate the cable to prevent it from coming into contact with the battery negative terminal.

6  Some vehicle systems (alarm system, power seats, power door locks, etc.) require battery power all the time, either to enable their operation or to maintain control unit memory (Powertrain Control Module, automatic transmission control module, etc.), which would be lost if the battery were to be disconnected. So before you disconnect the battery, note the following points:

a) *Before connecting or disconnecting the cable from the negative battery terminal, make sure that you turn the ignition key and the lighting switch to their OFF positions. Failure to do so could damage semiconductor components.*

b) *On a vehicle with power door locks, it is a wise precaution to remove the key from the ignition and to keep it with you, so that it does not get locked inside if the power door locks should engage accidentally when the battery is reconnected!*

c) *The engine management system's PCM has some learning capabilities that allow it to adapt or make corrections in response to minor variations in the fuel system in order to optimize driveability and idle characteristics. However, the PCM might lose some or*

*all of this information when the battery is disconnected. The PCM must go through a relearning process before it can regain its former driveability and performance characteristics. Until it relearns this lost data, you might notice a difference in driveability, idle and/or (if you have an automatic) shift feel. In certain cases, the operating parameters might have to be reprogrammed using a proprietary scan tool at a dealer service department or other service facility equipped with the proper tool.*

## MEMORY SAVERS

7  Devices known as "memory savers" (typically, small, low current 9- or 12-volt batteries) can be used to avoid some of the above problems. A memory saver is usually plugged into the cigarette lighter, and allows you to disconnect the vehicle battery from the electrical system. The memory saver will deliver sufficient current to maintain security alarm codes and (maybe, but don't count on it) PCM memory. It will also run "unswitched" (always on) circuits such as the clock and radio memory, while isolating the car battery in the event that a short circuit occurs while the vehicle is being serviced.

> ✳✳ **WARNING:**
>
> **If you're going to work around any airbag system components, disconnect the battery and do not use a memory saver. If you do, the airbag could accidentally deploy and cause personal injury.**

> ✳✳ **CAUTION:**
>
> **Because memory savers deliver current to operate unswitched circuits when the battery is disconnected, make sure that the circuit that you're going to service is actually open before working on it!**

## AFTER RECONNECTING THE BATTERY, PERFORM THE FOLLOWING RELEARNING PROCEDURES:

### Re-synchronizing the power windows

➡**Note: After voltage to the power window modules has been interrupted, the modules can no longer determine the position of the windows, so re-synchronize each power window after reconnecting the battery. This procedure applies to all four windows.**

8  Push the button to raise the window (even if it's already raised) and keep it depressed for at least half a second after the window is fully closed. When the control module for the power window assembly detects a motor lock-up for at least 0.3 second, it sets the position recognition counter to zero. The power window is now synchronized.

9  Repeat this procedure for each power window.

### Reactivating the steering angle sensor

➡**Note: The steering angle sensor is a component of the Electronic Stability Program (ESP). You must reactivate the steering angle sensor after reconnecting the battery.**

10 When the voltage supply to the steering angle sensor has been interrupted, the Electronic Stability Program (ESP) control unit switches to its malfunction mode, and the message "EL. STAB. PROGRAM GO TO GARAGE" appears on the multi-function display.

11 Start the engine and allow it to idle.

12 Turn the steering wheel lock-to-lock (etreme left to extreme right). The message "EL. STAB. PROGRAM GO TO GARAGE" disappears from the multi-function display.

13 Turn off the engine.

### Re-synchronizing the pop-up roof

➡**Note: You must synchronize the pop-up roof after reconnecting the battery. When the voltage supply to the pop-up roof motor and the overhead control panel module has been interrupted, the overhead control panel module cannot determine the position of the pop-up roof.**

14 Open the pop-up roof with the roof system switch until the roof reaches its mechanical stop and continue activating the roof system switch (and therefore the roof motor) for about a second. When the overhead control module recognizes that the roof system motor has

been locked up for at least 0.5 second, it sets the position counter to zero. The pop-up roof is now re-synchronized.

### Recalibrating the power seats

➡**Note: You must recalibrate the power seats after reconnecting the battery. When the voltage supply to the power seat motors is interrupted, the power seat motors are "denormalized," meaning the memory inside each power seat adjustment control unit doesn't know the seat positions. This procedure applies to both front seats.**

15 Adjust the longitudinal seat adjustment switch all the way forward to its front stop position and hold for at least a second.

16 Adjust the seat angle adjustment switch to its lower stop position and hold for at least a second.

17 Adjust the seat height adjustment switch to its lower stop position and hold for at least a second.

18 Adjust the seat backrest adjustment switch to its front stop position and hold for at least a second.

19 Adjust the seat head restraint adjustment switch to its upper stop position and hold for at least a second.

20 The seat is now recalibrated.

---

## 2  Battery - emergency jump starting

Refer to the *Booster battery (jump) starting* procedure at the front of this manual.

---

## 3  Battery - check, removal and installation

---

### ✳✳ WARNING:

**Hydrogen gas is produced by the battery, so keep open flames and lighted cigarettes away from it at all times. Always wear eye protection when working around a battery. Rinse off spilled electrolyte immediately with large amounts of water.**

### ✳✳ CAUTION:

**Always disconnect the negative cable first and hook it up last or you might accidentally short the battery with the tool that you're using to loosen the cable clamps.**

## CHECK

1  A battery cannot be accurately tested until it is at or near a fully charged state. Disconnect the negative battery cable from the battery and perform the following tests:

### Open circuit voltage test

♦ **Refer to illustration 3.2**

2  Using a digital voltmeter, perform an open circuit voltage test (see illustration). Connect the negative probe of the voltmeter to the negative

battery post and the positive probe to the positive battery post. The battery voltage should be greater than 12.6 volts.

3  If the battery is less than the specified voltage, charge the battery before proceeding to the next test. Do not proceed with the battery load test until the battery is fully charged.

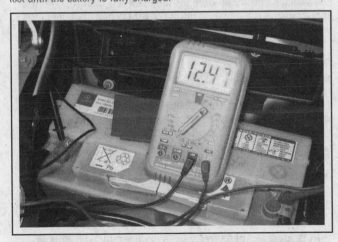

**3.2  To test the open circuit voltage of the battery, connect the positive (red) probe to the positive terminal and the negative (black) probe of the voltmeter to the negative battery terminal. A fully charged battery should have at least 12.6 volts**

**3.4 Some battery load testers are equipped with an ammeter, which enables the battery load to be precisely dialed in. Less expensive testers like this one only have a load switch and a voltmeter**

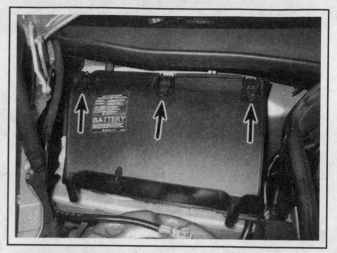

**3.6 To remove the battery cover, flip open these three retainer clips, then carefully pull off the cover**

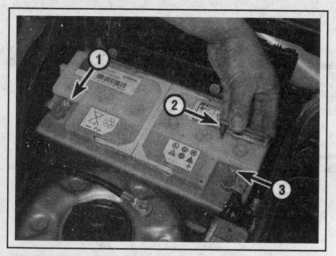

**3.8 When disconnecting the battery cables, always disconnect the cable from the negative terminal (1) first, then remove the red plastic terminal cover (2) and disconnect the cable from the positive terminal (3)**

### Battery load test

▶ **Refer to illustration 3.4**

4  An accurate check of the battery condition can only be performed with a load tester (available at most auto parts stores). This test evaluates the ability of the battery to operate the starter and other accessories during periods of heavy amperage draw (load). Connect a battery load-testing tool to the battery terminals (see illustration). This tool increases the load demand (amperage draw) on the battery. Maintain the load on the battery for 15 seconds and observe that the battery voltage does not drop below 9.6 volts. If the battery condition is weak or defective, the tool will indicate this condition immediately.

➡ **Note: Cold temperatures will cause the minimum voltage reading to drop slightly. Follow the chart given in the tool manufacturer's instructions to compensate for cold climates. Minimum load voltage for freezing temperatures (32-degrees F/0-degrees C) should be approximately 9.1 volts.**

### Battery drain test

5  This test will indicate whether there's a constant drain on the vehicle's electrical system that can cause the battery to discharge. Make sure all accessories are turned off. If the vehicle has an underhood light, verify that it's working properly, then disconnect it. Connect one lead of a digital ammeter to the disconnected negative battery cable clamp and the other lead to the negative battery post. A drain of approximately 100 milliamps or less is considered normal (due to the engine control computers, clocks, digital radios and other components that normally cause a key-off battery drain). An excessive drain (approximately 500 milliamps or more) will cause the battery to discharge. The problem circuit or component can be located by removing the fuses, one at a time, until the excessive drain stops and normal drain is indicated on the meter.

## REPLACEMENT

▶ **Refer to illustrations 3.6, 3.8, 3.9 and 3.11**

### ✳✳ CAUTION:

**You'll need a memory saver for this procedure. Before you disconnect the battery cables, be sure to hook up the memory saver in accordance with the manufacturer's instructions**

6  Remove the battery cover (see illustration).
7  Connect a memory saver in accordance with the manufacturer's instructions.
8  Disconnect the cable from the negative battery terminal, then disconnect the cable from the positive terminal (see illustration).
9  Remove the two nuts that retain the battery hold-down bracket (see illustration) and remove the hold-down bracket.
10  Lift out the battery. Be careful - it's heavy.

➡ **Note: Battery straps and handles are available at most auto parts stores for a reasonable price. They make it easier to remove and carry the battery.**

11  While the battery is out, inspect the battery tray for corrosion deposits. Clean the battery tray, then use a baking soda/water solu-

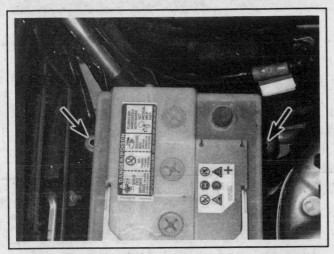

**3.9 To remove the battery hold-down bracket, remove these two nuts**

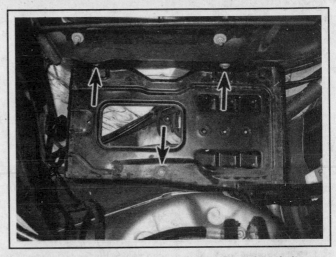

**3.11 To remove the battery tray, remove these three bolts**

tion to neutralize any deposits to prevent further oxidation. If the metal around the tray is also corroded, clean it as well and spray the area with a rust-inhibiting paint. If any corrosion has leaked down past the battery tray, remove the tray (see illustration) and use baking soda and water to neutralize the deposits on the components located under the tray.

12 If you're replacing the battery, make sure you get an identical unit, with the same dimensions, amperage rating, cold cranking rating, etc.

13 Installation is the reverse of removal. After reconnecting the battery, be sure to perform the relearning procedures outlined in Section 1.

## 4 Battery cables - check, general information and replacement

### CHECK

1 Periodically inspect the entire length of each battery cable for damage, cracked or burned insulation and corrosion. Poor battery cable connections can cause starting problems and decreased engine performance.

2 Check the cable-to-terminal connections at the ends of the cables for cracks, loose wire strands and corrosion. The presence of white, fluffy deposits under the insulation at the cable terminal connection is a sign that the cable is corroded and should be replaced. Check the terminals for distortion, missing mounting bolts and corrosion.

### GENERAL INFORMATION

3 When removing the cables, always disconnect the cable from the negative battery terminal first and hook it up last to prevent the battery from being accidentally shorted by the tool you're using to loosen the cable clamps. Even if you're only replacing the cable for the positive terminal, be sure to disconnect the cable from the negative battery terminal first.

4 When buying new battery cables, take the old cables with you. It is critical that you replace the old cables with identical replacement cables. Battery cables have characteristics that make them easy to identify: positive cables are usually red and larger in cross-section; ground cables are usually black and smaller in cross-section.

5 Clean the threads of the solenoid terminals and/or ground terminals with a wire brush to remove rust and corrosion. Apply a light coat of battery terminal corrosion inhibitor or petroleum jelly to the threads to prevent future corrosion.

6 Attach the cable to the solenoid or ground connection and tighten the mounting nut/bolt securely.

7 Before connecting a new cable to the battery, make sure that it reaches the battery post without having to be stretched.

8 Connect the positive cable first, followed by the negative cable.

### REPLACEMENT

**Ground cable**

▶ **Refer to illustrations 4.10**

9 Remove the battery cover (see illustration 3.6).

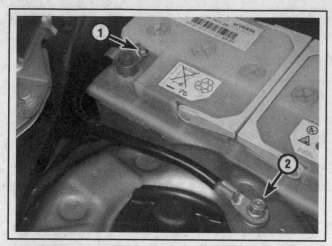

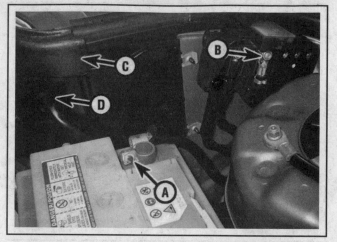

**4.10 To remove the battery ground cable, disconnect it from the negative battery terminal (1), then disconnect it from the vehicle body (2)**

**4.13 Disconnect the battery negative cable, then loosen the clamp nut (A), remove nut (B) at the junction block and detach the positive cable, then remove the trim (C) and the cable grommet (D), raise the front of the vehicle, trace the cable to the starter and alternator and disconnect it from both components**

10 Disconnect the ground cable from the negative battery terminal and from the right strut tower (see illustration).

11 Installation is the reverse of removal.

### Positive cable and alternator/starter cable

▸ **Refer to illustration 4.13**

➡**Note: Before removing the alternator/starter cable, make a sketch or take a few digital photos of the routing of the cable.**

12 Disconnect the cable from the negative battery terminal, then disconnect the battery cable from the positive terminal (see illustration 3.8).

13 Disengage the cable grommet from the sheetmetal between the battery and the engine compartment (see illustration), then disengage the cable from the harness clip that secures it to the right side of the engine compartment. (You might find it easier to disengage the harness from this clip from underneath, after you've raised the vehicle in the next step.)

14 Raise the front of the vehicle and place it securely on jackstands.

15 Trace the path of the cable forward, along the right side of the engine, to the alternator. Remove the rubber cover and disconnect the battery cable from the B+ terminal on the alternator (see Section 10).

16 Trace the cable harness back to the starter motor, remove the rubber cover and disconnect the cable from the terminal on the starter motor solenoid (see Section 14).

17 Installation is the reverse of removal.

---

## 5   Ignition system - general information

All engines are equipped with a distributorless Motor Electronics (ME) ignition control system, which includes the following components:

*Accelerator Pedal Position (APP) sensor*
*Altitude sensor (supercharged engines)*
*Battery*
*Camshaft Position (CMP) sensor*
*Crankshaft Position (CKP) sensor*
*Electronic throttle body*
*Engine Coolant Temperature (ECT) sensor*
*Intake Air Temperature (IAT) sensor*
*Ignition coils*
*Ignition switch*
*Knock sensor(s)*
*Manifold Absolute Pressure (MAP) sensor*
*Mass Air Flow (MAF) sensor*
*Park/Neutral Position (PNP) switch*
*Powertrain Control Module (PCM)*
*Spark plugs*
*Throttle Position (TP) sensor*
*Wheel speed sensors*

The PCM uses input voltage signals from the information sensors listed above to calculate and control ignition timing under all operating conditions. The PCM calculates the optimum timing in response to engine speed, coolant temperature, throttle position and other parameters, each of which varies in accordance with the operating conditions such as cranking, warm-up, idle, acceleration, deceleration, etc. The PCM and the CKP sensor are the key components of the EI system. If the PCM or the CKP sensor is defective, the ME system will not operate and the engine will not start. For more information about the information sensors, refer to Chapter 6.

2001 through 2005 V6 engines are equipped with six individual coils, each of which is mounted on top of the valve cover and connected to twin spark plugs by short high-tension plug wires. All other engines use a coil-over-plug system, which consists of an individual coil above, and connected directly to, each spark plug. The PCM fires the coils in firing order sequence by turning the ground paths for their primary circuits on and off.

## 6    Ignition system - check

▶ Refer to illustration 6.5

1    Before proceeding with the ignition system, check the following items:

    a) *Make sure the battery cable clamps, where they connect to the battery, are clean and tight.*

    b) *Test the condition of the battery (see Section 3). If it does not pass all the tests, replace it with a new battery.*

    c) *Check the ignition system wiring and connections for tightness, damage, corrosion or any other signs of a bad connection.*

    d) *Check the related fuses inside the engine compartment fuse and relay box (see Chapter 12). If they're burned, determine the cause and repair the circuit.*

2    If the engine turns over but won't start or has a severe misfire, perform the following steps using a calibrated ignition tester to make sure there is sufficient secondary ignition voltage to fire the spark plugs.

3    Make sure the ignition is turned to the Off position, and the key is removed, then remove the engine cover(s).

4    Disable the fuel system by removing the fuel pump fuse, which is located in the fuse and relay box in the trunk (see illustration 2.1 in Chapter 4).

5    On 2001 through 2005 V6 engines, there are two spark plugs per cylinder. The coil packs are mounted on top of the valve covers with short spark plug leads connecting them to the plugs. Disconnect one of the spark plug leads from the cylinder being tested (see Chapter 1) and connect the tester inline between the between the plug wire boot and the spark plug (see illustration).

6    On 2006 and later V6 engines and on all four-cylinder engines, there is one centrally mounted spark plug per cylinder. The ignition coils are mounted directly over the plugs. Remove each ignition coil from the spark plug (see Section 7), then connect the spark tester inline between the high-tension terminal underneath the coil and the spark plug.

7    Crank the engine and see if the tester body flashes.

8    If the tester flashes during cranking, sufficient voltage is reaching the plug to fire it. Repeat this test for each spark plug to verify that all the coils are OK.

9    If no flashes occur during cranking at any one cylinder, inspect the primary wire connection at the coil that isn't functioning. Make sure that it's clean and tight.

10   If the coil is operating but a cylinder still has a misfire condition, a spark plug might be fouled. So remove and inspect the suspect plug (see Chapter 1), then retest.

11   If no sparks or intermittent sparks occur during cranking at all cylinders, the Powertrain Control Module (PCM) might be defective. Have the PCM checked out by a dealer service department or other qualified repair shop (testing the PCM is beyond the scope of the do-it-yourselfer because it requires expensive special tools). Any additional testing of the ignition system must be done by a dealer service department or other qualified repair shop with the proper tools.

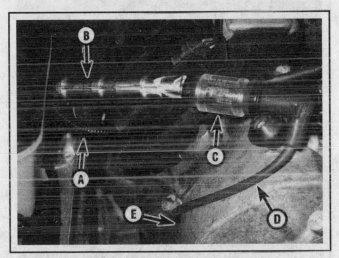

**6.5  To use a calibrated ignition tester on a 2001 through 2005 V6 engine, trace each spark plug wire (A) down to its corresponding spark plug and disconnect plug wire boot (B) from the plug. Connect the tester (C) to the plug wire boot and connect the tester lead (D) to the spark plug (E, not visible in this photo)**

## 7    Ignition coil - check and replacement

### CHECK

1    If a coil seems to be misfiring or not firing at all, or is causing the Powertrain Control Module (PCM) to set a Diagnostic Trouble Code (DTC) that indicates a misfire, try swapping it with an adjacent coil. If the suspect coil was causing a DTC for one cylinder, it will likely set the same DTC when it's installed above another cylinder. If this is the case, the coil is probably defective, because it's unlikely that the harnesses for two adjacent ignition coils would both be defective. At any rate, no further testing is possible at home. If you're not sure whether you should replace the coil at this point, consult a dealer service department or other qualified repair shop.

## REPLACEMENT

### V6 engines

♦ **Refer to illustrations 7.4a, 7.4b and 7.5**

2  Disconnect the cable from the negative battery terminal (see Section 1).

3  On models with an integral engine cover/air filter housing, remove the engine cover/air filter housing (see *Air filter housing - removal and installation* in Chapter 4). On 2001 through 2005 models with a remote air filter housing, remove the engine cover and, if you're removing a coil from the right valve cover, remove the air intake duct (see *Air filter housing - removal and installation* in Chapter 4).

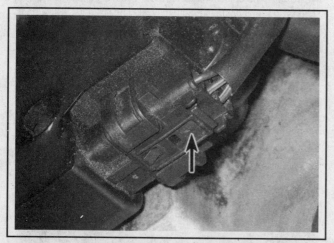

**7.4a  To disconnect the electrical connector from an ignition coil on a 2001 through 2005 V6 model, depress the release tab and pull off the connector**

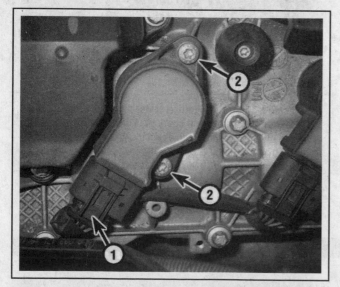

**7.4b  To disconnect the electrical connector from an ignition coil on a 2006 and later model, depress the release tab (1) and pull off the connector. To detach the coil from the valve cover, remove the two bolts (2)**

4  Disconnect the electrical connector from the ignition coil (see illustrations).

5  On 2001 through 2005 models, disconnect the spark plug wires from the ignition coil (see illustration).

6  On 2001 through 2005 models, remove the ignition coil mounting bolt (see Illustration 7.5) and remove the coil. On 2006 and later models, remove the coil mounting bolts (see illustration 7.4b) and remove the coil by pulling it up and off the spark plug.

7  On 2006 and later models, inspect the condition of the rubber boot that seals the connection between the coil high tension tower and the spark plug. If it's cracked, torn or deteriorated, replace it.

8  Installation is the reverse of removal.

9  When you're done, be sure to perform the relearn procedures outlined in Section 1.

### Four-cylinder engines

♦ **Refer to illustrations 7.14a and 7.14b**

10  Disconnect the cable from the negative battery terminal (see Section 1).

11  On 2002 models, remove the ignition coil cover screws and remove the cover from the valve cover.

12  On 2003 through 2005 models, remove the engine cover.

13  Disconnect the electrical connector from the ignition coil.

14  Remove the ignition coil mounting bolts and remove the coil (see illustrations).

15  Inspect the condition of the rubber boot that seals the connection between the coil high tension tower and the spark plug. If it's cracked, torn or deteriorated, replace it.

16  Installation is the reverse of removal.

17  When you're done, be sure to perform the relearn procedures outlined in Section 1.

**7.5  Before disconnecting the spark plug wires from the ignition coil on a 2001 through 2005 model, label the upper boot A and the lower boot B to ensure that they're reconnected correctly. "A" corresponds with the forward spark plug and "B" with the rear spark plug. To remove an ignition coil, remove the coil mounting bolt (C)**

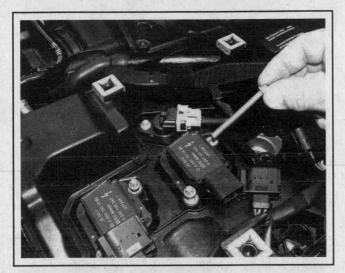

**7.14a  Remove the mounting bolts . . .**

**7.14b . . . then twist and remove the coil from the valve cover**

## 8  Charging system - general information and precautions

The charging system supplies electrical power for the ignition system, all lighting and audio-visual components, etc. The charging system consists of the alternator and an integral IC voltage regulator, the ignition switch, the battery, the charge warning light, the voltage gauge and the wiring between all the components. The alternator is driven by a serpentine drivebelt at the front of the engine.

The charging system doesn't ordinarily require periodic maintenance. However, you should inspect the drivebelt, the battery, the charging system wiring harness and all connections at the intervals outlined in Chapter 1. Be very careful when making electrical circuit connections to the alternator or the charging system circuit and note the following:

a)  Never disconnect the battery while the engine is running.
b)  When reconnecting wires to the alternator from the battery, be sure to note the polarity.

c)  Before using arc-welding equipment to repair any part of the vehicle, disconnect the wires from the alternator and the battery terminals.
d)  Never start the engine with a battery charger connected.
e)  Always disconnect both battery cables before using a battery charger.
f)  The alternator is turned by an engine drivebelt, which could cause serious injury if your hands, hair or clothes become entangled in it with the engine running.
g)  Because the alternator is connected directly to the battery, it could arc or cause a fire if overloaded or shorted out.
h)  Before steam-cleaning the engine, wrap a plastic bag over the alternator and secure it with rubber bands.

## 9  Charging system - check

▶ **Refer to illustration 9.3**

➡**Note: These vehicles are equipped with an On-Board Diagnostic-II (OBD-II) system that is useful for detecting charging system problems because it can provide you with the Diagnostic Trouble Code (DTC) that will indicate the general nature of the problem. Refer to Chapter 6 for a list of the DTCs used by the Powertrain Control Module (PCM) on these vehicles and for the procedure you'll need to use to obtain DTCs.**

1   If a malfunction occurs in the charging circuit, do not immedi-

ately assume that the alternator is causing the problem. First check the following items:

a)  The battery cables where they connect to the battery. Make sure the connections are clean and tight.
b)  The battery electrolyte specific gravity (by observing the charge indicator on the battery). If it is low, charge the battery.
c)  Inspect the external alternator wiring and connections.
d)  Check the drivebelt condition and tension (see Chapter 1).
e)  Check the alternator mounting bolts for tightness.
f)  Run the engine and check the alternator for abnormal noise.

2    Using a voltmeter, check the battery voltage with the engine off (see illustration 3.2). It should be at least 12.6 volts with a fully charged battery.

3    Start the engine and check the battery voltage again (see illustration). It should now be at least 13 volts, but should not read more than 15 volts.

4    If the indicated voltage reading is less or more than the specified charging voltage, have the charging system checked at a dealer service department or other properly equipped repair facility. The voltage regulator on these models is contained within the alternator and cannot be adjusted.

**9.3  To test the charging voltage, connect a voltmeter to the battery terminals. A healthy charging system should put out at least 13 volts, but not more than 15 volts**

## 10  Alternator - removal and installation

➡ **Note 1: If you are replacing the alternator, take the old one with you when purchasing a replacement unit. Make sure the new/rebuilt unit looks identical to the old alternator. Look at the terminals - they should be the same in number, size and location as the terminals on the old alternator. Finally, look at the identification numbers - they will be stamped into the housing or printed on a tag attached to the housing. Make sure the numbers are the same on both alternators.**

➡ **Note 2: Many new and remanufactured alternators do not have a pulley installed, so you may have to switch the pulley from the old unit to the new/rebuilt one. When buying an alternator, find out the shop's policy regarding pulleys; some shops will perform this service free of charge.**

### 2001 THROUGH 2005 V6 MODELS

▶ **Refer to illustrations 10.4 and 10.5**

1    Disconnect the cable from the negative terminal of the battery

(see Section 1).

2    Remove the engine cover/air filter housing (see *Air filter housing - removal and installation* in Chapter 4).

3    Remove the accessory drivebelt (see Chapter 1).

4    Remove the upper and lower alternator mounting bolts (see illustration).

5    Pull the alternator forward and disconnect the electrical connector from the alternator (see illustration). Also remove the nut that secures the battery cable to the B+ terminal and disconnect the cable.

6    Installation is the reverse of removal.

### 2006 AND LATER V6 MODELS

▶ **Refer to illustrations 10.14**

7    Disconnect the cable from the negative terminal of the battery (see Section 1).

8    Remove the right air intake duct (see *Air filter housing - removal and installation* in Chapter 4).

**10.4  Alternator upper and lower mounting bolts (2001 through 2005 V6 models)**

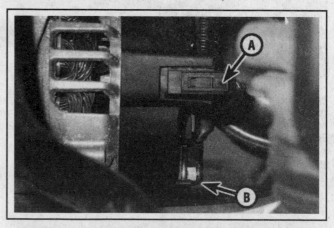

**10.5  Depress the release tab (A) and pull off the electrical connector, then remove the cover from the B+ terminal, remove the nut (B) and detach the cable from the B+ terminal**

9   Remove the accessory drivebelt (see Chapter 1).

10  Raise the vehicle and place it securely on jackstands.

11  Remove the engine under-cover.

12  Remove the battery (B+) terminal nut and disconnect the battery cable from the B+ terminal.

13  Disconnect the electrical connector from the alternator.

14  Remove the lower alternator mounting bolts (see illustration).

15  Lower the vehicle.

16  Remove the engine cover bracket and set the air pump switchover valve to one side.

17  Remove the electric air pump (see *Secondary air injection - description and component replacement* in Chapter 6).

18  Remove the shutoff valve from the right cylinder head (see *Secondary air injection - description and component replacement* in Chapter 6).

19  Remove the upper alternator mounting bolts and remove the alternator.

20  Installation is the reverse of removal.

## 2002 FOUR-CYLINDER MODELS

→**Note: The alternator is located on the lower right side of the engine block.**

21  Disconnect the cable from the negative terminal of the battery (see Section 1).

22  Raise the vehicle and remove the engine under-cover.

23  Remove the alternator drivebelt.

24  Remove the battery (B+) terminal nut (and disconnect the battery cable).

25  Disconnect the electrical connector from the alternator.

26  Remove the alternator mounting bolts and remove the alternator.

27  Installation is the reverse of removal.

## 2003 THROUGH 2005 FOUR-CYLINDER MODELS

→**Note: The alternator is located on the lower right side of the**

10.14  Alternator lower mounting bolts (2006 and later V6 models)

engine block.

28  Disconnect the cable from the negative terminal of the battery (see Section 1).

29  Remove the fresh air intake duct (see *Air filter housing - removal and installation* in Chapter 4).

30  Raise the vehicle and remove the engine under cover.

31  Remove the alternator drivebelt.

32  Remove the battery (B+) terminal nut (and disconnect the battery cable).

33  Remove the upper alternator mounting bolts.

34  Disconnect the electrical connector from the alternator.

35  Remove the lower alternator mounting bolts and remove the alternator.

36  Installation is the reverse of removal.

## 11  Voltage regulator/brushes - replacement

▶  **Refer to illustrations 11.2, 11.3, 11.5a and 11.5b**

1   Remove the alternator (see Section 10).

2   Remove the voltage regulator cover bolts (see illustration) and remove the cover.

3   Remove the regulator mounting bolts (see illustration) and remove the regulator.

4   Measure the length of the alternator brushes and compare your measurement to the specified minimum length listed in this Chapter's Specifications. If the brushes are too short, replace the voltage regulator.

5   To hold the brushes in the retracted position for installation, push them in all the way and pull back on the plastic cover to keep them there (see illustration). Install the voltage regulator/brush holder assembly and tighten the bolts securely, then push down on the plastic cover to release the brushes (see illustration).

6   Install the cover over the end frame and tighten the bolts securely.

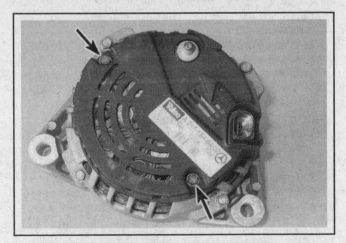

11.2  To remove the voltage regulator cover, remove these two bolts (on some covers, you must remove a collar nut, a nut and a retaining bolt to detach the cover)

**11.3 To detach the voltage regulator/ brush holder from the alternator, remove these bolts**

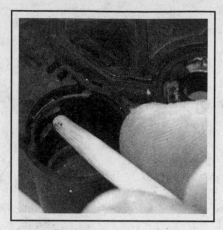

**11.5a Push the brushes in all the way, then slide the plastic cover back to hold them in the retracted position**

**11.5b After installing the voltage regulator/brush holder, push down on the plastic cover to release the brushes**

## 12 Starting system - general description and precautions

### GENERAL DESCRIPTION

All starter motors are located on the lower part of the engine, near the transmission bellhousing, where they can engage the ring gear on the driveplate.

The starting system consists of the following components:

*Ignition switch*
*Battery and battery cables*
*Starter relay (inside the engine compartment fuse and relay box)*
*Starter fuse (inside the engine compartment fuse and relay box)*
*Starter solenoid/starter motor assembly*
*Clutch interlock switch (manual transmission models)*
*Park-Neutral Position (PNP) switch function, inside the Transmission Control Module (TCM) (automatic transmission models)*
*The wiring harnesses connecting these components*

The starting system has two separate circuits: A low-amperage control circuit and a high-amperage supply circuit between the battery and the starter motor. The low-amp control circuit includes the:

*Ignition switch*
*Starter relay (inside the engine compartment fuse and relay box)*
*Clutch interlock switch (manual transmission models)*
*Transmission Control Module (TCM) (automatic transmission models)*
*Coil winding (inside the starter solenoid)*
*Wire harnesses connecting these components*

The high-amperage supply circuit consists of the:

*Battery starter cable*
*Contact disc (inside the starter solenoid)*
*Starter motor*

On models with an automatic transmission, the Park/Neutral Position (PNP) switch (Mercedes calls it the starter lockout contact), which is not an external component but rather an integral component of the electrical control unit, energizes the starter relay only when the shift lever is in PARK or NEUTRAL. The PNP switch is normally open to prevent the starter relay from being energized unless the shift lever is in the PARK or NEUTRAL position. When the ignition switch is turned to START, battery voltage is supplied through the low-amperage control circuit to the starter relay coil if the shift lever is in the PARK or NEUTRAL position. If it isn't, the starter circuit remains open and the engine won't start.

On models with a manual transmission, the clutch pedal switch at the clutch pedal energizes the starter relay only when the clutch pedal is depressed. The clutch pedal switch is normally open to prevent the starter relay from being energized. When the ignition switch is turned to START, battery voltage is supplied through the low-amperage control circuit to the starter relay coil if the clutch pedal is depressed. If it isn't, the starter circuit remains open and the engine won't start.

When the starter relay coil is energized, the normally-open relay contacts close, which energize the windings of the starter solenoid pull-in coil, which pulls in the solenoid plunger, which pulls the shift lever in the starter motor, which engages the starter's overrunning clutch and pinion gear with the starter's ring gear. As the solenoid plunger reaches the end of its travel, the solenoid contact disc completes the high-current starter supply circuit and energizes the solenoid plunger hold-in coil. Current flows from the solenoid battery terminal to the starter motor and energizes the starter.

The starter motors used on the vehicles covered in this manual are not rebuildable. They're available only as new or remanufactured units. If any part of the starter motor fails, including the starter solenoid, replace the entire starter assembly.

### PRECAUTIONS

Always observe the following precautions when working on the starting system:

a) *Excessive cranking of the starter motor can overheat it and cause serious damage. Never operate the starter motor for more than 15 seconds at a time without pausing to allow it to cool for at least two minutes.*

b) *The starter is connected directly to the battery and could arc or cause a fire if mishandled, overloaded or shorted.*

c) *Always detach the cable(s) from the negative terminal of the battery before working on the starting system.*

## 13 Starter motor and circuit - check

▶ **Refer to illustrations 13.3 and 13.4**

1  If a malfunction occurs in the starting circuit, do not immediately assume that the starter is causing the problem. First, check the following items:

   a) *Make sure the battery cable clamps, where they connect to the battery, are clean and tight.*

   b) *Check the condition of the battery cables (see Section 4). Replace any defective battery cables with new parts.*

   c) *Test the condition of the battery (see Section 3). If it does not pass all the tests, replace it with a new battery.*

   d) *Check the starter motor wiring and connections.*

   e) *Check the starter motor mounting bolts for tightness.*

   f) *Check the starter fuse in the engine compartment fuse box (see Chapter 12). If the fuse is blown, determine the cause and repair the circuit.*

   g) *Check to see if the S terminal on the starter motor receives voltage when the ignition key is turned to the Start position.*

   h) *Check the starter relay (see Chapter 12).*

2  If the starter does not activate when the ignition switch is turned to the start position, check for battery voltage to the starter solenoid. This will determine if the solenoid is receiving the correct voltage from the ignition switch. Connect a 12-volt test light or a voltmeter to the starter solenoid positive terminal. While an assistant turns the ignition switch to the start position, observe the test light or voltmeter. The test light should shine brightly or battery voltage should be indicated on the voltmeter. If voltage is not available to the starter solenoid, refer to the wiring diagrams in Chapter 12 and check the fuses and starter relay in series with the starting system. If voltage is available but there is no movement from the starter motor, remove the starter from the engine (see Section 14) and bench test the starter (see Step 4).

3  If the starter turns over slowly, check the starter cranking voltage and the current draw from the battery. This test must be performed with the starter assembly on the engine. Crank the engine over (for 10 seconds or less) and observe the battery voltage. It should not drop below 9.6 volts. Also, observe the current draw with an inductive type ammeter (see illustration). Typically a starter should not exceed 160 amps. If the starter motor amperage draw is excessive, have it tested by a dealer service department or other qualified repair shop. There are several conditions that may affect the starter cranking potential. The battery must be in good condition and the battery cold-cranking rating must not be under-rated for the particular application. Be sure to check the battery specifications carefully. The battery terminals and cables must be clean and not corroded. Also, in cases of extreme cold temperatures, make sure the battery and/or engine block is warmed before performing the tests.

4  If the starter is receiving voltage but does not activate, remove and check the starter motor assembly on the bench (see illustration). Most likely the solenoid is defective. In some rare cases, the engine may be seized so be sure to try and rotate the crankshaft pulley (see Chapter 2) before proceeding. With the starter assembly mounted in a vise on the bench, install one jumper cable from the positive terminal of a test battery to the B+ terminal on the starter. Install another jumper cable from the negative terminal of the battery to the body of the starter. Install a starter switch and apply battery voltage to the solenoid S terminal (for 10 seconds or less) and observe the solenoid plunger, shift lever and overrunning clutch extend and rotate the pinion drive. If the pinion drive extends but does not rotate, the solenoid is operating but the starter motor is defective. If there is no movement but the solenoid clicks, the solenoid and/or the starter motor is defective. If the solenoid plunger extends and rotates the pinion drive, the starter assembly is operating properly.

**13.3  Use an inductive ammeter to measure starter current draw**

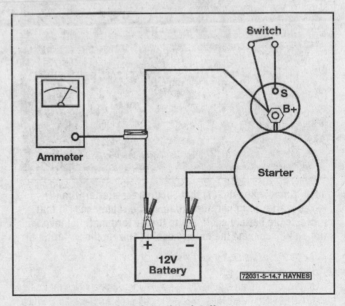

**13.4  Starter motor bench-testing details**

## 14 Starter motor - removal and installation

### V6 MODELS

▶ **Refer to illustrations 14.5 and 14.7**

➡**Note: The starter motor is located on the right lower side of the block.**

1  Disconnect the cable from the negative terminal of the battery (see Section 1).

2  Raise the vehicle and support it securely on jackstands.

3  Remove the engine undercover.

4  Remove the exhaust system (see Chapter 4).

5  Remove the nut that secures the starter wire to the starter terminal on the starter motor solenoid (see illustration).

6  Remove the rubber cap that protects the battery starter cable to the B+ terminal stud (see illustration 14.5) and disconnect the battery cable from the B+ terminal.

7  Remove the two starter motor mounting bolts (see illustration).

8  Note that the lower starter mounting bolt also secures a hose bracket. Remove the bracket, push the hose aside and remove the starter motor.

9  Installation is the reverse of removal. Be sure to tighten the starter motor mounting bolts to the torque listed in this Chapter's Specifications.

### FOUR-CYLINDER MODELS

➡**Note: The starter motor is located on the left side of the engine block.**

10  Disconnect the cable from the negative terminal of the battery (see Section 1).

11  Raise the vehicle and support it securely on jackstands.

12  Remove the engine undercover.

13  On 2003 through 2005 models, remove the two bolts that secure the air conditioning hose bracket to the transmission bellhousing and push the hose aside.

14  On 2003 through 2005 models, disconnect the steering shaft coupler from the steering gear (see *Steering gear - removal and installation* in Chapter 10).

15  On 2003 through 2005 models, remove the intake muffler (see *Supercharger system [four-cylinder models] – description and component removal and installation* in Chapter 4).

16  Disconnect the electrical connections from the starter motor solenoid.

17  Remove the starter motor mounting bolts and remove the starter.

18  Installation is the reverse of removal.

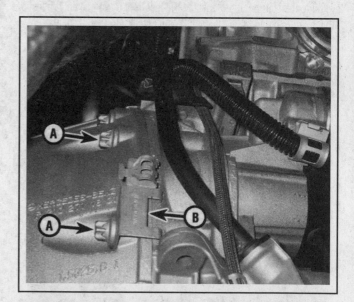

**14.5  Remove the nut (1) that secures the starter wire (2) to the starter terminal, then remove the rubber cap (3) that protects the battery cable nut to the B+ terminal. Remove the nut and disconnect the battery cable (4) from the B+ terminal**

**14.7  To remove the starter motor, remove these two bolts (A). Note that the lower mounting bolt also secures a hose clip (B); don't forget to install this clip when installing the lower starter bolt**

## Specifications

### General

| | |
|---|---|
| Battery voltage | |
|     Engine off | At least 12.66 volts |
|     Engine running | 13.5 to 14.5 volts |
| Firing order | |
|     Four-cylinder models | 1-3-4-2 |
|     V6 models | 1-4-3-6-2-5 |
| Voltage regulator minimum brush length | 13/64-inch (5 mm) |

**Notes**

# 6

## EMISSIONS AND ENGINE CONTROL SYSTEMS

**Section**

**Reference to other Chapters**

CHECK ENGINE light on - See Section 2

## 1   General information

♦ **Refer to illustration 1.7**

To prevent pollution of the atmosphere from incompletely burned and evaporating gases, and to maintain good driveability and fuel economy, a number of emission control systems are incorporated on the vehicles covered by this manual. These emission control systems and their components are an integral part of the engine management system. The engine management system also includes all the government mandated diagnostic features of the second generation of on-board diagnostics, which is known as On-Board Diagnostics II (OBD-II).

At the center of the engine management and OBD-II systems is the on-board computer, which is known as the Powertrain Control Module (PCM). Using a variety of information sensors, the PCM monitors all of the important engine operating parameters (temperature, speed, load, etc.). It also uses an array of output actuators - such as the ignition coils, the fuel injectors, the electronic throttle control system, the Torque Converter Clutch (TCC) and various solenoids and relays - to respond to and alter these parameters as necessary to maintain optimal performance, economy and emissions. The principal emission control systems used on the vehicles covered in this manual include the:

*Catalytic converters*
*Evaporative Emission Control (EVAP) system*
*Exhaust Gas Recirculation (EGR) system*
*Positive Crankcase Ventilation (PCV) system*
*Secondary air injection system*
*Torque Converter Clutch (TCC) system*

The Sections in this Chapter include general descriptions and component replacement procedures for most of the information sensors and output actuators, as well as the important components that are part of the systems listed above. Refer to Chapter 4 for more information on the air induction, fuel delivery and injection systems and exhaust systems, and to Chapter 5 for information on the ignition system. Refer to Chapter 1 for any scheduled maintenance for emission-related systems and components.

The procedures in this Chapter are intended to be practical, affordable and within the capabilities of the home mechanic. The diagnosis of most engine and emission control functions and driveability problems requires specialized tools, equipment and training. When servicing emission devices or systems becomes too difficult or requires special test equipment, consult a dealer service department or other qualified repair shop.

Although engine and emission control systems are very sophisticated on late-model vehicles, you can do most of the regular maintenance and some servicing at home with common tune-up and hand tools and relatively inexpensive digital multimeters. Because of the

Federally mandated extended warranty that covers the emission control system, check with a dealer about warranty coverage before working on any emission-related systems. After the warranty has expired, you might want to perform some of the component replacement procedures in this Chapter to save money. Remember that the most frequent cause of emission and driveability problems is a loose electrical connector or a broken wire or vacuum hose, so before jumping to conclusions, the first thing you should always do is to inspect all electrical connections, electrical wiring and vacuum hoses related to a system. You'll find a vacuum hose routing diagram label under the hood.

Pay close attention to any special precautions given in this Chapter. Remember that illustrations of various system components might not exactly match the component installed on the vehicle on which you're working because of changes made by the manufacturer during production or from year to year.

A Vehicle Emission Control Information (VECI) label (see illustration) is located under the hood. This label contains emission-control and engine tune-up specifications and adjustment information. It also includes a vacuum hose routing diagram for emission-control components. When servicing the engine or emission systems, always check the VECI label in your vehicle. If any information in this manual contradicts what you read on the VECI label on your vehicle, always defer to the information on the VECI label.

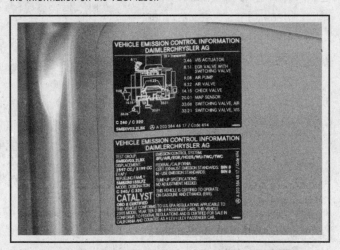

**1.7  The Vehicle Emission Control Information (VECI) label, which is located on the underside of the hood, includes a vacuum hose routing diagram for your engine and information about the emission devices installed on your vehicle**

## 2   On-Board Diagnostic (OBD) system and Diagnostic Trouble Codes (DTCs)

### SCAN TOOL INFORMATION

♦ **Refer to illustrations 2.1 and 2.2**

1   Hand-held scanners are handy for analyzing the engine management systems used on late-model vehicles. Because extracting the Diagnostic Trouble Codes (DTCs) from an engine management system is now the first step in troubleshooting many computer-controlled systems and components, even the most basic generic code readers are capable of accessing a computer's DTCs (see illustration). More powerful scan tools can also perform many of the diagnostics once associated with expensive factory scan tools. If you're planning to obtain a generic scan tool for your vehicle, make sure that it's compatible with OBD-II systems. If you don't plan to purchase a code reader or scan tool and don't have access to one, you can have the codes extracted by a dealer service department or by an independent repair shop.

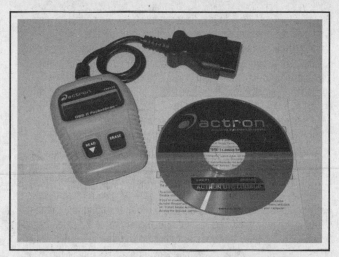

**2.1 Simple code readers are an economical way to extract trouble codes when the CHECK ENGINE light comes on**

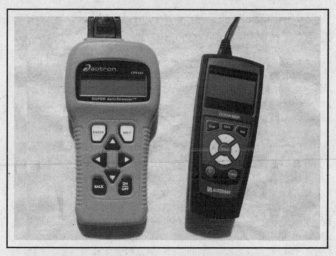

**2.2 Scanners like these from Actron and AutoXray are powerful diagnostic aids - they can tell you just about anything that you want to know about your engine management system**

➡ **Note: Before purchasing an aftermarket generic scan tool, verify that it will work properly with the OBD-II system you want to scan. If necessary, of course, you can always have the codes extracted by a dealer service department or an independent repair shop with a professional scan tool. Some auto parts stores even provide this service for free.**

2   With the advent of the Federally mandated emission control system known as On-Board Diagnostics-II (OBD-II), specially designed scanners were developed. Several tool manufacturers have released OBD-II scan tools for the home mechanic (see illustration).

## OBD-II SYSTEM

3   All vehicles covered by this manual are equipped with the OBD-II system. This system consists of the on-board computer, known as the Powertrain Control Module (PCM) and information sensors that monitor various functions of the engine and send a constant stream of data to the PCM during engine operation. Unlike earlier on-board diagnostics systems, the OBD-II system doesn't just monitor everything, store Diagnostic Trouble Codes (DTCs) and illuminate a Check Engine light or Malfunction Indicator Light (MIL) when there's a problem. (This warning light was referred to as the "Check Engine" light prior to OBD-II, and many do-it-yourselfers and professional technicians still use this term. However, its name was changed to "Malfunction Indicator Light," or simply "MIL," as part of the Society of Automotive Engineers' standard terminology that was introduced in 1996 to encourage all manufacturers to use the same terms when referring to the same components.)

4   The PCM is the brain of the electronically controlled OBD-II system. It receives data from a number of information sensors and switches. Based on the data that it receives from the sensors, the PCM constantly alters engine operating conditions to optimize driveability, performance, emissions and fuel economy. It does so by turning on and off and by controlling various output actuators such as relays, solenoids, valves and other devices. The PCM can only be accessed with an OBD-II scan tool plugged into the 16-pin Data Link Connector (DLC), which is located underneath the driver's end of the dashboard, near the steering column.

5   If your vehicle is still under warranty, virtually every fuel, ignition and emission control component in the OBD-II system is covered by a

Federally mandated emissions warranty that is longer than the warranty covering the rest of the vehicle. Vehicles sold in California and in some other states have even longer emissions warranties than other states. Read your owner's manual for the terms of the warranty protecting the emission-control systems on your vehicle. It isn't a good idea to do-it-yourself at home while the vehicle emission systems are still under warranty because owner-induced damage to the PCM, the sensors and/or the control devices might VOID this warranty. So as long as the emission systems are still under warranty, take the vehicle to a dealer service department if there's a problem.

## INFORMATION SENSORS

6   **Accelerator Pedal Position (APP) sensor** - The APP sensor (or "pedal value sensor," as Mercedes Benz calls it) is located at the upper end of (and is an integral component of) the accelerator pedal assembly. The APP sensor provides the PCM with a variable voltage signal that's proportional to the position (angle) of the accelerator pedal. The PCM uses this data to control the position of the throttle plate inside the electronic throttle body.

7   **Altitude sensor** - The altitude sensor, which is used on 2003 through 2005 four-cylinder models, is located on the front left part of the air filter housing. The altitude sensor monitors the atmospheric pressure of ambient (outside) air and sends a voltage signal to the PCM, which uses this information to help it calculate the correct air-fuel mixture ratio.

8   **Camshaft Position (CMP) sensor** - The CMP sensor produces a signal which the PCM uses to monitor the position of the camshaft, which in turn enables the Powertrain Control Module (PCM) to determine the identification and position of each piston. This data enables the PCM to time the firing sequence of the fuel injectors. The PCM also uses the signal from the CMP sensor and the signal from the Crankshaft Position (CKP) sensor to distinguish between fuel injection and spark timing. In the event that the CKP sensor fails, the PCM uses the CMP sensor to provide the cylinder identification necessary for controlling spark timing as well.

On 2001 through 2005 V6 models, the CMP sensor is located on the front end of the right cylinder head. On 2006 and later V6 models, there are four CMP sensors, all of which are located on the front ends of the cylinder heads. On these models, there is one CMP sensor for each intake camshaft and one sensor for each exhaust camshaft. On 2002 four-cylinder engines, the CMP sensor is located on the left side of the valve cover. On 2003 through 2005 four-cylinder engines, there are two CMP sensors, one for each camshaft. The CMP sensor for the intake camshaft is located on the inner left rear side of the valve cover, to the left of the ignition coil for cylinder No. 3. The CMP sensor for the exhaust camshaft is located on the right front side of the valve cover, near the timing cover.

9 **Crankshaft Position (CKP) sensor** - The PCM uses data from the CKP sensor to calculate engine speed and crankshaft position, which enables it to synchronize ignition timing with fuel injector timing, to control spark knock and to detect misfires.

On V6 models, the CKP sensor is located at the back of the engine, behind and below the left valve cover, at the rear edge of the block, just ahead of the transmission bellhousing. On four-cylinder models, the CKP sensor is located on the left rear side of the engine block, at the end of the block next to the transmission bellhousing, above the starter motor.

10 **Engine Coolant Temperature (ECT) sensor** - The ECT sensor is a Negative Temperature Coefficient (NTC) thermistor (temperature-sensitive variable resistor). In an NTC-type thermistor, the resistance of the thermistor decreases as the coolant temperature increases, so the voltage output of the ECT sensor increases. Conversely, the resistance of the thermistor increases as the coolant temperature decreases, so the voltage of the ECT sensor decreases. The PCM uses this variable voltage signal to calculate the temperature of the engine coolant. The ECT sensor tells the PCM when the engine is sufficiently warmed up to go into closed-loop operation and helps the PCM control the air/fuel mixture ratio and ignition timing.

On 2001 through 2005 V6 models, the ECT sensor is located at the front of the engine block, ahead of the intake manifold, near the right cylinder head. On 2006 and later V6 models, the ECT sensor is located on the back end of the left cylinder head, directly above the CKP sensor. On 2002 four-cylinder models, the ECT sensor is located on the thermostat housing at the front of the engine, right in front of the forward end of the valve cover. On 2003 through 2005 four-cylinder models, the ECT sensor is located on the right front side of the cylinder head.

11 **Fuel tank pressure sensor** - The fuel tank pressure sensor, which is part of the Evaporative Emissions Control (EVAP) system, monitors the pressure of evaporative gases inside the fuel tank. The pressure sensor sends a voltage signal to the PCM that increases as the pressure increases. When the signal reaches a specified threshold, the PCM energizes the EVAP canister purge solenoid, which allows the evaporative emissions to be drawn into the intake manifold. The EVAP system pressure sensor is located on the underside of the mounting flange for the fuel level sensor, which itself is located in the left side of the fuel tank. (The fuel tank is essentially two tanks, left and right. The fuel level sensor is located in the left half and the fuel pump/fuel pressure regulator is located in the right half.)

12 **Inlet Air Temperature (IAT) sensor** - The IAT sensor is a Negative Temperature Coefficient (NTC) thermistor (temperature-sensitive variable resistor) that monitors the temperature of the air entering the engine and sends a variable voltage signal to the PCM. (See the explanation for how an NTC-type thermistor works in the ECT sensor description above.) The voltage signal from the IAT sensor is one of the parameters used by the PCM to determine injector pulse-width (the duration of each injector's on-time) and to adjust spark timing (to prevent spark knock). On V6 models and 2002 four-cylinder models, the IAT sensor is an integral component of the Mass Air Flow (MAF) sensor. See *Mass Air Flow/Intake Air Temperature (MAF/IAT) sensor* below.

On 2003 through 2005 four-cylinder models, the IAT sensor is located on the left side of the engine, directly behind the throttle body.

13 **Knock sensor** - The knock sensor is a piezoelectric crystal that oscillates in proportion to engine vibration. (The term piezoelectric refers to the property of certain crystals that produce a voltage when subjected to a mechanical stress.) The oscillation of the piezoelectric crystal produces a voltage output that is monitored by the PCM, which retards the ignition timing when the oscillation exceeds a certain threshold. When the engine is operating normally, the knock sensor oscillates consistently and its voltage signal is steady. When detonation occurs, engine vibration increases, and the oscillation of the knock sensor exceeds a design threshold. (Detonation is an uncontrolled explosion, after the spark occurs at the spark plug, which spontaneously combusts the remaining air/fuel mixture, resulting in a pinging or slapping sound.) If allowed to continue, the engine could be damaged. On V6 models, there are two knock sensors and they're located on top of the block, in the valley between the cylinder heads, under the intake manifold. On four-cylinder models, the knock sensor is located on the left side of the block, above and ahead of the starter motor.

14 **Manifold Absolute Pressure (MAP) sensor** - The MAP sensor monitors the pressure or vacuum downstream from the throttle plate, inside the intake manifold. The MAP sensor measures intake manifold pressure and vacuum on the absolute scale - from zero instead of from sea-level atmospheric pressure (14.7 psi). The MAP sensor converts the absolute pressure into a variable voltage signal that changes with the pressure. The PCM uses this data to determine engine load so that it can alter the ignition advance and fuel enrichment. On 2001 through 2005 V6 models, the MAP sensor is located at the right front corner of the intake manifold, near the right valve cover. On 2006 and later V6 models, the MAP sensor is located on top of the left valve cover. On 2003 through 2005 four-cylinder models, the MAP sensor is located at the left rear corner of the intake manifold.

15 **Mass Air Flow/Intake Air Temperature (MAF/IAT) sensor** - The MAF/IAT sensor is used by the PCM to measure the amount of intake air drawn into the engine. It uses a hot-wire sensing element to measure the amount of air entering the engine. The wire is constantly maintained at a specified temperature above the ambient temperature of the incoming air by electrical current. As intake air passes through the MAF sensor and over the hot wire, it cools the wire, and the control system immediately corrects the temperature back to its constant value. The current required to maintain the constant value is used by the PCM to determine the amount of air flowing through the MAF sensor. The MAF sensor also includes an integral Intake Air Temperature (IAT) sensor. The two components cannot be serviced separately; if either sensor is defective, replace the MAF/IAT sensor.

On 2001 through 2005 V6 models with a remote air filter housing, the MAF/IAT sensor is located between the air filter housing and the air intake duct. On 2001 through 2005 V6 models with an integral engine cover/air filter housing, the MAF/IAT sensor is located below the air filter housing and above the throttle body. On these models, the filter housing is connected directly to the MAF/IAT sensor, which in turn is connected to the throttle body by a short elbow-shaped duct that Mercedes Benz calls the "air intake connection." On 2006 and later V6 models, the MAF/IAT sensor is located below the air filter housing and above the throttle body. The air filter housing is connected directly to the MAF/IAT sensor, which in turn is connected to the throttle body by a short, elbow-shaped duct, which Mercedes Benz refers to as the "air duct housing." On 2002 four-cylinder models, the MAF/IAT sensor is located on the left side of the engine, between the left charge line (the air duct that routes pressurized intake air from the intercooler to the MAF/IAT sensor) and the air scoop (the short horn-shaped air intake duct between the MAF/IAT sensor and the throttle body). On 2003 through 2005 four-cylinder models, the MAF/IAT sensor is located between the air filter housing and the air intake duct that connects the air filter housing to the intake muffler.

16 **Oxygen sensors** - An oxygen sensor is a galvanic battery that generates a small variable voltage signal in proportion to the difference between the oxygen content in the exhaust stream and the oxygen content in the ambient air. The PCM uses the voltage signal from the upstream oxygen sensor to maintain a stoichiometric air/fuel ratio of 14.7:1 by constantly adjusting the on-time of the fuel injectors.

On 2001 through 2005 V6 models, the upstream sensors are located directly below the exhaust manifold flanges, on the short sections of exhaust pipes that connect the flanges to the catalytic converters. The downstream sensors are located on the pipes directly behind the catalysts. On 2006 and later V6 models, the upstream sensors are located in the same place as on earlier models - on the short sections of exhaust pipes that connect the flanges to the converters. The downstream sensors are located on the catalytic converters themselves (not behind the catalysts as on earlier models). On 2002 four-cylinder models, there are two oxygen sensors: one upstream and one downstream. You have to raise the vehicle to access either of them. The upstream sensor is located in the front exhaust pipe below the flange and ahead of the catalytic converter. The downstream sensor is located just behind the catalyst. On 2003 through 2005 four-cylinder models, there are two oxygen sensors: one upstream and one downstream. On these models, the catalytic converter is an integral component of the exhaust manifold. The upstream sensor is located on the upper end of the catalyst and the downstream sensor is located on the lower end of the catalyst. You might be able to access the upstream sensor from above, but you'll need to raise the vehicle to access the downstream sensor.

## POWERTRAIN CONTROL MODULE (PCM)

17 The PCM is a computer. Think of it as the brain of the engine management system. Like all computers, the PCM receives data inputs, processes the data and outputs commands. The PCM receives data from all of the information sensors described above (input), compares the data to its program and calculates the appropriate responses (processing), then turns the output actuators on or off, or changes their pulse width or duty cycle (output) to keep everything running smoothly, cleanly and efficiently. On 2001 through 2005 V6 models and on 2002 four-cylinder models, the PCM is located in the left rear corner of the engine compartment. On 2006 and later V6 models, the PCM is located on top of the intake manifold, in the center of the engine cover/air filter housing. On 2003 through 2005 four-cylinder models, the PCM is located on the left side of the air filter housing.

## OUTPUT ACTUATORS

18 **Electronic accelerator/cruise control/idle speed control actuator** - In this manual we refer to this device as the "throttle body" because its function is similar to that of a conventional mechanically operated throttle body except that it's electronically controlled by the PCM. The throttle body consists of a throttle valve motor, the throttle valve, a throttle return spring, a pair of potentiometers and the cast aluminum throttle body housing. The Powertrain Control Module (PCM) operates the throttle valve motor to open and close the throttle valve in accordance with the position of the accelerator pedal and driving conditions. The two potentiometers monitor the position of the throttle valve. The PCM compares their signals for rationality. In the event of

a potentiometer failure, a Diagnostic Trouble Code is set, but the other potentiometer allows you to drive the vehicle to a dealership for repairs. The throttle body cannot be disassembled, so none of its components are separately replaceable.

19 **EVAP canister purge solenoid** - The EVAP canister purge solenoid is a PCM-controlled solenoid that controls the purging of evaporative emissions from the EVAP canister to the intake manifold. The EVAP purge solenoid is never turned on during cold start warm-ups or during hot start time delays. But once the engine reaches a specified temperature and enters closed-loop operation the PCM energizes the canister purge solenoid under certain open-throttle operating conditions (acceleration, high speed cruising, etc.). When the solenoid is energized by the PCM, it allows fuel vapors stored in the EVAP canister to be drawn into the intake manifold, where they're mixed with intake air, then burned along with the normal air/fuel mixture. The PCM regulates the flow rate of the vapors by controlling the pulse-width of the solenoid (the length of time during which the solenoid is turned on) in accordance with operating conditions. The EVAP canister purge solenoid is located in the left rear corner of the engine compartment, near the ABS hydraulic control unit.

20 **EVAP canister shutoff valve** - The EVAP canister shutoff valve, which is used only for diagnosis of the EVAP system, is normally open, allowing ventilation of the EVAP system. When the solenoid inside the shutoff valve is energized by the PCM, it closes the shutoff valve, which depressurizes the EVAP system and enables the PCM to conduct a leak test of the EVAP system components. The canister shutoff valve is located on top of the EVAP canister, so you'll have to remove the EVAP canister to replace it.

21 **Exhaust Gas Recirculation (EGR) valve** - When the engine is put under a load (hard acceleration, passing, going up a steep hill, pulling a trailer, etc.), combustion chamber temperature increases. When combustion chamber temperature exceeds 2500 degrees, excessive amounts of oxides of nitrogen (NOx) are produced. NOx is a precursor of photochemical smog. When combined with hydrocarbons (HC), other reactive organic compounds (ROCs) and sunlight, it forms ozone, nitrogen dioxide and nitrogen nitrate and other nasty stuff. The PCM-controlled EGR valve allows exhaust gases to be recirculated back to the intake manifold where they dilute the incoming air/fuel mixture, which lowers the combustion chamber temperature and decreases the amount of NOx produced during high-load conditions.

On 2001 through 2005 V6 models, the EGR valve is located at the right rear corner of the engine, on the back end of the right cylinder head. On four-cylinder models, the EGR valve is located at the right front corner of the cylinder head. 2003 through 2005 four-cylinder models use an air injection/exhaust gas recirculation valve instead of a conventional EGR valve. Depending on what it's ordered to do by the PCM, this valve either redirects spent gases to the intake manifold or injects pressurized air into the exhaust stream. For more information about the Exhaust Gas Recirculation (EGR) valve, refer to *Exhaust Gas Recirculation (EGR) system - description and component replacement* in this Chapter.

22 **Fuel Injectors** - The fuel injectors spray fuel into the intake ports, where it mixes with air being drawn into the combustion chambers, in the same firing order as the spark plugs. The injector valves are opened and closed by PCM-controlled inductive coils in the injector bodies. The injectors are installed between the fuel rail and the intake manifold. For more information about the injectors, see Chapter 4.

23 **Ignition coils** - The ignition coils are controlled by the Powertrain Control Module (PCM). There is no separate ignition control module. This function is handled inside the PCM, which controls the ground path for the primary side of each coil. On 2001 through 2005

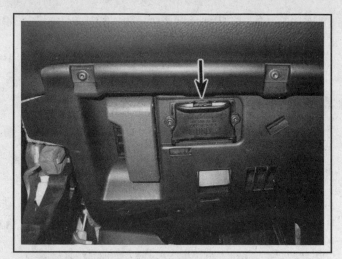

**2.26a  The Data Link Connector (DLC), or diagnostic connector, is located in the left underside of the instrument panel**

**2.26b  To access the diagnostic connector, flip open this small hinged door, then plug in the scan tool**

V6 models, the ignition coils are located on top of the valve covers and are connected to the spark plugs by short spark plug wires (on these models there are two spark plugs per cylinder, so each coil has two short plug wires). On 2006 and later V6 models, the ignition coils are mounted on top of the valve covers; each coil is mounted directly on top of a centrally-located spark plug. On four-cylinder models, the ignition coils are also mounted on top of the valve cover, with each coil mounted directly on top of a centrally-mounted spark plug. For more information about the ignition coils refer to Chapter 5.

24 **Secondary air injection system** - All models are equipped with a PCM-controlled secondary air injection system that is turned on for the first 90 seconds (V6) or up to 150 seconds (four-cylinder) during a cold-start warm-up to quickly bring the catalytic converter(s) up to operating temperature, which reduces emissions during the catalyst warm-up phase. The secondary air injection system consists of an air injection relay, a check valve, a switchover valve, one (four) or two (V6) shutoff valves and an air pump. If the engine temperature is between 50 and 140 degrees F (10 to 60 degrees C) when the engine is started, the PCM energizes the air injection relay and the switchover valve. The switchover valve admits intake manifold vacuum to the two shutoff valves (V6 models) or single shutoff valve (four-cylinder models). The shutoff valve(s) open and the air pump pumps air into the exhaust stream through drilled passages in the cylinder head. Once mixed with the exhaust stream, this extra air reacts with hot exhaust gases, oxidizing them and reducing carbon monoxide (CO) and hydrocarbons (HC). And it also increases the exhaust gas temperature, which heats up the catalyst(s) more quickly to operating temperature. The check valve, which is located upstream in the vacuum line between the intake manifold and switchover valve admits intake manifold vacuum to the switchover valve but prevents pressurized intake air from escaping when the manifold if pressurized under boost conditions.

On V6 models, the check valve, switchover valve, two shutoff valves and air pump are all located on top and at the front of the engine, directly below the front engine cover. On 2002 four-cylinder models, the air pump is located at the lower right front corner of the engine block, directly below the alternator, and the check valve, switchover valve and shutoff valve are located at the back of the intake manifold.

On 2003 through 2005 four-cylinder models there is no air pump. Instead, an air injection/exhaust gas recirculation valve does double duty, redirecting some of the pressurized air from the duct between the supercharger and the intercooler into the exhaust stream. The air injection/exhaust gas recirculation valve, as its name indicates, also redirects spent exhaust gases into the intake manifold when the EGR system is energized by the PCM (see *Exhaust Gas Recirculation [EGR] valve* above). On these models, the check valve, switchover valve and air injection/exhaust gas recirculation valve are located at the right front corner of the valve cover.

For more information on the various secondary air injection systems used on these vehicles, refer to *Secondary air injection system - description and component replacement* in this Chapter.

## OBTAINING AND CLEARING DIAGNOSTIC TROUBLE CODES (DTCS)

25  All models covered by this manual are equipped with on-board diagnostics. When the PCM recognizes a malfunction in a monitored emission control system, component or circuit, it turns on the Malfunction Indicator Light (MIL) on the dash. The PCM will continue to display the MIL until the problem is fixed and the Diagnostic Trouble Code (DTC) is cleared from the PCM's memory. You'll need a scan tool to access any DTCs stored in the PCM. Before outputting any DTCs stored in the PCM, thoroughly inspect ALL electrical connectors and hoses. Make sure that all electrical connections are tight, clean and free of corrosion. And make sure that all hoses are correctly connected, fit tightly and are in good condition (no cracks or tears).

### Accessing the DTCs

▶ **Refer to illustrations 2.26a and 2.26b**

26  On the vehicles covered in this manual, all of which are equipped with On-Board Diagnostic II (OBD-II) systems, the Diagnostic Trouble Codes (DTCs) can only be accessed with a scan tool or code reader. Simply plug the connector of the scan tool into the Data Link Connector (DLC) or diagnostic connector, which is located in the left underside of the instrument panel (see illustration). To access the diagnostic connector, flip open the small hinged door (see illustration). Then connect the scan tool connector and follow the instructions included with the scan tool to extract the DTCs.

27  Once you have outputted all of the stored DTCs, look them up on the accompanying DTC chart.

28  After troubleshooting the source of each DTC, make any necessary repairs or replace the defective component(s).

## Clearing the DTCs

29  Clear the DTCs with the scan tool in accordance with the instructions provided by the scan tool's manufacturer.

## DIAGNOSTIC TROUBLE CODES

30  The accompanying tables are a list of the Diagnostic Trouble Codes (DTCs) that can be accessed by a do-it-yourselfer working at home (there are many more DTCs available to professional service technicians with proprietary scan tools and software, but those codes cannot be accessed by a generic scan tool). If, after you have checked and repaired the connectors, wire harness and vacuum hoses (if applicable) for an emission-related system, component or circuit, the problem persists, have the vehicle checked by a dealer service department.

## OBD-II DIAGNOSTIC TROUBLE CODES (DTCS)

➡Note: Not all trouble codes apply to all models. Also, some codes have multiple definitions. Your generic scan tool will tell you which definition applies to the engine management system that you are scanning.

| Code | Probable cause |
| --- | --- |
| P0100 | Mass Air Flow (MAF) sensor |
| P0105 | Manifold Absolute Pressure (MAP) sensor |
| P0110 | Intake Air Temperature (IAT) sensor |
| P0115 | Engine Coolant Temperature (ECT) sensor |
| P0115 | Coolant thermostat |
| P0120 | Throttle valve actuator adjustment |
| P0120 | Throttle valve actuator, actual value potentiometer |
| P0120 | Accelerator Pedal Position (APP) sensor, voltage difference between signals 1 and 2 |
| P0120 | Accelerator Pedal Position (APP) sensor, interruption at signal path 1 |
| P0120 | Accelerator Pedal Position (APP) sensor, short circuit at signal path 1 |
| P0120 | Accelerator Pedal Position (APP) sensor, interruption at signal path 2 |
| P0120 | Accelerator Pedal Position (APP) sensor, short circuit signal path 2 |
| P0120 | Accelerator Pedal Position (APP) sensor, voltage supply for APP sensor |
| P0130 | Oxygen sensor signal, right upstream oxygen sensor, electrical fault |
| P0133 | Aging downstream oxygen sensor, right upstream oxygen sensor, period duration |
| P0135 | Oxygen sensor heater, left or right upstream oxygen sensor, internal resistor |

## OBD-II DIAGNOSTIC TROUBLE CODES (DTCS) (CONTINUED)

➡Note: Not all trouble codes apply to all models. Also, some codes have multiple definitions. Your generic scan tool will tell you which definition applies to the engine management system that you are scanning.

| Code | Probable cause |
| --- | --- |
| P0135 | Oxygen sensor heater, left or right upstream oxygen sensor, voltage supply |
| P0136 | Oxygen sensor signal, left or right downstream oxygen sensor, electrical fault |
| P0141 | Oxygen sensor heater, left or right downstream oxygen sensor, internal resistor |
| P0141 | Oxygen sensor heater, left or right downstream oxygen sensor, voltage supply |
| P0150 | Oxygen sensor signal, left or right upstream oxygen sensor, electrical fault |
| P0153 | Aging downstream oxygen sensor, left upstream oxygen sensor, period duration |
| P0155 | Oxygen sensor heater, left upstream oxygen sensor, internal resistor |
| P0156 | Oxygen sensor signal, left downstream oxygen sensor, electrical fault |
| P0161 | Oxygen sensor heater, left downstream oxygen sensor, internal resistor |
| P0170 | Adaptation of air/fuel ratio at limit, at idle or at partial load, right cylinder bank |
| P0170 | Adaptation of air/fuel ratio at limit, between idle and partial load, right cylinder bank |
| P0170 | Coolant anti-boil protection |
| P0173 | Adaptation of air/fuel ratio at limit, at idle or partial load, left cylinder bank |
| P0173 | Adaptation of air/fuel ratio at limit, between idle and partial load, left cylinder bank |
| P0201 | Fuel injector, cylinder 1 |
| P0202 | Fuel injector, cylinder 2 |
| P0203 | Fuel injector, cylinder 3 |
| P0204 | Fuel injector, cylinder 4 |
| P0205 | Fuel injector, cylinder 5 |
| P0206 | Fuel injector, cylinder 6 |
| P0221 | Powertrain Control Module (PCM), fault in function monitoring |
| P0300 | Misfire |
| P0301 | Misfire, cylinder 1 |
| P0302 | Misfire, cylinder 2 |

| Code | Probable cause |
|------|----------------|
| P0303 | Misfire, cylinder 3 |
| P0304 | Misfire, cylinder 4 |
| P0305 | Misfire, cylinder 5 |
| P0306 | Misfire, cylinder 6 |
| P0335 | Crankshaft Position (CKP) sensor |
| P0341 | Camshaft Position (CMP) sensor |
| P0370 | Deviation of camshaft position relative to crankshaft position |
| P0400 | Exhaust Gas Recirculation (EGR) malfunction |
| P0403 | Exhaust Gas Recirculation (EGR) pressure transducer |
| P0410 | Air injection malfunction |
| P0410 | Air injection relay |
| P0412 | Air injection pump switchover valve |
| P0422 | Catalytic converter efficiency too low, right catalytic converter |
| P0422 | EVAP system, micro leak or minor leak |
| P0432 | Catalytic converter efficiency too low, left catalytic converter |
| P0440 | EVAP system, leak |
| P0442 | EVAP system, micro leak or minor leak |
| P0443 | EVAP system, purge control valve |
| P0446 | EVAP canister shut-off valve, voltage supply |
| P0446 | EVAP canister shut-off valve, plausibility |
| P0450 | Fuel tank pressure sensor, plausibility |
| P0455 | EVAP system, major leak |
| P0460 | Fuel tank fill level |
| P0500 | Controller Area Network (CAN) fault detection, left front or rear wheel speed signal |
| P0507 | Idle speed control |
| P0560 | Control unit voltage supply |

## OBD-II DIAGNOSTIC TROUBLE CODES (DTCS) (CONTINUED)

➥**Note: Not all trouble codes apply to all models. Also, some codes have multiple definitions. Your generic scan tool will tell you which definition applies to the engine management system that you are scanning.**

| Code | Probable cause |
|---|---|
| P0600 | Controller Area Network (CAN) fault detection, CAN message from ABC control unit |
| P0600 | Controller Area Network (CAN) fault detection, CAN message from electronic selector lever module control unit |
| P0600 | Controller Area Network (CAN) fault detection, CAN message from ESP control unit |
| P0600 | Controller Area Network (CAN) fault detection, CAN message from ETC control unit |
| P0600 | Controller Area Network (CAN) fault detection, CAN message from instrument cluster |
| P0600 | Controller Area Network (CAN) fault detection, CAN message from steering column module |
| P0700 | Gear implausible or leak in transmission |
| P0700 | Command valve jams in pressure position |
| P0702 | Electronic Transmission Control (ETC) control unit, internal transmission fault |
| P0702 | Electronic Transmission Control (ETC) control unit, implausible torque request from ETC control unit |
| P0702 | Electronic Transmission Control (ETC) control unit, CAN transmission error for torque request from ETC control unit |
| P0702 | Supply voltage to valves |
| P0705 | Electronic Transmission Control (ETC) control unit, selector lever module incorrectly coded |
| P0715 | Supply voltage and speed sensors function |
| P0720 | Electronic Transmission Control (ETC) unit |
| P0720 | Electronic Transmission Control (ETC) unit, CAN message from rear wheels from ESP control unit missing or incorrect |
| P0730 | Gear comparison negative too many times |
| P0740 | Torque converter lock-up clutch |
| P0743 | Torque converter lock-up solenoid valve |
| P0748 | Modulating pressure control solenoid valve |
| P0748 | Shift pressure control solenoid valve |
| P0753 | 1-2/4-5 shift solenoid valve |
| P0758 | 2-3 shift solenoid valve |
| P0763 | 3-4 shift solenoid valve |

## 3  Accelerator Pedal Position (APP) sensor - replacement

▶ Refer to illustration 3.2a, 3.2b, 3.2c and 3.3

➡Note: The Accelerator Pedal Position (APP) sensor is located at the upper end of the accelerator pedal assembly. The APP sensor is an integral component of the accelerator pedal assembly; to replace the APP sensor, you must replace the pedal assembly.

1  Remove the knee bolster trim panel (see Chapter 11).
2  Remove the APP sensor assembly mounting nut (see illustra-

tions), lift the sensor/pedal assembly off its mounting stud and pull the assembly down to disengage the mounting tab at the top (see illustration) from its mounting slot.

3  Disconnect the electrical connector from the APP sensor (see illustration) and remove the APP sensor assembly.

4  Installation is the reverse of removal. Make sure that the mounting tab at the top of the sensor/pedal assembly is correctly aligned with its mounting slot.

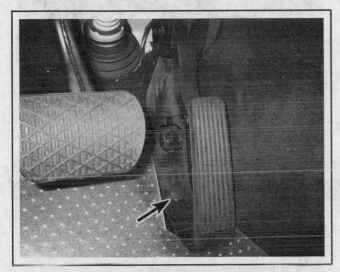

3.2a  To detach the lower end of the APP sensor/accelerator pedal assembly, remove this trim cover . . .

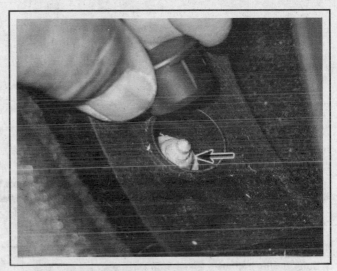

3.2b  . . . and remove the mounting nut. To access the APP sensor electrical connector, lift the APP sensor/accelerator pedal assembly off its mounting stud . . .

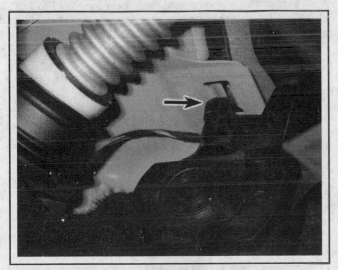

3.2c  . . . then pull down the sensor/pedal assembly to disengage the mounting tab at the top from its mounting slot. When installing the sensor/pedal assembly, make sure that this tab is correctly aligned with its slot

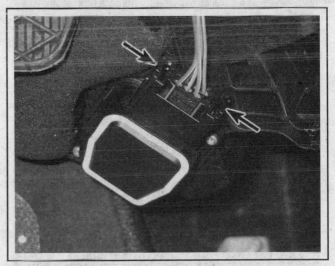

3.3  To disconnect the electrical connector from the APP sensor, depress these two release tabs

## 4 Altitude sensor - replacement

▶ Refer to illustration 4.1

➡ Note: The altitude sensor, which is used on 2003 through 2005 models, is located on the left side of the air filter housing, above the throttle body.

1  Disconnect the electrical connector from the altitude sensor (see illustration).

2  Remove the sensor mounting screws and detach the sensor.

3  Installation is the reverse of removal.

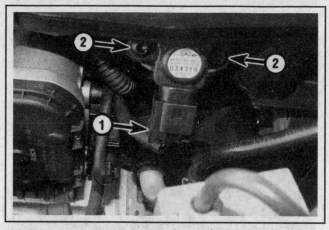

4.1  To remove the altitude sensor from the air filter housing, depress the release tab (1) and disconnect the electrical connector, then remove the two sensor mounting screws (2) (2003 through 2005 four-cylinder models)

## 5 Camshaft Position (CMP) sensor - replacement

### 2001 THROUGH 2005 V6 MODELS

▶ Refer to illustrations 5.2 and 5.4

➡ Note: The CMP sensor is located on the front end of the right cylinder head.

1  Remove the engine cover.

2  Disconnect the electrical connector from the CMP sensor (see illustration).

3  Remove the sensor mounting bolt and remove the CMP sensor.

4  Remove and replace the old CMP sensor O-ring (see illustration). Whether you're installing the old CMP sensor or a new unit, be sure to use a new O-ring.

5  Installation is the reverse of removal.

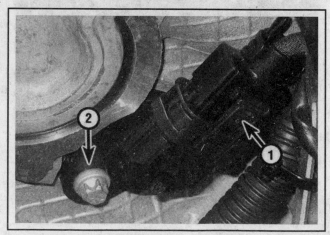

5.2  To remove the CMP sensor from a 2001 through 2005 V6 model, depress the release tab (1) and disconnect the electrical connector, then remove the mounting bolt (2)

### 2006 AND LATER V6 MODELS

▶ Refer to illustrations 5.7a and 5.7b

➡ Note: The CMP sensors are located at the front end of the cylinder heads. There are four CMP sensors, one for each intake camshaft and one for each exhaust camshaft.

6  Remove the front engine cover, then remove the left or right fresh air intake duct (see *Air filter housing - removal and installation* in Chapter 4).

7  Disconnect the electrical connector from the CMP sensor (see illustrations).

8  Remove the CMP sensor mounting bolt and remove the CMP sensor.

5.4  Even if you plan to reuse the old CMP sensor, be sure to remove and replace the O-ring

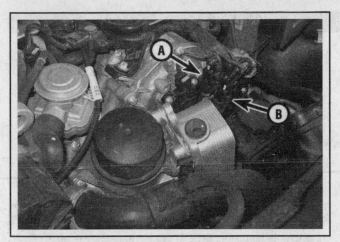

5.7a The intake CMP sensor (A) and the exhaust CMP sensor (B) for the left cylinder head are located on the front of the head (2006 and later V6 models)

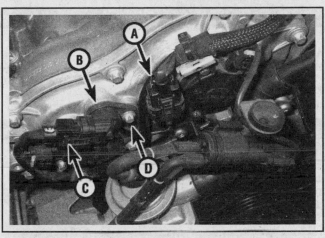

5.7b The intake CMP sensor (A) and the exhaust CMP sensor (B) for the right cylinder head are located on the front of tho head. To remove any of the four CMP sensors, simply depress the release tab (C) and pull off the connector, then remove the sensor mounting bolt (D) (2006 and later V6 models)

9 Remove and replace the old CMP sensor O-ring. Whether you're installing the old CMP sensor or a new unit, be sure to use a new O-ring.

10 Installation is the reverse of removal.

## 2002 FOUR-CYLINDER MODELS

➡Note: The CMP sensor is located on the top of the valve cover, on the left side of the cover.

11 Remove the engine cover.
12 Disconnect the electrical connector from the CMP sensor.
13 Remove the CMP sensor mounting bolt and remove the sensor.
14 Remove and replace the old CMP sensor O-ring. Whether you're installing the old CMP sensor or a new unit, be sure to use a new O-ring.
15 Installation is the reverse of removal.

## 2003 THROUGH 2005 FOUR-CYLINDER MODELS

▶ Refer to illustrations 5.17a and 5.17b

16 There are two CMP sensors on these models. The intake CMP sensor is located on top of the valve cover, to the left of the ignition coil for cylinder No. 3. The exhaust CMP sensor is located on the right side of the cylinder head, in the middle of the head, just below the right side of the valve cover.
17 Disconnect the electrical connector from the CMP sensor (see illustrations).
18 Remove the CMP sensor mounting bolt and remove the sensor.
19 Remove and replace the old CMP sensor O-ring. Whether you're installing the old CMP sensor or a new unit, be sure to use a new O-ring.
20 Installation is the reverse of removal.

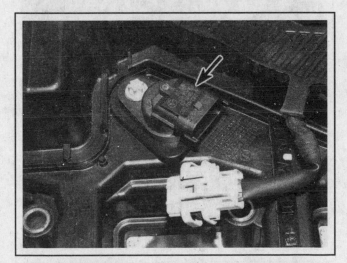

5.17a Intake CMP sensor, located on the top of the valve cover on the left side (2003 through 2005 four-cylinder engines)

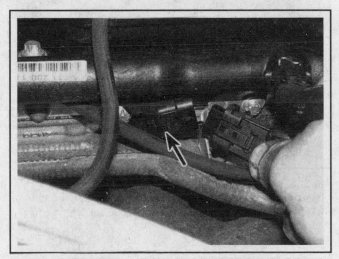

5.17b Exhaust CMP sensor, located on the right side of the cylinder head, just below the valve cover (2003 through 2005 four-cylinder engines)

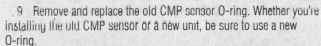

**6    Crankshaft Position (CKP) sensor - replacement**

## V6 MODELS

◆ **Refer to illustrations 6.3 and 6.4**

✳✳ **CAUTION:**

**According to Mercedes Benz, if you're replacing the old CKP sensor with a new sensor, the new unit must be re-initialized by a STAR DIAGNOSIS unit (a factory scan tool). So, you can remove and install the old CKP sensor, but if you replace this sensor at home, the engine might not run correctly when you start it up.**

➥**Note: The CKP sensor is located on the upper left rear edge of the engine block, behind and below the back end of the left cylinder head. It is extremely difficult to access because of the tight clearance between the engine block and the cowl, and extensive component removal is required to reach it.**

1    On 2001 through 2005 models with an integral engine cover/air filter housing, and on all 2006 and later models, remove the front cover, then remove the engine cover/air filter housing (see *Air filter housing - removal and installation* in Chapter 4).

2    You should be able to access the CKP sensor from the left side of the engine, between the back end of the left cylinder head and the firewall. But if you're unable to do so, remove the Mass Air Flow/Intake Air Temperature (MAF/IAT) sensor (see Section 12) and, if that still doesn't give you enough room, the elbow-shaped air intake duct between the MAF/IAT sensor and the throttle body (see *Throttle body -*

*removal and installation* in Chapter 4).

3    Disconnect the electrical connector from the CKP sensor (see illustration).

4    Remove the CKP sensor mounting bolt (see illustration) and remove the sensor from the engine.

5    Installation is the reverse of removal.

## FOUR-CYLINDER MODELS

✳✳ **CAUTION:**

**According to Mercedes Benz, if you're replacing the old CKP sensor with a new sensor, the new unit must be re-initialized by a STAR DIAGNOSIS unit (a factory scan tool). So, you can remove and install the old CKP sensor, but if you replace this sensor at home, the engine might not run correctly when you start it up.**

➥**Note: The CKP sensor is located on the upper left rear edge of the engine block, slightly to the left of the back end of the cylinder head.**

6    Raise the vehicle and place it securely on jackstands.

7    Remove the lower engine cover.

8    Disconnect the electrical connector from the CKP sensor.

9    Remove the CKP sensor mounting bolt and remove the sensor from the engine.

10   Installation is the reverse of removal.

6.3  To disconnect the electrical connector from the CKP sensor, depress this release tab and pull off the connector (2001 through 2005 V6 model shown; 2006 and later models similar)

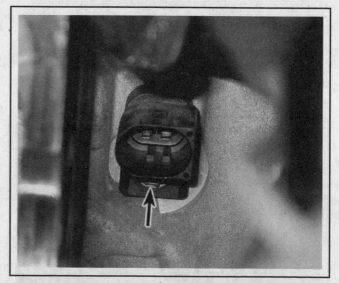

6.4  To detach the CKP sensor from the engine block, remove the sensor mounting bolt

## 7  Engine Coolant Temperature (ECT) sensor - replacement

**✳✳ WARNING:**

**Wait until the engine is completely cool before beginning this procedure.**

### 2001 THROUGH 2005 V6 MODELS

▶ Refer to illustrations 7.3, 7.4 and 7.5

➡Note: The ECT sensor is located at the front of the engine, on top of the timing chain cover, just to the right of the thermostat housing.

1   Remove the front engine cover.
2   Drain the engine coolant to a level below that of the ECT sensor (see Chapter 1).
3   Disconnect the electrical connector from the ECT sensor (see illustration).
4   Using a small screwdriver, carefully pry up the wire retainer clip that secures the ECT sensor (see illustration).
5   Remove and replace the old ECT sensor O-ring (see illustration). Even if you're planning to install the old sensor, make sure that you replace the O-ring.
6   Installation is otherwise the reverse of removal.
7   Refill the cooling system (see Chapter 1).

### 2006 AND LATER V6 MODELS

➡Note: The ECT sensor is located on the back end of the left cylinder head. It is extremely difficult to access because of the tight clearance between the head and the cowl.

8   Remove the front cover and the air filter housing/engine cover (see *Air filter housing - removal and installation* in Chapter 4).
9   Remove the Mass Air Flow/Intake Air Temperature (MAF/IAT) sensor (see Section 12) and the elbow-shaped air intake duct between the MAF/IAT sensor and the throttle body.
10  Drain the coolant below the level of the cylinder heads (see Chapter 1).
11  Disconnect the ECT sensor electrical connector.
12  Remove the ECT sensor mounting bolt and remove the sensor.
13  Remove and replace the old ECT sensor O-ring. Even if you're planning to install the old sensor, make sure that you replace the O-ring.

7.3  To disconnect the electrical connector from the ECT sensor, depress this release tab and pull off the connector (2001 through 2005 V6 models)

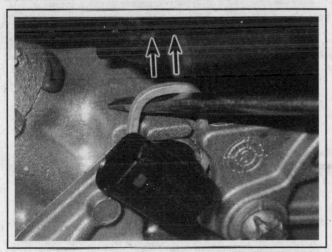

7.4  Carefully pry up on this wire retainer with a small screwdriver, then pull out the ECT sensor (2001 through 2005 V6 models)

7.5  Be sure to replace the old ECT sensor O-ring whether you're installing the old sensor or a new unit (2001 through 2005 V6 models)

14 Installation is otherwise the reverse of removal.

15 Refill the cooling system (see Chapter 1).

## 2002 FOUR-CYLINDER MODELS

➡**Note: The ECT sensor is located on the thermostat housing at the front of the engine, directly in front of the forward end of the valve cover.**

16 Remove the engine cover.

17 Drain the coolant below the level of the thermostat housing (see Chapter 1).

18 Disconnect the electrical connector from the ECT sensor.

19 Unscrew and remove the ECT sensor.

20 Wrap the threads of the new ECT sensor with Teflon tape to prevent leaks. Even if you're planning to reuse the old ECT sensor, wrap the threads with Teflon tape.

21 Installation is the reverse of removal.

22 Refill the cooling system.

## 2003 THROUGH 2005 FOUR-CYLINDER MODELS

▶ **Refer to illustration 7.24**

➡**Note: The ECT sensor is located on the right side of the cylinder head, behind the secondary air injection/exhaust gas recirculation combination valve.**

23 Drain the coolant below the level of the sensor (see Chapter 1).

24 Disconnect the ECT sensor electrical connector (see illustration).

25 Remove the ECT sensor from the cylinder head.

26 Installation is the reverse of removal.

27 Refill the cooling system.

**7.24 On 2003 through 2005 four-cylinder models, the ECT sensor is located on the right side of the cylinder head**

## 8   Fuel Tank Temperature (FTT) sensor - replacement

The FTT sensor is an integral component of the fuel pump/fuel level sensor module. To replace it you have to replace the fuel pump/fuel level sensor module (see Chapter 4).

## 9   Intake Air Temperature (IAT) sensor - replacement

The IAT sensor is an integral component of the Mass Air Flow (MAF) sensor (see Section 12).

## 10   Knock sensor - replacement

### V6 MODELS

▶ **Refer to illustration 10.4**

➡**Note: There are two knock sensors on these models and they're located on top of the block, in the valley between the cylinder heads, underneath the intake manifold.**

1 Remove the engine cover/air filter housing (see *Air filter housing - removal and installation* in Chapter 4).

2 Remove the fuel rail and fuel injector assembly (see Chapter 4).

3 Remove the intake manifold (see Chapter 2A).

4 Disconnect the electrical connector from the knock sensor (see illustration).

5 Remove the knock sensor mounting bolt and remove the knock sensor.

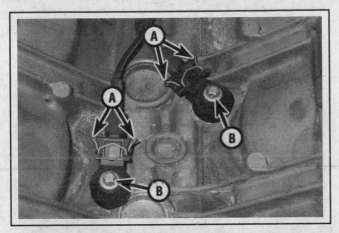

**10.4 To remove either knock sensor, squeeze the wire retainers (A) and pull off the electrical connector, then remove the sensor retaining bolt (B)**

6 Installation is the reverse of removal. Be sure to tighten the knock sensor mounting bolt to the torque listed in this Chapter's Specifications.

**✵✵ CAUTION:**

Over- or under-tightening the knock sensor mounting bolt(s) will affect knock sensor performance, which might affect the PCM's spark control ability.

## FOUR-CYLINDER MODELS

➡Note: The knock sensor is located on the left side of the engine block, slightly above and near the front of the starter solenoid.

7 Raise the vehicle and place it securely on jackstands.
8 Remove the supercharger (see Chapter 4).
9 Disconnect the electrical connector from the knock sensor.
10 Remove the knock sensor mounting bolt and remove the knock sensor.
11 Installation is the reverse of removal. Be sure to tighten the knock sensor mounting bolt to the torque listed in this Chapter's Specifications.

**✵✵ CAUTION:**

Over- or under-tightening the knock sensor mounting bolt(s) will affect knock sensor performance, which might affect the PCM's spark control ability.

---

## 11 Manifold Absolute Pressure (MAP) sensor - replacement

### 2001 THROUGH 2005 V6 MODELS

⬦ Refer to illustrations 11.2 and 11.4

➡Note: The MAP sensor is located at the front of the engine, on a bracket bolted to the upper right corner of the timing chain cover.

1 Remove the front engine cover.
2 Disconnect the electrical connector from the MAP sensor (see illustration).
3 Remove the MAP sensor retaining bolt.
4 Pull the MAP sensor forward, off its mounting bracket, disconnect the vacuum hose (see illustration) and remove the sensor.
5 Installation is the reverse of removal.

**11.2 To detach the MAP sensor from its mounting bracket, depress the release tab (1) and disconnect the electrical connector, then remove the MAP sensor retaining bolt (2) (2001 through 2005 V6 models)**

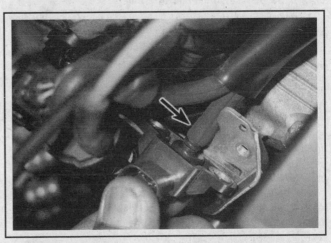

**11.4 Pull the MAP sensor forward, off its mounting bracket, and disconnect the vacuum hose (2001 through 2005 V6 models)**

## 2006 AND LATER V6 MODELS

♦ **Refer to illustration 11.7**

➡**Note: The MAP sensor is located at the front of the engine, at the right front corner of the left valve cover.**

6  Remove the front engine cover.

7  Disconnect the electrical connector from the MAP sensor (see illustration).

8  Spread the retaining tangs apart and detach the MAP sensor from its bracket.

9  Disconnect the vacuum hose from the pipe on the underside of the sensor and remove the sensor.

10  Installation is the reverse of removal.

## FOUR-CYLINDER MODELS

➡**Note: The MAP sensor is located at the left rear corner of the intake manifold.**

11  Disconnect the electrical connector from the MAP sensor.

12  Remove the MAP sensor mounting bolts and remove the MAP sensor.

13  Installation is the reverse of removal.

**11.7  MAP sensor details (2006 and later V6 models):**

*A  Depress the release tab and disconnect the electrical connector*

*B  Spread the tangs to detach the sensor from the bracket, then detach the hose from the underside*

## 12  Mass Air Flow/Intake Air Temperature (MAF/IAT) sensor - replacement

## V6 MODELS

♦ **Refer to illustrations 12.2a, 12.2b, 12.3, 12.4a, 12.4b and 12.5**

➡**Note: The MAF/IAT sensor is located at the rear of the engine, underneath the back end of the engine cover/air filter housing and above the elbow-shaped air intake duct that connects it to the throttle body below. The photos accompanying this Section depict a typical MAF/IAT sensor used on 2001 through 2005 models, but the MAF/IAT sensor used on 2005 and later models is virtually identical to the one shown here.**

1  Remove the engine cover/air filter housing (see Air filter housing - removal and installation in Chapter 4). Disconnect the air intake duct from the MAF/IAT sensor and from the air intake resonator, then remove it (see *Air filter housing - removal and installation* in Chapter 4).

2  Disconnect the electrical connector from the MAF/IAT sensor (see illustrations).

3  Disengage the PCV hose from the hose clip on the right side of the MAF/IAT sensor (see illustration).

4  Detach the MAF/IAT sensor from the intake manifold (see illustrations).

5  Using a flashlight, locate the metal spring clamp on the lower end of the MAF/IAT sensor (it's in the back, on the firewall side). This clamp secures the lower end of the MAF/IAT sensor to the elbow-shaped air intake duct that connects the sensor to the throttle body. Using a screwdriver, pry the clamp to the rear (see illustration) to disengage it from the MAF/IAT sensor.

6  Grasp the MAF/IAT sensor firmly and pull it straight up to disengage it from the elbow-shaped air intake duct.

7  The sensor and the duct are sealed by a large rubber seal located inside the inlet mouth of the duct. Remove this seal and inspect it for cracks, tears and deterioration. If the seal is damaged in any way, replace it.

8  Installation is the reverse of removal. When installing the large clamp for the MAF/IAT sensor, make sure that the two support brackets of the clamp are fully engaged with the lugs on the back of the intake manifold (see illustration 12.4b).

## FOUR-CYLINDER MODELS

### 2002 models

➡**Note: The MAF/IAT sensor is located on the left side of the engine, between the left charge air line (carries pressurized intake air from the intercooler to the MAF/IAT sensor) and the rubber duct that connects the sensor to the air scoop (the short horn-shaped piece between the rubber air duct and the throttle body).**

9  Remove the engine cover.

10  Disconnect the electrical connector from the MAF/IAT sensor.

11  Loosen the hose clamp that secures the air scoop (the short horn-shaped air intake duct between the MAF/IAT sensor and the throttle body) to the short connection hose between the MAF/IAT sensor and the air scoop, then unbolt the air scoop from the throttle body and remove the air scoop.

12  Remove the hose clamp that secures the short connection hose to the MAF/IAT sensor and remove the hose.

13  Remove the two bolts that secure the MAF/IAT sensor to the air intake duct and remove the MAF/IAT sensor.

14  Installation is the reverse of removal.

12.2a  To disconnect the electrical connector from the MAF/IAT sensor . . .

12.2b  . . . grasp the connector firmly, depress the two release tabs and pull off the connector (2001 through 2005 V6 models)

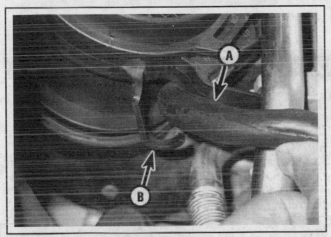

12.3  Disengage the PCV hose (A) from the hose clip (B) on the right side of the MAF/IAT sensor

12.4a  To detach the MAF/IAT sensor from the intake manifold, unlock this clamp with a screwdriver . . .

12.4b  . . . then disengage the clamp support brackets from these two lugs on the back of the intake manifold. When installing the MAF/IAT sensor, make sure that the clamp brackets are correctly engaged with these two lugs (intake manifold and MAF/IAT sensor removed for clarity)

12.5  To disengage the MAF/IAT sensor from the elbow-shaped air intake duct below the sensor, pry this metal spring clamp (on the sensor's lower end, near the firewall) from the sensor with a large screwdriver

## 2003 through 2005 models

▶ Refer to illustration 12.16

➡Note: The MAF/IAT sensor is located on the left side of the engine, at the back (inlet) end of the air filter housing.

15  Remove the engine cover.

16  Disconnect the electrical connector from the MAF sensor (see illustration).

17  Remove the air filter housing (see Chapter 4).

18  Remove the bolts that secure the MAF/IAT sensor to the air intake duct and remove the sensor.

19  Installation is the reverse of removal.

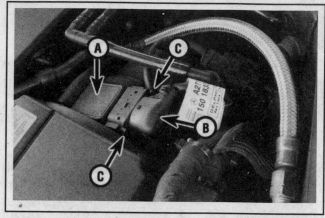

**12.16  On 2003 through 2005 four-cylinder models the MAF/IAT sensor (A) is located at the back of the air filter housing. To disconnect the electrical connector (B), depress these two release tabs (C)**

## 13  Oxygen sensors - description and replacement

### DESCRIPTION

1  An oxygen sensor is a galvanic battery. Unburned oxygen in the exhaust reacts with elements inside the oxygen sensor to produce a voltage output that varies from 0.1 volt (high oxygen, lean mixture) to 0.9 volt (low oxygen, rich mixture). The upstream oxygen sensors, which are located on the exhaust manifolds, ahead of the catalytic converters, provide feedback signals to the PCM that indicate the amount of leftover oxygen in the exhaust. The PCM monitors this variable voltage to determine the correct fuel injector pulse width (the duration of the time interval during which each injector sprays fuel) required to support complete combustion. A mixture ratio of 14.7 parts air to 1 part fuel is the ideal ratio for complete combustion and minimum exhaust emissions, as well as the best combination for fuel economy and engine performance. Using the input signals from the oxygen sensors, the PCM tries to maintain this air/fuel ratio of 14.7:1 at all times.

2  The downstream sensors, which are mounted on the catalytic converters, are identical to the upstream sensors and operate in the same way. But the downstream oxygen sensors have no effect on PCM control of the air/fuel ratio. Instead, the PCM uses the downstream oxygen sensor signals to monitor the efficiency of the catalytic converters. Downstream oxygen sensors produce an output voltage signal that fluctuates more slowly, which reflects the lower oxygen content of the catalyzed exhaust gases. As a catalyst ages, its efficiency diminishes and the signal produced by a downstream oxygen sensor starts to fall outside the expected range. The PCM uses this degraded signal to calculate and predict failure of the catalytic converter.

3  On V6 models, there are four oxygen sensors. The two upstream sensors (1/1 and 2/1) are located below the exhaust manifolds, on the exhaust pipes that connect the exhaust manifolds to the catalytic converters. The two downstream sensors (1/2 and 2/2) are located on the exhaust pipes right behind the catalytic converters. On four-cylinder models, there are two oxygen sensors. On 2002 four-cylinder models, the upstream sensor is located in the exhaust pipe that connects the exhaust manifold to the catalytic converter; the downstream sensor is located in the pipe just behind the catalyst. On 2003 through 2005 four-cylinder models, the catalytic converter is an integral component of the exhaust manifold. The upstream sensor is located on the upper end of the catalyst; the downstream sensor is located on the lower end of the catalyst.

4  An oxygen sensor produces no voltage when it is below its normal operating temperature of about 600-degrees F. During this warm-up period, the PCM operates in an open-loop fuel control mode. It does not use the oxygen sensor signal as a feedback indication of residual oxygen in the exhaust. Instead, the PCM controls fuel metering based on the inputs of other sensors and its own programs.

5  An oxygen sensor depends on three conditions in order to operate correctly:

a)  *Electrical* - *The low voltage generated by the sensor requires good, clean connections. Always check the connectors whenever an oxygen sensor problem is suspected or indicated.*

b)  *Correct operating temperature* - *The PCM will not react to the sensor signal until the sensor reaches approximately 600-degrees F. This factor must be considered when evaluating the performance of the sensor.*

c)  *Unleaded fuel* - *Unleaded fuel is essential for correct sensor operation.*

6  The PCM can detect several different oxygen sensor problems and set Diagnostic Trouble Codes (DTCs) to indicate the specific fault (see Section 2). When an oxygen sensor DTC occurs, the PCM disregards the oxygen sensor signal voltage and reverts to open-loop fuel control as described previously.

## REPLACEMENT

◆ Refer to illustrations 13.8, 13.9a, 13.9b and 13.9c

**✳✳ WARNING:**

Be careful not to burn yourself during the following procedure.

➡ **Note 1:** Since the exhaust pipe contracts when cool, the oxygen sensor may be difficult to unscrew. To make sensor removal easier, start the engine and let it run for a minute or two, then turn it off.

➡ **Note 2:** On V6 models, the two upstream sensors (1/1 and 2/1) are located below the exhaust manifolds, on the exhaust pipes that connect the exhaust manifolds to the catalytic converters. The connectors for the upstream sensors are located below the transmission bellhousing and both the upstream and downstream sensors are accessed from underneath the vehicle.

➡ **Note 3:** On 2002 four-cylinder models, the upstream sensor is located in the exhaust pipe that connects the exhaust manifold to the catalytic converter; the downstream sensor is located in the pipe just behind the catalyst. On 2003 through 2005 four-cylinder models, the catalytic converter is an integral component of the exhaust manifold. The upstream sensor is located on the upper end of the catalyst; the downstream sensor is located on the lower end of the catalyst.

7   Raise the front of the vehicle and place it securely on jackstands.

8   Locate the electrical connector for the oxygen sensor that you want to replace (see illustration), then disconnect it.

9   Locate the oxygen sensor that you want to replace (V6 upstream sensors, see illustration; V6 downstream sensors, see illustration 13.8; four-cylinder sensors, see illustration) and unscrew it with an oxygen sensor socket (see illustration) or an open wrench. If there's enough room, you should use an oxygen sensor socket to remove an oxygen sensor. On some models there isn't enough room to use a socket-style oxygen sensor socket, though you might be able to use the type that employs a shallow socket. The larger style oxygen sensor sockets are available at most auto parts stores; oxygen sensor sockets with a shal-

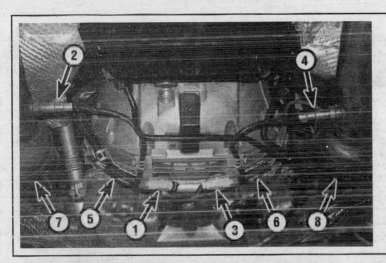

**13.8 Typical oxygen sensor and connector locations (2001 through 2005 V6 model shown, 2006 and later V6 models similar)**

1   Electrical connector for left downstream oxygen sensor
2   Left downstream oxygen sensor
3   Electrical connector for right downstream oxygen sensor
4   Right downstream oxygen sensor
5   Electrical connector for left upstream oxygen sensor
6   Electrical connector for right upstream oxygen sensor
7   Left catalytic converter
8   Right catalytic converter

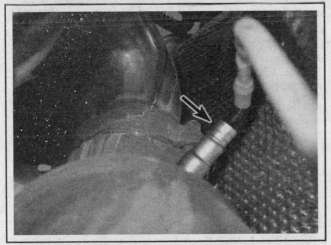

**13.9a  The right upstream oxygen sensor (shown) and the left upstream oxygen sensor (not shown) are located on the exhaust pipe right below the exhaust manifold flange and right above the upper end of the catalytic converter (V6 models)**

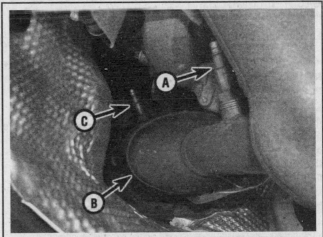

**13.9b  On a four-cylinder model, the upstream oxygen sensor (A) is located right above the catalytic converter (B) and the downstream sensor (C) is located on the catalyst. You can access the upstream sensor from the engine compartment, but you might find it easier to access the downstream sensor from underneath the vehicle**

**13.9c To protect an oxygen sensor from damage during removal and installation, use an oxygen sensor socket**

lower socket are generally available only from specialty tool suppliers.

10 Clean the threads inside the sensor mounting hole in the exhaust manifold with a tap.

11 If you're installing the old sensor, clean off the threads, then apply a coat of anti-seize compound (such as Loctite® 771-64 or a suitable equivalent) to the threads before installing the sensor. If you're installing a new sensor, do not apply anti-seize compound; new sensors are already coated with anti-seize.

12 Installation is otherwise the reverse of removal. Be sure to tighten the oxygen sensor to the torque listed in this Chapter's Specifications.

## 14 Powertrain Control Module (PCM) - removal and installation

### ✳✳ CAUTION:

You can remove the PCM to access some other component(s), but do NOT replace the PCM at home. If you ever see a Diagnostic Trouble Code (DTC) that indicates a problem with the PCM, have it replaced by a dealer. A new PCM must be reprogrammed with a factory scan tool by a dealership service department, so if you were to replace the old PCM with a new unit, it wouldn't work until the vehicle was towed to a dealer for programming.

### 2001 THROUGH 2005 V6 MODELS AND 2002 FOUR-CYLINDER MODELS

▶ Refer to illustrations 14.2, 14.3, 14.4a, 14.4b and 14.4c

➡ Note 1: The PCM is located in a watertight plastic box in the left rear corner of the engine compartment, just to the left of the power brake booster/brake master cylinder assembly.

➡ Note 2: The following procedure depicts complete removal of the PCM. If you're simply removing the PCM to access the brake master cylinder and/or power brake booster assembly, it's not necessary to actually disconnect the electrical connectors from the PCM. Simply dislodge the large grommets for the PCM harnesses, lift out the PCM and set it aside.

1 Disconnect the cable from the negative battery terminal (see Chapter 5, Section 1).

2 Remove the cover (see illustration).

3 Disengage the two windshield wiper arm links (see illustration).

4 Lift up the PCM and disconnect the electrical connectors (see illustrations).

5 Installation is the reverse of removal.

### 2006 AND LATER V6 MODELS

▶ Refer to illustrations 14.8 and 14.9

➡ Note: The PCM is located on top of the intake manifold, in the center of the engine cover/air filter housing.

6 Disconnect the cable from the negative battery terminal (see Chapter 5, Section 1).

7 Remove the engine cover/air filter housing assembly (see *Air filter housing - removal and installation* in Chapter 4).

8 Disconnect the electrical connectors from the PCM (see illustration).

9 To remove the PCM, simply disengage its four ball-type locator pins from its left and right mounting brackets (see illustration). While the PCM is out, inspect the condition of the insulator grommets for the locator pins. If they're cracked, torn or otherwise deteriorated, replace them.

10 Installation is the reverse of removal.

**14.2 Unsnap the two wire retainers and remove the cover (2001 through 2005 V6 and 2002 four-cylinder models)**

14.3  Use a pair of needle nose pliers or a trim removal tool to separate the two windshield wiper links, then push the links out of the way (2001 through 2005 V6 and 2002 four-cylinder models)

14.4a  Lift up the PCM to provide better access to the electrical connectors . . .

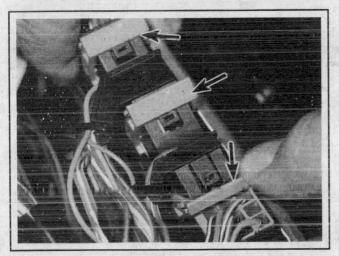

14.4b  . . . flip the lever forward to unlock each of the three large electrical connectors, disconnect all three of them . . .

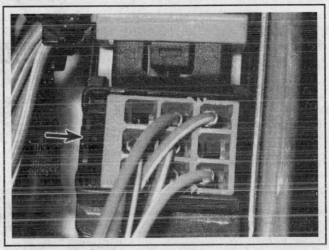

14.4c  . . . depress this release tab and disconnect the smaller, forward electrical connector, then remove the PCM (2001 through 2005 V6 and 2002 four-cylinder models)

14.8  To unlock the PCM connectors from the PCM, pull out the sliding catches (2006 and later V6 models)

14.9  Grasp the PCM firmly and pull straight up to disengage the PCM locator pins (2006 and later V6 models)

## 2003 THROUGH 2005 FOUR-CYLINDER MODELS

▶ **Refer to illustration 14.12**

➡**Note: The PCM is located on the left side of the air filter housing.**

11  Disconnect the cable from the negative battery terminal (see Chapter 5, Section 1).

12  Disconnect the electrical connectors from the PCM (see illustration).

13  Remove the air filter housing and PCM as a single assembly (see *Air filter housing - removal and installation* in Chapter 4).

14  Remove the four PCM mounting bolts to detach the PCM from the air filter housing.

15  Installation is the reverse of removal.

**14.12  To disconnect the electrical connectors from the PCM, pull out the sliding catches (2003 through 2005 four-cylinder models)**

## 15  Catalytic converter - description, check and replacement

➡**Note: Because of a Federally-mandated extended warranty which covers emission-related components such as the catalytic converter, check with a dealer service department before replacing the converter at your own expense.**

### GENERAL DESCRIPTION

1  A catalytic converter (or catalyst) is an emission control device in the exhaust system that reduces certain pollutants in the exhaust gas stream. There are two types of converters. An oxidation catalyst reduces hydrocarbons (HC) and carbon monoxide (CO). A reduction catalyst reduces oxides of nitrogen (NOx). A catalyst that can reduce all three pollutants is known as a "Three-Way Catalyst" (TWC).

2  All V6 models covered by this manual are equipped with two catalysts (see illustration 13.8), one below each exhaust manifold flange. The upper end of each catalyst has a short inlet pipe with a mounting flange that bolts to the exhaust manifold flange. The lower end of each catalyst has a short outlet pipe with a flange that bolts to the Y-pipe that connects the two catalysts to the remainder of the exhaust system. All four-cylinder models use a single catalyst. On 2002 models, it's located near the rear end, and is an integral component, of the front exhaust pipe. On 2003 through 2005 models, it's directly below the exhaust manifold (see illustration 13.9b). On some of the later four-cylinder models, the catalyst is an integral component of the exhaust manifold and cannot be replaced separately from the exhaust manifold.

### CHECK

3  The test equipment for a catalytic converter (a loaded-mode dynamometer and a 5-gas analyzer) is expensive. If you suspect that the converter on your vehicle is malfunctioning, take it to a dealer or authorized emission inspection facility for diagnosis and repair.

4  Whenever you raise the vehicle to service underbody components, inspect the converter for leaks, corrosion, dents and other damage. Carefully inspect the welds and/or flange bolts and nuts that attach the front and rear ends of the converter to the exhaust system. If you note any damage, replace the converter.

5  Although catalytic converters don't break too often, they can become clogged or even plugged up. The easiest way to check for a restricted converter is to use a vacuum gauge to diagnose the effect of a blocked exhaust on intake vacuum.

a) *Connect a vacuum gauge to an intake manifold vacuum source (see Chapter 2B).*

b) *Warm the engine to operating temperature, place the transaxle in PARK (automatic transmission) or NEUTRAL (manual transmission) and apply the parking brake.*

c) *Note the vacuum reading at idle and write it down.*

d) *Quickly open the throttle to near its wide-open position, then quickly get off the throttle and allow it to close. Note the vacuum reading and write it down.*

e) *Do this test three more times, recording your measurement after each test.*

f) *If your fourth reading is more than one in-Hg lower than the reading that you noted at idle, the exhaust system might be restricted (the catalytic converter could be plugged, OR an exhaust pipe or muffler could be restricted).*

### REPLACEMENT

▶ **Refer to illustrations 15.7a and 15.7b**

✳✳ **WARNING:**

**Make sure that the exhaust system is completely cooled down before proceeding. If the vehicle has just been driven, the catalytic converter can be hot enough to cause serious burns.**

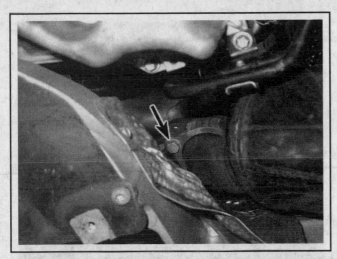

**15.7a To disconnect the upper end of each front exhaust pipe from the exhaust manifold flange, remove the flange bolts (other bolt not visible)**

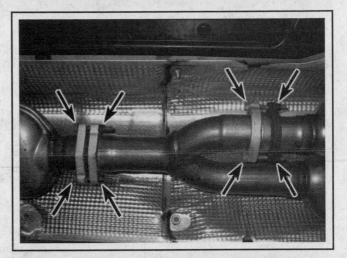

**15.7b To disconnect the back end of the front exhaust pipe/catalytic converter assembly from the rear exhaust pipes, remove these fasteners from these two flanges**

6   Raise the vehicle and place it securely on jackstands.

7   Spray a liberal amount of penetrating oil onto the threads of the fasteners at the exhaust manifold flange and at the flanges behind the catalysts (see illustrations). Wait awhile for the penetrant to loosen things up.

8   While you're waiting for the penetrant to do its work, disconnect the electrical connectors for the upstream and downstream oxygen sensors and remove all four oxygen sensors (see Section 13).

9   Once the penetrant has done its work, loosen and remove all fasteners and remove the catalytic converter/front exhaust pipe assembly. Remove and discard the old flange gaskets. Replace any damaged fasteners. (It's a good idea to replace all of the fasteners.)

10  Installation is the reverse of removal. Be sure to use new flange gaskets. Coat the threads of the bolts with anti-seize compound and tighten all fasteners securely.

## 16  Evaporative Emissions Control (EVAP) system - description and component replacement

### GENERAL DESCRIPTION

1   The Evaporative Emissions Control (EVAP) system prevents fuel system vapors (which contain unburned hydrocarbons) from escaping into the atmosphere. On warm days, vapors trapped inside the fuel tank expand. When the pressure reaches a certain threshold, these vapors are routed from the fuel tank through the fuel vapor vent valve and the fuel vapor control valve to the EVAP canister, where they're stored temporarily, until they can be consumed by the engine during normal operation. Under certain conditions (engine warmed up, vehicle up to speed, moderate or heavy loads, etc.) the Powertrain Control Module (PCM) opens the canister purge solenoid, which allows intake vacuum to pull fuel vapors from the EVAP canister into the intake manifold, where they mix with the air/fuel mixture before being consumed in the combustion chambers. This system is complex and very difficult to troubleshoot without the right tools and training. However, the following description should give you a good idea of how the system works and where the components are located:

2   The **EVAP canister**, which contains activated charcoal, is the repository for storing fuel vapors produced by gasoline as it heats up inside the fuel tank. You'll have to raise the vehicle to inspect or replace the canister, but the canister is designed to be maintenance-free and should last the life of the vehicle. The EVAP canister is located in the

right rear corner of the vehicle, behind the right rear wheel. You'll have to raise the vehicle and remove the small splash shield behind the right rear wheel to access the EVAP canister.

3   **Fuel tank pressure sensor** - The pressure sensor monitors the pressure of evaporative gases inside the fuel tank. The pressure sensor sends a voltage signal to the PCM that increases as the pressure increases. When the signal reaches a specified threshold, the PCM energizes the EVAP canister purge solenoid, which allows the evaporative emissions to be drawn into the intake manifold by intake manifold vacuum. The pressure sensor is located inside the left half of the fuel tank, on the underside of the fuel level sensor mounting flange. This sensor is an integral component of the fuel level sensor and cannot be replaced separately. If it's bad, replace the fuel level sensor assembly (see Chapter 4).

4   **EVAP canister shutoff valve** - The canister shutoff valve, which is used only for diagnosis of the EVAP system, is open under normal conditions, which means that ambient air pressure (14.7 psi) is allowed to enter (but not exit) the space above the fuel level inside the fuel tank and throughout the rest of the EVAP system. When energized by the PCM, the shutoff valve closes, which creates a closed system and a relative vacuum inside the fuel tank and EVAP system, so that the PCM can diagnose the EVAP system for leaks. The shutoff valve solenoid is located on top of the EVAP canister and is not separately replaceable. If the shutoff valve is bad you have to replace the EVAP canister.

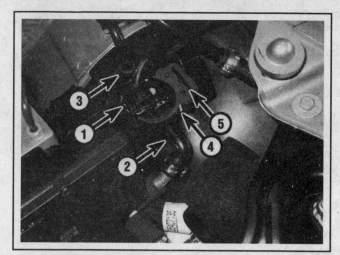

**16.9 To remove the EVAP canister purge solenoid, depress the wire retainer (1) and disconnect the electrical connector, disconnect the rubber inlet (2) and outlet (3) elbows from the solenoid, then pull the solenoid mounting insulator (4) straight up and off the mounting bracket (5)**

5  **EVAP canister purge solenoid** - The EVAP canister purge solenoid is a PCM-controlled solenoid that controls the purging of evaporative emissions from the EVAP canister to the intake manifold. The EVAP purge solenoid is never turned on during cold start warm-ups or during hot start time delays. But once the engine reaches a specified temperature and enters closed-loop operation, the PCM energizes the canister purge solenoid under certain open-throttle operating conditions (acceleration, high speed cruising, etc.). When the solenoid is energized by the PCM, it allows fuel vapors stored in the EVAP canister to be drawn into the intake manifold, where they're mixed with intake air, then burned along with the normal air/fuel mixture. The PCM regulates the flow rate of the vapors by controlling the pulse-width of the solenoid (the length of time during which the solenoid is turned on) in accordance with operating conditions. The EVAP canister purge solenoid is located in the right front corner of the engine compartment.

## GENERAL SYSTEM CHECKS

6  The most common symptom of a faulty EVAP system is a strong fuel odor (particularly during hot weather). If you smell fuel while driving or (more likely) right after you park the vehicle and turn off the engine, check the fuel filler cap first. Make sure that it's screwed onto the fuel filler neck all the way.

7  If the odor persists, inspect all EVAP hose connections, both in the engine compartment and under the vehicle. You'll have to raise the vehicle and place it securely on jackstands to inspect most of the EVAP system, since it's located under the vehicle. Be sure to inspect each hose attached to the canister for damage and leakage along its entire length. Repair or replace as necessary. Inspect the canister for damage and look for fuel leaking from the bottom. If fuel is leaking or the canister is otherwise damaged, replace it.

8  Poor idle, stalling, and poor driveability can be caused by a defective fuel vapor vent valve or canister purge solenoid, a damaged canister, cracked hoses, or hoses connected to the wrong tubes. Fuel loss or fuel odor can be caused by fuel leaking from fuel lines or hoses, a cracked or damaged canister, or a defective vapor valve.

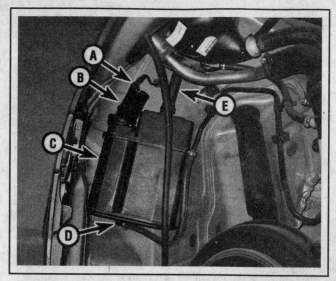

**16.15  The EVAP canister/shutoff valve assembly is mounted behind the right rear wheel (splash shield removed)**

| | |
|---|---|
| A | Shutoff valve electrical connector |
| B | Shutoff valve (not separately replaceable) |
| C | EVAP canister |
| D | EVAP purge hose (to purge solenoid in engine compartment) |
| E | EVAP vent hose (from fuel tank) |

## COMPONENT REPLACEMENT

### EVAP canister purge solenoid

▶ **Refer to illustration 16.9**

➡**Note: The EVAP canister purge solenoid is located in the left front corner of the engine compartment, on a small bracket attached to the right strut tower.**

·9  Disconnect the electrical connector from the EVAP canister purge solenoid (see illustration).

10  Clearly label the EVAP inlet and outlet hoses (see illustration 16.9), then disconnect them from the EVAP canister purge solenoid.

11  To detach the EVAP canister purge solenoid from its mounting bracket, pull it straight up.

12  Installation is the reverse of removal.

### EVAP canister/shutoff valve

▶ **Refer to illustration 16.15**

➡**Note: The EVAP canister/shutoff valve assembly is located behind the right rear wheel well, above a small splash shield.**

13  Loosen the right rear wheel lug nuts, raise the vehicle and place it securely on jackstands. Remove the right rear wheel.

14  Remove the splash shield from the wheel well (see Chapter 11).

15  Disconnect the electrical connector from the EVAP canister shutoff valve (see illustration).

16  Disconnect the hoses from the EVAP canister.

17  Firmly grasp the EVAP canister and push up to disengage it from its mounting bracket.

18  Installation is the reverse of removal.

## 17 Exhaust Gas Recirculation (EGR) system - description and component replacement

### DESCRIPTION

1   Oxides of nitrogen (or simply NOx) is a compound that is formed in the combustion chambers when the oxygen and nitrogen in the incoming air mix together. NOx is a natural byproduct of high combustion chamber temperatures. When NOx is emitted from the tailpipe, it mixes with reactive organic compounds (ROCs), hydrocarbons (HC) and sunlight to form ozone and photochemical smog. The EGR system reduces oxides of nitrogen by recirculating exhaust gases from the exhaust manifold, through the EGR valve and intake manifold, then back to the combustion chambers, where it mixes with the incoming air/fuel mixture before being consumed. These recirculated exhaust gases dilute the incoming air/fuel mixture, which cools the combustion chambers, thereby reducing NOx emissions.

2   The EGR system consists of the Powertrain Control Module (PCM), the EGR valve, the EGR vacuum transducer and various information sensors that the PCM uses to determine when to open the EGR valve. When engine coolant temperature is between 140 and 230 degrees F (60 and 110 degrees C), engine speed is less than 3500 rpm and the engine is under a partial load, the PCM switches on the transducer, allowing vacuum to draw exhaust gases through the EGR valve.

The PCM-controlled vacuum transducer stabilizes intake manifold vacuum by means of a pulse width-modulated signal from the PCM.

### COMPONENT REPLACEMENT

▶ **Refer to illustrations 17.4 and 17.6**

3   Remove the air filter housing/engine cover (see Chapter 4).

4   Using a small screwdriver, disengage the clip for the battery cable from the dipstick tube support bracket (see illustration).

5   Remove the bolt that secures the dipstick tube to the bracket and pull the dipstick tube back, toward the firewall, so there's enough room to remove the EGR valve/transducer assembly.

6   Remove the EGR tube (see illustration).

7   Disconnect the electrical connector from the EGR valve.

8   Remove the EGR valve mounting bolts and remove the EGR valve.

9   Remove and discard the old EGR valve gasket.

10   When installing the EGR valve, be sure to use a new gasket and tighten the EGR valve mounting bolts, the EGR tube-to-intake manifold bolts and the EGR valve tube nut to the torque listed in this Chapter's Specifications. Installation is otherwise the reverse of removal.

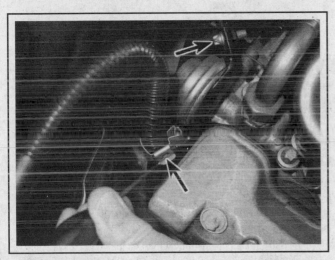

**17.4  Use a small screwdriver to disengage the clip securing the battery cable. Also remove the bolt securing the dipstick tube to the bracket**

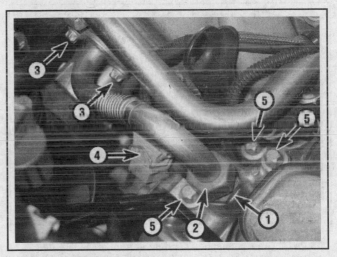

**17.6  EGR valve and tube details**

| | | | |
|---|---|---|---|
| 1 | Fitting | 4 | Vacuum transducer |
| 2 | Tube nut | | electrical connector |
| 3 | EGR tube-to-intake | 5 | EGR valve mounting bolts |
| | manifold nuts | | |

## 18 Positive Crankcase Ventilation (PCV) system - description and check

### DESCRIPTION

1   The Positive Crankcase Ventilation (PCV) system reduces hydrocarbon emissions by scavenging crankcase vapors, which are rich in unburned hydrocarbons. A PCV valve regulates the flow of gases into the intake manifold in proportion to the amount of intake vacuum available. At idle, when intake vacuum is very high, the PCV valve restricts the flow of vapors so the engine doesn't run poorly. As the throttle plate opens and intake vacuum begins to diminish, the PCV valve opens more to allow vapors to flow more freely.

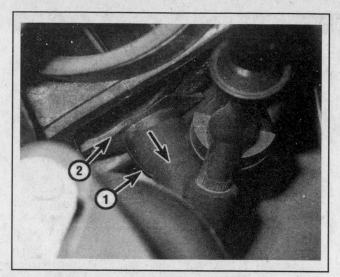

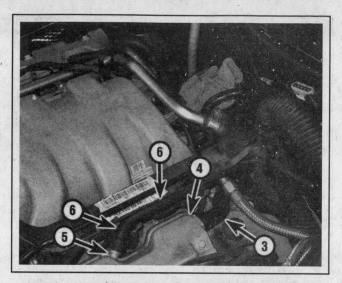

**18.2a** On V6 engines, the PCV fresh air inlet hose (1) begins at the air intake connection (2) between the Mass Air Flow/ Intake Air Temperature (MAF/IAT) sensor (removed for clarity) and the throttle body. Filtered air from the air filter housing enters the fresh air inlet hose here . . .

**18.2b** . . . and is routed through the fresh air hose (3) to a pipe on the back end of the breather box (4) on the left valve cover. Crankcase vapors are drawn by intake manifold vacuum through a fixed orifice in the wall of the breather box, through another pipe (5) into the left cylinder head crankcase ventilation hose (6), which is routed to . . .

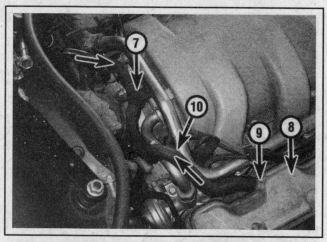

**18.2c** . . . this connection (7) right in front of the throttle body (where intake vacuum is high). The right valve cover also has a breather box (8) from which crankcase vapors are drawn through another fixed orifice and pipe (9) and then through another crankcase ventilation hose (10) to the same connection at the throttle body

## 2001 through 2005 V6 models

▶ Refer to illustrations 18.2a, 18.2b and 18.2c

2   The PCV system consists of the fresh air inlet hose, two PCV fixed orifices (one in each valve cover breather box) and a pair of crankcase ventilation hoses (or PCV hoses). The fresh air inlet hose connects the elbow-shaped air intake duct (between the MAF/IAT sensor and the throttle body) to a pipe on the back end of the left valve cover breather

box (see illustrations). Each crankcase ventilation hose (or PCV hose) connects a PCV fixed orifice in the cylinder head breather box to a connection plumbed into the rear of the intake manifold, just downstream from the throttle plate inside the throttle body (see illustration). There is no actual PCV valve. A fixed orifice in each valve cover breather box controls the flow of crankcase vapors to the intake manifold.

## 2006 and later V6 models

▶ Refer to illustrations 18.3a and 18.3b

3   These models use a conventional breather box or oil separator for part-throttle ventilation, and a centrifugal oil separator for ventilation at higher load levels. The breather box or oil separator (see illustration) is located on top and at the front end of the left valve cover. The crankcase ventilation hose (PCV hose) is routed from a pipe on the upper back end of the intake manifold to a pipe on the separator. The centrifugal oil separator (see illustration) is located on the back end of the right cylinder head. The hose for the centrifugal oil separator is routed from the separator to the underside of the air guide housing (the elbow-shaped air intake duct between the MAF/IAT sensor and the throttle body).

## 2003 through 2005 four-cylinder models

4   The PCV crankcase ventilation system is integrated into the underside of the valve cover. Blow-by gases from the crankcase enter the right center part of the valve cover, travel forward slightly, make a U-turn, travel through the volume separator to the back of the valve cover, travel from the right to left side of the valve cover through the dome (taper), head forward through a labyrinth separator and enter the cyclone or spiral separator before exiting through a pipe, from which they're drawn into the intake manifold. Replacing the PCV system means replacing the valve cover.

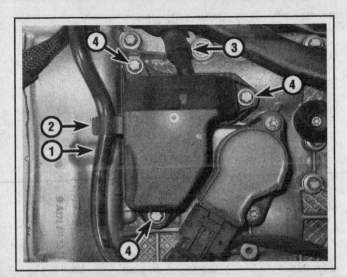

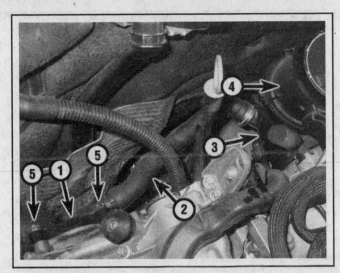

**18.3a  To remove the breather box (or oil separator) on 2006 and later V6 engines:**

1   Detach this tubing . . .
2   . . . from this clip
3   Disconnect the PCV hose from the breather box
4   Remove the three mounting bolts and remove the box from the left valve cover

**18.3b  To remove the centrifugal oil separator on 2006 and later V6 engines:**

1   Centrifugal oil separator cover
2   Full-throttle PCV ventilation hose
3   The ventilation hose is connected to the elbow-shaped air intake duct . . .
4   . . . between the Mass Air Flow/Intake Air Temperature (MAF/IAT) sensor above and the throttle body below (not visible)
5   Centrifugal oil separator cover bolts (third bolt not visible in this photo)

## INSPECTION

5   An engine that is operated without a properly functioning crankcase ventilation system can be damaged. Anytime you're servicing the engine, be sure to inspect the PCV system hose(s) for cracks, tears, deterioration and other damage. Disconnect the hose(s) and inspect it/them for damage and obstructions. If a hose is clogged, clean it out. If you're unable to clean it satisfactorily, replace it.

6   A plugged PCV hose might cause any or all of the following conditions: A rough idle, stalling or a slow idle speed, oil leaks or sludge in the engine. So if the engine is running roughly, stalling and idling at a lower than normal speed, or is losing oil, or has oil in the throttle body or air intake manifold plenum, or has a build-up of sludge, a PCV system hose might be clogged. Repair or replace the hose(s) as necessary.

7   A leaking PCV hose might cause any or all of the following conditions: a rough idle, stalling or a high idle speed. So if the engine is running roughly, stalling and/or idling at a higher-than-normal speed, a PCV system hose might be leaking. Repair or replace the hose(s) as necessary.

8   Here's an easy functional check of the PCV system on a vehicle with a fresh air inlet hose and crankcase ventilation hoses (2001 through 2005 V6 models):

a)  Disconnect a crankcase ventilation hose (PCV hose) from the breather box.
b)  Start the engine and let it warm up to its normal idle.
c)  Cover the end of the PCV hose with your thumb and verify that there is vacuum. If there is no vacuum, look for a plugged hose or a clogged port or pipe on the intake manifold. Also look for a hose that collapses when it's blocked (that is, when vacuum is applied). Replace clogged or deteriorated hoses.
d)  Remove the engine oil dipstick (or plug, if there is no dipstick) and install a vacuum gauge on the upper end of the dipstick tube.
e)  Pinch off or plug the PCV system's fresh air inlet hose.
f)  Run the engine at 1500 rpm for 30 seconds, then read the vacuum gauge while the engine is running at 1500 rpm.
g)  If there's vacuum present, the crankcase ventilation system is operating correctly.
h)  If there's NO vacuum present, the engine might be drawing in outside air. The PCV system won't function correctly unless the engine is a sealed system. Inspect the valve cover(s), oil pan gasket or other sealing areas for leaks.
i)  If the vacuum gauge indicates positive pressure, look for a plugged hose or engine blow-by.
j)  Repeat this procedure for the other PCV hose.

9   If the PCV system is functioning correctly, but there's evidence of engine oil in the throttle body or air filter housing, it could be caused by excessive crankcase pressure. Have the crankcase pressure tested by a dealer service department.

10   In the PCV system, excessive blow-by (caused by worn rings, pistons and/or cylinders, or by constant heavy loads) is discharged into the intake manifold and consumed. If you discover heavy sludge deposits or a dilution of the engine oil, even though the PCV system is functioning correctly, look for other causes (see Troubleshooting and Chapter 2B) and correct them as soon as possible.

## 19 Secondary air injection system - description and component replacement

### DESCRIPTION

♦ **Refer to illustration 19.2**

1   All models are equipped with a PCM-controlled secondary air injection system that is turned on for the first 90 seconds (V6) or up to 150 seconds (four-cylinder) during a cold-start warm-up to quickly bring the catalytic converter(s) up to operating temperature, which reduces emissions during the catalyst warm-up phase. The secondary air injection system consists of an air injection relay, a check valve, a switchover valve, one (four) or two (V6) shutoff valves and an air pump. If the engine temperature is between 50 and 140 degrees F (10 to 60 degrees C) when the engine is started, the PCM energizes the air injection relay and the switchover valve. The switchover valve admits intake manifold vacuum to the two shutoff valves (V6 models) or single shutoff valve (four-cylinder models). The shutoff valve(s) open and the air pump pumps air into the exhaust stream through drilled passages in the cylinder head. Once mixed with the exhaust stream, this extra air reacts with hot exhaust gases, oxidizing them and reducing carbon monoxide (CO) and hydrocarbons (HC). And it also increases the exhaust gas temperature, which heats up the catalyst(s) more quickly to operating temperature. All systems use a check valve, which is located upstream in the vacuum line between the intake manifold and switchover valve. The check valve admits intake manifold vacuum to the switchover valve but prevents pressurized intake air from escaping when the manifold is pressurized under boost conditions.

2   On V6 models, the check valve, switch-over valve, two shutoff valves and air pump are all located on top and at the front of the engine, right below the front engine cover (see illustration).

3   On 2002 four-cylinder models, the air pump is located at the lower right front corner of the engine block, right below the alternator. The check valve, switchover valve and shutoff valve are located on the right side of the engine, just below the rear mounting bracket for the fuel rail.

4   On 2003 through 2005 four-cylinder models, there is no air pump. Instead, an air injection/exhaust gas recirculation valve - which is located on the right side of the engine, at the front of the exhaust manifold - redirects pressurized air from the duct between the supercharger and the intercooler into the exhaust stream. As its name indicates, the air injection/exhaust gas recirculation valve also redirects spent exhaust gases into the intake manifold when the EGR system is energized by the PCM. On these models, the check valve and switchover valve are located on the intake manifold, near the throttle body, and the air injection/exhaust gas recirculation valve is located at the right front corner of the valve cover.

### COMPONENT REPLACEMENT

#### V6 models

##### Air pump switchover valve

♦ **Refer to illustrations 19.5a and 19.5b**

➡**Note: On 2001 through 2005 models, the switchover valve is located at the front of the engine on a small bracket that's bolted to the water pump housing. On 2006 and later models, the switchover valve is also mounted at the front of the engine on a similar small bracket, which is located right in front of the intake camshaft**

5   Disconnect the electrical connector from the switchover valve (see illustrations).

6   Clearly label the vacuum hoses connected to the switchover valve, then disconnect them from the valve.

7   To remove the switchover valve from its mounting bracket, simply pull it off the bracket.

8   Installation is the reverse of removal.

##### Shutoff valves

♦ **Refer to illustrations 19.10a, 19.10b, 19.10c and 19.13**

➡**Note: On 2001 through 2005 models, the shutoff valves are located at the front of the engine, on either side of the air injection pump. The photo of a 2001 through 2005 model accompanying this Section depicts the right shutoff valve, but the removal procedure is the same for either shutoff valve. On 2006 and later models, the shutoff valves are also located at the front of the engine, but in slightly different locations: The left shutoff valve is located directly behind the oil filter, and the right shutoff valve is located below the Camshaft Position (CMP) sensors on the front of the right cylinder head.**

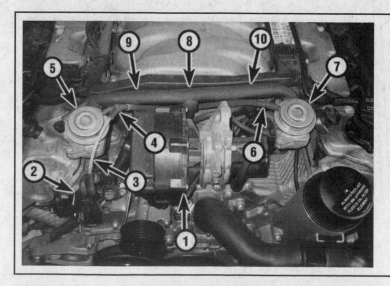

**19.2 Secondary air injection system (2001 through 2005 V6 model shown, 2006 and later V6 models similar):**

1   *Secondary air injection pump*
2   *Switchover valve*
3   *Vacuum hose to shutoff valves*
4   *Junction for vacuum hose to right and left shutoff valves*
5   *Right shutoff valve*
6   *Vacuum hose to left shutoff valve*
7   *Left shutoff valve*
8   *Air pump-to-air injection hose connection*
9   *Air injection hose to right shutoff valve*
10  *Air injection hose to left shutoff valve*

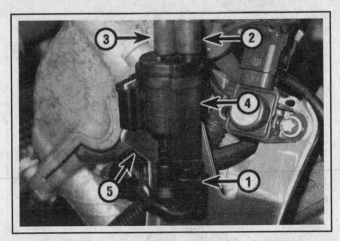

**19.5a Switchover valve assembly (2001 through 2005 V6 models):**

1  Electrical connector
2  Vacuum hose to the two shutoff valves
3  Vacuum supply hose from the intake manifold
4  Switchover valve
5  Switchover valve mounting bracket

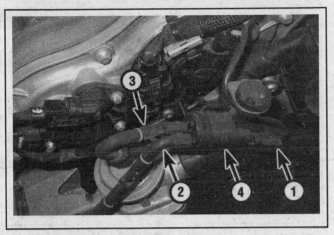

**19.5b Switchover valve assembly (2006 and later V6 models):**

1  Electrical connector
2  Vacuum hose to the two shutoff valves
3  Vacuum supply hose from the intake manifold
4  Switchover valve

9  Remove the front engine cover. On 2006 and later models, you'll also need to remove the air filter housing to remove the left shutoff valve (see *Air filter housing - removal and installation* in Chapter 4).

10  Disconnect the vacuum hose from the shutoff valve (see illustrations).

11  Remove the air injection hose from the shutoff valve.

12  On 2001 through 2005 models, remove the shutoff valve mounting bolt and remove the shutoff valve. On 2006 and later models, remove the shutoff valve mounting bolts; the left shutoff valve has two mounting bolts and the right shutoff valve has three mounting bolts.

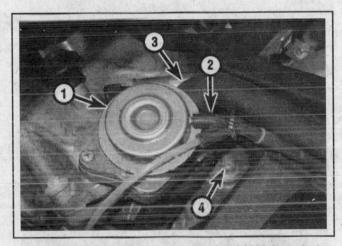

**19.10a To remove a shutoff valve (1) from a 2001 through 2005 V6 model, disconnect the vacuum hose (2), detach the air hose (3) and remove the mounting bolt (4) (right shutoff valve shown, left shutoff valve identical)**

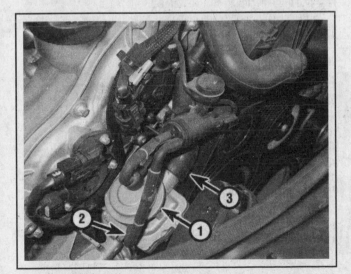

**19.10b To remove the right shutoff valve (1) from a 2006 or later V6 model, disconnect the vacuum hose (2) and the air hose (3), then remove the three mounting bolts underneath at the mounting flange (not visible in this photo)**

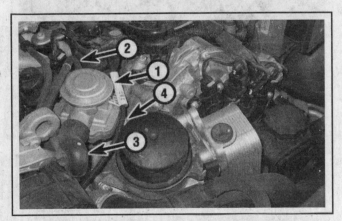

**19.10c To remove the left shutoff valve (1) from a 2006 or later model, disconnect the vacuum hose (2) and the air hose (3), then remove the two mounting bolts (4) (other bolt not visible in this photo)**

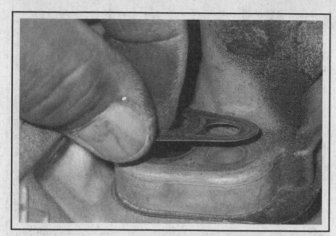

**19.13  Be sure to remove and discard the old shutoff valve gasket (2001 through 2005 V6 model shown). Always use a new gasket when installing the shutoff valve**

13 Remove and discard the old shutoff valve gasket (see illustration).

14 Installation is the reverse of removal. Be sure to use a new gasket and tighten the shutoff valve mounting bolt(s) securely.

### Air injection pump (2001 through 2005 models)

▶ **Refer to illustration 19.16**

➡ **Note:** The air injection pump is located at the front of the intake manifold, on top of the timing chain cover.

15 Remove the front cover.

16 Disconnect the electrical connector from the air injection pump (see illustration).

17 Remove the injection pump clamp bolt. Note that the pump harness is grounded at this bolt.

**19.22  Air injection pump and mounting bracket assembly (2006 and later V6 models):**

| | | | |
|---|---|---|---|
| 1 | Electrical connector | 4 | Air supply hose - right |
| 2 | Air intake hose | | shutoff valve |
| 3 | Air supply hose - left | 5 | Air injection pump |
| | shutoff valve | 6 | Bracket bolts. |
| | | 7 | Mounting bracket |

**19.16  Secondary air injection pump details (2001 through 2005 V6 models)**

| | | | |
|---|---|---|---|
| 1 | Electrical connector | 4 | Air hose |
| 2 | Clamp bolt | 5 | Clamp |
| 3 | Ground wire | | |

18 Disconnect the air hose from the pipe on the back of the pump.

19 Tilt the front part of the clamp forward and remove the air injection pump.

20 Installation is the reverse of removal. Don't forget to attach the harness ground to the clamp bolt.

### Air injection pump (2006 and later models)

▶ **Refer to illustrations 19.22 and 19.25**

21 Remove the front cover.

22 Disconnect the electrical connector from the air injection pump (see illustration).

23 Disconnect the air intake hose (see illustration 19.22) from the air injection pump.

24 Disconnect the air supply hoses from the pump (see illustration 19.22).

25 Unbolt the air injection pump mounting bracket from the cylinder head and from the timing chain cover (see illustration).

26 Remove the air injection pump and mounting bracket as a single assembly.

27 Unbolt the mounting bracket from the air injection pump (see illustration 19.22) and separate the bracket from the pump.

28 Installation is the reverse of removal.

### Four-cylinder models

▶ **Air injection pump (2002 models)**

➡ **Note:** The electric air injection pump is located on the right side of the engine, below the alternator. (There is no air injection pump on 2003 through 2005 models, which use pressurized air from the supercharger instead.)

29 Raise the vehicle and place it securely on jackstands.

30 Remove the engine undercover.

31 Disconnect the air hose from the air injection pump.

32 Disconnect the electrical connector from the pump.

33 Remove the three pump mounting bolts and remove the pump.

34 While the pump is removed, inspect the condition of the mounting bolt sleeves and rubber insulators. If the insulators are cracked, torn or otherwise deteriorated, replace them.

35 Installation is the reverse of removal.

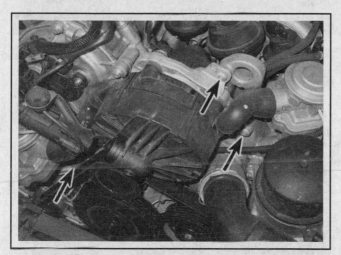

**19.25  To detach the air injection pump and mounting bracket from the cylinder head, remove these two upper bolts; to detach it from the timing chain cover, remove this lower bolt (bolt not visible in this photo) (2006 and later V6 models)**

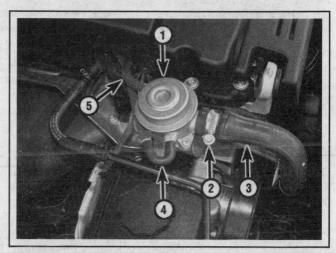

**19.46  Air injection/exhaust gas recirculation combination valve details (2003 through 2005 four-cylinder models)**

| | | | |
|---|---|---|---|
| 1 | Air injection/exhaust gas recirculation combination valve | 3 | Pressurized air hose |
| 2 | Hose clamp | 4 | Ambient air hose |
| | | 5 | Vacuum hose |

### Check valve (2002 models)

➡Note: The check valve is located at the back of the intake manifold. (The check valve used on 2003 through 2005 models is simply installed in line with the vacuum source line to the switchover valve, and is located on top of the valve cover, a few inches away from the switchover valve.)

36  Remove the engine cover.

37  Loosen and remove the hose clamp that secures the hose to the check valve and disconnect the hose from the check valve.

38  Unscrew and remove the check valve.

39  Remove and discard the O-ring.

40  Installation is the reverse of removal. Be sure to use a new O-ring and tighten the check valve to the torque listed in this Chapter's Specifications.

### Switchover valve

➡Note: On 2002 models the switchover valve is located on the left side of the engine, right below the rear mounting bracket for the fuel rail. On 2003 through 2005 models the switchover valve is located on top of the valve cover.

41  Remove the engine cover.

42  Disconnect the electrical connector from the switchover valve.

43  Disconnect the vacuum hoses from the switchover valve.

44  To remove the switchover valve from its mounting bracket, simply pull it off.

45  Installation is the reverse of removal.

### Air injection/exhaust gas recirculation combination valve (2003 through 2005 models)

▶ Refer to illustration 19.46

➡Note: The air injection/exhaust gas recirculation combination valve is located at the right front corner of the engine, just ahead of the exhaust manifold.

46  Loosen the hose clamp and disconnect the pressurized air hose from the air injection/exhaust gas recirculation combination valve (see illustration).

47  Clearly label the two smaller hoses and disconnect them from the air injection/exhaust gas recirculation combination valve.

48  Remove the two air injection/exhaust gas recirculation combination valve mounting bolts on the valve mounting flange at the lower end of the unit and remove the combination valve.

49  Remove and discard the old combination valve gasket.

50  Installation is the reverse of removal.

## 20  Electric throttle control and idle speed control systems - description

1  The electric throttle control and idle speed control system consists of the Powertrain Control Module (PCM), the Accelerator Pedal Position (APP) sensor, the electronic throttle body, the Throttle Position (TP) sensors and a number of other engine sensors. The PCM controls the electric throttle control actuator.

2  The PCM controls the electric throttle control actuator (the throttle body). A solenoid motor in the actuator controls the throttle plate in response to commands from the PCM.

3  The PCM also controls the Idle Speed Control (ISC) system, which dispenses with the conventional idle speed control valve or idle speed control motor. Instead, the PCM controls the electric throttle control actuator to maintain the lowest possible idle speed at which the engine can operate smoothly and steadily. This speed varies somewhat in accordance with engine operating conditions such as warm-up, deceleration and engine load, which varies with air conditioning, power steering, cooling fan operation, etc.

4  The electric throttle control actuator (throttle body) is covered in Chapter 4. The PCM is covered in Section 14 of this Chapter. The Throttle Position (TP) sensors are integrated into the throttle body and cannot be replaced separately.

## 21 Variable intake manifold - description and component replacement

## DESCRIPTION

### 2001 through 2005 V6 models

1 The PCM-controlled variable intake manifold optimizes engine torque by switching back and forth between two different intake manifold lengths. Each cylinder has its own dedicated variable intake runner, the length of which is controlled by a flap that's opened and closed by the variable intake manifold switchover diaphragm unit, which rotates a shaft that opens or closes three spring-loaded flaps for one cylinder head. The shaft for the three spring-loaded flaps for the other cylinder head is linked to the primary shaft by a connecting link, so when the diaphragm unit opens the flaps for one head it does the same for the other head. Vacuum to the diaphragm unit is PCM-controlled by the variable intake manifold switchover valve (a vacuum solenoid). Here's how it works:

2 At lower engine speeds and loads, the springs keep the flaps open, sending intake air through the shorter intake runners, which decreases frictional losses inside the intake manifold and improves cylinder filling and therefore torque.

3 When the engine load exceeds 50 percent (between about 1750 and 3900 rpm) the PCM-controlled switchover valve is energized by the PCM, sending intake vacuum to the diaphragm unit, which opens the flaps, sending intake air through the longer intake runners. Now intake air flows through the longer intake runners, so that the pressure waves produced by the pistons arrive at the open intake valves at just the right moment for the next induction stroke, which improves cylinder charging (filling) and therefore increases torque. (The intake vacuum that actuates the diaphragm is delivered from a vacuum reservoir through a one-way check valve. There's enough vacuum for about five operations without renewing the vacuum inside the reservoir, which can only be re-evacuated with high intake manifold vacuum.)

4 When engine rpm exceeds 3900 rpm, the PCM de-energizes the switchover valve, which cuts vacuum to the diaphragm unit and allows the spring-loaded flaps to open under spring pressure, which again sends intake air through the shorter intake runners, which allows the pressure waves to arrive in time even at higher engine speeds before the intake valves close, again promoting better cylinder filling and improving horsepower and torque.

### 2006 and later V6 models

5 The variable intake manifold on these models is similar in concept to earlier models with a couple of refinements:

6 Like the earlier intake manifold, the newer manifold uses variable flaps to control the path of the incoming air through the manifold, except that there are two diaphragm units (Mercedes Benz calls them "aneroid capsules"), one for each flap shaft. Both variable flap diaphragm units are controlled by a single switchover valve.

7 The other addition is a series of six tumble flaps or turbulence flaps, each of which is situated in the end of an intake runner, directly above the fuel injector nozzle. At low speeds, the tumble flaps are deployed (sticking out into the intake air), which speeds up the incoming air, which produces turbulence as the air tumbles past the flap. The result is a more even distribution of the air/fuel mixture and therefore better and faster combustion.

8 At part-throttle, when the mixture is leaner because of EGR operation, the increased combustion speed helps produce lower fuel consumption. At higher engine speeds, the flaps are retracted, and

flush with the intake runner walls, because the speed of incoming air is sufficient to produce good turbulence and mixing on its own. The tumble flaps are actuated by the intake manifold tumble flap switchover valve, another aneroid capsule (diaphragm unit), which uses a bell crank assembly to rotate the tumble flap shafts to open and close the tumble flaps. The tumble flap diaphragm unit is controlled by the PCM-controlled tumble flap switchover valve.

## COMPONENT REPLACEMENT

### 2001 through 2005 V6 models

**Switchover valve**

▸ Refer to illustrations 21.10 and 21.11

➡ **Note: The switchover valve is located at the left front corner of the intake manifold, directly above the diaphragm unit.**

9 Remove the front engine cover.
10 Disconnect the electrical connector from the switchover valve (see illustration).
11 Disconnect the two vacuum hoses from the switchover valve (see illustration).
12 Remove the retainer and remove the switchover valve.
13 Inspect the condition of the retainer. If it's too distorted to reuse, replace it.
14 Installation is the reverse of removal.

**Diaphragm unit**

▸ Refer to illustration 21.16

➡ **Note: The diaphragm unit is located at the left front corner of the intake manifold, directly below the switchover valve.**

15 Remove the front engine cover.
16 Disconnect the vacuum signal hose from the diaphragm unit (see illustration).
17 Using a small screwdriver, carefully pry loose the ball socket on the end of the vacuum unit's actuator arm from the spherical bearing on the end of the crank arm for the variable flap shaft.
18 Remove the two diaphragm unit mounting bolts.
19 Remove the diaphragm unit.
20 Installation is the reverse of removal.

### 2006 and later V6 models

**Diaphragm units**

▸ Refer to illustration 21.21

➡ **Note: This procedure applies to any of the three diaphragm units.**

21 Remove the front engine cover. The two variable flap diaphragm units and the tumble flap diaphragm unit are located on the front end of the intake manifold (see illustration). The two switchover valves are located below the diaphragm units. To access any of these components, you must remove the intake manifold (see Chapter 2A).

22 Disconnect the vacuum signal hose from the diaphragm unit (see illustration 21.21).

23 Using a small screwdriver, carefully pry the ball socket on the end

of the actuator arm loose from the spherical bearing on the end of the crank arm for the variable flap shaft or tumble flap shaft.

24 Pry off the retainer and remove the diaphragm unit.

25 Installation is the reverse of removal.

**Switchover valves**

➡**Note: This procedure applies to either switchover valve.**

26 Remove the front engine cover. The two switchover valves are located on the front end of the intake manifold, below the three diaphragm units. To access either of these components you must remove the intake manifold (see Chapter 2A).

27 Disconnect the electrical connector from the switchover valve.

28 Clearly label the vacuum hoses connected to the switchover valve, then disconnect them from the valve.

29 Remove the switchover valve retainer and remove the valve.

30 Installation is the reverse of removal.

21.10 To disconnect the electrical connector from the switchover valve, depress these two wire retainers and pull off the connector (2001 through 2005 V6 models)

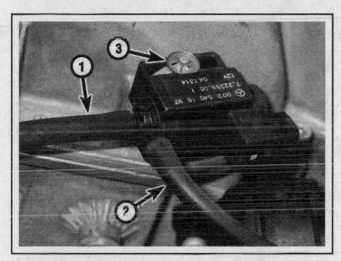

21.11 To remove the switchover valve, disconnect the vacuum supply hose (1) and the vacuum signal hose (2), then pry off the retainer (3) (2001 through 2005 V6 models) (intake manifold removed for clarity)

21.16 To remove the diaphragm unit, disconnect the vacuum signal hose (1), carefully pry off the ball socket on the end of the arm (2) from the spherical bearing on the end of the crank arm for the variable flap shaft, then remove the two mounting bolts (3) and remove the unit (2001 through 2005 V6 models) (intake manifold removed for clarity)

21.21 The three diaphragm actuator units for the variable intake manifold, and the two switchover valves (not shown) below them, are all located on the front of the manifold, which must be removed to access any of these five components

A   Diaphragm actuator unit for left variable flap
B   Vacuum signal hose for left variable flap diaphragm unit
C   Diaphragm actuator unit for right variable flap
D   Vacuum signal hose for right variable flap diaphragm unit
E   Diaphragm actuator unit for tumble flap
F   Vacuum signal hose for tumble flap diaphragm unit

| Torque specifications | Ft-lbs (unless otherwise indicated) | Nm |
|---|---|---|

➡**Note: One foot-pound (ft-lb) of torque is equivalent to 12 inch-pounds (in-lbs) of torque. Torque values below approximately 15 ft-lbs are expressed in inch-pounds, since most foot-pound torque wrenches are not accurate at these smaller values.**

| | Ft-lbs | Nm |
|---|---|---|
| Secondary air injection system check valve | | |
|     (2002 four-cylinder models) | 25 | 34 |
| Exhaust Valve Recirculation (EGR) valve | | |
|     EGR valve mounting bolts | 180 in-lbs | 20 |
|     EGR valve tube nut | 30 | 40 |
|     EGR tube-to-intake manifold flange bolts | 84 in-lbs | 9 |
| Knock sensor mounting bolt | 180 in-lbs | 20 |
| Oxygen sensors | | |
|     V6 models | | |
|         2001 through 2005 | 33 | 45 |
|         2006 and later | 37 | 50 |
|     Four-cylinder models | 37 | 50 |

## Section

1   General information
2   Shift lever - removal and installation
3   Manual transmission - removal and installation
4   Manual transmission overhaul - general information

## Reference to other Chapters

CHECK ENGINE light on - See Chapter 6
Manual transmission lubricant - change - See Chapter 1
Manual transmission lubricant level - check - See Chapter 1
Oil seal - replacement - See Chapter 7B
Transmission mount - check and replacement - See Chapter 7B

# 7A

## MANUAL TRANSMISSION

## 1  General information

The Type 716 transmission is a fully-synchronized, six-speed manual transmission with an overdrive sixth gear.

All model years have an optional Sequentronic six-speed manual transmission that has an electro/hydraulic-operated clutch and shifting system. The result is a transmission that is conventional in its gears and internal components, but which is operated without a clutch pedal; the clutch is operated instead in response to commands from the shifter through the TCU, so in shifting it operates more like an automatic transmission. The manufacturer calls it an "automated manual transmission." Some models with Sequentronic transmission have a floor shift, while another option is shift buttons on the steering wheel that allow the driver to upshift or downshift without taking his/her hands from the steering wheel.

Information on the manual transmission is included in this Part of Chapter 7. Information on the automatic transmissions can be found in Part B of this Chapter. You'll also find certain procedures common to both transmissions - such as oil seal replacement - in Part B.

Depending on the expense involved in having a transmission over-hauled, it might be a better idea to consider replacing it with either a used or rebuilt unit. Your local dealer or transmission shop should be able to supply information concerning cost, availability and exchange policy. Regardless of how you decide to remedy a transmission problem, you can still save a lot of money by removing and installing the unit yourself.

## 2  Shift lever - removal and installation

1   Position the shift lever into Neutral. Refer to Chapter 11 for removal of the trim panel surrounding the shifter upper boot. The boot around the shifter will remain attached to the shifter and the trim cover. Release the two clips underneath the console trim panel to separate the boot from the cover.

2   To remove the shift knob, turn the boot inside-out and pull it upward over the shift knob. Beneath the boot, twist the clamp on the shifter counterclockwise to loosen it, then remove the knob and boot.

3   Push down on the spring-loaded washer on the shift lever and extract the retaining pin.

4   Pull up the rubber cup and the shift lever together and remove them from the vehicle.

5   Installation is the reverse of the removal procedure.

## 3  Manual transmission - removal and installation

### REMOVAL

1   Disconnect the cable from the negative battery terminal (see Chapter 5, Section 1).

2   Place the transmission in NEUTRAL.

3   Raise the vehicle and support it securely on jackstands.

4   Remove the shifter (see Section 2).

5   Remove the driveshaft (see Chapter 8).

6   Disconnect the clutch hydraulic line (see Chapter 8, Section 5).

7   Remove the air intake/engine cover (see Chapter 4), and the engine underside splash panels (see Chapter 1).

8   Remove the exhaust system (see Chapter 4).

9   Remove the starter motor (see Chapter 5).

10  On models through 2005, disconnect the electrical connector at the backup-light switch.

11  On models with Sequentronic transmission, remove the two bolts securing the connector cover, then disconnect the two large electrical connectors on the right side of the transmission.

12  In the engine compartment, remove the bolts securing the refrigerant line to the top of the transmission.

### ✳✳ WARNING:

**Do not disconnect the refrigerant line.**

13  Support the engine from below with a floor jack. Put a block of wood between the jack head and the engine oil pan to protect the pan.

14  Support the transmission with a transmission jack (available at most auto parts stores and at equipment rental yards) or with a large, heavy duty floor jack. Safety chains should be used to secure the transmission to the jack.

15  Raise the transmission slightly to take the weight off the crossmember.

16  Remove the transmission crossmember-to-body bolts (see Chapter 7B, Section 6).

17  Remove the transmission mount-to-transmission bolts and the ground strap, then remove the crossmember.

18  Remove the engine-to-transmission and transmission-to-engine bolts. Lowering the jack will make access to the upper transmission bolts easier.

19  Make a final check that all wires have been disconnected from

the transmission, then move the transmission and jack toward the rear of the vehicle until the transmission input shaft is clear of the clutch or clutch housing. If the transmission input shaft is difficult to disengage from the clutch hub, use a prybar to separate the transmission from the engine. Keep the transmission level as you pull it to the rear.

20 Once the input shaft is clear, lower the transmission and remove it from under the vehicle.

## ❋❋ CAUTION:

**Do not depress the clutch pedal while the transmission is out of the vehicle.**

21 Inspect the clutch components. Generally speaking, new clutch components should always be installed whenever the transmission is removed (see Chapter 8).

## INSTALLATION

22 Install the clutch components, if they were removed (see Chapter 8). Apply a thin film of high-temperature grease to the splines of the transmission input shaft and to the inner surface of the pilot bearing.

23 With the transmission secured to the jack, raise it into position behind the engine and carefully slide it forward, engaging the input shaft with the clutch plate hub. Do not use excessive force to install

the transmission - if the input shaft won't slide into place, readjust the angle of the transmission or turn the input shaft so the splines engage properly with the clutch.

24 Once the transmission is flush with the engine, install the transmission-to-engine bolts. Tighten the bolts to the torque listed in this Chapter's Specifications.

## ❋❋ CAUTION:

**Don't use the bolts to force the transmission and engine together. If the transmission doesn't slide up to the engine easily, find out what's wrong before proceeding.**

25 Install the transmission mount and crossmember. Tighten all nuts and bolts to the torque listed in this Chapter's Specifications.

26 Remove the jacks supporting the transmission and the engine.

27 Install the various components removed previously. To connect the clutch hydraulic line and bleed the clutch hydraulic system, refer to Chapter 8.

28 Make a final check to verify all wires and hoses have been reconnected and the transmission has been filled with lubricant to the proper level (see Chapter 1). Lower the vehicle.

29 Reconnect the shift linkage.

30 Connect the negative battery cable. Road test the vehicle and check for leaks. Make sure the shifter operates smoothly in all gears.

## 4   Manual transmission overhaul - general Information

Overhauling a manual transmission is a difficult job for the do-it-yourselfer. It involves the disassembly and reassembly of many small parts. Numerous clearances must be precisely measured and, if necessary, changed with select fit spacers and snap-rings. As a result, if transmission problems arise, it can be removed and installed by a competent do-it-yourselfer, but overhaul should be left to a transmission repair shop. Rebuilt transmissions may be available - check with your dealer parts department and auto parts stores. At any rate, the time and money involved in an overhaul is almost sure to exceed the cost of a rebuilt unit.

Nevertheless, it's not impossible for an inexperienced mechanic to rebuild a transmission if the special tools are available and the job is done in a deliberate step-by-step manner so nothing is overlooked.

The tools necessary for an overhaul include internal and external snap-ring pliers, a bearing puller, a slide hammer, a set of pin punches, a dial indicator and possibly a hydraulic press. In addition, a large, sturdy workbench and a vise or transmission stand will be required.

During disassembly of the transmission, make careful notes of how each piece comes off, where it fits in relation to other pieces and what holds it in place.

Before taking the transmission apart for repair, it will help if you have some idea what area of the transmission is malfunctioning. Certain problems can be closely tied to specific areas in the transmission, which can make component examination and replacement easier. Refer to the *Troubleshooting* Section at the front of this manual for information regarding possible sources of trouble.

| Torque specifications | Ft-lbs (unless otherwise indicated) | Nm |
|---|---|---|

➡Note: One foot-pound (ft-lb) of torque is equivalent to 12 inch-pounds (in-lbs) of torque. Torque values below approximately 15 ft-lbs are expressed in inch-pounds, since most foot-pound torque wrenches are not accurate at these smaller values.

| | | |
|---|---|---|
| Backup light switch (models through 2005) | 89 in-lbs | 10 |
| Drain plug | 22 | 30 |
| Driveshaft joint flange nut | | |
|     Step 1 | 148 | 200 |
|     Step 2 | Loosen | |
|     Step 3 | 118 | 160 |
| Filler plug | 26 | 35 |
| Shift housing cross-brace-to-floor bolts | 17 | 23 |
| Shift cable housing-to-floor bolts | 53 in-lbs | 6 |
| Shift unit-to-transmission | 71 in-lbs | 8 |
| Transmission crossmember-to-chassis bolts | 32 to 40 | 43 to 55 |
| Transmission-to-engine bolts | 30 | 40 |
| Transmission mount-to-crossmember bolts | 22 | 30 |
| Transmission mount-to-transmission bolts | 37 | 50 |

## Section

## Reference to other Chapters

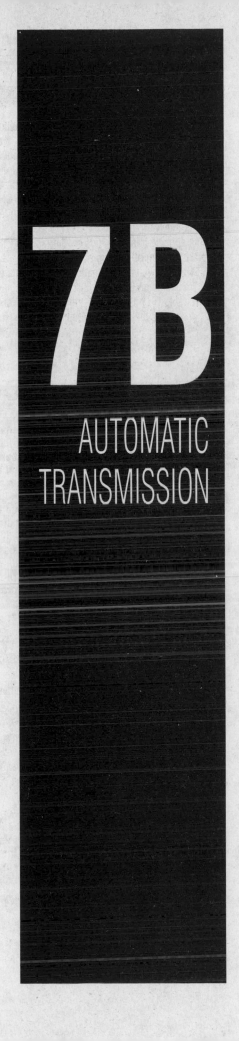

# 7B

## AUTOMATIC TRANSMISSION

## 1 General information

The vehicles covered in this manual are equipped with a five-speed (Model 722) or seven-speed (Model 722.9, 2006 and later models only) automatic transmission. All transmissions are equipped with a Torque Converter Clutch system that increases fuel economy. The TCC engages In Drive and Overdrive modes. The TCC system consists of a solenoid, controlled by the Powertrain Control Module (PCM), which locks the torque converter when the vehicle is cruising on level ground and the engine is fully warmed up.

All automatic transmissions covered in this Chapter are equipped with transmission oil coolers which are part of the radiator.

All vehicles with an automatic transmission are equipped with a Brake Transmission Shift Interlock (BTSI) system that locks the shift lever in the PARK position and prevents the driver from shifting out of PARK unless the brake pedal is depressed. The BTSI system also pre-vents the ignition key from being turned to the LOCK or ACCESSORY position unless the shift lever is in the PARK position.

Due to the complexity of the automatic transmissions covered in this manual and the need for specialized equipment to perform most service operations, this Chapter is limited to general diagnosis, routine mainte-. nance, adjustments and removal and installation procedures.

If the transmission requires major repair work, leave it to a dealer service department or a transmission repair shop. However, even if a transmission shop does the repairs, you can save some money by removing and installing the transmission yourself. Keep in mind that a faulty transmission should not be removed before the vehicle has been diagnosed by a knowledgeable technician equipped with the proper tools, as troubleshooting must be performed with the transmission installed in the vehicle.

## 2 Diagnosis - general

➡**Note: Automatic transmission malfunctions may be caused by five general conditions: poor engine performance, incorrect adjustments, hydraulic malfunctions, mechanical malfunctions or malfunctions in the computer or its signal network. Diagnosis of these problems should always begin with a check of the easily repaired items: fluid level and condition (see Chapter 1) and shift cable adjustment. Next, perform a road test to determine if the problem has been corrected or if more diagnosis is necessary. If the problem persists after the preliminary tests and corrections are completed, additional diagnosis should be done by a dealer service department or transmission repair shop. Refer to the Troubleshooting section at the front of this manual for information on symptoms of transmission problems.**

### PRELIMINARY CHECKS

1   Drive the vehicle to warm up the transmission to its normal operating temperature.

2   Check the fluid level as described in Chapter 1:

a)   *If the fluid level is unusually low, add enough fluid to bring the level to the correct mark (see Chapter 1, then check for external leaks - see below). The manufacturer states that routine checks of the automatic transmission fluid are not necessary; the procedure in Chapter 1 should only be used when refilling the transmission after the fluid has been drained, unless an obvious leak has been detected. Low fluid level can lead to slipping or loss of drive, while overfilling can cause foaming and loss of fluid.*

➡**Note: To check the fluid level you'll have to obtain a dipstick (part number 9336), through a dealer parts department (unlike most vehicles, a dipstick is not present in the transmission filler tube). A scan tool capable of reading the temperature of the automatic transmission fluid will also be required.**

b)   *If the fluid level is abnormally high, it might have been overfilled. Drain off the excess.*

c)   *If the fluid is foaming, drain it and refill the transmission, then check for coolant in the fluid that was drained. If coolant is present, the transmission fluid cooler in the radiator is faulty.*

3   Check the engine idle speed.

➡**Note: If the engine is malfunctioning, do not proceed with the preliminary checks until it has been repaired and runs normally.**

4   Inspect the shift rod (see Section 3). Make sure it's properly adjusted and that it operates smoothly.

### FLUID LEAK DIAGNOSIS

5   Most fluid leaks are usually easy to locate because they leave a visible stain and/or wet spot. Most repairs are simply a matter of replacing a seal or gasket. If a leak is more difficult to find, the following procedure will help.

6   Identify the fluid. Make sure that it's transmission fluid, not engine oil or brake fluid. One way to positively identify Automatic Transmission Fluid (ATF) is by its red color.

7   Try to pinpoint the source of the leak. Drive the vehicle several miles, then park it over a large sheet of cardboard. After a minute or two, you should be able to locate the leak by determining the source of the fluid dripping onto the cardboard.

8   Make a careful visual inspection of the suspected component and the area immediately around it. Pay particular attention to gasket mating surfaces. A flashlight and mirror are often helpful for finding leaks in areas that are hard to see.

9   If you still can't find the leak, thoroughly clean the suspected area with a degreaser or solvent, then dry it off.

10   Drive the vehicle for several miles at normal operating temperature and varying speeds. After driving the vehicle, visually inspect the suspected component again.

11   Once you have located the leak, you must determine the source before you can repair it properly. For example, if you replace a pan gasket but the sealing flange is warped or bent, the new gasket won't stop the leak. The flange must first be straightened.

12   Before attempting to repair a leak, verify that the following conditions are corrected or they might cause another leak.

➡**Note: Some of the following conditions cannot be fixed without highly specialized tools and expertise. Such problems must be referred to a transmission repair shop or a dealer service department.**

## Gasket leaks

13 Inspect the pan periodically. Make sure that the bolts are tight, that no bolts are missing, that the gasket is in good condition and that the pan is flat (dents in the pan might indicate damage to the valve body inside).

14 If the pan gasket is leaking, the fluid level or the fluid pressure might be too high, the vent might be plugged, the pan bolts might be too tight, the pan sealing flange might be warped, the sealing surface of the transmission housing might be damaged, the gasket might be damaged or the transmission casting might be cracked or porous. If sealant instead of gasket material has been used to form a seal between the pan and the transmission housing, it may be the wrong type sealant.

## Seal leaks

15 If a transmission seal is leaking, the fluid level or pressure might be too high, the vent might be plugged, the seal bore might be dam-aged, the seal itself might be damaged or incorrectly installed, the surface of the shaft protruding through the seal might be damaged or a loose bearing might be causing excessive shaft movement.

16 Make sure that the dipstick tube seal is in good condition and that the tube is correctly seated.

## Case leaks

17 If the case itself appears to be leaking, the casting is porous. A porous casting must be repaired or replaced.

18 Make sure that the oil cooler hose fittings are tight and in good condition.

## Fluid comes out vent pipe or fill tube

19 If this condition occurs, the transmission is overfilled, there is coolant in the fluid, the case is porous, the dipstick is incorrect, the vent is plugged or the drain-back holes are plugged.

---

## 3  Shift rod - check, adjustment and replacement

### ✳✳ WARNING:

**The models covered by this manual are equipped with a Supplemental Restraint System (SRS), more commonly known as airbags. Always disable the airbag system before working in the vicinity of any airbag system component to avoid the possibility of accidental deployment of the airbag(s), which could cause personal injury (see Chapter 12). Do not use a memory saving device to preserve the PCM or radio memory when working on or near airbag system components.**

## CHECK

1  Firmly apply the parking brake and try to momentarily operate the starter in each shift lever position. The starter should only operate when the shift lever is in the PARK or NEUTRAL positions. If the starter operates in any position other than PARK or NEUTRAL, adjust the shift rod (see below). If, after adjustment, the starter still operates in positions other than PARK or NEUTRAL, the Transmission Range (TR) sensor may be defective (see Chapter 6).

## ADJUSTMENT

▶ **Refer to illustration 3.4**

2  Raise the vehicle and support it securely on jackstands.

➡**Note: The vehicle must remain level during the shift rod adjustment.**

3  Have an assistant in the vehicle hold the shift lever in Drive during the adjustment procedure.

4  From below, loosen the bolt at the shifter-end of the shift rod (see illustration).

5  While pushing up against the bolt, tighten it. Do not twist the rod or the rod holder.

6  Lower the vehicle.

7  If the linkage appears to be adjusted correctly, but the starter still operates in any other position(s) besides PARK and NEUTRAL, the Transmission Range (TR) sensor might be faulty (see Chapter 6).

**3.4  Shift rod-to-shifter details: (A) is the retaining clip, (B) is the adjustment lock bolt**

## REPLACEMENT

♦ **Refer to illustration 3.10**

8  Place the shift lever in the PARK position.

9  Raise the vehicle and support it securely on jackstands.

10 Working under the vehicle, use needle-nose pliers to remove the clip securing the shift rod to the arm on the transmission (see illustration).

11 At the floor shift end of the rod, loosen the adjustment bolt (see illustration 3.4) and slide the shift rod out of its bracket at the bottom of the shift arm.

12 Installation is the reverse of removal. When you're done, adjust the rod (see Steps 2 through 6).

**3.10  Lift this tab to release the clip and separate the shift rod from the arm on the transmission**

## 4  Brake Transmission Shift Interlock (BTSI) system

### ✳✳ WARNING:

**The models covered by this manual are equipped with a Supplemental Restraint System (SRS), more commonly known as airbags. Always disable the airbag system before working in the vicinity of any airbag system component to avoid the possibility of accidental deployment of the airbag(s), which could cause personal injury (see Chapter 12). Do not use a memory saving device to preserve the PCM or radio memory when working on or near airbag system components.**

➡ **Note: The shift lever and BTSI solenoid is one complete assembly. In the event of failure, replace the shift lever assembly as a complete unit. Check with a dealer parts department or other qualified automotive parts distributor.**

### DESCRIPTION

1  The Brake Transmission Shift Interlock (BTSI) system is designed to prevent the vehicle from being started unless the transmission is in Park and the brake pedal is depressed. When the system is functioning correctly, the only way to unlock the shift lever and move it out of PARK is to depress the brake pedal. The BTSI system also prevents the ignition key from being turned to the LOCK or ACCESSORY position unless the shift lever is fully locked into the PARK position.

### CHECK

2  Verify that the ignition key can be removed only in the PARK position.

3  When the shift lever is in the PARK position, you should be able to rotate the ignition key from OFF to LOCK. But when the shift lever is in any gear position other than PARK (including NEUTRAL), you should not be able to rotate the ignition key to the LOCK position.

4  You should not be able to move the shift lever out of the PARK position when the ignition key is turned to the OFF position.

5  You should not be able to move the shift lever out of the PARK position when the ignition key is turned to the RUN or START position until you depress the brake pedal.

6  You should not be able to move the shift lever out of the PARK position when the ignition key is turned to the ACC or LOCK position (brake pedal NOT depressed).

7  Once in gear, with the ignition key in the RUN position, you should be able to move the shift lever between gears, or put it into NEUTRAL or PARK, without depressing the brake pedal.

8  If the BTSI system doesn't operate as described, try adjusting it (see Steps 9 through 17).

### BTSI SYSTEM ADJUSTMENT

♦ **Refer to illustration 4.15**

9  On most models, there are two cables attached to a bracket on the brake pedal. One cable connects to the ignition/steering column lock, and the other cable is routed to the transmission. When they are adjusted properly, the cables prevent the key from turning unless the brake pedal is depressed.

10 Move the shift lever to the Park position.

11 A spring is connected to either side of the bracket on the brake pedal, and each cable end is equipped with a pushbutton lock. Adjust

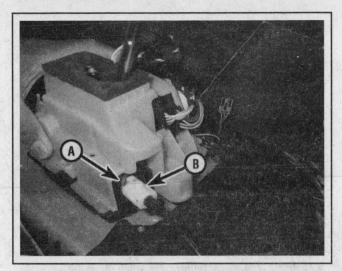

**4.15  To disconnect the BTSI cable at the shifter, depress the tab (A) then twist the cable (B) counterclockwise**

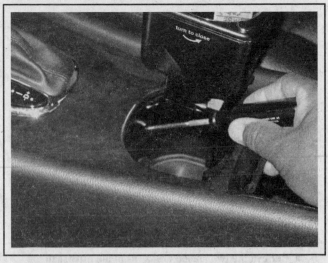

**4.19  To override the BTSI system, pull the cupholder out and depress the button with a screwdriver**

the cable to the steering column by applying some preload pressure by hand on the spring, then with the key in the Off position, push in and release the button on the adjuster located at the cable housing end near the pedal bracket.

12  Perform the same procedure on the spring and adjuster on the cable that leads to the transmission. The adjuster button is close to the case of the transmission.

13  On some models with ESM (Electronic Shift Module), there is only one BTSI cable, connected at the shifter housing and the ignition switch.

14  On ESM models, there is no mechanical adjustment of the cable, but its performance can be checked with a scan tool if you suspect a problem.

15  To replace the cable on ESM models, disconnect the cable at the shifter by depressing the tab and twisting the cable end a quarter-turn counterclockwise (see illustration).

16  The other end of the cable is secured to the back of the ignition switch (see Chapter 12). Unscrew the retaining ring and pull the cable off.

17  Installation is the reverse of the removal procedure. Check with a scan tool to ensure that no trouble codes exist.

## SHIFT LOCK OVERRIDE FEATURE

**Refer to illustration 4.19**

18  In the event the Brake Transmission Shift Interlock (BTSI) system fails and the shift lever cannot be moved out of gear, the system is equipped with an override feature.

19  Pull up the cupholder at the center of the console, just rearward of the shifter. Depress the brake pedal (and keep it depressed) and start the engine (or, if you just want to shift out of PARK without starting the engine, turn the ignition key to the ACC position). Locate the button at the front of the cupholder cavity and depress it with a screwdriver, then move the shifter out of the PARK position (see illustration).

20  Repair the BTSI system (or have it repaired) as soon as possible.

## 5  Extension housing oil seal - replacement

▶ **Refer to illustrations 5.4a and 5.4b**

1  Oil leaks frequently occur due to wear of the extension housing oil seal. Replacement of this seal is relatively easy, since the repair can be performed without removing the transmission from the vehicle.

2  If you suspect a leak at the extension housing seal, raise the vehicle and support it securely on jackstands. The extension housing seal is located at the rear end of the transmission, where the driveshaft is attached. If the extension housing seal is leaking, transmission lubricant will be evident on the front of the driveshaft and may be dripping from the rear of the transmission.

3  Remove the driveshaft (see Chapter 8).

**5.4a  Relieve the two staked areas (A) of the driveshaft flange retaining nut before attempting to remove the nut - (B) is the oil seal in the housing**

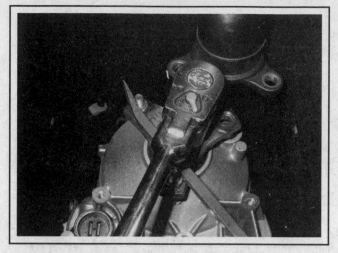

**5.4b  Use a long prybar for leverage when removing the retaining nut; it's on very tight**

4   Position the shift lever into PARK, if not already done. Before attempting to remove the large nut securing the driveshaft flange to the transmission shaft, use a small drift and hammer to undo the two staked areas of the nut in the depressions (see illustrations).

➡**Note: If you can't do this with a punch, use a small die grinder. Use a two-jaw puller to remove the driveshaft flange from the output shaft.**

5   Using a screwdriver, prybar or seal removal tool, carefully pry out the extension housing seal. Do not damage the splines on the transmis-

sion output shaft.

6   Using a seal driver or a large deep socket with an outside diameter the same as that of the seal, install the new extension housing seal. Drive it into the bore squarely and make sure it's completely seated.

7   Install the output shaft flange and nut and tighten it to the torque listed in this Chapter's Specifications.

8   Use a punch to stake the flange nut to the output shaft to prevent rotation.

9   Install the driveshaft (see Chapter 8).

## 6   Transmission mount - check and replacement

### CHECK

▶ **Refer to illustration 6.2**

1   Raise the vehicle and support it securely on jackstands.

2   Insert a large screwdriver or prybar into the space between the transmission extension housing and the crossmember and try to pry the transmission up slightly (see illustration).

3   The transmission should not move much at all and the rubber in the center of the mount should fully insulate the center of the mount from the mount bracket around it.

### REPLACEMENT

▶ **Refer to illustrations 6.4a and 6.4b**

4   Support the transmission with a jack, remove the bolts attaching the mount to the crossmember and the bolts attaching the mount to the transmission (see illustrations).

5   Raise the transmission slightly with the jack and remove the mount.

6   Installation is the reverse of the removal procedure. Be sure to tighten all fasteners to the Specifications listed in this Chapter.

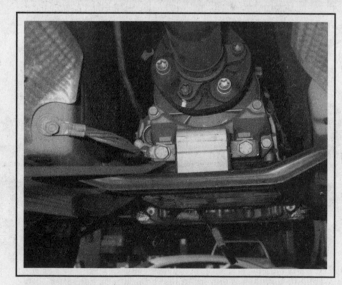

**6.2  To check the transmission mount, insert a large screwdriver between the extension housing and the crossmember and try to lever the transmission up**

6.4a  Transmission mount-to-transmission bolts

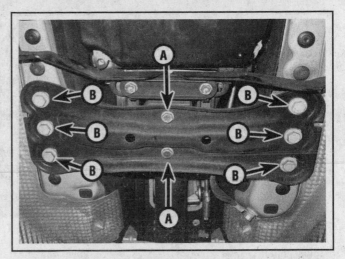

6.4b  Location of the crossmember-to-mount bolts (A) and the crossmember-to-frame mounting bolts (B)

## 7   Transmission Control Module (TCM) - general information

※※ **WARNING:**

The models covered by this manual are equipped with a Supplemental Restraint System (SRS), more commonly known as airbags. Always disable the airbag system before working in the vicinity of any airbag system component to avoid the possibility of accidental deployment of the airbag(s), which could cause personal injury (see Chapter 12). Do not use a memory saving device to preserve the PCM or radio memory when working on or near airbag system components.

※※ **CAUTION:**

The TCM is an Electro-Static Discharge (ESD) sensitive electronic device, meaning a static electricity discharge from your body could possibly damage electrical components. Be sure to properly ground yourself and the TCM before handling it. Avoid touching the electrical terminals of the TCM.

→Note: Do not interchange TCMs from different year vehicles. Whenever the TCM is replaced with a new unit, it must be programmed with a scan tool by a dealership service department or other qualified repair shop. This may require having the vehicle towed to the facility that will perform this procedure.

The transmission control module on these models is incorporated in the valve body of the transmission. Due to the complicated and labor-intensive work required to service the module, it is suggested that the procedure be done at a dealership service department. If you are having trouble with the automatic transmission and you know the fluid level is correct, have a dealership or other repair shop check your vehicle with a scan tool for Diagnostic Trouble Codes relating to the transmission.

## 8   Automatic transmission - removal and installation

▸ **Refer to illustrations 8.3, 8.8, 8.9, 8.13, 8.17, 8.21a and 8.21b**

※※ **CAUTION:**

The transmission and torque converter must be removed as a single assembly. If you try to leave the torque converter attached to the driveplate, the converter driveplate, pump bushing and oil seal will be damaged. The driveplate is not designed to support the load, so none of the weight of the transmission should be allowed to rest on the driveplate during removal.

1   Disconnect the cable from the negative terminal of the battery (see Chapter 5, Section 1).
2   Raise the vehicle and support it securely on jackstands.
3   Remove the rearmost engine splash shield (see illustration).
4   Remove the driveshaft (see Chapter 8).
5   Remove the starter (see Chapter 5).
6   Disconnect the oxygen sensor connectors, unbolt the exhaust system fasteners and the exhaust brace at the transmission, then remove the exhaust system (see Chapter 4).
7   Drain the transmission fluid, then reinstall the fluid pan (see Chapter 1).

8.3  Front (A) and rear (B) engine splash shields

8.8  Remove the torque converter cover from the transmission

8.9  Turn the lock ring and disconnect the electrical connector from the transmission

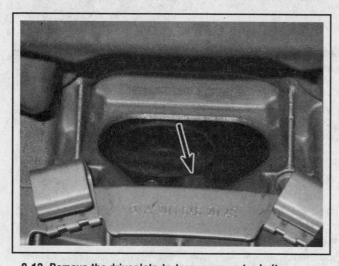

8.13  Remove the driveplate-to-torque converter bolts

8.17  Remove the banjo bolts (A) and separate the transmission fluid cooler lines from the transmission. Also remove the mounting clamp (B)

8  Remove the torque converter access cover (see illustration).

9  Disconnect the electrical harness plug on the transmission (see illustration).

10  Remove the air filter/air intake and the MAF/IAT sensor housing (see Chapter 4).

11  Remove the transmission heat shield, if equipped.

12  Mark the relationship of the torque converter to the driveplate to ensure that their dynamic balance is maintained when the converter is reattached to the driveplate.

13  Remove the driveplate-to-torque converter bolts (see illustration). Turn the crankshaft clockwise for access to each bolt, using a socket and breaker bar placed on the crankshaft pulley bolt.

14  Disconnect the shift rod from the transmission (see Section 3).

15  Support the transmission with a transmission jack (available at most equipment rental facilities) and secure the transmission to the jack with safety chains.

16  Unbolt and remove the transmission crossmember (see illustration 6.4b).

17  Clean the area around the transmission fluid line banjo bolts, then disconnect the transmission cooler lines from the transmission (see illustration). Plug the ends of the lines to prevent fluid from leaking out after you disconnect them.

18  Unbolt the transmission fluid fill pipe from the engine oil pan and pull the pipe from the transmission.

19  Lower the jack supporting the transmission and allow it and the engine to angle down as far as possible (if you're using a transmission jack, you'll have to readjust the angle of the jack head).

20  Support the engine with a jack. Use a block of wood under the oil pan to spread the load.

21  Remove the bolts securing the transmission to the engine (see illustrations). A long extension and a U-joint socket will greatly simplify this step.

22  Move the transmission to the rear to disengage it from the engine block dowel pins. Make sure the torque converter is detached from the driveplate and stays with the transmission. Lower the transmission with the jack.

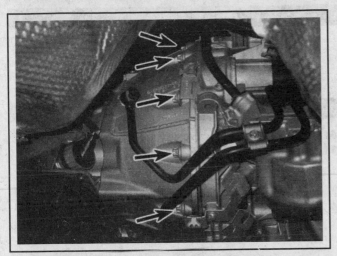

8.21a  Transmission-to-engine bolts seen from the right side . . .

8.21b  . . . and the left side

## INSTALLATION

23 Installation is the reverse of the removal procedure, noting the following points:

a) Prior to installation, make sure the torque converter is securely engaged in the pump. If you've removed the converter, spread transmission fluid on the torque converter rear hub, where the transmission front seal rides. With the front of the transmission facing up, rotate the converter back and forth. It should drop down into the transmission front pump in stages. To make sure the converter is fully engaged, lay a straightedge across the transmission-to-engine mating surface and make sure the converter lugs are at least 3/4-inch below the straightedge.

b) When mating the transmission to the engine, turn the torque converter to line up the marks on the torque converter and driveplate made during removal.

c) Move the transmission forward carefully until the dowel pins and the transmission are engaged. Make sure the transmission mates with the engine with no gap. If there's a gap, make sure there are no wires or other objects pinched between the engine and transmission and also make sure the torque converter is completely engaged in the transmission front pump. Try to rotate the converter - if it doesn't rotate easily, it's probably not fully engaged in the pump. If necessary, lower the transmission and install the converter fully.

d) Install the transmission-to-engine bolts and tighten them to the torque listed in this Chapter's Specifications. As you're tightening the bolts, make sure that the engine and transmission mate completely at all points. If not, find out why. Never try to force the engine and transmission together with the bolts or you'll break the transmission case!

e) Install the driveplate-to-torque converter bolts. Tighten them to the torque listed in this Chapter's Specifications.

➡ **Note: Install all of the bolts before tightening any of them.**

f) The remainder of installation is the reverse of removal.

g) When you're done, refill the transmission with the specified fluid (see Chapter 1), run the engine and check for fluid leaks.

## 9  Automatic transmission overhaul - general information

In the event of a fault occurring, it will be necessary to establish whether the fault is electrical, mechanical or hydraulic in nature, before repair work can be contemplated. Diagnosis requires detailed knowledge of the transmission's operation and construction, as well as access to specialized test equipment, and so is deemed to be beyond the scope of this manual. It is therefore essential that problems with the automatic transmission are referred to a dealer service department or other qualified repair facility for assessment.

Note that a faulty transmission should not be removed before the vehicle has been assessed by a knowledgeable technician equipped with the proper tools, as troubleshooting must be performed with the transmission installed in the vehicle.

## Specifications

### General

Transmission fluid type       See Chapter 1

| Torque specifications | Ft-lbs (unless otherwise indicated) | Nm |
|---|---|---|

→**Note:** One foot-pound (ft-lb) of torque is equivalent to 12 inch-pounds (in-lbs) of torque. Torque values below approximately 15 ft-lbs are expressed in inch-pounds, since most foot-pound torque wrenches are not accurate at these smaller values.

| | Ft-lbs | Nm |
|---|---|---|
| Output shaft flange nut | 148 | 200 |
| Driveplate-to-torque converter bolts | 31 | 42 |
| Shift rod adjuster bolt | 106 in-lbs | 12 |
| Transmission fluid cooler lines-to-transmission banjo bolts | | |
|   Step 1 | 44 in-lbs | 5 |
|   Step 2 | Tighten an additional 90-degrees | |
| Transmission mount-to-transmission bolts | | |
|   2005 and earlier models | 22 | 30 |
|   2006 and later models | 30 | 40 |
| Transmission crossmember-to-mount bolts | | |
|   2005 and earlier models | 17 | 23 |
|   2006 and later models | 21 | 28 |
| Transmission-to-engine block bolts | 28 | 38 |
| Transmission-to-engine oil pan bolts | | |
|   V6 models | 28 | 38 |
|   Four-cylinder models | | |
|     M6 bolts | 80 in-lbs | 9 |
|     M8 bolts | 177 in-lbs | 20 |

## Section

# 8

## CLUTCH AND DRIVELINE

## 1 Clutch - description and check

1   All vehicles with a manual transmission use a single dry plate, diaphragm spring type clutch. The clutch disc has a splined hub which allows it to slide along the splines of the transmission input shaft. The clutch and pressure plate are held in contact by spring pressure exerted by the diaphragm in the pressure plate.

2   The clutch release system is operated by hydraulic pressure. The hydraulic release system consists of the clutch pedal, a master cylinder and fluid reservoir, the hydraulic line, a release (or slave) cylinder which actuates the clutch release (or throwout) bearing.

3   When pressure is applied to the clutch pedal to release the clutch, a pushrod pushes against brake fluid inside the master cylinder, applying hydraulic pressure to the release cylinder, which pushes the release bearing against the diaphragm fingers of the clutch pressure plate, which in turn releases the clutch plate.

4   Terminology can be a problem when discussing the clutch components because common names are in some cases different from those used by the manufacturer. For example, the driven plate is also called the clutch plate or disc, the clutch release bearing is sometimes called a throwout bearing, the release cylinder is sometimes called the operating or slave cylinder.

5   Other than to replace components with obvious damage, some preliminary checks should be performed to diagnose clutch problems.

*a) The first check should be of the fluid level in the brake fluid reservoir. If the fluid level is excessively low, add fluid as necessary and inspect the hydraulic system for leaks (fluid level will actually rise as the clutch wears).*

*b) To check clutch spin-down time, run the engine at normal idle speed with the transmission in Neutral (clutch pedal up - engaged). Disengage the clutch (pedal down), wait several seconds and shift the transmission into Reverse. No grinding noise should be heard. A grinding noise would most likely indicate a problem in the pressure plate or the clutch disc.*

*c) To check for complete clutch release, run the engine (with the parking brake applied to prevent movement) and hold the clutch pedal approximately 1/2-inch from the floor. Shift the transmission between First gear and Reverse several times. If the shift is hard or the transmission grinds, component failure is indicated.*

## 2 Clutch hydraulic system - bleeding

1   Bleed the hydraulic system whenever any part of the system has been removed or the fluid level has fallen so low that air has been drawn into the master cylinder. The bleeding procedure is very similar to bleeding a brake system.

2   Fill the brake master cylinder reservoir with new brake fluid of the proper type (see Chapter 1).

### ✳✳ CAUTION:

**Do not re-use any of the fluid coming from the system during the bleeding operation or use fluid which has been inside an open container for an extended period of time.**

3   Working at the transmission, remove the cap from the bleeder valve and attach a length of clear hose to the valve. Place the other end of the hose into a container partially filled with clean brake fluid.

4   Have an assistant depress the clutch pedal and hold it. Open the bleeder valve on the hydraulic line, allowing fluid and any air to escape. Close the bleeder valve when the flow of fluid (and bubbles) ceases. Once closed, have your assistant release the pedal.

5   Continue this process until all air is evacuated from the system, indicated by a solid stream of fluid being ejected from the bleeder valve each time with no air bubbles. Keep a close watch on the fluid level inside the brake master cylinder reservoir - if the level drops too far, air will get into the system and you'll have to start all over again.

➥**Note: Wash the area with water to remove any spilled brake fluid.**

6   Check the brake fluid level again, and add some, if necessary, to bring it to the appropriate level. Check carefully for proper operation before placing the vehicle into normal service.

## 3 Clutch master cylinder - removal and installation

### REMOVAL

1   Disconnect the cable from the negative terminal of the battery (see Chapter 5, Section 1).

2   Remove the driver's side knee bolster (see Chapter 11).

3   Unplug the electrical connector from the brake light switch.

4   Remove the clip that attaches the clutch fluid hydraulic line to the clutch master cylinder. Have rags handy, as some fluid will be lost as the line is removed. Also have a plug ready and immediately plug the line to prevent leakage.

5   Remove the nuts attaching the pedal assembly to the firewall, then remove the pedal assembly. Pull out the hydraulic line from the clutch master cylinder, then plug the line to prevent leakage.

6   Remove the clip securing the clutch pedal pivot pin. Pull out the pin.

7   Remove the pins securing the clutch master cylinder to the pedal assembly. Remove the master cylinder from the pedal assembly.

### INSTALLATION

8   Installation is the reverse of removal. If the fluid level is extremely low, fill the brake master cylinder reservoir with the fluid recommended in the Chapter 1 Specifications Section. Don't add too much, though, because the fluid level actually rises as the clutch components wear.

## 4 Clutch components - removal, inspection and installation

### ✳✳ WARNING:

Dust produced by clutch wear and deposited on clutch components is hazardous to your health. DO NOT blow it out with compressed air and DO NOT inhale it. DO NOT use gasoline or petroleum-based solvents to remove the dust. Brake system cleaner should be used to flush the dust into a drain pan. After the clutch components are wiped clean with a rag, dispose of the contaminated rags and cleaner in a covered, marked container.

### REMOVAL

▶ Refer to illustration 4.4

1  Access to the clutch components is normally accomplished by removing the transmission, leaving the engine in the vehicle. If, of course, the engine is being removed for major overhaul, then check the clutch for wear and replace worn components as necessary. However, the relatively low cost of the clutch components compared to the time and trouble spent gaining access to them warrants their replacement anytime the engine or transmission is removed, unless they are new or in near perfect condition. The following procedures are based on the assumption the engine will stay in place.

2  Referring to Chapter 7 Part A, remove the transmission from the vehicle. Support the engine while the transmission is out. Preferably, an engine hoist or support fixture should be used to support it from above. However, if a jack is used underneath the engine, make sure a piece of wood is positioned between the jack and oil pan to spread the load.

### ✳✳ CAUTION:

The pickup for the oil pump is very close to the bottom of the oil pan. If the pan is bent or distorted in any way, engine oil starvation could occur.

3  To support the clutch disc during removal, install a clutch alignment tool through the clutch disc hub.

4  Carefully inspect the flywheel and pressure plate for indexing marks. The marks are usually an X, an O or a white letter. If they cannot be found, scribe marks yourself so the pressure plate and the flywheel will be in the same alignment during installation (see illustration).

5  Turning each bolt only 1/4-turn at a time, loosen the pressure plate-to-flywheel bolts. Work in a criss-cross pattern until all spring pressure is relieved. Then hold the pressure plate securely and completely remove the bolts, followed by the pressure plate and clutch disc.

### INSPECTION

▶ Refer to illustrations 4.9, 4.11a and 4.11b

6  Ordinarily, when a problem occurs in the clutch, it can be attributed to wear of the clutch driven plate assembly (clutch disc). However, all components should be inspected at this time.

7  Inspect the flywheel for cracks, heat checking, grooves and other obvious defects. If the imperfections are slight, a machine shop can machine the surface flat and smooth, which is highly recommended regardless of the surface appearance. Refer to Chapter 2 for the flywheel removal and installation procedure.

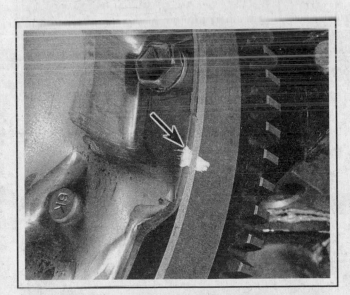

**4.4  Be sure to mark the pressure plate and flywheel in order to insure proper alignment during installation (this won't be necessary if a new pressure plate is to be installed)**

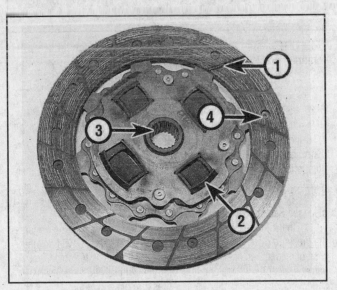

**4.9  The clutch disc**

1  *Lining* - this will wear down in use
2  *Springs or dampers* - check for cracking and deformation
3  *Splined hub* - the splines must not be worn and should slide smoothly on the transmission input shaft splines
4  *Rivets* - these secure the lining and will damage the flywheel or pressure plate if allowed to contact the surfaces

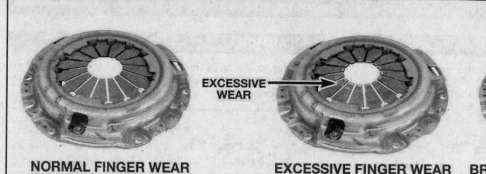

**NORMAL FINGER WEAR**  **EXCESSIVE FINGER WEAR**  **BROKEN OR BENT FINGERS**

**EXCESSIVE WEAR**

**4.11a  Replace the pressure plate if excessive wear is noted**

**4.11b  Examine the pressure plate friction surface for score marks, cracks and evidence of overheating**

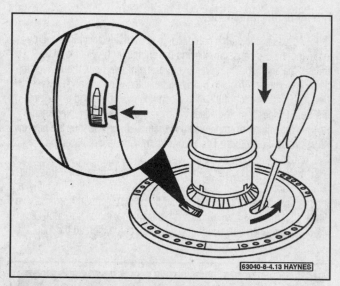

**4.13  Rotate the adjustment ring counterclockwise to the marking**

8   Inspect the pilot bearing (see Section 6).

9   Inspect the lining on the clutch disc. There should be at least 1/16-inch of lining above the rivet heads. Check for loose rivets, distortion, cracks, broken springs and other obvious damage (see illustration). As mentioned above, ordinarily the clutch disc is routinely replaced, so if in doubt about the condition, replace it with a new one.

10   The release bearing should also be replaced along with the clutch disc (see Section 5).

11   Check the machined surfaces and the diaphragm spring fingers of the pressure plate (see illustrations). If the surface is grooved or otherwise damaged, replace the pressure plate. Also check for obvious damage, distortion, cracking, etc. Light glazing can be removed with sandpaper or emery cloth. If a new pressure plate is required, new and factory-rebuilt units are available.

## INSTALLATION

▶ **Refer to illustration 4.13 and 4.14**

12   Before installation, clean the flywheel and pressure plate machined surfaces with brake system cleaner. It's important that no oil or grease is on these surfaces or the lining of the clutch disc. Handle the parts only with clean hands.

13   If you're reusing the pressure plate, reset the adjustment ring. Position the pressure plate in a hydraulic press, with a block of wood or some other suitable support placed under the central portion of the pressure plate, directly below the diaphragm spring fingers (not on the friction face). Apply pressure to the diaphragm spring fingers until the adjusting ring is loose. While still applying pressure, use a suitable tool and rotate the adjustment ring counterclockwise to the marking (see illustration). Hold the adjustment ring, then release the pressure on the diaphragm spring fingers.

14 Position the clutch disc and pressure plate against the flywheel with the clutch held in place with an alignment tool (see illustration). Make sure it's installed properly (most replacement clutch plates will be marked "flywheel side" or something similar - if not marked, install the clutch disc with the damper springs toward the transmission).

15 Tighten the pressure plate-to-flywheel bolts only finger tight, working around the pressure plate.

16 Center the clutch disc by ensuring the alignment tool extends through the splined hub and into the pilot bearing in the crankshaft. Wiggle the tool up, down or side-to-side as needed to bottom the tool in the pilot bearing. Tighten the pressure plate-to-flywheel bolts a little at a time, working in a criss-cross pattern to prevent distorting the cover. After all of the bolts are snug, tighten them to the torque listed in this Chapter's Specifications. Remove the alignment tool.

17 Using high-temperature grease, lubricate the inner groove of the release bearing.

18 Install the transmission (see Chapter 7A).

**4.14  Center the clutch disc using a clutch alignment tool**

---

## 5    Clutch release cylinder and bearing - removal and installation

**✳✳ WARNING:**

**Dust produced by clutch wear and deposited on clutch components is hazardous to your health. DO NOT blow it out with compressed air and DO NOT inhale it. DO NOT use gasoline or petroleum-based solvents to remove the dust. Brake system cleaner should be used to flush the dust into a drain pan. After the clutch components are wiped clean with a rag, dispose of the contaminated rags and cleaner in a covered, marked container.**

1    Disconnect the cable from the negative battery terminal (see Chapter 5, Section 1).

2    Using a small screwdriver, remove the clip that attaches the clutch fluid hydraulic line to the clutch release cylinder on the side of the transmission. Have rags handy, as some fluid will be lost as the line is removed. Also have a plug ready and immediately plug the line to prevent leakage.

3    Remove the transmission (see Chapter 7, Part A).

4    On some models it may be necessary to remove a clip securing the release cylinder hydraulic line to the transmission bellhousing. Disconnect the release cylinder electrical connector, if equipped.

5    Remove the fasteners securing the release cylinder to the transmission and slide the release cylinder assembly off the transmission input shaft.

6    Installation is the reverse of the removal procedure.

---

## 6    Pilot bearing - inspection and replacement

▶ **Refer to illustrations 6.5 and 6.6**

1    The clutch pilot bearing is pressed into the rear of the crankshaft. It is greased at the factory and does not require additional lubrication. Its primary purpose is to support the front of the transmission input shaft. The pilot bearing should be inspected whenever the clutch components are removed from the engine. Due to its inaccessibility, if you are in doubt as to its condition, replace it with a new one.

➡ **Note: If the engine has been removed from the vehicle, disregard the following steps which do not apply.**

2    Remove the transmission (see Chapter 7 Part A).

3    Remove the clutch components (see Section 4).

4    Inspect for any excessive wear, scoring, lack of grease, dryness or obvious damage. If any of these conditions are noted, the bearing should be replaced. A flashlight will be helpful to direct light into the recess.

**6.5 A small slide-hammer puller is handy for removing the pilot bearing**

**6.6 If available, use a bearing driver to install the pilot bearing**

5    Removal can be accomplished with a slide hammer fitted with a puller attachment (see illustration), which are available at most auto parts stores or equipment rental yards.

6    To install the new bearing, lightly lubricate the outside surface with multi-purpose grease, then drive it into the recess with a hammer and bearing/bushing driver (see illustration). Make sure the bearing seal faces toward the transmission. If you don't have a bearing driver, carefully tap it into place with a hammer and a socket.

**❋❋ CAUTION:**

**Be careful not to let the bearing become cocked in the bore.**

7    Install the clutch components, transmission and all other components removed previously, tightening all fasteners properly.

## 7    Clutch pedal position switch - check and replacement

### CHECK

1    The clutch pedal position switch, which is part of the starter relay circuit, is mounted on the clutch pedal. The switch closes the starter relay circuit only when the clutch pedal is fully depressed.

2    To test the switch, verify that the engine will not crank over when the clutch pedal is in the released position, and that it does crank over with the pedal depressed.

3    If the engine starts without depressing the clutch pedal, replace the switch.

### REPLACEMENT

4    Remove the driver side knee bolster (see Chapter 11).

5    Unplug the electrical connector from the clutch pedal position switch.

6    Release the clip that attaches the clutch pedal switch to the pedal, then rotate the switch and remove it from the pedal.

7    Installation is the reverse of removal.

## 8    Driveshaft(s) - general information

The driveshaft is of tubular construction and may be of a one or two-section type. The front driveshaft on AWD models is bolted to a flange at the front axle pinion and the transfer case. The attachment of the rear driveshaft to the transmission or transfer case and the rear axle pinion flange are connected by bolted flange. The shaft is supported near its forward end on a ball bearing which is flexibly mounted in a bracket.

## 9  Driveshaft(s) - removal and installation

➡Note: The manufacturer recommends replacing driveshaft fasteners with new ones when installing the driveshaft.

### REAR DRIVESHAFT

#### Removal

▶ Refer to illustrations 9.3, 9.4, 9.5, 9.7 and 9.8

➡Note: Where a two-piece driveshaft is involved, the rear shaft must be removed before the front shaft.

1  Raise the vehicle and support it securely on jackstands.
2  Remove the rear portion of the exhaust system (see Chapter 4).

3  Remove the exhaust heat shield (see illustration).
4  Use chalk or a scribe to index the relationship of the driveshaft to the differential axle assembly mating flange. This ensures correct alignment when the driveshaft is reinstalled (see illustration).
5  Remove the bolts securing the driveshaft flange to the differential pinion flange (see illustration). Turn the driveshaft (or wheels) as necessary to bring the bolts into the most accessible position, then separate the driveshaft from the differential pinion flange.
6  If equipped, remove the rear engine crossmember.
7  Mark the relationship of the center support bearing to the support bracket, then loosen the bolts securing the center support bearing, but don't remove them at this time (see illustration).

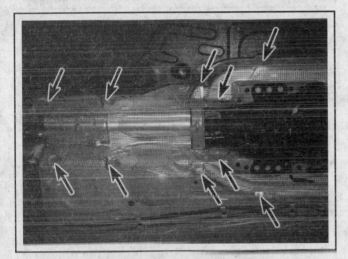

9.3  Remove the fasteners securing the heat shield

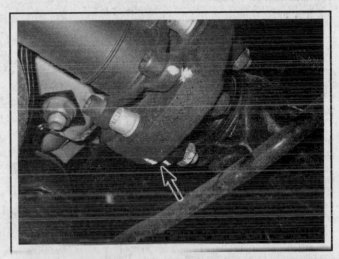

9.4  Mark the relationship of the driveshaft to the pinion flange

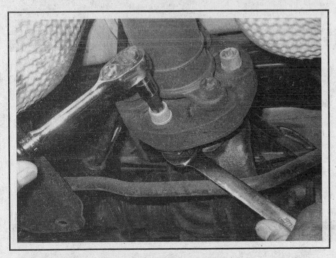

9.5  Remove the bolts securing the driveshaft flange to the differential pinion flange

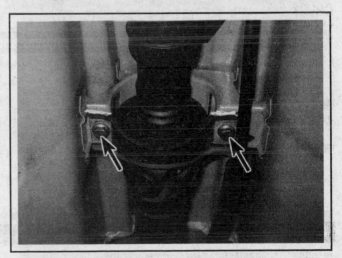

9.7  Loosen the two fasteners securing the center support bearing

8   Mark the relationship of the driveshaft to the transmission companion flange, then remove the bolts (see illustration).

9   Remove the fasteners securing the center support bearing and lower the driveshaft.

### Installation

10  Inspect the center support bearing, if equipped. If it's rough or noisy, replace it (see Section 10).

11  Connect the front end of the driveshaft assembly to the transmission extension housing.

12  Raise the center support bearing and bolt it loosely into place. Raise the rear end of the rear shaft into position and make sure the alignment marks are in alignment. If not, turn the pinion flange until they are aligned.

13  Tighten the fasteners and center support bearing bolts to the torque listed in this Chapter's Specifications.

14  The remainder of installation is the reverse of the removal procedure.

## FRONT DRIVESHAFT (AWD MODELS)

### Removal

15  Remove the right side intake air duct (see Chapter 4).

16  Remove the fastener(s) securing the upper portion of the exhaust shielding plate.

17  Raise the vehicle and support it securely on jackstands.

18  Remove the lower engine cover(s).

19  Remove the right side downstream oxygen sensor (see Chapter 6). Unclip the oxygen sensor wiring harness from its retaining clips.

20  Remove the fastener(s) securing the lower portion of the exhaust shielding plate. Then remove the shield.

21  Use chalk or a scribe to mark the relationship of the driveshaft to the differential axle assembly mating flange. This ensures correct alignment when the driveshaft is reinstalled.

**9.8  Remove the bolts securing the driveshaft flange to the transmission pinion flange**

22  Remove the bolts that secure the front end of the driveshaft to the differential mating flange.

23  Make alignment marks on the driveshaft and transfer case flanges. Unbolt the flange that secures the driveshaft universal joint to the transfer, then remove the driveshaft.

### Installation

24  Installation is the reverse of removal. If the shaft cannot be lined up due to the components of the differential or transfer case having been rotated, put the vehicle in Neutral or rotate one wheel to allow the original alignment to be achieved. Make sure the universal joint caps are properly placed in the flange seat. Tighten the fasteners to the torque listed in this Chapter's Specifications.

## 10  Driveshaft center support bearing - removal and installation

1   Raise the vehicle and support it securely on jackstands.

2   Remove the driveshaft assembly (see Section 9). Mark the relationship of the front portion of the driveshaft to the rear portion of the driveshaft.

3   Separate the rear driveshaft and the front driveshaft at the slide connection.

4   Take the driveshaft and center bearing to an automotive machine shop and have the old bearing pressed off and a new bearing pressed on.

5   Installation is the reverse of removal. Be sure the match marks line up so the driveshaft is properly phased.

## 11  Driveshaft rubber couplings - removal and installation

➡**Note: The manufacturer recommends replacing the coupling retaining nuts with new ones when installing the rubber coupling.**

1   Remove the driveshaft as described in Section 9.

2   Make alignment marks between the coupling and driveshaft.

3   Unscrew the retaining nuts and washers, then withdraw the bolts and remove the coupling from the driveshaft.

4   Check the centering sleeve in the center of the coupling for signs of wear or damage. If necessary, the centering sleeve can be pressed out of position and replaced.

5   Before installing the rubber coupling to the shaft, fill the centering sleeve cavity with multi-purpose grease.

6   Place the new rubber coupling to the shaft, insert the retaining bolts then new retaining nuts and washers, and tighten them to the specified torque.

7   Install the driveshaft as described in Section 9.

## 12  Driveaxles - removal and installation

### ✳✳ WARNING:

Clean all mounting bolts of old thread-locking compound as necessary and apply thread-locking compound (blue/medium) during installation. Clean threaded holes with a thread chasing tool, or equivalent, before installing bolts in them. Replace all self-locking fasteners as equipped.

## FRONT (AWD MODELS)

### Removal

▶ Refer to illustration 12.1

1   Remove the cover from the center of the wheel (see illustration), then break the driveaxle bolt loose with a socket and large breaker bar.

➡Note: If the wall of your socket is too thick to fit through the hole, you'll have to loosen the bolt after removing the wheel. To prevent the hub from turning, you can insert a large punch into the vanes of the brake disc and allow it to rest against the caliper mounting bracket (floating calipers) or the caliper itself (fixed calipers).

2   Loosen the wheel bolts, raise the vehicle and support it securely on jackstands, then remove the wheel and the driveaxle bolt.

3   Separate the tie-rod end from the steering knuckle (see Chapter 10).

4   Remove the bolt and nut securing the balljoint to the steering knuckle, then pry the lower control arm down to separate the components (see Chapter 10).

5   Swing the knuckle/hub assembly out (away from the vehicle) until the end of the driveaxle is free of the hub.

➡Note: If the driveaxle splines stick in the hub, tap on the end of the driveaxle with a plastic hammer. Support the outer end of the driveaxle with a piece of wire to avoid unnecessary strain on the inner CV joint.

6   If you're working on the left-side axle, carefully tap the inner end of the driveaxle off the intermediate shaft using a hammer and long drift positioned against the CV joint housing. If you're working on the right-side axle, carefully pry the inner end of the driveaxle out using a large screwdriver or prybar positioned between the differential and the CV joint housing. Support the CV joints and carefully remove the driveaxle from the vehicle.

### Installation

7   Pry the old spring clip from the inner end of the driveaxle (right-side driveaxle) or intermediate shaft (left-side driveaxle) and install a new one. Lubricate the differential seal with multi-purpose grease and raise the driveaxle into position while supporting the CV joints.

8   Insert the splined end of the inner CV joint into the differential side gear (right-side driveaxle), or the CV joint onto the intermediate shaft (left-side driveaxle) and make sure the spring clip seats in its groove.

9   Grasp the inner CV joint housing (not the driveaxle) and pull out to make sure the spring clip has seated securely.

10  Apply a light coat of multi-purpose grease to the outer CV joint splines, pull out on the strut/steering knuckle assembly and install the stub axle into the hub.

11  Reconnect the balljoint to the lower control arm and tighten the

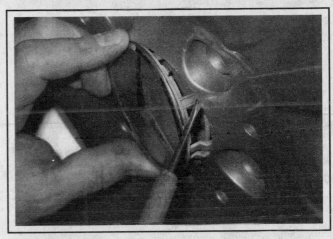

**12.1  Remove the wheel center cap for access to the hub bolt**

nuts (see the torque specifications in Chapter 10).

12  Install the driveaxle bolt. Tighten the bolt securely, but don't try to tighten it to the actual torque specification until you've lowered the vehicle to the ground.

➡Note: If the wall of your socket is too thick to fit through the hole in the center of the wheel, you'll have to tighten the bolt before installing the wheel. To prevent the hub from turning, you can insert a large punch into the vanes of the brake disc and allow it to rest against the caliper mounting bracket (floating calipers) or the caliper itself (fixed calipers).

13  Install the wheel and wheel bolts, then lower the vehicle.

14  Tighten the wheel bolts to the torque listed in the Chapter 1 Specifications. Tighten the hub bolt to the torque listed in this Chapter's Specifications (see illustration).

15  Check the differential lubricant level and top it up, if necessary (see Chapter 1).

## INTERMEDIATE SHAFT (FRONT, AWD MODELS)

16  Remove the left-front driveaxle.

17  Remove the snap-ring retaining the intermediate shaft at the engine oil pan.

18  Slide the intermediate shaft out from the oil pan.

19  If necessary, the support bearing on the end of the shaft can be removed by removing its snap-ring.

20  Installation is the reverse of removal.

➡Note: Check the condition of the snap-rings, replacing them as necessary.

## REAR

### Removal

21  Remove the cover from the center of the wheel (see illustration 12.1), then break the driveaxle nut loose with a socket and large breaker bar.

➡Note: If the wall of your socket is too thick to fit through the hole, you'll have to loosen the bolt after removing the wheel. To prevent the hub from turning, you can install two wheel bolts and brace a large prybar across them.

22 Loosen the wheel bolts, then raise the vehicle and support it securely on jackstands. Remove the wheel.

23 Remove the brake disc (see Chapter 9).

24 Remove the wheel speed sensor from the rear knuckle (see Chapter 9).

25 Disconnect the stabilizer bar link, radius rod, camber strut, tierod and thrust arm from the rear knuckle (see Chapter 10).

26 Carefully fold back the knuckle and pull the driveaxle out of the rear knuckle. Make sure you don't damage the lip of the inner rear knuckle seal. If the splines on the outer CV joint spindle hang up on the splines in the hub, knock them loose with a hammer and punch.

## ✳✳ CAUTION:

**Don't let the driveaxle hang by the inner CV joint.**

27 Carefully pry the inner end of the driveaxle from the differential using a large screwdriver or prybar positioned between the differential and the CV joint housing. Support the CV joints and carefully remove the driveaxle from the vehicle.

## Installation

28 Pry the old spring clip from the inner end of the driveaxle and install a new one. Lubricate the differential seal with multi-purpose grease and raise the driveaxle into position while supporting the CV joints.

29 Insert the splined end of the inner CV joint or the intermediate shaft into the differential and make sure the spring clip locks in its groove.

30 Grasp the inner CV joint housing (not the driveaxle) and pull out to make sure the driveaxle has seated securely in the transaxle.

31 Apply a light coat of multi-purpose grease to the outer CV joint splines, pull out on the rear knuckle assembly and install the stub axle into the hub.

32 Reconnect the control arms to the rear knuckle (see the torque specifications in Chapter 10).

33 Install the driveaxle/hub nut. Tighten the nut securely, but don't try to tighten it to the actual torque specification until you've lowered the vehicle to the ground.

➡**Note: If the wall of your socket is too thick to fit through the hole in the center of the wheel, you'll have to tighten the nut before installing the wheel. To prevent the hub from turning, you can install two wheel bolts and brace a large prybar across them.**

34 Install the wheel and wheel bolts, then lower the vehicle.

35 Tighten the wheel bolts to the torque listed in the Chapter 1 Specifications. Tighten the driveaxle/hub nut to the torque listed in this Chapter's Specifications.

36 Check the differential lubricant level and top it up, if necessary (see Chapter 1).

## 13 Driveaxle boot - replacement

➡**Note: If the CV joints exhibit wear, indicating the need for an overhaul (usually due to torn boots), explore all options before beginning the job. Complete rebuilt driveaxles may be available on an exchange basis, which eliminates a lot of time and work. Whatever is decided, check on the cost and availability of parts before disassembling the joints.**

1 Loosen the wheel bolts. Raise the vehicle and support it securely on jackstands, then remove the wheel.

2 Remove the driveaxle (see Section 12).

## REAR DRIVEAXLES

### Inner CV joint

#### Disassembly

▶ **Refer to illustrations 13.6, 13.7, 13.12a and 13.12b**

3 Mount the driveaxle in a bench vise with wood blocks to protect it.

## ✳✳ CAUTION:

**Do not overtighten the vise.**

4 Remove the boot retaining clamps and slide the inner boot back onto the shaft.

5 Wipe the excess grease from the joint.

6 Mark the relative position of the bearing cage, inner race and housing (see illustration).

7 Mount the CV joint in the vise with wood blocks to protect the stub shaft. Push down one side of the cage and remove the ball bearing from the opposite side (see illustration). The balls may have to be pried out.

8 Repeat this procedure until all of the balls are removed.

9 Remove the inner race from the shaft by tapping on the inner race (not the cage) with a hammer and brass drift.

10 Remove the boot from the shaft.

11 Clean all of the parts with solvent and dry them with compressed air (if available).

**13.6  Mark the bearing cage, inner race and housing relationship after removing the grease (driveaxle shaft removed for clarity)**

**13.7  With the cage and inner race tilted, the balls can be removed one at a time (driveaxle shaft removed for clarity)**

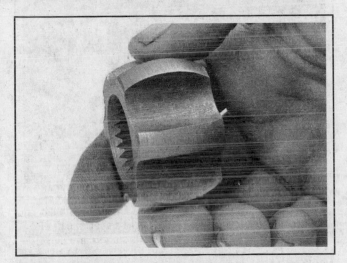

**13.12a  Check the inner race lands and grooves for pitting and score marks**

**13.12b  Check the cage for cracks, pitting and score marks (shiny spots are normal and don't affect operation)**

12  Inspect the housing, splines, balls and races for damage, corrosion, wear and cracks. Check the inner race for wear and scoring. If any of the components are not serviceable, the entire CV joint assembly must be replaced with a new one (see illustrations).

### Assembly

▶ **Refer to illustrations 13.13, 13.21 and 13.22**

13  Wrap the splines of the shaft with tape to prevent damage to the boot, then install the small boot clamp and boot onto the shaft (see illustration).

14  Install the inner race on the shaft by tapping on the inner race (not the cage) with a hammer and brass drift.

15  Rotate the inner race into position in the housing. The marks made during disassembly should face out and be aligned.

16  Pack the lubricant from the kit into the ball races and grooves.

17  Install the balls into the holes, one at a time, until they are all in position. Fill the joint with grease.

18  Apply the remainder of the grease into the boot. Position the large-diameter end of the boot over the edge of the housing and seat the lip of the boot into the locating groove at the edge of the housing

19  Insert the lip of the small-diameter end of the boot into the locating groove on the shaft.

20  Adjust the length of the joint by positioning it mid-way through its travel.

**13.13 Wrap the driveshaft splines with electrical tape to prevent damaging the boot as it's slid onto the shaft**

21 Insert a small screwdriver between the boot and the housing to equalize the pressure inside the boot (see illustration)

22 Tighten the boot clamps (see illustration).

## Outer CV joint

### Disassembly

23 Remove the inner CV joint (see Steps 3 through 10).

24 Mount the driveaxle in a bench vise with wood blocks to protect it.

### ✳✳ CAUTION:

**Do not overtighten the vise.**

25 Remove the boot retaining clamps and slide the outer boot back off of the shaft.

26 Wipe the excess grease from the joint.

27 Mark the relative position of the bearing cage, inner race and housing (see illustration 13.6).

28 Push down one side of the cage and remove the ball bearing from the opposite side (see illustration 13.7). The balls may have to be pried out.

29 Repeat this procedure until all of the balls are removed.

30 Clean all of the parts with solvent and dry them with compressed air (if available).

31 Inspect the housing, splines, balls and races for damage, corrosion, wear and cracks. Check the inner race for wear and scoring. If any of the components are not serviceable, the entire CV joint assembly must be replaced with a new one (see illustrations).

### Assembly

32 Wrap the splines of the shaft with tape to prevent damage to the boot, then install the small boot clamp and boot onto the shaft (see illustration 13.13).

33 Rotate the inner race into position in the housing. The marks made during disassembly should face out and be aligned.

34 Pack the lubricant from the kit into the ball races and grooves.

35 Install the balls into the holes, one at a time, until they are all in position. Fill the joint with grease.

36 Apply the remainder of the grease into the boot. Position the large-diameter end of the boot over the edge of the housing and seat the lip of the boot into the locating groove at the edge of the housing.

37 Insert the lip of the small-diameter end of the boot into the locat-

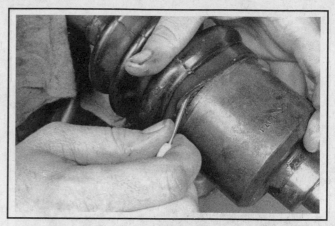

**13.21 After positioning the joint mid-way through its travel, equalize the pressure inside the boot by inserting a small, dull screwdriver between the boot and the CV joint housing**

**13.22 Depending on the type of clamps furnished with the replacement boot, you'll most likely need a special pair of clamp tightening pliers (most auto parts stores carry these)**

ing groove on the shaft.

38 Adjust the length of the joint by positioning it mid-way through its travel.

39 Insert a small screwdriver between the boot and the housing to equalize the pressure inside the boot (see illustration 13.21).

40 Tighten the boot clamps (see illustration 13.22).

41 Install the inner CV joint and boot (see Steps 13 through 22).

## FRONT DRIVEAXLES (AWD MODELS)

### Outer CV joint

▶ **Refer to illustrations 13.43a through 13.43j**

42 Mount the driveaxle in a bench vise with wood blocks to protect it.

### ✳✳ CAUTION:

**Do not overtighten the vise.**

43 Refer to the accompanying illustrations and perform the outer CV joint boot replacement procedure (see illustrations 13.43a through 13.43j).

13.43a Cut off the band retaining the boot to the shaft, then slide the boot toward the center of the shaft

13.43b Clamp the driveaxle in a vise, pull back the boot, then strike the inner race of the CV joint with a hammer and drift to dislodge it from the axle

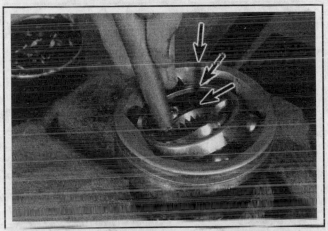

13.43c Tilt one side of the inner race, then remove the balls one at a time to disassemble the CV joint and clean it. Be sure to mark the relationship of the housing, cage and inner race. Once everything is clean, reassemble the joint, lining up the marks

13.43d Apply CV joint grease through the splined hole, then insert a wooden dowel (slightly smaller in diameter than the hole) into the hole and push down - the dowel will force the grease into the joint. Repeat this until the joint is packed

13.43e Wrap the splined area of the axleshaft with tape to prevent damage to the boot when installing it

13.43f Install the small clamp and the boot on the driveaxle and apply grease to the inside of the axle boot until . . .

**13.43g** . . . the level is up to the end of axle

**13.43h** Install a new circlip into the groove at the end of the driveaxle. Position the CV joint assembly on the driveaxle, aligning the splines . . .

**13.43i** . . . then use a hammer and brass punch to carefully drive the joint onto the driveaxle disassembly

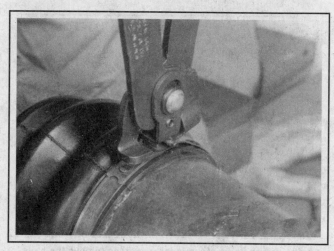

**13.43j** Seat the inner end of the boot in the groove and install the retaining clamp, then do the same on the other end of the boot - tighten the boot clamps with the special tool

## 14 Differential pinion oil seal - replacement

▶ Refer to illustrations 14.4a and 14.4b

➡Note: This procedure applies to the front and rear pinion oil seals.

1   Loosen the wheel bolts. Raise the front (for front differential) or rear (for rear differential) of the vehicle and support it securely on jackstands. Block the opposite set of wheels to keep the vehicle from rolling off the stands. Set the parking brake.

2   Drain the differential lubricant (see Chapter 1).

3   Disconnect the driveshaft from the differential pinion flange and support it out of the way with a piece of wire or rope (see Section 9).

4   Before attempting to remove the large nut securing the driveshaft flange to the differential shaft, use a small drift and hammer to undo the two staked areas of the clutch in the depressions (see illustrations).

➡Note: If you can't do this with a punch, use a small die grinder. Use a three-jaw puller to remove the flange from the pinion shaft.

5   Using a screwdriver, prybar or seal removal tool, carefully pry out the seal. Do not damage the splines on the shaft.

6   Using a seal driver or a large deep socket with an outside diameter the same as that of the seal, install the new seal. Drive it into the bore squarely and make sure it's completely seated.

7   Install the flange and nut and tighten it to the torque listed in this Chapter's Specifications.

8   Use a punch to stake the flange nut to the output shaft to prevent rotation.

9   Install the driveshaft (see Section 9). Tighten all fasteners to the torque values listed in this Chapter's Specifications.

10  Fill the differential with the proper lubricant (see Chapter 1).

14.4a Relieve the two staked areas (A) of the driveshaft flange retaining nut before attempting to remove the nut - (B) is the oil seal in the housing

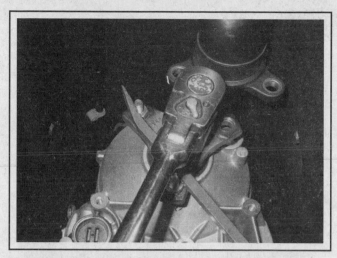

14.4b Use a long prybar for leverage when removing the retaining nut; it's on very tight

## 15 Differential assembly - removal and installation

### REAR DIFFERENTIAL ASSEMBLY

♦ Refer to illustrations 15.5a and 15.5b

1   Raise the rear of the vehicle and support it securely on jackstands. Place the transaxle in Neutral with the parking brake off. Block the front wheels to prevent the vehicle from rolling.

2   Drain the differential lubricant (see Chapter 1).

3   Remove the driveaxles (see Section 12).

4   Mark the relationship of the driveshaft to the pinion flange, then unbolt the driveshaft from the flange (see Section 5). Suspend the driveshaft with a piece of wire (don't let it hang by the center support bearing).

5   Support the differential with a floor jack, then remove the differential mounting bolts (see illustrations).

6   Slowly lower the jack and remove the differential out from under the vehicle.

7   Installation is the reverse of the removal procedure. Tighten all fasteners to the torque values listed in this Chapter's Specifications. Fill the differential with the proper lubricant (see Chapter 1).

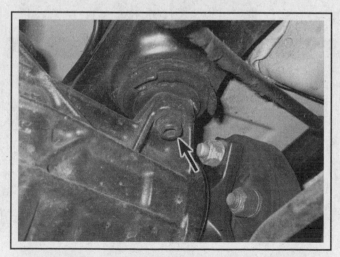

15.5a Remove the fastener at the front of the differential . . .

15.5b . . . then remove the ones at the rear

## FRONT DIFFERENTIAL ASSEMBLY (AWD MODELS)

8 Remove the right side intake air duct (see Chapter 4).

9 Remove the fastener(s) securing the upper portion of the exhaust shielding plate.

10 Raise the front of the vehicle and support it with jackstands.

➡**Note: Support the vehicle by placing the jackstands under the frame (unibody) and not under the suspension components or subframe.**

11 Remove the front wheels.

12 Remove the driveaxles and intermediate shaft (see Section 12).

13 Remove the front driveshaft (see Section 9).

14 Disconnect the return line for the steering gear from the bottom of the differential.

15 Detach the front stabilizer bar from the link rods (see Chapter 10).

16 Remove the fasteners securing the heat shield above the steering gear's right boot.

17 At the bottom of the differential, remove the engine mount.

18 Remove the steering gear retaining plate and pull the steering gear slightly back.

19 Use a transmission jack to support the rear portion of the subframe. Secure the subframe by attaching it to the jack with ratchet type tie-down straps or equivalent. Use an additional floor jack under the front center portion of the subframe.

20 Lower the subframe (see Chapter 10).

21 Detach the differential lower mount.

22 Remove the fasteners securing the differential to the subframe and remove it from the subframe.

23 Installation is the reverse of the removal procedure. Tighten all fasteners to the torque values listed in this Chapter's Specifications. Fill the differential with the proper lubricant (see Chapter 1).

## 16 Driveaxle oil seals - replacement

➡**Note 1: This procedure applies to both the front and rear driveaxle oil seals.**

➡**Note 2: Replacement of the front left-side driveaxle oil seal requires opening the differential housing and removing the differential assembly to gain access to the side seal. This is deemed to be beyond the scope of this manual.**

1 Raise the vehicle and support it securely on jackstands.

2 The driveaxle oil seals are located in the sides of the differential, where the driveaxles are attached. If leakage at the seal is suspected, raise the vehicle and support it securely on jackstands. If the seal is leaking, fluid will be found on the sides of the differential.

3 Remove the driveaxle(s) (see Section 12).

4 Use a screwdriver or prybar to carefully pry the oil seal out of the differential bore.

5 If the oil seal cannot be removed with a screwdriver or prybar, a special oil seal removal tool (available at auto parts stores) is required.

6 Compare the old seal to the new one to be sure it's the correct one.

7 Using a seal installer or a large deep socket as a drift, install the new oil seal. Drive it into the bore squarely and make sure it's completely seated.

8 Lubricate the lip of the new seal with multi-purpose grease, then install the driveaxle. Be careful not to damage the lip of the new seal.

9 Check the differential lubricant level and add some, if necessary, to bring it to the appropriate level (see Chapter 1).

## 17 Transfer case (AWD models) - removal and installation

1 Raise the front of the vehicle and support it securely on jackstands.

2 Mark the relationship of the rear driveshaft to the transfer case flange, then unbolt the driveshaft from the flange (see Section 9). Suspend the driveshaft with a piece of wire (don't let it hang by the center support bearing).

3 Drain the transaxle lubricant (see Chapter 1).

4 Support the transmission with a transmission jack.

5 Remove the fasteners securing the crossmember at the rear of the engine, then remove the crossmember.

6 Mark the relationship of the front driveshaft to the transfer case flange, then unbolt the driveshaft from the flange (see Section 9). Suspend the driveshaft with a piece of wire (don't let it hang by the center support bearing).

7 Lower the transmission slightly, then remove the bolts securing the transfer case to the transaxle. Carefully remove the transfer case from the transaxle.

8 Installation is the reverse of removal, noting the following points:

a) *Coat the plug-type splines in the transfer case with grease.*

b) *Tighten the mounting fasteners to the torque listed in this Chapter's Specifications.*

c) *Refill the transaxle with the proper type and amount of lubricant (see Chapter 1).*

## Specifications

### General

| | |
|---|---|
| Clutch hydraulic fluid type | See Chapter 1 |
| Clutch disc lining thickness (minimum) | 1/16 inch (1.5 mm) above rivet |

| Torque specifications | Ft-lbs (unless otherwise indicated) | Nm |
|---|---|---|

➡ **Note: One foot-pound (ft-lb) of torque is equivalent to 12 inch-pounds (in-lbs) of torque. Torque values below approximately 15 ft-lbs are expressed in inch-pounds, since most foot-pound torque wrenches are not accurate at these smaller values.**

**Clutch**

| | Ft-lbs | Nm |
|---|---|---|
| Pressure plate-to-flywheel bolts | 18 | 25 |
| Clutch release cylinder mounting nuts | 84 in-lbs | 10 |
| Flywheel bolts | See Chapter 2 | |

**Differential**

| | Ft-lbs | Nm |
|---|---|---|
| Front differential (AWD) | | |
|     Front axle-to-engine oil pan collar bolt | 48 | 65 |
|     Differential mount-to-differential assembly collar bolt(s) | 17 | 22 |
| Rear differential | | |
|     Upper mounting bolts | 81 | 110 |
|     Front center section mounting bolt | 33 | 45 |
|     Pinion nut | 37 | 50 |

**Driveshaft**

| | Ft-lbs | Nm |
|---|---|---|
| Front driveshaft-to-differential companion flange | 22 | 30 |
| Front driveshaft-to-transfer case companion flange | 22 | 30 |
| Rear driveshaft-to-differential companion flange | | |
|     M10 | 30 | 40 |
|     M12 | 44 | 60 |
| Rear driveshaft-to-transmission companion flange | | |
|     M10 | 30 | 40 |
|     M12 | 44 | 60 |
| Center support bearing bolts | 22 | 30 |

**Driveaxles**

| | Ft-lbs | Nm |
|---|---|---|
| Front driveaxle/hub bolt | | |
|     Step 1 | 81 | 110 |
|     Step 2 | Tighten an additional 60-degrees | |
| Rear driveaxle/hub nut | 162 | 220 |
| Transfer case mounting nuts/bolts | 23 | 30 |

**Notes**

**Section**

**Reference to other Chapters**

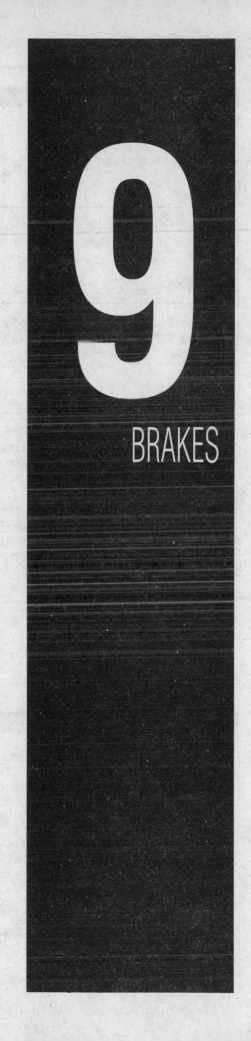

9

BRAKES

## 1 General information

The vehicles covered by this manual are equipped with hydraulically operated front and rear disc brake systems. These disc type brakes are self-adjusting and automatically compensate for pad wear.

## HYDRAULIC SYSTEM

The hydraulic system consists of two separate circuits. In the event of a leak or failure in one hydraulic circuit, the other circuit will remain operative.

## POWER BRAKE BOOSTER

The power brake booster is mounted on the firewall in the engine compartment. It typically uses engine manifold vacuum and atmospheric pressure to provide assistance to the hydraulically operated brakes.

## PARKING BRAKE

The parking brake actuates a pair of parking brake shoes mounted inside the drum (hub) portion of each rear brake disc. The parking brake cable tension is adjusted automatically and requires no service.

## SERVICE

After completing any operation involving disassembly of any part of the brake system, always test-drive the vehicle to check for proper braking performance before resuming normal driving. When testing the brakes, perform the tests on a clean, dry, flat surface. Conditions other than these can lead to inaccurate test results.

Test the brakes at various speeds with both light and heavy pedal pressure. The vehicle should stop evenly without pulling to one side or the other. Avoid locking the brakes, because this slides the tires and diminishes braking efficiency and control of the vehicle.

Tires, vehicle load and wheel alignment are other factors that affect braking performance as well.

## PRECAUTIONS

There are some general cautions and warnings concerning brake system components:

a) *Use only the proper type of brake fluid (see Chapter 1).*

b) *The brake pads and linings contain fibers which are hazardous to your health if inhaled. Whenever you work on brake system components, clean all parts with brake system cleaner. Do not allow the fine dust to become airborne. Also, wear an approved filtering mask.*

c) *Safety should be paramount whenever any servicing of the brake components is performed. Do not use parts or fasteners which are not in perfect condition, and be sure that all clearances and torque specifications are adhered to. If you are at all unsure about a certain procedure, seek professional advice. Upon completion of any brake system work, test the brakes carefully in a controlled area before putting the vehicle into normal service. If a problem is suspected in the brake system, don't drive the vehicle until it's fixed.*

d) *Used brake fluid is considered a hazardous waste and it must be disposed of in accordance with federal, state and local laws. DO NOT pour it down the sink, into septic tanks or storm drains, or on the ground.*

e) *Clean up any spilled brake fluid immediately and wash the area with large amounts of water. This is especially true for any finished or painted surfaces.*

## 2 Anti-lock Brake System (ABS) and Electronic Stability Program (ESP) - general information

1   The Anti-lock Brake System (ABS) and Electronic Stability Program (ESP) is designed to help maintain vehicle steerability, directional stability and optimum deceleration under severe braking conditions and on most road surfaces. The ABS system is primarily designed to prevent wheel lockup during heavy or panic braking situations. It works by monitoring the rotational speed of each wheel and controlling the brake line pressure to each wheel when engaged. Data provided by the ABS wheel speed sensors is shared with the Electronic Stability Program. This very sophisticated system helps with traction control, over/under-steering and acceleration control under all driving conditions when the system is on. Overall, these systems aid in vehicle control and handling. Another system added to vehicles with ESP is the Brake Assist System (BAS). This system works with the ABS system to maximize brake system application during panic braking situations.

## COMPONENTS

### Actuator assembly

◗ **Refer to illustration 2.2**

2   The actuator assembly is mounted in the engine compartment and consists of an electric hydraulic pump and solenoid valves (see illustration).

a) *The electric pump provides hydraulic pressure to charge the reservoirs in the actuator, which supplies pressure to the braking system. The pump and reservoirs are housed in the actuator assembly.*

b) *The solenoid valves modulate brake line pressure during ABS and ESP operation.*

### Wheel speed sensors

3   There is a wheel speed sensor for each wheel. Each sensor generates a signal in the form of a low-voltage electrical current or a frequency when the wheel is turning. A variable signal is generated as a result of a square-toothed ring (tone-ring, exciter-ring, reluctor, etc.) that rotates very close to the sensor. The signal is directly proportional to the wheel speed and is interpreted by an electronic module (computer).

4   The front sensors are mounted in the steering knuckles. The tone-rings are located at the back of the wheel hubs (2WD) or on the outboard CV joints of the front driveaxles (AWD).

5   The rear sensors are mounted in the rear suspension knuckles. The tone-rings are mounted onto the outboard CV joints of the rear driveaxles.

### ABS/ESP computer

6   The ABS/ESP computer is mounted with the actuator and is the brain of these systems. The function of the computer is to accept and process information received from the wheel speed sensors to control the hydraulic line pressure, avoiding wheel lock up or wheel spin. The computer also constantly monitors the system, even under normal driving conditions, to find faults within the system.

## DIAGNOSIS AND REPAIR

7   If a dashboard warning light comes on and stays on while the vehicle is in operation, the ABS or ESP system requires attention. Although special electronic diagnostic testing tools are necessary to properly diagnose the system, you can perform a few preliminary checks before taking the vehicle to a dealer service department.

a)  Check the brake fluid level in the reservoir.
b)  Verify that the computer electrical connectors are securely connected.
c)  Check the electrical connectors at the hydraulic control unit.
d)  Check the fuses.
e)  Follow the wiring harness to each wheel and verify that all connections are secure and that the wiring is undamaged.

8   If the above preliminary checks do not rectify the problem, the vehicle should be diagnosed by a dealer service department or other qualified repair shop. Due to the complexity of this system, all actual repair work must be done by a qualified automotive technician.

### ❋❋ WARNING:

Do NOT try to repair an ABS/ESP wiring harness. These systems are sensitive to even the smallest changes in resistance. Repairing the harness could alter resistance values and cause the system to malfunction. If the wiring harness is damaged in any way, it must be replaced.

### ❋❋ CAUTION:

Make sure the ignition is turned off before unplugging or reattaching any electrical connections.

## WHEEL SPEED SENSOR - REMOVAL AND INSTALLATION

▶ Refer to illustrations 2.11 and 2.12

### ❋❋ CAUTION:

Clean all mounting bolts and use thread-locking compound (blue/medium) during installation. Clean the holes with a thread chasing tool or equivalent before installing the mounting bolts.

9   Loosen the wheel bolts, raise the vehicle and support it securely on jackstands. Remove the wheel.

10  Make sure the ignition key is turned to the Off position.

11  Trace the wiring back from the sensor, detaching all brackets and clips while noting its correct routing, then disconnect the electrical connector (see illustration).

12  Remove the mounting bolt and carefully pull the sensor out from the knuckle (see illustration).

13  Installation is the reverse of the removal procedure. Tighten the mounting fastener securely.

14  Install the wheel and bolts, tightening them securely. Lower the vehicle and tighten the bolts to the torque listed in the Chapter 1 Specifications.

2.2  The ABS/ESP actuator assembly is mounted in the left-front area of the engine compartment

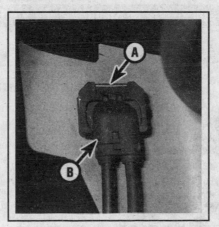

2.11  Press the spring (A) down to release the wheel speed sensor electrical connector (B)

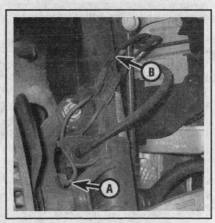

2.12  A front wheel speed sensor (A) and wire harness (B) (rear is similar)

### 3  Disc brake pads - replacement

### ❋❋ WARNING 1:

Disc brake pads must be replaced on both front or on both rear wheels at the same time - never replace the pads for only one wheel. Also, the dust created by the brake system is harmful to your health. Never blow it out with compressed air and don't inhale any of it. An approved filtering mask should be worn when working on the brakes. Do not, under any circumstances, use petroleum-based solvents to clean brake parts. Use brake system cleaner only!

### ❋❋ WARNING 2:

Clean all mounting bolts and use thread-locking compound (blue/medium) during installation. Clean the holes with a thread chasing tool or equivalent before installing the mounting bolts.

➥Note 1: Most models have floating calipers on the front and fixed calipers on the rear. Some models may have fixed calipers all around. Distinguishing the difference between the two types of calipers is based on the piston configuration and how the calipers are mounted. Fixed-type calipers have one or two pistons on each side of the disc and bolt up directly to the steering knuckle. Floating-type calipers have one or two pistons on one side of the disc only and bolt-up to a mounting bracket that is bolted to the steering knuckle.

➥Note 2: When approaching pad replacement, take a moment to note how many brake pad wear sensors may exist for each caliper on your particular model before doing any disassembly. This can be done by observing the number of small sensor connectors on the back of each caliper (see illustration 3.6b). Replacement brake pads must be able to accommodate the number of sensors installed on your model.

1  Remove the cap from the brake fluid reservoir and remove enough fluid to bring the level to the MIN mark on the reservoir.

2  Loosen the wheel bolts, raise the front or rear of the vehicle and support it securely on jackstands. Block the wheels at the opposite end.

3  Remove the wheels. Work on one brake assembly at a time, using the assembled brake for reference if necessary.

4  Inspect the brake disc carefully as outlined in Section 5. If machining is necessary, follow the information in that Section to remove the disc, at which time the pads can be removed as well.

## FLOATING CALIPERS (FRONT ONLY)

▶ Refer to illustrations 3.5 and 3.6a through 3.6s

5  Push the piston back into its bore to provide room for the new brake pads. A C-clamp can be used to accomplish this (see illustration). As the piston is depressed to the bottom of the caliper bore, the fluid in the master cylinder will rise. Make sure that it doesn't overflow. If necessary, siphon off some of the fluid.

6  Follow the accompanying photos (see illustrations 3.6a through 3.6s) for the actual pad replacement procedure. Be sure to stay in order and read the caption under each illustration.

7  When reinstalling the caliper, be sure to tighten the mounting bolts to the torque listed in this Chapter's Specifications. After the job has been completed, depress the brake pedal a few times to bring the pads into contact with the disc. Check the level of the brake fluid, adding some if necessary.

3.5  Before removing the caliper, slowly depress the piston into the caliper bore by using a large C-clamp between the outer brake pad and the back of the caliper

3.6a  Always wash the brakes with brake cleaner before disassembling anything

3.6b  Disconnect the pad wear sensor electrical connector(s) (as equipped, some calipers may have one or two sensors, while others may not have any)

3.6c Remove the caliper mounting bolts

3.6d Lift the caliper up and secure it with a piece of wire; do not allow the caliper to hang by the flexible brake hose

3.6e Remove the outer pad . . .

3.6f . . . and the inner pad

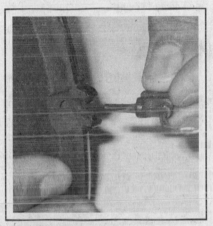

3.6g Remove the wear sensor(s) from the pad(s) and inspect them (as equipped). If any are worn, replace them

3.6h Remove the upper and lower anti-rattle clips; make sure they fit tightly and aren't worn. Replace them if necessary

3.6i Install the clean or new anti-rattle clips

3.6j Pull out the upper and lower guide pins. Clean and inspect them for wear. Be careful not to tear the boots when removing them; replace any boots that are worn or damaged . . .

3.6k . . . apply a coat of high-temperature grease to the pins and reinstall them. When installing them, seat the boots onto the caliper mounting bracket

3.6l Clean the threads of the guide pins to remove any old locking compound

3.6m The inner pad has a shim attached that matches with the caliper piston (a circular pattern). Lubricate the contact areas with an anti-seize compound approved for disc brake use (Mercedes Benz brake pad paste shown)

3.6n Install the pad wear sensor(s) into the pad(s) (as equipped)

3.6o Install the inner pad, making sure that the ends are seated correctly into the anti-rattle clips . . .

3.6p . . . then install the outer pad

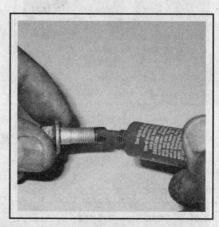

3.6q Apply thread-locking compound (blue/medium) to the caliper mounting bolts

3.6r Place the caliper back into position over the brake pads and match it to the caliper mounting bracket, install the caliper mounting bolts and tighten them to the torque listed in this Chapter's Specifications. Note: Make sure the flats of the guide pins engage the flat portions of the caliper (arrows)

3.6s Connect the brake pad wear sensor electrical connector(s)

## FIXED CALIPERS (FRONT OR REAR)

◗ **Refer to illustrations 3.8a through 3.8p**

8   Follow the accompanying photos (see illustrations 3.8a through 3.8p) for the actual pad replacement procedure. Be sure to stay in order and read the caption under each illustration.

9   After the job has been completed, depress the brake pedal a few times to bring the pads into contact with the disc. Check the level of the brake fluid, adding some if necessary.

## ALL CALIPERS

10   Install the wheels, then lower the vehicle to the ground. Tighten the wheel bolts to the torque listed in the Chapter 1 Specifications. Pump the brake pedal a few times and check the fluid level again, making sure it is correct (see Chapter 1). Check the operation of the brakes carefully before placing the vehicle into normal service.

**3.8a** Always wash the brakes with brake cleaner before disassembling anything

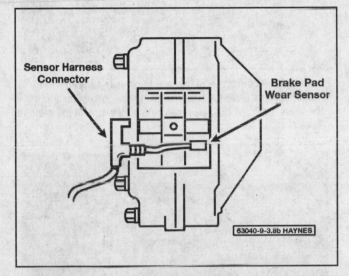

**3.8b** Disconnect the pad wear sensor electrical connector(s) (as equipped, some calipers may have one or two sensors, while others may not have any)

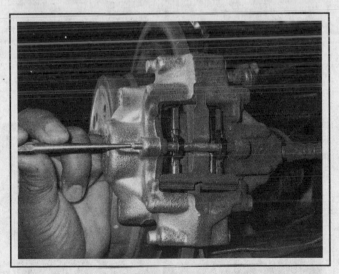

**3.8c** Use a punch to remove the brake pad retaining pin (rear shown)

**3.8d** Front calipers have two brake pad retaining pins that are removed in the same way

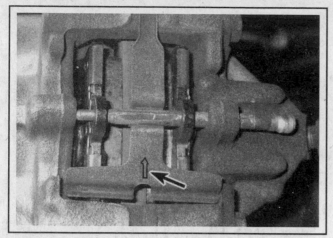

3.8e  Note the direction of the spring on rear calipers. The factory springs have an arrow showing the correct installed direction. On front calipers, just note which side of the spring faces out

3.8f  Remove the spring as the retaining pin(s) are removed

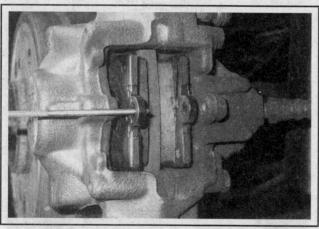

3.8g  Pry the outer pad from the caliper or pull it out using needle-nose pliers while leaving the inner pad in place

3.8h  Push the piston back into the caliper bore. On four-piston front calipers, (two on each side), push both pistons in simultaneously so that one is not forced out while the other is being pushed in. Check the brake fluid level and remove some if necessary

3.8i  Remove the inner pad

3.8j  Use a tool to hold the piston(s) on the outboard side in place while pushing the piston(s) on the inboard side back into the caliper bore(s) (rear caliper shown - front caliper similar)

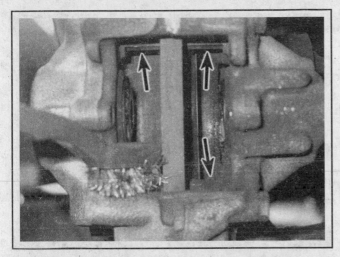

3.8k With all of the pistons pressed back into their bores, clean the surfaces that contact the brake pad plates with a wire brush, followed by brake system cleaner

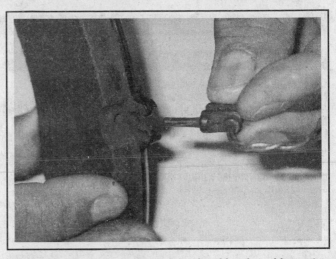

3.8l Remove all wear sensors from the old pads and inspect them (as equipped). If any are worn, replace them. Install the sensors onto the new pads

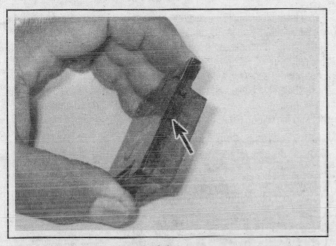

3.8m On rear calipers only, lubricate each brake pad plate on both contact edges with an anti-seize compound approved for disc brakes (or Mercedes Benz brake pad paste). DO NOT get any lubricant on the pad lining

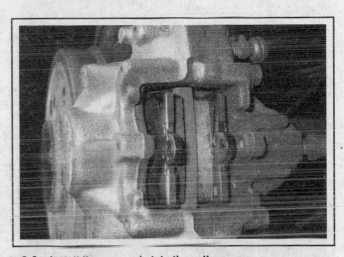

3.8n Install the new pads into the caliper

3.8o Place the spring into position and insert the retaining pin(s)

3.8p Use a punch to seat the retaining pin(s) into position

## 4  Disc brake caliper - removal and installation

**✳✳ WARNING:**

Dust created by the brake system is harmful to your health. Never blow it out with compressed air and don't inhale any of it. An approved filtering mask should be worn when working on the brakes. Do not, under any circumstances, use petroleum-based solvents to clean brake parts. Use brake system cleaner only!

➡ Note: Always replace the calipers in pairs - never replace just one of them.

### REMOVAL

♦ Refer to illustrations 4.3a and 4.3b

1   Loosen the wheel bolts, raise the vehicle and support it securely on jackstands. Remove the wheels.

2   Disconnect any electrical connectors and detach the wire harnesses for the brake pad wear sensors from the caliper as equipped (see illustration 4.3a).

3   Detach the brake hose from the brake line and bracket (see Section 7). Plug or cap the brake line (on the chassis side) and the brake hose to prevent fluid leakage and to keep contaminants out of the brake system. Using a flare-nut wrench, loosen the brake hose fitting from the caliper (see illustrations).

➡ Note: If you're just removing the caliper for access to other components, don't detach the hose from the brake line or loosen the hose fitting at the caliper.

4   Remove the caliper mounting bolts, then lift the caliper from the bracket or steering knuckle. If you're just removing the caliper for access to other components and the hose is still attached, support it with a length of wire.

### INSTALLATION

**✳✳ WARNING:**

Clean all mounting bolts and use thread-locking compound (blue/medium) during installation. Clean the holes with a thread chasing tool or equivalent before installing the mounting bolts.

5   Install the caliper by reversing the removal procedure. Tighten the caliper mounting bolts, the brake hose fitting and brake line-to-brake hose fitting (if removed), in that order, to the torque values listed in this Chapter's Specifications. Tighten the brake pad wear sensor harness connector(s) securely, as equipped.

6   Bleed the brake system if a hose was disconnected (see Section 8).

7   Install the wheels and bolts. Lower the vehicle and tighten the bolts to the torque listed in the Chapter 1 Specifications.

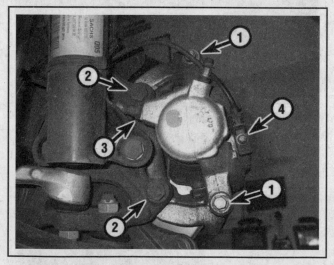

**4.3a  Floating-type brake caliper mounting details:**

1   Caliper mounting bolts
2   Caliper mounting bracket bolts
3   Brake hose fitting
4   Harness connector fastener for the brake pad wear sensor

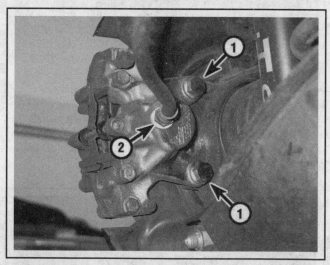

**4.3b  Fixed-type brake caliper mounting details (rear shown - front similar):**

1   Caliper mounting bolts
2   Brake hose fitting

## 5   Brake disc - inspection, removal and installation

### INSPECTION

▶ **Refer to illustrations 5.4, 5.5, 5.6a, 5.6b, 5.7a and 5.7b**

### ✷✷ WARNING:

**Clean all mounting bolts and use thread-locking compound (blue/medium) during installation. Clean the holes with a thread chasing tool or equivalent before installing the mounting bolts.**

➡**Note: Some models covered in this manual are equipped with cross-drilled front brake discs. These discs have a series of holes through them created to cool the discs during extreme braking. Drilled discs cannot be resurfaced (machined) on typical brake lathes used by automotive brake repair shops. If a disc is warped or defective, replacement may be the easiest and most cost effective solution.**

1   Loosen the wheel bolts, raise the vehicle and support it securely on jackstands. Remove the wheel.

2   Remove the brake caliper as outlined in Section 4. It's not necessary to disconnect the brake hose for this procedure. After removing the caliper bolts, suspend the caliper out of the way with a piece of wire. Don't let the caliper hang by the hose and don't stretch or twist the hose.

3   Reinstall a few wheel bolts to hold the disc securely against the hub, if necessary. It may be necessary to install washers between the disc and the wheel bolts to take up space.

4   Visually check the disc surface for score marks, cracks and other damage. Light scratches and shallow grooves are normal after use and may not always be detrimental to brake operation. Hairline cracks that are 25 mm (1 inch) or less in length can be considered acceptable. If any cracks intersect a hole on cross-drilled rotors, include the hole's width when measuring the crack. Deep score marks or wide cracks may require disc refinishing by an automotive machine shop or disc replacement (see illustration). Be sure to check both sides of the disc. If the brake pedal pulsates during brake application, suspect disc runout.

➡**Note: The most common symptoms of damaged or worn brake discs are pulsation in the brake pedal when the brakes are applied or loud grinding noises caused from severely worn brake pads. If these symptoms are extreme, it is very likely that the disc(s) will need to be replaced.**

5   On cross-drilled discs, inspect the holes, making sure they are not plugged with brake dust. Clear the holes with a small rod or a 4 mm (5/32 inch) drill bit and drill if necessary. Do not enlarge the holes (see illustration).

6   To check disc runout, place a dial indicator at a point about 1/2-inch from the outer edge of the disc (see illustration). Set the indicator to zero and turn the disc. Although the manufacturer doesn't give a runout specification, an indicator reading that exceeds 0.003 of an inch could cause pulsation upon brake application and will require disc refinishing by an automotive machine shop or disc replacement.

➡**Note: If disc refinishing or replacement is not necessary, you can deglaze the brake pad surface on the disc with emery cloth or sandpaper (use a swirling motion to ensure a non-directional finish) (see illustration).**

**5.4  The brake pads on this vehicle were obviously neglected, as they wore down completely and cut deep grooves into the disc - wear this severe means the disc must be replaced**

**5.5  Cross-drilled discs have holes for added cooling that can get plugged with brake dust**

**5.6a  Use a dial indicator to check disc runout; if the reading exceeds the maximum allowable runout limit, the disc will have to be machined or replaced**

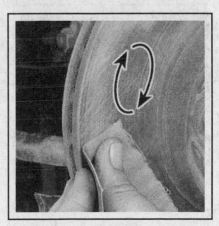

**5.6b  Using a swirling motion, remove the glaze from the disc surface with sandpaper or emery cloth**

7 The disc must not be machined to a thickness less than the specified minimum refinish thickness. The minimum wear (or discard) thickness is cast into either the front or backside of the disc (see illustration). The disc thickness can be checked with a micrometer (see illustration).

## REMOVAL AND INSTALLATION

▸ **Refer to illustrations 5.9, 5.10a and 5.10b**

➡**Note: Clean all mounting bolts and use thread-locking compound (blue/medium) during installation. Clean the holes with a thread chasing tool or equivalent before installing the mounting bolts.**

8 Remove the brake caliper and suspend it out of the way with a piece of wire (don't disconnect the hose). Remove the caliper mounting bracket on floating type calipers (see Section 4).

9 Remove the disc retaining screw and any wheel bolts installed during inspection, then remove the disc (see illustration). If it's stuck, use a mallet to loosen it from the hub.

➡**Note: On rear discs, make sure the parking brake is released. Adjust the parking brake shoes away from the drum section of the disc if the brake shoes will not allow the disc to come off (see Section 10).**

10 Clean the hub flange and the inside of the brake disc thoroughly; removing any rust or corrosion (see illustrations). Apply a thin layer of anti-seize compound between the hub flange and inside of the disc to prevent rust and corrosion prior to the next brake service.

11 Install the disc onto the hub and tighten the retaining screw to the torque listed in this Chapter's Specifications.

12 Install the brake caliper mounting bracket (floating-type calipers) and tighten the bolts to the torque listed in this Chapter's Specifications.

13 Install the brake pads (floating-type calipers) and caliper, tightening the bolts to the torque listed in this Chapter's Specifications.

14 Install the wheel, then lower the vehicle to the ground. Tighten the wheel bolts to the torque listed in the Chapter 1 Specifications. Depress the brake pedal a few times to bring the brake pads into contact with the disc. Bleeding of the system will not be necessary unless the brake hose was disconnected from the caliper. Check the operation of the brakes carefully before placing the vehicle into normal service.

**5.7a  The minimum wear dimension is typically cast or etched into the disc. Inspect all areas (front, back, edges, etc.) of the disc closely to find this information**

**5.7b  Use a micrometer to measure disc thickness**

**5.9  A disc retaining screw holds the disc to the hub flange**

**5.10a  Clean any rust and corrosion from the areas of the hub flange that contact the disc. A wire brush or sanding tool, designed to be used with a power drill, can make the job a lot easier**

**5.10b  Clean any rust or corrosion from the area inside the disc that contacts the hub flange. Again, power tools are very useful for this job**

## 6 Master cylinder - removal and installation

### REMOVAL

▶ Refer to illustrations 6.3, 6.6 and 6.8

### ※ CAUTION:

**Brake fluid will damage paint or finished surfaces. Cover all body parts and be careful not to spill fluid during this procedure. Clean up any spilled brake fluid immediately and wash the area with large amounts of water.**

1   Disconnect the cable from the negative battery terminal (see Chapter 5, Section 1).
2   Firmly depress the brake pedal several times to remove all vacuum from the power brake booster.
3   Remove the cover over the master cylinder (see illustration).
4   Place some rags under the master cylinder, then clean the area around the hydraulic line fittings with brake system cleaner.

### ※ CAUTION:

**Don't get brake cleaner on any painted surfaces.**

5   Remove as much fluid as possible from the reservoir with a syringe or equivalent.
6   Unplug the electrical connector for the brake fluid level warning switch (see illustration).
7   On manual transmission models, detach the brake fluid line attached to the fluid reservoir for the clutch master cylinder (see illustration 6.6). Place rags under the fittings and prepare caps or plastic

bags to cover the ends of the lines once they are disconnected.
8   Loosen the fittings at the ends of the brake lines where they enter the master cylinder. To prevent rounding off the corners on the fittings, use a flare-nut wrench (see illustration).
9   Carefully move the brake lines away from the master cylinder and plug the ends to prevent contamination.
10  Disconnect the electrical connector for the electronic stability program (ESP) brake pressure sensor that's on the side of the master cylinder (see illustration 6.8).

➡**Note: Some models are equipped with two sensors; one on the side and one under the front. Disconnect the one on the front after the master cylinder is loose, if equipped.**

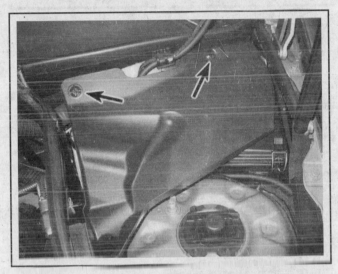

6.3  Turn the fasteners 1/4-turn and remove the cover

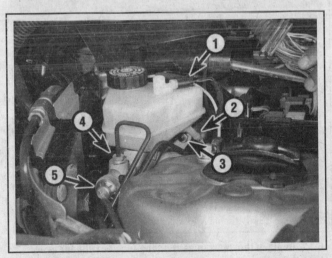

6.6  Master cylinder details (angled view):

1   Fluid level switch electrical connector
2   Clutch master cylinder hose fitting (manual transmission models)
3   Mounting nut (one hidden from view in this photo - located on the other side of the mounting flange)
4   Brake line fitting (one hidden from view in this photo)
5   Spring nut

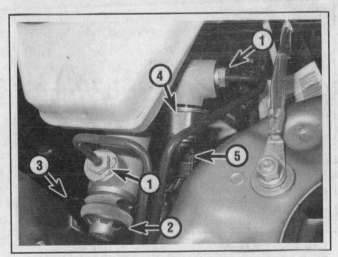

6.8  Master cylinder details (top view):

1   Brake line fittings
2   Spring nut
3   Front bracket
4   ESP brake pressure sensor
5   Electrical connector

11 Remove the sensor on the side of the master cylinder. Be prepared for brake fluid to leak from the fitting when the sensor is removed.

12 Remove the spring nut on the end of the master cylinder, then remove the front bracket by tilting it off the master cylinder and pulling it up from the frame (see illustration 6.8).

➡**Note: A replacement spring nut will be needed for installation.**

13 Remove the master cylinder mounting nuts. Carefully remove the master cylinder from the studs by pulling it directly out, then turning it to the side while keeping it level to free it. Again, be careful not to spill fluid or bend the brake lines as this is done.

❄❄ **CAUTION:**

**Tilting the master cylinder up could cause damage to the pushrod in the power brake booster.**

14 With the master cylinder separated from the power brake booster, disconnect the electrical connector for the electronic stability program (ESP) brake pressure sensor that is on the bottom-front of the master cylinder, if equipped.

## INSTALLATION

◆ **Refer to illustrations 6.16, 6.17 and 6.22**

15 Install the brake pressure sensor(s) onto the new master cylinder.
16 Bench bleed the new master cylinder before installing it:
 a) *Mount the master cylinder in a vise with soft jaws.*
 b) *Attach a pair of master cylinder bleeder tubes to the outlet ports of the master cylinder (see illustration).*
 c) *Fill the reservoir with brake fluid of the recommended type (see Chapter 1).*

➡**Note: If the replacement master cylinder is not equipped with a reservoir, remove the reservoir from the old master cylinder and place it on the new one using new seals.**

 d) *Slowly push the pistons into the master cylinder (a large Phillips screwdriver can be used for this) - air will be expelled from the pressure chambers and into the reservoir. Because the tubes are submerged in fluid, air can't be drawn back into the master cylinder when you release the pistons.*
 e) *Repeat the procedure until no more air bubbles are present.*
 f) *Remove the bleed tubes, one at a time, and install plugs in the open ports to prevent fluid leakage and air from entering.*

17 Install a new vacuum seal on the master cylinder (see illustration).

❄❄ **WARNING:**

**This must be done every time the master cylinder is removed.**

18 Install the reservoir cover, connect the electrical connector(s), then install the master cylinder over the studs on the power brake booster and tighten the attaching nuts only finger tight at this time.

19 Thread the brake line fittings into the master cylinder. Since the master cylinder is still a bit loose, it can be moved slightly in order for the fittings to thread in easily. Do not cross-thread or strip the threads as the fittings are tightened.

20 Tighten the mounting nuts to the torque listed in this Chapter's Specifications and tighten the brake line fittings securely.

21 Place the front bracket back into position and install a new spring-nut on the end of the master cylinder. The spring-nut thread should be about 5 mm or 1/4 of an inch from the end of the master cylinder.

**6.16 Place the master cylinder in a vise by its mounting flange, attach the bleed tubes as shown and push the piston with a blunt tool several times to bench bleed the master cylinder (typical shown)**

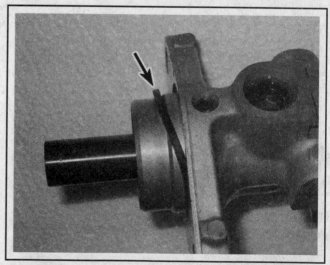

**6.17 Replace the vacuum seal on the master cylinder every time the cylinder is removed (typical shown)**

22 Fill the master cylinder reservoir with the correct fluid (see Chapter 1), then bleed the brake system as described in Section 8. To bleed the master cylinder on the vehicle, have an assistant pump the brake pedal several times slowly, then hold the pedal to the floor. Loosen the line fittings one at a time to allow air and fluid to escape. Repeat this procedure on both fittings until the fluid is clear of air bubbles (see illustration).

### ☀☀ CAUTION:

**Have plenty of rags on hand to catch the fluid - brake fluid will ruin painted surfaces.**

23 The remainder of installation is the reverse of removal. Test the operation of the brake system carefully before placing the vehicle into normal service.

### ☀☀ WARNING:

**Do not operate the vehicle if you are in doubt about the effectiveness of the brake system. It is possible for air to become trapped in the ABS hydraulic control unit, so, if the pedal continues to feel spongy after repeated bleedings or the BRAKE or ABS light stays on, have the vehicle towed to a dealer service department or a qualified repair shop to be bled with the aid of a scan tool.**

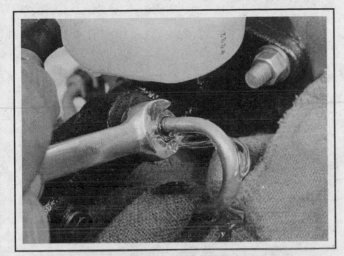

**6.22 With the brake pedal depressed, loosen a fitting on the master cylinder to bleed it when it is installed on the vehicle. Bleed the lines one at a time (typical shown)**

## 7 Brake hoses and lines - inspection and replacement

### INSPECTION

1 About every six months, with the vehicle raised and supported securely on jackstands, the rubber hoses which connect the steel brake lines with the front and rear brake assemblies should be inspected for cracks, chafing of the outer cover, leaks, blisters and other damage. These are important and vulnerable parts of the brake system and inspection should be complete. A light and mirror will be helpful for a thorough check. If a hose exhibits any of the above conditions, replace it with a new one.

### REPLACEMENT

#### Front brake hose

▶ **Refer to illustrations 7.3 and 7.4**

2 Loosen the wheel bolts, raise the vehicle and support it securely on jackstands. Remove the wheel.

3 At the frame bracket, note how the small tabs of the hose fitting sit in the bracket and keep it from rotating (see illustration).

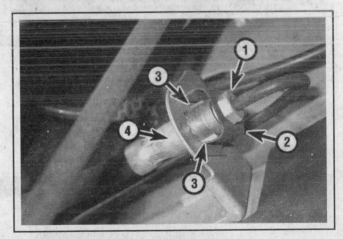

**7.3 Front brake hose/line fitting details:**

1  *Line fitting tube nut (remove with a flare-nut wrench)*
2  *Spring*
3  *Hose fitting tabs and frame bracket grooves*
4  *Hose fitting (support with a wrench during removal)*

4  Support the hose fitting with an open-end wrench, then unscrew the brake line fitting from the hose (see illustration 7.3 and the accompanying illustration). Use a flare-nut wrench to prevent rounding off the corners of the nut and be careful not to lose the spring on the end of the line fitting.

5  At the caliper end of the hose, use a flare nut wrench to separate the hose fitting from the caliper.

6  Remove the grommet from the bracket at the lower end of the strut, then pull the hose through the bracket.

7  To install the hose, place the grommet on the hose, thread the hose through the bracket on the strut, then connect the hose fitting to the caliper and tighten it with a flare-nut wrench. Seat the grommet back into the bracket on the strut.

8  Place the brake hose fitting into the frame bracket while making sure the hose isn't twisted between the caliper and the frame bracket.

9  Place the small spring on the line fitting and connect it to the hose fitting, starting the threads by hand, then tighten the fitting securely.

10  Bleed the caliper (see Section 8).

11  Install the wheel and bolts, lower the vehicle and tighten the bolts to the torque listed in the Chapter 1 Specifications.

### Rear brake hose

▶ **Refer to illustration 7.12**

12  The rear brake hose has a fitting and a bracket that is fastened to the rear frame (see illustration). Otherwise, refer to the previous steps for front brake hose replacement.

### Metal brake lines

13  When replacing brake lines, be sure to use the correct parts. Don't use copper tubing for any brake system components. Purchase genuine steel brake lines from a dealer or auto parts store.

14  Prefabricated brake line, with the tube ends already flared and fittings installed, is available at auto parts stores and dealer parts departments.

15  When installing the new line, make sure it's securely supported in the brackets and has plenty of clearance between moving or hot components.

16  After installation, check the master cylinder fluid level and add fluid as necessary. Bleed the brake system (see Section 8) and test the brakes carefully before driving the vehicle in traffic.

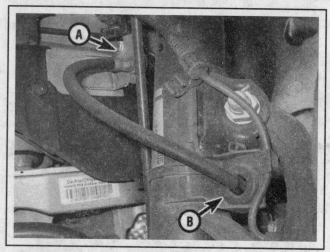

**7.4  Front brake hose frame bracket (A) and strut bracket and grommet (B)**

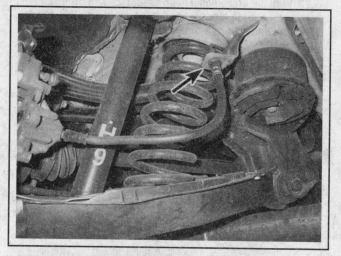

**7.12  Rear brake hose/line fitting at the frame bracket**

## 8    Brake hydraulic system - bleeding

▶ **Refer to illustration 8.8**

### ❊❊ WARNING:

**Wear eye protection when bleeding the brake system. If the fluid comes in contact with your eyes, immediately rinse them with water and seek medical attention.**

➥Note: Bleeding the hydraulic system is necessary to remove any air that manages to find its way into the system when it's been opened during removal and installation of a hose, line, caliper or master cylinder. It is also a part of regular maintenance (see Chapter 1).

1  You'll probably have to bleed the system at all four brakes if air has entered it due to low fluid level, or if the brake lines have been disconnected at the master cylinder.

2  If a brake line was disconnected only at a wheel, then only that caliper must be bled. If a brake line is disconnected at a fitting located between the master cylinder and any of the brakes, that part of the system served by the disconnected line must be bled.

3  Raise the vehicle about one foot and support it securely on jackstands.

➥Note: If you can access the bleeder valves without raising the vehicle, then you may skip this step.

4  Remove any residual vacuum from the brake power booster by pressing the brake pedal several times with the engine off.

5  Remove the master cylinder reservoir cover and fill the reservoir with brake fluid. Reinstall the cover.

➡Note: Continue to add fluid while bleeding the system to prevent the fluid level from dropping too low; if this happens, air will enter the master cylinder.

6  Have an assistant on hand, as well as a supply of new brake fluid, a clear container partially filled with clean brake fluid, a length of tubing to fit over the bleeder valve and a wrench to open and close the bleeder valve.

7  Beginning at the right rear wheel, loosen the bleeder valve slightly, then tighten it to a point where it's snug but can still be loosened quickly and easily.

➡Note: Use a six-point box-end wrench or socket to loosen the bleeder valve. For bleeder valves that appear to be stuck, clean the area where the valve screws into the caliper with a small wire brush. Tap on the valve with a hammer and attempt to use the wrench or socket again.

8  Place one end of the tubing over the bleeder valve and submerge the other end in brake fluid in the container (see illustration)

9  Have the assistant depress the brake pedal slowly, then hold the pedal down firmly.

10  While the pedal is held down, open the bleeder valve just enough to allow a flow of fluid to leave the valve. Watch for air bubbles to exit the submerged end of the tube. When the fluid flow slows after a couple of seconds, close the valve and have your assistant release the pedal.

11  Repeat Steps 9 and 10 until no more air is seen leaving the tube, then tighten the bleeder valve and proceed to the left rear wheel, the right front wheel and the left front wheel, in that order, and perform the same procedure. Be sure to check the fluid in the master cylinder reservoir frequently

12  Never use old brake fluid. It contains moisture that can boil, rendering the brake system inoperative.

13  Refill the master cylinder with fluid at the end of the operation.

14  Check the operation of the brakes. The pedal should feel solid when depressed, with no sponginess. If necessary, repeat the entire process.

## ✳✳ WARNING:

Do not operate the vehicle if you are in doubt about the effectiveness of the brake system. It's possible for air to become trapped in the ABS hydraulic control unit, so, if the pedal continues to feel spongy after repeated bleedings or the BRAKE or ABS light stays on, have the vehicle towed to a dealer service department or other qualified repair shop to be bled with the aid of a scan tool.

8.8  When bleeding the brakes, a hose is connected to the bleeder valve at the caliper and the other end is submerged in brake fluid. Air will be seen as bubbles in the tube and container. All air must be expelled before moving to the next wheel (typical shown)

## 9  Power brake booster - check, removal and installation

➡Note: On some V6 engine models, a small vacuum pump may have been added to the power brake booster system. The pump is the vacuum source for the booster. It is mounted to a bracket just behind the right headlamp housing and has a large diameter vacuum hose coming off the side that is routed to the brake booster. Vehicles equipped with a brake booster vacuum pump require diagnosis by a dealer service department if the system appears to be defective.

### OPERATING CHECK

1  Depress the brake pedal several times with the engine off and make sure there's no change in the pedal reserve distance.

2  Depress the pedal and start the engine. If the pedal goes down slightly, operation is normal.

### AIRTIGHTNESS CHECK

3  Start the engine and turn it off after one or two minutes. Depress the brake pedal slowly several times. If the pedal depresses less each time, the booster is airtight.

4  Depress the brake pedal while the engine is running, then stop the engine with the pedal depressed. If there's no change in the pedal reserve travel after holding the pedal for 30 seconds, the booster is airtight.

## REMOVAL

▶ **Refer to illustrations 9.9, 9.11, 9.12, 9.15, 9.16 and 9.17**

➡**Note: The power brake booster is not serviceable; replace it with a new or rebuilt unit if it's defective.**

5   With the engine off, press the brake pedal several times to remove any stored vacuum in the power brake booster.

6   Move the driver's seat to the rearmost position, then disconnect the cable from the negative battery terminal (see Chapter 5, Section 1).

7   Remove the windshield wiper motor and linkage (see Chapter 12).

8   Remove the brake master cylinder (see Section 6).

9   Pull the vacuum hose fitting from the brake booster (see illustration).

➡**Note: Leave the vacuum hose attached to the fitting.**

10   Remove the electrical connectors from the sensors and switches mounted to the power brake booster, if equipped (see illustration 9.9).

➡**Note: Vehicle models equipped with ESP will have electrical components mounted to the power brake booster. These components will need to be transferred to the replacement booster.**

11   Release any wire harnesses from the separator inside the engine compartment and from the side of the fuse and relay box (see illustration).

12   On models with the Powertrain Control Module (PCM) inside the engine compartment fuse and relay box (near the booster), the PCM will need to be pulled out of the box to give its harness enough slack for the booster to come out. Do not disconnect the harness from the PCM. Simply move the PCM up away from the box as necessary (see illustration).

13   Remove the lower instrument panel insulator below the driver's side knee bolster for access (see Chapter 11).

14   Inside the vehicle, remove the brake light switch, if equipped (see Section 12).

15   Remove the plastic cover over the brake pedal (see illustration).

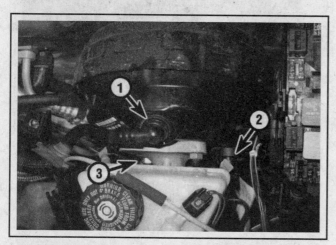

**9.9  Power brake booster details (engine compartment):**

*1   Vacuum hose, fitting and grommet*
*2   ESP BAS release switch and electrical connector*
*3   ESP BAS diaphragm travel sensor and electrical connector (hidden*

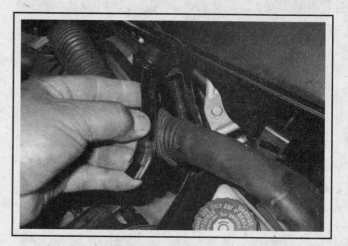

*from view in this photo - it is located directly below the master cylinder)*
**9.11  Detach the PCM wire harness bracket from the separator rail in the engine compartment**

**9.12  Create slack in the PCM wire harness by pulling the PCM out of the fuse and relay box. Be careful not to disturb any electrical connections to the PCM**

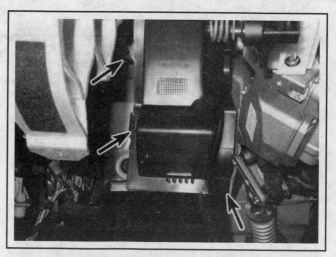

**9.15  Pull the cover directly out to release the cover retainers, then guide it down and out of the vehicle**

16 Carefully pry the retaining clip off of the brake pedal pin, pull the pin from the brake pedal and pushrod clevis, then disconnect the booster pushrod (see illustration).

17 Remove the booster mounting nuts (see illustration).

18 From the engine compartment, slide the booster straight out from the firewall until the studs clear the holes, then remove it.

## INSTALLATION

19 Installation procedures are essentially the reverse of removal, noting the following points:

a) Replace the seal that goes between the power booster and the firewall (over the booster's mounting studs).

b) Be especially careful not to drop anything into the replacement power booster when transferring sensors and switches on ESP equipped models. This will ruin the replacement booster.

c) Tighten the booster mounting nuts to the torque listed in this Chapter's Specifications.

d) Install the retaining clip securing the booster pushrod to the brake pedal pin.

e) Reinstall and bleed the master cylinder (see Section 6).

f) Bleed the brake system (see Section 8) and test the operation of the brakes before putting the vehicle into normal service.

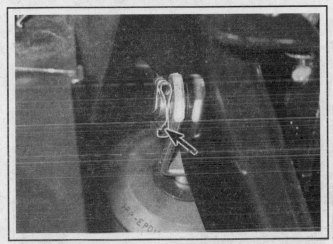

**9.16  Use a small screwdriver to pry the retaining clip off the brake pedal pin**

**9.17  Brake booster mounting nuts**

## 10  Parking brake shoes - replacement

▶ Refer to illustrations 10.2, 10.3 and 10.4a through 10.4u

**❋❋ WARNING 1:**

Dust created by the brake system is hazardous to your health. Never blow it out with compressed air and don't inhale any of it. An approved filtering mask should be worn when working on the brakes. Do not, under any circumstances, use petroleum-based solvents to clean brake parts. Use brake system cleaner only!

**❋❋ WARNING 2:**

Parking brake shoes must be replaced on both wheels at the same time - never replace the shoes on only one wheel.

1  Remove the brake disc (see Section 5).

2  Wash the parking brake assembly (see illustration). Check the lining thickness of parking brake shoes and compare it to the values in this Chapter's Specifications.

**10.2  Wash the parking brake assembly with brake cleaner. Use a pan or rags underneath to catch the runoff. DO NOT USE COMPRESSED AIR TO BLOW BRAKE DUST OFF THE PARTS!**

3  If it is necessary to remove the backing plate from the knuckle for other procedures on the vehicle, remove the brake cable bracket retaining bolt and pull the cable out of the backing plate when the expanding lock has been separated from the cable (see illustration 10.4j and the accompanying illustration). When re-installing the bracket, tighten the retaining bolt securely.

4  Follow the accompanying illustrations for the brake shoe replacement procedure (see illustrations 10.4a through 10.4u). Be sure to stay in order and read the caption under each illustration.

5  Install the brake disc and caliper (see Sections 4 and 5). Proceed to replace the shoes on the opposite rear wheel.

6  With both sides complete, install the wheels using only four wheel bolts on each wheel. It is necessary to leave one wheel bolt uninstalled to adjust the brake shoe clearance.

7  Perform a parking brake shoe adjustment on each rear wheel (see Section 11).

8  Set the parking brake and confirm proper operation. Re-adjust the parking brake again if necessary.

9  Lower the vehicle and tighten the wheel bolts to the torque listed in the Chapter 1 Specifications.

10  Check the parking brake for proper operation. If they are not fully operational, perform a break-in procedure.

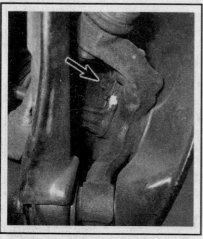

**10.3  The location of the parking brake cable bracket and retaining bolt**

**10.4a  Turn the star-wheel on the adjuster until it's at its shortest setting**

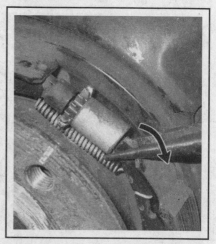

**10.4b  Pry the lower shoe and adjuster apart to remove the adjuster**

**10.4c  Using brake spring pliers, remove the lower return spring. Note the larger hook on one end of the spring after it's removed**

**10.4d  Release the lower shoe hold-down spring by grasping the center of the spring firmly with needle-nose pliers while pushing it in and turning it**

10.4e Remove the lower shoe while unhooking the adjuster spring from it

10.4f Unhook the adjuster spring from the upper shoe and remove it

10.4g Remove the upper shoe hold-down spring

10.4h Remove the upper shoe

10.4i Clean the backing plate thoroughly, then lubricate the brake shoe contact areas on the plate with high-temperature brake grease (not all contact areas can be viewed in this photo)

10.4j Move the expanding lock and remove the pin that connects it to the cable. Lubricate the moving parts of the lock and pin with high-temperature brake grease and place it back into position

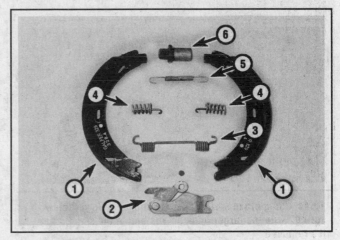

10.4k Parking brake assembly details:

| | | |
|---|---|---|
| 1 | Brake shoes | 4 Hold-down springs |
| 2 | Expanding lock and pin (above) | 5 Adjuster spring |
| 3 | Lower return spring | 6 Adjuster assembly |

10.4l Lubricate the screw threads in the adjuster assembly with high-temperature brake grease

10.4m Lubricate the outer wall of the star-wheel adjuster in the adjuster assembly with high-temperature brake grease

10.4n Place the upper shoe into position . . .

10.4o . . . and install the upper shoe hold-down spring

10.4p Hook the adjuster spring into the upper shoe . . .

10.4q . . . and then into the lower shoe and place the shoe into position

10.4r Install the lower shoe hold-down spring

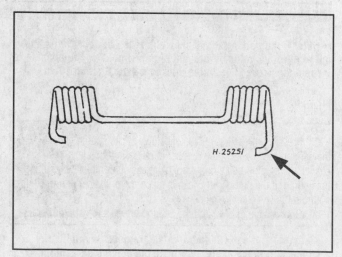

10.4s Note the longer hook on one end of the lower return spring. This end is intended to fit into the upper shoe

**10.4t Install the lower return spring**

**10.4u Install the adjuster assembly**

11 Break-in the new shoes by performing the following procedure.

a) *Set and release the parking brake a few times.*

b) *Drive the vehicle to approximately 30 miles (50 kilometers) per hour.*

c) *While holding the parking brake release handle, apply the parking brake two to three times, eventually braking to a stop.*

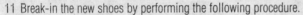

### ✳✳ WARNING:

**Be aware that your brake lights will not go on and you will need to warn other drivers that you are slowing down. Use extreme caution while performing this procedure.**

d) *Allow the parking brake shoes and disc/drum to cool for at least 10 minutes.*

e) *Repeat the break-in steps again if necessary. Do not shorten the cooling period between driving cycles.*

12 Check the parking brake adjustment and adjust it again if necessary (see Section 11).

13 If the parking brake does not fully release or pulls to one side after the break-in procedure, inspect the brake shoes and other components. Also, check the parking brake cables and replace any components as necessary.

## 11 Parking brake - check and adjustment

➡**Note: If the parking brake shoe clearance or cable adjusting nut require a significant amount of adjustment, it is advisable to inspect the brake shoe lining thickness (see Section 10).**

### CHECK

1 Pressing the parking brake pedal five clicks should engage the parking brake fully. If the number of clicks is much less, there's a chance the parking brake might not be releasing completely resulting in brake drag. If the number of clicks is much more, the parking brake may not hold the vehicle on an incline.

2 One method of checking the parking brake is to park the vehicle on a steep hill with the parking brake set and the transmission in Neutral (be sure to stay in the vehicle for this check!). If the parking brake cannot prevent the vehicle from rolling, it's in need of adjustment.

### ADJUSTMENT

▶ **Refer to illustrations 11.5a, 11.5b, 11.9 and 11.10**

3 There are two areas of adjustment for the parking brake: the star-wheel adjuster at the top of the shoes for each wheel and the adjusting nut on the front brake cable. Adjustment at the shoes is performed first.

4 Block the front wheels, raise the rear of the vehicle and support it securely on jackstands. Remove one wheel bolt from each rear wheel.

5   Using a flashlight, turn the wheel and align the hole with the star-wheel adjuster in the brake assembly (see illustrations). This will allow you to adjust the parking brake shoe-to-drum clearance.

6   Turn the star-wheel adjuster until the wheel cannot be rotated, then reverse the adjuster eight notches. Adjust both wheels the same amount.

➡**Note 1: Turn the adjuster wheel from the bottom to top on the right-rear wheel, and from the top to bottom on the left-rear wheel to spread the brake shoes and cause the wheel not to rotate.**

➡**Note 2: Place duct tape around the wheel bolt hole to protect the wheel from scratches if necessary.**

7   Set the parking brake fully and compare the number of clicks to those specified in Step one. If more adjustment is necessary, move on to the next adjustment at the parking brake cable assembly.

8   Remove the rear passenger seat cushion (see Chapter 11).

9   Remove the fasteners for the brake cable adjuster cover (see illustration).

10  Locate the adjusting nut on the assembly and either tighten or loosen it to achieve the proper number of clicks when the parking brake is set (see illustration). Tightening the nut (turning it clockwise) decreases the number of clicks, while the opposite is achieved by loosening the nut (turning it counterclockwise).

11  Confirm that the parking brake is fully engaged within the number of clicks stated in Step one.

12  Release the parking brake and confirm that the brakes don't drag when the rear wheels are turned.

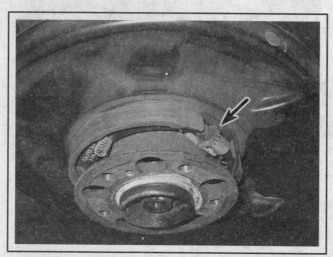

11.5a  The location of the star-wheel adjuster (left-rear shown with the wheel and brake disc removed for clarity)

11.5b  With the wheel bolt hole aligned with the star-wheel adjuster, you can reach through the wheel and brake disc with a long screwdriver and adjust the parking brake shoe-to-drum clearance

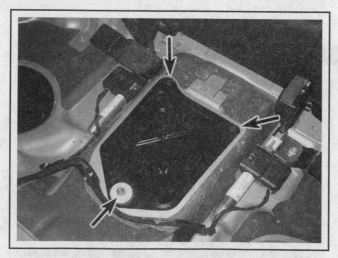

11.9  Remove these fasteners to remove the brake cable adjuster cover

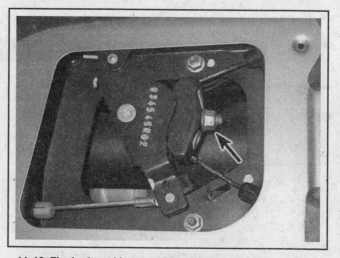

11.10  The brake cable assembly adjusting nut

## 12 Brake light switch - removal and installation

▶ Refer to illustrations 12.4 and 12.6

➡ **Note: 2002 and later model vehicles are not equipped with a brake light switch. ESP components are used for brake light operation (see illustration 9.9).**

1  Remove the lower instrument panel insulator below the driver's side knee bolster for access (see Chapter 11).

2  Locate the brake light switch near the top of the brake pedal arm or on the outside cover over the pedal arm.

3  Depress and hold the brake pedal.

4  Press the small release tab on the switch where it meets the mounting bracket. Rotate the switch and remove it from its bracket (see illustration).

5  Disconnect the electrical connector.

6  Before installing the switch, pull the plunger on the switch out fully (see illustration).

7  Depress the brake pedal as far as it will go, then install the switch in its bracket in the opposite manner that it was removed.

8  Release the brake pedal and gently pull up on it to make sure it is fully released.

9  Connect the electrical connector. Confirm that the brake lights are operating properly.

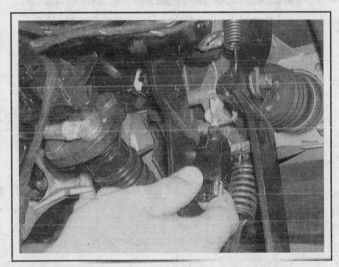

12.4  Press the small release tab and rotate the switch to remove it

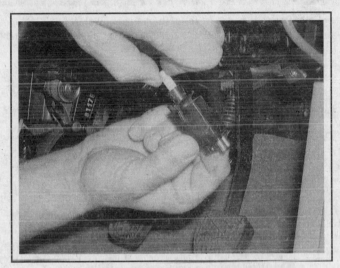

12.6  Pull the plunger on the switch out fully to reset it

### General

| | |
|---|---|
| Brake fluid type | See Chapter 1 |

### Disc brakes

| | |
|---|---|
| Minimum brake pad thickness | See Chapter 1 |
| Disc minimum thickness | Cast into disc |
| Disc runout limit | Not specified (see Section 5 of this Chapter) |
| Parking brake shoe minimum thickness | 0.040 inch (1 mm) |

| Torque specifications | Ft-lbs (unless otherwise indicated) | Nm |
|---|---|---|

➡ **Note: One foot-pound (ft-lb) of torque is equivalent to 12 inch-pounds (in-lbs) of torque. Torque values below approximately 15 ft-lbs are expressed in inch-pounds, since most foot-pound torque wrenches are not accurate at these smaller values.**

| | | |
|---|---|---|
| Caliper mounting bolts | | |
|     Floating (front) | 18 | 25 |
|     Fixed | | |
|         Front | 85 | 115 |
|         Rear | 45 | 55 |
| Caliper mounting bracket bolts | | |
|     (floating front calipers only) | 85 | 115 |
| Brake disc retaining screw | 88 in-lbs | 10 |
| Brake hose fitting-to-caliper | 159 in-lbs | 18 |
| Brake line-to-brake hose fitting | 148 in-lbs | 14 |
| Master cylinder-to-brake booster nuts | 177 in-lbs | 20 |
| Power brake booster mounting nuts | 159 in-lbs | 18 |
| Wheel bolts | See Chapter 1 | |

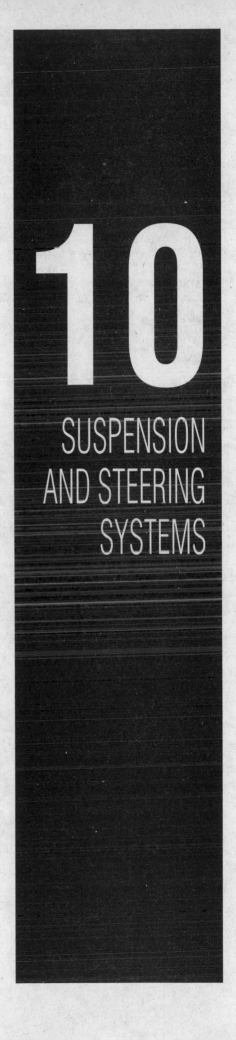

10

SUSPENSION
AND STEERING
SYSTEMS

**Section**

## 1 General information

### FRONT SUSPENSION

▶ **Refer to illustration 1.1**

Most models are equipped with an independent, multi-link, front suspension system with McPherson strut type assemblies. A stabilizer bar controls body roll. The 4MATIC models (AWD) utilize a lower control arm instead of individual links or suspension struts. McPherson struts and lower suspension struts (or arms) with integral balljoints position the steering knuckles (see illustration).

### REAR SUSPENSION

▶ **Refer to illustration 1.2**

All models are equipped with an independent, multi-link rear suspension consisting of shock absorbers and coil springs. Additionally, all models incorporate a stabilizer bar to control body roll (see illustration).

### STEERING

The steering system consists of a rack-and-pinion steering gear and two adjustable tie-rods. Power assist is standard.

### PRECAUTIONS

Many of the bolts and threaded holes used for suspension components will have to be cleaned of old locking compound in order to be used again. Most of the bolts had threads that were pretreated with locking compound before they were installed. Bolts used with self-locking nuts do not require any cleaning, but the nuts must be replaced anytime they are removed. Most of the nuts used for the suspension are self-locking and designed to be used only once.

Frequently, when working on the suspension or steering system components, you may come across fasteners which seem impossible to loosen. These fasteners on the underside of the vehicle are continually subjected to water, road grime, mud, etc., and can become rusted or

**1.1 Front suspension and steering components**

| | | | | | |
|---|---|---|---|---|---|
| 1 | Steering gear | 4 | Torque strut | 6 | Subframe |
| 2 | Cross strut | 5 | Suspension strut | 7 | Stabilizer bar |
| 3 | Tie-rod end | | | | |

frozen, making them extremely difficult to remove. In order to unscrew these stubborn fasteners without damaging them (or other components), be sure to use lots of penetrating oil and allow it to soak in for a while. Using a wire brush to clean exposed threads will also ease removal of the nut or bolt and prevent damage to the threads. Sometimes a sharp blow with a hammer and punch is effective in breaking the bond between a nut and bolt threads, but care must be taken to prevent the punch from slipping off the fastener and ruining the threads. Heating the stuck fastener and surrounding area with a torch sometimes helps too, but isn't recommended because of the obvious dangers associated with fire. Long breaker bars and extension, or cheater, pipes will increase leverage, but never use an extension pipe on a ratchet - the ratcheting mechanism could be damaged. Sometimes, turning the nut or bolt in the tightening (clockwise) direction first will help to break it loose. Fasteners that require drastic measures to unscrew should always be replaced with new ones.

Since most of the procedures that are dealt with in this Chapter involve jacking up the vehicle and working underneath it, a good pair of jackstands will be needed. A hydraulic floor jack is the preferred type of jack to lift the vehicle, and it can also be used to support certain components during various operations.

### ❊❊ WARNING:

**Never, under any circumstances, rely on a jack to support the vehicle while working on it. Also, whenever any of the suspension or steering fasteners are loosened or removed they must be inspected and, if necessary, be replaced with new ones of the same part number or of original equipment quality and design. Torque specifications must be followed for proper reassembly and component retention. Never attempt to heat or straighten any suspension or steering components. Instead, replace any bent or damaged part with a new one.**

**1.2 Rear suspension components**

| | | | | | |
|---|---|---|---|---|---|
| 1 | Stabilizer bar | 4 | Thrust arm | 6 | Coil spring |
| 2 | Spring link (beneath cover) | 5 | Shock absorber | 7 | Subframe |
| 3 | Track rod | | | | |

## 2   Strut assembly (front) - removal, inspection and installation

### ❄ WARNING:

Always replace the struts and/or coil springs in pairs - never replace just one strut or one coil spring (this could cause dangerous handling peculiarities).

➡ Note: It is possible to replace the struts or coil springs individually but the unit will have to be disassembled by a qualified repair shop with the proper equipment. This will add considerable cost to the project. You can compare the cost of replacing the complete assemblies yourself to the cost of replacing individual components (with the help of a shop).

### REMOVAL

▶ **Refer to illustration 2.3**

1   Loosen the wheel bolts, raise the front of the vehicle and support it securely on jackstands. Remove the front wheels.

➡ Note: Support the vehicle by placing the jackstands under its frame and not any of the suspension components.

2   Remove the wheel speed sensors from the steering knuckle (see Chapter 9).

3   Remove the brake hose and wire harness bracket from the strut, as equipped (see illustration).

4   Detach the stabilizer bar link from the strut (see Section 3).

### Rear-wheel drive models

▶ **Refer to illustrations 2.5 and 2.7**

5   Remove the strut-to-knuckle fasteners (see illustration).

6   Separate the strut from the steering knuckle. Be careful not to let the steering knuckle fall outward, as the brake hose and wire harnesses could be damaged. If necessary, support the steering knuckle by placing a jack under the cross strut balljoint at the steering knuckle.

➡ Note: If necessary, disconnect the wire harnesses or other electrical components before separating the strut and steering knuckle to protect them from damage.

7   Pry the small plastic cap off the piston rod nut (see illustration).

8   Have an assistant hold the strut assembly from below. Hold the piston rod with an Allen wrench and remove the piston rod nut and rebound stop (see illustration 2.7). Remove the assembly from the fenderwell.

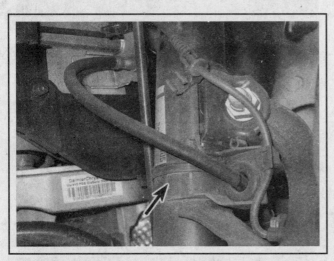

**2.3  Location of the brake hose and harness bracket**

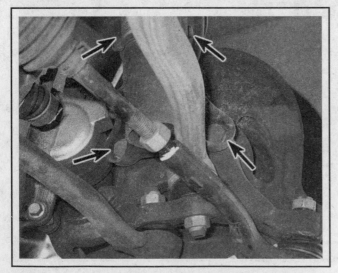

**2.5  Location of the lower strut mounting fasteners (some hidden from view - vicinity given)**

**2.7  Mounting details at the upper strut:**

| 1 | Piston rod nut | 2 | Rebound stop |

## 4MATIC models

▶ **Refer to illustration 2.10**

9   Remove the brake caliper and secure it aside (see Chapter 9).

10  Mark the relationship of the strut to the knuckle (these marks will be used during installation to maintain wheel alignment). Remove the strut-to-knuckle nuts and discard them. Knock the bolts out with a hammer and punch (see illustration).

11  Separate the strut from the steering knuckle. Be careful not to overextend the inner CV joint. Also, don't let the steering knuckle fall outward, as the brake hose and wire harnesses could be damaged.

➡**Noto: If necessary, disconnect the wire harnesses or other electrical components before separating the strut and steering knuckle to protect them from damage.**

12  Have an assistant hold the strut assembly from below, then remove the three upper mounting bolts at the top of the strut in the engine compartment. Remove the assembly from the fenderwell. Make certain that the struts are marked left or right if both are being removed.

## INSPECTION

13  Check the strut body for leaking fluid, dents, cracks and other obvious damage that would warrant repair or replacement.

14  Check the coil spring for chips or cracks in the spring coating (this can cause premature spring failure due to corrosion). Inspect the spring seat and other rubber parts for cuts, hardness and general deterioration.

15  If any undesirable conditions exist, replace the strut assembly entirely or any failed components with the help of a qualified repair shop (see **Note** above).

## INSTALLATION

> ✱✱✱ **WARNING:**
>
> **Clean all mounting bolts of old thread-locking compound as necessary and apply thread-locking compound (blue/medium) during installation. Clean threaded holes with a thread chasing tool, or equivalent, before installing bolts in them. Replace all self-locking nuts as equipped.**

## Rear-wheel drive models

16  With the help of an assistant, guide the strut assembly into position, then install the rebound stop and piston-rod nut until its finger tight; final tightening will occur with the vehicle lowered.

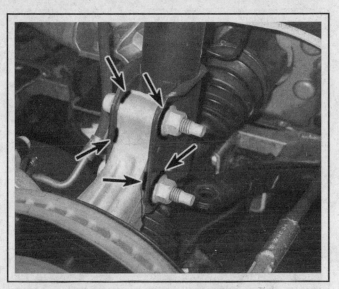

**2.10  Mark the relationship of the strut to the steering knuckle (typical shown)**

17  Attach the strut to the steering knuckle, then tighten the fasteners to the torque listed in this Chapter's Specifications.

## 4MATIC models

18  With the help of an assistant, guide the strut assembly into position and install the upper mounting bolts through the holes in the strut tower; final tightening will occur with the vehicle lowered.

19  Carefully slide the steering knuckle into the strut flange and install the two bolts using a soft-face hammer or mallet. Install new self-locking nuts, align the marks made in Step 10, then tighten the nuts to the torque listed in this Chapter's Specifications.

20  Install the brake caliper (see Chapter 9).

## All models

21  Install the brake hose and wire harness bracket on the using a new cable-tie if necessary.

22  Install the wheels, then lower the vehicle and tighten the wheel bolts to the torque listed in the Chapter 1 Specifications.

23  On rear-wheel drive models, hold the piston rod with an Allen wrench and tighten the piston-rod nut to the torque listed in this Chapter's Specifications.

24  On 4MATIC models, tighten the strut's upper mounting bolts to the torque listed in this Chapter's Specifications.

25  Have the front wheel alignment checked and, if necessary, adjusted.

## 3   Stabilizer bar, bushings and links (front) - removal and installation

▶ **Refer to illustrations 3.3 and 3.4**

1   Raise the front of the vehicle and support it securely on jackstands. Remove the front wheels.

➡**Note: Support the vehicle by placing the jackstands under its frame and not any of the suspension components.**

2   Remove the engine splash shield from under the vehicle (see Chapter 2).

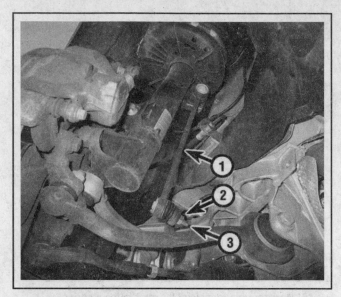

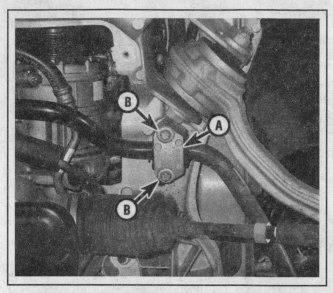

**3.3 Stabilizer bar link mounting details**

1   *Stabilizer bar link*
2   *Link nut (lower)*
3   *Link ballstud (hold with wrench while loosening or tightening link nuts)*

**3.4 Stabilizer bar bracket (A) and fasteners (B) (rear wheel drive shown - 4MATIC similar)**

3   Remove the lower nut from each stabilizer bar link, then remove them from the bar (see illustration). Inspect the small boots on the links for damage or deterioration. Replace the links if necessary.

➥**Note: The stabilizer bar links can be removed entirely by separating them from the strut assemblies.**

4   Remove the stabilizer bar bracket fasteners and remove the brackets (see illustration).

✳✳ **CAUTION:**

**Models equipped with bi-xenon headlamps, with range adjustment, are equipped with a sensor and linkage that is mounted to the stabilizer bar. Mark the position of the sensor linkage in relation to the stabilizer bar, then carefully remove the linkage from the bar. Do this before removing the stabilizer bar brackets.**

## REAR-WHEEL DRIVE MODELS

5   Remove the stabilizer bar, then remove the rubber bushings from the stabilizer bar.

## 4MATIC MODELS

6   The stabilizer bar removal on 4MATIC models involves lowering the subframe from under the vehicle while supporting the engine from

above. This is an extensive procedure and important safety precautions must be observed. Refer to Section 9 of this Chapter regarding subframe removal. It is important to note that the need to remove the stabilizer bar, from a vehicle of this design, is usually due to damage from an accident. If this is the case, it is highly likely that other major components (such as the subframe itself) have also been damaged. We recommend having the vehicle inspected by a qualified body repair shop before replacing the stabilizer bar.

## ALL MODELS

✳✳ **WARNING:**

**Clean all mounting bolts of old thread-locking compound as necessary and apply thread-locking compound (blue/medium) during installation. Clean threaded holes with a thread chasing tool, or equivalent, before installing bolts in them. Replace all self-locking nuts as equipped.**

7   Clean the stabilizer bar where the bushings contact it. Inspect all bushings for wear and damage. If any of the rubber parts are cracked, torn or generally deteriorated, replace them.

8   Check each stabilizer link for signs of excessive wear and replace them as necessary.

9   Installation is the reverse of removal. Be sure to tighten all the fasteners to the torque listed in this Chapter's Specifications.

## 4   Suspension links (front) - removal and installation

➡Note 1: The following procedure applies to rear-wheel drive models only.

➡Note 2: All of the fasteners and related hardware that attach the struts to the subframe must be returned to their original positions in order to preserve the front wheel alignment.

## REMOVAL

1   Loosen the front wheel bolts. Raise the front of the vehicle and support it securely on jackstands. Remove the front wheel.

➡Note: Support the vehicle by placing the jackstands under its frame and not any of the suspension components.

2   Remove the engine splash shield from under the vehicle (see Chapter 2).

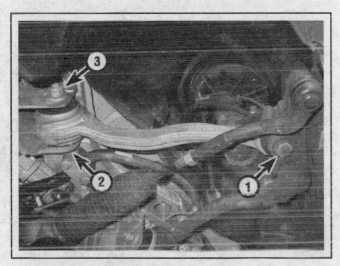

**4.4a  Torque strut mounting details:**

1   *Balljoint stud nut*
2   *Torque strut-to-subframe mounting bolt (hidden from view - vicinity given) (hold the bolt with a wrench and remove the nut - DO NOT turn the bolt)*
3   *Mounting nut (replace)*

### Torque strut

▶ **Refer to illustrations 4.4a, 4.4b, 4.5 and 4.6**

3   Remove the stabilizer bar from the subframe (see Section 3). The stabilizer bar links may stay attached.

4   Separate the balljoint on the torque strut from the steering knuckle (see illustrations).

## ✱✱ CAUTION:

**Be careful not to damage the balljoint seal during this Step.**

➡Note: Balljoint separating tools are available at most auto parts stores.

5   Inspect the torque strut-to-subframe mounting bolt for grooves by looking at the end where the threads can be seen (see illustration).

➡Note: Grooved mounting bolts may or may not be installed on the vehicle you're working on. They are installed for wheel alignment adjustment when necessary (see Section 24).

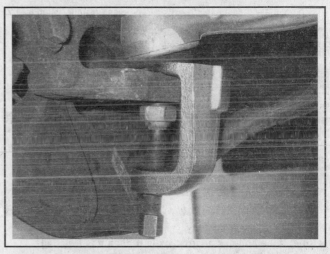

**4.4b  To separate the strut mounted balljoint from the steering knuckle, loosen the balljoint stud nut, then install the tool as shown**

**4.5  The torque strut may have a grooved mounting bolt like the one illustrated**

25027-10-04.04.HAYNES

6   Hold the torque strut-to-subframe mounting bolt while loosening the nut (see illustration 4.4a).

## ❋❋ CAUTION:

**DO NOT turn the torque strut mounting bolt, as this could damage the small lugs in the center of the strut's bushing (see illustration).**

7   Remove the nut and slowly withdraw the bolt while noting its placement in the bushing (see illustration 4.6).

➡️**Note: If the bolt has no grooves in it, then it is installed between the lugs in the center of the bushing.**

8   Remove the torque strut, then proceed to Step 14.

### Cross strut

▶ **Refer to illustrations 4.9a and 4.9b**

9   Loosen the cross strut balljoint nut, then separate the balljoint from the steering knuckle by using a drift and striking the knuckle to break loose the taper of the ballstud (see illustration).

10   Inspect the cross strut-to-subframe mounting bolt for grooves by looking at the end where the threads can be seen (see illustration 4.5).

➡️**Note: Grooved mounting bolts may or may not be installed on the vehicle you're working on. They are installed for wheel alignment adjustment when necessary (see Section 24).**

11   Hold the cross strut-to-subframe mounting bolt while loosening the nut (see illustration 4.9a).

## ❋❋ CAUTION:

**DO NOT turn the cross strut mounting bolt, as this could damage the small lugs in the center of the strut's bushing (see illustration 4.6).**

12   Remove the nut and slowly withdraw the bolt while noting its placement in the lugged portion of the bushing (see illustration 4.6).

➡️**Note: If the bolt has no grooves in it, then it is installed between the lugs in the center of the bushing.**

**4.6   The torque strut and cross strut have lugs in the center of the bushing that engage grooved mounting bolts. Regular (non-grooved) mounting bolts are placed in between the lugs (directly in the center). Grooved bolts are placed on one side or the other (cross strut shown - torque strut is similar)**

13   Remove the cross strut.

## INSTALLATION

14   Inspect the center bushing for wear or deterioration. The bushing can be replaced on all cross struts, but only on some torque struts. For bushing replacement, you'll need the assistance of a dealer service department or other qualified repair shop due to the special tools and knowledge required.

15   Installation is the reverse of removal. Use a new balljoint stud nut. Tighten all fasteners to the torque listed in this Chapter's Specifications. Use new self-locking nuts where equipped. Hold the mounting bolt while tightening the torque or cross strut-to-frame nut.

➡️**Note: Before tightening the torque or cross strut-to-subframe nut, carefully raise the steering knuckle with a floor jack to simulate normal ride height.**

16   Install the wheel, remove the jackstands and lower the vehicle.

17   Tighten the wheel bolts to the torque listed in the Chapter 1 Specifications.

18   Have the front-end alignment checked, and if necessary, adjusted.

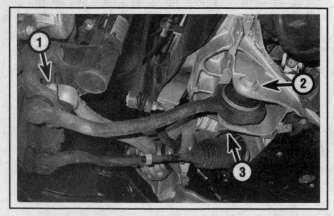

**4.9a   Cross strut mounting details:**

1   *Balljoint stud nut*
2   *Cross strut-to-subframe mounting bolt (hold the bolt with a wrench and remove the nut - DO NOT turn the bolt)*
3   *Mounting nut (replace) (hidden from view - vicinity given)*

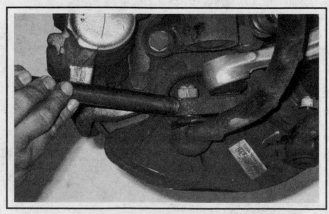

**4.9b   To separate the cross strut-mounted balljoint from the steering knuckle, loosen the balljoint stud nut, then strike the knuckle using a large drift or equivalent to break the taper loose**

### 5   Lower control arm - removal and installation

➥**Note 1: The following procedure applies to 4MATIC (AWD) models only.**

➥**Note 2: All of the fasteners and related hardware that attach the lower control arm to the subframe must be returned to their original positions in order to preserve the front wheel alignment.**

## REMOVAL

♦ **Refer to illustrations 5.4 and 5.7**

1   Loosen the wheel bolts, raise the front of the vehicle and support it securely on jackstands. Remove the wheel.

➥**Note: Support the vehicle by placing the jackstands under its frame and not any of the suspension components.**

2   Remove the engine splash shield from under the vehicle (see Chapter 2).

3   On models equipped with range adjustable bi-xenon headlamps, remove the sensor's linkage from the lower control arm (right side only).

4   Mark the front and rear mounting (pivot) fasteners on the arm (see illustration).

5   Disconnect the tie-rod end from the steering knuckle (see Section 18).

6   Disconnect the lower control arm balljoint from the steering knuckle using the same technique as the tie-rod end.

➥**Note: Balljoint separating tools are available at most auto parts stores.**

7   Inspect the lower control arm-to-subframe pivot bolts for a groove by looking at the end of each bolt where the threads can be seen (see illustration).

➥**Note: Grooved mounting bolts may or may not be installed on the vehicle you're working on. They are installed for wheel alignment adjustment when necessary (see Section 24).**

8   Hold the lower control arm-to-subframe mounting bolt while loosening the nut (see illustrations 5.4 and 5.7).

### ✳✳ CAUTION:

**DO NOT turn the control arm mounting bolts, as this could damage the small lugs in the center of the arm's bushing.**

9   Remove the nut and slowly withdraw the bolt while noting its placement in the lugged portion of the bushing and the related washers (shims) along with their exact position.

➥**Note 1: If the bolt has no grooves in it, then it is installed between the lugs in the center of the bushing.**

➥**Note 2: When removing the rear pivot bolt (on either arm), swivel the tie-rod upwards and have the steering wheel turned to the extreme opposite side that you're working on. This will provide the necessary clearance to remove the bolt.**

10   Remove the lower control arm by sliding it out of the subframe bracket.

## INSTALLATION

11   Installation is the reverse of removal. Use a new balljoint stud nut. Be sure to tighten all fasteners to the torque values listed in this Chapter's Specifications. Use new self-locking nuts where equipped.

➥**Note: Raise the lower control arm with a floor jack to simulate normal ride height before tightening the lower control arm mounting nuts at the subframe.**

12   Install the wheel. Lower the vehicle and tighten the wheel bolts to the torque listed in the Chapter 1 Specifications.

13   Have the front end alignment checked and, if necessary, adjusted.

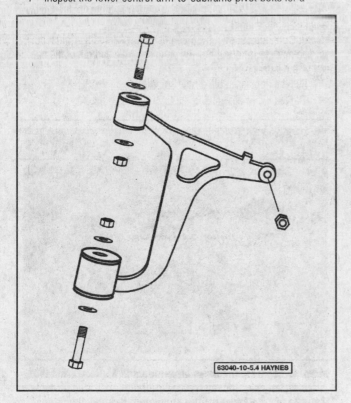

**5.4  Lower control arm and mounting fasteners**

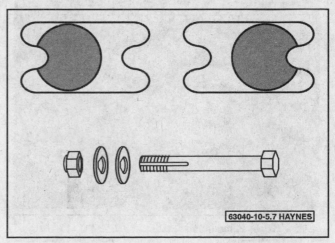

**5.7  Grooved bolts may be installed for wheel alignment. Turning them with a wrench will cause damage to the control arm bushing**

## 6  Balljoints - check and replacement

1   Inspect the balljoint boots for signs of damage, wear, or leaks. The balljoints and boots are not serviceable. The components that they are integrated with must be replaced if a boot or balljoint is defective. Check for looseness anytime suspension components are separated from the steering knuckle. See if you can turn the ballstud in its socket with your fingers. If the balljoint is loose, or if the ballstud can be turned easily, replace the component. One method of checking the balljoints with the suspension assembled is by carefully prying on the suspension components near the balljoints.

2   Loosen the front wheel bolts, raise the front of the vehicle and support it securely on jackstands, then remove the wheel.

➡Note: Support the vehicle by placing the jackstands under its frame and not any of the suspension components.

3   Using a large prybar, attempt to pry the components directly away from the steering knuckle. Look for up-and-down movement between the ballstud and the joint casing.

### ✳✳ WARNING:

Do not damage any balljoint boots while checking them for looseness.

4   Replace components as necessary.

## 7  Hub and wheel bearings (front) - removal, service, installation and adjustment

### ✳✳ WARNING:

The dust created by the brake system is harmful to your health. Never blow it out with compressed air and don't inhale any of it. Do not, under any circumstances, use petroleum-based solvents to clean brake parts. Use brake system cleaner only.

## REAR WHEEL DRIVE MODELS

### Removal

◆ Refer to illustrations 7.3 and 7.4

➡Note: Because of the design of these hubs and bearings, removal of the inner bearing causes damage to it. Therefore, wheel bearing inspection or repacking is not feasible. If you are going to remove the inner bearing, it must be replaced with a new one along with a new grease seal.

1   Loosen the wheel bolts, raise the front of the vehicle and support it securely on jackstands. Remove the wheel.

➡Note: Support the vehicle by placing the jackstands under its frame and not any of the suspension components.

2   Remove the brake disc (see Chapter 9).
3   Remove the dust cap (see illustration).
4   Loosen the locking bolt on the clamping hub nut, then unscrew the nut (see illustration).
5   Pull the hub out slightly, then push it back into its original position. The outer bearing will now be on the spindle and out of the hub. Remove the outer bearing.
6   Pull the hub assembly off the spindle.

7.3  Carefully remove the dust cover using a sharp chisel or suitable tool

7.4  Loosen the locking bolt (A) and unscrew the clamping hub nut (B)

## Service

▸ **Refer to illustrations 7.7, 7.8 and 7.9**

7   Using a suitable drift, gently tap out the inner wheel bearing and grease seal from the hub (see illustration).

➡**Note: The tone-ring for the ABS wheel speed sensor is integral with the grease seal, so the seal should always be replaced when removed. A replacement tone-ring will come with the new seal.**

8   Use high-temperature front wheel bearing grease to pack the bearings. Work the grease completely into the bearings, forcing it between the rollers, cone and cage from the back side (see illustration).

9   Coat the spindle and the bearing contact surfaces with grease (see illustration).

10   Apply a thick layer of grease to the inside wall of the hub.

11   Place the inner bearing into the rear of the hub, then add a little more grease on top of the bearing.

12   Install a new grease seal into the hub (and over the inner bearing)

by tapping it evenly into place until it's flush with the hub.

➡**Note: On vehicles equipped with wheel speed sensors (see Chapter 9), the tone-ring on the grease seal can become damaged when coming into contact with metal. Use a mallet or equivalent to tap the seal into the hub.**

## Installation

▸ **Refer to illustration 7.14**

13   Carefully place the hub assembly onto the spindle, push the outer bearing into position and install the clamping hub nut (finger tight only).

➡**Note: Excess grease will be pushed out of the hub and bearings while installing the hub onto the spindle. Simply move your finger around the edge of the hub and remove it.**

14   Rotate the hub in a forward direction while tightening the spindle nut using only needle-nose pliers. Repeat this about three or four times. This will coat the bearings and remove excess grease (see illustration).

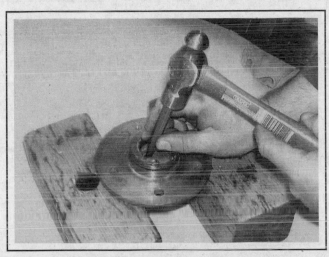

**7.7  Set the hub between two blocks of wood. Use a drift to remove the inner bearing and grease seal from the hub**

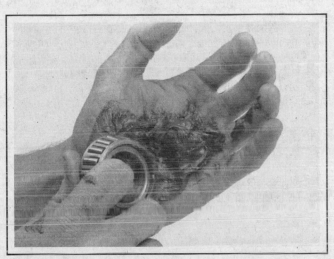

**7.8  Place a good amount of grease in your hand, work the grease into the bearing by repeatedly pressing a section of the bearing against your hand. Grease will come out the other end when done correctly**

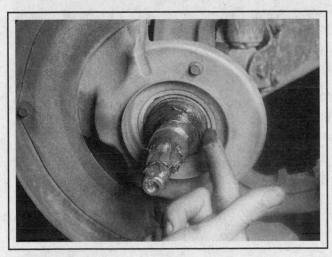

**7.9  Coat the entire spindle with high-temperature brake grease**

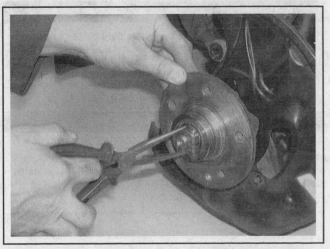

**7.14  Rotate the hub forward while tightening the clamping hub nut. Repeat this a few times**

## Adjustment

◆ **Refer to illustration 7.16**

15  Loosen the locking bolt on the clamping hub nut (if not done previously) (see illustration 7.4). If bearing replacement was performed, make sure that the hub and bearings are free of excess grease. Loosen and tighten the clamping hub nut with needle-nose pliers a few times to feel for a point just before torque resistance is felt on the nut. Attempt to achieve almost no wheel bearing play by lightly tightening the clamping hub nut. Rotate the hub and confirm that the movement is smooth with no resistance.

16  Mount a dial indicator to the hub and measure the play between the spindle and the hub (see illustration). The amount of wheel bearing play should be within the values listed in this Chapter's Specifications.

17  When the proper amount of play is achieved, tighten the locking bolt on the clamping hub nut to the torque listed in this Chapter's Specifications; be careful not to move the hub nut in the process.

18  Recheck the amount of wheel bearing play and re-adjust if necessary. Rotate the hub to confirm that it turns freely with no noticeable free play.

19  Install the dust cap, lightly tapping it into place with a hammer.

20  Install the brake disc and caliper in the reverse order of removal (see Chapter 9).

21  Install the wheel on the hub and tighten the wheel bolts.

22  Lower the vehicle and tighten the wheel bolts to the torque listed in this Chapter's Specifications.

## 4MATIC MODELS

23  The front wheel bearings and hubs on 4MATIC models are non-serviceable assemblies requiring no maintenance or adjustment. An assembly is replaced if found to be defective. Due to the special tools

**7.16  Mount a dial indicator as shown and set it to zero. Grip the top and bottom of the hub and attempt to pivot (or rock) it on the spindle. Note the movement of the gauge's needle to measure the amount of wheel bearing play (similar hub design shown)**

and expertise required to press the hub and bearing from the steering knuckle, the job requires a professional mechanic. However, the steering knuckle may be removed and taken to an automotive machine shop or a qualified repair facility to have the assembly replaced. See Section 8 for the steering knuckle removal procedures.

## 8   Steering knuckle - removal and installation

### ✳✳ WARNING 1:

**The dust created by the brake system is harmful to your health. Never blow it out with compressed air and don't inhale any of it. Do not, under any circumstances, use petroleum-based solvents to clean brake parts. Use brake system cleaner only.**

### ✳✳ WARNING 2:

**Clean all mounting bolts of old thread-locking compound as necessary and apply thread-locking compound (blue/medium) during installation. Clean threaded holes with a thread chasing tool, or equivalent, before installing bolts in them. Replace all self-locking nuts as equipped.**

1   Loosen the wheel bolts, raise the front of the vehicle and support it securely on jackstands. Remove the wheel.

➡**Note: Support the vehicle by placing the jackstands under its frame and not any of the suspension components.**

2   Remove the brake disc, the wheel speed sensor and brake wear sensor(s), as equipped (see Chapter 9).

3   On rear wheel drive models, remove the hub from the steering knuckle (see Section 7).

4   On 4MATIC (AWD) models, remove the driveaxle/hub nut from the axle shaft (see Chapter 8). Push the axle shaft through the hub just enough to make sure that it's loose. If it is stuck, put the hub nut on the shaft until its flush with the end. Use a mallet and strike the end of the shaft to break it loose from the hub. If this doesn't work, install a puller on the hub and shaft (see Chapter 8).

5   Disconnect the tie-rod end from the steering knuckle (see Section 18).

6   Separate the strut assembly from the steering knuckle (see Section 2).

7   On rear wheel drive models, separate the suspension struts from the steering knuckle (see Section 4).

8  On 4MATIC (AWD) models, separate the lower control arm from the steering knuckle (see Section 5).

9  Carefully inspect the steering knuckle for cracks, especially around the steering arm and spindle area. Also inspect the balljoint stud holes. If they're elongated, or if you find any cracks in the knuckle, replace the steering knuckle.

10  Remove the brake dust shield(s) as necessary for replacement.

11  Installation is the reverse of removal. Be sure to tighten all suspension fasteners to the torque values listed in this Chapter's Specifications. Refer to the torque values listed in the Chapter 9 Specifications for brake related fasteners and Chapter 8 for the driveaxle hub nut.

12  Tighten the wheel bolts to the torque listed in the Chapter 1 Specifications.

13  Have the front end alignment checked and, if necessary, adjusted.

## 9  Subframe assembly (front) - removal and installation

### ✳✳ WARNING 1:

**Make sure the steering wheel is not turned or the angle of the front wheels is changed while the steering shaft is disconnected or you could damage the airbag system clockspring. To prevent the shaft from turning, turn the ignition key to the lock position before beginning work, and run the seat belt through the steering wheel and clip it into its latch.**

### ✳✳ WARNING 2:

**Clean all mounting bolts of old thread-locking compound as necessary and apply thread-locking compound (blue/medium) during installation. Clean threaded holes with a thread chasing tool, or equivalent, before installing bolts in them. Replace all self-locking nuts as equipped.**

➡ **Note: New subframe mounting bolts will be necessary.**

1  Park the vehicle with the wheels pointing straight ahead.

2  Move the steering column to its outermost position. Deactivate the easy entry and exit function, if equipped.

➡ **Note: The easy entry/exit function creates more room to enter and exit the vehicle by moving the steering column and driver's seat automatically. It is controlled by buttons on the steering wheel and the multi-function display**

3  Drain the power steering fluid from the reservoir (see Section 21).

4  Raise the engine slightly and support it with an engine support fixture or equivalent (see Chapter 2).

5  Loosen the front wheel bolts, raise the front of the vehicle, support it securely on jackstands and remove the front wheels.

➡ **Note: Support the vehicle by placing the jackstands under the frame (unibody) and not under any of the suspension components or subframe.**

### REAR WHEEL DRIVE MODELS

▶ **Refer to illustration 9.8**

6  Detach the lower mounting fasteners for the strut/coil spring assemblies (see Section 2).

7  Remove the stabilizer bar and links (see Section 3).

8  Remove the heat shields from the subframe (see illustration).

### 4MATIC MODELS

9  Remove both front driveaxles (see Chapter 8).

10  Reattach the lower control arm to the steering knuckle (see Section 5).

11  Remove the heat shields from above the right boot and the steering shaft coupler of the steering gear.

### ALL MODELS

▶ **Refer to illustrations 9.18, 9.20a and 9.20b**

12  Remove the engine mount bolts from the subframe (see Chapter 2).

13  Separate the steering shaft coupler from the lower steering shaft (see Section 20).

14  Disconnect the fluid lines from the steering gear and plug or cap all openings (see Section 20).

15  Disconnect the brake lines from the brake hoses and plug or cap all openings (see Chapter 9).

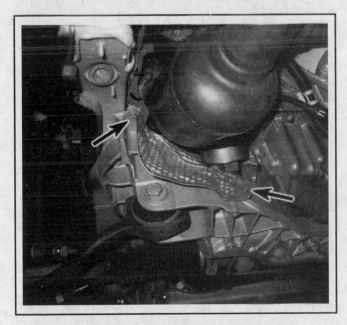

**9.8  Remove the fasteners for the heat shields that are attached to each side of the subframe**

16 Disconnect the wheel speed and brake pad wear sensors from the steering knuckles and brake calipers, then remove them (see Chapter 9).

➡**Note: The wire harnesses for these sensors are vulnerable to damage. Use care when removing them.**

17 Inspect the subframe for any attached wire harness or hoses and detach them and move them aside so the subframe can be lowered.

18 Use a transmission jack to support the rear part of the subframe and suspension components. Secure the subframe by attaching it to the jack with ratchet type tie-down straps or equivalent. Use an additional floor jack under the front center portion of the subframe. (see illustration).

19 Place jackstands under the subframe in addition to the transmission jack and floor jacks.

20 Remove the four mounting bolts for the subframe and discard them (see the accompanying illustrations and illustration 9.18).

**✱✱ WARNING:**

**Do not work below any part of the subframe unless it is supported by jackstands.**

21 With the help of an assistant, remove the jackstands and slowly lower the transmission jack and floor jack. Place two-by-fours underneath the brake discs to protect them and the dust shields from damage as the subframe is lowered completely.

**✱✱ WARNING:**

**The subframe and suspension components are awkward, heavy and easily unbalanced. Do not attempt this procedure alone.**

22 When reinstalling the subframe, slowly and carefully raise the subframe with the jacks while guiding the steering shaft coupler towards the steering shaft. It can be engaged after the subframe is mounted.

➡**Note: Inspect the stabilizer bar and subframe bushings before reinstalling the subframe.**

23 Line up the subframe using the mounting holes on the chassis and use the jacks and jackstands to support it.

24 Use new bolts (purchased from a dealership service depart-

9.18 Subframe details (rear wheel drive model shown - 4MATIC models similar):

1 *Mounting bolt locations (vicinity shown)*
2 *Location for transmission jack placement*
3 *Location for floor jack placement*

ment) for mounting the subframe. Install them with hand tools only and tighten them to the torque listed in this Chapter's Specifications.

**✱✱ CAUTION:**

**The bolts are self-tapping; be careful not to cut cross-threads into the mounting hole during installation.**

25 The remainder of the installation is the reverse of removal. Make sure any wire harnesses or brackets that were removed to lower the subframe are reattached.

26 Install the wheels then lower the vehicle. Tighten the wheel bolts to the torque listed in the Chapter 1 Specifications.

27 Have the front end alignment checked and, if necessary, adjusted.

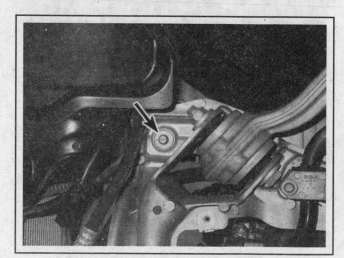

9.20a Location of the left-front mounting bolt (rear wheel drive model shown - 4MATIC models similar)

9.20b Location of the left-rear mounting bolt (rear wheel drive model shown - 4MATIC models similar)

### 10  Shock absorber (rear) - removal and installation

▶ Refer to illustrations 10.1a, 10.1b, 10.2, 10.4 and 10.5

### ✳✳ WARNING:

**Replace all self-locking nuts as equipped.**

1   In the trunk compartment, remove the rear trim panel and lining fasteners and pull the carpeting aside for access to the shock absorber's upper mounting nut (see illustrations).

➡**Note 1: For round-headed fasteners with a circle in the center, simply pry the center out then pull the entire fastener out. If there is no small circle in the center, pry the entire fastener out. For small flat rectangular fasteners, pry them up using the small slots on the sides.**

➡**Note 2: For wagon models, remove the rear-most storage compartment covers on each side of the cargo area.**

2   Remove the upper mounting nut and hardware by holding the damper rod and loosening the mounting nut (see illustration). Discard the nut.

3   Raise the rear of the vehicle and support it securely on jackstands.

➡**Note: Support the vehicle by placing the jackstands under its frame and not any of the suspension components.**

4   Remove the cover from the spring link (see illustration).

5   Remove the fasteners that attach the lower end of the shock to the spring link (see illustration). If the fasteners appear to be frozen, apply some penetrating oil and allow some time for it to work.

6   Installation is the reverse of removal. Use new self-locking mounting nuts. Tighten the mounting nuts to the torque listed in this Chapter's Specifications.

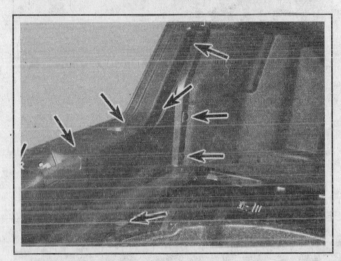

**10.1a  Fastener locations for the rear trim panel (some locations are out of view in this photo - sedan shown)**

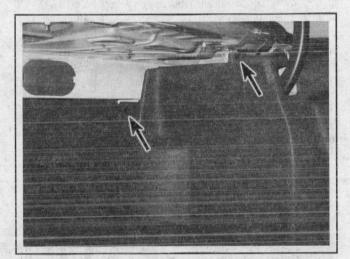

**10.1b  Fasteners for the carpet lining in the trunk on the right side (sedan shown)**

**10.2  Location of the upper mounting nut and hardware for the shock absorber (sedan shown)**

**10.4  Remove the two screws and then unclip the cover from the spring link**

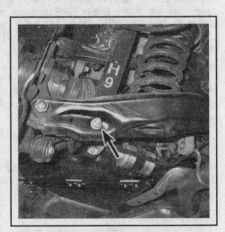

**10.5  Location of the lower mounting fasteners for the shock absorber**

## 11  Stabilizer bar, bushings and links (rear) - removal and installation

▸ **Refer to illustration 11.2**

※※ **WARNING:**

Clean all mounting bolts of old thread-locking compound as necessary and apply thread-locking compound (blue/medium) during installation. Clean threaded holes with a thread chasing tool, or equivalent, before installing bolts in them. Replace all self-locking nuts as equipped.

1　Raise the rear of the vehicle and support it securely on jackstands.

➡Note: Support the vehicle by placing the jackstands under its frame and not any of the suspension components.

2　Remove the lower nut from each stabilizer bar link, then remove the links from the bar (see illustration). Inspect the small boots on the links for damage or deterioration. Replace the links if necessary.

➡Note: The stabilizer bar links can be removed entirely by separating them from the rear knuckles.

3　Remove the stabilizer bar bracket fasteners and remove the brackets.

4　Remove the stabilizer bar, then remove the rubber bushings from the stabilizer bar.

5　Clean the stabilizer bar where the bushings contact it. Inspect all bushings for wear and damage. If any of the rubber parts are cracked, torn or generally deteriorated, replace them.

6　Check each stabilizer link for signs of excessive wear and replace them as necessary.

7　Installation is the reverse of removal. Be sure to tighten all the fasteners to the torque listed in this Chapter's Specifications.

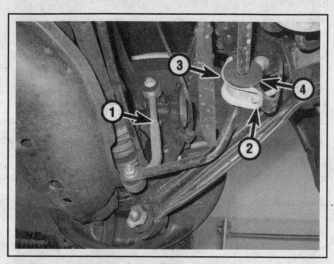

**11.2  Stabilizer bar details (rear):**

1　Stabilizer bar link
2　Stabilizer bar bracket mounting bolt (one shown - top bolt hidden from view)
3　Stabilizer bar bracket
4　Stabilizer bar bushing

## 12  Suspension links (rear) - removal and installation

※※ **WARNING:**

Clean all mounting bolts of old thread-locking compound as necessary and apply thread-locking compound (blue/medium) during installation. Clean threaded holes with a thread chasing tool, or equivalent, before installing bolts in them. Replace all self-locking nuts as equipped.

➡Note: The subframe must be lowered to remove the radius rod; a good floor jack, jackstands and wood blocks will be necessary.

1　Loosen the wheel bolts, raise the rear of the vehicle and support it securely on jackstands. Remove the wheel.

➡Note: Support the vehicle by placing the jackstands under its frame and not any of the suspension components.

### THRUST ARM

▸ **Refer to illustration 12.2**

2　Remove the thrust arm mounting fasteners from the knuckle (see illustration).

**12.2  Thrust arm mounting fastener locations**

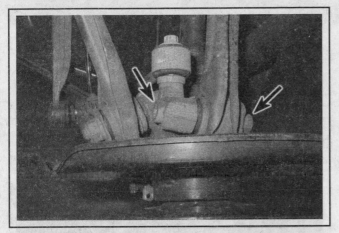

12.8  Camber strut mounting fasteners at the rear knuckle

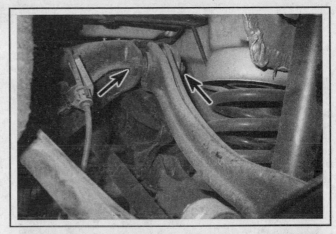

12.9  Camber strut mounting fasteners at the rear subframe

9   Remove the camber strut mounting fasteners at the subframe (see illustration).

10  Inspect all rubber bushings for wear and damage. If any of the rubber parts are cracked, torn or generally deteriorated, replace the strut.

11  Installation is the reverse of removal. Tighten the mounting fasteners to the torque listed in this Chapter's Specifications.

➡Note: Raise the spring link with a floor jack to simulate normal ride height before tightening the camber strut mounting fasteners (see illustration 12.36).

### RADIUS ROD

▸ **Refer to illustrations 12.15, 12.24, 12.26 and 12.27**

12.15  Location of the wheel speed sensor and brake pad wear sensor electrical connectors

3   Remove the thrust arm mounting fasteners from the subframe and remove the arm.

4   Inspect all rubber bushings for wear and damage. If any of the rubber parts are cracked, torn or generally deteriorated, replace the arm. The plastic cover can be unclipped from the arm and replaced if necessary.

5   Installation is the reverse of removal. Tighten the mounting fasteners to the torque listed in this Chapter's Specifications.

➡Note: Raise the spring link with a floor jack to simulate normal ride height before tightening the thrust arm mounting fasteners (see illustration 12.36).

### CAMBER STRUT

▸ **Refer to illustrations 12.8 and 12.9**

6   Mark the strut so you will know which side faces forward and which end faces inward/outward.

7   Remove the radius rod mounting fasteners from the knuckle (see illustration 12.26).

8   Remove the camber strut mounting fasteners at the knuckle (see illustration). Move the radius rod so that you can remove the camber strut bolt.

---

**✳✳ WARNING**

**The removal of the radius rod involves lowering the subframe and drivetrain components. This job is very involved and can be considered hazardous even with the proper equipment. Use extreme caution throughout the following procedures to avoid injury.**

---

➡Note 1: A transmission jack or equivalent is necessary for the following procedure.

➡Note 2: It is recommended that additional help from an assistant be used during this procedure.

12  Disconnect the cable from the negative battery terminal (see Chapter 5, Section 1).

13  Loosen the wheel bolts, raise the rear of the vehicle and support it securely on jackstands placed under the frame rails. Remove the rear wheels.

➡Note: Support the vehicle by placing the jackstands under its frame and not any of the suspension components.

14  Detach the parking brake cables from the equalizer and remove them from the bracket attached to the body (see Chapter 9) (see illustrations 11.9 in Chapter 9 and 7.11 in Chapter 4).

15  Disconnect the wheel speed and brake pad wear sensor electrical connectors located above the rear differential, as equipped (see illustration).

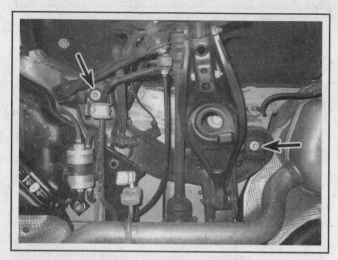

**12.24 Location of the subframe mounting bolts on the left side**

**12.26 Radius rod mounting fasteners at the rear knuckle**

16 Remove the two under covers (see illustrations 6.3a and 6.3b in Chapter 4).

17 Remove the rear portion of the exhaust system (see Chapter 4).

18 Remove the heat shield that is mounted above the rear muffler.

19 Disconnect the driveshaft from the rear differential (see Chapter 8).

20 Remove the stabilizer bar from the subframe brackets and stabilizer bar links; leaving the links attached to the rear knuckles (see Section 11).

21 Remove the brake calipers and secure them so that the brake hoses will not be affected when the subframe is lowered (see Chapter 9).

22 Remove the coil spring (see Steps 36 through 42).

23 Place a transmission jack (or equivalent) under the differential and attach it securely.

24 Position jackstands under the subframe (along with the transmission jack) to secure the differential and subframe, then remove the subframe mounting bolts (see illustration).

### ✽✽ WARNING:

**Do not work below any part of the subframe unless it is supported by jackstands.**

25 With the help of an assistant, remove the jackstands, then slowly lower the subframe while pulling it rearward.

### ✽✽ WARNING:

**The subframe and suspension components are awkward, heavy and easily unbalanced. Do not attempt this procedure alone.**

26 Remove the radius rod mounting fasteners at the knuckle (see illustration).

27 Note the position of the radius rod, then remove the mounting fasteners at the subframe and remove the rod (see illustration).

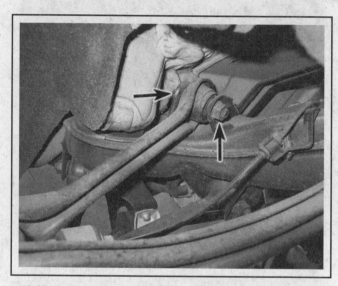

**12.27 Radius rod mounting fasteners at the rear subframe**

28 Inspect all rubber bushings for wear and damage. If any of the rubber parts are cracked, torn or generally deteriorated, replace the rod.

29 Installation is the reverse of removal noting the following points:

a) *The subframe mounting bolt holes must be re-tapped and cleaned thoroughly of all old adhesive before the bolts are installed.*

b) *When installing the subframe, it must be guided forward while raising it into position.*

c) *Tighten the subframe mounting bolts to the torque listed in this Chapter's Specifications.*

d) *Make sure to reinstall the brake, driveline and exhaust system components.*

e) *Raise the spring link with a floor jack to simulate normal ride height before tightening any suspension component mounting fasteners (see illustration 12.36).*

f) *Be sure to tighten all suspension fasteners to the torque values listed in this Chapter's Specifications.*

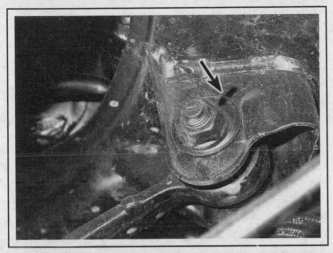

**12.30 Mark the relationship of the toe adjusting cam bolt to the subframe to preserve the rear wheel alignment when the fasteners are reinstalled**

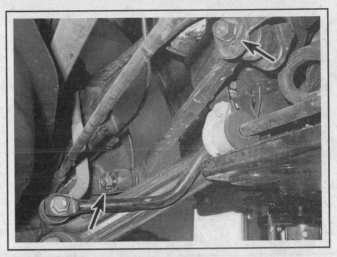

**12.31 Track rod mounting fasteners**

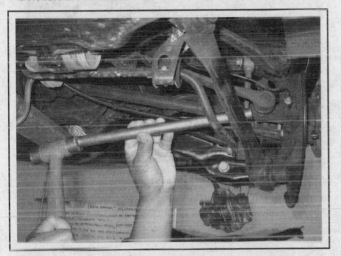

**12.32 To separate the link-mounted balljoint from the rear knuckle, loosen the balljoint stud nut, then strike the knuckle using a large brass drift or equivalent to break the taper loose**

**12.36 Use a floor jack to raise, lower or support the spring link**

## TRACK ROD

▶ **Refer to illustrations 12.30, 12.31 and 12.32**

30 Mark the relationship of the toe-adjusting cam bolt to the subframe (see illustration).

31 Loosen the ballstud nut on the track rod balljoint at the rear knuckle (see illustration).

32 Separate the balljoint on the track rod from the rear knuckle by using a drift and striking the knuckle to break the taper of the ballstud (see illustration).

33 Hold the cam bolt while loosening the track rod mounting nut from the rear subframe. Note the position of the link, then remove it.

34 Inspect all rubber bushings for wear and damage. If any of the rubber parts are cracked, torn or generally deteriorated, replace the track rod.

➡**Note: The bushing on the inboard end of the track rod can be replaced. Due to the special tools and expertise required, the job requires a professional mechanic. Take the track rod to dealer service department or a qualified repair facility for service.**

35 Installation is the reverse of removal. Tighten the mounting fasteners to the torque listed in this Chapter's Specifications.

➡**Note: Raise the spring link with a floor jack to simulate normal ride height before tightening the link mounting fasteners (see illustration 12.36).**

## SPRING LINK (AND COIL SPRING)

▶ **Refer to illustrations 12.36, 12.38 and 12.40**

36 Support the spring link and coil spring tension with a floor jack (see illustration).

37 Remove the shock absorber lower mounting fasteners (see Section 10).

38 Remove the link mounting fasteners from the rear knuckle and loosen the fasteners at the subframe (see illustration).

39 Slowly lower the spring link with the floor jack until the spring tension is relieved.

40 Note the position of the coil spring in the spring link as well as the position of any seats (or insulators), then remove them (see illustration).

41 Remove the spring link mounting fasteners at the subframe, then remove the link.

42 Inspect the coil spring seats (insulators) and the link bushing for wear and damage. If any of the rubber parts are cracked, torn or generally deteriorated, replace them.

➡Note: For bushing replacement, you'll need the assistance of a dealer service department or a qualified repair shop due to the special tools and expertise required.

43 Installation is the reverse of removal. Be sure to place the coil spring and seats in their originals positions. Tighten the mounting fasteners to the torque listed in this Chapter's Specifications.

➡Note: Raise the spring link with a floor jack to simulate normal ride height before tightening the link mounting fasteners (see illustration 12.27).

## ALL LINKS

44 Install the wheel(s) and lower the vehicle. Tighten the wheel bolts to the torque listed in the Chapter 1 Specifications.

45 Have the wheel alignment checked and, if necessary, adjusted.

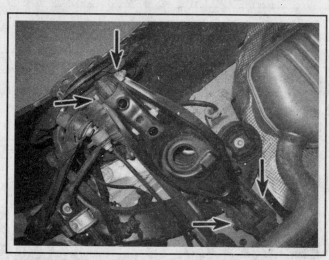

**12.38  Spring link mounting fasteners**

**12.40  With the coil spring tension relieved, remove the spring and seats**

## 13  Coil spring (rear) - removal and installation

### ✳✳ WARNING:

**Always replace coil springs in pairs - never replace just one of them.**

Refer to Section 12, Steps 36 through 43 for the coil spring removal and installation procedure.

## 14  Knuckle (rear) - removal and installation

### ✳✳ WARNING 1:

**The dust created by the brake system is harmful to your health. Never blow it out with compressed air and don't inhale any of it. Do not, under any circumstances, use petroleum-based solvents to clean brake parts. Use brake system cleaner only.**

### ✳✳ WARNING 2:

**Clean all mounting bolts of old thread-locking compound as necessary and apply thread-locking compound (blue/medium) during installation. Clean threaded holes with a thread chasing tool, or equivalent, before installing bolts in them. Replace all self-locking nuts as equipped.**

1  Remove the driveaxle hub nut (see Chapter 8).

2  Loosen the wheel bolts, raise the rear of the vehicle and support it securely on jackstands. Remove the wheel.

➡**Note: Support the vehicle by placing the jackstands under its frame and not any of the suspension components.**

3  Remove the brake disc, the wheel speed and brake wear sensor(s) as equipped (see Chapter 9).

4  Remove the rear parking brake shoes and disconnect the parking brake cable from the knuckle (see Chapter 9).

5  Remove the stabilizer bar link from the knuckle (see Section 11).

6  Remove the coil spring (see Section 12).

7  Detach the track rod, thrust arm and radius rod links from the knuckle (see Section 12).

8  Push the axle shaft through the hub, pivot the rear knuckle up and remove the driveaxle from the knuckle (see Chapter 8).

➡**Note: Secure the driveaxle aside and be careful not to over extend any of the CV joints.**

### ✳✳ CAUTION:

**When withdrawing the driveaxle from the hub and bearing assembly, be careful not to damage the tone-ring for the wheel speed sensor.**

9  Detach the camber strut from the rear knuckle, then remove the knuckle.

10  Carefully inspect the steering knuckle for cracks, especially around the steering arm and spindle area. Also inspect the balljoint stud hole for the track rod. If it's elongated, or if you find any cracks in the knuckle, replace the knuckle.

11  Remove brake dust shield as necessary for replacement.

12  Installation is the reverse of removal. Be sure to tighten all suspension fasteners to the torque values listed in this Chapter's Specifications. Refer to the torque values listed in the Chapter 9 Specifications for brake related fasteners.

➡**Note: Raise the spring link with a floor jack to simulate normal ride height, then tighten the suspension component mounting fasteners to the torque listed in this Chapter's Specifications (see illustration 12.26).**

13  Tighten the wheel bolts to the torque listed in the Chapter 1 Specifications.

## 15  Hub and wheel bearings (rear) - removal and installation

The rear hub and wheel bearings require no maintenance or adjustment and are replaced if found to be defective. Due to the special tools and expertise required to press the hub and bearing from the rear knuckle, the job requires a professional mechanic. However, the knuckle may be removed and taken to an automotive machine shop or a qualified repair facility for service. See Section 14 for the rear knuckle removal procedures.

## 16  Steering wheel - removal and installation

### ✳✳ WARNING:

**These models are equipped with airbags. Always disable the airbag system whenever working in the vicinity of any airbag system component to avoid the possibility of accidental airbag deployment, which could cause personal injury (see Chapter 12).**

## REMOVAL

▸ **Refer to illustrations 16.4, 16.5a, 16.5b, 16.6, 16.7, 16.8a, 16.8b and 16.9**

➡**Note: A new steering wheel retaining bolt is necessary for installation.**

1  Park the vehicle with the front wheels in the straight-ahead position.

### ✳✳ WARNING:

**Do NOT turn the steering shaft during or after steering wheel removal. If the shaft is turned while the steering wheel is removed, a mechanism known as the clockspring can be damaged. The clockspring maintains a continuous electrical circuit between the wiring harness and the airbag module and consists of a flat, ribbon-like electrically conductive tape which winds and unwinds as the steering wheel is turned.**

2  Extend the steering wheel to its outermost position towards you. On vehicles with electrically adjustable steering columns, leave the ignition key in the ACC position.

3  Disconnect the cable from the negative terminal of the battery (see Chapter 5, Section 1).

4   Remove the two airbag module fasteners (see illustration) and carefully lift the airbag module from the steering wheel.

5   Unplug the electrical connectors for the airbag module, horn and other components as equipped, then remove the module (see illustrations).

> ☀ **WARNING:**
>
> **Carry the airbag module with the trim cover (upholstered side) facing away from you, and set the airbag module in a safe location with the trim cover facing up.**

6   Remove the steering wheel retaining bolt and mark the relationship of the steering wheel hub to the steering shaft before removing the steering wheel (see illustration).

➡ **Note: The steering wheel hub is keyed to the steering shaft in two places. Slide the steering wheel off the shaft while guiding the clockspring wire harness through the steering wheel hub.**

7   Loosen one of the clockspring mounting screws to keep the clockspring from rotating and in the centered position (see illustration).

> ☀ **CAUTION:**
>
> **If the clockspring is rotated and the steering wheel is installed, the clockspring will be damaged and the airbag system will be disabled.**

8   If it's necessary to remove the clockspring, remove the steering column module by loosening the mounting bolt and pulling the module from the steering column (see illustrations).

➡ **Note: On models manufactured prior to July 7, 2002, leave the module on the steering column.**

9   Remove the clockspring from the steering column module by loosening its mounting screws, removing all of the switches (see Chapter 12 for additional information) and the module cover. Start disassembly by fully loosening the front clockspring mounting screws (see illustration 16.7). Then, remove the module cover fasteners from the rear of the module (see illustration). Also, note the position of the mod-

**16.4  Remove the airbag module fasteners**

**16.5a  Lift the airbag off the steering wheel and unplug the electrical connectors for the airbag, horn, etc.**

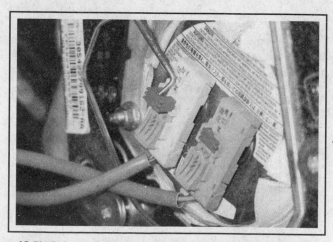

**16.5b  Release the locks on the connectors to unplug them from the module**

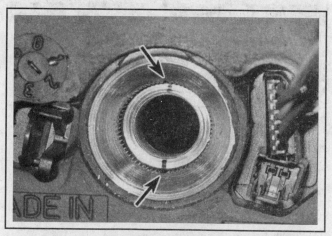

**16.6  After removing the retaining bolt, note the keyed area of the steering wheel hub and mark its relationship to the steering shaft**

ule's mounting bolt in the back of the clockspring; except on models prior to July 7, 2002.

**➡Note: On models manufactured prior to July 7, 2002, loosen the three clockspring mounting screws (on the front) fully, then carefully pry it from the module around the edges. No other disassembly is necessary.**

## INSTALLATION

10 Reassemble the steering column module as necessary and reinstall it to the steering column.

11 Before installing the steering wheel, make absolutely sure that the airbag clockspring is centered and the front wheels are pointing straight ahead (see illustration 16.7). This shouldn't be a problem as long as you have not turned the steering shaft while the wheel was removed or rotated the clockspring. If necessary, center the clockspring as follows:

a) Rotate the clockspring counterclockwise until it stops (don't apply

too much force, though).

b) Rotate the clockspring clockwise about 3 to 3-1/2 turns until the mounting screws and top rotating part of the clockspring line-up. Look for a small window on the clockspring with contrasting colors, as equipped.

12 Installation is the reverse of removal, noting the following points:

a) Make sure the airbag clockspring is centered before installing the steering wheel (see Step 11).

b) When installing the steering wheel, carefully feed the clockspring wire harness through the wheel, engage the steering wheel hub with the raised portions (tabs) of the clockspring and place it on the steering shaft using the reference marks made earlier.

c) Install a NEW steering wheel retaining bolt and tighten it to the torque listed in this Chapter's Specifications.

d) Install the airbag module on the steering wheel and tighten the fasteners to the torque listed in this Chapter's Specifications.

e) Enable the airbag system (see Chapter 12).

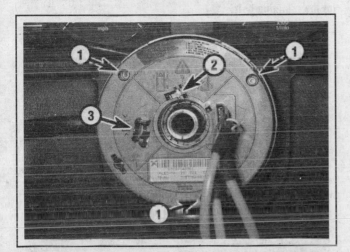

**16.7 Centered clockspring details (2005 model shown - others are similar):**

1    Mounting screws (loosen one to hold in centered position)
2    Centering window (contrasting colors visible when centered)
3    Tab that engages with steering wheel hub

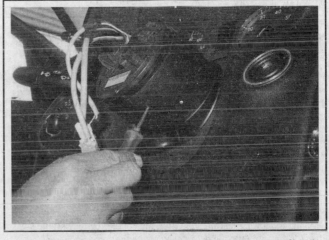

**16.8a Loosen the steering column module mounting bolt**

**16.8b Pull the module from the steering column**

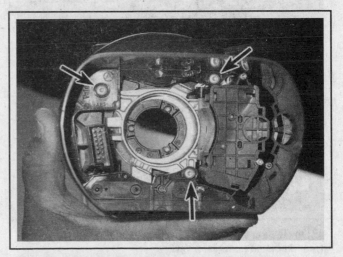

**16.9 Steering module cover fasteners (rear of module)**

## 17 Steering column - removal and installation

### ※※ WARNING 1:

These models are equipped with airbags. Always disable the airbag system whenever working in the vicinity of any airbag system component to avoid the possibility of accidental airbag deployment, which could cause personal injury (see Chapter 12).

### ※※ WARNING 2:

Clean all mounting bolts of old thread-locking compound as necessary and apply thread-locking compound (blue/medium) during installation. Clean threaded holes with a thread chasing tool, or equivalent, before installing bolts in them. Replace all self-locking nuts as equipped.

### REMOVAL

♦ Refer to illustrations 17.3a, 17.3b, 17.4, 17.6, and 17.10 through 17.15

1   Raise the front of the vehicle and support it securely.

➡Note: Drive-on (ramp style) supports are ideal for this procedure as they keep the wheels pointed forward while supporting the vehicle.

2   Remove the engine splash shields from under the vehicle (see Chapter 2).

3   Remove the small exhaust shield located just above the steering shaft coupler (see illustrations).

4   Mark the lower steering shaft (that comes through the firewall) in relation to the steering shaft coupler, then remove the retaining bolt. Separate the lower steering shaft from the coupler by moving the shaft upwards (towards the inside of the vehicle) and removing the small plate between them (see illustration).

### ※※ CAUTION:

If it is necessary to rotate the lower steering shaft slightly to get to the retaining bolt, be sure to move the shaft and coupler back to the centered position to avoid damage to the clockspring.

➡Note 1: On 4MATIC models, the steering shaft coupler resembles a universal joint and uses a pinch bolt to hold it to the lower steering shaft; it doesn't have a long shaft like the coupler used on rear wheel drive models. The coupler on the 4MATIC models is removed similarly; mark its relationship to the lower steering shaft (that comes through the firewall), remove the pinch bolt and separate the coupler from the lower steering shaft.

➡Note 2: On rear wheel drive models, the manufacturer recommends replacing the small plate between the lower steering shaft and steering shaft coupler because it incorporates the nut for the retaining bolt.

17.3a  The steering shaft coupler (rear wheel drive model shown)

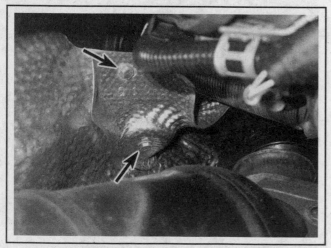

17.3b  The small exhaust shield and mounting fasteners (rear wheel drive model shown)

17.4  Mark the relationship of the lower steering shaft to the shaft coupler (A) and remove the retaining bolt (B)

5   Remove the lower instrument cluster trim panel located just above the brake and accelerator pedals (see Chapter 11).

6   On vehicles equipped with an electric steering column lock (an anti-theft mechanism), remove the motor assembly from the column as follows:

  a) *Place the ignition key in the ACC position (the first position clockwise from OFF).*

  b) *Disconnect the cable from the negative battery terminal, (see Chapter 5, Section 1).*

  c) *Remove the retaining bolt (recessed) that attaches the motor assembly to the steering column (see illustration).*

  d) *Move the motor assembly towards the firewall to remove it from the steering column (move it in the opposite direction for installation).*

  e) *Detach the electrical connector for the motor assembly.*

7   Remove the steering wheel (see Section 16).

8   Remove the steering column switches (see Chapter 12) and clockspring (see Section 16).

➡**Note: On models manufactured after July 7, 2002, the steering column switches and clockspring can be removed as an assembly (referred to as the steering column module). Refer to Step 8 in Section 16 to remove the steering column module.**

9   Remove the instrument cluster (see Chapter 12).

10  Remove any insulation from around the steering column (see illustration).

11  Move the small lock to release the lever used to adjust the steering column. Push down on the adjustment lever and disengage it from the steering column (see illustration).

12  Release the clip on the top part of the steering column cover, then remove the cover (see illustration).

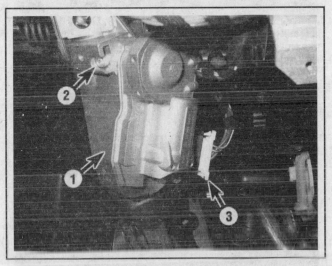

**17.6  Electric steering lock motor details:**

| | |
|---|---|
| *1   Motor assembly* | *3   Electrical connector* |
| *2   Recessed retaining bolt* | |

**17.10  Insulation on the left side of the steering column**

**17.11  Move the small lock to release the column adjustment lever**

**17.12  The retaining clip for the steering column cover**

13 Detach the electrical wiring harness (see illustration).

14 Remove the lower steering column mounting bolt (see illustration).

15 Remove the upper steering column mounting bolts, then pull the column and lower steering shaft upwards and out of the boot at the firewall to remove it (see illustration).

### ❊❊ CAUTION:

**Handle the steering column with care to avoid damaging it.**

## INSTALLATION

16 Guide the steering column into position with the lower steering shaft going through the boot at the firewall. Install the mounting fasteners, but don't tighten them yet.

➡Note: Lubricate the boot's shaft contact areas with all-purpose grease.

17 Confirm the alignment of the steering column, then tighten the mounting fasteners to the torque listed in this Chapters Specifications.

18 The remainder of installation is the reverse of removal. Make sure to match the lower steering shaft with the steering shaft coupler using

**17.13  Remove the wiring harness and connector from the column**

the index marks made in Step 4. Also, secure the wire harness to the steering column in the same manner as it was originally installed.

**17.14  The location of the lower steering column mounting bolt**

**17.15  The location of the upper steering column mounting bolts**

## 18  Tie-rod ends - removal and installation

## REMOVAL

◆ **Refer to illustrations 18.2, 18.3, and 18.4**

1 Loosen the wheel bolts, raise the front of the vehicle and support it securely on jackstands. Apply the parking brake. Remove the wheel.

➡Note: Support the vehicle by placing the jackstands under its frame and not any of the suspension components.

2 Loosen the tie-rod end jam nut (see illustration).

3 Mark the relationship of the tie-rod end to the threaded portion of the tie-rod (see illustration). The reference mark will help restore the front wheel alignment toe setting upon reassembly.

4 Loosen (but don't remove) the nut on the tie-rod end ballstud and disconnect the tie-rod end from the steering knuckle arm (see illustration).

➡Note: If the ballstud turns while loosening the nut, hold the ballstud with a wrench while removing the nut.

5   If you're replacing the tie-rod end, unscrew the tie-rod end from the tie-rod, then thread the new tie-rod end onto the tie-rod to the marked position.

## INSTALLATION

6   Connect the tie-rod end to the steering knuckle arm. Install a new nut on the ballstud and tighten it to the torque listed in this Chapter's Specifications. Install the wheel. Lower the vehicle and tighten the wheel bolts to the torque listed in the Chapter 1 Specifications.

7   Have the front end alignment checked and, if necessary, adjusted.

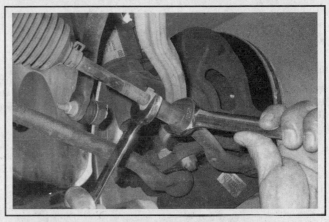

18.2  Hold the tie-rod with a wrench while loosening the jam nut

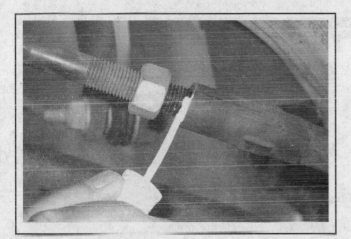

18.3  Mark the position of the tie-rod end in relation to the threads

18.4  Loosen the ballstud nut a few turns, then separate the tie-rod end from the steering knuckle with a balljoint separator tool or puller (leaving the nut on the ballstud will prevent the tie-rod end from separating violently)

## 19  Steering gear boots - replacement

▶ Refer to illustration 19.5

1   Loosen the wheel bolts, raise the front of the vehicle and support it securely on jackstands. Remove the wheel.

➡Note: Support the vehicle by placing the jackstands under its frame and not any of the suspension components.

2   Remove the engine splash shields (see Chapter 2).

3   On 4MATIC models, remove the heat shield over the right boot as necessary.

4   Remove the tie-rod end and jam nut (see Section 18).

5   Remove the steering gear boot clamps and slide the boot off (see illustration).

➡Note: Check for the presence of power steering fluid in the boot. If there is a substantial amount, it means the steering gear seals are leaking and the power steering gear should be replaced with a new or rebuilt unit.

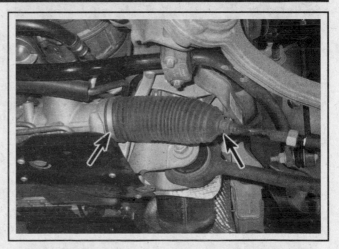

19.5  Remove both clamps to remove the steering gear boot

6    Before installing the new boot, wrap the threads and serrations on the end of the steering rod with a layer of tape so the small end of the new boot isn't damaged.

7    Slide the new boot into position on the steering gear until it seats in the grooves, then install new clamps.

➡**Note: The inboard boot clamp is a crimp-type clamp, similar to those used on CV joint boots. Refer to Chapter 8 for information on installing these types of clamps.**

8    Remove the tape and install the tie-rod end (see Section 18).

9    The remainder of installation is the reverse of removal.

10   Install the engine splash shields (see Chapter 2).

11   Install the wheel. Lower the vehicle and tighten the wheel bolts to the torque listed in the Chapter 1 Specifications.

12   Have the front end alignment checked and, if necessary, adjusted.

## 20  Steering gear - removal and installation

▸ **Refer to illustrations 20.6, 20.8, 20.10 and 20.12**

### ✳✳ WARNING 1:

**Make sure the steering wheel is not turned while the steering gear is removed or you could damage the airbag system clockspring. To prevent the steering shaft from turning, turn the ignition key to the lock position before beginning work, and run the seat belt through the steering wheel and clip it into its latch.**

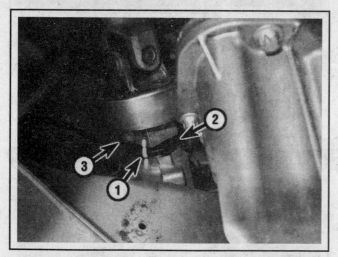

**20.6  Steering shaft coupler details (rear wheel drive shown - 4MATIC similar):**

*1    Index mark for matching steering gear input shaft position to steering shaft coupler position*

*2    Small plastic cap (also used for centering the steering gear)*

*3    Steering shaft coupler pinch bolt*

### ✳✳ WARNING 2:

**Clean all mounting bolts of old thread-locking compound as necessary and apply thread-locking compound (blue/medium) during installation. Clean threaded holes with a thread chasing tool, or equivalent, before installing bolts in them. Replace all self-locking nuts as equipped.**

1    Park the vehicle with the wheels pointing straight ahead and apply the parking brake.

2    Move the steering column to its outermost position. Deactivate the "easy entry and exit" function, if equipped.

➡**Note: The "easy entry/exit" function creates more room to enter and exit the vehicle by moving the steering column and driver's seat automatically. It is controlled by buttons on the steering wheel and the multifunction display.**

3    Remove the power steering fluid from the reservoir (see Section 21).

4    Loosen the front wheel bolts, raise the front of the vehicle, support it securely on jackstands and remove the front wheels.

➡**Note: Support the vehicle by placing the jackstands under its frame and not any of the suspension components.**

5    Remove the engine splash shields from under the vehicle (see Chapter 2).

6    Refer to Steps 3 and 4 in Section 17 to separate the steering shaft coupler from the lower steering shaft.

➡**Note: The steering shaft coupler can be removed from the steering gear also. The relationship of the coupler to the steering gear's input shaft needs to be marked before removing the coupler (see illustration). The small plastic cap that is seated around the steering gear's input shaft is vulnerable to damage; be careful when removing the coupler and do not pry against it. If the steering gear is being replaced, it should come equipped with a new cap. Install the steering coupler in the same position as it was on the original steering gear.**

7    Detach the tie-rod ends from the steering knuckles (see Section 18).

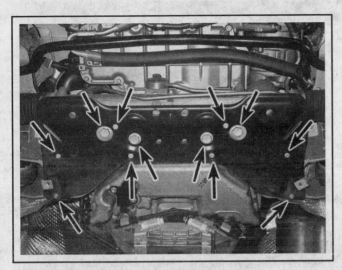

20.8 The retaining plate and steering gear mounting fasteners

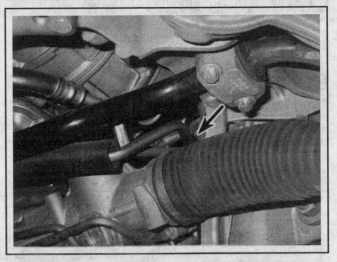

20.10 The line fitting is on the steering gear valve body housing (vicinity shown)

8   Remove the retaining plate and the steering gear mounting fasteners (see illustration).

➡Note: On rear wheel drive models, there is a small plate on top of the steering gear that the mounting bolts thread into that the manufacturer states to replace. On 4MATIC models, individual nuts are used.

9   Move the steering gear forward and down enough to access the line fitting and retaining bolt. Use rope or equivalent to support the steering gear while removing the line fitting.

➡Note: Some models may have an electrical connector located on the steering gear valve body housing. Disconnect the connector before moving the steering gear, if equipped.

10  Position a drain pan under the steering gear. Disconnect the line fitting retaining bolt and pull the fitting from the steering gear (see illustration). Cap the lines and openings to prevent leakage.

11  Inspect all rubber bushings for wear and damage. If any of the rubber or plastic parts are cracked, torn or generally deteriorated, replace them.

12  Installation is the reverse of removal, noting the following points:

a)  *When installing the steering gear, make sure that it is in its centered position when the steering shaft coupler and the lower steering shaft are reconnected (see illustration).*

b)  *Tighten the steering gear mounting bolts and the coupler bolt(s) to the torque values listed in this Chapter's Specifications.*

c)  *Tighten the wheel bolts to the torque listed in the Chapter 1 Specifications.*

d)  *Add power steering fluid to bring it to the proper level (see Chapter 1), then bleed the system as described in Section 22.*

e)  *Re-check the power steering fluid level.*

f)  *Have the front end alignment checked and, if necessary, adjusted.*

20.12 An example of a centered steering gear using the protrusions on the small plastic cap and the steering gear housing

## 21 Power steering pump - removal and installation

♦ Refer to illustrations 21.3 and 21.5

### ✳ WARNING:

**Clean all mounting bolts of old thread-locking compound as necessary and apply thread-locking compound (blue/medium) during installation. Clean threaded holes with a thread chasing tool, or equivalent, before installing bolts in them. Replace all self-locking nuts as equipped.**

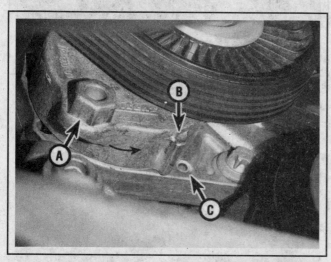

**21.3  To lock the auto-tensioner, rotate it counterclockwise by using a tool on the lug (A). When the protrusion (B) is just past the hole (C), insert a small drift or equivalent into the hole and allow the pump to settle clockwise until the spring tension is relieved**

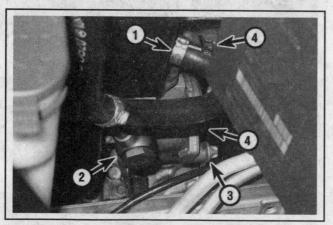

**21.5  Side view of power steering pump mounting details (2005 model shown, others similar):**

1   *Supply hose and clamp (crimp type - replace with traditional hose clamp)*
2   *Pressure line fitting (banjo type - replace sealing washers after removal)*
3   *Ground cable*
4   *Rear mounting bolts (one hidden from view - vicinity given)*

1   Disconnect the cable from the negative battery terminal, (see Chapter 5, Section 1).
2   On V6 engine models, remove the left air intake duct (see Chapter 4).
3   Remove the drivebelt (see Chapter 1). Rotate the auto-tensioner counterclockwise and lock it into position (see illustration).

➡**Note: It is not necessary to lock the auto-tensioner on four-cylinder engine models.**

4   Using a large syringe or suction gun, suck as much fluid out of the power steering fluid reservoir as possible.
5   Position a drain pan under the power steering pump, detach the pressure line fitting (banjo bolt) and the supply hose at the reservoir (carefully cut crimp-type hose clamps) (see illustration). Plug the openings to prevent excessive fluid loss and the entry of contaminants.

➡**Note: On V6 engine models, perform Steps 6 and 7 first.**

## V6 ENGINE MODELS

### 2006 and later models

♦ Refer to illustrations 21.6 and 21.7

6   Using a long hooked tool, pull the circlip from the fitting on the rear of the reservoir (see illustration).

➡**Note: Before removing the circlip, attach a magnetic pick-up tool to it. The tool will help prevent losing the clip when pulling it off.**

7   Remove the three mounting bolts for the reservoir and remove it from the pump (see illustration). Discard the seal.
8   Disconnect the electrical connector from the pump that is next to the pipe for the reservoir.

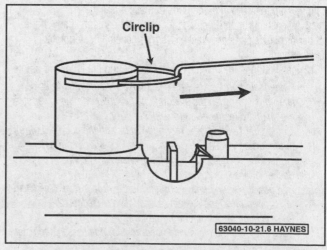

63040-10-21.6 HAYNES

**21.6  Reach in back of the reservoir with a long hooked tool and pull the circlip that retains the reservoir to the pump**

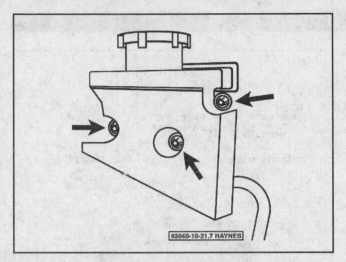

**21.7  Reservoir mounting bolt locations**

**21.13  Front view of power steering pump mounting details (2005 model shown, others similar):**

1   *Reservoir-to-engine bracket bolt*
2   *Front mounting bolts*

9   Remove the air conditioning compressor (see Chapter 3).

10   Detach the ground cable from the back of the pump.

11   Remove the mounting bolt on the back of the pump that is near the bottom.

12   Remove the two front mounting bolts from the left side of the pump (just left of the pulley) and carefully remove it.

### 2005 and earlier models

#### Refer to illustration 21.13

13   Remove the bolt that secures the reservoir to the engine bracket (see illustration).

14   Remove the ground wire from the rear of the pump and remove the mounting bolts on the front and rear of the pump (see illustrations 21.5 and 21.13).

➡**Note: The rear mounting bolts are longer than the front bolts.**

15   Slide the pump and reservoir forward from the engine, being careful not to let any power steering fluid drip on the vehicle's paint.

16   Remove the reservoir from the pump by removing the circlip from the pipe fitting between the reservoir and the pump (see illustration 21.6). Discard the seal.

### FOUR-CYLINDER ENGINE MODELS

17   Remove the alternator wire harness from the pump's heat shield.

18   Remove the eight screws securing the heat shield to the pump, then remove it.

19   Remove the mounting bolts located on the front and rear of the pump, then carefully remove the pump.

### ALL MODELS

20   The pulley can be removed from the pump if necessary. Special tools for this are available at most auto parts stores.

21   Installation is the reverse of removal. Be sure to tighten the mounting bolts and pressure line fitting (banjo-type) bolt to the torque values listed in this Chapter's Specifications. Use a new hose clamp (if cut) on the supply hose at the reservoir and use a new seal when installing the reservoir onto the pump. Use new sealing washers on the banjo-type pressure line fitting. Fill the power steering reservoir with the recommended fluid (see Chapter 1) and bleed the system following the procedure described in Section 22. Re-check the power steering fluid level.

## 22  Power steering system - bleeding

1   The power steering system must be bled whenever a line is disconnected. Bubbles can be seen in power steering fluid that has air in it and the fluid will often have a milky appearance. Low fluid level can cause air to mix with the fluid, resulting in a noisy pump as well as foaming of the fluid.

2   Open the hood and check the fluid level in the reservoir, adding the specified fluid necessary to bring it up to the proper level (see Chapter 1).

3   Start the engine and slowly turn the steering wheel several times from left-to-right and back again. Turn the wheel completely from lock-to-lock, but do not hold it in the extreme position on either side. Check the fluid level, topping it up as necessary until it remains steady and no more bubbles are visible.

## 23 Wheels and tires - general information

▸ **Refer to illustration 23.1**

All models covered by this manual are equipped with radial tires (see illustration). Use of other size or type of tires may affect the ride and handling of the vehicle. Don't mix different types of tires, such as radials and bias belted tires, on the same vehicle - handling may be seriously affected. It's recommended that tires be replaced in pairs on the same axle, but if only one tire is being replaced, be sure it's the same size, structure and tread design as the other tire on the same axle.

Because tire pressure has a substantial effect on handling and wear, the pressure of all tires should be checked at least once a month or before any extended trips are taken (see Chapter 1).

Wheels must be replaced if they are bent, dented, leak air, have elongated bolt holes, are heavily rusted, out of vertical symmetry or if the wheel bolts won't stay tight. Wheel repairs that use welding or peening are not recommended.

Tire and wheel balance are important to the overall handling, braking and performance of the vehicle. Unbalanced wheels can adversely affect handling and ride characteristics as well as tire life. Whenever a tire is installed on a wheel, the tire and wheel should be balanced by a shop with the proper equipment and expertise.

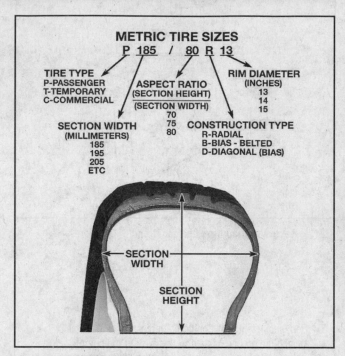

**23.1 Metric tire size code**

## 24 Wheel alignment - general information

▸ **Refer to illustration 24.1**

➡**Note: Since wheel alignment requires special equipment and techniques, it is beyond the scope of this manual. This Section is intended only to familiarize the reader with the basic terms used and procedures followed during a typical wheel alignment.**

The three basic checks made when aligning a vehicle's front wheels are camber, caster and toe-in (see illustration).

Camber and caster are the angles at which the wheels and suspension are inclined in relation to a vertical centerline. Camber is the angle of the wheel in the lateral, or side-to-side plane, while caster is the tilt between the steering axis and the vertical plane, as viewed from the side. Camber angle affects the amount of tire tread which contacts the road and compensates for changes in suspension geometry as the vehicle travels around curves and over bumps. Caster angle affects the self-centering action of the steering, which governs straight-line stability.

Toe-in is the amount the front wheels are angled in relationship to the center line of the vehicle. For example, in a vehicle with zero toe-in, the distance measured between the front edges of the wheels and the distance measured between the rear edges of the wheels are the same. In other words, the wheels are running parallel with the centerline of the vehicle. Toe-in is adjusted by lengthening or shortening the tie-rods. Incorrect toe-in will cause the tires to wear improperly by allowing them to scrub against the road surface.

Proper wheel alignment is essential for safe steering and even tire wear. Symptoms of alignment problems are pulling of the steering to one side or the other and uneven tire wear. If these symptoms are present, check for the following before having the alignment adjusted:

a) Loose steering gear mounting bolts
b) Damaged or worn steering gear mounts
c) Worn or damaged wheel bearings
d) Bent tie-rods
e) Worn balljoints
f) Improper tire pressures
g) Mixing tires of different construction

Front wheel alignment should be left to an alignment shop with the proper equipment and experienced personnel.

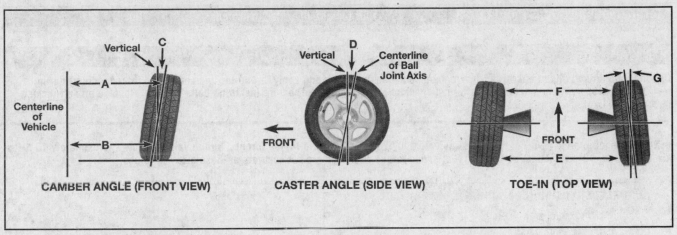

**24.1 Wheel alignment details:**

*A minus B = C (degrees camber)*          *D = degrees caster*          *E minus F = toe-in (measured in inches)*

## Specifications

### Front wheel bearing

Wheel bearing play adjustment          0.0004 to 0.001 inch (0.01 to 0.02 mm)

| Torque specifications | Ft-lbs (unless otherwise indicated) | Nm |
|---|---|---|

**※ WARNING:**

Clean all mounting bolts of old thread-locking compound as necessary and apply thread-locking compound (blue/medium) during installation. Clean threaded holes with a thread chasing tool, or equivalent, before installing bolts in them. Replace all self-locking nuts as equipped.

➡Note: One foot-pound (ft-lb) of torque is equivalent to 12 inch-pounds (in-lbs) of torque. Torque values below approximately 15 ft-lbs are expressed in inch-pounds, since most foot-pound torque wrenches are not accurate at these smaller values.

### Front suspension

| | | |
|---|---|---|
| Clamping hub nut lock bolt | 96 in-lbs | 11 |
| Cross strut | | |
| Strut-to-subframe nut | 110 | 150 |
| Balljoint-to-steering knuckle nut | 59 | 80 |

| Torque specifications (continued) | Ft-lbs (unless otherwise indicated) | Nm |
|---|---|---|

**✳✳ WARNING:**

Clean all mounting bolts of old thread-locking compound as necessary and apply thread-locking compound (blue/medium) during installation. Clean thrcaded holes with a thread chasing tool, or equivalent, before installing bolts in them. Replace all self-locking nuts as equipped.

➡ Note: One foot-pound (ft-lb) of torque is equivalent to 12 inch-pounds (in-lbs) of torque. Torque values below approximately 15 ft-lbs are expressed in inch-pounds, since most foot-pound torque wrenches are not accurate at these smaller values.

### Front suspension (continued)

| | Ft-lbs | Nm |
|---|---|---|
| Lower control arm | | |
|     Arm-to-subframe nut | 81 | 110 |
|     Balljoint-to-steering knuckle nut | | |
|         Step 1 | 22 | 30 |
|         Step 2 | Tighten an additional 120-degrees | |
| Stabilizer bar | | |
|     Link nuts | 44 | 60 |
|     Bracket bolts | 30 | 40 |
| Strut assembly | | |
|     Rear wheel drive models | | |
|         Upper mounting nut | 44 | 60 |
|         Lower mounting nut/bolt (top of knuckle) | | |
|             Step 1 | 89 | 120 |
|             Step 2 | Tighten an additional 90-degrees | |
|         Bottom mounting bolts | 81 | 110 |
|     4MATIC (all-wheel drive) models | | |
|         Upper mounting bolts | 37 | 50 |
|         Lower mounting nut/bolt | | |
|             Step 1 | 74 | 100 |
|             Step 2 | Tighten an additional 80-degrees | |
| Subframe mounting bolts | 74 | 100 |
| Torque strut | | |
|     Strut-to-subframe nut | 110 | 150 |
|     Balljoint-to-steering knuckle nut | 59 | 80 |

### Rear suspension

| | Ft-lbs | Nm |
|---|---|---|
| Camber strut | | |
|     Strut-to-subframe nut/bolt | 52 | 70 |
|     Strut-to-knuckle nut/bolt | 52 | 70 |
| Radius rod | | |
|     Rod-to-subframe nut/bolt | 52 | 70 |
|     Rod-to-knuckle nut/bolt | 52 | 70 |
| Shock absorber | | |
|     Upper mounting nut | 22 | 30 |
|     Lower mounting nut/bolt | 41 | 55 |
| Spring link | | |
|     Link-to-subframe nut/bolt | 52 | 70 |
|     Link-to-knuckle nut/bolt | 89 | 120 |

| Torque specifications | Ft-lbs (unless otherwise indicated) | Nm |
|---|---|---|
| **Rear suspension (continued)** | | |
| Stabilizer bar | | |
|     Link nut/bolt-to-stabilizer bar | 30 | 40 |
|     Link bolt-to-knuckle | 30 | 40 |
|     Bracket bolts | 22 | 30 |
| Subframe mounting bolts | | |
|     Step 1 | 30 | 40 |
|     Step 2 | Tighten an additional 90-degrees | |
| Thrust arm | | |
|     Arm-to-subframe nut/bolt | 52 | 70 |
|     Arm-to-knuckle nut/bolt | 52 | 70 |
| Track rod | | |
|     Rod-to-subframe nut/bolt | 52 | 70 |
|     Rod-to-knuckle nut/bolt | 22 | 30 |
| **Steering** | | |
| Airbag module-to-steering wheel bolts | 72 in-lbs | 8 |
| Lower steering shaft-to-coupler bolt | 22 | 30 |
| Power steering pump mounting bolts | 180 in-lbs | 20 |
| Pressure line fitting (banjo-type) bolt | 33 | 45 |
| Steering wheel retaining bolt | 59 | 80 |
| Steering column mounting bolts | 180 in-lbs | 20 |
| Steering shaft coupler-to-steering gear input shaft | | |
|     Rear wheel drive | | |
|         Nut/bolt | 10 | 25 |
|     4MATIC | | |
|         Pinch bolt | 18 | 25 |
| Steering gear mounting bolts | | |
|     Rear wheel drive | 63 | 85 |
|     4MATIC | | |
|         Step 1 | 37 | 50 |
|         Step 2 | Tighten an additional 60-degrees | |
| Tie-rod-to-steering knuckle (ballstud) nut | 52 | 70 |
| Wheel bolts | See Chapter 1 | |

**Notes**

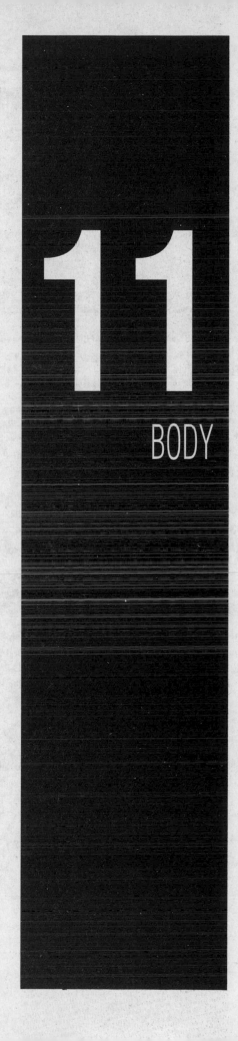

**11**

BODY

## 1  General information

The Mercedes C-class models covered by this manual feature unibody construction, in which the major body components, floor pan and front and rear frame side rails are welded together to create a rigid structure which supports the remaining body components, drivetrain, front and rear suspension and other components.

Certain components are particularly vulnerable to accident damage and can be unbolted and repaired or replaced. Among these parts are the body moldings, bumpers, front fenders, doors, the hood and trunk lid. Only general body maintenance practices and body panel repair procedures within the scope of the do-it-yourselfer are included in this Chapter.

Although all models are very similar, some procedures may differ somewhat from one body to another.

## 2  Body - maintenance

1  The condition of your vehicle's body is very important, because the resale value depends a great deal on it. It's much more difficult to repair a neglected or damaged body than it is to repair mechanical components. The hidden areas of the body, such as the wheel wells, the frame and the engine compartment, are equally important, although they don't require as frequent attention as the rest of the body.

2  Once a year, or every 12,000 miles, it's a good idea to have the underside of the body steam cleaned. All traces of dirt and oil will be removed and the area can then be inspected carefully for rust, damaged brake lines, frayed electrical wires, damaged cables and other problems.

3  At the same time, clean the engine and the engine compartment with a steam cleaner or water-soluble degreaser.

4  The wheel wells should be given close attention, since undercoating can peel away and stones and dirt thrown up by the tires can cause the paint to chip and flake, allowing rust to set in. If rust is found, clean down to the bare metal and apply an anti-rust paint.

5  The body should be washed about once a week. Wet the vehicle thoroughly to soften the dirt, then wash it down with a soft sponge and plenty of clean soapy water. If the surplus dirt is not washed off very carefully, it can wear down the paint.

6  Spots of tar or asphalt thrown up from the road should be removed with a cloth soaked in solvent.

7  Once every six months, wax the body and chrome trim. If a chrome cleaner is used to remove rust from any of the vehicle's plated parts, remember that the cleaner also removes part of the chrome, so use it sparingly. After cleaning chrome trim, apply paste wax to preserve it.

## 3  Vinyl trim - maintenance

Don't clean vinyl trim with detergents, caustic soap or petroleum-based cleaners. Plain soap and water works just fine, with a soft brush to clean dirt that may be ingrained. Wash the vinyl as frequently as the rest of the vehicle. After cleaning, application of a high-quality rubber and vinyl protectant will help prevent oxidation and cracks. The protectant can also be applied to weatherstripping, vacuum lines and rubber hoses, which often fail as a result of chemical degradation, and to the tires.

## 4  Upholstery and carpets - maintenance

1  Every three months, remove the floormats and clean the interior of the vehicle (more frequently if necessary). Use a stiff whiskbroom to brush the carpeting and loosen dirt and dust, then vacuum the upholstery and carpets thoroughly, especially along seams and crevices.

2  Dirt and stains can be removed from carpeting with basic household or automotive carpet shampoos available in spray cans. Follow the directions and vacuum again, then use a stiff brush to bring back the nap of the carpet.

3  Most interiors have cloth or vinyl upholstery, either of which can be cleaned and maintained with a number of material-specific cleaners or shampoos available in auto supply stores. Follow the directions on the product for usage, and always spot-test any upholstery cleaner on an inconspicuous area (bottom edge of a backseat cushion) to ensure that it doesn't cause a color shift in the material.

4  After cleaning, vinyl upholstery should be treated with a protectant.

➡**Note: Make sure the protectant container indicates the product can be used on seats - some products may make a seat too slippery.**

✳✳ **CAUTION:**

**Do not use protectant on vinyl-covered steering wheels.**

5   Leather upholstery requires special care. It should be cleaned regularly with saddlesoap or leather cleaner. Never use alcohol, gasoline, water, nail polish remover or thinner to clean leather upholstery.

6   After cleaning, regularly treat leather upholstery with a leather conditioner, rubbed in with a soft cotton cloth. Never use car wax on leather upholstery.

7   In areas where the interior of the vehicle is subject to bright sunlight, cover leather seating areas of the seats with a sheet if the vehicle is to be left out for any length of time.

## 5   Body repair - minor damage

## REPAIR OF SCRATCHES

1   If the scratch is superficial and does not penetrate to the metal of the body, repair is very simple. Lightly rub the scratched area with a fine rubbing compound to remove loose paint and built-up wax. Rinse the area with clean water.

2   Apply touch-up paint to the scratch, using a small brush. Continue to apply thin layers of paint until the surface of the paint in the scratch is level with the surrounding paint. Allow the new paint at least two weeks to harden, then blend it into the surrounding paint by rubbing with a very fine rubbing compound. Finally, apply a coat of wax to the scratch area.

3   If the scratch has penetrated the paint and exposed the metal of the body, causing the metal to rust, a different repair technique is required. Remove all loose rust from the bottom of the scratch with a pocket knife, then apply rust inhibiting paint to prevent the formation of rust in the future. Using a rubber or nylon applicator, coat the scratched area with glaze-type filler. If required, the filler can be mixed with thinner to provide a very thin paste, which is ideal for filling narrow scratches. Before the glaze filler in the scratch hardens, wrap a piece of smooth cotton cloth around the tip of a finger. Dip the cloth in thinner and then quickly wipe it along the surface of the scratch. This will ensure that the surface of the filler is slightly hollow. The scratch can now be painted over as described earlier in this Section.

## REPAIR OF DENTS

▶ **See photo sequence**

4   When repairing dents, the first job is to pull the dent out until the affected area is as close as possible to its original shape. There is no point in trying to restore the original shape completely as the metal in the damaged area will have stretched on impact and cannot be restored to its original contours. It is better to bring the level of the dent up to a point which is about 1/8-inch below the level of the surrounding metal. In cases where the dent is very shallow, it is not worth trying to pull it out at all.

5   If the back side of the dent is accessible, it can be hammered out gently from behind using a soft-face hammer. While doing this, hold a block of wood firmly against the opposite side of the metal to absorb the hammer blows and prevent the metal from being stretched.

6   If the dent is in a section of the body which has double layers, or some other factor makes it inaccessible from behind, a different technique is required. Drill several small holes through the metal inside the damaged area, particularly in the deeper sections. Screw long, self tapping screws into the holes just enough for them to get a good grip in the metal. Now the dent can be pulled out by pulling on the protruding heads of the screws with locking pliers.

7   The next stage of repair is the removal of paint from the damaged area and from an inch or so of the surrounding metal. This is easily done with a wire brush or sanding disk in a drill motor, although it can be done just as effectively by hand with sandpaper. To complete the preparation for filling, score the surface of the bare metal with a screwdriver or the tang of a file or drill small holes in the affected area. This will provide a good grip for the filler material. To complete the repair, see the Section on Filling and painting.

## REPAIR OF RUST HOLES OR GASHES

8   Remove all paint from the affected area and from an inch or so of the surrounding metal using a sanding disk or wire brush mounted in a drill motor. If these are not available, a few sheets of sandpaper will do the job just as effectively.

9   With the paint removed, you will be able to determine the severity of the corrosion and decide whether to replace the whole panel, if possible, or repair the affected area. New body panels are not as expensive as most people think and it is often quicker to install a new panel than to repair large areas of rust.

10   Remove all trim pieces from the affected area except those which will act as a guide to the original shape of the damaged body, such as headlight shells, etc. Using metal snips or a hacksaw blade, remove all loose metal and any other metal that is badly affected by rust. Hammer the edges of the hole on the inside to create a slight depression for the filler material.

11   Wire brush the affected area to remove the powdery rust from the surface of the metal. If the back of the rusted area is accessible, treat it with rust inhibiting paint.

12   Before filling is done, block the hole in some way. This can be done with sheet metal riveted or screwed into place, or by stuffing the hole with wire mesh.

13   Once the hole is blocked off, the affected area can be filled and painted. See the following subsection on Filling and painting.

## FILLING AND PAINTING

14   Many types of body fillers are available, but generally speaking, body repair kits which contain filler paste and a tube of resin hardener are best for this type of repair work. A wide, flexible plastic or nylon applicator will be necessary for imparting a smooth and contoured finish to the surface of the filler material. Mix up a small amount of filler on a clean piece of wood or cardboard (use the hardener sparingly). Follow the manufacturer's instructions on the package, otherwise the filler will set incorrectly.

15   Using the applicator, apply the filler paste to the prepared area. Draw the applicator across the surface of the filler to achieve the desired contour and to level the filler surface. As soon as a contour that

These photos illustrate a method of repairing simple dents. They are intended to supplement Body repair - mlnor damage in this Chapter and should not be used as the sole instructions for body repair on these vehicles.

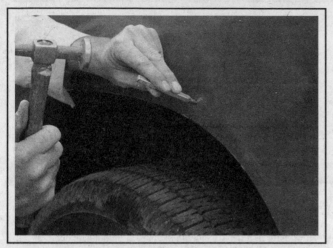

1  If you can't access the backside of the body panel to hammer out the dent, pull it out with a slide-hammer-type dent puller. In the deepest portion of the dent or along the crease line, drill or punch hole(s) at least one inch apart . . .

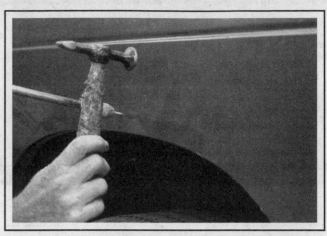

2  . . . then screw the slide-hammer into the hole and operate it. Tap with a hammer near the edge of the dent to help 'pop' the metal back to its original shape. When you're finished, the dent area should be close to its original contour and about 1/8-inch below the surface of the surrounding metal

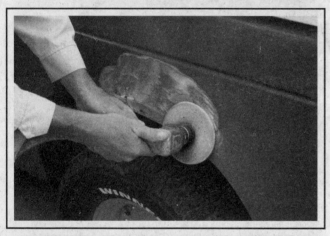

3  Using coarse-grit sandpaper, remove the paint down to the bare metal. Hand sanding works fine, but the disc sander shown here makes the job faster. Use finer (about 320-grit) sandpaper to feather-edge the paint at least one inch around the dent area

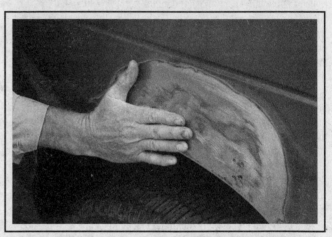

4  When the paint is removed, touch will probably be more helpful than sight for telling if the metal is straight. Hammer down the high spots or raise the low spots as necessary. Clean the repair area with wax/silicone remover

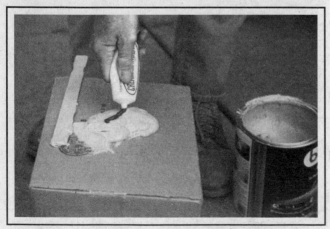

5  Following label instructions, mix up a batch of plastic filler and hardener. The ratio of filler to hardener is critical, and, if you mix it incorrectly, it will either not cure properly or cure too quickly (you won't have time to file and sand it into shape)

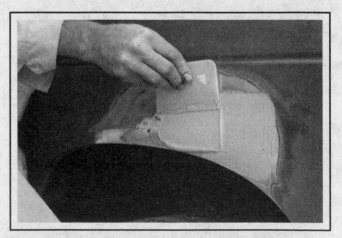

6  Working quickly so the filler doesn't harden, use a plastic applicator to press the body filler firmly into the metal, assuring it bonds completely. Work the filler until it matches the original contour and is slightly above the surrounding metal

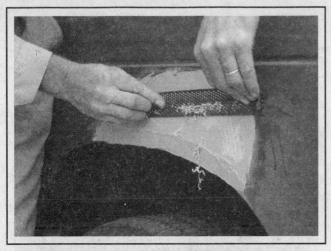

7  Let the filler harden until you can just dent it with your fingernail. Use a body file or Surform tool (shown here) to rough-shape the filler

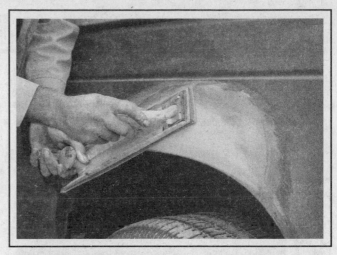

8  Use coarse-grit sandpaper and a sanding board or block to work the filler down until it's smooth and even. Work down to finer grits of sandpaper - always using a board or block - ending up with 360 or 400 grit

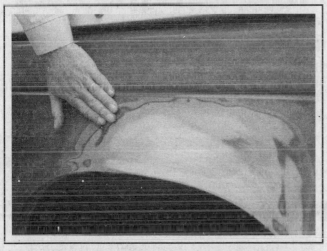

9  You shouldn't be able to feel any ridge at the transition from the filler to the bare metal or from the bare metal to the old paint. As soon as the repair is flat and uniform, remove the dust and mask off the adjacent panels or trim pieces

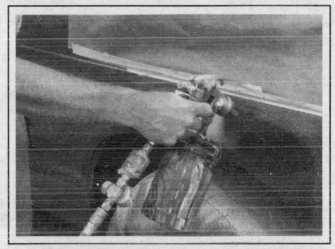

10  Apply several layers of primer to the area. Don't spray the primer on too heavy, so it sags or runs, and make sure each coat is dry before you spray on the next one. A professional-type spray gun is being used here, but aerosol spray primer is available inexpensively from auto parts stores

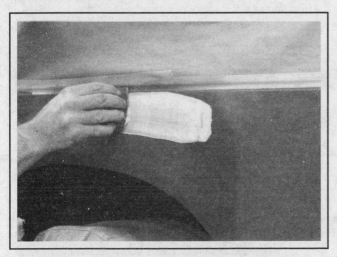

11  The primer will help reveal imperfections or scratches. Fill these with glazing compound. Follow the label instructions and sand it with 360 or 400-grit sandpaper until it's smooth. Repeat the glazing, sanding and respraying until the primer reveals a perfectly smooth surface

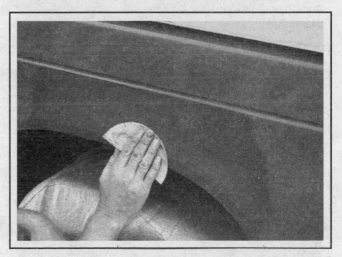

12  Finish sand the primer with very fine sandpaper (400 or 600-grit) to remove the primer overspray. Clean the area with water and allow it to dry. Use a tack rag to remove any dust, then apply the finish coat. Don't attempt to rub out or wax the repair area until the paint has dried completely (at least two weeks)

approximates the original one is achieved, stop working the paste. If you continue, the paste will begin to stick to the applicator. Continue to add thin layers of paste at 20-minute intervals until the level of the filler is just above the surrounding metal.

16 Once the filler has hardened, the excess can be removed with a body file. From then on, progressively finer grades of sandpaper should be used, starting with a 180-grit paper and finishing with 600-grit wet-or-dry paper. Always wrap the sandpaper around a flat rubber or wooden block, otherwise the surface of the filler will not be completely flat. During the sanding of the filler surface, the wet-or-dry paper should be periodically rinsed in water. This will ensure that a very smooth finish is produced in the final stage.

17 At this point, the repair area should be surrounded by a ring of bare metal, which in turn should be encircled by the finely feathered edge of good paint. Rinse the repair area with clean water until all of the dust produced by the sanding operation is gone.

18 Spray the entire area with a light coat of primer. This will reveal any imperfections in the surface of the filler. Repair the imperfections with fresh filler paste or glaze filler and once more smooth the surface with sandpaper. Repeat this spray-and-repair procedure until you are satisfied that the surface of the filler and the feathered edge of the paint are perfect. Rinse the area with clean water and allow it to dry completely.

19 The repair area is now ready for painting. Spray painting must be carried out in a warm, dry, windless and dust free atmosphere. These conditions can be created if you have access to a large indoor work area, but if you are forced to work in the open, you will have to pick the day very carefully. If you are working indoors, dousing the floor in the work area with water will help settle the dust which would otherwise be in the air. If the repair area is confined to one body panel, mask off the surrounding panels. This will help minimize the effects of a slight mismatch in paint color. Trim pieces such as chrome strips, door handles, etc., will also need to be masked off or removed. Use masking tape and several thickness of newspaper for the masking operations.

20 Before spraying, shake the paint can thoroughly, then spray a test area until the spray painting technique is mastered. Cover the repair area with a thick coat of primer. The thickness should be built up using several thin layers of primer rather than one thick one. Using 600-grit wet-or-dry sandpaper, rub down the surface of the primer until it is very smooth. While doing this, the work area should be thoroughly rinsed with water and the wet-or-dry sandpaper periodically rinsed as well. Allow the primer to dry before spraying additional coats.

21 Spray on the top coat, again building up the thickness by using several thin layers of paint. Begin spraying in the center of the repair area and then, using a circular motion, work out until the whole repair area and about two inches of the surrounding original paint is covered. Remove all masking material 10 to 15 minutes after spraying on the final coat of paint. Allow the new paint at least two weeks to harden, then use a very fine rubbing compound to blend the edges of the new paint into the existing paint. Finally, apply a coat of wax.

## 6  Body repair - major damage

1  Major damage must be repaired by an auto body shop specifically equipped to perform body and frame repairs. These shops have the specialized equipment required to do the job properly.

2  If the damage is extensive, the body must be checked for proper alignment or the vehicle's handling characteristics may be adversely affected and other components may wear at an accelerated rate.

3  Due to the fact that all of the major body components (hood, fenders, etc.) are separate and replaceable units, any seriously damaged components should be replaced rather than repaired. Sometimes the components can be found in a wrecking yard that specializes in used vehicle components, often at considerable savings over the cost of new parts.

## 7  Hinges and locks - maintenance

Once every 3000 miles, or every three months, the hinges and latch assemblies on the doors, hood and trunk should be given a few drops of light oil or lock lubricant. The door latch strikers should also be lubricated with a thin coat of grease to reduce wear and ensure free movement. Lubricate the door and trunk locks with spray-on graphite lubricant.

## 8  Windshield and fixed glass - replacement

Replacement of the windshield and fixed glass requires the use of special fast-setting adhesive/caulk materials and some specialized tools and techniques. These operations should be left to a dealer service department or a shop specializing in glass work.

## 9   Hood - removal, installation and adjustment

### REMOVAL AND INSTALLATION

▶ **Refer to illustrations 9.2 and 9.4**

➡**Note: The hood is somewhat awkward to remove and install; at least two people should perform this procedure.**

1   Open the hood, then place blankets or pads over the fenders and cowl area of the body. This will protect the body and paint as the hood is lifted off.

2   Make marks or scribe a line around the hood hinge to ensure proper alignment during installation (see illustration).

3   Disconnect any cables or wires that will interfere with removal.

4   Support one side of the hood while an assistant supports the other. Pry open the clip on one end of each hood support strut and remove the struts (see illustration). Remove the hinge-to-hood bolts and lift off the hood.

5   Installation is the reverse of removal. Align the hinge bolts with the marks made in Step 2.

### ADJUSTMENT

▶ **Refer to illustration 9.9**

6   Fore-and-aft and side-to-side adjustment of the hood is done by moving the hood after loosening the hinge bolts or nuts.

7   Scribe a line around the entire hinge plate so you can determine the amount of movement.

8   Loosen the bolts or nuts and move the hood into correct alignment. Move it only a little at a time. Tighten the hinge bolts and carefully lower the hood to check the position.

9   Adjust the hood bumpers so the hood is flush with the fenders when closed (see illustration).

10  The hood latch hinges should be periodically lubricated with white lithium-base grease to prevent sticking and wear.

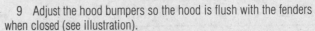
❊❊ **WARNING:**

**Do not lubricate the hood latches or safety catches. If they stick, replace them.**

**9.2  Before removing the hood, draw a mark around each hinge**

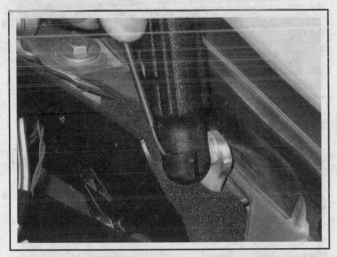

**9.4  Use a small screwdriver to pry the clip out of its locking groove, then detach the end of the strut**

**9.9  Adjust the hood closing height by turning the hood bumpers in or out**

**10  Hood release latches, cable and safety catch - removal and installation**

## LATCHES

▶ **Refer to illustrations 10.2 and 10.4**

1  Open the hood to the normal open position.

2  Draw a mark around both lower latches to aid alignment when installing, then detach the latch retaining bolts from the radiator support (see illustration) and remove the latches. If you're working on the passenger-side latch, disconnect its electrical connector.

3  Disengage the hood release cable from the latches.

4  To remove the safety catch, mark its position on the hood and remove the mounting bolts (see illustration).

5  Installation is the reverse of the removal procedure.

## CABLE

▶ **Refer to illustrations 10.9 and 10.10**

6  Disconnect the hood release cable from the latch assembly as described above.

7  Remove the lower left cover from the instrument panel (see Section 24).

8  Working in the left rear corner of the engine compartment, detach the fuse and relay box from the vehicle and move it out of the way without detaching any electrical connectors.

9  Attach a piece of stiff wire to the end of the cable, trace the cable back to the firewall and detach all cable retaining clips. Note that the cable is made in two sections with a connector between them at the left front corner of the engine compartment (see illustration).

10  Working in the passenger compartment, disconnect the cable from the hood release lever (see illustration).

11  Pull the old cable into the passenger compartment until you can see the stiff wire that you attached to the cable. A grommet insulates the cable hole in the firewall from the elements. The new cable should have a new grommet, so you can remove and discard the old cable grommet. Make sure the new grommet is already on the new cable (if not, slip the old grommet onto the new cable), then detach the old cable from the wire and attach the new cable to the wire.

12  Working from the engine compartment side of the firewall, pull the wire through the cable hole in the firewall.

13  Installation is otherwise the reverse of the removal. Working from the passenger compartment side, push the grommet into place with your fingers. Make sure it's fully seated in the hole in the firewall.

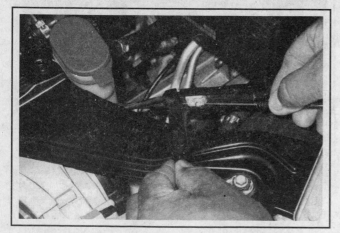

**10.2  Mark the latch position and remove the bolts**

**10.4  Mark the position of the safety catch and remove its bolts**

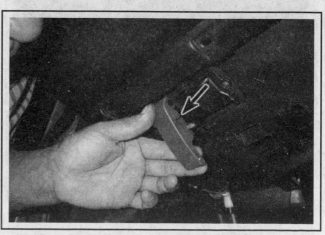

**10.9  Flip open the connector and separate the cables**

**10.10  Disconnect the cable from the slot in the hood release lever**

## 11 Bumper covers - removal and installation

### FRONT

▶ **Refer to illustrations 11.2a, 11.2b, 11.3 and 11.5**

1   Remove the screws from the forward section of the front fender liner (see Section 12).

2   Working inside the fender, unbolt the bumper cover mount and the connecting bracket that secures the bumper cover to the front fender (see illustration). Take the connecting bracket off (see illustration).

3   Remove the sensor for the outside temperature indicator (see illustration). Disconnect the fog lamp electrical connectors (see Chapter 12).

4   Remove the side marker lamp sockets from the lamps.

5   Remove the license plate mounting plate (see illustration). Remove the bumper cover mounting bolts from the front and top and remove the bumper cover from the vehicle.

6   Installation is the reverse of the removal steps.

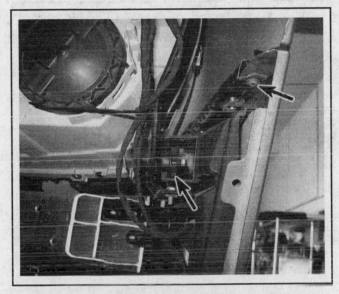

11.2a  Unbolt the bumper bracket (upper arrow) and note how the bumper fits on the adjuster (lower arrow) . . .

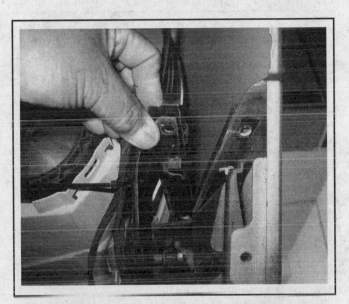

11.2b  . . . pivot the bracket sideways, away from the bumper and fender, and take it out

11.3  Disconnect the outside temperature sensor electrical connector, then unclip the sensor and remove it

11.5  Remove the license plate holder and bumper cover bolts

### REAR

▶ **Refer to illustrations 11.7a, 11.7b, 11.8, 11.12a, 11.12b and 11.12c**

7  Open the trunk. Remove the clips and screws that secure the side and rear trim panels and floor panel (see illustrations).

8  Outside the vehicle, remove the clips that secure the inner fender panel to the bumper (see illustration).

9  If the vehicle is equipped with Parktronic, disconnect the system electrical connector from the rear bumper.

10  Remove the rear exhaust pipe mounting screw.

11  Remove the taillight housing (see Chapter 12).

12  Detach the clips on each side of the bumper (see illustrations). Remove the mounting screw from each side of the bumper (see illustration).

13  With the help of an assistant, pull the bumper out and away from the vehicle.

14  Installation is the reverse of removal. Be sure to align the mounting brackets on each end of the bumper with the guide on the vehicle body (see illustration 11.12c).

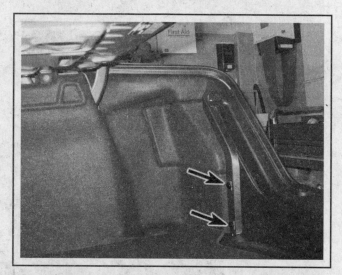

**11.7a  Inside the trunk, remove the trim cover fasteners at the rear of the trunk . . .**

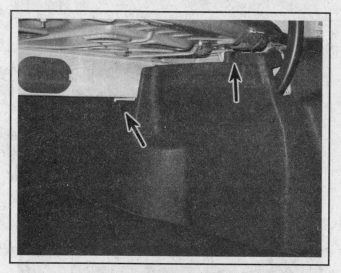

**11.7b  . . . in the corners and on the sides**

**11.8  Remove the clips that secure each inner rear fender panel to the bumper**

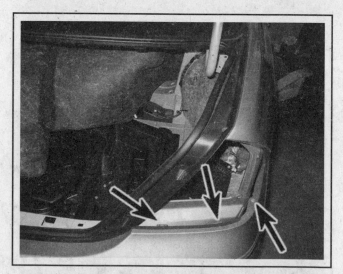

**11.12a  Detach the mounting clips and remove the screw from each side of the bumper on the top . . .**

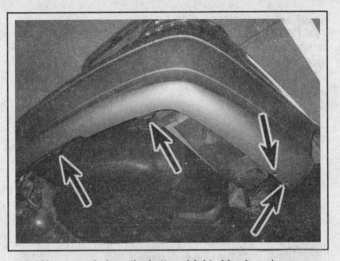

11.12b . . . and along the bottom (right side shown)

11.12c Remove the screw (upper arrow) and when the bumper cover is completely detached, slide it off the guide (lower arrow)

## 12  Front fender - removal and installation

▶ Refer to illustrations 12.3a, 12.3b, 12.5, 12.7, 12.8a and 12.8b

1    Open the hood to the full upright position

2    Loosen the front wheel lug nuts, raise the vehicle and support it securely on jackstands. Remove the wheel.

3    Remove the inner fender splash shield from the wheel housing (see illustrations).

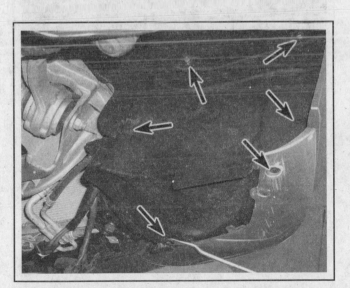

12.3a  Remove the forward section of the inner fender splash shield . . .

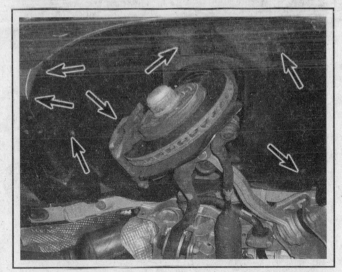

12.3b  . . . and the main section (not all fasteners visible in this photo)

4   Remove the connecting bracket bolt (see illustrations 11.2a and 11.2b). Detach the bracket and take it out.

5   Remove the underbody paneling bolts (see illustration).

6   Remove the trim molding from the door sill (see Section 14).

7   Disengage the clips and move the underbody panel enough to expose the fender nuts (see illustration). Remove the nuts.

8   Remove the fender mounting bolts along the upper edge and at the upper rear corner (see illustrations).

9   Detach the fender. It's a good idea to have an assistant support the fender while it's being moved away from the vehicle to prevent damage to the surrounding body panels.

10  Installation is the reverse of removal. If you're installing a new fender, remove the plastic liner so you can install a new gasket.

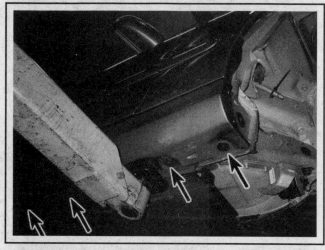

**12.5  Remove the panel bolts along the underbody (not all bolts are visible in photo)**

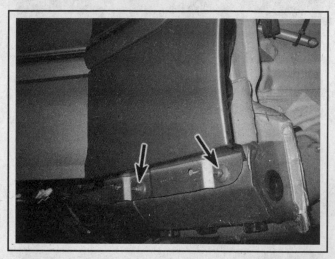

**12.7  Remove the nuts at the lower rear of the fender**

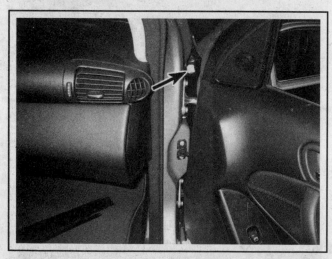

**12.8a  Open the door and remove the fender bolt at the upper rear corner . . .**

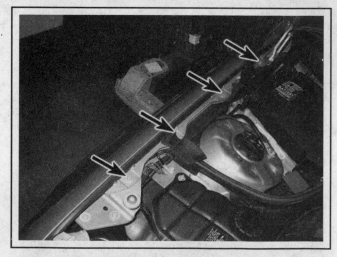

**12.8b  . . . and along the upper edge of the fender**

## 13  Door trim panels - removal and installation

▶ Refer to illustrations 13.1, 13.2, 13.3, 13.4, 13.6, 13.7a, 13.7b and 13.11

### ❊❊ WARNING:

**Models covered by this manual are equipped with a Supplemental Restraint System (SRS), more commonly known as airbags. Always disable the airbag system before working in the vicinity of any airbag system component to avoid the possibility of accidental deployment of the airbag, which could cause personal injury (see Chapter 12).**

1  Pry the upper end of the grab handle trim, then the lower end, away from the door using a door panel removal tool (see illustration).
2  Remove the SRS (airbag) emblem from the door (see illustration).
3  Remove the screws from the door panel (two securing the armrest and one behind the SRS emblem) (see illustration).
4  Separate the foot lamp from the door and disconnect its electrical connector (see illustration).

5  Remove the radio speaker from the door forward of the window (if equipped) (see Chapter 12).
6  Unscrew the door latch trim with a Torx bit (see illustration).

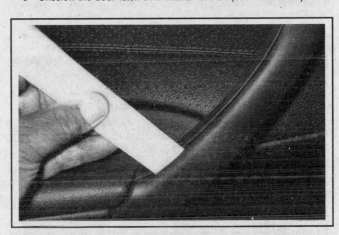

**13.1  Pry the grab handle trim away from the door with a trim stick**

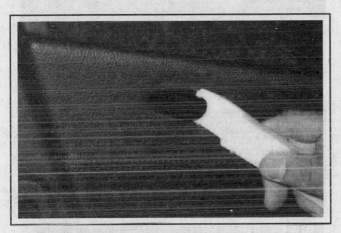

**13.2  Pry the SRS emblem out of the door panel**

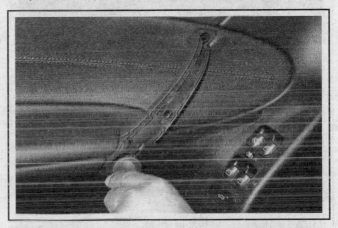

**13.3  Remove the door panel screws from the armrest and from behind the SRS emblem**

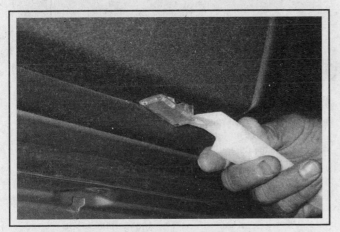

**13.4  Take out the foot lamp and unplug its connector**

**13.6  Unscrew the door latch trim**

7   Remove the door trim panel using a door panel removal tool (see illustration). Lift the panel free of the door (see illustration).

8   Unlatch the actuating cable from the door handle lever. Disconnect the electrical connectors that attach the trim panel to components inside the door.

9   Once the panel is fully detached, carefully remove it from the door.

10   Carefully pry the power window switch trim piece out of the door panel using a door panel removal tool. Remove the switch screws (if equipped) and remove the switch from the trim panel. On models with the seat adjustment switch mounted in the door panel, release the latches and take the seat adjustment switch out of the panel.

11   If necessary for access to other components, remove the watershield from the door. This requires drilling out the pop rivets to remove the handle mounting bracket (see illustration).

12   Before installing the door trim panel, inspect the condition of all clips and reinstall any clips which may have fallen out.

13   The remainder of installation is the reverse of the removal procedure. If you removed the handle mounting bracket, secure it with new pop rivets.

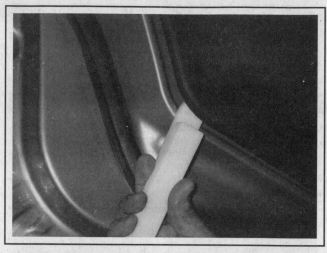

**13.7a   Start from the bottom of the trim panel and work around the perimeter until all the fasteners have been released from the door . . .**

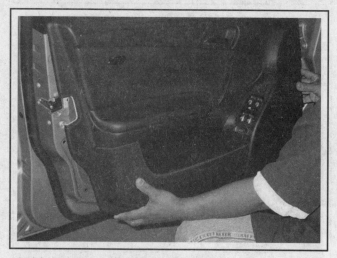

**13.7b   . . . then lift the trim panel off**

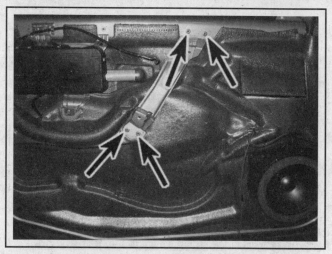

**13.11   If the watershield is to be removed, drill out the pop rivets to remove the handle mounting bracket**

## 14   Door - removal and installation

◆ **Refer to illustrations 14.8a and 14.8b**

➡Note: The door is heavy and somewhat awkward to remove and install - at least two people should perform this procedure.

1   Open the window. Open the door all the way and support it on jacks or blocks covered with rags to prevent damaging the paint.

2   Remove the door trim panel as described in Section 13.

3   Remove the door sill molding.

4   Remove the edge trim from the A-pillar cover (front door) or B-pillar cover (rear door). Remove the screw, release the clip at the cover cap and take the cover out.

5   Unplug all electrical connections at the A-pillar.

➡Note: It is a good idea to label all connections to aid the reassembly process.

6   Free the protective conduit from its clips using a door panel removal tool, then pull the door wiring harness through the A-pillar.

7   Mark around the door hinges with a pen or a scribe to facilitate

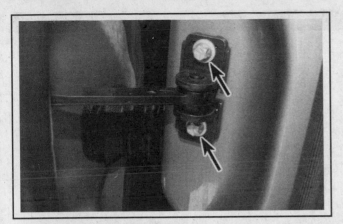

**14.8a Remove the door stop bolts**

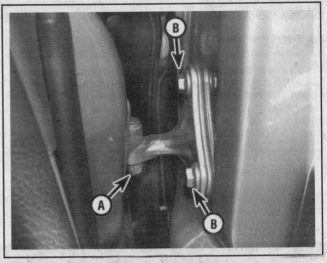

**14.8b Remove the nuts (A) from the door hinge pivot bolts and lift the door off - unbolt the hinge from the pillar if necessary (B) (front door upper hinge shown, others similar)**

realignment during reassembly.

8　With an assistant holding the door, remove the door stop bolts and the nut from the hinge pivot bolt and lift off the door (see illustrations).

9　If necessary, unbolt the hinges from the door pillar and take them off.

10　Installation is the reverse of removal.

## 15  Door handles, key lock cylinder and latch - removal and installation

### ✳✳ WARNING:

**Models covered by this manual are equipped with a Supplemental Restraint System (SRS), more commonly known as airbags. Always disable the airbag system before working in the vicinity of any airbag system component to avoid the possibility of accidental deployment of the airbag, which could cause personal injury (see Chapter 12).**

1　Raise the window, then remove the door trim panel and watershield (see Section 13). Remove the radio speaker (just the left-hand speaker on models with dual door speakers (see Chapter 12).

2　Remove the door airbag (see Chapter 12).

### KEY LOCK CYLINDER

3　Free the weatherstripping from its clips in the area around the lock mechanism.

4　Remove the lock cylinder retaining screw from the handle. Pull the lock cylinder partway out, disengage it from the latch, then remove the lock cylinder from the handle.

5　Installation is the reverse of removal.

### OUTSIDE HANDLE

6　Remove the lock cylinder as described above.

7　Slide the door handle rearward to disengage it from the bearing bracket, then pull it straight out of the holes.

8　Installation is the reverse of removal.

### DOOR LATCH

**✦ Refer to illustration 15.10**

9　Drill out the rivets that secure the rear power window lift rail and detach it.

10　Disconnect the door latch cable and free it from its retainers. Remove the three screws securing the latch to the door, then remove the latch assembly from the door (see illustration).

11　Disconnect the electrical connectors from the latch mechanism.

12　Installation is the reverse of removal.

**15.10 Remove the latch retaining screws from the end of the door**

## 16 Door window glass - removal and installation

### ※※ WARNING:

Models covered by this manual are equipped with a Supplemental Restraint System (SRS), more commonly known as airbags. Always disable the airbag system before working in the vicinity of any airbag system component to avoid the possibility of accidental deployment of the airbag, which could cause personal injury (see Chapter 12).

1  Lower the window glass about halfway into the door.

2  Remove the window inside sealing strip.
3  Remove the door trim panel (see Section 13).
4  Remove the door speaker(s) (see Chapter 12).
5  Carefully detach the lower edge of the watershield from the door (see Section 13). Fold it up and secure it out of the way.
6  Remove the window glass retainer bolts.
7  Remove the glass by carefully pulling it up and out.
8  Installation is the reverse of removal. Raise the window all the way and hold the switch in the UP position for at least 1/2 second to adjust the automatic shut-off.

## 17 Door window glass regulator and motor - removal and installation

### ※※ WARNING:

Models covered by this manual are equipped with a Supplemental Restraint System (SRS), more commonly known as airbags. Always disable the airbag system before working in the vicinity of any airbag system component to avoid the possibility of accidental deployment of the airbag, which could cause personal injury (see Chapter 12).

1  Remove the door trim panel and the watershield (see Section 13).
2  Remove the door window glass (see Section 16).
3  Detach the window glass from the regulator.
4  Drill out the regulator rivets.
5  Detach the regulator from the door and pull it through the service hole in the door frame to remove it. Unplug the electrical connector from the window regulator motor.
6  Installation is the reverse of removal.

## 18 Outside mirrors - removal and installation

▶ Refer to illustration 18.2a and 18.2b

### ※※ WARNING:

Models covered by this manual are equipped with a Supplemental Restraint System (SRS), more commonly known as airbags. Always disable the airbag system before working in the vicinity of any airbag system component to avoid the possibility of accidental deployment of the airbag, which could cause personal injury (see Chapter 12).

1  Remove the door trim panel (see Section 13). If the watershield has a removable section behind the mirror, remove it. Otherwise, work the upper front corner of the watershield free of the door for access to the mirror retaining fasteners.
2  Unplug the mirror electrical connectors from the control unit, then remove the mirror retaining fasteners (see illustrations).
3  Detach the mirror from the vehicle.
4  Installation is the reverse of removal.

**18.2a  Unplug the mirror electrical connectors from the control unit in the door panel . . .**

**18.2b  . . . then fold the mirror back to expose the bolts and remove them**

## 19  Trunk lid or tailgate - removal and installation

### TRUNK LID (SEDAN)

▶ **Refer to illustrations 19.1a, 19.1b, 19.1c, 19.1d, 19.1e and 19.2**

➡**Note: The trunk lid is heavy and somewhat awkward to remove and install - at least two people should perform this procedure.**

1   Open the trunk lid and cover the edges of the trunk compartment with pads or cloths to protect the painted surfaces when the lid is removed. Remove the trim covers from the trunk hinges. Also remove the trunk lid trim panel (see illustrations).

2   Disconnect any cables or wire harness connectors attached to the trunk lid that would interfere with removal (see illustration).

3   Make alignment marks around the hinge mounting fasteners with a marking pen.

4   While an assistant supports the trunk lid, remove the lid-to-hinge fasteners on both sides and lift it off.

5   Installation is the reverse of removal.

➡**Note: When reinstalling the trunk lid, align the lid-to-hinge fasteners with the marks made during removal.**

### TAILGATE (STATION WAGON)

➡**Note: The tailgate is heavy and somewhat awkward to remove and install - at least two people should perform this procedure.**

6   Open the tailgate. Detach the headliner from the rear section of the vehicle roof and remove the trim panel from the tailgate.

7   Follow the tailgate wring harnesses to the electrical connectors and unplug them.

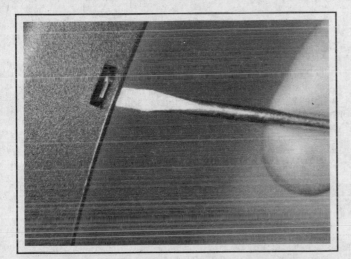

**19.1a  Release the clips that secure the retaining straps to the trunk lid hinges . . .**

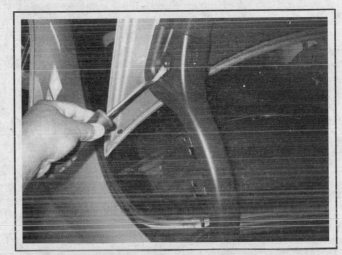

**19.1b  . . . pull out the center post on the pushpins and remove the hinge trim pieces**

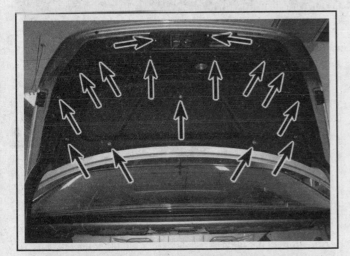

**19.1c  Remove the screws holding the latch trim and the pushpins that secure the trim panel to the inside of the trunk lid . . .**

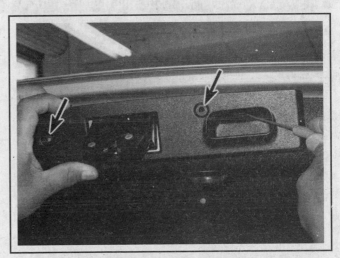

**19.1d  . . . release the clip inside the handhold and remove the screws . . .**

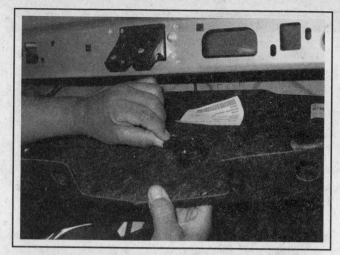

**19.1e . . . lower the trim away from the trunk lid and unplug the electrical connector from the emergency release button**

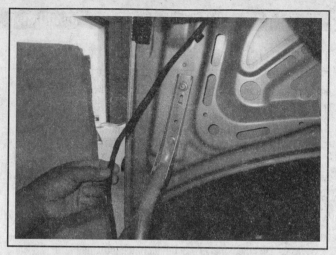

**19.2 Move the wiring harness out of the way, mark around the hinge bolts on each side and remove the bolts**

8  Open the retaining clip on the upper end of one of the tailgate struts, then pull the strut off the pivot ball. Disconnect the lower end of the strut in the same way. Detach the strut from one side of the door. Leave the other strut attached for now.

9  Make alignment marks around the hinge mounting fasteners with a marking pen.

10  Place padding, such as a sheet of cardboard, between the tailgate and the roof.

11  While an assistant supports the tailgate, detach the remaining strut. Remove the tailgate-to-hinge fasteners on both sides and lift it off.

12  Installation is the reverse of removal.

➡**Note: When reinstalling the tailgate, align the lid-to-hinge fasteners with the marks made during removal.**

## 20  Trunk lid latch - removal and installation

▶ **Refer to illustrations 20.2, 20.3 and 20.4**

1  Open the trunk. Remove the road warning reflector triangle (if equipped) from the underside of the trunk lid, then remove its storage bracket. Remove the trunk lid trim panel (see Section 19).

2  Disconnect the latch electrical connector (see illustration).

3  Remove the trunk lid latch retaining bolts, then remove the latch (see illustration).

4  To remove the pushbutton lock, remove its mounting bolts and unplug its electrical connectors (see illustration). Remove the lock cover, disconnect the cable and remove the lock.

5  Installation is the reverse of removal.

**20.2 Unplug the electrical connector from the trunk latch . . .**

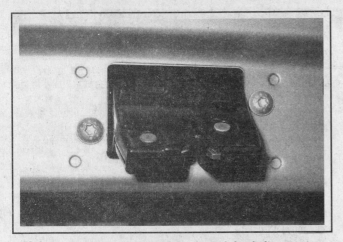

**20.3** . . . and remove the trunk latch retaining bolts

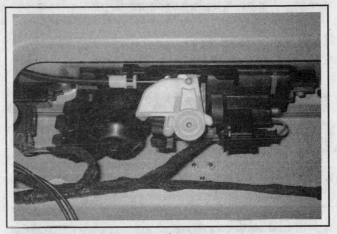

**20.4 Unplug the electrical connector and disconnect the latch cable from the lock solenoid**

## 21 Cowl cover - removal and installation

▶ **Refer to illustrations 21.3, 21.4a and 21.4b**

1    Open the hood, then depress the button on the driver's side support strut and raise the hood to the fully open position.

2    Remove the windshield wiper arms (see Chapter 12). Also peel off the weatherstripping from the cowl.

3    Remove the cowl screws (see illustration). Free any wiring harnesses that would interfere with removal.

4    Detach the windshield molding from each end of the cowl cover (see illustration), then remove the cowl cover from the vehicle (see illustration)

5    Installation is the reverse of removal.

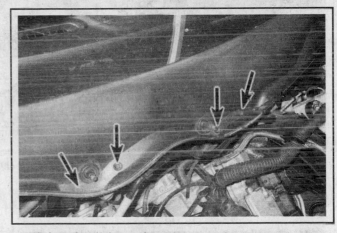

**21.3 Location of the cowl screws**

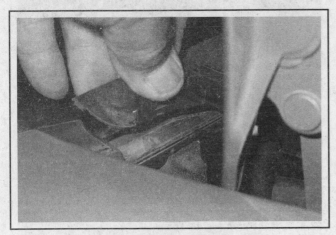

**21.4a Pull back the molding from each end of the cowl cover . . .**

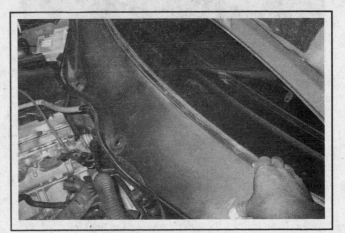

**21.4b . . . then lift off the cowl cover**

## 22 Center console - removal and installation

◆ Refer to illustrations 22.1a, 22.1b, 22.1c, 22.5a, 22.5b, 22.6, 22.7, 22.8, 22.9, 22.10 and 22.11

### ✳✳ WARNING:

**Models covered by this manual are equipped with a Supplemental Restraint System (SRS), more commonly known as airbags. Always disable the airbag system before working in the vicinity of any airbag system component to avoid the possibility of accidental deployment of the airbag, which could cause personal injury (see Chapter 12).**

1   If the vehicle has a soft gearshift boot, carefully pry it up using a trim tool (see illustration). Pry the surrounding panel up with the same tool, then lift the panel, disconnect its wiring connectors and take it off (see illustrations).

2   If the vehicle has a manual transmission, place the shift lever in second gear.

3   If the vehicle has an automatic transmission, turn the ignition key to the On position, depress the brake pedal, then place the shifter in the rearmost position.

4   Disconnect the cable from the battery negative terminal (see Chapter 5, Section 1).

5   Open the cup holder, remove the rubber liner from the bottom, remove the screw from the bottom (see illustrations).

6   Pry the console trim panel out with a trim stick, then lift it out and off the shift lever, together with the cup holder (see illustration).

7   Open the ashtray housing, disengage the retaining tangs and lift the housing out (see illustration). Disconnect its electrical connector and remove it from the vehicle.

8   Remove the trim piece from each side of the ashtray cavity (see illustration).

9   Rotate the two cam-lock fasteners counterclockwise at the upper front of the console, one on each side (see illustration).

22.1a  Using a trim stick, carefully pry up the shift lever boot

22.1b  Release the clips and lift off the trim panel . . .

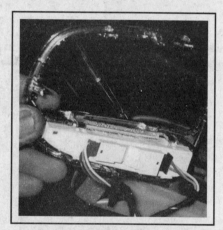

22.1c  . . . then turn it over and disconnect the wiring harnesses

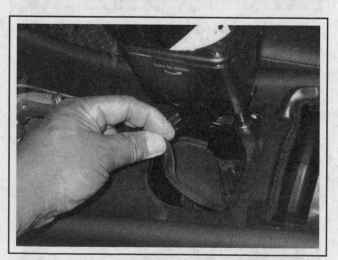

22.5a  Open the cup holder and remove the liner from the bottom . . .

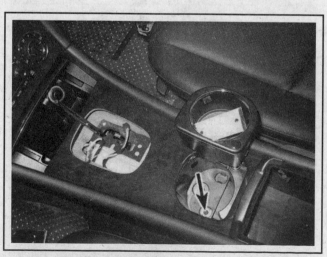

22.5b  . . . then remove the screw

10 Open the armrest, remove the carpet from the bottom of the storage compartment and unscrew the console bolts (see illustration).

11 Disengage the console from the studs at the upper right and left (see illustration). Carefully lift the console up and over the shifter, disconnect any electrical connectors, then remove it from the vehicle.

12 Installation is the reverse of removal.

13 Move the shift lever back into the Park position (automatic transmission), turn the ignition key to Off, then reconnect the cable to the negative terminal of the battery.

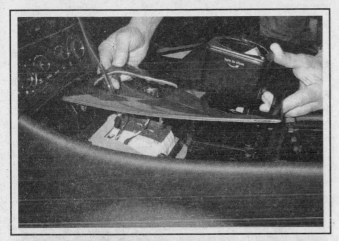

**22.6  Carefully pry the shift lever trim panel out and remove it together with the cup holder**

**22.7  Release the ashtray housing tangs and remove the housing**

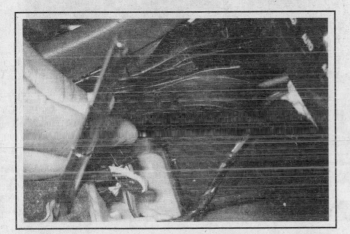

**22.8  Remove the trim piece on each side . . .**

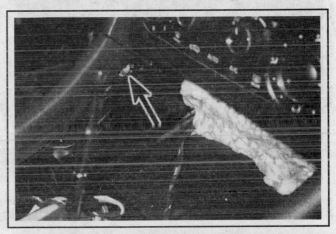

**22.9  . . . and turn the cam-lock fasteners counterclockwise to unlock them**

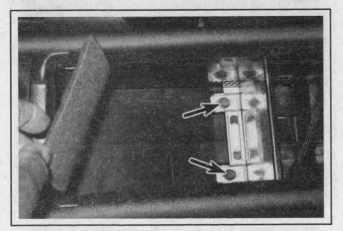

**22.10  Open the lid to the console bin, remove the mat, then remove the bolts**

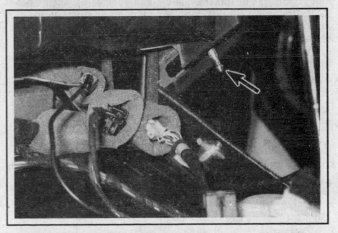

**22.11  Disengage the console from the studs on either side (these are what the cam-lock fasteners engage) and lift it out**

## 23 Steering column cover - removal and installation

▸ **Refer to illustration 23.3a and 23.3b**

❊❊ **WARNING:**

Models covered by this manual are equipped with a Supplemental Restraint System (SRS), more commonly known as airbags. Always disable the airbag system before working in the vicinity of any airbag system component to avoid the possibility of accidental deployment of the airbag, which could cause personal injury (see Chapter 12).

1   Disconnect the cable from the negative terminal of the battery (see Chapter 5, Section 1).
2   Remove the steering wheel (see Chapter 10).
3   Loosen the Torx screw and pull the cover off the steering column (see illustrations).
4   Installation is the reverse of removal.

❊❊ **CAUTION:**

Make sure the clockspring is centered before installing the steering wheel (see Chapter 10, Section 16).

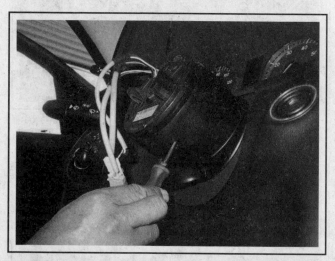

**23.3a  Loosen the Torx screw from the lower cover . . .**

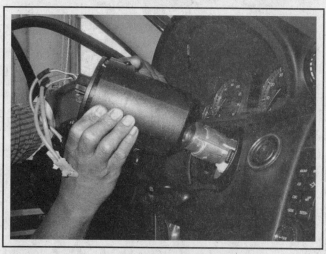

**23.3b  . . . then slide the cover and switches off the steering column**

## 24 Dashboard trim panels - removal and installation

❊❊ **WARNING:**

Models covered by this manual are equipped with a Supplemental Restraint System (SRS), more commonly known as airbags. Always disable the airbag system before working in the vicinity of any airbag system component to avoid the possibility of accidental deployment of the airbag, which could cause personal injury (see Chapter 12).

1   Disconnect the cable from the negative battery terminal (see Chapter 5, Section 1).

### INSTRUMENT CLUSTER TRIM PANEL

▸ **Refer to illustrations 24.4, 24.5, 24.8a and 24.8b**

2   Remove the center console (see Section 22). Remove the center trim panel as described below.
3   Remove the radio and GPS display (see Chapter 12).
4   Free the CAN connector from the left side lower trim cover and pass it through the cover (see illustration).

**24.4  Remove the CAN connector (upper arrow) from the trim panel; unplug the diagnostic connector (lower arrow) after the panel is lowered**

5   Unbolt the hood latch lever from the cover and pass it through the cover (see illustration).

6   Remove the screws from the left side lower trim cover and lower it away from the instrument panel. Disengage the data link connector from the cover (see illustration 24.4) and remove the cover from the vehicle.

7   Remove the headlight switch from the instrument cluster trim panel (see Chapter 12).

8   Remove the panel mounting bolts (see illustrations).

9   Free the lower edge of the panel with a trim stick. Pull the panel out far enough to access the ignition switch and parking brake pedal.

10   Remove the ignition switch from the panel (see Chapter 12).

11   Disconnect the cable from the parking brake pedal, then take the panel out.

12   Installation is the reverse of the removal procedure.

## AIR VENTS

▶ **Refer to illustrations 24.13a, 24.13b, 24.13c, 24.14a and 24.14b**

13   On center air vents, disengage the lower stops inside the air vents (see illustration). Pivot the vents upward to expose the screws and remove the screws (see illustration). Disengage the upper stops and pivot the vents downward (see illustration), press down on the retaining tangs in the top of the vents (see illustration) and take the vents out as an assembly with their housing.

24.5  Unbolt the hood release lever; the bolt is hidden under the lever

24.8a  Remove the screws on the left and center of the panel . . .

24.8b  . . . and along the right side

24.13a  Center air vent stops:

A   Pry the lower stop toward the center of the vent to allow the vent to pivot upward

B   Pry the upper stop toward the center of the vent to allow the vent to pivot downward

24.13b  Once the vents have been pivoted upward, remove the screws (left center vent shown)

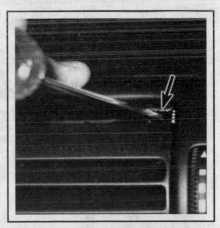

24.13c  Once the vents have been pivoted downward, pry the retaining tangs down and remove the vent and housing assembly from the instrument panel (right-side tang shown)

14 On side air vents, reach inside the vent and release the latch (see illustration). Pivot the vent downward, release the clips in the top of the vent and take it out (see illustration).

## CENTER TRIM PANEL

### One-piece center trim

▶ Refer to illustration 24.15

15 Some models have a one-piece center trim panel surrounding the radio and air conditioning controls (see illustration). Remove the center air vents as described in Step 13. Remove the ashtray housing from the center console (see Section 22). Release the center panel latches inside

the ashtray housing opening. Pivot the panel away from the instrument panel, unplug its wiring connectors and take it out as a unit, complete with the ventilation and air conditioning control assemblies. Installation is the reverse of the removal procedure.

### Two-piece center trim

### Lower section

▶ Refer to illustrations 24.16a and 24.16b

16 Remove the console and ashtray housing (see Section 22). Remove the screws and carefully pry the trim panel out along with the HVAC control panel (see illustrations). Unplug the electrical connectors from the back of the panel. Installation is the reverse of removal.

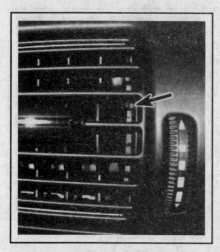

24.14a  On side vents, pry the stop toward the center of the vent . . .

24.14b  . . . then pivot the vent down and release the two retaining tangs by prying them downward

24.15  On some models, a single trim panel surrounds the center switches, radio and air conditioning controls

24.16a  Remove the screws from the bottom of the lower center trim panel . . .

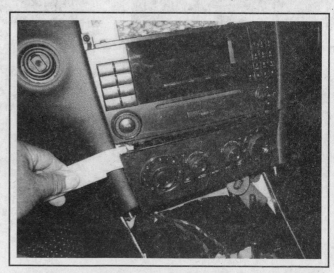

24.16b  . . . then carefully pry the panel out

## Upper section

▶ **Refer to illustrations 24.17a and 24.17b**

17 Remove the center air vents as described in Step 13. Remove the screws, then carefully pry the panel out (see illustrations).

## GLOVE BOX

▶ **Refer to illustrations 24.20, 24.22, 24.24a, 24.24b, 24.24c, 24.25a and 24.25b**

18 Remove the center console (see Section 22).

19 Remove the center trim panel(s) as described above. Also remove the radio (see Chapter 12).

20 Remove the screws that secure the cover under the right side of the instrument panel and lower the cover down (see illustration).

21 Detach the side cover from the right side of the instrument panel as described in Step 27.

22 Unplug the electrical connector for the glove compartment light (see illustration).

23 Remove the radio and center navigation panel (see Chapter 12)

24 Remove the upper center console cover (see illustrations).

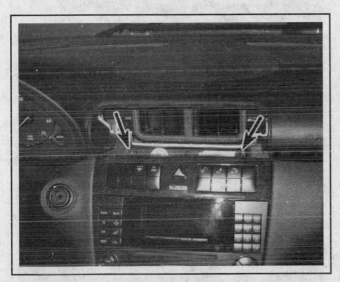

**24.17a  Remove the screws from the top of the upper center trim panel . . .**

**24.17b  . . . then carefully pry the panel out**

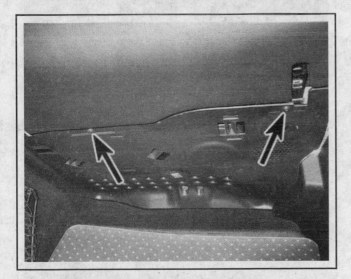

**24.20  Remove the panel fasteners and lower it away**

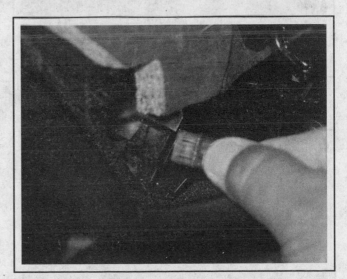

**24.22  Disconnect the wiring for the glove compartment light**

25 Remove the bolts that secure the glove compartment to the instrument panel (see illustrations).

26 Installation is the reverse of the removal procedure.

## SIDE COVERS

▶ **Refer to illustration 24.27**

27 Carefully pry the side cover away from the instrument panel with a trim stick (see illustration).

28 To install, simply press the side cover back into place.

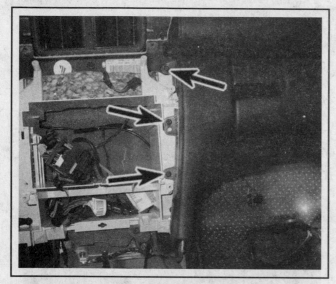

**24.24a  Remove the screws at the center of the trim piece . . .**

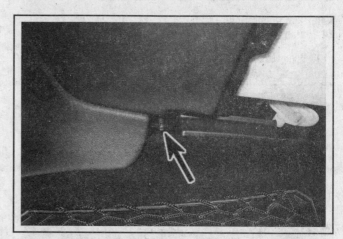

**24.24b  . . . at the bottom . . .**

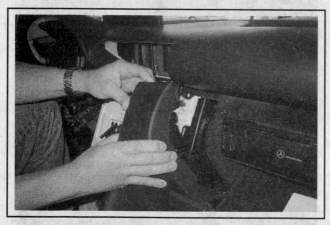

**24.24c  . . . and take the trim piece out**

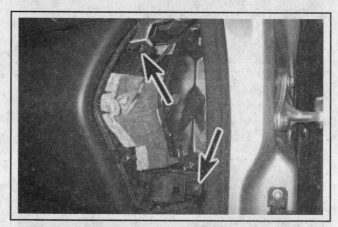

**24.25a  Remove the two bolts at the side of the glove compartment . . .**

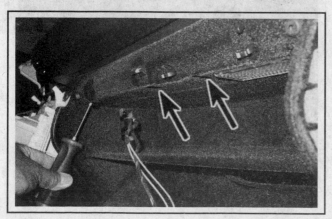

**24.25b  . . . and three along the top, then lower the glove compartment**

**24.27  If the end trim piece doesn't have a finger pull slot, use a trim stick to pry it off**

## 25  Seats - removal and installation

### ✳✳ WARNING 1:

Models covered by this manual are equipped with a Supplemental Restraint System (SRS), more commonly known as airbags. Always disable the airbag system before working in the vicinity of any airbag system component to avoid the possibility of accidental deployment of the airbag, which could cause personal injury (see Chapter 12).

### ✳✳ WARNING 2:

The front seat belts on some models are equipped with pre-tensioners, which are pyrotechnic (explosive) devices designed to retract the seat belts in the event of a collision. On models equipped with pre-tensioners, do not remove the front seat belt retractor assemblies, and do not disconnect the electrical connectors leading to the assemblies. Problems with the pre-tensioners will turn on the SRS (airbag) warning light on the dash. If any pre-tensioner problems are suspected, take the vehicle to a dealer service department. Also on these models, be sure to disable the airbag system (see Chapter 12).

## FRONT SEAT

▶ **Refer to illustrations 25.3 and 25.4**

1   If you're working on the driver's seat, move the adjustable steering wheel all the way forward.

2   If the outer end of the seat belt is attached to the seat, remove the trim cover from the side of the seat, then remove the seat belt anchor bolt.

3   Position the seat all the way forward to access the rear retaining bolts. Detach any bolt trim covers and remove the retaining bolts (see illustration).

4   Position the seat all the way rearward to access the front retaining bolts. Detach any bolt trim covers and remove the retaining bolts (see illustration).

5   Tilt the seat upward to access the under side. Disconnect any electrical connectors and lift the seat from the vehicle.

6   Installation is the reverse of removal.

## REAR SEAT

▶ **Refer to illustration 25.8**

7   Lift up on the rear of the seat cushion and pivot it forward.

8   Detach the retaining bolts at the lower edge of the seat back, and if necessary, remove the seat belt anchor bolts (see illustration).

9   Lift up on the seat back and remove it from the vehicle.

10   Installation is the reverse of removal.

**25.3  With the seat positioned all the way back, remove the front retaining bolts and unplug the electrical connector(s)**

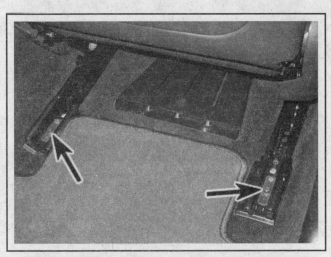

**25.4  With the seat positioned all the way forward, remove the rear retaining bolts**

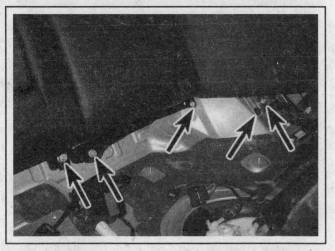

**25.8  Detach the retaining bolts at the lower edge of the seat back**

## 26 Rear shelf trim panel - removal and installation

▶ **Refer to illustration 26.2**

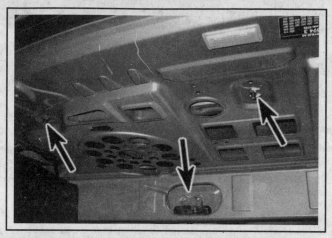

1   If the rear seat can be lowered to load cargo into the trunk (through-loading feature), lower it and remove the seat back side cushion. Working in the trunk, detach the seat lock from the seat back rest lock and remove the shelf mounting nuts (see illustration).

2   If the seat can't be lowered to load cargo into the trunk, remove the rear seat back (see Section 25).

3   Release the latches on either side of the shelf and remove the clips.

4   Detach the seat lock knobs (seats with the through-loading feature).

5   Remove the trim panel fasteners. Some models have nuts in the trunk and bolts beneath.

6   Installation is the reverse of removal.

**26.2  Remove the nuts (center and left side shown) and release the seatback latches**

**Section**

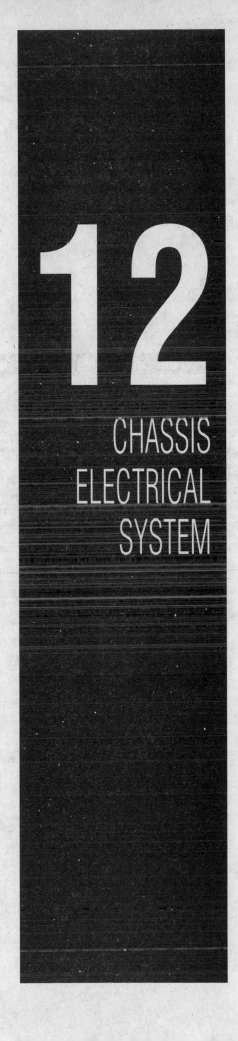

# 12

## CHASSIS
## ELECTRICAL
## SYSTEM

## 1   General information

The electrical system is a 12-volt, negative ground type. Power for the lights and all electrical accessories is supplied by a lead/acid-type battery, which is charged by the alternator.

This Chapter covers repair and service procedures for the various electrical components not associated with the engine. Information on the battery, alternator and starter motor can be found in Chapter 5.

It should be noted that when portions of the electrical system are serviced, the negative battery cable should be disconnected from the battery to prevent electrical shorts and/or fires.

## 2   Electrical troubleshooting - general information

▶ **Refer to illustrations 2.5a and 2.5b**

1   A typical electrical circuit consists of an electrical component, any switches, relays, motors, fuses, fusible links or circuit breakers related to that component and the wiring and connectors that link the component to both the battery and the chassis. To help you pinpoint an electrical circuit problem, wiring diagrams are included at the end of this Chapter.

2   Before tackling any troublesome electrical circuit, first study the appropriate wiring diagrams to get a complete understanding of what makes up that individual circuit. Noting whether other components related to the circuit are operating correctly, for instance, can often narrow down the location of potential trouble spots. If several components or circuits fail at one time, chances are the problem is in a fuse or ground connection, because several circuits are often routed through the same fuse and ground connections.

3   Electrical problems usually stem from simple causes, such as loose or corroded connections, a blown fuse, a melted fusible link or a failed relay. Visually inspect the condition of all fuses, wires and connections in a problem circuit before troubleshooting the circuit.

4   If test equipment and instruments are going to be utilized, use the diagrams to plan ahead of time where you will make the necessary connections in order to accurately pinpoint the trouble spot.

5   For electrical troubleshooting, you'll need a circuit tester, voltmeter or a 12-volt bulb with a set of test leads, a continuity tester and a jumper wire, preferably with a circuit breaker incorporated, which can be used to bypass electrical components (see illustrations). Before attempting to locate a problem with test instruments, use the wiring diagram(s) to decide where to make the connections.

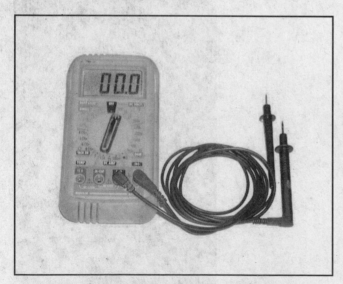

**2.5a  The most useful tool for electrical troubleshooting is a digital multimeter that can check volts, amps, and test continuity**

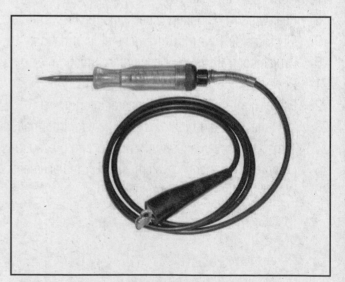

**2.5b  A simple test light is a very handy tool for testing voltage**

## VOLTAGE CHECKS

▶ **Refer to illustration 2.6**

6   Voltage checks should be performed if a circuit is not functioning properly. Connect one lead of a circuit tester to either the negative battery terminal or a known good ground. Connect the other lead to a connector in the circuit being tested, preferably nearest to the battery or fuse (see illustration). If the bulb of the tester lights, voltage is present, which means that the part of the circuit between the connector and the battery is problem free. Continue checking the rest of the circuit in the same fashion. When you reach a point at which no voltage is present, the problem lies between that point and the last test point with voltage. Most of the time the problem can be traced to a loose connection.

➡**Note: Keep in mind that some circuits receive voltage only when the ignition key is in the ACC or RUN position.**

## FINDING A SHORT

7   One method of finding shorts in a live circuit is to remove the fuse and connect a test light in place of the fuse terminals (fabricate two jumper wires with small spade terminals, plug the jumper wires into the fuse box and connect the test light). There should be no voltage present in the circuit. Move the suspected wiring harness from side-to-side while watching the test light. If the bulb goes on, there is a short to ground somewhere in that area, probably where the insulation has rubbed through.

## GROUND CHECK

8   Perform a ground test to check whether a component is properly grounded. Disconnect the battery and connect one lead of a continuity tester or multimeter (set to the ohm scale), to a known good ground. Connect the other lead to the wire or ground connection being tested. If the resistance is low (less than 5 ohms), the ground is good. If the bulb on a self-powered test light does not go on, the ground is not good.

## CONTINUITY CHECK

▶ **Refer to illustration 2.9**

9   A continuity check determines whether there are any breaks in a circuit (whether it can no longer carry current from the voltage source to ground). With the circuit off (no power in the circuit), a self-powered continuity tester or multimeter can be used to check the circuit. Connect the test leads to both ends of the circuit (or to the power end and a good ground), and if the test light comes on the circuit is passing current properly (see illustration). If the resistance is low (less than 5 ohms), there is continuity; if the reading is 10,000 ohms or higher, there is a break somewhere in the circuit. The same procedure can be used to test a switch, by connecting the continuity tester to the switch terminals. With the switch turned to ON, the test light should come on (or low resistance should be indicated on a meter).

## FINDING AN OPEN CIRCUIT

10  When diagnosing for possible open circuits, it is often difficult to locate them by sight because the connectors hide oxidation or terminal misalignment. Merely wiggling a connector on a sensor or in the wiring harness may correct the open circuit condition. Remember this when an open circuit is indicated when troubleshooting a circuit. Intermittent problems may also be caused by oxidized or loose connections.

11  Electrical troubleshooting is simple if you keep in mind that all electrical circuits are basically electricity running from the battery, through the wires, switches, relays, fuses and fusible links to each electrical component (light bulb, motor, etc.) and to ground, from which it is passed back to the battery. Any electrical problem is an interruption in the flow of electricity to and from the battery.

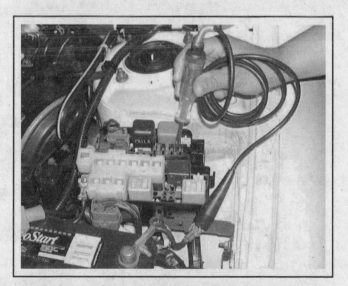

**2.6  In use, a basic test light's lead is clipped to a known good ground, then the pointed probe can test connectors, wires or electrical sockets - if the bulb lights, the circuit being tested has battery voltage**

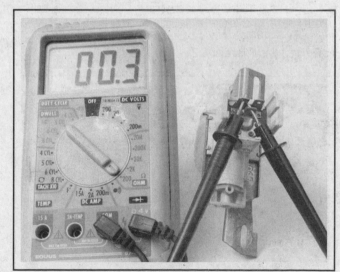

**2.9  With a multimeter set to the ohm scale, resistance can be checked across two terminals - when checking for continuity, a low reading indicates continuity, a high reading or infinity indicates high resistance or lack of continuity**

## CONNECTORS

12 Most electrical connections on these vehicles are made with multi-wire plastic connectors. The mating halves of many connectors are secured with locking clips molded into the plastic connector shells. The mating halves of large connectors, such as some of those under the instrument panel, are held together by a bolt through the center of the connector.

13 To separate a connector with locking clips, use a small screwdriver to pry the clips apart carefully, then separate the connector halves. Pull only on the shell; never pull on the wiring harness as you may damage the individual wires and terminals inside the connectors. Look at the connector closely before trying to separate the halves. Often the locking clips are engaged in a way that is not immediately clear. Additionally, many connectors have more than one set of clips.

14 Each pair of connector terminals has a male half and a female half. When you look at the end view of a connector in a diagram, be sure to understand whether the view shows the harness side or the component side of the connector. Connector halves are mirror images of each other, and a terminal that is shown on the right side end-view of one half will be on the left side end view of the other half.

## 3   Fuses and fusible links - general information

### FUSES

▶ **Refer to illustrations 3.1a through 3.1g and 3.2**

The electrical circuits of the vehicle are protected by a combination of fuses, circuit breakers and fusible links. Fuse and relay boxes are located in the engine compartment, trunk and inside the left end of the instrument panel (see illustrations 3.1a through 3.1f). Spare fuses are located in the tool kit in the trunk (see illustration 3.1g). Each of the fuses is designed to protect a specific circuit, and the various circuits are identified on a chart located in the passenger compartment fuse box. If the fuse chart is difficult to read, or missing, you can also refer to your owner's manual, which includes a complete guide to all fuses and relays in all three fuse/relay boxes.

Miniaturized fuses are employed in the fuse blocks. If an electrical component fails, always check the fuse first. The best way to check a fuse is with a test light. Check for power at the exposed terminal tips of each fuse. If power is present on one side of the fuses but not the other, the fuse is blown. A blown fuse can also be confirmed by visually inspecting it (see illustration 3.2).

Be sure to replace blown fuses with the correct type. Fuses of different ratings are physically interchangeable, but only fuses of the proper rating should be used. Replacing a fuse with one of a higher or lower value than specified is not recommended. Each electrical circuit needs a specific amount of protection. The amperage value of each fuse is molded into the fuse body.

If the replacement fuse immediately fails, don't replace it again until the cause of the problem is isolated and corrected. In most cases, this will be a short circuit in the wiring caused by a broken or deteriorated wire.

### FUSIBLE LINKS

Some circuits are protected by fusible links. The links are used in circuits which carry high current.

Cartridge-type fusible links are located in the engine compartment fuse/relay box and are similar to a large fuse (see illustration 3.1c). After disconnecting the negative battery cable, simply unplug the fusible link and replace it with a fusible link of the same amperage.

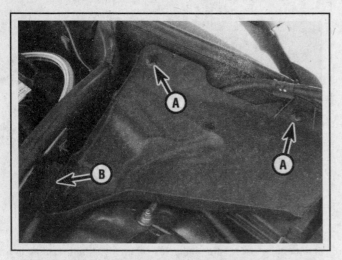

**3.1a  To detach the cover from over the engine compartment fuse and relay box, rotate the two clips 1/4-turn (A) and slide the cover out of the slot (B)**

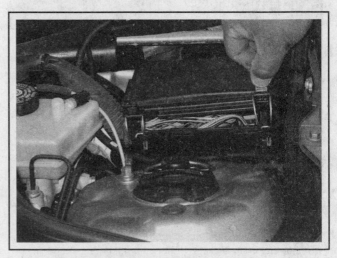

**3.1b  Release the clips and lift the lid . . .**

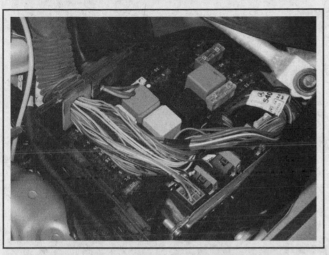

3.1c  . . . for access to the fuses and relays

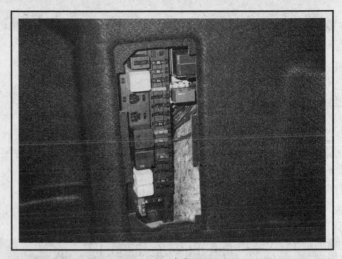

3.1d  There's a fuse box on the left side of the trunk, under a cover

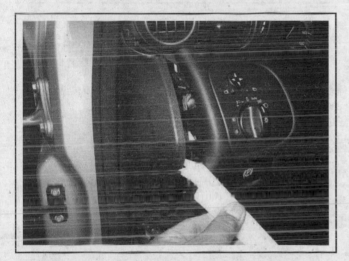

3.1e  If there's a finger slot in the instrument panel cover, pull it off; if not, use a trim tool to pry it off . . .

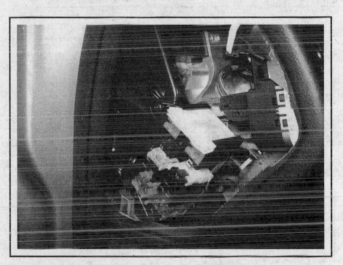

3.1f  . . . there's a fuse panel under the cover

3.1g  Spare fuses are in the tool kit on the right side of the trunk

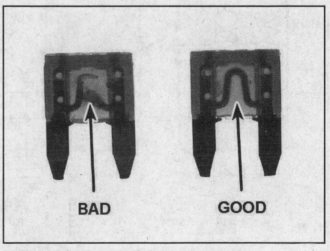

3.2  When a fuse blows, the element between the terminals melts

## 4  Circuit breakers - general information

Circuit breakers protect certain circuits, such as the power windows or heated seats. Depending on the vehicle's accessories, there may be one or two circuit breakers, located in the fuse/relay box in the engine compartment.

Because the circuit breakers reset automatically, an electrical overload in a circuit-breaker-protected system will cause the circuit to fail momentarily, then come back on. If the circuit does not come back on, check it immediately.

For a basic check, pull the circuit breaker up out of its socket on the fuse panel, but just far enough to probe with a voltmeter. The breaker should still contact the sockets.

With the voltmeter negative lead on a good chassis ground, touch each end prong of the circuit breaker with the positive meter probe. There should be battery voltage at each end. If there is battery voltage only at one end, the circuit breaker must be replaced.

Some circuit breakers must be reset manually.

## 5  Relays - general information and testing

### GENERAL INFORMATION

1   Several electrical accessories in the vehicle, such as the fuel injection system, horns, starter, and fog lamps use relays to transmit the electrical signal to the component. Relays use a low-current circuit (the control circuit) to open and close a high-current circuit (the power circuit). If the relay is defective, that component will not operate properly. Most relays are mounted in the engine compartment fuse/relay box. If a faulty relay is suspected, it can be removed and tested using the procedure below or by a dealer service department or repair shop. Defective relays must be replaced as a unit.

### TESTING

▶ **Refer to illustrations 5.2a and 5.2b**

2   Most of the relays used in these vehicles are of a type often called "ISO" relays, which refers to the International Standards Organization. The terminals of ISO relays are numbered to indicate their usual circuit connections and functions. There are two basic layouts of terminals on the relays used in these vehicles (see illustrations).

3   Refer to the wiring diagram for the circuit to determine the proper connections for the relay you're testing. If you can't determine the correct connection from the wiring diagrams, however, you may be able to determine the test connections from the information that follows.

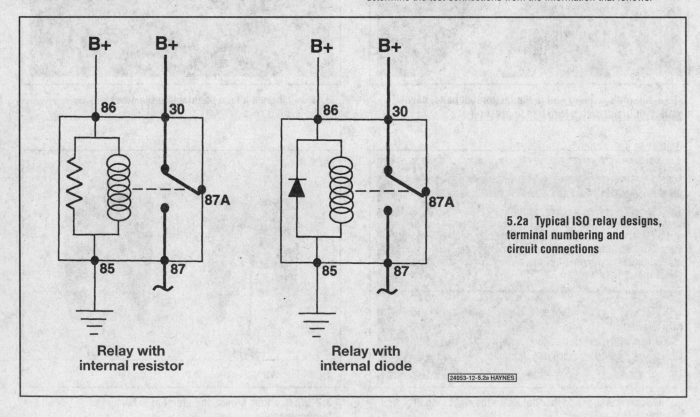

**5.2a  Typical ISO relay designs, terminal numbering and circuit connections**

Relay with internal resistor

Relay with internal diode

24053-12-5.2a HAYNES

**5.2b  Most relays are marked on the outside to easily identify the control circuits and the power circuits (four terminal type shown)**

4   Two of the terminals are the relay control circuit and connect to the relay coil. The other relay terminals are the power circuit. When the relay is energized, the coil creates a magnetic field that closes the larger contacts of the power circuit to provide power to the circuit loads.

5   Terminals 85 and 86 are normally the control circuit. If the relay contains a diode, terminal 86 must be connected to battery positive (B+) voltage and terminal 85 to ground. If the relay contains a resistor, terminals 85 and 86 can be connected in either direction with respect to

B+ and ground.

6   Terminal 30 is normally connected to the battery voltage (B+) source for the circuit loads. Terminal 87 is connected to the circuit leading to the component being powered. If the relay has several alternate terminals for load or ground connections, they usually are numbered 87A, 87B, 87C, and so on.

7   Use an ohmmeter to check continuity through the relay control coil.

    *a) Connect the meter according to the polarity shown in illustration 5.2a for one check; then reverse the ohmmeter leads and check continuity in the other direction.*

    *b) If the relay contains a resistor, resistance will be indicated on the meter, and should be the same value with the ohmmeter in either direction.*

    *c) If the relay contains a diode, resistance should be higher with the ohmmeter in the forward polarity direction than with the meter leads reversed.*

    *d) If the ohmmeter shows infinite resistance in both directions, replace the relay.*

8   Remove the relay from the vehicle and use the ohmmeter to check for continuity between the relay power circuit terminals. There should be no continuity between terminal 30 and 87 with the relay de-energized.

9   Connect a fused jumper wire to terminal 86 and the positive battery terminal. Connect another jumper wire between terminal 85 and ground. When the connections are made, the relay should click.

10  With the jumper wires connected, check for continuity between the power circuit terminals. Now, there should be continuity between terminals 30 and 87.

11  If the relay fails any of the above tests, replace it.

## 6   Turn signal/multi-function switch - replacement

▶ **Refer to illustration 6.2, 6.3a and 6.3b**

### ❊❊ WARNING:

**The models covered by this manual are equipped with a Supplemental Restraint System (SRS), more commonly known as airbags. Always disarm the airbag system before working in the vicinity of any airbag system component to avoid the possibility of accidental deployment of the airbag, which could cause personal injury (see Section 24).**

1   Remove the steering wheel and steering column trim piece (see Chapters 10 and 11).

2   Remove the switch mounting screws and take the airbag clockspring off the trim piece (see illustration).

**6.2  Remove the screws and clockspring . . .**

6.3a . . . then separate the switches from the clockspring. . .

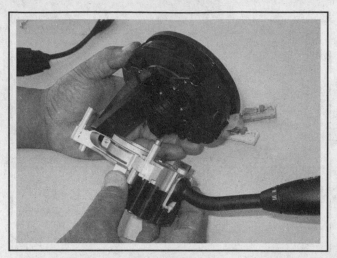

6.3b . . . noting how they engage it

3   Remove the switches from the back of the clockspring (see illustrations) and remove the switch.

4   Installation is the reverse of removal.

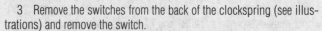

**✱✱ WARNING:**

**Before installing the airbag clockspring, make sure it's centered (see Chapter 10, "Steering wheel - removal and installation").**

## 7   Steering lock and ignition switch - replacement

**✱✱ WARNING:**

**The models covered by this manual are equipped with a Supplemental Restraint System (SRS), more commonly known as airbags. Always disarm the airbag system before working in the vicinity of any airbag system component to avoid the possibility of accidental deployment of the airbag, which could cause personal injury (see Section 24).**

### STEERING LOCK

▶ **Refer to illustration 7.4**

1   Insert the ignition key in the key lock cylinder and turn the key to the 1 (unlocked) position.

2   Disconnect the cable from the negative terminal of the battery (see Chapter 5, Section 1).

3   Remove the lower left instrument panel cover (see Chapter 11).

4   Turn the special bolt that secures the steering lock to align its tab with the slot, then remove it (see illustration). Slide the lock away from the steering column, unplug its electrical connector and remove it from the vehicle.

5   Installation is the reverse of removal.

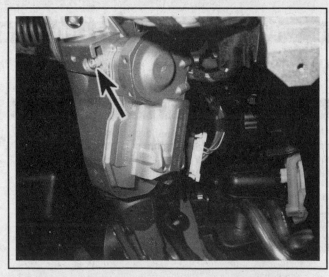

7.4  Remove the special bolt and detach the steering lock from the column

## IGNITION SWITCH

▶ **Refer to illustrations 7.9 and 7.11**

6   Disconnect the cable from the negative terminal of the battery (see Chapter 5, Section 1).

7   Lower the steering column all the way.

8   Remove the trim panel from under the instrument panel (see Chapter 11).

9   Unscrew the nut that secures the ignition switch, using a four-pronged tool or a pair of needle-nose pliers (see illustration).

10  Remove the screws that secure the underside of the trim panel in which the switch is mounted. Pull downward on the panel, taking care not to damage it, and remove the switch.

11  If the vehicle has an automatic transmission, detach the shift interlock cable from the switch (see illustration). Disconnect the electrical connectors from the switch and take it out.

12  Installation is the reverse of removal.

**7.9  If you don't have a special socket, a pair of needle-nose pliers can be used to unscrew the ignition switch nut**

**7.11  Unplug the electrical connectors from the ignition switch, and if the vehicle has an automatic transmission, squeeze the tangs and detach the shift interlock cable**

## 8   Dashboard and overhead switches - replacement

**❊❊ WARNING:**

The models covered by this manual are equipped with a Supplemental Restraint System (SRS), more commonly known as airbags. Always disarm the airbag system before working in the vicinity of any airbag system component to avoid the possibility of accidental deployment of the airbag, which could cause personal injury (see Section 24).

1   Disconnect the cable from the negative terminal of the battery (see Chapter 5, Section 1).

### HEADLIGHT SWITCH

▶ **Refer to illustrations 8.3, 8.4 and 8.5**

2   Remove the left instrument panel side cover (see Section 3).

3   Pull out the parking brake release handle to expose the headlight switch screw behind it and remove the screw (see illustration).

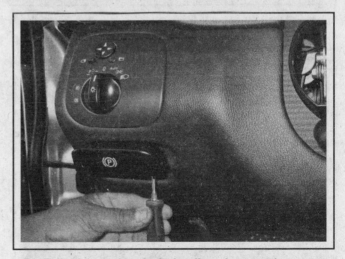

**8.3  Pull out the parking brake handle and remove the screw from the underside of the headlight switch . . .**

4   Using your fingers, release the clips and pull out the headlight switch (see illustration).

5   Disconnect the electrical connector from the headlight switch (see illustration).

6   Detach the headlight range adjuster from the switch.

7   Installation is the reverse of removal. When installing the headlight switch, make sure that it snaps back into place.

## OVERHEAD SWITCH

▶ **Refer to illustration 8.8, 8.9a, 8.9b and 8.9c**

8   Carefully pry the lens off the dome light (see illustration).

9   Using your fingers, release the latches under the lens (see illustration). Lower the unit away from the headliner and unplug the electrical connectors (see illustrations).

➡**Note: When releasing the latches, it is sometimes necessary to carefully pry the rear of the housing down with a wide-bladed, plastic trim tool.**

10  Installation is the reverse of removal. When installing the switch, make sure that the switch snaps into place.

8.4 . . . disengage the clips and pull the switch out of the dash . . .

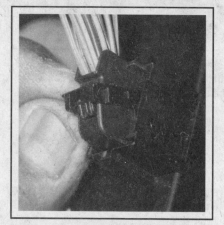

8.5 . . . then swing the lock up and unplug the electrical connector

8.8 Carefully pry the lens downward . . .

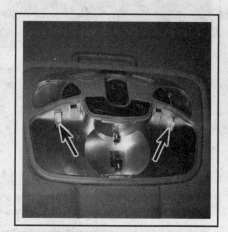

8.9a . . . pull the latches back . . .

8.9b . . . lower the switch unit out of the headliner . . .

8.9c . . . and disconnect its electrical connectors

## 9 Instrument cluster - removal and installation

▶ Refer to illustrations 9.2a, 9.2b, 9.2c and 9.3

### ❄❄ WARNING:

The models covered by this manual are equipped with a Supplemental Restraint System (SRS), more commonly known as airbags. Always disarm the airbag system before working in the vicinity of any airbag system component to avoid the possibility of accidental deployment of the airbag, which could cause personal injury (see Section 24).

1  Disconnect the cable from the negative terminal of the battery (see Chapter 5, Section 1).
2  Insert a pair of removal hooks (you can use picks or small screwdrivers with the ends bent at 90-degrees) into the slots on each side of the instrument panel until they reach the stops (about 3-5/32 inches) (see illustration). Use the hooks to disengage the cluster hood release latches and remove the hood (see illustration). Use the hooks to disengage the cluster latches and pull the hooks toward you to pull the cluster out of the instrument panel (see illustration).
3  Disconnect the electrical connector (see illustration) and remove the cluster.
4  Installation is the reverse of removal.

9.2a  Insert hooked removal tools into the removal slots . . .

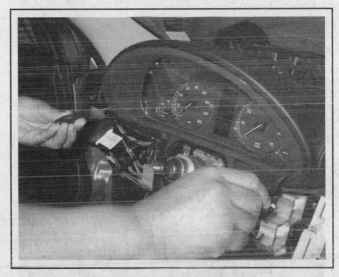

9.2b  . . . push them back until they stop . . .

9.2c  . . . release the latches and pull the cluster out . . .

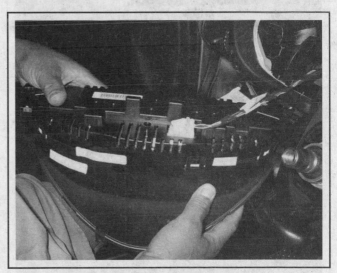

9.3  . . . then disconnect its electrical connector

## 10 Radio and speakers - removal and installation

### ⁂ WARNING:

The models covered by this manual are equipped with a Supplemental Restraint System (SRS), more commonly known as airbags. Always disarm the airbag system before working in the vicinity of any airbag system component to avoid the possibility of accidental deployment of the airbag, which could cause personal injury (see Section 24).

### ⁂ CAUTION:

Do not bend the fiber optic cable into a loop tighter than one inch. Cover the end of the cable with a clean rag to keep out light.

5   Disconnect the electrical connectors from the radio and remove it from the vehicle.
6   Installation is the reverse of removal.

### RADIO

1   Disconnect the cable from the negative terminal of the battery (see Chapter 5, Section 1).

#### Audio 10 or Audio 30 radio

2   Remove the center console cover (see Chapter 11).
3   Unscrew the Torx bolts that secure the radio.
4   Pull the radio out and disconnect the fiber optic cable.

#### Audio 20 radio

▶ **Refer to illustrations 10.8a, 10.8b, 10.8c, 10.8d, 10.10a and 10.10b**

7   Remove the center air vent from the instrument panel. Remove the shift lever cover and ashtray (see Chapter 11).
8   Remove the upper panel control unit screws and take the unit out (see illustrations).
9   Remove the air conditioning control unit (see Chapter 3).

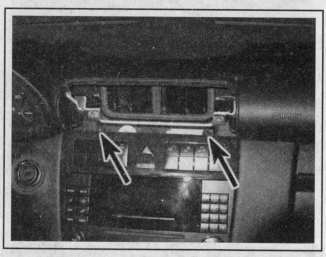

10.8a  Remove the screws that secure the switch unit . . .

10.8b  . . . carefully pry it out with a trim stick . . .

10.8c  . . . disengaging the clips on the underside . . .

10.8d  . . . and unplug the electrical connector

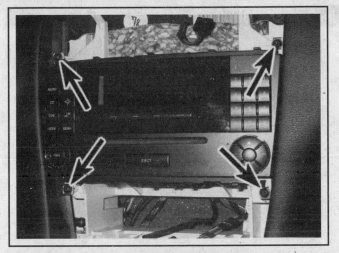

**10.10a Unscrew the radio mounting screws . . .**

**10.10b . . . then pull the radio out of the dash and unplug the fiber optic cables and wiring**

10 Remove the radio mounting screws (see illustration). Pull the radio out and disconnect the fiber optic cables (see illustration).

> **✻✻ CAUTION:**
>
> Do not bend the fiber optic cable into a loop tighter than one inch. Cover the end of the cable with a clean rag to keep out light.

11 Disconnect the electrical connectors from the radio and remove it from the vehicle.

12 Installation is the reverse of removal.

## SPEAKERS

### Mirror triangle speakers

▸ Refer to illustration 10.14

13 Free the molded rear edge of the speaker cover from the door, then slide the speaker cover forward to separate it from the door.

14 Turn the cover around and unplug the speaker electrical connector (see illustration).

15 Unclip the speaker from the holder and take it out.

16 Installation is the reverse of removal.

### Front door speakers

17 Remove the front door trim panel (see Chapter 11).

18 Remove the speaker housing mounting screws.

19 Note which side of the speaker is upward. Release the speaker clips, pull out the speaker and disconnect the electrical connector.

20 Installation is the reverse of removal.

### Rear door speakers

21 Remove the rear door trim panel (see Chapter 11).

22 Disconnect the speaker electrical connector.

23 Remove the speaker housing cover screws and cover. Remove the speaker housing screws and remove the housing.

24 Note which side of the speaker is upward. Release the speaker clips and pull out the speaker.

25 If necessary, detach the small speaker from the large speaker.

**10.14 Remove the trim piece and unplug the wiring connector from the speaker**

26 Installation is the reverse of removal.

### Front upper speaker

27 Using a trim removal tool, remove the instrument panel upper center cover.

28 Remove the upper center air vent from the instrument panel (see Chapter 11).

29 Disconnect the electrical connector, then release the speaker clips and detach the speaker.

30 Installation is the reverse of removal.

### Rear speaker

31 Remove the rear shelf trim panel (see Chapter 11).

32 Disconnect the electrical connector from the rear speaker.

33 Squeeze the two mounting tabs and push them up through their mounting holes, then push up on the speaker and remove it together with its housing.

34 Unbolt the speaker from the housing.

35 Installation is the reverse of removal.

## 11 Antenna - general information

### WINDSHIELD AND REAR WINDOW ANTENNAS

#### Windshield antenna

1   On some models the antennas are mounted in the windshield and on the inside of the rear window. The windshield antenna is an integral component of the windshield; it's installed between the inner and outer layers of glass. To replace a windshield antenna you must replace the windshield.

#### Rear window antenna

2   The rear window antenna is a grid baked onto the glass surface, just like the rear window defroster heater grid. If the rear window antenna is damaged, you might be able to repair it the same way that you would repair the rear window heater grid (see Section 18).

### ROOF-MOUNTED ANTENNA

3   On models with cellular navigation and/or digital satellite radio systems, the antenna is mounted on the roof. To replace it, you must remove the headliner and, on vehicles equipped with side-curtain airbags, the side-curtain airbag modules as well. We therefore recommend that you have this type of antenna replaced by a dealer service department or other qualified repair shop.

## 12 Windshield wiper motor - replacement

♦ **Refer to illustrations 12.2a, 12.2b, 12.3, 12.4a, 12.4b, 12.4c, 12.6a, 12.6b, 12.7a, 12.7b, 12.8 and 12.10**

### ✳ WARNING:

**Remove the ignition key when working on the wipers to prevent them from starting accidentally and causing injury.**

1   Place the wipers in the parked position. Open the hood, push the button on the left support strut and raise the hood to the fully open position.

2   Remove the windshield wiper arm retaining nuts and washers (see illustrations). Mark the position of each wiper arm in relation to its shaft, then remove the wiper arms.

3   Remove the outer cover from the engine compartment fuse and relay box (see Section 3). Unplug the electrical connector at the back of the box and free the harness (see illustration).

4   Remove the gasket from the water collector and free the wiper wiring harnesses from their retainers (see illustration). Remove the clips that secure the water collector to the windshield base and disconnect the drain tubes (see illustrations).

5   On models with convenience automatic air conditioning, disconnect the electrical connector from the sensor mounted in the center of the water collector.

6   Remove the screws that secure the water collector near the wiper arm shafts and remove the end pieces from the water collector (see illustrations).

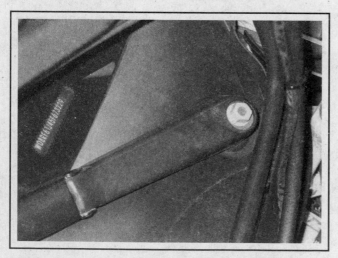

**12.2a  Remove the nut from the driver's side wiper arm . . .**

**12.2b  . . . and both nuts from the passenger side - note the L mark**

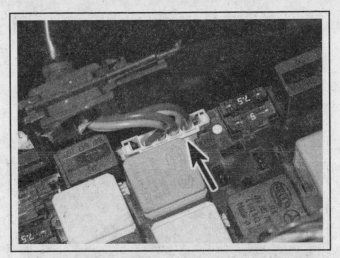

12.3  Unplug the wiper motor wiring connector and free its grommet from the fuse box

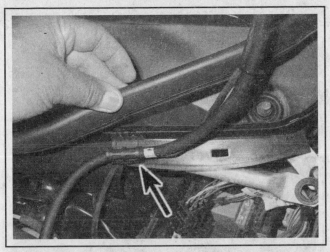

12.4a  Pull the gasket off the water deflector and free the wiring harness from the retainer

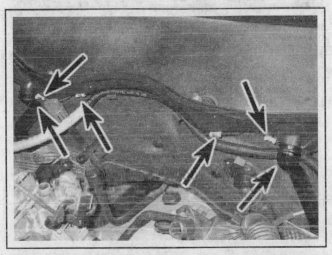

12.4b  Free the water deflector from the clips and disconnect the drain hoses . . .

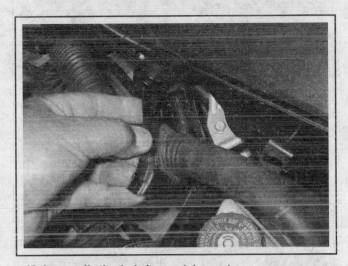

12.4c  . . . slip the drain hose retainer out . . .

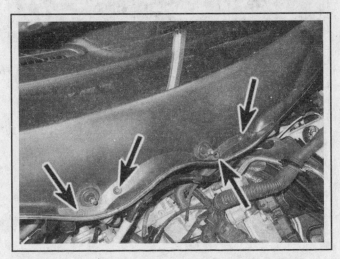

12.6a  . . . remove the bolts near the passenger side wiper arm shafts . . .

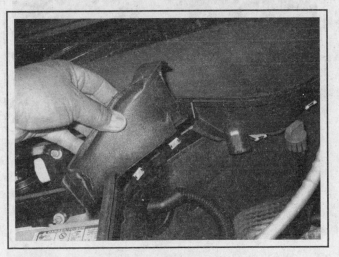

12.6b  . . . and remove the end pieces

7  Pull the water collector upward to detach it from the molding on the windshield frame, then remove it from the vehicle (see illustrations).

8  Remove the wiper linkage bolts (see illustration). Take the linkage out and remove the bracket.

9  Cut the tie wrap(s) that secure the wiper motor wiring harness to the linkage (see illustration 12.8). Using a trim removal tool or a large screwdriver, carefully pry the linkage off the wiper motor crank arm.

10  Remove the nut that attaches the actuator arm to the motor shaft (see illustration).

11  Mark the relationship of the actuator arm to the motor shaft, then remove the actuator arm from the shaft.

12  Remove the motor mounting bolts and remove the motor (see illustration 12.10).

13  Installation is the reverse of removal. Be sure to align the marks you made on the actuator arm and the motor shaft, and on the windshield wiper arms and the wiper arm shafts.

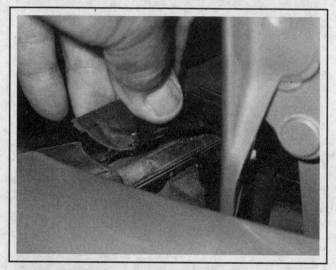

**12.7a  Detach the ends of the water collector from the molding**

**12.7b  . . . and lift the water protector out**

**12.8  Remove the wiper linkage mounting bolts and cut the tie wrap that secures the wiring harness**

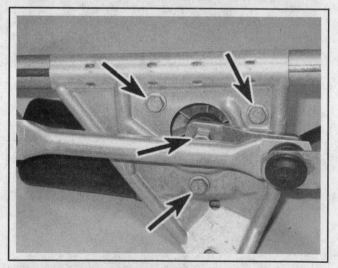

**12.10  Remove the actuator arm nut and motor mounting bolts**

## 13  Headlight housing - replacement

▶ Refer to illustrations 13.2a and 13.2b

### ✳✳ WARNING:

**Some models use High Intensity Discharge (HID) bulbs instead of conventional halogen bulbs. According to the manufacturer, the high voltages produced by this system can be fatal in the event of a shock. Also, the voltage can remain in the circuit even after the headlight switch has been turned to OFF and the ignition key has been removed. Therefore, for your safety, we don't recommend that you try to perform this procedure yourself if your vehicle is equipped with xenon headlight bulbs. Instead, have this service performed by a dealer service department or other qualified repair shop.**

1   Open the hood and prop it up all the way. If you're just removing one headlight housing, loosen the bumper on that side of the vehicle, then cover it with shop towels to prevent scratches. If you're removing both headlight housings, remove the bumper cover (see Chapter 11).

2   Remove the headlight housing bolts (see illustrations). Pull out the headlight housing and disconnect the electrical connector. If the vehicle has xenon headlights, disconnect the vacuum line from the bottom of the housing.

3   Installation is the reverse of removal.

4   Have the headlight adjustment checked when you're done (see Section 14).

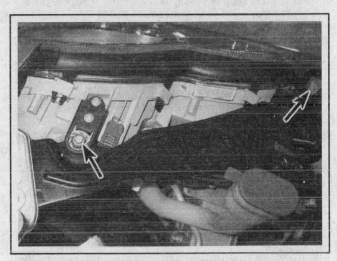

13.2a  Remove the headlight housing upper mounting bolts . . .

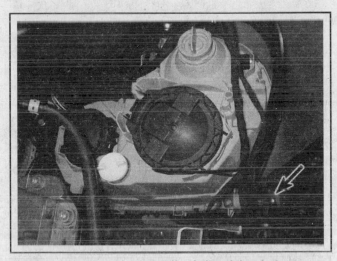

13.2b  . . . and the lower mounting bolt and thumbwheel

## 14  Headlights - adjustment

The headlights must be aimed correctly. If adjusted incorrectly they could blind the driver of an oncoming vehicle and cause a serious accident or seriously reduce your ability to see the road. The headlights should be checked for proper aim every 12 months and any time a new headlight is installed or front end bodywork is performed. The headlights are adjusted by an automatic aiming system. If adjustment is not correct, take the vehicle to a dealer service department or other qualified shop.

**15  Headlight bulb - replacement**

### ⁕⁕ WARNING:

Halogen gas-filled bulbs are under pressure and can shatter if the surface is scratched or the bulb is dropped. Wear eye protection and handle the bulbs carefully, grasping only the base whenever possible. Do not touch the surface of the bulb with your fingers because the oil from your skin could cause it to overheat and fail prematurely. If you do touch the bulb surface, clean it with rubbing alcohol.

## CONVENTIONAL (HALOGEN) HEADLIGHTS

1  Make sure the headlight switch is in the OFF position and open the hood.

### Low beam

▶ Refer to illustrations 15.2, 15.3a and 15.3b

2  Open the bulb housing cover on the back of the headlight housing (see illustration).

3  Disconnect the low beam headlight bulb electrical connector (see illustration). Twist the bulb retaining ring counterclockwise and remove the bulb from the socket (see illustration). When installing the bulb, be sure it aligns properly with the housing before twisting the retaining ring clockwise to lock it in place.

### High beam

▶ Refer to illustration 15.4

4  Open the bulb housing cover on the back of the headlight housing (see illustration).

5  Disconnect the high beam headlight bulb electrical connector. Twist the bulb retaining ring counterclockwise and remove the bulb from the socket (see illustration). When installing the bulb, be sure it aligns properly with the housing before twisting the retaining ring

clockwise to lock it in place (the flat part of the bulb flange must be positioned at the top).

## DUAL XENON (HID) HEADLIGHTS

### ⁕⁕ WARNING:

Some models use High Intensity Discharge (HID) bulbs instead of conventional halogen bulbs. According to the manufacturer, the high voltages produced by this system can be fatal in the event of a shock. Also, the voltage can remain in the circuit even after the headlight switch has been turned to OFF and the ignition key has been removed. Therefore, for your safety, we don't recommend that you try to replace one of these bulbs yourself. Instead, have this service performed by a dealer service department or other qualified repair shop.

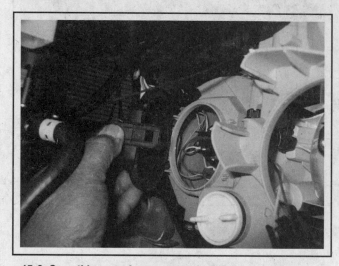

**15.2  Open this cover for access to the low beam bulb**

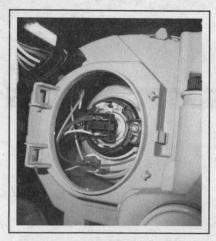

**15.3a  The headlight bulb is on top and the parking light bulb is below it. To disconnect the electrical connector from the headlight bulb, pull it straight off**

**15.3b  Turn the bulb retaining ring counterclockwise until it stops, then remove the bulb**

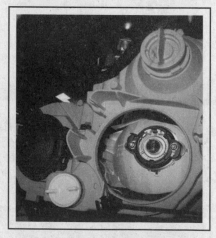

**15.4  The conventional high beam bulb is located behind the larger cover**

## 16  Bulb replacement

### EXTERIOR LIGHTS

#### Front side marker light bulbs

▶ **Refer to illustrations 16.1 and 16.2**

1  Carefully pry the bulb housing out of the bumper cover with a trim stick (see illustration).

2  Twist the bulb socket and remove it from the housing, then remove the bulb from the socket (see illustration). Installation is the reverse of removal.

#### Front parking light bulbs

3  Open the hood.

4  Open the low beam bulb cover on the back of the headlight housing (see illustration 15.3a). Pull the front parking light bulb holder out of the headlight housing.

5  To remove the old bulb from its holder, pull it straight out.

6  To install a new bulb in the bulb holder, push it straight into the socket until it stops.

7  Installation is otherwise the reverse of removal.

#### Front turn signal lights

▶ **Refer to illustrations 16.9 and 16.10**

8  Open the hood.

9  Turn the turn signal bulb socket counterclockwise and remove it from the back of the headlight housing (see illustration).

10  Press the bulb into its socket, turn counterclockwise and remove it (see illustration).

11  Align the nubs on the side of the bulb with the slots in the socket, then push the bulb in and turn it clockwise to lock it in place. Note that the nubs are staggered; the one at the bottom of the bulb must go in the deeper slot.

12  Installation is otherwise the reverse of removal.

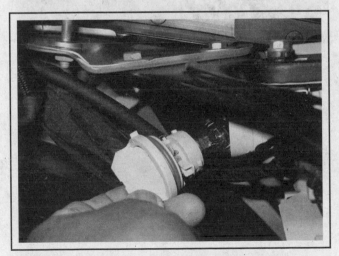

**16.1  Carefully pry the side marker light assembly out with a trim stick . . .**

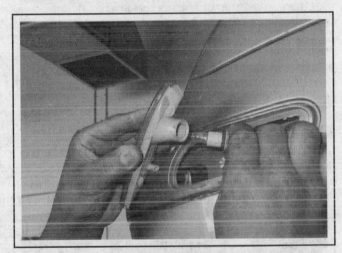

**16.2  . . . then turn the bulb socket to remove it from the housing and pull the bulb out of the socket**

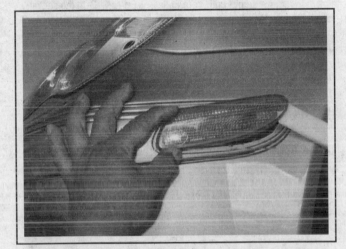

**16.9  Twist the turn signal bulb socket and pull it out of the housing . . .**

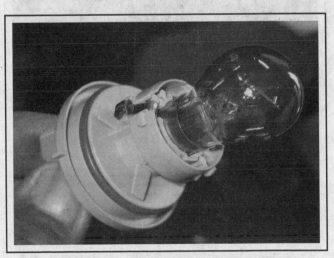

**16.10  . . . then push in on the bulb, turn it about 1/8-turn counterclockwise and remove it from the socket**

**High beam flasher bulb (xenon HID headlights)**

## Fog lights

▶ **Refer to illustration 16.13**

13 Working inside the front bumper, remove the bulb holder from the housing (see illustration).

14 Unplug the electrical connector from the bulb holder

15 The bulb and bulb holder are a single assembly. No further disassembly is necessary. The new bulb includes its own new holder.

## Center high-mounted brake light

▶ **Refer to illustration 16.17**

16 Open the trunk and remove the trim from the underside of the trunk lid (see Chapter 11).

17 Remove the center high-mounted brake light housing mounting bolts at the retaining clips (see illustration).

18 Disengage the retaining clips, remove the center high-mounted brake light assembly and disconnect the electrical connector.

19 The center high-mounted brake light housing, lens and bulb(s) are a one-piece assembly. No further disassembly is possible.

20 Installation is the reverse of removal.

## License plate light bulbs

▶ **Refer to illustration 16.21**

21 Remove the license plate lamp screws and take the lamp out of the vehicle body (see illustration). The bulb will come out with the lens

22 Remove the old bulb from the lens and install the new one. Line up the terminals of the bulb with the contacts, then push the lens into place and tighten the screws.

## Taillight bulbs

▶ **Refer to illustrations 16.24, 16.25, 16.26 and 16.27**

23 Open the trunk and fold the trim panel out of the way to expose the taillight housing.

24 To detach the taillight bulb carrier from the vehicle, twist the plastic latch counterclockwise (see illustration).

25 Pull out the bulb carrier (see illustration).

26 Lay the bulb carrier on a clean surface and refer to the accompanying taillight bulb guide (see illustration).

27 To remove an old bulb from the carrier, press it into the socket, turn it counterclockwise and pull it out of the housing (see illustration).

28 Installation is the reverse of removal.

➥**Note: On dual-filament bulbs the locating nubs on the bulb are staggered; the one at the bottom of the bulb must go in the deeper slot.**

## INTERIOR LIGHTS

## Dome light bulbs

▶ **Refer to illustrations 16.29a, 16.29b, 16.30a and 16.30b**

29 Pry off the dome light lens (see illustration).

**16.13 Remove the fog light bulb and holder from the housing (the bulb can't be separated from its holder)**

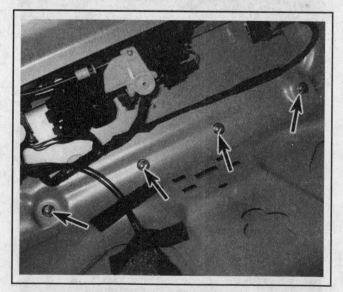

**16.17 Remove the bolts and remove the high-mounted brake light from the trunk lid**

**16.21  The license plate light bulb will come out with the lens**

**16.24  Twist the latch . . .**

**16.25  . . . and take the taillight bulb carrier out of the housing**

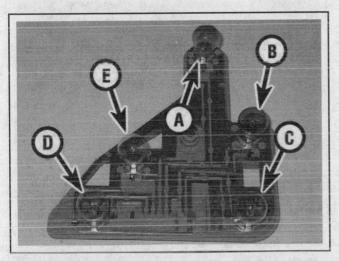

**16.26  Taillight unit bulbs**

A  Brake light
B  Turn signal
C  Parking/side marker light
D  Tail/parking light, rear fog lamp (driver's side only)
E  Back-up light

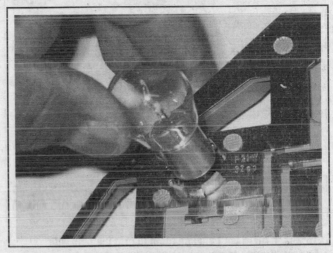

**16.27  Remove the bulb from the socket**

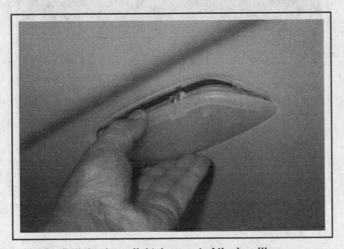

**16.29a  Pull the dome light down out of the headliner . . .**

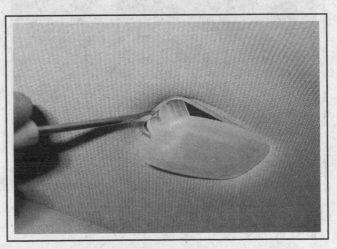

**16.29b  . . . prying it carefully if necessary**

30 Remove the bad light bulb from the terminals in the lens (see illustration).

### ❋❋ WARNING:

**If it's necessary to pry a bulb out, pry only on the metal terminal ends.**

31 To install a new bulb, push it up between the conductors until it snaps into place.

32 When installing the lens, make sure that it snaps into place.

## Map light bulbs

▶ **Refer to illustration 16.34**

33 Remove the overhead switch assembly from the headliner (see Section 8).

34 Twist the bulb counterclockwise to align the tabs with the slots, then pull out the bulb (see illustration).

35 Installation is the reverse of the removal steps.

## Glove compartment light

▶ **Refer to illustration 16.36**

36 Open the glove compartment and carefully pry the lens downward (see illustration). Pull the bulb out of its clips and install a new one.

## Illuminated door sills

37 Replacement of the illuminated door sills is a complicated procedure that should be done by a dealer service department or other qualified shop.

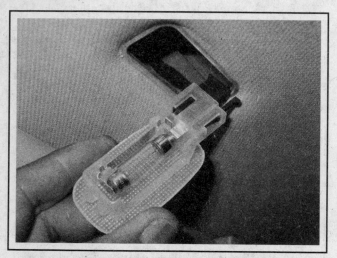

**16.30a** If there isn't enough room to grip the bulb with fingers, be sure to pry only against the metal ends

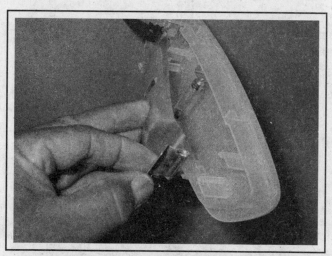

**16.30b** Pivot the reflector (if equipped) out of the way for access to the bulb

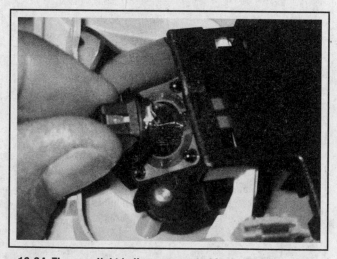

**16.34** The map light bulbs are mounted in the forward edge of the overhead switch housing

**16.36** Pull the glove compartment light lens down for access to the bulb

## 17  Horn - replacement

▶ **Refer to illustration 17.2**

➡**Note: The horns are located in front of the radiator grille.**

1  Open the hood.

2  Locate the horns (see illustration).

3  Disconnect the electrical connector from the horns.

4  Remove the horn mounting nut and remove the two horns and the mounting bracket as a single assembly.

5  Once the horns and mounting bracket are removed, you can detach either or both horns as necessary from the mounting bracket by unbolting them.

6  Installation is the reverse of removal.

17.2  Remove the nut and unplug the electrical connectors to remove the horns

## 18  Rear window defogger - check and repair

1  The rear window defogger consists of a number of horizontal elements baked onto the glass surface.

2  Small breaks in the element can be repaired without removing the rear window.

### CHECK

▶ **Refer to illustrations 18.4, 18.5 and 18.7**

3  Turn the ignition switch and defogger system switches to the ON position. Using a voltmeter, place the positive probe against the defogger grid positive terminal and the negative probe against the ground terminal. If battery voltage is not indicated, check the fuse, defogger switch and related wiring. If voltage is indicated, but all or part of the defogger doesn't heat, proceed with the following tests.

4  When measuring voltage during the next two tests, wrap a piece of aluminum foil around the tip of the voltmeter positive probe and press the foil against the heating element with your finger (see illustration). Place the negative probe on the defogger grid ground terminal.

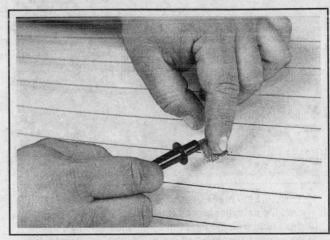

18.4  When measuring the voltage at the rear window defogger grid, wrap a piece of aluminum foil around the positive probe of the voltmeter and press the foil against the wire with your finger

5   Check the voltage at the center of each heating element (see illustration). If the voltage is 5 or 6-volts, the element is okay (there is no break). If the voltage is zero, the element is broken between the center of the element and the positive end. If the voltage is 10 to 12-volts the element is broken between the center of the element and ground. Check each heating element.

6   Connect the negative lead to a good body ground. The reading should stay the same. If it doesn't, the ground connection is bad.

7   To find the break, place the voltmeter negative probe against the defogger ground terminal. Place the voltmeter positive probe with the foil strip against the heating element at the positive terminal end and slide it toward the negative terminal end. The point at which the voltmeter deflects from several volts to zero is the point at which the heating element is broken (see illustration).

## REPAIR

▶ **Refer to illustration 18.13**

8   Repair the break in the element using a repair kit specifically recommended for this purpose, available at most auto parts stores. Included in this kit is plastic conductive epoxy.

9   Prior to repairing a break, turn off the system and allow it to cool off for a few minutes.

10   Lightly buff the element area with fine steel wool, then clean it thoroughly with rubbing alcohol.

11   Use masking tape to mask off the area being repaired.

12   Thoroughly mix the epoxy, following the instructions provided with the repair kit.

13   Apply the epoxy material to the slit in the masking tape, overlapping the undamaged area about 3/4-inch on either end (see illustration).

14   Allow the repair to cure for 24 hours before removing the tape and using the system.

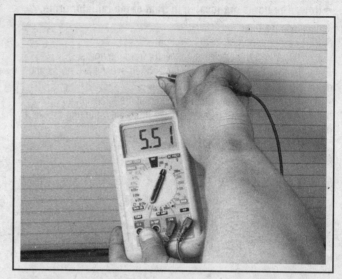

**18.5  To determine if a heating element has broken, check the voltage at the center of each element; if the voltage is 5 or 6-volts, the element is unbroken, but if the voltage is 10 or 12-volts, the element is broken between the center and the ground side. If there is no voltage, the element is broken between the center and the positive side**

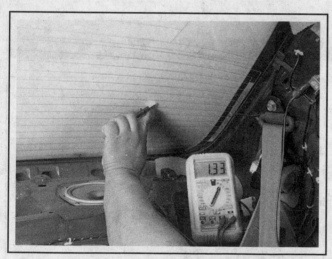

**18.7  To find the break, place the voltmeter negative lead against the defogger ground terminal, place the voltmeter positive lead with the foil strip against the heating element at the positive terminal end and slide it toward the negative terminal end. The point at which the voltmeter reading changes abruptly is the point at which the element is broken**

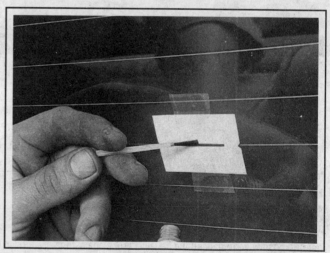

**18.13  To use a defogger repair kit, apply masking tape to the inside of the window at the damaged area, then brush on the special conductive coating**

## 19  Electric side view mirrors - general information

1   Most electric rear view mirrors use two motors to move the glass; one for up and down adjustments and one for left-right adjustments.

2   The control switch has a selector portion that sends voltage to the left or right side mirror. With the ignition ON but the engine OFF, roll down the windows and operate the mirror control switch through all functions (LEFT-RIGHT and UP-DOWN) for both the left and right side mirrors.

3   Listen carefully for the sound of the electric motors running in the mirrors.

4   If the motors can be heard but the mirror glass doesn't move, there's a problem with the drive mechanism inside the mirror.

5   If the mirrors do not operate and no sound comes from the mirrors, check the fuse (see Section 3).

6   If the fuse is OK, remove the mirror control switch. Have the switch continuity checked by a dealership service department or other qualified automobile repair facility.

7   Make sure the mirror is properly grounded.

8   If the mirror still doesn't work, remove the mirror and check the wires at the mirror for voltage.

9   If there's not voltage in each switch position, check the circuit between the mirror and control switch for opens and shorts.

10 If there's voltage, remove the mirror and test it off the vehicle with jumper wires. Replace the mirror if it fails this test.

## 20  Cruise control system - general information

There are no conventional cruise control system components on these vehicles. The cruise control system is an integral subsystem of the electronic throttle body, which is controlled by the Powertrain Control Module (PCM). If the cruise control system isn't functioning correctly, take the vehicle to a dealer service department or other qualified repair shop for diagnosis.

## 21  Power window system - general information

1   The power window system operates electric motors, mounted in the doors, which lower and raise the windows. The system consists of the control switches, the motors, regulators, glass mechanisms and associated wiring.

2   The power windows can be lowered and raised from the master control switch by the driver or by remote switches located at the individual windows. Each window has a separate motor, which is reversible. The position of the control switch determines the polarity and therefore the direction of operation.

3   The circuit is protected by a fuse and a circuit breaker. Each motor is also equipped with an internal circuit breaker; this prevents one stuck window from disabling the whole system.

4   The power window system will only operate when the ignition switch is ON. In addition, many models have a window lockout switch at the master control switch which, when activated, disables the switches at the rear windows and, sometimes, the switch at the passenger's window also. Always check these items before troubleshooting a window problem.

5   These procedures are general in nature, so if you can't find the problem using them, take the vehicle to a dealer service department or other properly equipped repair facility.

6   If the power windows won't operate, always check the fuse and circuit breaker first.

7   If only the rear windows are inoperative, or if the windows only operate from the master control switch, check the rear window lockout switch for continuity in the unlocked position. Replace it if it doesn't have continuity.

8   Check the wiring between the switches and fuse panel for continuity. Repair the wiring, if necessary.

9   If only one window is inoperative from the master control switch, try the other control switch at the window.

➤Note: This doesn't apply to the driver's door window.

10 If the same window works from one switch, but not the other, check the switch for continuity.

11 If the switch tests OK, check for a short or open in the circuit between the affected switch and the window motor.

12 If one window is inoperative from both switches, remove the trim panel from the affected door and check for voltage at the switch and at the motor while the switch is operated.

13 If voltage is reaching the motor, disconnect the glass from the regulator (see Chapter 11). Move the window up and down by hand while checking for binding and damage. Also check for binding and damage to the regulator. If the regulator is not damaged and the window moves up and down smoothly, replace the motor. If there's binding or damage, lubricate, repair or replace parts, as necessary.

14 If voltage isn't reaching the motor, check the wiring in the circuit for continuity between the switches and motors. You'll need to consult the wiring diagram for the vehicle. If the circuit is equipped with a relay, check that the relay is grounded properly and receiving voltage.

## 22 Power door lock system - general information

1   A power door lock system operates the door lock actuators mounted in each door. The system consists of the switches, actuators, a control unit and associated wiring. Diagnosis can usually be limited to simple checks of the wiring connections and actuators for minor faults that can be easily repaired.

2   Power door lock systems are operated by bi-directional solenoids located in the doors. The lock switches have two operating positions: Lock and Unlock. When activated, the switch sends a ground signal to the door lock control unit to lock or unlock the doors. Depending on which way the switch is activated, the control unit reverses polarity to the solenoids, allowing the two sides of the circuit to be used alternately as the feed (positive) and ground side.

3   Some vehicles may have an anti-theft system incorporated into the power locks. If you are unable to locate the trouble using the following general Steps, consult a dealer service department or other qualified repair shop.

4   Always check the circuit protection first. Some vehicles use a combination of circuit breakers and fuses.

5   Operate the door lock switches in both directions (Lock and Unlock) with the engine off. Listen for the click of the solenoids operating.

6   Test the switches for continuity. Remove the switches and have them checked by a dealer service department or other qualified automobile repair facility.

7   Check the wiring between the switches, control unit and solenoids for continuity. Repair the wiring if there's no continuity.

8   Check for a bad ground at the switches or at the control unit.

9   If all but one of the lock solenoids operate, remove the trim panel from the door with the problem (see Chapter 11) and check for voltage at the solenoid while the lock switch is operated. One of the wires should have voltage in the Lock position; the other should have voltage in the Unlock position.

10   If the inoperative solenoid is receiving voltage, replace the solenoid.

11   If the inoperative solenoid isn't receiving voltage, check the relay for an open or short in the wire between the lock solenoid and the control unit.

## 23 Daytime Running Lights (DRL) - general information

The Daytime Running Lights (DRL) system illuminates the low beam headlights whenever the engine is running. In low light, the tail, parking, side marker and license plate lights also turn on automatically. On US models, the system can be turned on or off (the vehicle comes from the manufacturer with the system set to Off). On Canadian models, it's on at all times.

## 24 Airbag system - general information and precautions

### GENERAL INFORMATION

1   All models are equipped with two front airbags and four side airbags, formally known as the Supplemental Restraint System (SRS). This system is designed to protect the driver and the front seat passenger from serious injury in the event of a frontal collision. It consists of an array of external and internal (inside the control unit) information sensors (decelerometers), the control unit, the inflator modules (a driver's airbag in the steering wheel, a passenger airbag in the dash and side-impact airbags in each door) and the wiring and connectors tying all these components together.

### AIRBAG/INFLATOR MODULES

**Driver's airbag/inflator module**

2   The airbag inflator module in the steering wheel consists of a housing, the cushion (airbag), an initiating device and a canister of gas-generating material. The initiator is part of the inflator module deployment loop. When a collision occurs, the control unit sends current through the deployment loop to the initiator. Current passing through the initiator ignites the material in the canister, producing a rapidly expanding gas, which inflates the airbag almost instantaneously. Seconds after the airbag inflates, it deflates almost as quickly through airbag vent holes and/or the airbag fabric.

3   When the control unit sends current to the initiator, it travels through the airbag circuit to the steering column. From there, a clockspring on the steering wheel delivers the current to the module initiator. This clockspring assembly, which is the final segment of the airbag ignition circuit, functions as the bridge between the end of the airbag circuit on the (fixed) steering column and the beginning of the circuit on the (rotating) steering wheel. It's designed to maintain a closed circuit between the steering column and the steering wheel regardless of the position of the steering wheel. For this reason, remov-

ing and installing the clockspring is critical to the performance of the driver's side airbag. For information on how to remove and install the driver's side airbag, refer to *Steering wheel - removal and installation* in Chapter 10.

### Passenger's airbag/inflator module

4   The passenger's airbag/inflator module is mounted above the glove compartment. It's similar in design to the driver's airbag except that it doesn't use a clockspring. When deployed by the control unit, the passenger's airbag bursts through the dashboard above the glove box. Although this area looks like it's simply part of the dashboard, it's actually a trim cover with a perforated seam that allows the cover to separate from the dash when the passenger's airbag inflates.

### Side impact airbags

5   The side-impact airbag/inflator modules are mounted in the front and rear doors (one airbag for each door) behind the trim panels. The letters SRS are molded into the module cover portion of each door trim panel. Each module consists of a housing, an inflatable airbag, an initiator and a canister of gas-generating material. Each module employs its own side impact sensor (SIS), which contains a sensing device that monitors changes in vehicle acceleration and velocity. This data is sent to the control unit, which compares it with its program. When the data exceeds a certain threshold, the SDM determines that the vehicle has been hit hard enough on one side or the other to warrant deployment of the side airbag on that side. The SDM doesn't deploy the side airbags on both sides, just on the side being hit. Then the SDM sends current to the initiator to inflate the airbag, ripping open the trim as it deploys to protect the occupant(s) on the left or right side of the vehicle.

## CONTROL UNIT

6   The control unit, mounted on the transmission tunnel under the console, is the computer module that controls the airbag system. Besides a microprocessor, the control unit also includes an array of sensors. Some of them are inside the unit itself. Other external sensors are located throughout the vehicle. All of the sensors, internal and external, send a continuous voltage signal to the control unit, which compares this data to values stored in its memory. When these signals exceed a threshold value - when the control unit determines that the vehicle is decelerating more quickly than the threshold value - the control unit allows current to flow through the circuit to the appropriate airbag module(s), which initiates deployment of the airbag(s).

7   For more information about the airbag system in your vehicle, refer to your owner's manual.

## DISARMING THE SYSTEM AND OTHER PRECAUTIONS

**⁑ WARNING:**

**Failure to follow these precautions could result in accidental deployment of the airbag and personal injury.**

8   Whenever working in the vicinity of the steering wheel, instru-

ment panel or any of the other SRS system components, the system must be disarmed. To disarm the system:
  a)   *Point the wheels straight ahead and remove the ignition key.*
  b)   *Disconnect the cable from the negative battery terminal. Refer to Chapter 5, Section 1 for the disconnecting procedure.*
  c)   *Wait at least two minutes for the back-up power supply to be depleted.*
  d)   *If you're working in the passenger compartment, disconnect the electrical connector from the control unit on the transmission tunnel.*

9   Whenever handling an airbag module, always keep the airbag opening (the upholstered side of front airbags) pointed away from your body. Never place the airbag module on a bench or other surface with the airbag opening facing the surface. Always place the airbag module in a safe location with the airbag opening (the upholstered side of front airbags) facing up.

10   Never measure the resistance of any SRS component or use any electrical test equipment on any of the wiring or components. An ohmmeter has a built-in battery supply that could accidentally deploy the airbag.

11   Never dispose of a live airbag/inflator module. Return it to a dealer service department or other qualified repair shop for safe deployment and disposal.

12   Never use electrical welding equipment in the vicinity of any airbag components. The connectors for the system are easy to spot because they're bright yellow. Do NOT disconnect or tamper with these connectors, or you run the risk of setting a Diagnostic Trouble Code (DTC) in the control unit. Like the PCM, the control unit has a malfunction indicator light, known as the AIRBAG indicator light, on the instrument cluster. When you turn the ignition key to ON, the control unit checks out all of the SRS components and circuits. If everything is okay, the AIRBAG indicator light goes off, just like the PCM's Malfunction Indicator Light (MIL). But if there's a problem somewhere, the light stays on, and will remain on until the problem is repaired and the DTC(s) cleared from the control unit's memory.

13   If an airbag is dropped from a height greater than 18 inches, it must be replaced with a new one. Dropped airbags must be safely disposed of and not reused.

14   Do not allow oil, grease or cleaning materials (solvent, etc.) to touch airbags or seat belt retractors.

## IMPACT SEAT BELT RETRACTORS

15   All models are equipped with pyrotechnic (explosive) units in the front and rear seat belt retracting mechanisms for both the lap and shoulder belts. During an impact that would trigger the airbag system, the airbag control unit also triggers the seat belt retractors. When the pyrotechnic charges go off, they accelerate the retractors to instantly take up any slack in the seat belt system to more fully prepare the driver and front seat passenger for impact.

16   The airbag system should be disabled any time work is done to or around the seats.

**⁑ WARNING:**

**Never strike the pillars or floorpan with a hammer or use an impact-driver tool in these areas unless the system is disabled.**

## 25 Remote keyless entry system - battery replacement

1  Here's how the transmitter inside the remote keyless entry fob should work:

a) *The vehicle comes from the factory with the key set to global unlocking (all the doors open when you press the Unlock button once).*

b) *The setting can be changed from global unlocking (all doors) to selective unlocking (driver's door and fuel filler cap) by holding down the Lock and Unlock buttons together for five seconds or more. In this case, when you press the UNLOCK button once, the driver's door and fuel filler cap unlock. If you press the UNLOCK button a second time, all the doors unlock.*

c) *When you press the remote TRUNK RELEASE button on the transmitter for 1/2-second, it releases the trunk lid. (The remote TRUNK RELEASE button doesn't work unless the transmission shift lever is in PARK.)*

d) *If a door or the trunk lid is open, you cannot lock the doors and trunk with the transmitter.*

### BATTERY REPLACEMENT

▶ **Refer to illustrations 25.3a, 25.3b and 25.4**

2  The transmitter batteries should last about four years. When the transmitter becomes weak, operation will become intermittent and require you to be closer to the vehicle for it to work. Eventually it won't work at all.

3  To replace the transmitter batteries, carefully open the keyless entry fob by removing the mechanical key that comes with the transmitter and inserting it into the notch near the end of the fob to disengage the lock and remove the battery holder (see illustration).

4  Remove the old batteries (see illustration).

5  Installation is the reverse of removal. Use a clean, lint-free cloth to avoid touching the new batteries. Make sure that the new battery is a CR2025 or equivalent.

**25.3a  Slide the lock (A) back and remove the mechanical key from the fob . . .**

**25.3b  . . . then insert the mechanical key into the end of the fob and push the lock to release the battery holder**

**25.4  Remove the old batteries from the holder and install new ones (the positive side of the batteries must face up)**

## 26 Wiring diagrams - general information

Since it isn't possible to include all wiring diagrams for every year covered by this manual, the following diagrams are those that are typical and most commonly needed.

Prior to troubleshooting any circuits, check the fuse and circuit breakers (if equipped) to make sure they're in good condition. Make sure the battery is properly charged and check the cable connections (see Chapter 1).

When checking a circuit, make sure that all connectors are clean, with no broken or loose terminals. When unplugging a connector, do not pull on the wires. Pull only on the connector housings themselves.

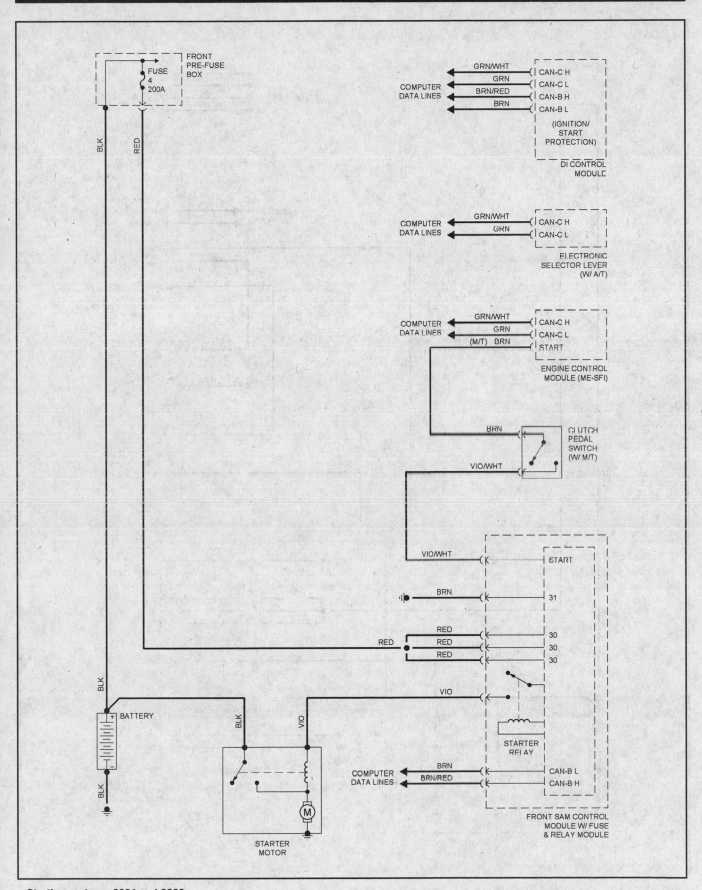

**Starting system - 2001 and 2002**

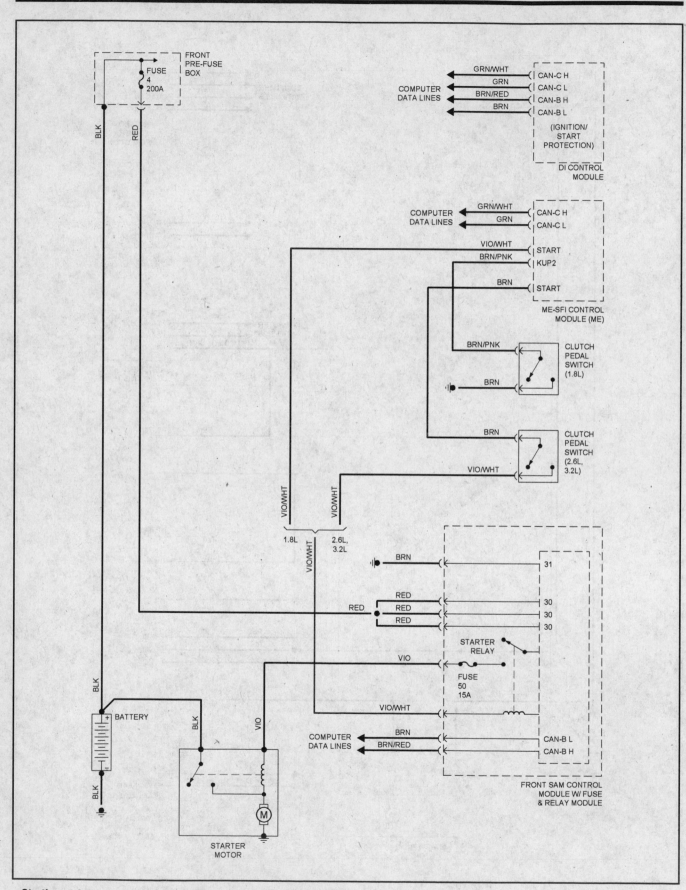

**Starting system - manual transmission models (2003 through 2005)**

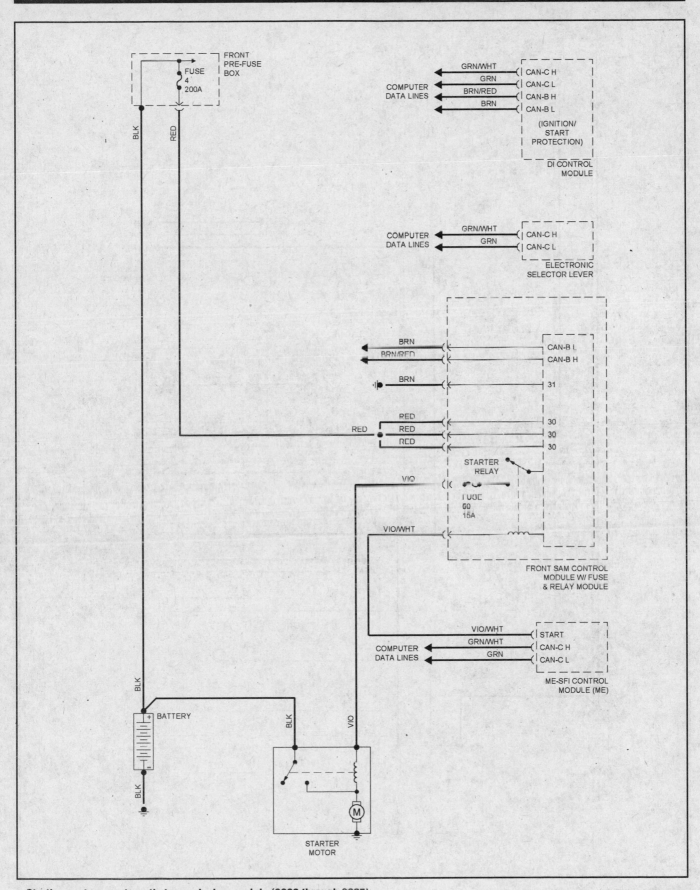

**Starting system - automatic transmission models (2003 through 2005)**

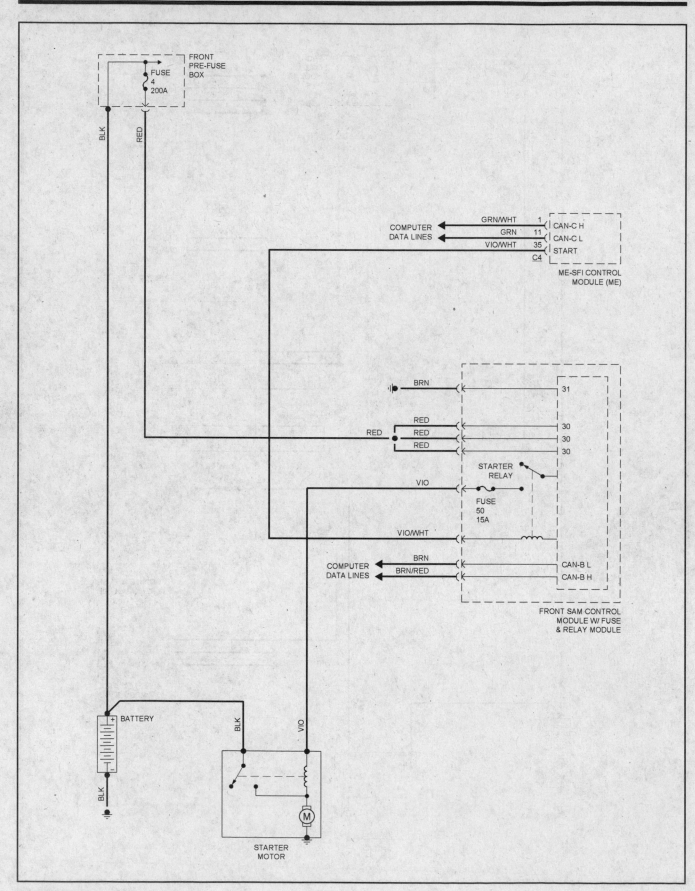

**Starting system - 2006 and later**

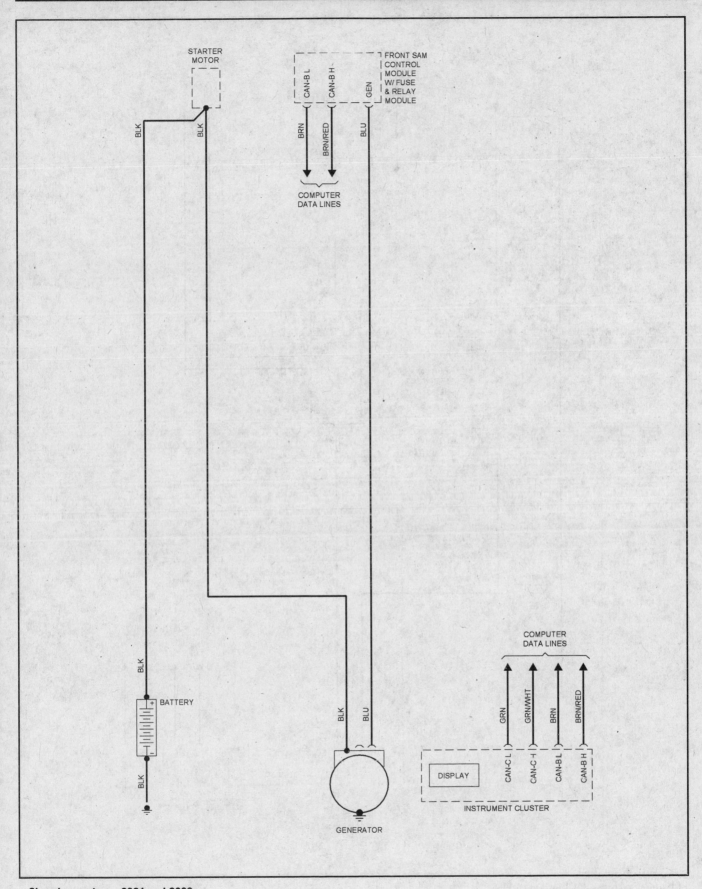

**Charging system - 2001 and 2002**

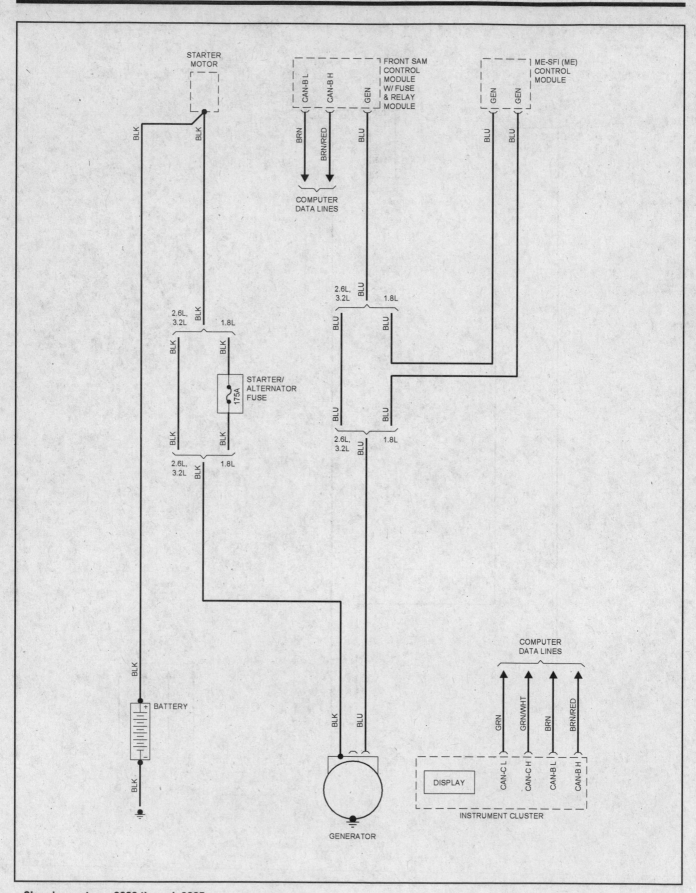

**Charging system - 2003 through 2005**

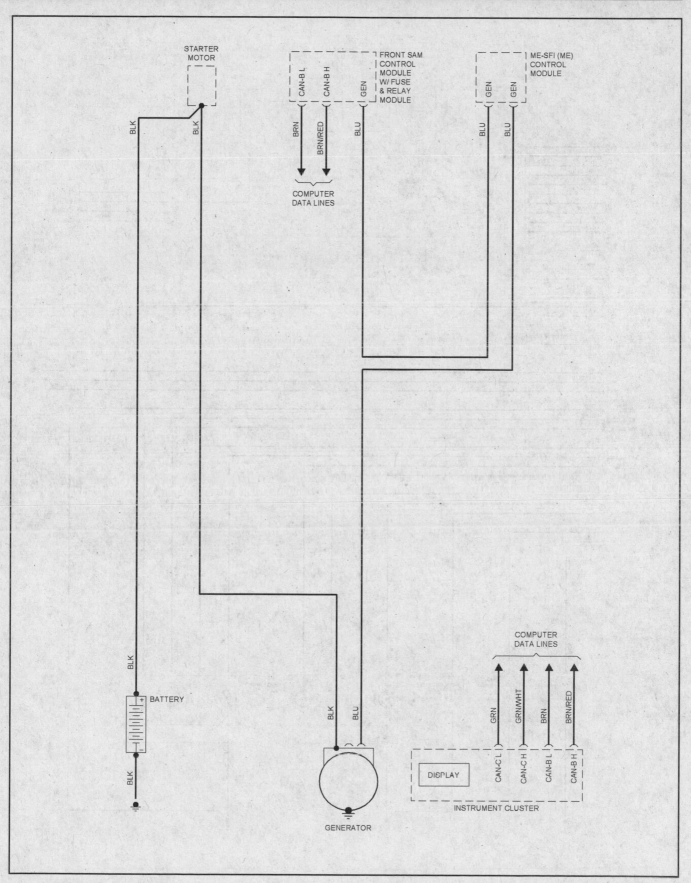

**Charging system - 2006 and later**

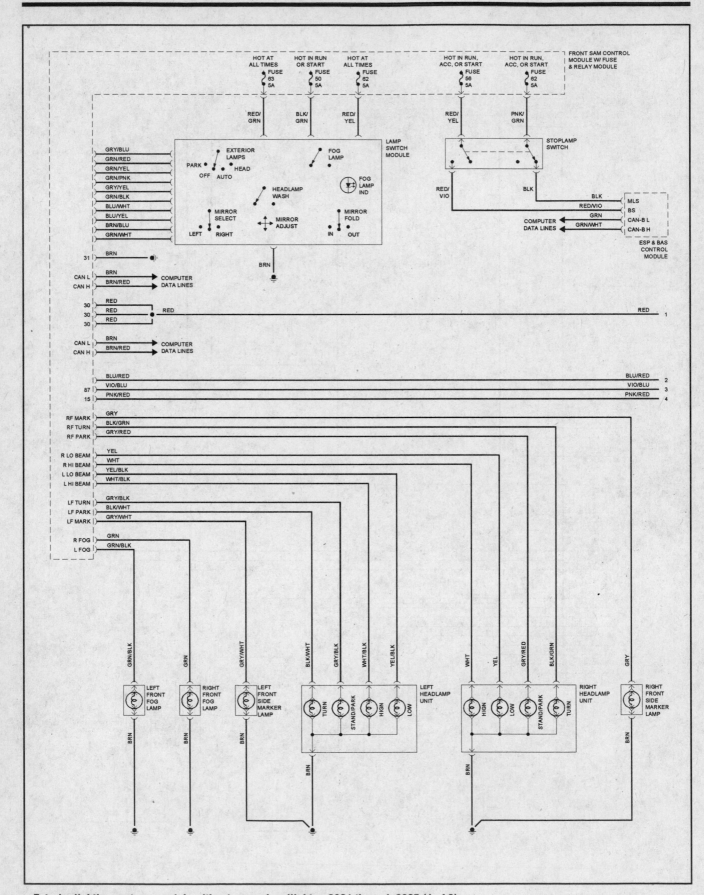

**Exterior lighting system, models without xenon headlights - 2001 through 2005 (1 of 2)**

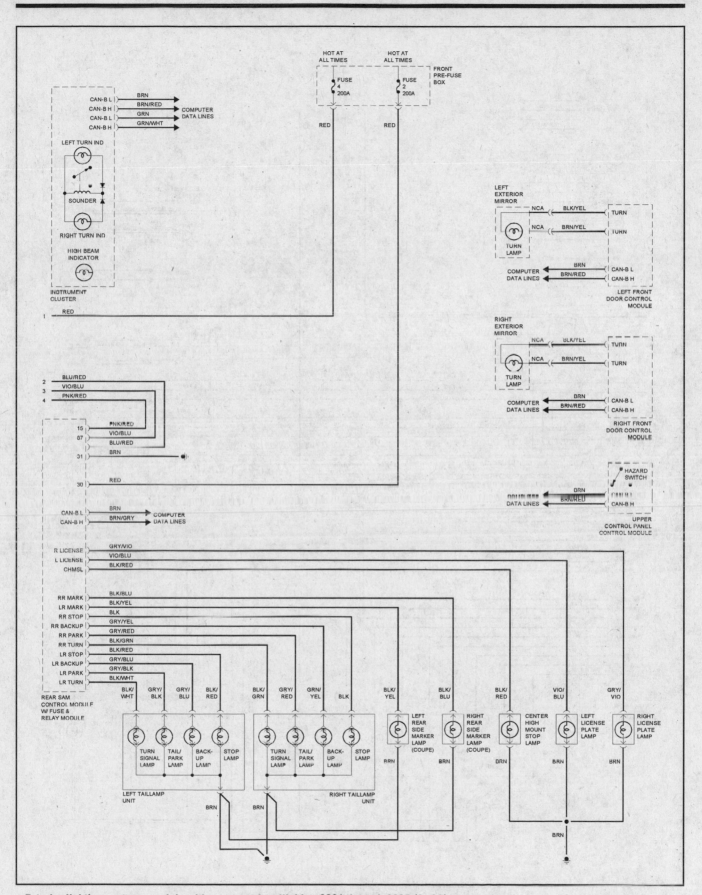

**Exterior lighting system, models without xenon headlights - 2001 through 2005 (2 of 2)**

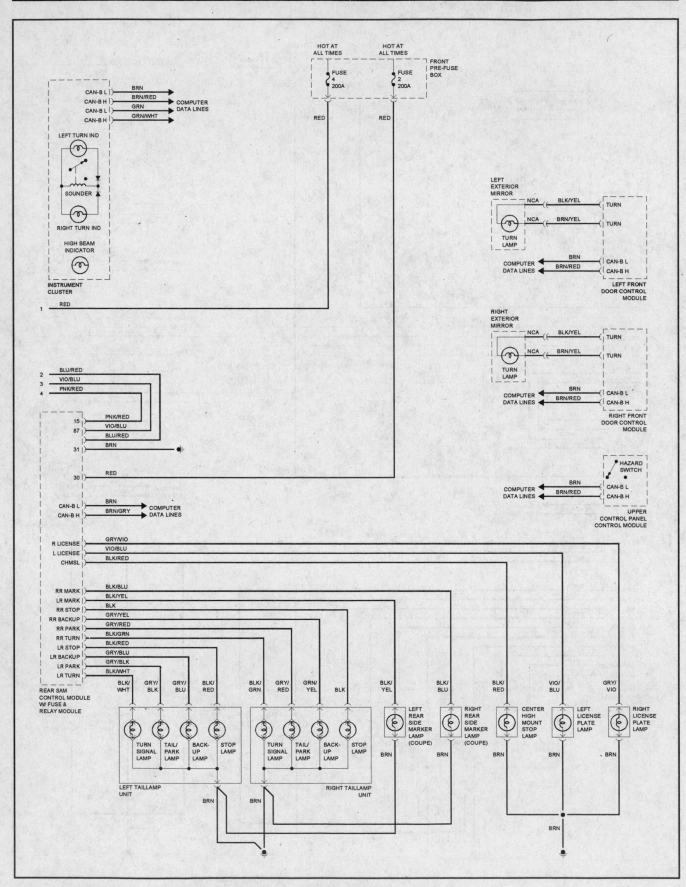

**Exterior lighting system, models with xenon headlights - 2001 through 2005 (1 of 2)**

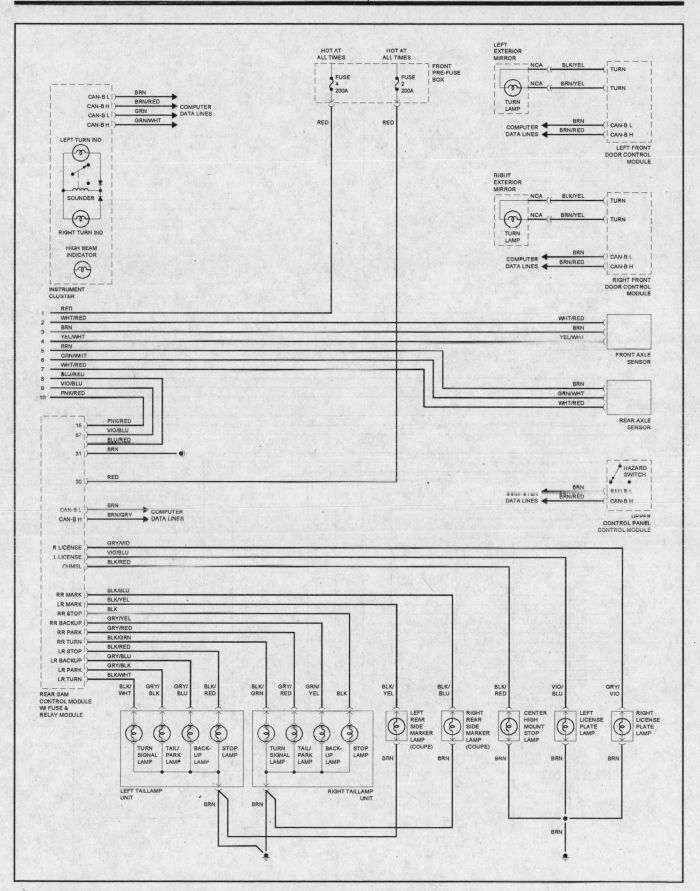

**Exterior lighting system, models with xenon headlights - 2001 through 2005 (2 of 2)**

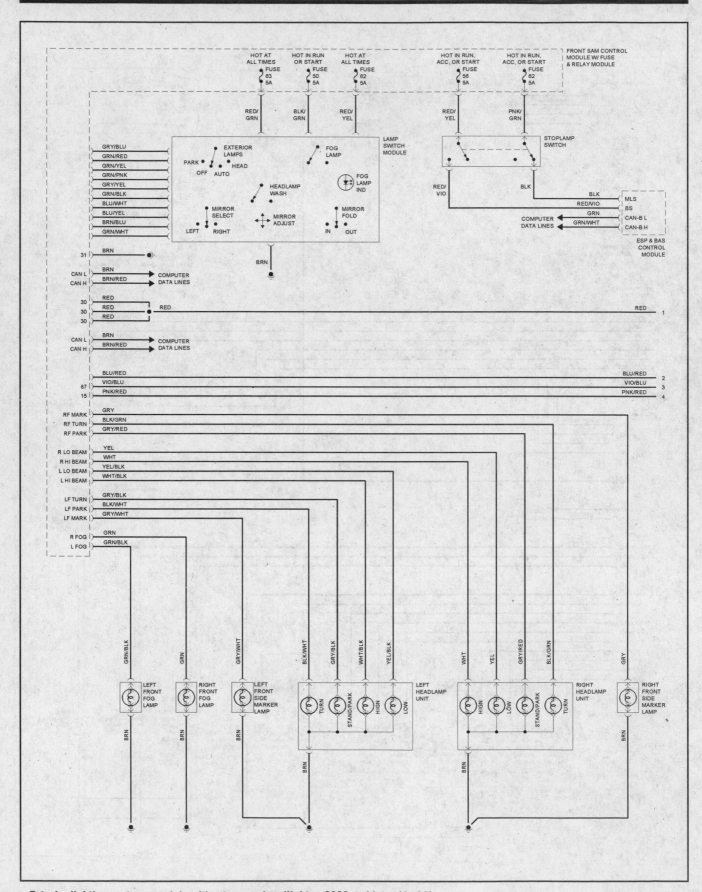

**Exterior lighting system, models without xenon headlights - 2006 and later (1 of 2)**

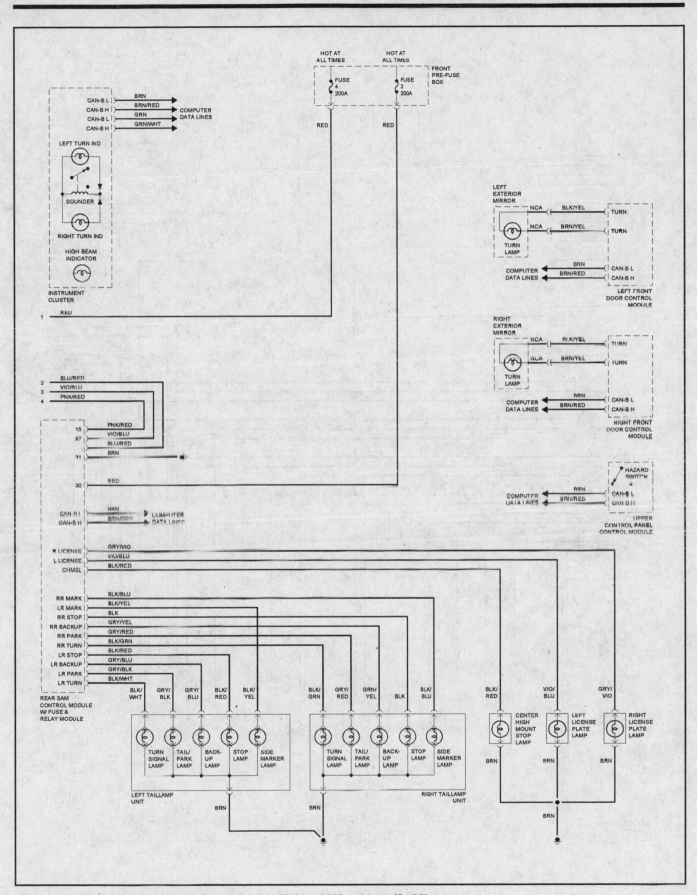

**Exterior lighting system, models without xenon headlights - 2006 and later (2 of 2)**

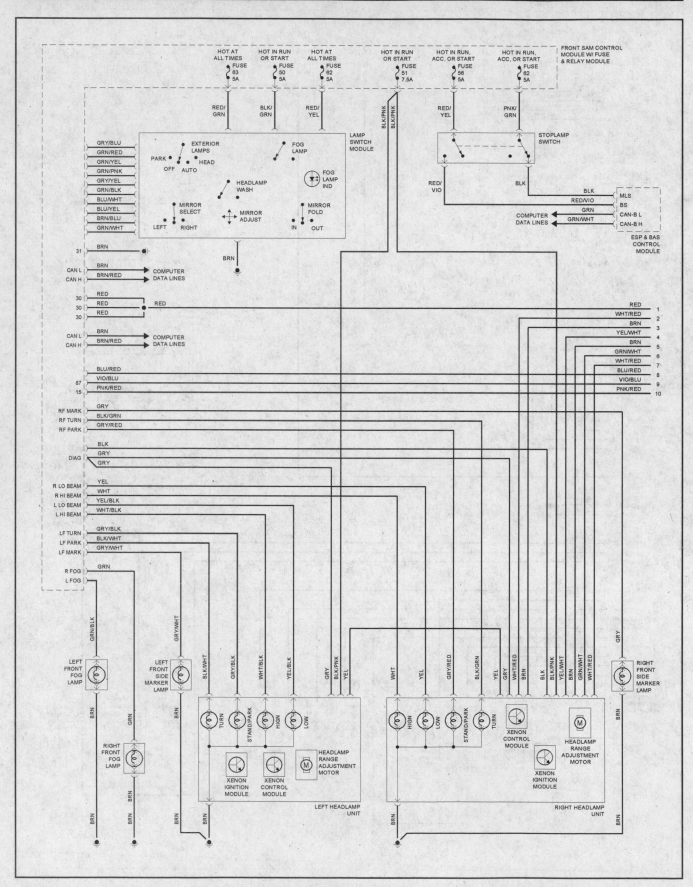

**Exterior lighting system, models with xenon headlights - 2006 and later (1 of 2)**

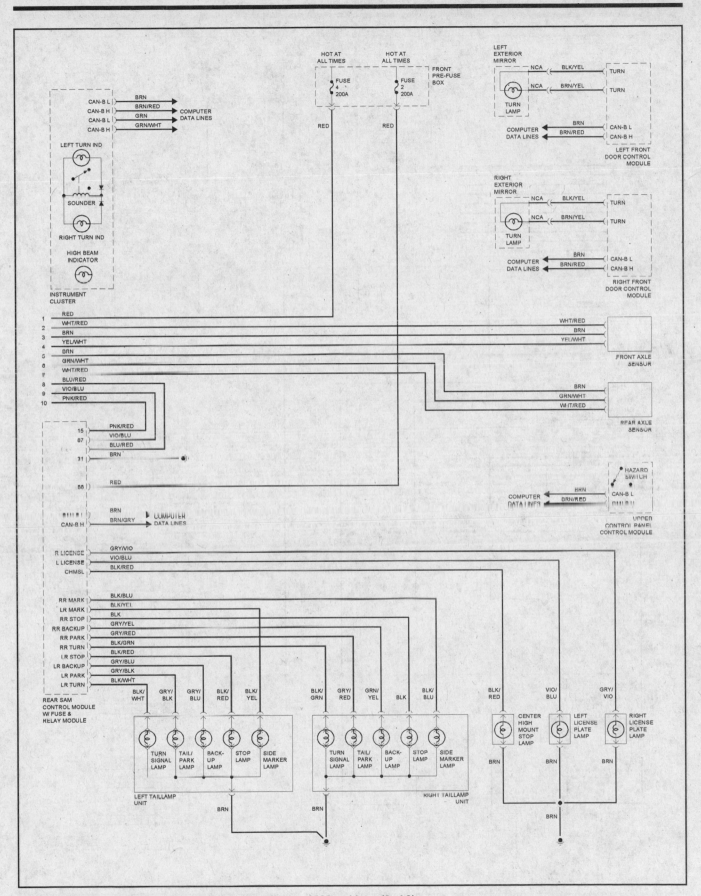

**Exterior lighting system, models with xenon headlights - 2006 and later (2 of 2)**

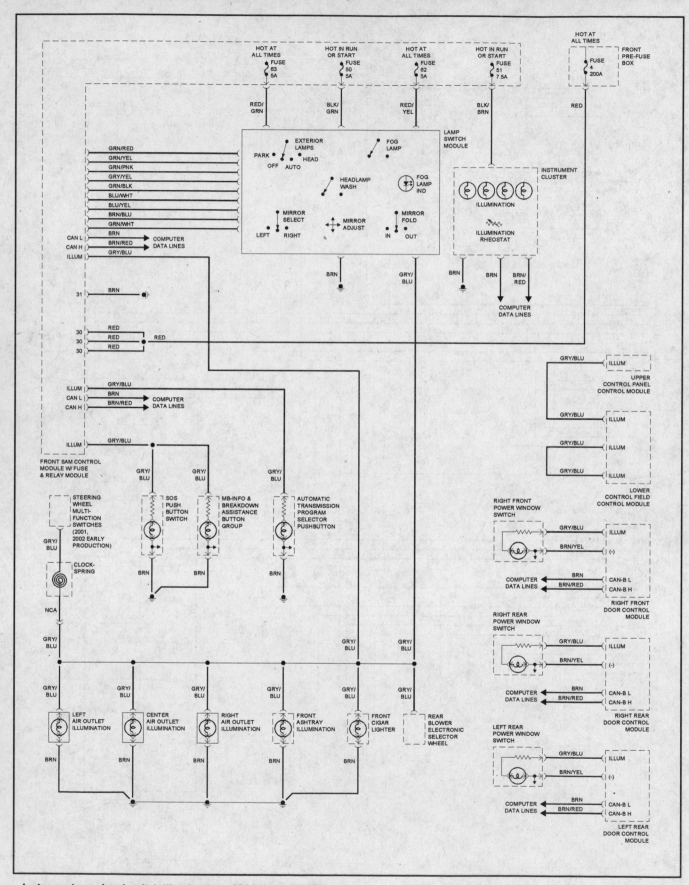

**Instrument panel and switch illumination - 2001 through 2005**

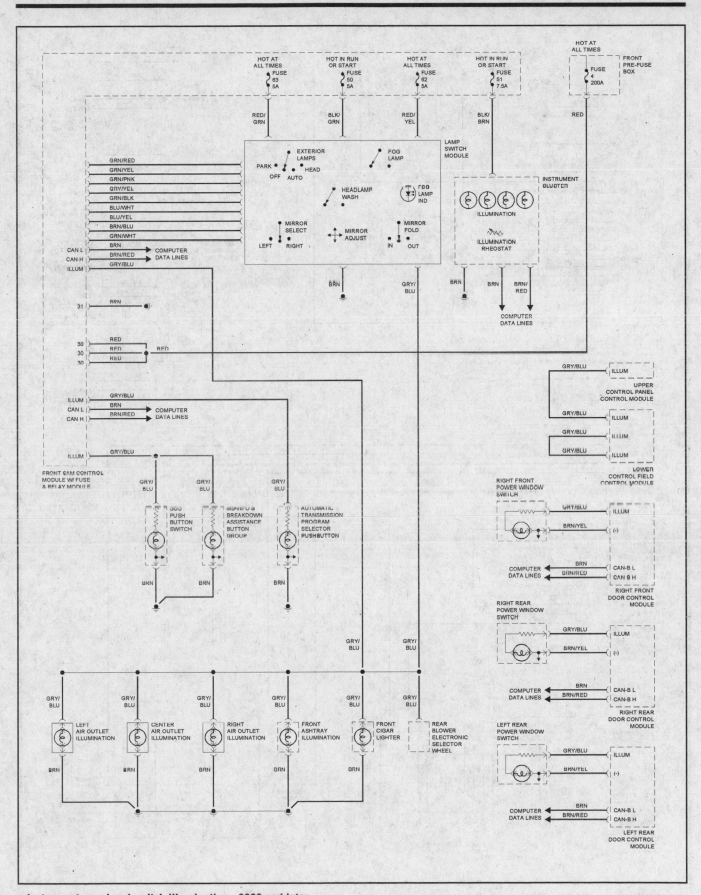

**Instrument panel and switch illumination - 2006 and later**

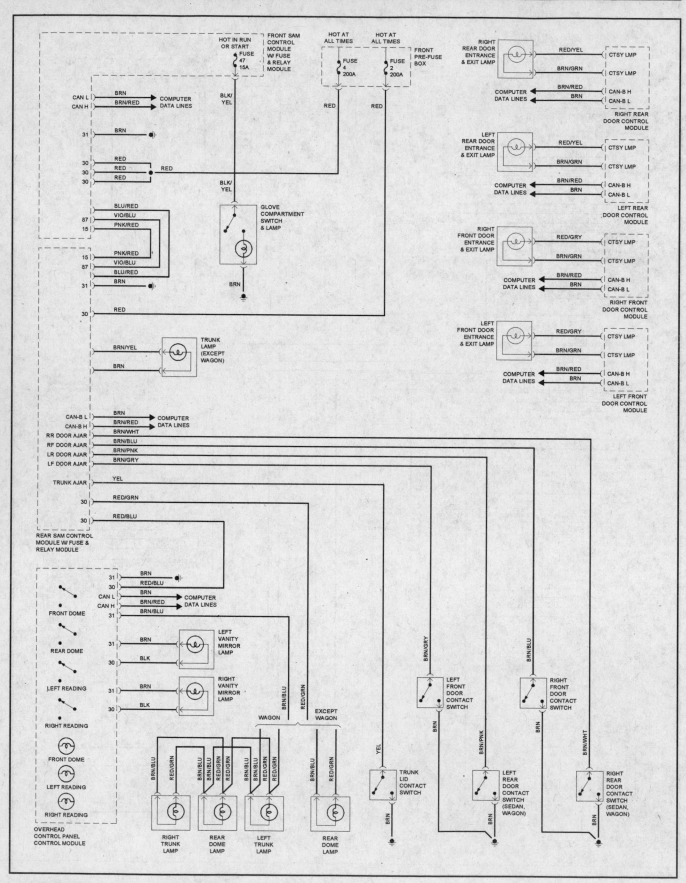

**Interior lighting system - 2001 through 2005**

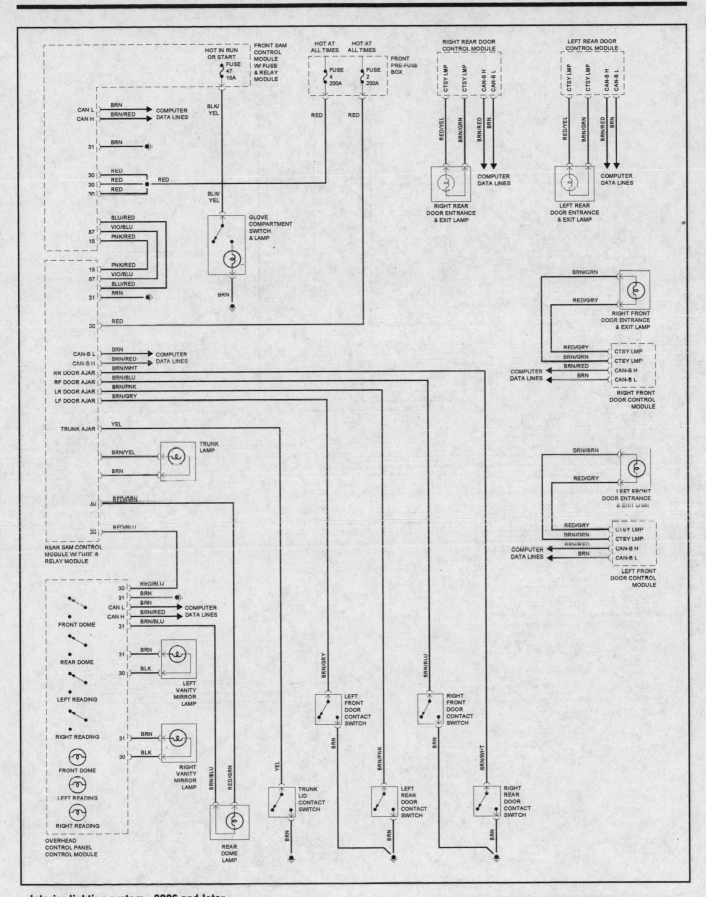

**Interior lighting system - 2006 and later**

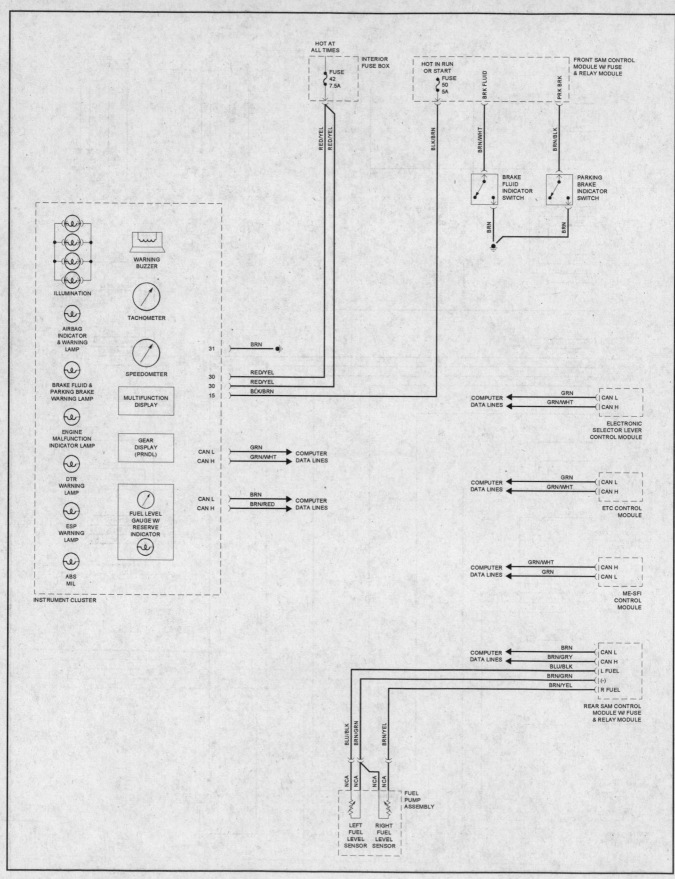

**Gauges and warning lights system - 2001 and 2002**

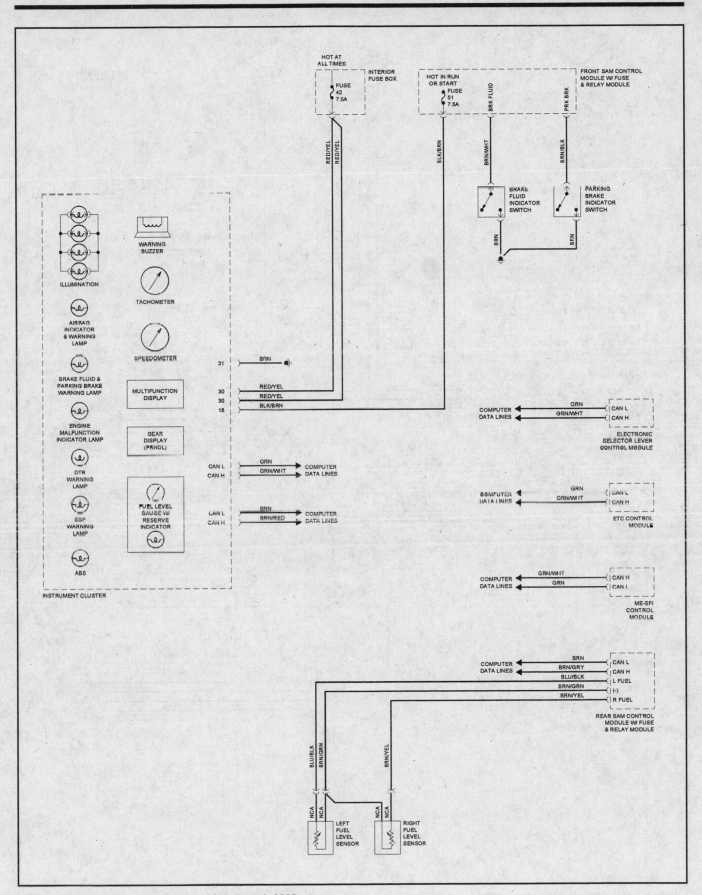

**Gauges and warning lights system - 2003 through 2005**

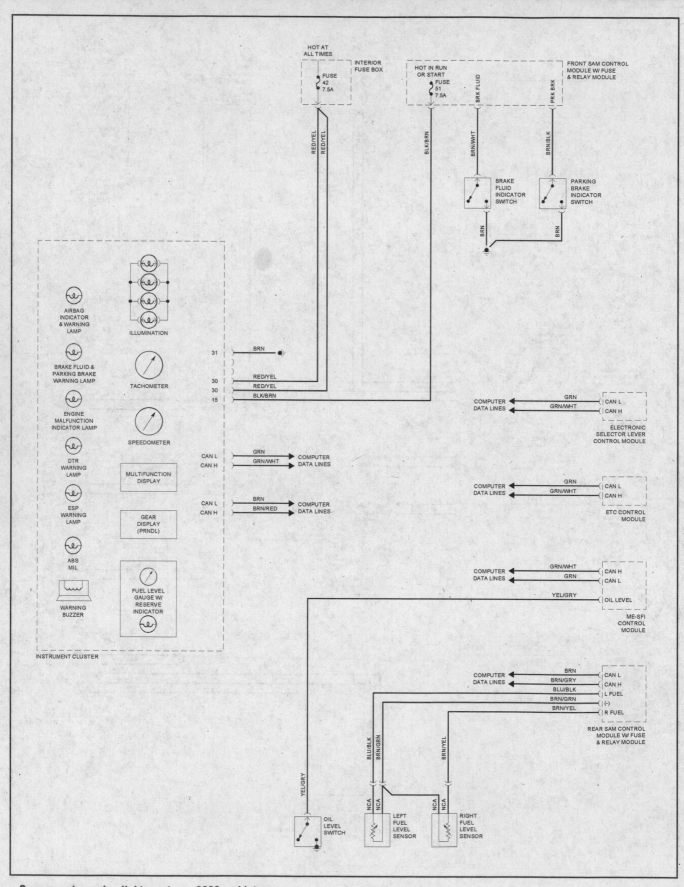

**Gauges and warning lights system - 2006 and later**

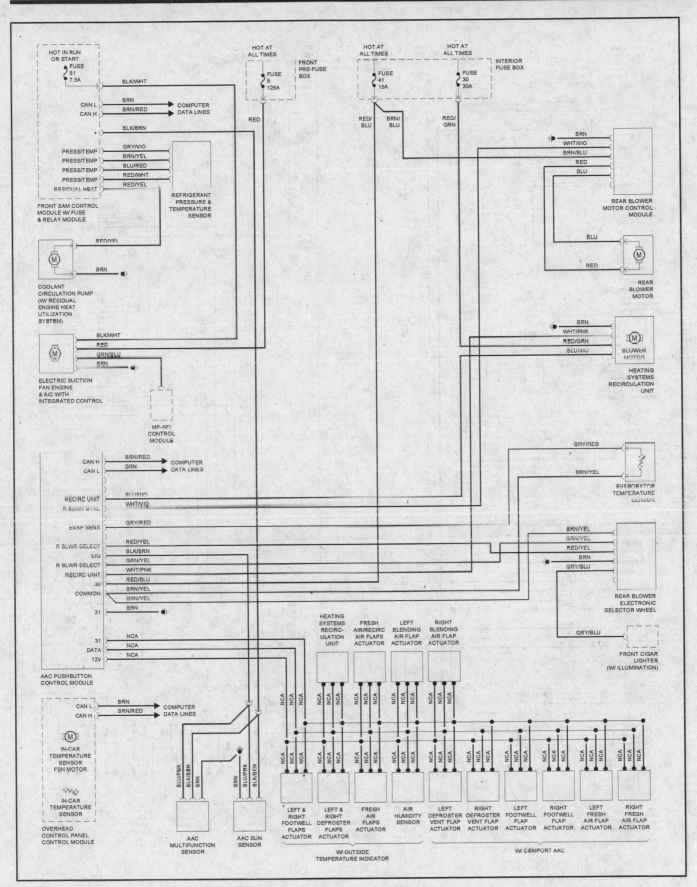

**Air conditioning and engine cooling fan system - 2001 and 2002**

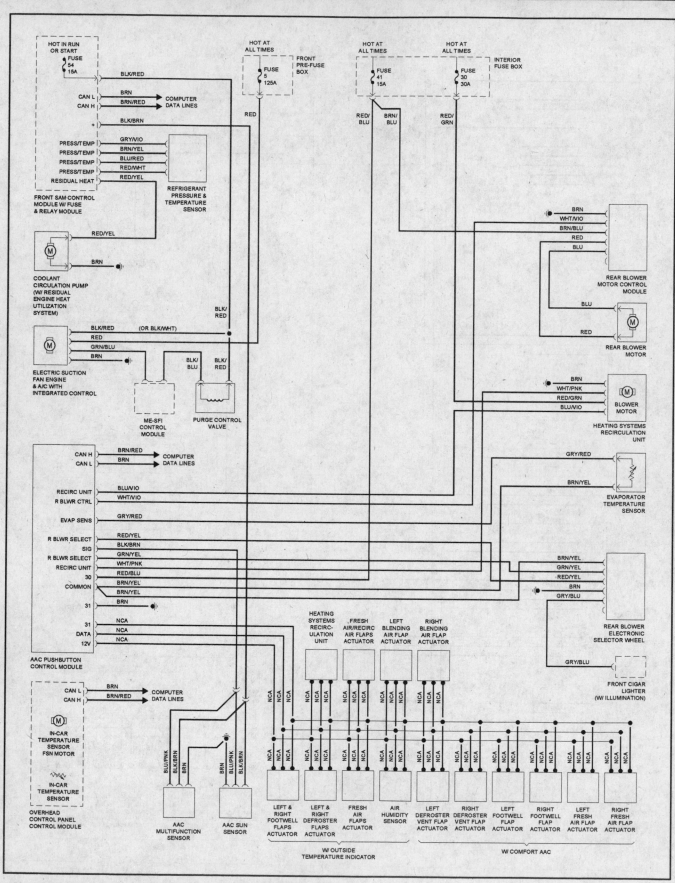

**Air conditioning and engine cooling fan system - 2003 through 2005**

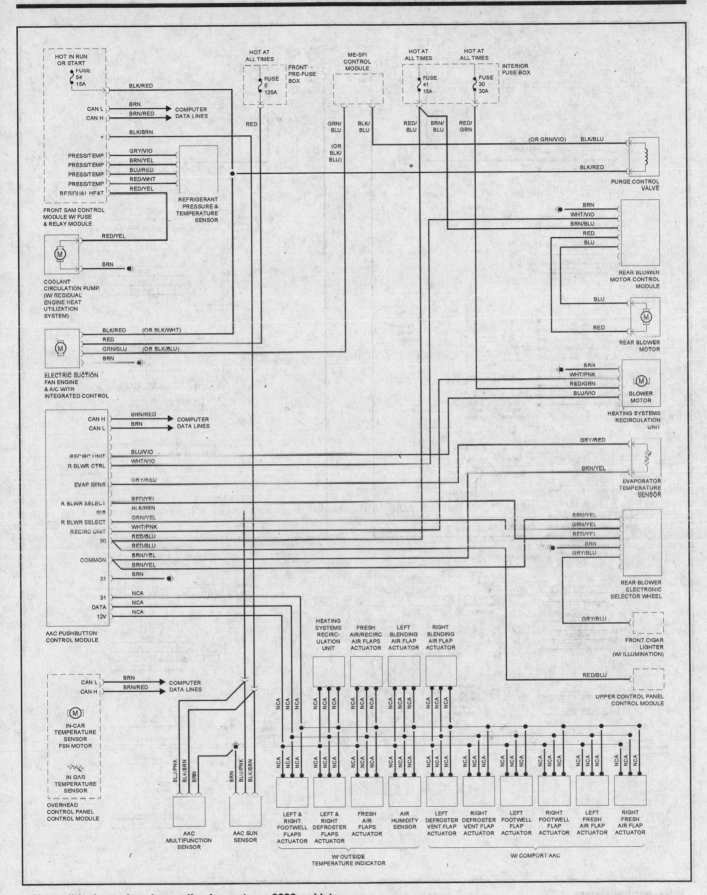

**Air conditioning and engine cooling fan system - 2006 and later**

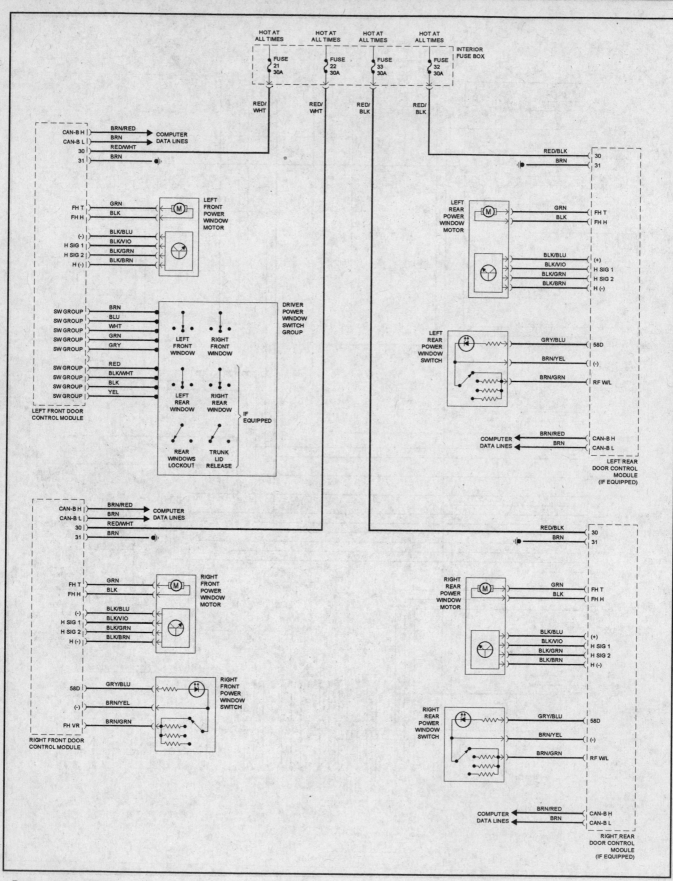

**Power window system**

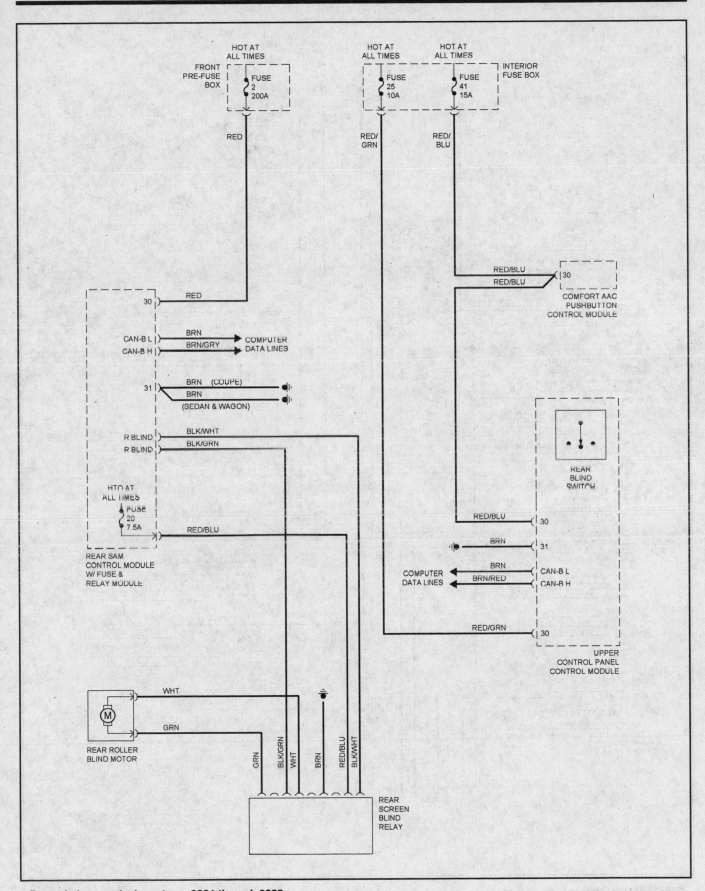

**Rear window sunshade system - 2001 through 2005**

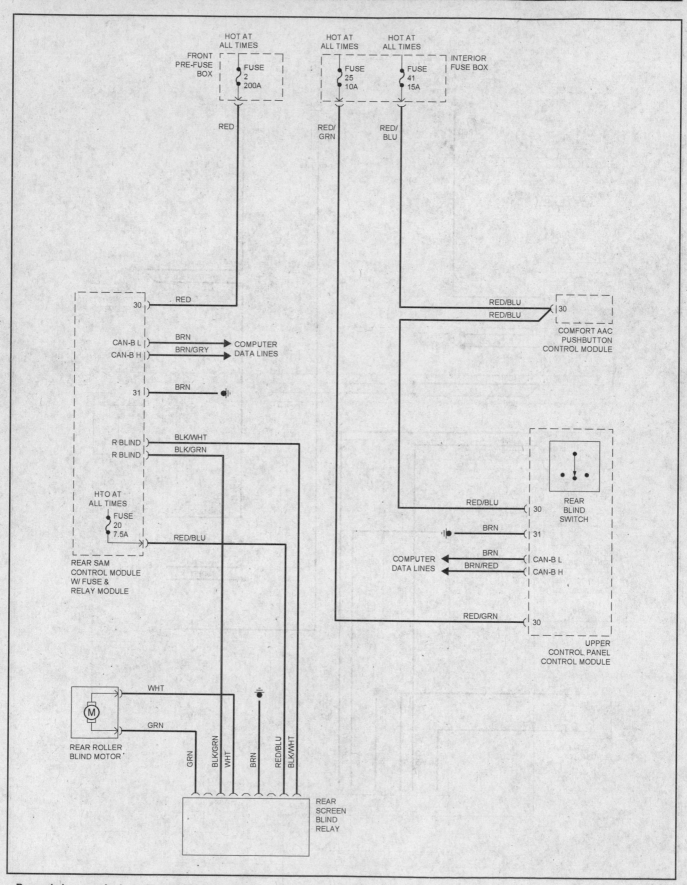

**Rear window sunshade system - 2006 and later**

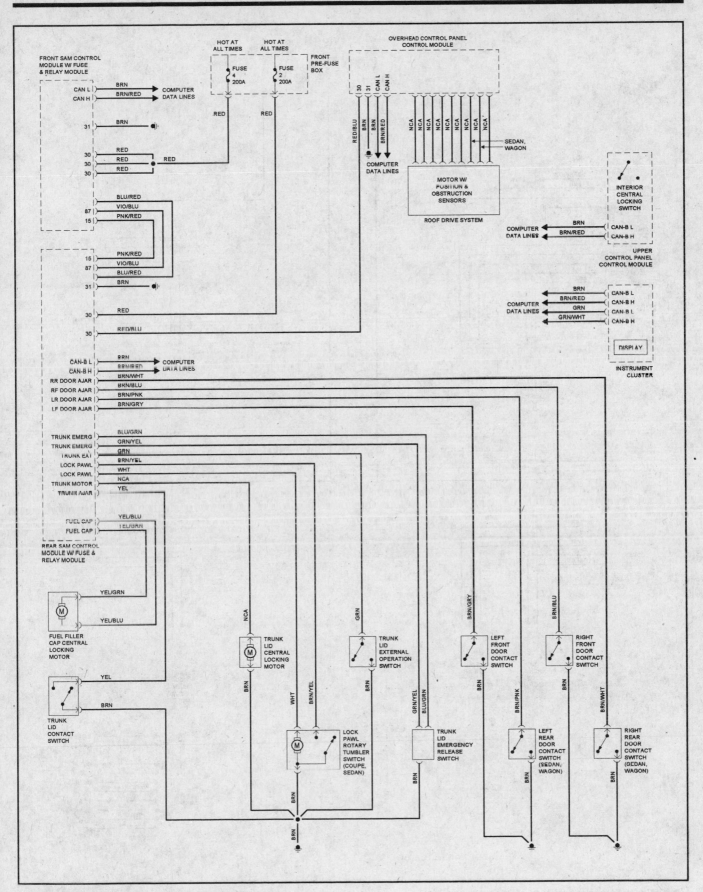

**Power door lock system - 2001 through 2005 (1 of 2)**

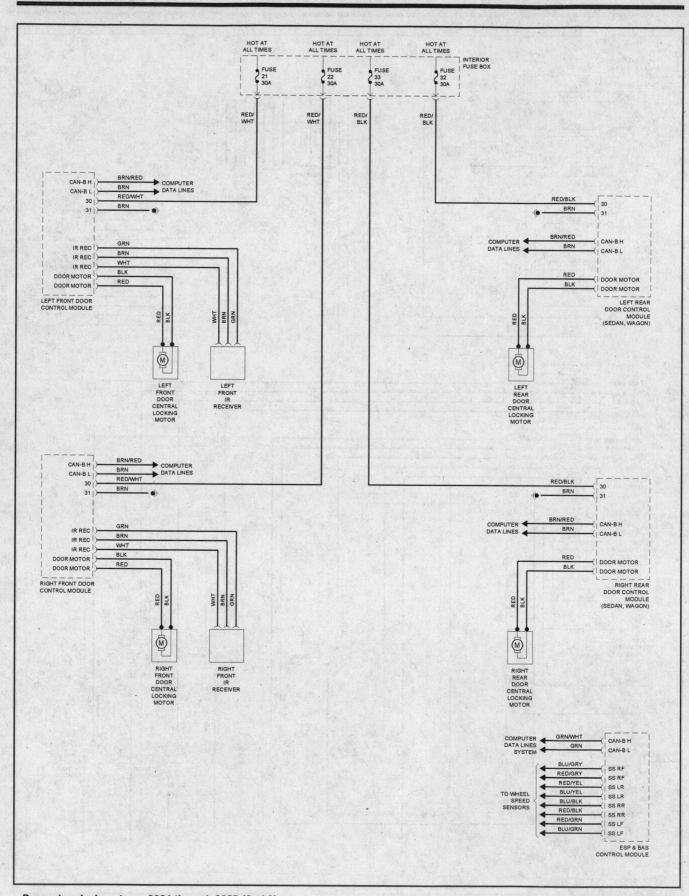

**Power door lock system - 2001 through 2005 (2 of 2)**

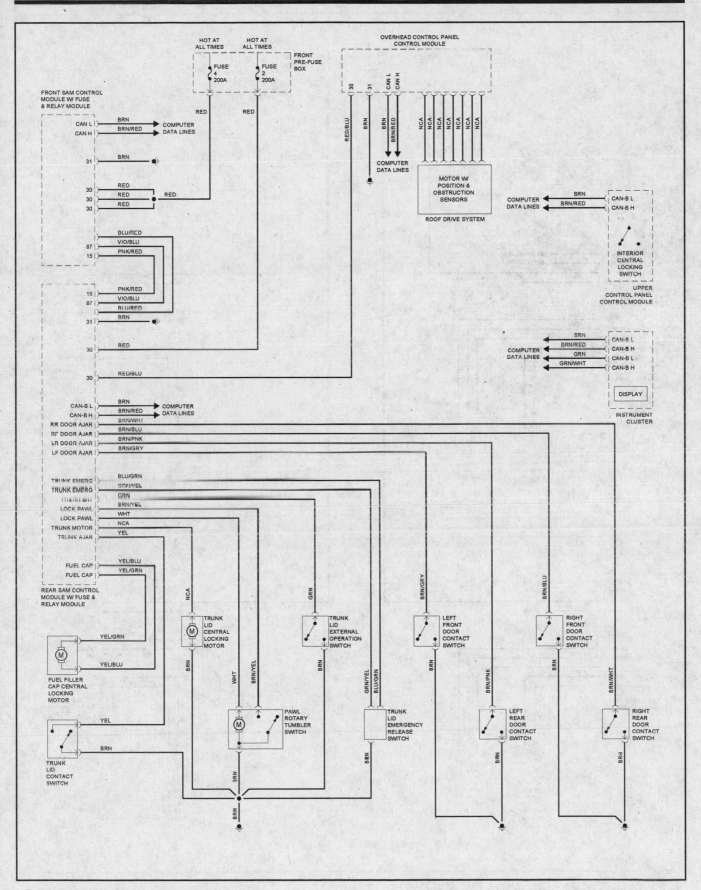

**Power door lock system - 2006 and later (1 of 2)**

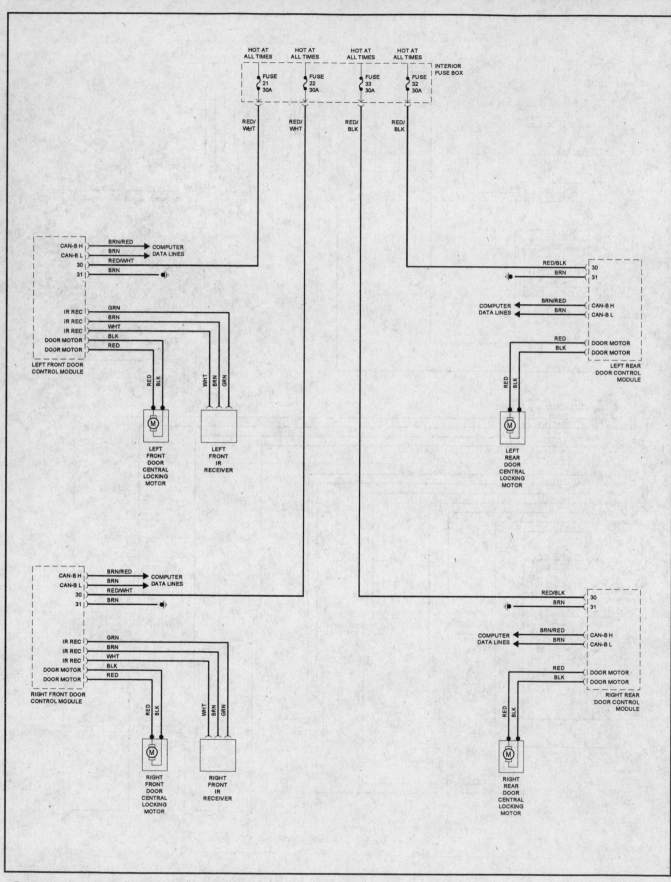

**Power door lock system - 2006 and later (2 of 2)**

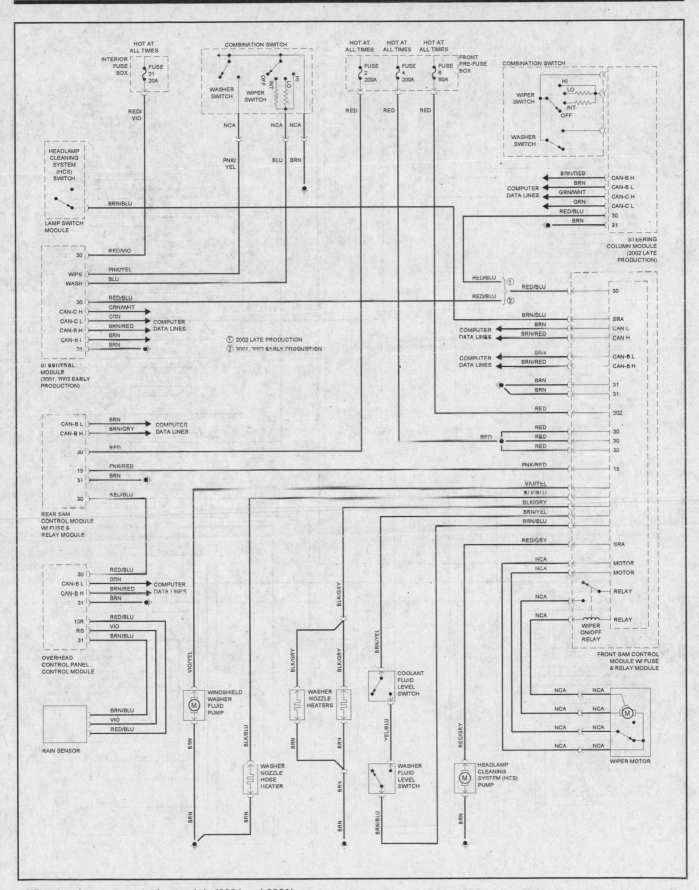

**Wiper/washer system - sedan models (2001 and 2002)**

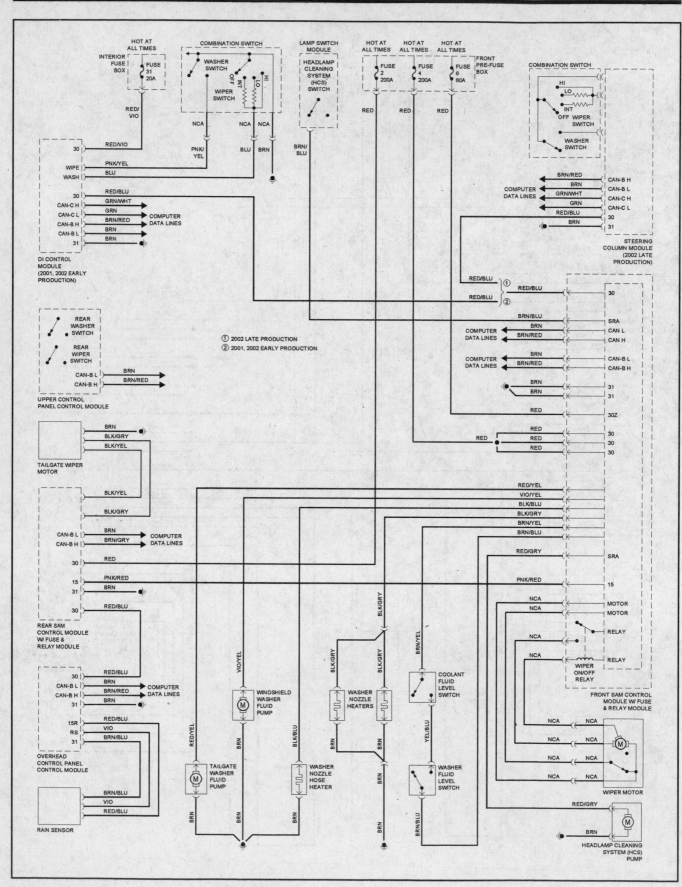

**Wiper/washer system - wagon models (2001 and 2002)**

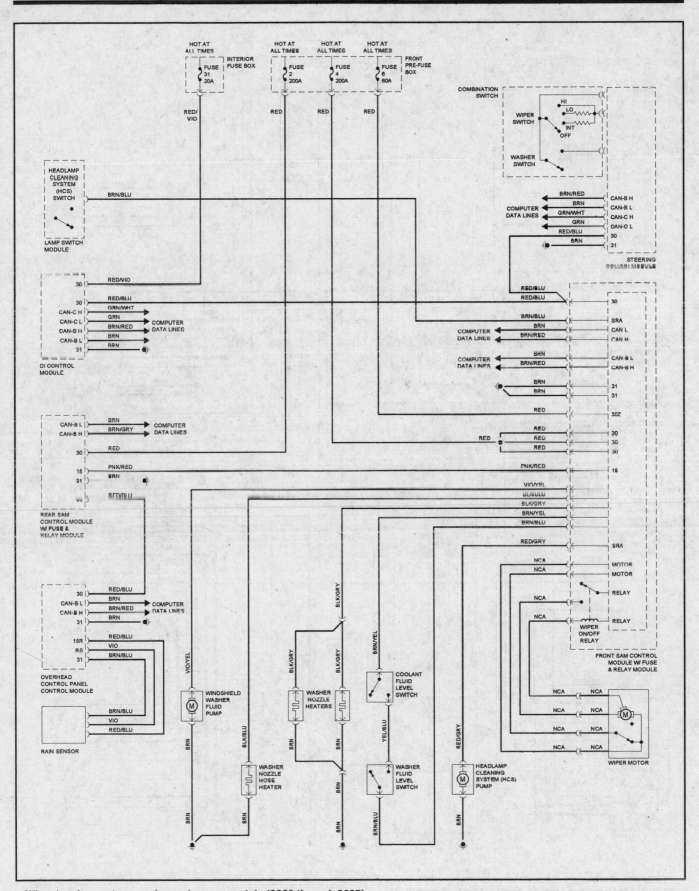

**Wiper/washer system - sedan and coupe models (2003 through 2005)**

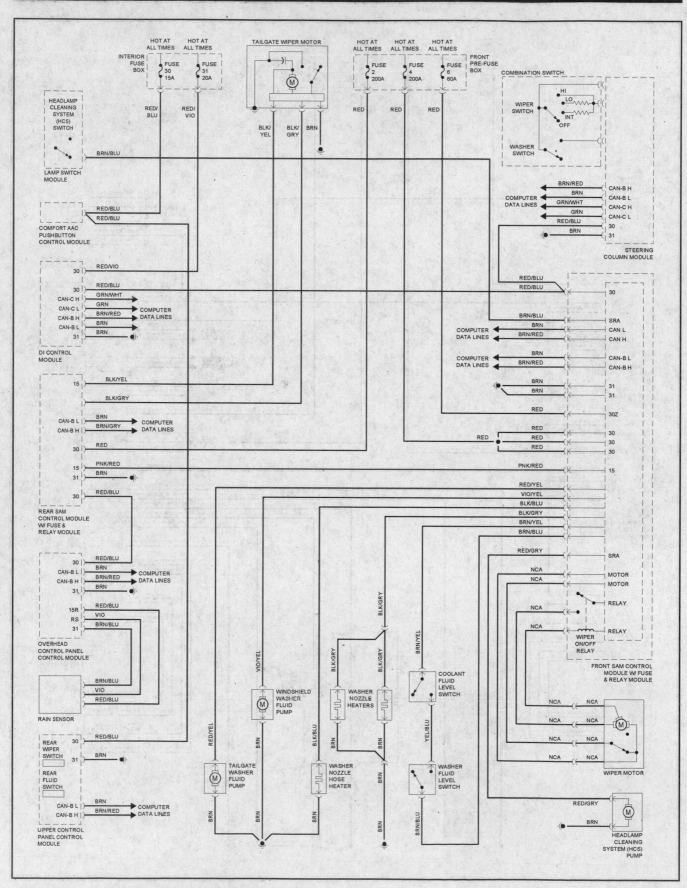

**Wiper/washer system - wagon models (2003 through 2005)**

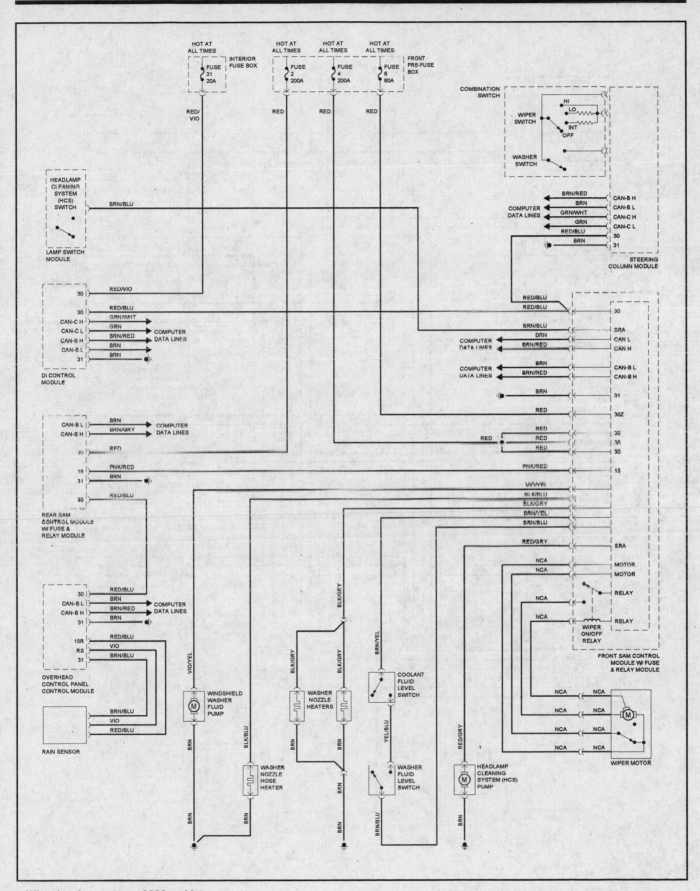

**Wiper/washer system - 2006 and later**

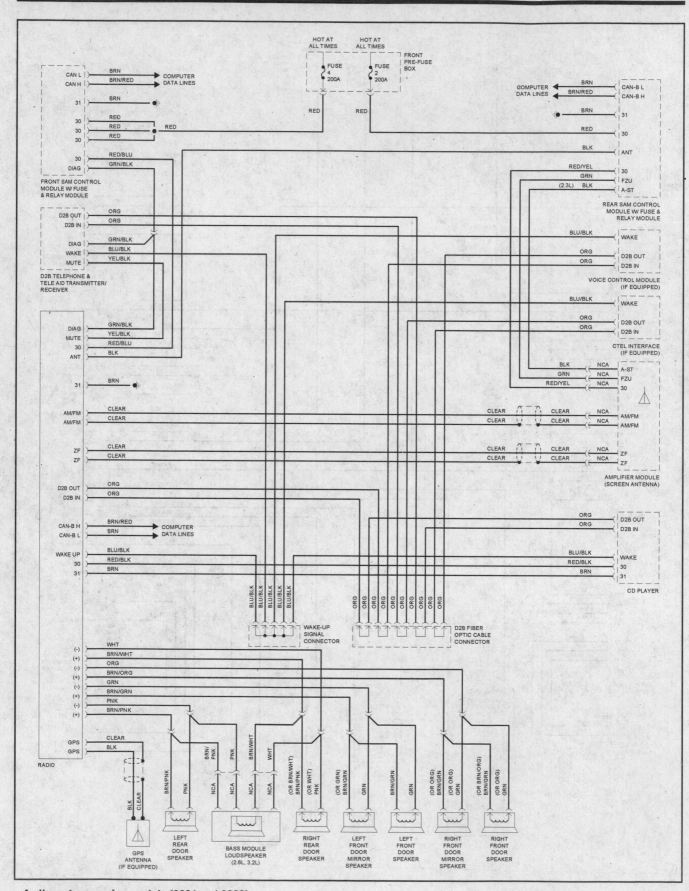

**Audio system - sedan models (2001 and 2002)**

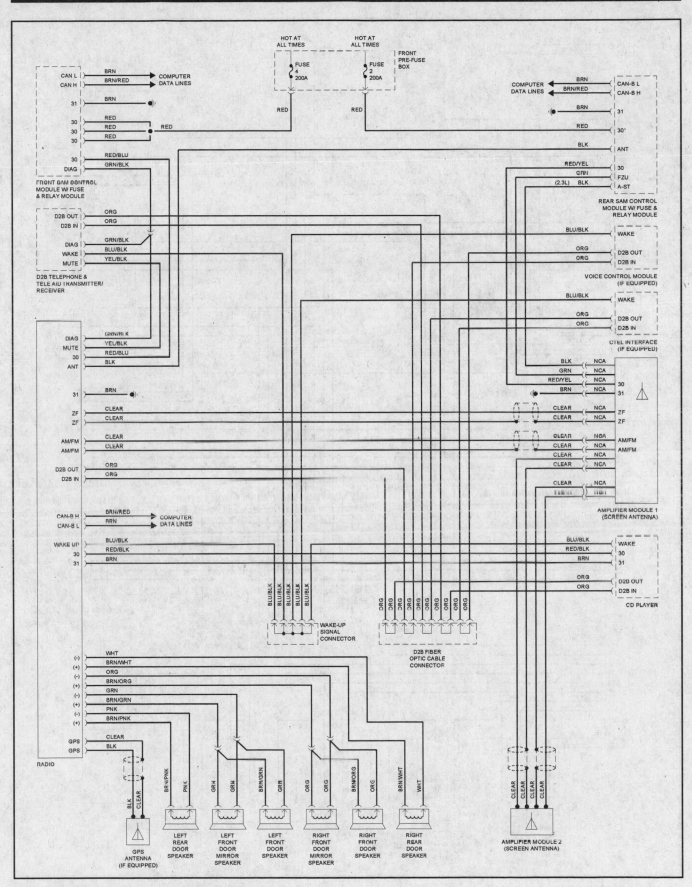

**Audio system - wagon models (2001 and 2002)**

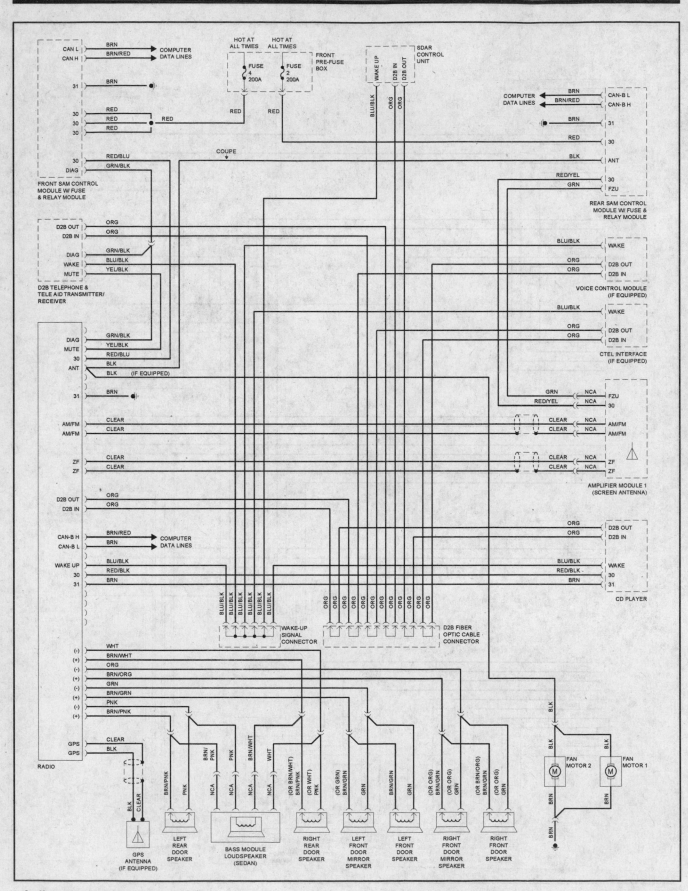

**Audio system - sedan models (2003)**

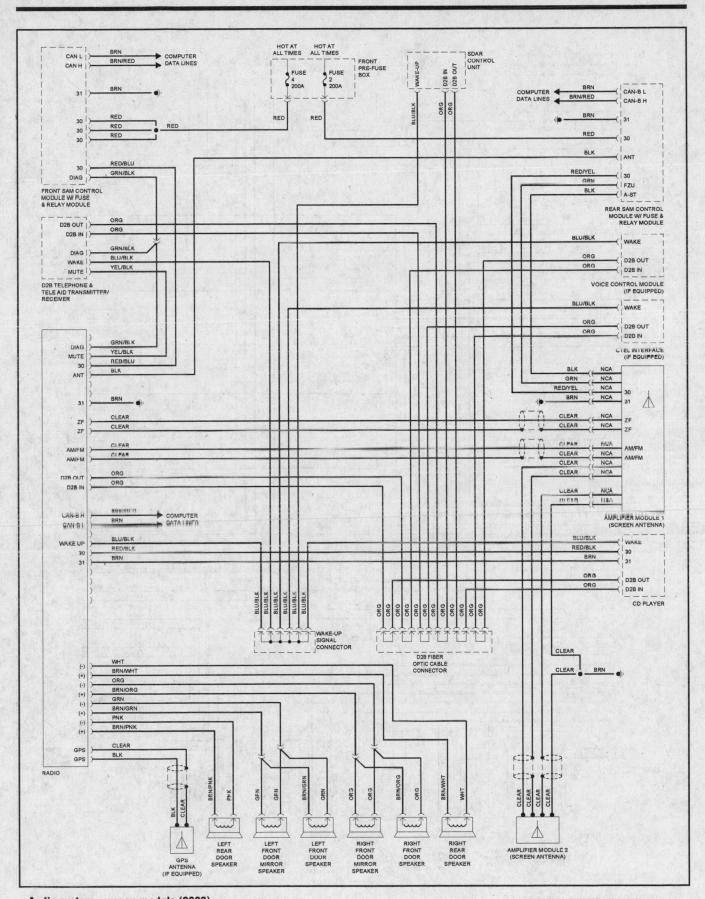

**Audio system - wagon models (2003)**

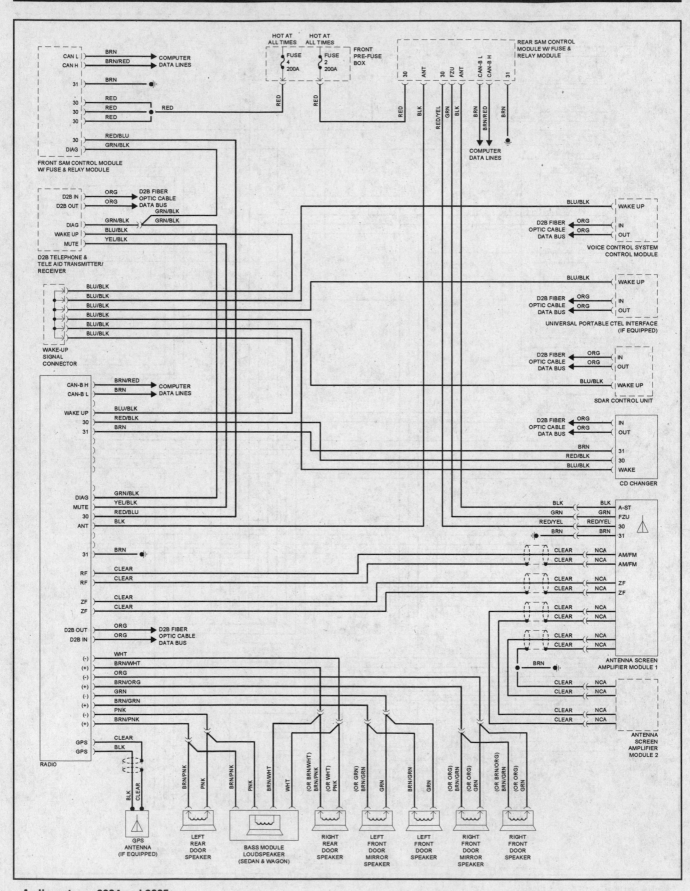

**Audio system - 2004 and 2005**

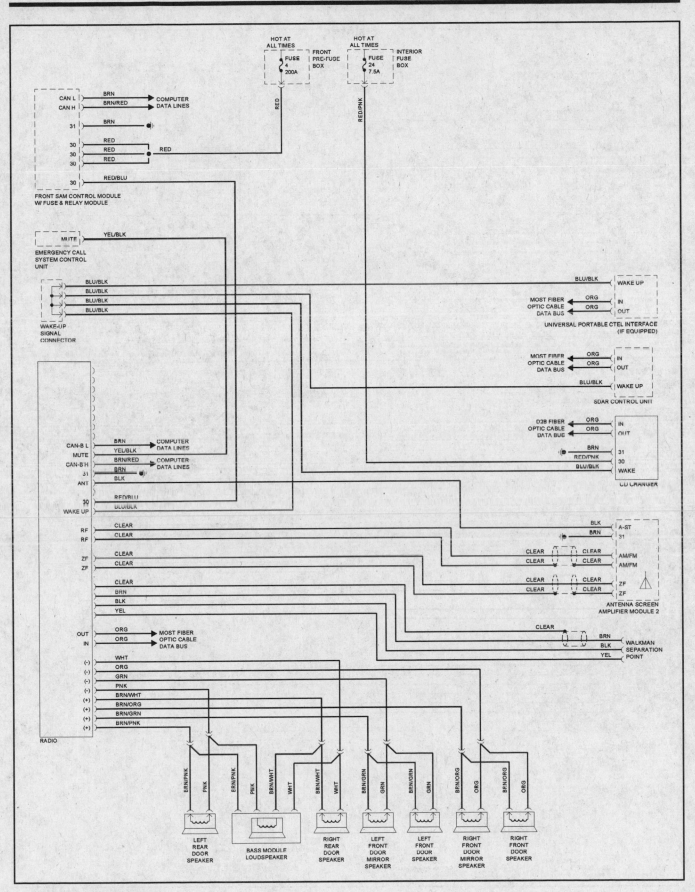

**Audio system - 2006 and later**

## Notes

## GLOSSARY

**AIR/FUEL RATIO:** The ratio of air-to-gasoline by weight in the fuel mixture drawn into the engine.

**AIR INJECTION:** One method of reducing harmful exhaust emissions by injecting air into each of the exhaust ports of an engine. The fresh air entering the hot exhaust manifold causes any remaining fuel to be burned before it can exit the tailpipe.

**ALTERNATOR:** A device used for converting mechanical energy into electrical energy.

**AMMETER:** An instrument, calibrated in amperes, used to measure the flow of an electrical current in a circuit. Ammeters are always connected in series with the circuit being tested.

**AMPERE:** The rate of flow of electrical current present when one volt of electrical pressure is applied against one ohm of electrical resistance.

**ANALOG COMPUTER:** Any microprocessor that uses similar (analogous) electrical signals to make its calculations.

**ARMATURE:** A laminated, soft iron core wrapped by a wire that converts electrical energy to mechanical energy as in a motor or relay. When rotated in a magnetic field, it changes mechanical energy into electrical energy as in a generator.

**ATMOSPHERIC PRESSURE:** The pressure on the Earth's surface caused by the weight of the air in the atmosphere. At sea level, this pressure is 14.7 psi at 32°F (101 kPa at 0°C).

**ATOMIZATION:** The breaking down of a liquid into a fine mist that can be suspended in air.

**AXIAL PLAY:** Movement parallel to a shaft or bearing bore.

**BACKFIRE:** The sudden combustion of gases in the intake or exhaust system that results in a loud explosion.

**BACKLASH:** The clearance or play between two parts, such as meshed gears.

**BACKPRESSURE:** Restrictions in the exhaust system that slow the exit of exhaust gases from the combustion chamber.

**BAKELITE:** A heat resistant, plastic insulator material commonly used in printed circuit boards and transistorized components.

**BALL BEARING:** A bearing made up of hardened inner and outer races between which hardened steel balls roll.

**BALLAST RESISTOR:** A resistor in the primary ignition circuit that lowers voltage after the engine is started to reduce wear on ignition components.

**BEARING:** A friction reducing, supportive device usually located between a stationary part and a moving part.

**BIMETAL TEMPERATURE SENSOR:** Any sensor or switch made of two dissimilar types of metal that bend when heated or cooled due to the different expansion rates of the alloys. These types of sensors usually function as an on/off switch.

**BLOWBY:** Combustion gases, composed of water vapor and unburned fuel, that leak past the piston rings into the crankcase during normal engine operation. These gases are removed by the PCV system to prevent the buildup of harmful acids in the crankcase.

**BRAKE PAD:** A brake shoe and lining assembly used with disc brakes.

**BRAKE SHOE:** The backing for the brake lining. The term is, however, usually applied to the assembly of the brake backing and lining.

**BUSHING:** A liner, usually removable, for a bearing; an anti-friction liner used in place of a bearing.

**CALIPER:** A hydraulically activated device in a disc brake system, which is mounted straddling the brake rotor (disc). The caliper contains at least one piston and two brake pads. Hydraulic pressure on the piston(s) forces the pads against the rotor.

**CAMSHAFT:** A shaft in the engine on which are the lobes (cams) which operate the valves. The camshaft is driven by the crankshaft, via a belt, chain or gears, at one half the crankshaft speed.

**CAPACITOR:** A device which stores an electrical charge.

**CARBON MONOXIDE (CO):** A colorless, odorless gas given off as a normal byproduct of combustion. It is poisonous and extremely dangerous in confined areas, building up slowly to toxic levels without warning if adequate ventilation is not available.

**CARBURETOR:** A device, usually mounted on the intake manifold of an engine, which mixes the air and fuel in the proper proportion to allow even combustion.

**CATALYTIC CONVERTER:** A device installed in the exhaust system, like a muffler, that converts harmful byproducts of combustion into carbon dioxide and water vapor by means of a heat-producing chemical reaction.

**CENTRIFUGAL ADVANCE:** A mechanical method of advancing the spark timing by using flyweights in the distributor that react to centrifugal force generated by the distributor shaft rotation.

**CHECK VALVE:** Any one-way valve installed to permit the flow of air, fuel or vacuum in one direction only.

**CHOKE:** A device, usually a moveable valve, placed in the intake path of a carburetor to restrict the flow of air.

**CIRCUIT:** Any unbroken path through which an electrical current can flow. Also used to describe fuel flow in some instances.

**CIRCUIT BREAKER:** A switch which protects an electrical circuit from overload by opening the circuit when the current flow exceeds a predetermined level. Some circuit breakers must be reset manually, while most reset automatically.

**COIL (IGNITION):** A transformer in the ignition circuit which steps up the voltage provided to the spark plugs.

**COMBINATION MANIFOLD:** An assembly which includes both the intake and exhaust manifolds in one casting.

**COMBINATION VALVE:** A device used in some fuel systems that routes fuel vapors to a charcoal storage canister instead of venting them into the atmosphere. The valve relieves fuel tank pressure and allows fresh air into the tank as the fuel level drops to prevent a vapor lock situation.

**COMPRESSION RATIO:** The comparison of the total volume of the cylinder and combustion chamber with the piston at BDC and the piston at TDC.

**CONDENSER:** 1. An electrical device which acts to store an electrical charge, preventing voltage surges. 2. A radiator-like device in the air conditioning system in which refrigerant gas condenses into a liquid, giving off heat.

**CONDUCTOR:** Any material through which an electrical current can be transmitted easily.

**CONTINUITY:** Continuous or complete circuit. Can be checked with an ohmmeter.

**COUNTERSHAFT:** An intermediate shaft which is rotated by a mainshaft and transmits, in turn, that rotation to a working part.

**CRANKCASE:** The lower part of an engine in which the crankshaft and related parts operate.

**CRANKSHAFT:** The main driving shaft of an engine which receives reciprocating motion from the pistons and converts it to rotary motion.

**CYLINDER:** In an engine, the round hole in the engine block in which the piston(s) ride.

**CYLINDER BLOCK:** The main structural member of an engine in which is found the cylinders, crankshaft and other principal parts.

**CYLINDER HEAD:** The detachable portion of the engine, usually fastened to the top of the cylinder block and containing all or most of the combustion chambers. On overhead valve engines, it contains the valves and their operating parts. On overhead cam engines, it contains the camshaft as well.

**DEAD CENTER:** The extreme top or bottom of the piston stroke.

**DETONATION:** An unwanted explosion of the air/fuel mixture in the combustion chamber caused by excess heat and compression, advanced timing, or an overly lean mixture. Also referred to as "ping".

**DIAPHRAGM:** A thin, flexible wall separating two cavities, such as in a vacuum advance unit.

**DIESELING:** A condition in which hot spots in the combustion chamber cause the engine to run on after the key is turned off.

**DIFFERENTIAL:** A geared assembly which allows the transmission of motion between drive axles, giving one axle the ability to turn faster than the other.

**DIODE:** An electrical device that will allow current to flow in one direction only.

**DISC BRAKE:** A hydraulic braking assembly consisting of a brake disc, or rotor, mounted on an axle, and a caliper assembly containing, usually two brake pads which are activated by hydraulic pressure. The pads are forced against the sides of the disc, creating friction which slows the vehicle.

**DISTRIBUTOR:** A mechanically driven device on an engine which is responsible for electrically firing the spark plug at a predetermined point of the piston stroke.

**DOWEL PIN:** A pin, inserted in mating holes in two different parts allowing those parts to maintain a fixed relationship.

**DRUM BRAKE:** A braking system which consists of two brake shoes and one or two wheel cylinders, mounted on a fixed backing plate, and a brake drum, mounted on an axle, which revolves around the assembly.

**DWELL:** The rate, measured in degrees of shaft rotation, at which an electrical circuit cycles on and off.

**ELECTRONIC CONTROL UNIT (ECU):** Ignition module, module, amplifier or igniter. See Module for definition.

**ELECTRONIC IGNITION:** A system in which the timing and firing of the spark plugs is controlled by an electronic control unit, usually called a module. These systems have no points or condenser.

**END-PLAY:** The measured amount of axial movement in a shaft.

**ENGINE:** A device that converts heat into mechanical energy.

**EXHAUST MANIFOLD:** A set of cast passages or pipes which conduct exhaust gases from the engine.

**FEELER GAUGE:** A blade, usually metal, or precisely predetermined thickness, used to measure the clearance between two parts.

**FIRING ORDER:** The order in which combustion occurs in the cylinders of an engine. Also the order in which spark is distributed to the plugs by the distributor.

**FLOODING:** The presence of too much fuel in the intake manifold and combustion chamber which prevents the air/fuel mixture from firing, thereby causing a no-start situation.

**FLYWHEEL:** A disc shaped part bolted to the rear end of the crankshaft. Around the outer perimeter is affixed the ring gear. The starter drive engages the ring gear, turning the flywheel, which rotates the crankshaft, imparting the initial starting motion to the engine.

**FOOT POUND (ft. lbs. or sometimes, ft.lb.):** The amount of energy or work needed to raise an item weighing one pound, a distance of one foot.

**FUSE:** A protective device in a circuit which prevents circuit overload by breaking the circuit when a specific amperage is present. The device is constructed around a strip or wire of a lower amperage rating than the circuit it is designed to protect. When an amperage higher than that stamped on the fuse is present in the circuit, the strip or wire melts, opening the circuit.

**GEAR RATIO:** The ratio between the number of teeth on meshing gears.

**GENERATOR:** A device which converts mechanical energy into electrical energy.

**HEAT RANGE:** The measure of a spark plug's ability to dissipate heat from its firing end. The higher the heat range, the hotter the plug fires.

**HUB:** The center part of a wheel or gear.

**HYDROCARBON (HC):** Any chemical compound made up of hydrogen and carbon. A major pollutant formed by the engine as a byproduct of combustion.

**HYDROMETER:** An instrument used to measure the specific gravity of a solution.

**INCH POUND (inch lbs.; sometimes in.lb. or in. lbs.):** One twelfth of a foot pound.

**INDUCTION:** A means of transferring electrical energy in the form of a magnetic field. Principle used in the ignition coil to increase voltage.

**INJECTOR:** A device which receives metered fuel under relatively low pressure and is activated to inject the fuel into the engine under relatively high pressure at a predetermined time.

**INPUT SHAFT:** The shaft to which torque is applied, usually carrying the driving gear or gears.

**INTAKE MANIFOLD:** A casting of passages or pipes used to conduct air or a fuel/air mixture to the cylinders.

**JOURNAL:** The bearing surface within which a shaft operates.

**KEY:** A small block usually fitted in a notch between a shaft and a hub to prevent slippage of the two parts.

**MANIFOLD:** A casting of passages or set of pipes which connect the cylinders to an inlet or outlet source.

**MANIFOLD VACUUM:** Low pressure in an engine intake manifold formed just below the throttle plates. Manifold vacuum is highest at idle and drops under acceleration.

**MASTER CYLINDER:** The primary fluid pressurizing device in a hydraulic system. In automotive use, it is found in brake and hydraulic clutch systems and is pedal activated, either directly or, in a power brake system, through the power booster.

**MODULE:** Electronic control unit, amplifier or igniter of solid state or integrated design which controls the current flow in the ignition primary circuit based on input from the pick-up coil. When the module opens the primary circuit, high secondary voltage is induced in the coil.

**NEEDLE BEARING:** A bearing which consists of a number (usually a large number) of long, thin rollers.

**OHM:** ($\Omega$) The unit used to measure the resistance of conductor-to-electrical flow. One ohm is the amount of resistance that limits current flow to one ampere in a circuit with one volt of pressure.

**OHMMETER:** An instrument used for measuring the resistance, In ohms, in an electrical circuit.

**OUTPUT SHAFT:** The shaft which transmits torque from a device, such as a transmission.

**OVERDRIVE:** A gear assembly which produces more shaft revolutions than that transmitted to it.

**OVERHEAD CAMSHAFT (OHC):** An engine configuration in which the camshaft is mounted on top of the cylinder head and operates the valve either directly or by means of rocker arms.

**OVERHEAD VALVE (OHV):** An engine configuration in which all of the valves are located in the cylinder head and the camshaft is located in the cylinder block. The camshaft operates the valves via lifters and pushrods.

**OXIDES OF NITROGEN (NOx):** Chemical compounds of nitrogen produced as a byproduct of combustion. They combine with hydrocarbons to produce smog.

**OXYGEN SENSOR:** Use with the feedback system to sense the presence of oxygen in the exhaust gas and signal the computer which can reference the voltage signal to an air/fuel ratio.

**PINION:** The smaller of two meshing gears.

**PISTON RING:** An open-ended ring with fits into a groove on the outer diameter of the piston. Its chief function is to form a seal between the piston and cylinder wall. Most automotive pistons have three rings: two for compression sealing; one for oil sealing.

**PRELOAD:** A predetermined load placed on a bearing during assembly or by adjustment.

**PRIMARY CIRCUIT:** the low voltage side of the ignition system which consists of the ignition switch, ballast resistor or resistance wire, bypass, coil, electronic control unit and pick-up coil as well as the connecting wires and harnesses.

**PRESS FIT:** The mating of two parts under pressure, due to the inner diameter of one being smaller than the outer diameter of the other, or vice versa; an interference fit.

**RACE:** The surface on the inner or outer ring of a bearing on which the balls, needles or rollers move.

**REGULATOR:** A device which maintains the amperage and/or voltage levels of a circuit at predetermined values.

**RELAY:** A switch which automatically opens and/or closes a circuit.

**RESISTANCE:** The opposition to the flow of current through a circuit or electrical device, and is measured in ohms. Resistance is equal to the voltage divided by the amperage.

**RESISTOR:** A device, usually made of wire, which offers a preset amount of resistance in an electrical circuit.

**RING GEAR:** The name given to a ring-shaped gear attached to a differential case, or affixed to a flywheel or as part of a planetary gear set.

**ROLLER BEARING:** A bearing made up of hardened inner and outer races between which hardened steel rollers move.

**ROTOR:** 1. The disc-shaped part of a disc brake assembly, upon which the brake pads bear; also called, brake disc. 2. The device mounted atop the distributor shaft, which passes current to the distributor cap tower contacts.

**SECONDARY CIRCUIT:** The high voltage side of the ignition system, usually above 20,000 volts. The secondary includes the ignition coil, coil wire, distributor cap and rotor, spark plug wires and spark plugs.

**SENDING UNIT:** A mechanical, electrical, hydraulic or electro-magnetic device which transmits information to a gauge.

**SENSOR:** Any device designed to measure engine operating conditions or ambient pressures and temperatures. Usually electronic in nature and designed to send a voltage signal to an on-board computer, some sensors may operate as a simple on/off switch or they may provide a variable voltage signal (like a potentiometer) as conditions or measured parameters change.

**SHIM:** Spacers of precise, predetermined thickness used between parts to establish a proper working relationship.

**SLAVE CYLINDER:** In automotive use, a device in the hydraulic clutch system which is activated by hydraulic force, disengaging the clutch.

**SOLENOID:** A coil used to produce a magnetic field, the effect of which is to produce work.

**SPARK PLUG:** A device screwed into the combustion chamber of a spark ignition engine. The basic construction is a conductive core inside of a ceramic insulator, mounted in an outer conductive base. An electrical charge from the spark plug wire travels along the conductive core and jumps a preset air gap to a grounding point or points at the end of the conductive base. The resultant spark ignites the fuel/air mixture in the combustion chamber.

**SPLINES:** Ridges machined or cast onto the outer diameter of a shaft or inner diameter of a bore to enable parts to mate without rotation.

**TACHOMETER:** A device used to measure the rotary speed of an engine, shaft, gear, etc., usually in rotations per minute.

**THERMOSTAT:** A valve, located in the cooling system of an engine, which is closed when cold and opens gradually in response to engine heating, controlling the temperature of the coolant and rate of coolant flow.

**TOP DEAD CENTER (TDC):** The point at which the piston reaches the top of its travel on the compression stroke.

**TORQUE:** The twisting force applied to an object.

**TORQUE CONVERTER:** A turbine used to transmit power from a driving member to a driven member via hydraulic action, providing changes in drive ratio and torque. In automotive use, it links the driveplate at the rear of the engine to the automatic transmission.

**TRANSDUCER:** A device used to change a force into an electrical signal.

**TRANSISTOR:** A semi-conductor component which can be actuated by a small voltage to perform an electrical switching function.

**TUNE-UP:** A regular maintenance function, usually associated with the replacement and adjustment of parts and components in the electrical and fuel systems of a vehicle for the purpose of attaining optimum performance.

**TURBOCHARGER:** An exhaust driven pump which compresses intake air and forces it into the combustion chambers at higher than atmospheric pressures. The increased air pressure allows more fuel to be burned and results in increased horsepower being produced.

**VACUUM ADVANCE:** A device which advances the ignition timing in response to increased engine vacuum.

**VACUUM GAUGE:** An instrument used to measure the presence of vacuum in a chamber.

**VALVE:** A device which control the pressure, direction of flow or rate of flow of a liquid or gas.

**VALVE CLEARANCE:** The measured gap between the end of the valve stem and the rocker arm, cam lobe or follower that activates the valve.

**VISCOSITY:** The rating of a liquid's internal resistance to flow.

**VOLTMETER:** An instrument used for measuring electrical force in units called volts. Voltmeters are always connected parallel with the circuit being tested.

**WHEEL CYLINDER:** Found in the automotive drum brake assembly, it is a device, actuated by hydraulic pressure, which, through internal pistons, pushes the brake shoes outward against the drums.

MASTER INDEX